P9-DBX-853

McDougal Littell
*L*iterature
and Language

• RED LEVEL •

DAYDREAMING   Raymond Lark   Collection of Mary Moran, New Jersey.
Photo courtesy, Edward Smith, Los Angeles.

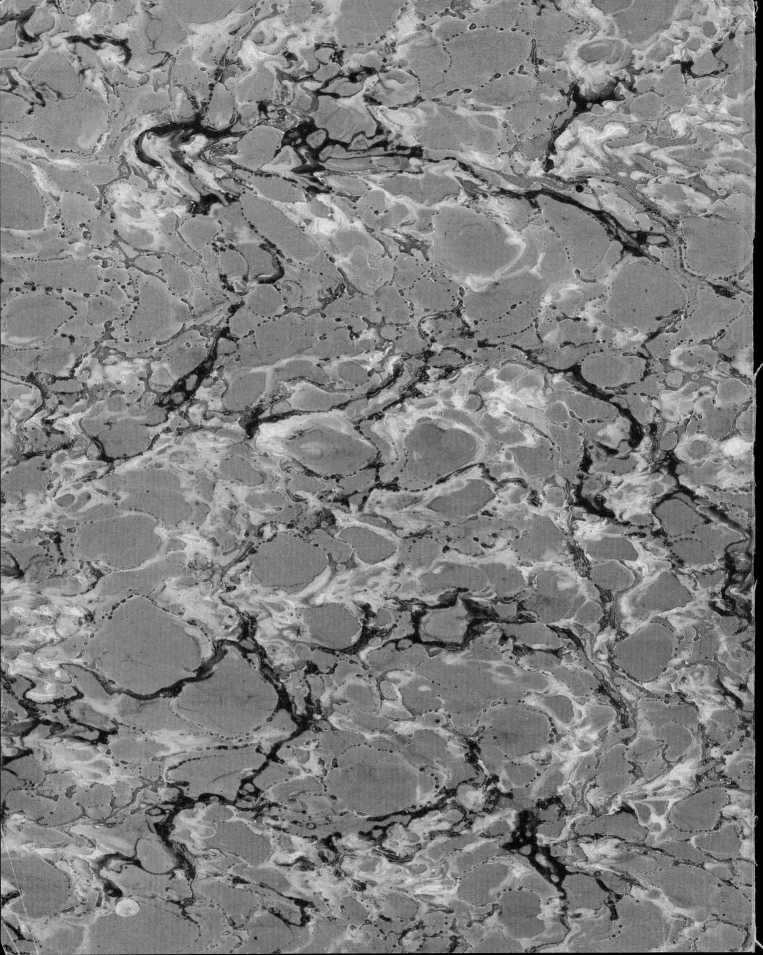

McDOUGAL LITTELL

LITERATURE AND LANGUAGE

Red Level

Senior Consultants

Arthur N. Applebee
State University of New York at Albany

Andrea B. Bermúdez
University of Houston–Clear Lake

Susan Hynds
Syracuse University, Syracuse, New York

Judith A. Langer
State University of New York at Albany

James Marshall
University of Iowa, Iowa City

Donna E. Norton
Texas A&M University, College Station

McDOUGAL LITTELL INC.
A Houghton Mifflin Company

Evanston, Illinois
Boston   Dallas   Phoenix

Acknowledgments

Ricardo E. Alegría: "Lazy Peter and His Three-Cornered Hat," from *The Three Wishes* by Ricardo E. Alegría. By permission of the author.

Terry D. Allen: "Looking North to Taos" by Rudy Bantista, from *Writer's Reader* (Fall 1970).

Américas/Organization of American States: "Formula" by Ana Maria Iza, from *Américas,* a bimonthly magazine published by the General Secretariat of the Organization of American States in English and Spanish.

Arte Publico Press: "Graduation Morning" by Pat Mora, from *Chants* (Houston: Arte Publico Press–University of Houston, 1984). "Primary Lessons" by Judith Ortiz Cofer, excerpted from *Silent Dancing:A Partial Remembrance of a Puerto Rican Childhood* by Judith Ortiz Cofer (Houston: Arte Publico Press, 1990).

Toni Cade Bambara: "The War of the Wall" by Toni Cade Bambara; copyright © 1981 by Toni Cade Bambara. By permission of the author.

Susan Bergholz Literary Services: "Bums in the Attic," from *The House on Mango Street* by Sandra Cisneros; copyright © 1989 by Sandra Cisneros. Published in the United States by Vintage Books, a division of Random House, Inc., New York, and distributed in Canada by Random House of Canada Limited, Toronto. Originally published in somewhat different form by Arte Publico Press in 1984 and revised in 1989. Reprinted by permission of Susan Bergholz Literary Services, New York.

BOA Editions, Ltd.: "in the inner city," from *good woman: poems and a memoir, 1969–1980* by Lucille Clifton; copyright © 1987 by Lucille Clifton. With the permission of BOA Editions, Ltd., 92 Park Avenue, Brockport, NY 14420.

Don Congdon Associates, Inc.: "All Summer in a Day" by Ray Bradbury, published in *Magazine of Fantasy and Science Fiction,* March 1954; copyright © 1954, renewed 1982 by Ray Bradbury. Reprinted by permission of Don Congdon Associates, Inc.

Copp Clark Pitman Ltd.: "Phaëthon" and "Echo and Narcissus," from *Myth* by Moira Kerr and John Bennett; copyright © 1966, Copp Clark Pitman Ltd. Used by permission of the publisher.

The Crisis/NAACP: "Wishes" by Georgia Douglas Johnson, from *The Crisis,* April 1927 issue. By permission of *The Crisis* magazine.

Continued on page 806

Cover Art
DAYDREAMING (detail) Raymond Lark Collection of Mary Moran, New Jersey. Photo courtesy, Edward Smith, Los Angeles. Background photograph by Andrew Lawson.

WARNING: No part of this book may be reproduced or transmitted in any form or by any means, electronic or mechanical, including photocopying, recording, or by any information storage and retrieval system without permission in writing from the Publisher.

ISBN: 0-8123-8042-8

Copyright © 1994 by McDougal Littell Inc.
Box 1667, Evanston, Illinois 60204

All rights reserved. Printed in the United States of America.

8 9 10-DWO-00 99

Senior Consultants

The senior consultants guided conceptual development for the *Literature and Language* series. They participated actively in shaping prototype materials for major components, and they reviewed completed prototypes and/or completed units to ensure consistency with current research and the philosophy of the series.

Arthur N. Applebee
Professor of Education, State University of New York at Albany; Director, Center for the Learning and Teaching of Literature; Senior Fellow, Center for Writing and Literacy

Andrea B. Bermúdez
Professor of Multicultural Education; Director, Research Center for Language and Culture, University of Houston–Clear Lake

Susan Hynds
Associate Professor and Director of English Education, Syracuse University, Syracuse, New York

Judith A. Langer
Professor of Education, State University of New York at Albany; Co-director, Center for the Learning and Teaching of Literature; Senior Fellow, Center for Writing and Literacy

James Marshall
Associate Professor of English and Education, University of Iowa, Iowa City; Executive Secretary, High School Task Force, National Standards Project for English Language Arts K-12.

Donna E. Norton
Professor of Children's Literature, Texas A & M University, College Station

Senior Writers

The senior writers participated in the conceptual development of the series and wrote all the lessons for the literature selections in this text.

Jane N. Beatty
Reading Specialist; formerly, Haverford High School, Haverford, Pennsylvania

William L. McBride, Ph.D.
Educational Materials Specialist; formerly Curriculum and Reading Specialist, Department of Defense Dependents School, Bonn, Germany

Writers

Susanna Nied (Workshops)
Educational Materials Consultant; formerly Instructor, Comparative Literature, San Diego State University, San Diego, California

Wordworks (Language Handbook)
Educational Publishing Services, Gloucester, Massachusetts

Multicultural Advisory Board

The multicultural advisors reviewed literature selections for appropriate content and made suggestions for teaching lessons in a multicultural classroom.

Andrea B. Bermúdez, Professor of Multicultural Education; Director, Research Center for Language and Culture, University of Houston–Clear Lake
Alice A. Kawazoe, Director of Curriculum and Staff Development, Oakland Unified School District, Oakland, California
Sandra Mehojah, Project Coordinator, Office of Indian Education, Omaha Public Schools, Omaha, Nebraska
Alexs D. Pate, Writer and columnist on multiculturalism, literature, and teaching; Adjunct faculty member, University of Minnesota and Macalester College

Manuscript Reviewers

The following educators reviewed prototype lessons and tables of contents during the development of the *Literature and Language* program.

Cheryl S. Archiable, Teacher, Shroder Paideia Middle School, Cincinnati Public Schools, Cincinnati, Ohio

William A. Battaglia, Teacher/Chairperson, Herman Intermediate School, Oak Grove School District, San Jose, California

Joanne Robertson Bizarro, Literature Teacher, St. Kevin's School, Catholic Diocese of Brooklyn, Flushing, New York

Martha W. Christian, Secondary English Department, Curriculum Specialist, Consultant, Southwestern Middle School, Southwestern Central School District, Jamestown, New York

Margaret J. Cummings, Language Arts Department Chairperson, William Chrisman High School, Independence Schools, Independence, Missouri

Kathleen Forslund, Principal, Aquinas Middle School, La Crosse, Wisconsin

Lorraine Gerhart, Reading Teacher, Chairperson and Team Leader, Elmbrook Middle School, Elmbrook Schools, Elm Grove, Wisconsin

Deborah Lynn Moeller, Teacher and Language Arts Department Chairperson, Attucks Middle School, Broward County Schools, Hollywood, Florida

Josephine Scott, Supervisor of Multicultural Education, Northgate Center, Columbus Public Schools, Columbus, Ohio

Elaine G. Sherman, Administrative Specialist, Secondary English and Reading, Division of Curriculum and Instruction, Clark County School District, Las Vegas, Nevada

Martha T. Stewart, Teacher and Chairperson of Language Arts, Turrentine Middle School, Burlington City Schools, Burlington, North Carolina

Sandra Childress Stringer, Principal, Lincoln Elementary School, Evanston District 65, Evanston, Illinois

Joel A. Turetzky, Ed.D., Teacher and Chairperson, Department of English, Raleigh Egypt Junior High School, Memphis City Schools, Memphis, Tennessee

Richard Wagner, Language Arts Curriculum Coordinator, Paradise Valley School District, Phoenix, Arizona

Virginia L. Woodley, English Department Chairperson, Brixner Junior High School, Klamath County School District, Klamath Falls, Oregon

Student Board

The student board members read and evaluated selections to assess their appeal for seventh-grade students.

Susana Arguijo, Saucedo Magnet School, Chicago, Illinois **Crystal Broch,** Swope Middle School, Reno, Nevada **Rosamond Elizabeth Carr,** Haven Middle School, Evanston, Illinois **Shannon Connor,** Beardon Middle School, Knoxville, Tennessee **John Dunbar,** A. B. Hart Junior High School, Cleveland, Ohio **Katrina L. Kalatzis,** Palms Junior High School, Los Angeles, California **Nathan Koering,** Valley Middle School, Apple Valley, Minnesota **David Leddy,** Pine Ridge Middle School, Naples, Florida **Vicky Lowe,** Chute Middle School, Evanston, Illinois **Roxana Old-Chapa,** Chute Middle School, Evanston, Illinois **Rajul Shah,** McKnight Middle School, Renton, Washington **Rolanda Shaw,** Chute Middle School, Evanston, Illinois **Brooke Skeen,** Turrentine Middle School, Burlington, North Carolina **Lara Alison Thoma,** Nichols Middle School, Evanston, Illinois **David C. Young,** Chute Middle School, Evanston, Illinois

Contents

Unit One

A MATTER OF PERSPECTIVE   12

Unit Two

SCALES OF JUSTICE 120

Unit Three

REACHING FOR THE STARS 248

Literature–based
Workshops

Unit Five

A QUESTION OF IDENTITY 468

Unit Six

THEMES IN WORLD FOLKLORE 580

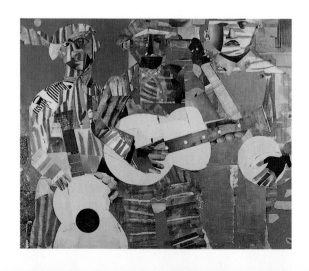

Handbook Section

Contents Overview

INTRODUCING
*L*ITERATURE
AND LANGUAGE

Literature and Language is different from other books you have used in two important ways. First, it is organized to help you tie together your study of the language arts—literature, writing, and language. The literature, chosen for its appeal to your life, serves as the starting point for all your learning. Students like you helped to select the stories, plays, articles, and poems that appear in this book (see their names on page vi). You'll find stories that have been favorites for many generations, as well as works by current writers.

Second, as you use this book, you will find that it does not present a "right" way to understand a story or to write a paper. Instead, it requires you to think for yourself. It asks you to form your own opinions and make your own decisions.

Unit Organization

All the parts of this book fit closely together. If you look at the Table of Contents, on pages vii–xviii, you will see that the book is divided into six units. Each unit is organized around a theme, such as "Scales of Justice" or "Reaching for the Stars," that connects to your life and the world around you. To narrow the focus of these broad themes, each unit is further divided into two subunits. For example, "Scales of Justice" is divided into "Victims or Victors?" and "Turning the Tables."

After the literature selections in each subunit, you will find a Writer's Workshop, a Language Workshop, and a third workshop that varies in content. These workshops are based upon the literature selections, so that all the parts of the subunit work together.

Organization of the Literature Lessons

Each literature lesson follows a carefully designed pattern, described below.

EXPLORE: Before You Read   An **Explore** page, marked by a green band at the top, appears before each selection. Its three parts prepare you for reading.

• **Examine What You Know** provides an activity or discussion question based on your own experiences to help you get into the selection.

• **Expand Your Knowledge** gives you useful background information about the selection.

• **Enrich Your Reading** or **Write Before You Read** provides a specific reading or writing activity to help you better understand the literature you are about to read.

Reading the Selection   Useful words that you should add to your vocabulary are underlined in the selection. These words are defined in a blue box at the bottom of the page where they first appear. Other difficult words and phrases are defined in footnotes, which appear beneath a black line at the bottom of the page.

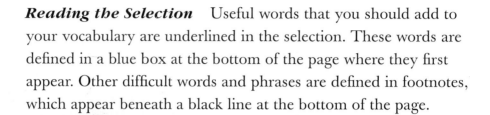

EXPLAIN: After You Read
You'll find one or two **Explain** pages at the end of the selection, marked by a red band at the top. This section starts with discussion questions about the literature. The questions, which have no "right" or "wrong" answers, help you develop your own ideas and interpretations.

After the discussion questions, a literary concept is presented to help you become aware of literary techniques and their importance. In addition, writing activities give you another way of thinking about the literature. Finally, a vocabulary practice is provided if the selection includes vocabulary words.

EXTEND: Beyond the Reading   This page, marked by a purple band at the top, gives you creative ways to display your understanding. These **Options for Learning** allow you to show what you have learned in many different ways such as group projects, dramatics, art, storytelling, and debates. An author biography also appears here.

Literature-based Workshops

Three workshops appear at the end of each subunit.

Writer's Workshop   Each Writer's Workshop guides you through an entire writing assignment closely related to the literature and theme of the subunit. Clear instructions, helpful hints, optional suggestions, examples from literature, and models of student writing will help you write your own compositions.

Language Workshop   Each Language Workshop focuses on skills that are related to your work in the Writer's Workshop as well as other writing that you do.

Related Skills Workshop   The third workshop gives you additional tips in reading, vocabulary, or speaking and listening.

Reading on Your Own

Two pages at the end of each unit suggest novels that tie in with the unit theme. The plot summaries of these novels will help you choose books to read on your own.

Handbook Section

At the back of the book, you'll find three reference handbooks to round out your language-arts studies—a **Reader's Handbook,** a **Writer's Handbook,** and a **Language Handbook.**

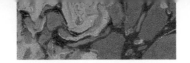

Strategies for

READING

Have you ever been so involved in reading that you ignored the world around you? A herd of elephants stampeding through your room, a flying saucer landing outside your window, or even your mom reminding you for the fifth time to take out the trash—none of these could tear you away from your book! When you are that excited about what you are reading, you are an active reader. Active readers not only step into the actions, times, and places of stories and poems but also become more involved in the issues and events they read about in magazines, news-papers, and textbooks. Try the strategies below. They describe the kinds of thinking good readers engage in as they read.

- **Questioning** Ask questions about what is happening. Exploring possible reasons for what is going on in the selection and how charac-ters feel can help you "get into" the selection. Also, make mental notes about words or statements that confuse you, but don't get side-tracked. Things may get clearer as you read further in the selection.

- **Connecting** Think of similarities between what is described in the selection you are reading and what you have experienced, heard about, or read about.

- **Predicting** Try to figure out what will happen next and how the selection might end.

- **Reviewing** Stop occasionally for a quick review of what you under-stand so far. Then draw conclusions about what is "between the lines," that is, what is suggested but not stated directly.

- **Evaluating** Form opinions about what you read, both during and after reading. Develop your own images of and ideas about characters and events.

The reading model on the next page shows how one reader used these strategies as she read the story "Charles." Naturally, your thoughts would be different from hers, since you think in your own way. You might have different questions, and you would make different connections based on your own experiences.

Charles

SHIRLEY JACKSON

CRAYON BOX II
David Brega
Courtesy, Alexander Gallery,
New York.

The day Laurie started kindergarten, he renounced corduroy overalls with bibs and began wearing blue jeans with a belt. I watched him go off the first morning with the older girl next door, seeing clearly that an era of my life was ended, my sweet-voiced nursery-school tot replaced by a long-trousered, swaggering character who forgot to stop at the corner and wave goodbye to me.

He came home the same way, the front door slamming open, his cap on the floor, and the voice suddenly become raucous shouting, "Isn't anybody *here?*"

At lunch he spoke insolently to his father, spilled Jannie's milk, and remarked that his teacher said that we were not to take the name of the Lord in vain.

"How *was* school today?" I asked, elaborately casual.

"All right," he said.

"Did you learn anything?" his father asked.

Laurie regarded his father coldly. "I didn't learn nothing," he said.

"Anything," I said. "Didn't learn anything."

"The teacher spanked a boy, though," Laurie said, addressing his bread and butter. "For being fresh," he added with his mouth full.

"What did he do?" I asked. "Who was it?"

Laurie thought. "It was Charles," he said. "He was fresh. The teacher spanked him and made him stand in a corner. He was awfully fresh."

"What did he do?" I asked again, but Laurie slid off his chair, took a cookie, and left, while his father was still saying, "See here, young man."

The next day Laurie remarked at lunch, as soon as he sat down, "Well, Charles was bad again today." He grinned enormously and said, "Today Charles hit the teacher."

▶ Why is this *boy* named Laurie?
(Questioning)

▶ Laurie's a bad boy!
(Evaluating)

▶ All parents correct their kids' language.
(Connecting)

▶ What does "being fresh" mean?
(Questioning)

▶ Laurie's rude.
(Evaluating)

▶ That's excessive—unless there's something wrong with Charles.
(Evaluating, Questioning)

"Good heavens," I said, mindful of the Lord's name, "I suppose he got spanked again?"

"He sure did," Laurie said. "Look up," he said to his father.

"What?" his father said, looking up.

"Look down," Laurie said. "Look at my thumb. Gee, you're dumb." He began to laugh insanely.

▶ That's typical of a kindergartner—stupid baby joke. *(Connecting)*

"Why did Charles hit the teacher?" I asked quickly.

"Because she tried to make him color with red crayons," Laurie said. "Charles wanted to color with green crayons, so he hit the teacher, and she spanked him and said nobody play with Charles; but everybody did."

The third day—it was Wednesday of the first week—Charles bounced a seesaw onto the head of a little girl and made her bleed, and the teacher made him stay inside all during recess. Thursday Charles had to stand in a corner during story time because he kept pounding his feet on the floor. Friday Charles was deprived of blackboard privileges because he threw chalk.

▶ Something's wrong with Charles. *(Evaluating)*

On Saturday I remarked to my husband, "Do you think kindergarten is too unsettling for Laurie? All this toughness and bad grammar, and this Charles boy sounds like such a bad influence."

"It'll be all right," my husband said reassuringly. "Bound to be people like Charles in the world. Might as well meet them now as later."

▶ That's true. (Dad's statement) *(Evaluating)*

On Monday Laurie came home late, full of news. "Charles," he shouted as he came up the hill; I was waiting anxiously on the front steps. "Charles," Laurie yelled all the way up the hill, "Charles was bad again."

"Come right in," I said, as soon as he came close enough. "Lunch is waiting."

"You know what Charles did?" he demanded, following me through the door. "Charles yelled so in school they sent a boy in from first grade to tell the teacher she had to make Charles keep quiet, and so Charles had to stay after school. And so all the children stayed to watch him."

"What did he do?" I asked.

"He just sat there," Laurie said, climbing into his chair at the table. "Hi, Pop, y'old dust mop."

▶ Sounds like Laurie is maturing too fast. *(Evaluating)*

"Charles had to stay after school today," I told my husband. "Everyone stayed with him."

"What does this Charles look like?" my husband asked Laurie. "What's his other name?"

"He's bigger than me," Laurie said, "and he doesn't ever wear a jacket."

Monday night was the first Parent-Teachers meeting, and only the fact that Jannie had a cold kept me from going; I wanted passionately to meet Charles's mother. On Tuesday Laurie remarked suddenly, "Our teacher had a friend come to see her in school today."

"Charles's mother?" my husband and I asked simultaneously.

"Naaah," Laurie said scornfully. "It was a man who came and made us do exercises. Look." He climbed down from his chair and squatted down and touched his toes. "Like this," he said. He got solemnly back into his chair and said, picking up his fork, "Charles didn't even *do* exercises."

"That's fine," I said heartily. "Didn't Charles want to do exercises?"

"Naaah," Laurie said. "Charles was so fresh to the teacher's friend he wasn't *let* do exercises."

"Fresh again?" I said.

"He kicked the teacher's friend," Laurie said. "The teacher's friend told Charles to touch his toes like I just did, and Charles kicked him."

"What are they going to do about Charles, do you suppose?" Laurie's father asked him.

Laurie shrugged elaborately. "Throw him out of school, I guess," he said.

Wednesday and Thursday were routine; Charles yelled during story hour and hit a boy in the stomach and made him cry. On Friday Charles stayed after school again and so did all the other children.

With the third week of kindergarten, Charles was an institution in our family. Jannie was being a Charles when she cried all afternoon. Laurie did a Charles when he filled his wagon full of mud and pulled it through the kitchen. Even my husband, when he caught his elbow in the telephone cord and pulled telephone, ash tray, and a bowl of flowers off the table, said, after the first minute,

▶ What does he mean by "his other name"?
(Questioning)

YOUTH WITH TOY   James Lloyd
Courtesy, Portal Gallery, London.

▶ Charles should just have been kicked out of school right away.
(Evaluating)

"Looks like Charles."

During the third and fourth weeks there seemed to be a reformation in Charles. Laurie reported grimly at lunch on Thursday of the third week, "Charles was so good today the teacher gave him an apple."

"What?" I said, and my husband added warily, "You mean Charles?"

"Charles," Laurie said. "He gave the crayons around and he picked up the books afterward, and the teacher said he was her helper."

"What happened?" I asked incredulously.

"He was her helper; that's all," Laurie said, and shrugged.

"Can this be true, about Charles?" I asked my husband that night. "Can something like this happen?"

"Wait and see," my husband said cynically. "When you've got a Charles to deal with, this may mean he's only plotting."

He seemed to be wrong. For over a week, Charles was the teacher's helper. Each day he handed things out, and he picked things up; no one had to stay after school.

"The PTA meeting's next week again," I told my husband one evening. "I'm going to find Charles's mother there."

"Ask her what happened to Charles," my husband said. "I'd like to know."

"I'd like to know myself," I said.

On Friday of that week things were back to normal. "You know what Charles did today?" Laurie demanded at the lunch table, in a voice slightly awed. "He told a little girl to say a word, and she said it; and the teacher washed her mouth out with soap, and Charles laughed."

"What word?" his father asked unwisely, and Laurie said, "I'll have to whisper it to you; it's so bad." He got down off his chair and went around to his father. His father bent his head down, and Laurie whispered joyfully. His father's eyes widened.

"Did Charles tell the little girl to say *that?*" he asked respectfully.

"She said it *twice,*" Laurie said. "Charles told her to say it *twice.*"

"What happened to Charles?" my husband asked.

▶ All of a sudden, Charles seems to change.
(Reviewing)

▶ Why doesn't she ask, "What did you do to make Charles's behavior change?"
(Questioning, Evaluating)

▶ Teacher should have washed *both* their mouths out with soap.
(Evaluating)

"Nothing," Laurie said. "He was passing out the crayons."

Monday morning Charles abandoned the little girl and said the evil word himself three or four times, getting his mouth washed out with soap each time. He also threw chalk.

My husband came to the door with me that evening as I set out for the PTA meeting. "Invite her over for a cup of tea after the meeting," he said. "I want to get a look at her."

"If only she's there," I said prayerfully.

"She'll be there," my husband said. "I don't see how they could hold a PTA meeting without Charles's mother."

At the meeting I sat restlessly, scanning each comfortable, matronly face, trying to determine which one hid the secret of Charles. None of them looked to me haggard enough. No one stood up in the meeting and apologized for the way her son had been acting. No one mentioned Charles.

After the meeting, I identified and sought out Laurie's kindergarten teacher. She had a plate with a cup of tea and a piece of chocolate cake; I had a plate with a cup of tea and a piece of marshmallow cake. We maneuvered up to one another cautiously and smiled.

"I've been so anxious to meet you," I said. "I'm Laurie's mother."

"We're all so interested in Laurie," she said.

"Well, he certainly likes kindergarten," I said. "He talks about it all the time."

"We had a little trouble adjusting, the first week or so," she said primly, "but now he's a fine little helper. With lapses, of course."

"Laurie usually adjusts very quickly," I said. "I suppose this time it's Charles's influence."

"Charles?"

"Yes," I said, laughing, "you must have your hands full in that kindergarten, with Charles."

"Charles?" she said. "We don't have any Charles in the kindergarten."

▶ Charles gets other people to do things for him while he still acts good.
(Reviewing)

▶ She's finally going to find out about Charles.
(Predicting)

▶ I like the ending. I was really involved with Charles when I found out it's really Laurie. Laurie's a good story-maker for his age.
(Evaluating)

A MATTER OF
PERSPECTIVE

It is difficult to see

the picture when you

are inside the frame.

R. S. Trapp

STOP LIGHT   1986   © C. J. Yao.
Courtesy, Styria Studio, New York.

FALSE IMPRESSIONS

A thirty-story building looks huge when seen from the ground. The same building looks tiny when seen from an airplane. The size of the building is a matter of perspective. It depends on your point of view. The same is true of people and situations. Your understanding of events and your opinions about people are also a matter of perspective—and the focus of Unit One.

Seeing things clearly is not always easy.

Have you ever been surprised to find out that your first impression of someone was totally false? You may have drawn the wrong conclusion because the person wanted to mislead you, or you may have simply made an error in judgment.

Sometimes we receive false impressions of others, and sometimes we give false impressions of ourselves. You will see both situations in the following selections.

Elements of
FICTION

When you read a story, you are reading a work of fiction. **Fiction** is writing that comes from an author's imagination. Although the author makes the story up, he or she might base it on real events.

Fiction writers write either short stories or novels. A **short story** usually revolves around a single idea and is short enough to be read at one sitting. A **novel** is much longer and more complex. In this textbook, the fiction selections that you will read are short stories. However, at the end of each unit you will find recommendations for novels that you can read on your own.

Understanding Fiction

Character **Characters** are the people, animals, or imaginary creatures that take part in the action of the story. Usually, a short story centers on events in the life of one person or animal. He or she is the **main character.** Generally, there are also one or more **minor characters** in the story. Minor characters sometimes provide part of the background for the story. More often, however, minor characters interact with the main character and with one another. Their words and actions help to move the plot along.

Setting The **setting** is the time and place in which the story happens. The time may be the past, present, or future; day or night; and any season. The place where the action of the story occurs may be imaginary or real.

Plot The sequence of events in a story is called the **plot.** The plot is the writer's blueprint for what happens, when it happens, and to whom it happens. One event causes another, which causes another, and so on until the end of the story.

Generally, plots are built around a **conflict**—a problem or struggle between two or more opposing forces. Conflicts can range from a life-or-death struggle to a disagreement between friends.

While the development of each plot is different, traditional works of fiction generally follow a pattern that includes the following stages:

• **Exposition** Exposition sets the stage for the story. Characters are introduced, the setting is described, and the conflict begins to unfold.

• **Complications** As the story continues, the plot gets more complex. While the characters struggle to find solutions to the conflict, suspense and a feeling of excitement and energy build.

• **Climax** The climax is the highest point of interest or suspense in the story. It is the turning point when the action reaches a peak and the outcome of the conflict is decided. The climax may occur because of a decision the characters reach or because of a discovery or an event that changes the situation. The climax usually results in a change in the characters or a solution to the problem.

• **Resolution** The resolution occurs at the conclusion of the story. Loose ends are tied up and the story ends.

Theme The **theme** of a story is the main message the writer wishes to share with the reader. This message might be a lesson about life or a belief about people and their actions. Most themes are not stated directly. They are like hidden messages that the reader must decode. You will find, however, as you discuss literature, that different readers discover different themes in the same selection. The following suggestions will help you unlock the theme.

• Review what happened to the main character. Did he or she change during the story? What did he or she learn about life?

• Skim the selection for key phrases and sentences—statements that move beyond the action of the story to say something important about life or people.

• Think about the title of the selection. Does it have a special meaning that could lead you to the main idea of the piece?

S*trategies for Reading Fiction*

1. **Preview** a story before you read it by looking at the title and the pictures, or even skimming through the pages, reading some words here and there.

2. Try to **visualize** the setting and the characters. Can you picture a similar place in your mind? Can you "see" the action and the characters?

3. As you read, **make connections.** Do any of the characters have the same thoughts or experiences that you have had? Does the story remind you of an event or person you've heard of or read about?

4. While you read, **question** events, characters, and ideas. "Why is the door unlocked?" "Why is she so rude?" Asking good questions is at the heart of good reading.

5. During your reading, stop occasionally and **predict** what might happen next and how the story will end.

6. As you read, **build** on what you're learning about the characters and events in the story. Let your thoughts change and grow as you learn more about the situation.

7. Continually **evaluate** the story as you read. Think about your feelings toward the characters and their actions. Also consider how well the author is telling his or her story.

When you have finished reading, discuss your understandings and questions about the story with someone else.

Remember, a story never tells you everything. It leaves room for you to build your own ideas. When you read, you are left with first impressions, but you need to be able to elaborate and explain them based on the story, your own experiences, and other stories you have read.

Fiction

Seventh Grade

GARY SOTO

Examine What You Know

How do seventh graders try to impress each other? Think about what you and your friends do to make others admire you. Create a chart that lists ways seventh graders show off. An example of such a chart is shown below. Share your ideas with your classmates.

Words or Actions	Appearance
bragging	designer jeans

Expand Your Knowledge

For some students, wearing the right clothes is a way to gain admiration and acceptance. They often work summer jobs in order to purchase a back-to-school wardrobe. The main character in the next story earns his clothing money by picking grapes near his home in Fresno. Fresno is an important farming center in central California. One of the largest crops grown in the Fresno area is grapes, a seasonal crop that requires thousands of workers to harvest. During summers, both migrant workers, those who follow harvests from one town to another, and residents pick grapes for money.

Write Before You Read

In your journal or notebook, write about a time you used clothing, money, or actions to impress someone. What did you do? What were the results?

■ *Author biography on Extend page*

Seventh Grade

GARY SOTO

On the first day of school, Victor stood in line half an hour before he came to a wobbly card table. He was handed a packet of papers and a computer card on which he listed his one elective, French. He already spoke Spanish and English, but he thought someday he might travel to France, where it was cool; not like Fresno, where summer days reached 110 degrees in the shade. There were rivers in France, and huge churches, and fair-skinned people everywhere, the way there were brown people all around Victor.

Besides, Teresa, a girl he had liked since they were in catechism classes[1] at Saint Theresa's, was taking French, too. With any luck they would be in the same class. Teresa is going to be my girl this year, he promised himself as he left the gym full of students in their new fall clothes. She was cute. And good at math, too, Victor thought as he walked down the hall to his homeroom. He ran into his friend, Michael Torres, by the water fountain that never turned off.

They shook hands, *raza*-style[2], and jerked their heads at one another in a *saludo de vato*[3]. "How come you're making a face?" asked Victor.

"I ain't making a face, *ese*[4]. This *is* my face." Michael said his face had changed during the summer. He had read a *GQ* magazine that his older brother borrowed from the Book Mobile and noticed that the male models all had the same look on their faces. They would stand, one arm around a beautiful woman, and scowl. They would sit at a pool, their rippled stomachs dark with shadow, and *scowl*. They would sit at dinner tables, cool drinks in their hands, and *scowl*.

"I think it works," Michael said. He scowled and let his upper lip quiver. His teeth showed along with the ferocity of his soul. "Belinda Reyes walked by a while ago and looked at me," he said.

Victor didn't say anything, though he thought his friend looked pretty strange. They talked about recent movies, baseball, their parents, and the horrors of picking grapes in order to buy their fall clothes. Picking grapes was like living in Siberia,

---

1. **catechism classes:** formal classes in religious instruction.
2. ***raza*-style** (rä′ zä-) *Spanish*: in the familiar manner that local Hispanics greet each other.
3. ***saludo de vato*** (sä lo͞o dô dä vä′ tô) *Spanish*: greeting between Hispanic buddies.
4. ***ese*** (e′ sā) *Spanish*: a slang term used when addressing someone, as in "Hey, man."

Words to Know and Use	**elective** (ē lek′ tiv) *n.* a school subject or course chosen by the student rather than assigned **scowl** (skoul) *v.* to look angry by drawing the eyebrows together and frowning **ferocity** (fə räs′ ə tē) *n.* extreme fierceness; savagery

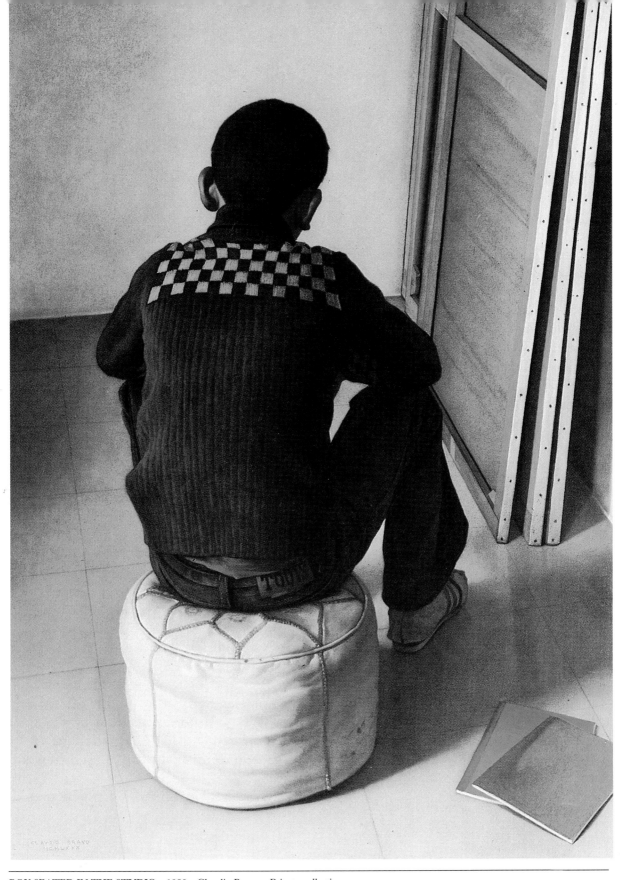

BOY SEATED IN THE STUDIO 1980 Claudio Bravo Private collection.
Courtesy, Marlborough Gallery, New York.

except hot and more boring.

"What classes are you taking?" Michael said, scowling.

"French. How 'bout you?"

"Spanish. I ain't so good at it, even if I'm Mexican."

"I'm not either, but I'm better at it than math, that's for sure."

A tinny, three-beat bell propelled students to their homerooms. The two friends socked each other in the arm and went their ways, Victor thinking, man, that's weird. Michael thinks making a face makes him handsome.

On the way to his homeroom, Victor tried a scowl. He felt foolish, until out of the corner of his eye he saw a girl looking at him. Umm, he thought, maybe it does work. He scowled with greater <u>conviction</u>.

In homeroom, roll was taken, emergency cards were passed out, and they were given a bulletin to take home to their parents. The principal, Mr. Belton, spoke over the crackling loudspeaker, welcoming the students to a new year, new experiences, and new friendships. The students squirmed in their chairs and ignored him. They were anxious to go to first period. Victor sat calmly, thinking of Teresa, who sat two rows away, reading a paperback novel. This would be his lucky year. She was in his homeroom, and would probably be in his English and math classes. And, of course, French.

The bell rang for first period, and the students herded noisily through the door. Only Teresa <u>lingered</u>, talking with the homeroom teacher.

"So you think I should talk to Mrs. Gaines?" she asked the teacher. "She would know about ballet?"

"She would be a good bet," the teacher said. Then added, "Or the gym teacher, Mrs. Garza."

Victor lingered, keeping his head down and staring at his desk. He wanted to leave when she did so he could bump into her and say something clever.

He watched her on the sly. As she turned to leave, he stood up and hurried to the door, where he managed to catch her eye. She smiled and said, "Hi, Victor."

He smiled back and said, "Yeah, that's me." His brown face blushed. Why hadn't he said, "Hi, Teresa," or "How was your summer?" or something nice?

As Teresa walked down the hall, Victor walked the other way, looking back, admiring how gracefully she walked, one foot in front of the other. So much for being in the same class, he thought. As he trudged to English, he practiced scowling.

In English they reviewed the parts of speech. Mr. Lucas, a portly man, waddled down the aisle, asking, "What is a noun?"

"A person, place, or thing," said the class in unison.

"Yes, now somebody give me an example of a person—you, Victor Rodriguez."

"Teresa," Victor said automatically. Some of the girls giggled. They knew he had a crush on Teresa. He felt himself blushing again.

"Correct," Mr. Lucas said. "Now provide

Words to Know and Use | **conviction** (kən vik′ shən) *n.* a strong belief
linger (liŋ′ gər) *v.* to continue to stay; delay leaving

me with a place."

Mr. Lucas called on a freckled kid who answered, "Teresa's house with a kitchen full of big brothers."

After English, Victor had math, his weakest subject. He sat in the back by the window, hoping that he would not be called on. Victor understood most of the problems, but some of the stuff looked like the teacher made it up as she went along. It was confusing, like the inside of a watch.

After math he had a fifteen-minute break, then social studies, and, finally, lunch. He bought a tuna casserole with buttered rolls, some fruit cocktail, and milk. He sat with Michael, who practiced scowling between bites.

Girls walked by and looked at him.

"See what I mean, Vic?" Michael scowled. "They love it."

"Yeah, I guess so."

They ate slowly, Victor scanning the horizon for a glimpse of Teresa. He didn't see her. She must have brought lunch, he thought, and is eating outside. Victor scraped his plate and left Michael, who was busy scowling at a girl two tables away.

The small triangle-shaped campus bustled with students talking about their new classes. Everyone was in a sunny mood. Victor hurried to the bag lunch area, where he sat down and opened his math book. He moved his lips as if he were reading, but his mind was somewhere else. He raised his eyes slowly and looked around. No Teresa.

He lowered his eyes, pretending to study, then looked slowly to the left. No Teresa. He turned a page in the book and stared at some math problems that scared him

because he knew he would have to do them eventually. He looked to the right. Still no sign of her. He stretched out lazily in an attempt to disguise his snooping.

Then he saw her. She was sitting with a girlfriend under a plum tree. Victor moved to a table near her and daydreamed about taking her to a movie. When the bell sounded, Teresa looked up, and their eyes met. She smiled sweetly and gathered her books. Her next class was French, same as Victor's.

They were among the last students to arrive in class, so all the good desks in the back had already been taken. Victor was forced to sit near the front, a few desks away from Teresa, while Mr. Bueller wrote French words on the chalkboard. The bell rang, and Mr. Bueller wiped his hands, turned to the class, and said, *"Bonjour."*[5]

"Bonjour," braved a few students.

"Bonjour," Victor whispered. He wondered if Teresa heard him.

Mr. Bueller said that if the students studied hard, at the end of the year they could go to France and be understood by the populace.

One kid raised his hand and asked, "What's 'populace'?"

"The people, the people of France."

Mr. Bueller asked if anyone knew French. Victor raised his hand, wanting to impress Teresa. The teacher beamed and said, *"Très bien. Parlez-vous français?"*[6]

Victor didn't know what to say. The teacher wet his lips and asked something else in French. The room grew silent. Victor felt all eyes staring at him. He tried to bluff

---

5. **Bonjour** (bōn zhōōr') *French*: Good day.
6. **Très bien. Parlez-vous français?** (tre byan pär' le vü frän' se) *French*: Very good. Do you speak French?

his way out by making noises that sounded French.

"La me vava me con le grandma," he said uncertainly.

Mr. Bueller, wrinkling his face in curiosity, asked him to speak up.

Great rosebushes of red bloomed on Victor's cheeks. A river of nervous sweat ran down his palms. He felt awful. Teresa sat a few desks away, no doubt thinking he was a fool. Without looking at Mr. Bueller, Victor mumbled, "Frenchie oh wewe gee in September."

Mr. Bueller asked Victor to repeat what he had said.

"Frenchie oh wewe gee in September," Victor repeated.

Mr. Bueller understood that the boy didn't know French and turned away. He walked to the blackboard and pointed to the words on the board with his steel-edged ruler.

"Le bateau," he sang.

"Le bateau," the students repeated.

"Le bateau est sur l'eau,"[7] he sang.

"Le bateau est sur l'eau."

Victor was too weak from failure to join the class. He stared at the board and wished he had taken Spanish, not French. Better yet, he wished he could start his life over. He had never been so embarrassed. He bit his thumb until he tore off a sliver of skin.

The bell sounded for fifth period, and Victor shot out of the room, avoiding the stares of the other kids, but had to return for his math book. He looked sheepishly at the teacher, who was erasing the board, then widened his eyes in terror at Teresa who stood in front of him. "I didn't know you knew French," she said. "That was good."

Mr. Bueller looked at Victor, and Victor looked back. Oh please, don't say anything, Victor pleaded with his eyes. I'll wash your car, mow your lawn, walk your dog—anything! I'll be your best student, and I'll clean your erasers after school.

Mr. Bueller shuffled through the papers on his desk. He smiled and hummed as he sat down to work. He remembered his college years when he dated a girlfriend in borrowed cars. She thought he was rich because each time he picked her up, he had a different car. It was fun until he had spent all his money on her and had to write home to his parents because he was broke.

Victor couldn't stand to look at Teresa. He was sweaty with shame. "Yeah, well, I picked up a few things from movies and books and stuff like that." They left the class together. Teresa asked him if he would help her with her French.

"Sure, anytime," Victor said.

"I won't be bothering you, will I?"

"Oh no, I like being bothered."

"Bonjour," Teresa said, leaving him outside her next class. She smiled and pushed wisps of hair from her face.

"Yeah, right, *bonjour,*" Victor said. He turned and headed to his class. The rosebushes of shame on his face became bouquets of love. Teresa is a great girl, he thought. And Mr. Bueller is a good guy.

He raced to metal shop. After metal shop there was biology, and after biology a long sprint to the public library, where he checked out three French textbooks.

He was going to like seventh grade. 🦤

---

7. *Le bateau est sur l'eau* (lə ba tō′ e sür lō) *French*: The boat is on the water.

Responding to Reading

First Impressions

1. What were your reactions to Victor? Jot down your ideas in your journal or on a sheet of paper.

Second Thoughts

2. Do you think Victor should feel proud or ashamed of his actions? Explain your answer.

> **Think about**
> - why he claimed to know French
> - what happens, or might happen, as a result of his claim

3. The French teacher, Mr. Bueller, realizes that Victor is faking his knowledge of French. Why do you think he keeps the truth to himself?

4. It seems that Victor succeeds in impressing Teresa. What is your opinion of Teresa? Support your answer with evidence from the story.

Broader Connections

5. Why do people feel the need to create false impressions of themselves? Are they always wrong to do so? Use the experiences you wrote about before reading to help you think through your response.

Literary Concept: Characterization

Characterization refers to the methods that writers use to make their characters seem real. Writers can use any of the following methods to make their characters come alive for readers.

1) Show the character in action or conversation.
2) Express the character's thoughts.
3) Describe his or her physical appearance.
4) Tell how other characters respond to him or her.

Look back through the story to find an example of each of the methods that Soto uses. Share your examples with your classmates.

Writing Options

1. Write the **note** Teresa might hand to her best friend describing what happened in French class and her reaction to Victor.

2. Extend the story by describing what might happen next. You might wish to create a **scene** between Victor and Teresa, or one between him and his friends.

3. Write an **advice column** to Victor and his friends, giving them suggestions on how to get a girl's attention.

4. Record your first impressions of seventh grade in your **journal.** Include what you expect to like about seventh grade as well as what you may not like about it or what worries you.

Vocabulary Practice

Exercise On your paper, write the word from the list that best completes the sentence.

1. Victor wanted to ___?___ in the hallway to see Teresa, even though he might be late for class.

2. Victor's friend changed his appearance because of his ___?___ that girls cared mainly for looks.

3. When a course is offered as an ___?___, students do not have to take it.

4. Most people probably would not consider a ___?___ to be more attractive than a smile.

5. Michael believed that a look of ___?___, not gentleness, would win the hearts of girls.

Words to Know and Use

conviction
elective
ferocity
linger
scowl

Options for Learning

1 • A Bunch of Trouble Grape pickers drew national attention in the 1960s and 1970s. Research the problems that grape pickers faced and their efforts to improve conditions. Report your findings to the class. Be sure to report both sides of the problems.

2 • A Tuneful Telling Write lyrics for a song that Victor might use to impress Teresa. The lyrics should boast about his imaginary achievements. You might want to include some fake French to impress her.

3 • On Stage With other students, act out one scene from "Seventh Grade" for your class. Study the story carefully for details about the characters.

4 • In Another Language Ask at least twenty students which foreign language they are most interested in learning. It may be one that they have already begun studying. Chart the results and share your findings with your class.

FACT FINDER SOCIAL STUDIES

What other crops are grown in the Fresno area?

Gary Soto
1952 –

Gary Soto grew up in a Mexican-American community in Fresno, California. His father worked for a raisin company, and his mother peeled potatoes at a food-processing company. At various times during his childhood, Soto wanted to be a priest, a hobo, and a paleontologist (a scientist who studies fossils).

In college he planned to study geography, until he discovered poetry. "I don't think I had any literary aspirations when I was a kid," says Soto. "In fact, we didn't have books, and no one encouraged us to read. So my wanting to write poetry was a sort of fluke."

He has been writing poetry, novels, and short stories for young readers and adults ever since college. A collection of autobiographical pieces, *Living Up the Street*, won an American Book Award. His recently published young adult novels include *Taking Sides, Pacific Crossing,* and *The Skirt*.

Soto lives with his wife and daughter in Berkeley, California, where he occasionally teaches at the University of California.

Fiction

The War of the Wall

TONI CADE BAMBARA

Examine What You Know

Is there a place in your neighborhood that seems to belong to young people? Perhaps it is a park or a schoolyard or a mall. Describe that place in your journal and tell how people feel about it.

Expand Your Knowledge

In the l960s, some African-American artists began the "wall of respect" movement. The artists began creating special places by painting walls within the community that became symbols of their respect for their own neighborhoods.

Walls have also been regarded as symbols for even larger ideas. The Berlin Wall was a negative symbol for the split between the Communist and free worlds. On the other hand, the Vietnam Veterans Memorial has a wall engraved with the name of every American killed or missing in action in the Vietnam conflict. It is a wall of honor.

Enrich Your Reading

Dialect Dialect is the particular type of language spoken in a particular place by a certain group of people. Dialect includes the way words are pronounced, as well as the colorful expressions used in informal conversation. The chart below explains some of the dialect used in the story.

Dialect	Meaning
pot likker:	liquid left after meat and/or vegetables have cooked
full of sky:	as if in another world
fix her wagon:	tell her off
hunching each other:	bumping someone with a shoulder or elbow
laying down a heavy rap:	saying something important
sounded very tall:	sounded proud

■ *Author biography on Extend page*

The War of the Wall

TONI CADE BAMBARA

Me and Lou had no time for courtesies. We were late for school. So we just flat out told the painter lady to quit messing with the wall. It was our wall, and she had no right coming into our neighborhood painting on it. Stirring in the paint bucket and not even looking at us, she mumbled something about Mr. Eubanks, the barber, giving her permission. That had nothing to do with it as far as we were concerned. We've been pitching pennies against that wall since we were little kids. Old folks have been dragging their chairs out to sit in the shade of the wall for years. Big kids have been playing handball against the wall since so-called integration[1] when the crazies 'cross town poured cement in our pool so we couldn't use it. I'd sprained my neck one time boosting my cousin Lou up to chisel Jimmy Lyons's name into the wall when we found out he was never coming home from the war in Vietnam to take us fishing.

"If you lean close," Lou said, leaning hip-shot against her beat-up car, "you'll get a whiff of bubble gum and kids' sweat. And that'll tell you something—that this wall belongs to the kids of Taliaferro Street." I thought Lou sounded very convincing. But the painter lady paid us no mind. She just snapped the brim of her straw hat down and hauled her bucket up the ladder.

"You're not even from around here," I hollered up after her. The license plates on her old piece of car said "New York." Lou dragged me away because I was about to grab hold of that ladder and shake it. And then we'd really be late for school.

Why is the narrator angry? *question*

When we came from school, the wall was slick with white. The painter lady was running string across the wall and taping it here and there. Me and Lou leaned against the gum ball machine outside the pool hall and watched. She had strings up and down and back and forth. Then she began chalking them with a hunk of blue chalk.

The Morris twins crossed the street, hanging back at the curb next to the beat-up car. The twin with the red ribbons was hugging a jug of cloudy lemonade. The one with yellow ribbons was holding a plate of dinner away from her dress. The painter lady began snapping the strings. The blue chalk dust measured off halves and quarters up and down and sideways too. Lou was about to say how hip it all was, but I dropped my book satchel on his toes to remind him we were at war.

---

1. **since so-called integration**: from the time in the 1960s when segregation, the separation of the races in public places, was outlawed. The narrator is being sarcastic, suggesting that integration never took effect.

SUNNY SIDE OF THE STREET   1950   Philip Evergood   Collection of The Corcoran Gallery of Art, Washington, D.C. Museum purchase, Anna E. Clark Fund.

Some good aromas were drifting our way from the plate leaking pot likker onto the Morris girl's white socks. I could tell from where I stood that under the tinfoil was baked ham, collard greens, and candied yams. And knowing Mrs. Morris, who sometimes bakes for my mama's restaurant, a slab of buttered cornbread was probably up under there too, sopping up some of the pot likker. Me and Lou rolled our eyes, wishing somebody would send us some dinner. But the painter lady didn't even turn around. She was pulling the strings down and prying bits of tape loose.

Side Pocket came strolling out of the pool hall to see what Lou and me were studying so hard. He gave the painter lady the once-over, checking out her paint-spattered jeans, her chalky T-shirt, her floppy-brimmed straw hat. He hitched up his pants and glided over toward the painter lady, who kept right on with what she was doing.

"Whatcha got there, sweetheart?" he asked the twin with the plate.

"Suppah," she said, all soft and country-like.

"For her," the one with the jug added, jerking her chin toward the painter lady's back.

Still she didn't turn around. She was rearing back on her heels, her hands jammed into her back pockets, her face squinched up like the masterpiece she had in mind was taking shape on the wall by magic. We could have been gophers crawled up into a rotten hollow for all she cared. She didn't even say hello to anybody. Lou was muttering something about how great her concentration was. I butt him with my hip, and his elbow slid off the gum machine.

"Good evening," Side Pocket said in his best ain't-I-fine voice. But the painter lady was moving from the milk crate to the step stool to the ladder, moving up and down fast, scribbling all over the wall like a crazy person. We looked at Side Pocket. He looked at the twins. The twins looked at us. The painter lady was giving a show. It was like those old-timey music movies where the dancer taps on the table top and then starts jumping all over the furniture, kicking chairs over, and not skipping a beat. She didn't even look where she was stepping. And for a minute there, hanging on the ladder to reach a far spot, she looked like she was going to tip right over.

"Ahh," Side Pocket cleared his throat and moved fast to catch the ladder. "These young ladies here have brought you some supper."

"Ma'am?" The twins stepped forward. Finally the painter turned around, her eyes "full of sky," as my grandmama would say. Then she stepped down like she was in a trance. She wiped her hands on her jeans as the Morris twins offered up the plate and the jug. She rolled back the tinfoil, then wagged her head as though something terrible was on the plate.

"Thank your mother very much," she said, sounding like her mouth was full of sky too. "I've brought my own dinner along." And then, without even excusing herself, she went back up the ladder, drawing on the wall in a wild way. Side Pocket whistled one of those oh-brother breathy whistles and went back into the pool hall. The Morris twins shifted their weight from one foot to the other, then crossed the street and went home. Lou had to drag me away, I was so mad. We couldn't wait to get to the firehouse to tell my daddy all about this rude woman who'd stolen our wall.

All the way back to the block to help my mama out at the restaurant, me and Lou kept asking my daddy for ways to run the painter lady out of town. But my daddy was busy talking about the trip to the country and telling Lou he could come too because Grandmama can always use an extra pair of hands on the farm.

Later that night, while me and Lou were in the back doing our chores, we found out that the painter lady was a liar. She came into the restaurant and leaned against the glass of the steam table, talking about how starved she was. I was scrubbing pots and Lou was chopping onions, but we could hear her through the service window. She was asking Mama was that a ham hock in the greens, and was that a neck bone in the pole beans, and were there any vegetables cooked without meat, especially pork.

"I don't care who your spiritual leader is," Mama said in that way of hers. "If you eat in the community, sistuh, you gonna eat pig by-and-by, one way or t'other."

review Why is Mama becoming annoyed?

Me and Lou were cracking up in the kitchen, and several customers at the counter were clearing their throats, waiting for Mama to really fix her wagon for not speaking to the elders when she came in. The painter lady took a stool at the counter and went right on with her questions. Was there cheese in the baked macaroni, she wanted to know? Were there eggs in the

salad? Was it honey or sugar in the iced tea? Mama was fixing Pop Johnson's plate. And every time the painter lady asked a fool question, Mama would dump another spoonful of rice on the pile. She was tapping her foot and heating up in a dangerous way. But Pop Johnson was happy as he could be. Me and Lou peeked through the service window, wondering what planet the painter lady came from. Who ever heard of baked macaroni without cheese, or potato salad without eggs?

"Do you have any bread made with unbleached flour?" the painter lady asked Mama. There was a long pause, as though everybody in the restaurant was holding their breath, wondering if Mama would dump the next spoonful on the painter lady's head. She didn't. But when she set Pop Johnson's plate down, it came down with a bang.

When Mama finally took her order, the starving lady all of a sudden couldn't make up her mind whether she wanted a vegetable plate or fish and a salad. She finally settled on the broiled trout and a tossed salad. But just when Mama reached for a plate to serve her, the painter lady leaned over the counter with her finger all up in the air.

"Excuse me," she said. "One more thing." Mama was holding the plate like a Frisbee, tapping that foot, one hand on her hip. "Can I get raw beets in that tossed salad?"

"You will get," Mama said, leaning her face close to the painter lady's, "whatever Lou back there tossed. Now sit down." And the painter lady sat back down on her stool and shut right up.

All the way to the country, me and Lou tried to get Mama to open fire on the

Urban artist Meg Fish portrays people from the neighborhood in her murals painted on Philadelphia buildings.
Mural in Philadelphia   1992   Meg Fish   Courtesy of the artist.

painter lady. But Mama said that seeing as how she was from the North, you couldn't expect her to have any manners. Then Mama said she was sorry she'd been so impatient with the woman because she seemed like a decent person and was simply trying to stick to a very strict diet. Me and Lou didn't want to hear that. Who did that lady think she was, coming into our neighborhood and taking over our wall?

"Welllll," Mama <u>drawled</u>, pulling into the filling station so Daddy could take the wheel, "it's hard on an artist, ya know. They can't always get people to look at their work. So she's just doing her work in the open, that's all."

Me and Lou definitely did not want to hear that. Why couldn't she set up an easel downtown or draw on the sidewalk in her own neighborhood? Mama told us to quit fussing so much; she was tired and wanted

to rest. She climbed into the back seat and dropped down into the warm hollow Daddy had made in the pillow.

All weekend long, me and Lou tried to <u>scheme</u> up ways to recapture our wall. Daddy and Mama said they were sick of hearing about it. Grandmama turned up the TV to drown us out. On the late news was a story about the New York subways. When a train came roaring into the station all covered from top to bottom, windows too, with writings and drawings done with spray paint, me and Lou slapped five. Mama said it was too bad kids in New York had nothing better to do than spray paint all over the trains. Daddy said that in the cities, even grown-ups wrote all over the trains and buildings too. Daddy called it "graffiti." Grandmama called it a shame.

We couldn't wait to get out of school on Monday. We couldn't find any black spray

Words to Know and Use

drawl (drôl) *v.* to speak in a slow manner, stretching the vowel sounds
scheme (skēm) *v.* to plot or plan in a secretive way

31

paint anywhere. But in a junky hardware store downtown we found a can of white epoxy[2] paint, the kind you touch up old refrigerators with when they get splotchy and peely. We spent our whole allowance on it. And because it was too late to use our bus passes, we had to walk all the way home lugging our book satchels and gym shoes, and the bag with the epoxy.

predict What are the kids planning to do?

When we reached the corner of Taliaferro and Fifth, it looked like a block party or something. Half the neighborhood was gathered on the sidewalk in front of the wall. I looked at Lou, he looked at me. We both looked at the bag with the epoxy and wondered how we were going to work our scheme. The painter lady's car was nowhere in sight. But there were too many people standing around to do anything. Side Pocket and his buddies were leaning on their cue sticks, hunching each other. Daddy was there with a lineman[3] he catches a ride with on Mondays. Mrs. Morris had her arms flung around the shoulders of the twins on either side of her. Mama was talking with some of her customers, many of them with napkins still at the throat. Mr. Eubanks came out of the barbershop, followed by a man in a striped poncho, half his face shaved, the other half full of foam.

"She really did it, didn't she?" Mr. Eubanks huffed out his chest. Lots of folks answered right quick that she surely did when they saw the straight razor in his hand.

Mama beckoned us over. And then we saw it. The wall. Reds, greens, figures outlined in black. Swirls of purple and orange. Storms of blues and yellows. It was something. I recognized some of the faces right off. There was Martin Luther King, Jr. And there was a man with glasses on and his mouth open like he was laying down a heavy rap. Daddy came up alongside and reminded us that that was Minister Malcolm X. The serious woman with a rifle I knew was Harriet Tubman because my grandmama has pictures of her all over the house. And I knew Mrs. Fannie Lou Hamer 'cause a signed photograph of her hangs in the restaurant next to the calendar.

Then I let my eyes follow what looked like a vine. It trailed past a man with a horn, a woman with a big white flower in her hair, a handsome dude in a tuxedo seated at a piano, and a man with a goatee holding a book. When I looked more closely, I realized that what had looked like flowers were really faces. One face with yellow petals looked just like Frieda Morris. One with red petals looked just like Hattie Morris. I could hardly believe my eyes.

"Notice," Side Pocket said, stepping close to the wall with his cue stick like a classroom pointer. "These are the flags of liberation," he said in a voice I'd never heard him use before. We all stepped closer while he pointed and spoke. "Red, black, and green," he said, his pointer falling on the leaflike

---

2. epoxy (i päk′ sē): a substance used to make glue or a tough lacquer.

3. lineman: a person who sets up and maintains telephone or electric power lines.

Words to Know and Use | **beckon** (bek′ ′n) *v.* to summon or call someone, usually by a gesture or nod
liberation (lib ər ā′ shən) *n.* the state of freedom reached after a struggle

flags of the vine. "Our liberation flag. And here Ghana, there Tanzania. Guinea-Bissau, Angola, Mozambique." Side Pocket sounded very tall, as though he'd been waiting all his life to give this lesson.

Mama tapped us on the shoulder and pointed to a high section of the wall. There was a fierce-looking man with his arms crossed against his chest guarding a bunch of children. His muscles bulged, and he looked a lot like my daddy. One kid was looking at a row of books. Lou hunched me 'cause the kid looked like me. The one that looked like Lou was spinning a globe on the tip of his finger like a basketball. There were other kids there with microscopes and compasses. And the more I looked, the more it looked like the fierce man was not so much guarding the kids as defending their right to do what they were doing.

Then Lou gasped and dropped the paint bag and ran forward, running his hands over a rainbow. He had to tiptoe and stretch to do it, it was so high. I couldn't breathe either. The painter lady had found the chisel marks and had painted Jimmy Lyons's name in a rainbow.

"Read the <u>inscription</u>, honey," Mrs. Morris said, urging little Frieda forward. She didn't have to urge much. Frieda marched right up, bent down, and in a loud voice that made everybody quit oohing and ahhing and listen, she read,

> *To the People of Taliaferro Street*
> *I Dedicate This Wall of Respect*
> *Painted in Memory of My Cousin*
> *Jimmy Lyons*

I N S I G H T

in the inner city
LUCILLE CLIFTON

in the inner city
or
like we call it
home
we think a lot about uptown
and the silent nights
and the houses straight as
dead men
and the pastel lights
and we hang on to our no place
happy to be alive
and in the inner city
or
like we call it
home

Words to Know and Use | **inscription** (in skrip' shən) *n.* a brief message permanently marked or engraved on a surface

33

Responding to Reading

First Impressions

1. Did your impressions of the painter change during the course of the story? In your journal or notebook, briefly describe your reactions.

Second Thoughts

2. Do you think the narrator was right to be upset with the painter when she first appeared? Why or why not?

3. An army of only two tries to wage war against the painter lady. Why do you think other family members or neighbors don't join the battle?

4. What do you think the artist accomplished by painting the mural?

   Think about
   - the people and faces on the wall
   - what the "wall of respect" means to the neighborhood
   - the impact that the wall has on various characters

Broader Connections

5. If an artist painted a mural in your neighborhood, which heroes do you think your neighbors would want represented? Why?

Literary Concepts: Plot and Setting

Plot is what happens in a story. You can think of the plot as a sequence of related actions. The actions center on a conflict—a problem or situation faced by the main character. The conflict builds up during the story. At the end, the conflict is usually settled. What is the main conflict of this story? How is the conflict settled?

Setting consists of the time and place of a story. Could this story occur in a rural rather than urban setting? Explain your opinion.

Writing Options

1. Put yourself in the shoes of the narrator and Lou. Write a **letter** they might send to the artist after seeing her work.

2. Think about the ways that the narrator and the narrator's mother respond to the painter. Make a list that shows the differences between their responses. Then make another list that shows similarities. Use your lists to write a **comparison** of their reactions.

3. Write an **explanation** that tells why you think the narrator of "The War of the Wall" would agree with the feelings expressed in the poem "in the inner city."

4. Think about the place in your neighborhood that seems to belong to the young people who live there—the one you wrote about earlier. Now write a **personal narrative** that illustrates the things that make this place special.

Vocabulary Practice

Exercise Some words seem to fit certain subjects or situations. For instance, you would expect to find the word *exercise* in a book about healthy living. Read each book title below. Choose a word from the list that you would expect to find in that book. Write the number and the word on your paper.

1. *The Speech Patterns of Slow Talkers*
2. *The True Story of a Million-Dollar Bank Robbery*
3. *Ways of Welcoming: A Study of Gestures and Their Meanings*
4. *Memoirs of a Former Slave*
5. *History Recorded on Tombstones*

Words to Know and Use

**beckon
drawl
inscription
liberation
scheme**

Options for Learning

1 • **Art Detective** Research public murals and mural artists from the past and present. Look under "murals" in an encyclopedia or "mural decoration" in the *Readers' Guide to Periodical Literature.* Share your findings with your class.

2 • **A Toast to Heroes** Read about one of the heroes of the wall: Martin Luther King, Jr., Malcolm X, Harriet Tubman, or Fannie Lou Hamer. Prepare and deliver a speech about that person's life.

3 • **Mural Maker** On a large sheet of paper or cardboard, paint or draw your own version of a mural. Like the mural in the story, your creation should reflect the people and heroes of your own neighborhood.

4 • **Dialect Dictionary** Create a dictionary of the words and expressions that are popular among students in your school. Illustrate some of the terms.

 FACT FINDER SOCIAL STUDIES

When was the Vietnam Veterans Memorial in Washington, D.C., dedicated?

Toni Cade Bambara
1939 –

Toni Cade Bambara has written numerous short stories, collected in *Gorilla, My Love* and *The Sea Birds Are Still Alive.* She is also a screenwriter and a novelist, having won an American Book Award for *The Salt Eaters.* She believes that writers "are everyday people who write stories that come out of their neighborhoods." "The War of the Wall" is inspired by her own memories. As a child, she and her companions created a park in a vacant city lot. One day they found a large advertisement there. "We were incensed," she recalls. "We went to city hall and got the billboard removed."

She has also worked in a welfare department, planned recreation for mentally ill patients, held community action workshops, and taught at a college. In recent years she has produced documentaries and videos for organizations that help needy people. One of her works, "The Bombing of Osage Avenue," won several awards. Bambara was born in New York City, has lived in Atlanta, and currently resides in Philadelphia.

Fiction

*H*earts and *H*ands

O. HENRY

*E*xamine *What You Know*

How much do you judge people by their appearance? How closely does a person's appearance reflect his or her personality? Share your ideas with your classmates.

*E*xpand *Your Knowledge*

In the late 1800s, the train was an important means of travel. Due to its speed and power, it won the affection of many Americans. It provided fast and comfortable transportation, and it often proved to be an interesting place to meet people from all walks of life. The odd mix of passengers often resulted in wealthy ladies in their finery sitting next to rough-looking characters who might even spit in the aisles.

*E*nrich *Your Reading*

Inferences   An inference is a logical guess based on the information that is known. For example, if you saw a man who was shabbily dressed, you might infer that he was poor. When reading this story, draw inferences about the three main characters. Base your judgment on how they appear and act. While you read, fill out a chart like the one started below. After finishing the selection, change each inference that you no longer agree with.

■ *Author biography in Reader's Handbook*

Character	Appearance	Inference
young woman	"dressed in elegance"	she's wealthy
Mr. Easton	a "bold" manner	he's confident
other man	"glum-faced"	he's unhappy

Hearts and Hands

O. HENRY

At Denver there was an influx of passengers into the coaches on the eastbound B. & M. express. In one coach there sat a very pretty young woman dressed in elegant taste and surrounded by all the luxurious comforts of an experienced traveler. Among the newcomers were two young men, one of handsome presence with a bold, frank countenance and manner; the other a ruffled, glum-faced person, heavily built and roughly dressed. The two were handcuffed together.

As they passed down the aisle of the coach the only vacant seat offered was a reversed one facing the attractive young woman. Here the linked couple seated themselves. The young woman's glance fell upon them with a distant, swift disinterest; then with a lovely smile brightening her countenance and a tender pink tingeing her rounded cheeks, she held out a little gray-gloved hand. When she spoke her voice, full, sweet, and deliberate, proclaimed that its owner was accustomed to speak and be heard.

"Well, Mr. Easton, if you *will* make me speak first, I suppose I must. Don't you ever recognize old friends when you meet them in the West?"

The younger man roused himself sharply at the sound of her voice, seemed to struggle with a slight embarrassment which he threw off instantly, and then clasped her fingers with his left hand.

"It's Miss Fairchild," he said, with a smile. "I'll ask you to excuse the other hand; it's otherwise engaged just at present."

He slightly raised his right hand, bound at the wrist by the shining "bracelet" to the left one of his companion. The glad look in the girl's eyes slowly changed to a bewildered horror. The glow faded from her cheeks. Her lips parted in a vague, relaxing distress. Easton, with a little laugh, as if amused, was about to speak again when the other forestalled him. The glum-faced man had been watching the girl's countenance with veiled glances from his keen, shrewd eyes.

"You'll excuse me for speaking, miss, but I see you're acquainted with the marshal here. If you'll ask him to speak a word for me when we get to the pen he'll do it, and it'll make things easier for me there. He's taking me to Leavenworth prison. It's seven years for counterfeiting."

"Oh!" said the girl, with a deep breath and returning color. "So that is what you are doing out here? A marshal!"

TRAIN INTERIOR   E. Boyd Smith   Collection of Oliver Jensen.

"My dear Miss Fairchild," said Easton, calmly, "I had to do something. Money has a way of taking wings unto itself, and you know it takes money to keep step with our crowd in Washington. I saw this opening in the West, and—well, a marshalship isn't quite as high a position as that of ambassador, but—"

"The ambassador," said the girl, warmly, "doesn't call anymore. He needn't ever have done so. You ought to know that. And so now you are one of these dashing Western heroes, and you ride and shoot and go into all kinds of dangers. That's different from the Washington life. You have been missed from the old crowd."

The girl's eyes, fascinated, went back, widening a little, to rest upon the glittering handcuffs.

"Don't you worry about them, miss," said the other man. "All marshals handcuff themselves to their prisoners to keep them from getting away. Mr. Easton knows his business."

"Will we see you again soon in Washington?" asked the girl.

"Not soon, I think," said Easton. "My butterfly days are over, I fear."

"I love the West," said the girl irrelevantly. Her eyes were shining softly. She looked away out the car window. She began to speak truly and simply, without the gloss of style and manner: "Mamma and I spent the summer in Denver. She went home a week ago because father was slightly ill. I could live and be happy in the West. I think the air here agrees with me. Money isn't everything. But people always misunderstand things and remain stupid—"

"Say, Mr. Marshal," growled the glum-faced man. "This isn't quite fair. I'm needin' a drink, and haven't had a smoke all day. Haven't you talked long enough? Take me in the smoker now, won't you? I'm half dead for a pipe."

The bound travelers rose to their feet, Easton with the same slow smile on his face.

"I can't deny a petition for tobacco," he said lightly. "It's the one friend of the unfortunate. Goodbye, Miss Fairchild. Duty calls, you know." He held out his hand for a farewell.

"It's too bad you are not going East," she said, reclothing herself with manner and style. "But you must go on to Leavenworth, I suppose?"

"Yes," said Easton, "I must go on to Leavenworth."

The two men sidled down the aisle into the smoker.

The two passengers in a seat nearby had heard most of the conversation. Said one of them: "That marshal's a good sort of chap. Some of these Western fellows are all right."

"Pretty young to hold an office like that, isn't he?" asked the other.

"Young!" exclaimed the first speaker, "why—Oh! didn't you catch on? Say—did you ever know an officer to handcuff a prisoner to his *right* hand?" ❧

Responding to Reading

First Impressions

1. What was your reaction to the ending of this story? Jot down a word or phrase to describe your response.

Second Thoughts

2. Review the inferences that you made about the characters. How did these inferences set the scene for the surprise ending?

   Think about
   • the appearance of Miss Fairchild and the men
   • what all three characters do and say

3. Based on what happens in the story, what can you infer about the personalities of Miss Fairchild and the two men?

4. A white lie is a lie about an unimportant matter, often told to spare someone's feelings. How does that term apply to the actions of the marshal and Mr. Easton? Why?

Literary Concept: Surprise Ending

A **surprise ending** is an unexpected twist in the plot at the end of a story. Most readers are surprised by the ending of "Hearts and Hands" because they have wrongly inferred that Mr. Easton is the marshal. However, there are clues earlier in the story that suggest the truth. Working with a partner, make a list of clues about the real identity of Mr. Easton.

Concept Review: Characterization Which method of characterization listed on page 23 does O. Henry use most in this story?

Writing Options

1. Give the marshal's account of what happened on the train. Write a **dialogue** to show how he tells his wife or his superior his version of the events.

2. Write two **descriptions** of Mr. Easton. One should be from Miss Fairchild's viewpoint. The other should be from the viewpoint of the passenger who speaks at the story's end.

Elements of
NONFICTION

While some readers enjoy getting lost in the imaginary world of fiction, others prefer the authenticity of stories from real life. **Nonfiction** is writing about real people, places, and events.

There are two broad categories of nonfiction. One category, called **informative nonfiction,** is mainly written to provide factual information. Nonfiction of this type includes science and history texts, informational books, encyclopedias, pamphlets, and most of the articles in magazines and newspapers.

The other category of nonfiction is called **literary nonfiction** because it is written to be read and experienced in much the same way you experience fiction. However, literary nonfiction differs from fiction in that real people take the place of fictional characters, and the settings and plots are not imagined but are actual places and true events.

The following are the types of literary nonfiction you will read in this book.

Understanding Nonfiction

Autobiography   An **autobiography** is the true story of a person's life, told by that person. It is almost always written using the first-person point of view. In this book you will read excerpts from several autobiographies. In each, the author focuses on a significant event in his or her life.

An autobiography is usually book length because it covers a long period of the writer's life. However, there are shorter types of autobiographical writing such as **journals, diaries,** and **memoirs.**

Biography   A **biography** is the true story of a person's life told by someone else. The writer, or **biographer,** interviews the subject if possible and also researches the person's life by reading letters, books, diaries, and any other information he or she can find. A short biography of Eleanor Roosevelt is included in this book.

As you will see, biographies and autobiographies often seem like fiction because they contain many of the same elements such as character, setting, and plot.

Essay   An **essay** is a short piece of nonfiction writing that deals with one subject. Essays are often found in newspapers and magazines. The writer might share an opinion, try to entertain or persuade the reader, or simply describe an incident that has special significance. These essays that explain how the author feels about a subject are called **informal,** or **personal,** essays. In this book, the selection "Homeless" is an example of an informal essay. **Formal essays** are serious and scholarly and are rarely found in literature textbooks.

Strategies for Reading Nonfiction

Nonfiction can be read as a piece of literature or as a source of information. The nonfiction you will read in this book has been included because of the interesting story it has to tell—because of its literary quality.

Use the following strategies when you read nonfiction.

1. **Preview** a selection before you read. Look at the title, pictures, diagrams, subtitles, and any terms in boldfaced print or italics. All of these will give you an idea of what the selection is about.

2. **Figure out the organization.** If the work is a biography or autobiography, the organization is probably chronological, that is, in the order that events happened. Other articles may be arranged around ideas the author wants to discuss. Understanding the organization can help you predict what to expect next.

3. **Separate facts and opinions.** Facts are statements that can be proved, such as "There are several autobiographies in this book." **Opinions** are statements that cannot be proved. They simply express the writer's beliefs, such as "*Boy* is the best autobiography in this book." Writers of nonfiction sometimes present opinions as if they were facts. Be sure you recognize the difference.

4. **Question** as you read. Why did things happen the way they did? How did people feel? What is the writer's opinion? Do you share the writer's opinion, or do you have different ideas on the subject?

5. During your reading, stop now and then and try to **predict** what will come next. Sometimes you will be surprised by what happens or by what the author has to say about an issue.

6. As you read, **build** on your understanding. Add new information to what you have already learned and see if your ideas and opinions change.

7. Continually **evaluate** what you read. Evaluation should be an ongoing process, not just something that is done when you have finished reading. Remember that evaluation means more than saying a selection is good or bad. Form opinions about people, events, and ideas that are presented. Decide whether or not you like the way the piece was written.

Finally, it is important to recognize that your understanding of a selection does not end when you stop reading. As you think more about what you have read and discuss it with others, you will find that your understanding continues to grow.

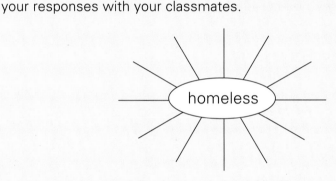

Nonfiction

Homeless

ANNA QUINDLEN

Examine What You Know

What are your impressions of the homeless people you have seen on the street or
on television? Draw a word web on a sheet
of paper, as shown below. On the spokes around the word *homeless,*
write the words that describe your impressions. Then share
your responses with your classmates.

homeless

Expand Your Knowledge

Every night in cities across the country, thousands of homeless
people sleep on sidewalks, in bus stations, in cardboard boxes, or in
other temporary shelters. In the last ten years, the number of homeless people has increased dramatically. Estimates of our nation's
homeless population range from a quarter of a million to three million.

People are homeless for a number of reasons. Many simply cannot
find low-cost housing. Others have lost their jobs, are mentally ill, or
are victims of abuse. The woman featured in this article lived in the
Port Authority Bus Terminal in New York City, a "home" for hundreds.

Enrich Your Reading

Author's Purpose   Authors write for many reasons: to entertain,
to explain or inform, to express an opinion, or to persuade the reader
to do or believe something. As you read this selection, think about
Quindlen's purpose for writing. What might she want to accomplish
by writing this essay? Do you think she has more than one goal?

■ *Author biography
in Reader's
Handbook*

Homeless

ANNA QUINDLEN

Her name was Ann, and we met in the Port Authority Bus Terminal several Januarys ago. I was doing a story on homeless people. She said I was wasting my time talking to her; she was just passing through, although she'd been passing through for more than two weeks. To prove to me that this was true, she rummaged through a tote bag and a manila envelope and finally unfolded a sheet of typing paper and brought out her photographs.

They were not pictures of family, or friends, or even a dog or cat, its eyes brown-red in the flashbulb's light. They were pictures of a house. It was like a thousand houses in a hundred towns, not suburb, not city, but somewhere in between, with aluminum siding and a chain-link fence, a narrow driveway running up to a one-car garage, and a patch of backyard. The house was yellow. I looked on the back for a date or a name, but neither was there. There was no need for discussion. I knew what she was trying to tell me, for it was something I had often felt. She was not adrift, alone, anonymous, although her bags and her raincoat with the grime shadowing its creases had made me believe she was. She had a house, or at least once upon a time had had one. Inside were curtains, a couch, a stove, potholders. You are where you live. She was somebody.

I've never been very good at looking at the big picture, taking the global view, and I've always been a person with an overactive sense of place, the legacy of an Irish grandfather. So it is natural that the thing that seems most wrong with the world to me right now is that there are so many people with no homes. I'm not simply talking about shelter from the elements, or three square meals a day, or a mailing address to which the welfare people can send the check—although I know that all these are important for survival. I'm talking about a home, about precisely those kinds of feelings that have wound up in cross-stitch and French knots on samplers[1] over the years.

Home is where the heart is. There's no place like it. I love my home with a ferocity totally out of proportion to its appearance or location. I love dumb things about it: the hot-water heater, the plastic rack you drain dishes in, the roof over my head, which occasionally leaks. And yet it is precisely those dumb things that make it what it is—a place of certainty, stability, predictability, privacy, for me and for my family. It is where I live. What more can you say about a place than that? That is everything.

Yet it is something that we have been

---

1. **cross-stitch and French knots on samplers:** two kinds of fancy stitches on hand-embroidered cloths.

SHADOW © Maureen Fennelli.

edging away from gradually during my life-time and the lifetimes of my parents and grandparents. There was a time when where you lived often was where you worked and where you grew the food you ate and even where you were buried. When that era passed, where you lived at least was where your parents had lived and where you would live with your children when you became enfeebled. Then, suddenly, where you lived was where you lived for three years, until you could move on to something else and something else again.

And so we have come to something else again, to children who do not understand what it means to go to their rooms because they have never had a room, to men and women whose fantasy is a wall they can paint a color of their own choosing, to old people reduced to sitting on molded plastic chairs, their skin blue-white in the lights of a bus station, who pull pictures of houses out of their bags. Homes have stopped being homes. Now they are real estate.

People find it curious that those without homes would rather sleep sitting up on benches or huddled in doorways than go to shelters. Certainly some prefer to do so because they are emotionally ill, because they have been locked in before and they are determined not to be locked in again. Others are afraid of the violence and trouble they may find there. But some seem to want something that is not available in shelters, and they will not compromise, not for a cot, or oatmeal, or a shower with special soap that kills the bugs. "One room," a woman with a baby who was sleeping on her sister's floor once told me, "painted blue." That was the crux[2] of it; not size or location, but pride of ownership. Painted blue.

This is a difficult problem, and some wise and compassionate people are working hard at it. But in the main I think we work around it, just as we walk around it when it is lying on the sidewalk or sitting in the bus terminal—the problem, that is. It has been customary to take people's pain and lessen our own participation in it by turning it into an issue, not a collection of human beings. We turn an adjective into a noun: the poor, not poor people; the homeless, not Ann or the man who lives in the box or the woman who sleeps on the subway grate.

Sometimes I think we would be better off if we forgot about the broad strokes and concentrated on the details. Here is a woman without a bureau. There is a man with no mirror, no wall to hang it on. They are not the homeless. They are people who have no homes. No drawer that holds the spoons. No window to look out upon the world. My God. That is everything. ❧

---

2. **crux:** the most important point.

Responding to Reading

First Impressions

1. What is the strongest feeling you had about Ann when you finished this selection? Share your ideas with your class.

Second Thoughts

2. Look back at your word web about homeless people. Does this essay change your impression of the homeless? Why or why not?

3. One of the ways the dictionary defines home is "a dwelling place." Compare Quindlen's thoughts and feelings about home with your own.

4. In your opinion, did Quindlen accomplish her purpose in writing this essay?

   Think about
   • why she focused on only one homeless person
   • why she described her own home and her feelings about it
   • what might have been her purpose for writing

Broader Connections

5. What is being done now to help homeless people like Ann? What other actions do you think should be taken?

Literary Concept: Essay

As you recall, an **essay** is a short nonfiction piece in which a writer gives her or his opinion on one subject. **Informal** or **personal** essays reflect a writer's feelings about a topic. Find places in Quindlen's essay where she expresses her own feelings and opinions about the homeless.

Writing Options

1. Work with a partner to brainstorm about ways students like you can help homeless people. Then write a student newspaper **editorial** that expresses these ideas.

2. Write an **essay** about the space or object in your home that you would miss most if you were homeless. Describe it so others will understand why it is so important to you.

Nonfiction

from Little by Little
A Writer's Education
JEAN LITTLE

Examine What You Know

Everyone has embarrassing moments. They are often hard to forget. Think of an embarrassing moment you've had. Remember what caused your embarrassment and how you felt? In small groups, talk about embarrassing moments and what causes them.

Expand Your Knowledge

As a child, Jean Little frequently faced embarrassment because of her poor eyesight. Not only was she born almost blind, she was also cross-eyed.

Cross-eye is a condition that most commonly occurs in children under the age of four who have poor vision. They sometimes force their pupils close together in an effort to see more clearly. Cross-eye can also be inherited or result from weak eye muscles. Usually the condition can be treated successfully. However, in Jean's case, it was not corrected, and in the fifth grade her eyesight was so poor that she could only make out the *E* at the top of the eye chart. In school she could not even read the words on the board.

Write Before You Read

Think about a time when you went out of your way to avoid being embarrassed. What did you do? In your journal, write about that time. As you read, compare your experience to the author's.

■ *Author biography on Extend page*

from *Little by Little*

A Writer's Education

JEAN LITTLE

I was eating my porridge when Hugh, hurrying too fast, fell down the back stairs. Before Mother could get up, he limped in, sniffling slightly, and displayed a bumped elbow for her inspection. Mother examined it gravely.

"A slight hematoma," she said in a serious voice. "And an <u>abrasion</u> almost invisible to the naked eye. You'll live."

Hugh, who always recovered with the speed of light and who won Mother's admiration with his bravery, chuckled at the impressive words.

"What does that mean?" he asked.

"A little bruise and a scrape I can hardly see."

I <u>glowered</u> at my oatmeal. Why did she have to smile at him like that? He was not so special. I searched my mind for something terrible he had done that I could tell her about.

"Jean, hurry up or you'll be late," Grandma said.

I did not want to go to school. We were going to have another mental arithmetic test, and I still did not know my times tables. If only I could fall down and break my leg . . .

Four-year-old Pat grinned at me.

"Huwwy up, Jean," she parroted. "You'll be late."

I wanted to slap the wide smile off her silly little face. Instead I scooped up a few drops of milk on the tip of my spoon and let fly. The tiny bit of milk splashed her on the nose. I laughed. Before anyone could stop her, Pat grabbed up her mug filled to the brim with milk and sent its entire contents sloshing over me, soaking me to the skin.

The next thing I knew, I was back upstairs changing out of my wet serge dress, cotton petticoat, long brown stockings, and underwear into clean, dry clothes. Not only was this going to make me really late, but Mother handed me the knitted suit Aunt Gretta had made for my tenth birthday. The ribbed blue skirt was sewn onto a sleeveless cotton vest. Over it went a horizontally striped blue and pink sweater with short sleeves. Nobody else in Miss Marr's class had a homemade knitted suit anything like it.

"I can't wear it," I said in <u>anguished</u> tones.

"It's lovely," my mother said calmly. "Gretta worked hard to make it for you.

Words to Know and Use

abrasion (ə brā′ zhən) *n.* a scrape on the skin
glower (glou′ ər) *v.* to stare in an angry way; scowl
anguished (aŋ′ gwisht) *adj.* filled with pain, mental or physical; extremely upset
  anguish *v.*

LE PETIT DEJEUNER 1986
Jennifer Hornyak
Courtesy, Gallery Claude Lafitte,
Montreal, Canada.

Don't be ridiculous. Of course you will wear it."

In ten minutes I was gobbling toast and honey, gulping down milk, and hating my cheerful little sister who was the cause of all the trouble and who got to stay home and be spoiled by everybody.

When I reached the street, it was <u>ominously</u> quiet. I really was going to be late, and it was all Pat's fault. I ran the first three blocks, but slowed down when I got a stitch[1] in my side. There was still not a single child in sight.

As I passed St. John's School, I could hear the grade four class singing "God Save the King." I sent the small building a look of longing. Mr. Johnston had not had these horrid mental arithmetic tests.

Then I stood stock still. When I got to school, Miss Marr would tell me to put my name on the board to stay after four. I didn't mind staying late—lots of the others got <u>detentions</u>—I wasn't sure what to write, though I had a strong suspicion that you did not write out your whole name. Did you just write your initials? Or one initial and your surname? Or your first name and your last initial?

I had to get it right. The others still called me names when no teacher was near enough to hear. The only game I had ever been invited to play was Crack the Whip, and they always made me go on the end. Then, when the big girl at the front swung

---

1. **stitch:** a sharp, sudden pain.

Words
to Know
and Use

ominously (ăm′ ə nəs lē) *adv.* in a threatening or evil way
detention (di ten′ shən) *n.* punishment of being held against one's will, as in having to stay after school

everybody around in a long *Crack!*, I ended up flying through the air and landing with a jarring crash on my hands and knees. As I picked myself up, I'd try to look as though I thought crash landings were fun. Nobody was fooled.

If I wrote my name up there differently than the others did, they would have a new thing to tease me about. I could hear the jeering voices already.

"You're not just cross-eyed, you're so *dumb* you don't even know how to write your name on the board!"

I stood there, thinking hard. How could I save myself? Once in a while, when a child brought a note from home, he got out of putting his name on the board. Well, my mother would not write me a note.

I had to invent the most convincing lie of my life.

Perhaps, if your parents were not at home, and some emergency cropped up and you had to deal with it, Miss Marr just might let you sit down without asking for a note. It would have to be a desperate emergency . . .

I began to walk again, taking my time. I had to invent the most convincing lie of my life. Bit by bit, I worked it out. As I imagined how it must have happened, it grew so real that I began to believe it myself. I had every detail ready as I turned the last corner. Then I began to run.

I knew it was essential that I be out of

breath when I arrived.

I dashed up the stairs, puffing hard. I opened the door, said a private prayer for help, and entered the grade five classroom. Miss Marr was at her desk. Out of the corner of my eye, I could see monitors collecting the test papers. So far so good.

"Jean," said my teacher, "you're late."

"Yes," I panted, facing her and opening my eyes wide so that I would look innocent and pitiful. "I know. I couldn't help it."

"Why are you late?" she asked.

I took a deep breath.

"Well, I was all ready in plenty of time. But just as I was going out the door, the telephone rang. I knew I should not go back to answer it, but you know my mother and father are both doctors, and I was afraid it might be an emergency."

Miss Marr opened her mouth to ask a question, but I rushed on, not giving her time to get a word in edgewise.

"The trouble was, you see, that nobody was home but me. So I took the receiver off the hook and I said, 'Dr. Littles' residence.'"

Everybody was listening now, even the boys who never paid attention. I kept going.

"MY DAUGHTER IS DYING! MY DAUGHTER IS DYING!"

I saw my teacher jump as I shrieked the words at the top of my lungs. Her eyes were wide with shock. The class gasped. I did not stop for effect. I could not give the teacher time to interrupt.

"It was a man's voice. He sounded frantic with worry. 'I'm sorry,' I told him, 'my par-

Words to Know and Use | **jeering** (jir′ iŋ) *adj.* mocking; rude, taunting **jeer** *v.*

ents are out. If you call back, they should be home in one hour.' 'No! Please, don't hang up,' he begged. 'You must come and save her life. If I wait for your parents, she will surely die.' 'Well, I guess if she is dying, I'd better come. Where do you live?' I asked him. '111 King Street,' he told me."

Miss Marr did not even try to ask a question as I paused to catch my breath. The entire class was sitting spellbound. The silence was absolute. Not a desk seat squeaked. Not a giggle broke the hush.

"I hurried in and got the right medicine from the office, and then I ran out the door. I didn't go the long way around by the Norwich Street bridge. I was afraid it would take too long. I went down London Road and across some stepping stones down there. When I got to King Street, there was the house. It was a log cabin with wind whistling through the cracks. And as I came up to it, I saw the door was standing open and there were a bunch of people in the doorway and they were all crying. 'What's wrong?' I asked them. 'You are too late,' they sobbed. 'She's dead already.' "

This time, as I snatched a breath, Miss Marr choked back a small sound. She made no attempt to stem the flood of my story. I pressed on.

" 'Oh, I am so sorry,' I told them. 'Take me to see her.' So they took me into the cabin, and there lay the girl on a trundle bed.[2] Her face was blue, and her eyes had rolled up till you could just see white, and her teeth were clenched. And her fingers and toes all curled over backwards."

I watched Miss Marr carefully at this point, because I was not absolutely sure what a dead person looked like. The last bit worried me especially. I had heard someone say that when people died, they turned their toes up. That could only mean that their toes curled over backwards, but I was not sure about the fingers.

Miss Marr's face quivered a little and her mouth twitched, but she did not speak. I hurried, eager to finish. It would be a relief to sit down. Even so, in spite of myself, I kept putting in extra bits as they occurred to me.

She's just on the point of death. I think I can save her.

" 'She's not quite dead,' I cried. 'She's just on the point of death. I think I can save her.' I hit her chin and her mouth opened. I poured in the medicine. She fluttered her lashes and turned a normal color and said weakly, 'Where am I?' I turned and hurried toward the door. But before I could escape, all the weeping people went down on their knees and grabbed hold of my skirt and they said, 'You saved her life! We want to give you a reward. Gold, silver, a bag of emeralds, a horse that will come when you whistle . . . tell us the one thing you want

---

2. **trundle bed:** a low bed on wheels that is stored under a larger bed when not needed.

Words to Know and Use | **spellbound** (spel' bound') *adj.* as if in a trance; fascinated
quiver (kwiv' ər) *v.* to tremble or shake

more than anything else in the world and you can have it.' "

I paused for effect this time. I knew no one would break the hush. I wanted my teacher to take in the next bit.

" 'The one thing I want more than anything else in the world,' I told them, 'is to be on time for school.' So they let me go, and I ran down the hill and across the stepping stones. When I got to the third last stone, though, I slipped and fell in the river and cut my knee. I had to get to shore, go home and bandage my knee and put on dry clothes. Then I hurried here as fast as I could. And that is why I am late."

There was a stunned silence in the classroom. Miss Marr and I stared at each other for a long, long minute. I waited for her to tell me to write my name on the board. Instead she pointed her finger at my desk. Speaking extremely slowly and wearily, she said, "Take . . . your . . . seat. Just . . . take . . . your . . . seat."

I tried to keep a solemn expression on my face. But it was hard not to grin. I sat down and did not turn my head as a buzz of whispers broke out behind me. I had missed the mental arithmetic test. I had not had to write my name on the board. And I had kept every single person <u>transfixed</u> with my exciting story.

At least three blissful minutes went by before I realized I had no cut on my knee and no bandage, either. Not only that, but I could not remember whether I had told her which knee I was supposed to have cut.

She had believed me. I was sure of that. Yet any second she was going to discover

Jean Little as a child.   Courtesy Jean Little.

that I had told her a <u>stupendous</u> lie.

I hooked one knee over the other and clasped my hands around the knee on top. I spent the entire morning that way. When I was required to write, I used only one hand. Miss Marr did not ask me a direct question. When recess time came and she said, "Class, stand," I stayed where I was.

"Jean, aren't you going out for recess?" she asked when the others had marched out and there I still sat.

"Oh, Miss Marr," I said in my smallest, most pathetic voice, "I am so tired from saving that girl's life that I have to stay in and have a rest."

Still clutching my knee with both hands, I

Words to Know and Use | **transfixed** (trans fikst′) *adj.* unable to move because of awe or fear **transfix** *v.*
stupendous (stoo pen′ dəs) *adj.* huge; tremendous

laid my head down on my desk and shut my eyes.

She did not say a word.

At noon, when she had her back turned, I ran out of the classroom, dashed home, sneaked bandaids from my parents' office and plastered them over both knees, to be on the safe side. When I returned to school, Miss Marr smiled and did not ask why both my knees were bandaged.

I sat through the afternoon thinking over what had happened. Did she really guess? The other kids did not seem to have figured out that I had lied. One girl had even smiled at me, as though she might be my friend. Nobody in my class had called me cross-eyed. A boy in grade seven had, though. If only I could shut him up the way I had hushed everybody that morning.

Then I remembered Hugh's knee. That night I asked Mother, "What are the long words for what's wrong with my eyes?"

I was standing beside her chair. She looked up at me.

"Why?" she asked.

"I want to know, that's all. They call me cross-eyed. I want to know the long words, the ones doctors use."

She rhymed off a whole list.

"Say it again. Slowly."

"Strabismus, nystagmus, corneal opacities, and eccentric pupils."[3]

I practiced.

The next day I was late coming out of school. The same grade-seven boy was waiting for me. He had his first snowball ready.

"Cross-eyed, cross-eyed," he chanted and waited for me to start running so that he could chase me, pelting me with hard-packed snowballs.

I turned on him instead.

"I am not cross-eyed," I said in a strong, clear voice. "I have corneal opacities and eccentric pupils."

I glared at him as I spoke, and my eyes were as crossed as ever. But he was so surprised that he stood there, his mouth gaping open like a fish's.

Then I turned my back and walked away. Perhaps his aim was off because he was so used to firing his missiles at a running target. But the first snowball flew past me harmlessly. The second exploded with a smack against a nearby tree.

I kept walking, chin in the air.

In the last two days, I had learned a lot about the power of words. Snowballs would hit me again, and I would run away and cry. I would be late, and, eventually, I would even have to write my name on the board.

But I had found out what mere words could do. I would not forget. ❧

---

3. **Strabismus** (strə biz′ məs), **nystagmus** (nis tag′ məs), **corneal opacities** (kôr′ nē əl ō pas′ ə tēs), **and eccentric pupils** (ək sen′ trik pyo͞o′ pəlz).

Responding to Reading

First Impressions

1. How did you feel about Jean Little? Jot down your thoughts in your journal or on a piece of paper.

Second Thoughts

2. Little hoped to invent "the most convincing lie" of her life to avoid standing at the board. Do you think she really convinced her classmates and teacher? Explain why or why not.

3. Imagine that you are Little's teacher or her parent. How would you respond to her invented story?

Think about
- how the rest of the class might react if she gets away with her lie
- the pride that she takes in her story

4. Little says that she "found out what mere words could do." Do you agree that words are important? Support your opinion with examples from the story and your own experience.

5. Compare Jean Little's embarrassing situation with the one you wrote about on page 48.

Broader Connections

6. What could have been done at Jean's school to help her deal with her disability? What is being done by your school and your community to help people with physical disabilities? Does more need to be done?

Literary Concept: Autobiography

An **autobiography** is the story of a person's life, written by that person. Even though it is based on real events, an autobiography shares many of the elements of fiction. In what ways is this chapter of Little's autobiography like a short story? How does it differ from a short story?

_W_riting Options

1. Suppose Jean Little moved to the "War of the Wall" neighborhood. How do you think she would be treated? Write a **diary entry** in which she tells about a typical day.

2. Work with a partner or a small group to write a **set of school rules** for treating disabled people respectfully and fairly.

3. What if the principal had listened to Little's invention and Miss Marr's response? Write a **script** of the conversation that the principal and the teacher might have had.

4. Describe an **incident** in your own life in which you experienced the power of words. You may describe a time when words gave you a sense of your own power or a time when words were used against you.

_V_ocabulary Practice

Exercise Write the letter of the word that is least like the other words in the set.

1. (a) jeering   (b) mocking   (c) cheering   (d) hissing
2. (a) fascinated   (b) bored   (c) spellbound   (d) interested
3. (a) worried   (b) calm   (c) upset   (d) anguished
4. (a) smile   (b) glower   (c) scowl   (d) stare
5. (a) great   (b) huge   (c) stupendous   (d) minor
6. (a) quiver   (b) shake   (c) tremble   (d) steady
7. (a) frozen   (b) transfixed   (c) motionless   (d) nervous
8. (a) reward   (b) punishment   (c) penalty   (d) detention
9. (a) threateningly   (b) encouragingly   (c) ominously   (d) evilly
10. (a) cut   (b) abrasion   (c) scrape   (d) paint

_Words
to Know
and Use_

____

**abrasion
anguished
detention
glower
jeering
ominously
quiver
spellbound
stupendous
transfixed**

Options for Learning

1 • **Read the Book** This selection is one chapter from Jean Little's autobiography. Read the rest of her book and share more anecdotes from her life with your class.

2 • **Debate the Question** Is it ever acceptable to tell a lie? Plan a debate with three students on each team. One team will argue the affirmative (yes), the other team the negative (no). Each group should list reasons to support its position and plan a concluding statement. Stage the debate and let the class vote for the winner.

3 • **Sight Technology** Find out what equipment is now available to help blind or nearly blind people lead lives closer to the lives of sighted people. Use your library or contact institutions that deal with the blind. Share your information with the class.

4 • **A Tall Tale** Create another story that Jean might tell to excuse her lateness. Tell your tale to your classmates.

 FACT FINDER SCIENCE

Use a dictionary to explain what a corneal opacity might be.

Jean Little
1932 –

Jean Little was born in Taiwan, where her parents, both doctors, were missionaries. She considers herself "very fortunate" that her parents never treated her as "the handicapped child," despite her eye problems. Her family settled in Guelph, Ontario, when she was in third grade. Continual teasing about her eyes forced her to the public library. "I read, I daydreamed and I lied prodigiously—so I prepared myself for becoming a writer."

Her first book, *Mine for Keeps,* won the Canadian Children's Book Award. Her other popular books include *Spring Begins in March* and *From Anna.* These books portray characters with physical disabilities.

Little's eye problems now prevent her from reading, though she continues to write by using a talking computer. She lives in Guelph with her guide dog. To young writers, she advises, "Read and write a lot. You have a storehouse in your head. If you don't put anything in it, there's nothing to draw on."

WRITER'S WORKSHOP

USE PERSONAL WRITING FOR
journals
logs
notes
letters
diaries
autobiographies

PERSONAL WRITING

Each of us remembers misunderstandings like those experienced by the characters in this subunit. We have all believed a false impression or have purposely or mistakenly created a false impression. In this workshop you will write about such an experience. Like Jean in *Little by Little*, you could write about a false impression you gave of yourself. Or, you can focus on a false impression you had of someone else. A personal experience of this kind is called an **autobiographical incident**. Writing about these experiences can help you understand them. You are sharing a moment in your life with readers—and with yourself.

> Here is one writer's PASSkey to this assignment.

GUIDED ASSIGNMENT: AUTOBIOGRAPHICAL INCIDENT

Write about a time when you either received or gave a false impression. Explain what happened as a result.

PURPOSE: To tell about a personal experience

AUDIENCE: Classmates, friends, family

SUBJECT: A false impression

STRUCTURE: Autobiographical incident

STUDENT MODEL

Before you write, read how one student responded to the assignment.

The pronoun *I* shows that this is personal or **autobiographical** writing.

> ### The Turnaround
> #### by Zachary Hurston
>
> I had to grin when Mike introduced us. "Your name is Eel-ya?" I asked. "Eel-ya?" The new kid's name sounded like a joke. Is he named after an eel, or what, I wondered. It was the first day of sixth grade, and he was sitting right behind me.
> "Ilya," he corrected in a fed-up voice. "It's a Russian name."
> "Oh—are you from Russia?" I was trying to be friendly.
> "No!" he snapped. "I'm American." He sure didn't sound Russian—but he did sound as if he

were talking to a pesky four-year-old. I knew right then that I wasn't going to like this guy. He looked like he didn't think much of me either.

Sure enough, when Ilya, Mike, and I were put in the same science-project group that week, Ilya turned out to be a pain. When Mike and I joked around, Ilya wouldn't even smile. It was like he was all brains and no fun. I wished I didn't have to sit in front of him for the whole year.

Now, finally, I'm in seventh grade. On the first day, I walked to school with my best friend—Ilya Penoff.

What caused the turnaround? For one thing, sometime during sixth grade, Ilya finally broke down and started laughing at my jokes. He admitted later that it had just about killed him to keep a straight face, but he thought I was a brainless clown and didn't want to get me going. For another thing, I started really listening to him. Ilya has a mind like some kind of wild video game, always coming up with new twists. Also I think he found out that I'm not exactly brainless myself. In fact, Mr. Sykes gave Ilya and me A's in science. We were the only two who earned them. My friend Ilya and I did learn a lot about science last year. We also learned a lot about judging people too quickly.

◀ Details about words, voices, and facial expressions help readers to imagine the incident.

◀ The writer uses time order to tell the story.

◀ Details show how the writer's original impressions were proved false.

◀ The writer explains reasons and results.

Now that you've read Zachary's paper, it's time to begin your own.

Prewrite and Explore

1 **Wake up your memory** To find ideas for personal writing, look in personal places. Rummaging is one way to waken memories. Look through family photo albums or watch family videos; check your old diaries, scrapbooks, notebooks, or calendars; swap memories with family members. Focus on times when you got—or gave—the wrong impression.

2 **Choose your topic and gather information**   By yourself or with a friend, sift through your memories. Which incident would be most fun to write about? Which one means the most to you today? Either would make a good topic. After you've chosen a topic, you can start gathering the details that will help you write.

STUDENT MODEL ▶

GATHERING INFORMATION

Try closing your eyes and reliving the incident you've chosen. Take your time. Think about why the incident happened and about the results it had. After you open your eyes, you can fill in an idea chain like the one below, which Zachary used. Jot down as many details as you can remember.

> **False Impression**
> Ilya seemed all brains, no fun.
> Like no one was home in there.
> Seemed like he felt so superior.

> **Reasons**
> When we first met,
>   Ilya treated me like
>   a little kid.
> I tried to be friendly,
>   and he got offended.
> He never laughed at my
>   jokes.

> **Results**
> I hated him at first.
>   Now we're tight.
> We both learned about
>   snap judgments.
> We both got A's!

Draft and Discover

1 **Begin drafting**   You don't have to start at the beginning of your incident. You can start with the part you're most interested in right now. When you run out of steam, your idea chain will remind you of what else to put in.

2 **Use paragraphs to organize**   You might write a paragraph for each main "link" in your idea chain, or you might write a paragraph for each main time segment in your story.

3 **Color your writing with details**   Adding details can turn a pale, washed-out piece of writing into a lively, interesting story. Details can include descriptive phrases, colorful verbs and nouns, and interesting comparisons. Look at this example.

> She was rearing back on her heels, her hands jammed into her back pockets, her face squinched up like the masterpiece she had in mind was taking shape on the wall by magic. We could have been gophers crawled up into a rotten hollow for all she cared.

◀ LITERARY MODEL
. . . .
from "The War of the Wall" by Toni Cade Bambara

Revise Your Writing

1 **Build on your pattern**   When you have finished drafting, notice the pattern your paragraphs make. They may follow **time order,** or they may follow the **cause-and-effect** order of your idea chain. (For cause-and-effect order, you first write about the reasons or causes of something, then you write about the results or effects.) If the order of your draft does not seem clear, you may have to move paragraphs or add information.

COMPUTER TIP
. . . .
On a word processor you can easily move blocks of text. So you can write two or three action beginnings, try each at the front of your draft, and decide which you like best.

2 **Write a strong beginning**   Now that you have a draft, you can write a "grabber" beginning for it. One way is to start with action rather than with explanation. For instance, reread the first part of Gary Soto's "Seventh Grade" on page 18. Notice that the author doesn't explain who Victor is. He just shows Victor moving through the registration line.

3 **Try a peer reader**   You might ask a friend to respond to your draft. The following questions can help.

◀ WRITER'S CHOICE
. . . .
If you don't feel ready to share your writing yet, you can use the For You questions as a guide for rethinking your work.

Revision Questions

For You

1. What's my favorite part of this writing?
2. Could I add details that would make other parts more like my favorite part?
3. Have I shown what this incident meant to me?

For a Peer Reader

1. Which part seemed most interesting to you?
2. Is there anything that confuses you?
3. How would you sum up the incident I wrote about?

Proofread

Check your work for errors in grammar, spelling, punctuation, and capitalization. If possible, ask a friend to check your writing. Pay special attention to personal pronouns.

THE EDITOR'S EYE: PERSONAL PRONOUNS

Use personal pronouns correctly in compound objects.

When you use pronouns as objects, you choose their object forms: *me, you, him, her, it, us,* and *them.* Sometimes you use two pronouns together, or a noun and a pronoun, as compound objects. Then it can be harder to choose the correct form. The object form is still the correct choice.

Problem	Mr. Sykes gave *Ilya and I* A's in science.
Revised	Mr. Sykes gave *Ilya and me* A's in science.
Also Correct	Mr. Sykes gave *him and me* A's in science.

NEED MORE HELP?

See the Language Workshop on pages 63–65 and pages 735–736 of the Language Handbook.

Publish and Present

Here is a suggestion for sharing your work with others.

Mime Show   With two or three friends, recast your autobiographical incidents as pantomimes. Plan how to convey your impressions using only gestures, props, and music. Then perform your pantomimes for the class.

Reflect on Your Writing

Briefly answer the following questions. Put your answers with your paper and add both to your portfolio.

FOR YOUR PORTFOLIO ▶

1. What surprised you as you worked on this assignment?
2. If you had more time to work on this assignment, which part would you change? Why?

LANGUAGE
WORKSHOP

USING PERSONAL PRONOUNS CORRECTLY

> **Personal pronouns** have three forms: subject, object, and possessive.

Personal Pronouns

When you do personal writing, as in an autobiographical incident, you use many personal pronouns. Choosing the correct forms of these pronouns can help to keep your writing clear. You probably remember that a **pronoun** is a word used to take the place of a noun or another pronoun. The pronouns underlined in the excerpt below are personal pronouns.

> Then <u>he</u> saw <u>her</u>. <u>She</u> was sitting with a girlfriend under a plum tree. . . . When the bell sounded, Teresa looked up, and <u>their</u> eyes met. <u>She</u> smiled sweetly and gathered <u>her</u> books.

◀ **LITERARY MODEL**
from "Seventh Grade" by Gary Soto

Each of the personal pronouns has a subject form, an object form, and a possessive form. The form that a personal pronoun takes depends on how the pronoun is used. Study the following chart.

Forms of Personal Pronouns

	Subject	Object	Possessive
Singular	I	me	my, mine
	you	you	your, yours
	she, he, it	her, him, it	her, hers, his, its
Plural	we	us	our, ours
	you	you	your, yours
	they	them	their, theirs

◀ **SPELLING TIP**
Notice that possessive pronouns are spelled without apostrophes: *hers, its, ours, yours, theirs.*

Exercise 1   Concept Check   Copy the personal pronouns that you find in each sentence. Above each, write *S, O,* or *P,* for subject form, object form, or possessive form.

1. Victor notices that his friend looks different.
2. "What did you do to your face?" asks Victor.
3. Victor's friend thinks that girls will like him if he scowls.
4. "See her? She looked at me!" he says. "It really works!"
5. As the boys talk, they watch girls watching them.
6. In their homeroom, Victor sees Teresa reading her novel.
7. He hopes that she will be his girlfriend.
8. To impress her, he pretends to speak French.
9. "If I have trouble with French, will you help me?" Teresa asks.
10. It might just be a great year for us, thinks Victor.

Using the Subject Form

You use the subject form for a personal pronoun that is the subject of a sentence. You also use the subject form for a **predicate pronoun**—a pronoun that follows a linking verb and renames, or refers to, the subject. Study the following examples.

Subject	Predicate Pronoun
<u>She</u> won the race.	The winner was <u>she</u>.
Tory and <u>I</u> visited the school.	The visitors were Tory and <u>I</u>.
Either <u>he</u> or <u>she</u> called.	The caller was either <u>he</u> or <u>she</u>.

Subject and predicate pronouns can be **compound**. One type of compound pronoun consists of two pronouns joined by *and, or,* or *nor.* Another type consists of a noun and a pronoun. In these cases, choosing the correct pronoun form can be confusing. However, as in the second and third examples above, the subject form is correct.

REMINDER

1. Predicate pronouns follow linking verbs such as *am, is, was,* and *were.*
2. Predicate pronouns rename or refer to the subject of the sentence.
3. A sentence with a predicate pronoun will make sense if the subject and the predicate pronoun are reversed.
The winner was *he.*
He was the winner.

Using the Object Form

The examples below show the three uses of object pronouns.

Direct Object	Lou saw <u>her</u>.
Indirect Object	The twins gave <u>her</u> some supper.
Object of Preposition	The children walked toward <u>her</u>.

You use the object form when the pronoun is a **direct object** or an **indirect object**—when the pronoun receives the action of a verb. You also use the object form when the pronoun is the **object of a preposition**—when it is part of a prepositional phrase.

Problems with object pronouns are most likely to occur when the object pronoun is part of a compound. Just remember—if the pronoun is used as an object, you must use the object form.

Direct Object	The painter ignored Lou and <u>me</u>.
Indirect Object	Mama gave <u>him</u> and <u>me</u> the dishes.
Object of Preposition	Daddy heard about <u>her</u> and <u>us</u>.

HELP!
Here's an easy way to choose the right pronoun for a compound. Take out one part of the compound and see how the sentence sounds with only the pronoun.
The teacher smiled at Teresa and (me, I).
The teacher smiled at I. (This sounds wrong, and it is!)
The teacher smiled at me. (This sounds better; it's correct!)

Exercise 2   Concept Check   For each sentence, choose the correct subject or object pronoun.

1. Lou stumbled when I nudged (he, him) in the ribs.
2. The first one to notice the painter lady was (I, me).
3. (She and I, Her and me) were enemies from the start.
4. (We, Us) and the twins stood around watching her work.
5. It was (they, them) who offered her some dinner.
6. I hoped my friends and (I, me) would get some cornbread.
7. Mama and (I, me) agreed that the lady was too fussy about her food.
8. Mama told (Lou and I, Lou and me) to stop criticizing her.
9. It was (we, us) who planned to spray paint the wall.
10. The finished mural amazed (he and I, him and me).

Exercise 3   Looking at Style   Professional writers sometimes use nonstandard pronoun forms. For example, in "The War of the Wall," "me and Lou" is the subject of several sentences.

◀ BREAKING THE RULES

1. Explain why "me and Lou" used as a subject is incorrect.
2. Do you think that the tone or mood of the story would change if it were rewritten with only correct pronoun forms? Why?
3. Why did the writer deliberately misuse pronouns?

Exercise 4   Revising Your Writing   Reread the autobiographical incident you wrote for the Writer's Workshop on pages 58–62, and lightly underline each personal pronoun you used. Correct any errors in the pronoun forms that you find.

LANGUAGE HANDBOOK
For review and practice: Section 5, Using Pronouns, pages 732–736.

READER'S WORKSHOP

INFERENCES

Making **inferences**—logical guesses based on facts—is an important reading skill. You already know how to do this mental detective work. As you were reading each selection, you picked up clues that let you understand what was going on. You made inferences about the setting, how the characters felt, and why they acted as they did.

For example, look at the paragraph below.

LITERARY MODEL
from "Homeless," by
Anna Quindlen

> Her name was Ann, and we met in the Port Authority Bus Terminal several Januarys ago. I was doing a story on homeless people. She said I was wasting my time talking to her; she was just passing through, although she'd been passing through for more than two weeks. To prove to me that this was true, she rummaged through a tote bag and a manila envelope and finally unfolded a sheet of typing paper and brought out her photographs.

From the fact that the narrator was "doing a story on homeless people," you can infer that she is a newspaper or magazine writer. What can you infer about Ann from this paragraph?

IN OTHER CLASSES
In science class, skill at making inferences can help you form reasonable hypotheses based on your experiments or reading.

Exercise   Drawing Inferences   Read the paragraph below. Then use inferences to answer the questions that follow it.

> The night my brother heard the ghost, he and I had gone to bed early. Our bedroom, crammed with Ghost-Slayer toys and posters, was just above the garage. I had read a comic book and dropped off to sleep, but my brother lay awake, excited because the next day was his birthday. Neither of us knew that our parents had bought him a puppy and hidden it in the garage. So, in the middle of the night, when the eerie yowling and the sound of clawing began, my brother immediately assumed the worst.

1. Was the narrator an adult or a child at the time of this incident? On which facts can you base your inference?
2. What can you infer about the cause of the noises? Which clues tell you this?
3. What can you infer about what the brother thought? What evidence supports your inference?

Tunnel Vision

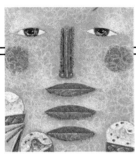

In medical terms, *tunnel vision* is a condition that limits what a person can see. People with this condition can only see what is directly in front of them—as if they were looking through a tube or a straw.

Sometimes, however, people act as if they have tunnel vision when their eyesight is perfectly normal. They seem to see the world from a very narrow point of view.

This kind of tunnel vision can be positive or negative—it can keep people focused on their goals, but it might also keep them from seeing something important that is right under their nose! In this subunit, you will discover many characters who have tunnel vision and you will decide whether it works for them or against them.

Fiction

Lose Now, Pay Later

CAROL FARLEY

Examine What You Know

Is there any one food that you simply cannot resist? For example, if a steaming hot pizza were put in front of you right now, could you turn away from it—even if you were on a diet? Think of your favorite foods and list them in your journal. Circle those that might cause you to lose your self-control.

Expand Your Knowledge

Dieting is one of our society's greatest passions. At any given time, more than 20 million people in the United States are on a diet. In 1992, the amount of money spent on diet products and weight loss programs in the United States was about 36 billion dollars. Although Americans lose millions of pounds every year, only two to five percent of dieters do not regain the weight they lost. Most dieters try to lose weight rapidly, usually resulting in only a temporary victory.

Enrich Your Reading

Predicting   Reading a story is more fun when you try to figure out what will happen next. For example, what do you think a story called "Lose Now, Pay Later" might be about? Use the title, pictures, and large blue quotes to make an educated guess. Then as you read the story, predict what the characters will do next. To make a prediction, think about what you've learned about the characters. Look for clues along the way. After you make your predictions, read on to see what actually happens.

■ *Author biography on Extend page*

Lose Now, Pay Later

CAROL FARLEY

I think my little brother is crazy. At least I hope he is. Because if his looney idea is right, then all of us are being used like a flock of sheep, and that's a pretty gruesome thought. Humans just can't be that stupid. My brother has a dumb idea, that's all. It's just a dumb idea.

This whole situation started about eight months ago. That's when I first knew anything about it, I mean. My best friend, Trinja, and I were shopping when we noticed a new store where an old insurance office used to be. It was a cubbyhole, really, at the far end of the mall where hardly anybody ever goes. We were there because we'd used that entrance as we came home from school.

"Swoodies!" Trinja said, pointing at the letters written across the display window. "What do you think they are, Deb?"

I stared through the glass. The place had always looked dim and dingy before, full of desks, half-dead plants, and bored-looking people; but now it was as bright and glaring as a Health Brigade Corp office. There weren't any people inside at all, but there were five or six gold-colored machines lining the walls. Signs were hung everywhere.

SWEETS PLUS GOODIES = SWOODIES, one said. Flavors were posted by each machine; peanut-butter-fudge-crunch . . . butter-rum-pecan . . . chocolate-nut-mint . . . Things like that. The biggest sign of all simply said FREE.

The place gave me the creeps . . .

I have to admit that the place gave me the creeps that first time I saw it. I don't know why. It just looked so bare and bright, so empty and clean, without any people or movement. The glare almost hurt my eyes. And I guess I was suspicious about anything that was completely free. Still, though, there was a terrific aroma drifting out of there—sort of a combination of all those flavors that were listed on the signs.

"Let's go in," Trinja said, grabbing my arm. I could see that the smell was getting to her too. She's always on a diet, so she thinks about food a lot.

"But it's so empty in there," I said, drawing away.

"They've just opened, that's all," she told me, yanking my arm again. "Besides, machines and robots run lots of the stores. Let's go inside and see what's in there."

Words to Know and Use

dingy (din' jē) *adj.* somewhat dark and unclean; shabby

69

SOFT FUR GOOD HUMOR 1963
Claes Oldenburg Courtesy,
BlumHelman Gallery, New York.

It was absolutely the neatest sensation I've had in my whole life. Swoodies aren't cold like ice cream or warm like cooked pudding, but they're a blending of both in temperature and texture. The flavor melts instantly, and your whole mouth and brain are flooded with tastes and impressions. Like that first swoodie I tried, coconut-almond-marshmallow; suddenly, as my mouth separated the individual tastes, my brain burst into memories associated with each flavor. I felt as if I were lying on a warm beach, all covered with coconut suntan oil—then I heard myself giggling and singing as a group of us roasted marshmallows around a campfire—then I relived the long-ago moments of biting into the special Christmas cookies my grandmother made with almonds when I was little.

"Wow!" Trinja looked at me, and I could see that she had just experienced the same kind of reactions. We scarfed up the rest of that swoodie in just a few more bites, and we moved on to another flavor. With each

Do you know that wonderful spurt of air that rushes out when you first open an expensive box of candy? The inside of that store smelled just like the inside of one of those boxes. For a few seconds we just stood there sniffing and grinning. My salivary glands started swimming.

Trinja turned toward the nearest machine. "Coconut-almond-marshmallow." She was almost drooling. "I've got to try one, Deb." She pressed the button, and a chocolate cone dropped down, like a coffee cup from a kitcho machine. Then a mixture, similar to the look of soft ice cream, filled it. "Want to try it with me?" she asked, reaching for the cone. We both took a taste.

one it was the same. I felt a combination of marvelous tastes and joyous thoughts. We tried every flavor before we finally staggered out into the mall again.

"I'll have to diet for a whole year now," Trinja said, patting her stomach.

"I feel like a blimp myself," I told her, but neither one of us cared. We both felt terrific. "Go ahead in there," I called to some grade-school kids who were looking at the store. "You'll love those swoodies."

"It's a publicity stunt, we think," Trinja told them. "Everything is free in there."

In no time at all the news about the swoodie shop had spread all over town. But days passed, and still everything was absolutely free. Nobody knew who the new owners were or why they were giving away their product. Nobody cared. The mall directors said a check arrived to pay for the rent, and that was all they were concerned about. The Health Brigade Corp said swoodies were absolutely safe for human consumption.

Swoodies were still being offered free a month later, but the shop owners had still not appeared. By then nobody cared. There were always long lines of people in front of the place, but the swoodies tasted so good nobody minded waiting for them. And the supply was endless. Soon more shops like the first one began opening in other places around the city, with machines running in the same quiet, efficient way. And everything was still absolutely free.

Soon all of us were gaining weight like crazy.

"It's those darn swoodies," Trinja told me as we left the mall after our daily binge. "I can't leave them alone. Each one must have a thousand calories, but I still pig out on them."

I sighed as I walked out into the sunshine. "Me too. If only there was some easy way to eat all the swoodies we want and still not gain any weight!"

The words were hardly out of my mouth when I noticed a new feature in the mall parking lot. Among all the usual heliobiles there was a tall white plastic box, sort of like those big telephone booths you see in old pictures. A flashing sign near the booth said THE SLIMMER. A short, thin woman was standing beside it. She was deeply tanned, and her head was covered with a green turban almost the same color as the jumpsuit she was wearing.

Trinja looked at the sign, then glanced at the woman. "What's that mean?"

"It means that this machine can make you slimmer," the woman answered. She had a deep, strange-sounding voice. "Just step inside, and you'll lose unwanted fat."

She seemed so serious and confident that I was startled. In the old days people thought they could lose weight in a hurry, but those of us who live in 2041 aren't that gullible. No pills or packs or wraps or special twenty-four-hour diets can work. There isn't any easy way to get rid of fat, and that's all there is to it. I knew this booth was a scam or a joke of some kind, but the woman acted as if it were a perfectly respectable thing. Her seriousness sort of unnerved me. I looked into the booth half

Words to Know and Use

consumption (kən sump′ shən) *n.* the act of eating or drinking
binge (binj) *n.* a period of uncontrolled eating or drinking
gullible (gul′ ə bəl) *adj.* easily fooled or tricked
unnerve (un nʉrv′) *v.* to take away courage; to make nervous

expecting someone to jump out laughing. But it was empty, <u>stark</u> white, and, except for some overhead grill work, it was completely smooth and bare.

"How can a thing like this make you slimmer?" I asked.

The woman shrugged. "A new process. Do you care to try? Twenty-five yen to lose one pound of body fat."

Trinja and I both burst into laughter. "And how long is it before the pound disappears?" she asked.

The woman never even cracked a smile. "Instantly. Body fat is gone instantly." She gestured to a small lever on the side nearest to her. "I regulate the power flow according to your payment."

M y mouth dropped open. "But that's impossible! No exercise? No chemicals? No starving on a retreat week?"

"No." The woman folded her arms and leaned against the smooth white sides of her <u>cubicle</u>, as if she didn't much care whether we tried her new process or not. Trinja and I stared at each other. I was wondering if the woman had tried her machine herself—she didn't have an ounce of fat.

"You got any money?" I asked Trinja. As she was shaking her head, I was rummaging through my pack. "I've got a hundred and thirty yen."

"Five pounds then," the woman said, taking my money with one hand and setting her lever with the other. She literally pushed me into the booth, and the door slammed behind me.

At first I wanted to scream because I was so scared.

At first I wanted to scream because I was so scared. The whole thing had happened too fast. I wanted to prove that this woman and her slimmer were a big joke, but suddenly I was trapped in a coffinlike structure as bare and as bright as an old microwave oven. My heart was hammering, and the hair on the back of my neck stood up straight. I opened my mouth, but before I could scream, there was a loud humming sound, and instantly the door flew open again. I saw Trinja's frightened face peering in at me.

"Are you all right, Deb? Are you okay? I guess she decided not to do anything after all. You ought to get your money back."

"Five pounds are gone," the woman said in her strange voice.

Trinja pulled me away. "I'll just bet!" she shouted back at the woman. "Somebody ought to report you and that phony machine! We might even call the Health Brigade Corp!" She leaned closer to me. "Are you really okay, Deb?"

I took a deep breath. "My jeans feel loose."

Frowning, Trinja shook her head. "It's just your imagination, that's all. What a fake! I think that woman was wacko, Debbie, really weird. The only thing slimmer after a treatment like that is your bank account. Nobody but nobody can lose weight that easily. We'll go to my house,

Words to Know and Use | **stark** (stärk) *adv.* entirely; completely
cubicle (kyōō′ bi kəl) *n.* a small compartment used for work or sleep

and you can weigh yourself. You haven't lost an ounce."

But Trinja was wrong. I really *was* five pounds lighter. I know it sounds impossible, but Trinja's calshow is never wrong. The two of us hopped and howled with joy. Then we ravaged her bedroom trying to find some more money. We ran all the way back to the mall, worrying all the way that the woman and her miracle machine might have disappeared. But the slimmer was still there. Within minutes Trinja had used up her three hundred yen, and she looked terrific.

"I can't believe it! I just can't believe it!" she kept saying as she notched her belt tighter. "Twelve pounds gone in seconds!"

"For safety's sake I'll have to prick your wrist, my dear," the woman said. "For every ten pounds you lose we give a tiny little mark. Nobody will ever notice it."

"It didn't even hurt," Trinja said as we walked home. And neither of us could see the tiny blue pinprick unless we looked closely. We were both so happy about the weight loss that we almost floated. All our worries and problems about calories and fat and diets were over forever.

Now there's hardly a fat person left . . .

In no time at all the slimmers were all over the city, near all the swoodie stores. They've been a real blessing. Everybody says so. Now there's hardly a fat person left

Illustration by Lynn Rowe Reed.

on the streets. A few people have so many blue marks on their wrists that you can see them, but most have just four or five pinpricks.

Nobody really understands how these slimmers work. The attendants, all just as strange sounding as the woman in our mall, get so technical in their explanations that none of us can follow the principles they're talking about, so we don't much worry about it. The process has something to do with invisible waves that can change fat cells into energy, which then radiates away from the body.

"I don't care how the slimmers work," Trinja says happily. "Now I can eat swoodies all day long if I want, and I never gain an ounce. That's all I care about."

Everybody feels that way, I guess. We're

too happy to want to upset anything by asking questions. Maybe that's why you don't hear about the swoodies or slimmers on the fax or the bodivision or read about them anywhere. Nobody understands them well enough to sound very intelligent about them. But people all over Earth are beginning to use them. My cousin in Tokyo faxed to say that they have them in her area now and people there are just as happy as we are.

Except for my brother, Trevor. He's not the least bit happy, he says. Of course, few ten-year-olds worry about weight, so he doesn't know the joy of being able to eat everything in sight and still stay thin.

"Suppose the swoodies and the slimmers are run by aliens from outer space," he says. "From lots farther than we've been able to go. Maybe they have big starships posted around Earth, and they're gathering up the energy from human fat that's sent up from the slimmers. Maybe the swoodies are here so people will get fat quicker so that there'll be more to harvest through the slimmer machines. Then they'll take the fat back to their planet and use it as fuel."

"That's the dumbest thing I ever heard of!" Trinja has told him. "Why don't we hear about the spaceships, then? Why doesn't the Health Brigade Corp tell us to stop doing this if it isn't good for us?"

Trevor thinks he has the answers. He says the spaceships are invisible to human detection, and he says the aliens have hypnotized our leaders into being as calm and placid as we all are. The blue marks on our wrists play a big role. He says maybe after each of us has had so many blue marks, we'll be culled from the flock because our fat content won't be as good anymore.

He's crazy, isn't he? He must think we all have the brains of sheep. Ten-year-old brothers can be a real pain. He simply doesn't know people yet, that's all. Humans would never sacrifice their freedom and dignity just so they could eat and still be thin. Even aliens ought to know that.

I could quit eating swoodies and using those slimmers any time I want to.

But all those little blue marks Trinja and I have are beginning to look like delicate tattooed bracelets, and we both think they look really neat on our wrists. ❧

Words to Know and Use

placid (plas′ id) *adj.* calm; at peace
cull (kul) *v.* to remove from a group something or someone that is not as good as the rest

Responding to Reading

First Impressions

1. What were your thoughts as you finished reading this story? Write your reactions in your journal.

Second Thoughts

2. Are Deb and Trinja right to reject Trevor's theory?

   Think about
   - how most of the people react to swoodies and slimmers
   - what Deb says about her little brother
   - the title of the story

3. At the end of the story, Deb says, "Humans would never sacrifice their freedom and dignity just so they could eat and still be thin." Do you agree? Explain your opinion using evidence from the story and your own experience.

4. Which **characters** in this story have tunnel vision? Explain the effects their tunnel vision has on them.

Broader Connections

5. Nowadays, there are advertisements in newspapers and on television for products that may be unhealthy or unsafe. While some people believe that these ads should be banned, others feel that consumers should make their own decisions. Explain your opinion on this issue, using examples from the story and your own experiences.

Literary Concept: Science Fiction

"Lose Now, Pay Later" is a work of **science fiction.** Science fiction stories are frequently based on possible scientific developments and are usually set in the future. Often, realistic characters with attitudes and values of present-day society are projected into an imaginary future world. This lets the reader examine current values in a different setting. What values of our society are reflected in this story? How do you know?

Concept Review: Setting   Science fiction writers sometimes use imaginary terms and inventions to set their stories in the future. Find several examples of this in "Lose Now, Pay Later."

Writing Options

1. If you were to write your own science fiction story, what would be the setting? Write **notes** that you could develop into a science fiction story of your own.

2. Assume that Trevor's theory is wrong. Write your own **explanation** of the swoodie and slimmer machines.

3. Assume that Trevor's theory is right. Write the **plan** that the aliens are using to obtain all the fat they need from humans. Add steps to the plan that Trevor was unable to guess.

4. Reread the description of how swoodies taste. Then write a detailed **description** of your own favorite snack for someone who has never tried the snack.

Vocabulary Practice

Exercise   Decide if the following pairs of words are synonyms (words that have the same meaning) or antonyms (words that have opposite meanings). On a separate sheet of paper, identify each pair as *Synonyms* or *Antonyms*.

1. gullible—suspicious
2. consumption—production
3. ravage—wreck
4. placid—disturbed
5. unnerve—comfort
6. stark—completely
7. cull—select
8. binge—spree
9. dingy—clean
10. cubicle—compartment

Words to Know and Use

binge
consumption
cubicle
cull
dingy
gullible
placid
ravage
stark
unnerve

Options for Learning

1 • Be Fat — Be Fit Plan and perform a radio ad for either swoodies or the slimmer. Use descriptive words that appeal to the senses.

2 • Mechanical Drawings Make a drawing or painting of one of the machines described in this story.

3 • Inventions of Tomorrow Think up your own marvelous invention for the future. Design and sketch your invention and present it to the class. Explain what it will do and how it will help people.

4 • Any Connection? Check through a current newspaper and count the total number of advertisements. As you go through the ads, jot down how many are related to weight-loss programs or products, and how many are for the food industry (restaurants, bakeries, supermarkets, and so on). Using a calculator, divide the number of each kind of ad by the total number of ads and multiply both results by 100. Report your final figures, which will be the percentages of the newspaper's ads that are devoted to food and weight loss in that paper.

 FACT FINDER SCIENCE

How many calories do you have to burn to lose one pound?

Carol Farley
1936-

For Carol Farley, writing is an extension of what she always loved about school. She says that her "happiest memories of school years are centered on classes I had in literature when we read fiction and talked about what we had read."

Farley has done many things besides write, however. She has taught school, picked fruit, and sold women's clothing. As an army wife, she once moved thirteen times in fifteen years. Her varied experiences have taught her that "we all look at life from our own viewpoint, often unaware or unconcerned about the views of others." Such concerns prompt her to write stories like "Lose Now, Pay Later" to show "that sometimes small children–like the boy in the story about the emperor's new clothes (or lack of them)–are the first to notice and report on something that is perfectly obvious."

Fiction

Stolen Day

SHERWOOD ANDERSON

*E*xamine What You Know

A missed day at school can be many things. You might be happy to miss school, or nervous about missing assignments, or you might just be too sick to care! Think about times when you have missed school. How did you feel? Compare your reactions with your classmates'.

*E*xpand Your Knowledge

In this selection, a neighbor of the narrator suffers from an illness called inflammatory rheumatism. Rheumatism is a general name for several painful conditions that make a person's joints and muscles hurt, swell up, and get stiff, so that it is hard to move. Although most people think only the elderly have rheumatism, children can get it too. When that happens, the children may have to miss weeks or months of school, as well as undergo special medical treatments.

*W*rite Before You Read

■ *Author biography in Reader's Handbook*

In your journal or on a separate piece of paper, tell about the last time you missed school. Include all the details—Why couldn't you go to school? What happened when you returned to class?

Stolen Day

SHERWOOD ANDERSON

It must be that all children are actors. The whole thing started with a boy on our street named Walter, who had inflammatory rheumatism. That's what they called it. He didn't have to go to school.

Still, he could walk about. He could go fishing in the creek or the waterworks pond. There was a place up at the pond where in the spring the water came tumbling over the dam and formed a deep pool. It was a good place. Sometimes you could get some big ones there.

I went down that way on my way to school one spring morning. It was out of my way but I wanted to see if Walter was there.

He was, inflammatory rheumatism and all. There he was, sitting with a fish pole in his hand. He had been able to walk down there all right.

It was then that my own legs began to hurt. My back, too. I went on to school but, at the recess time, I began to cry. I did it when the teacher, Sarah Suggett, had come out into the schoolhouse yard.

She came right over to me.

"I ache all over," I said. I did, too.

I kept on crying and it worked all right.

"You'd better go on home," she said.

So I went. I limped painfully away. I kept on limping until I got out of the schoolhouse street.

Then I felt better. I still had inflammatory rheumatism pretty bad but I could get along better.

I must have done some thinking on the way home.

"I'd better not say I have inflammatory rheumatism," I decided. "Maybe if you've got that, you swell up."

Why doesn't the boy want to say he has the disease?

review

I thought I'd better go around to where Walter was and ask him about that, so I did—but he wasn't there.

"They must not be biting today," I thought.

I had a feeling that, if I said I had inflammatory rheumatism, Mother or my brothers and my sister Stella might laugh. They did laugh at me pretty often, and I didn't like it at all.

"Just the same," I said to myself, "I have got it." I began to hurt and ache again.

I went home and sat on the front steps of our house. I sat there a long time. There wasn't anyone at home but Mother and the two little ones. Ray would have been four or five then and Earl might have been three.

It was Earl who saw me there. I had got tired of sitting and was lying on the porch. Earl was always a quiet, solemn little fellow.

He must have said something to Mother, for presently she came.

"What's the matter with you? Why aren't you in school?" she asked.

I came pretty near telling her right out that I had inflammatory rheumatism, but I thought I'd better not. Mother and Father had been speaking of Walter's case at the table just the day before. "It affects the heart," Father had said. That frightened me when I thought of it. "I might die," I thought. "I might just suddenly die right here; my heart might stop beating."

On the day before, I had been running a race with my brother Irve. We were up at the fairgrounds after school, and there was a half-mile track.

"I'll bet you can't run a half mile," he said. "I bet you I could beat you running clear around the track."

And so we did it and I beat him, but afterward my heart did seem to beat pretty hard. I remembered that, lying there on the porch. "It's a wonder, with my inflammatory rheumatism and all, I didn't just drop down dead," I thought. The thought frightened me a lot. I ached worse than ever.

"I ache, Ma," I said. "I just ache."

She made me go in the house and upstairs and get into bed.

It wasn't so good. It was spring. I was up there for perhaps an hour, maybe two, and then I felt better.

I got up and went downstairs. "I feel better, Ma," I said.

Mother said she was glad. She was pretty busy that day and hadn't paid much attention to me. She had made me get into bed upstairs and then hadn't even come up to see how I was.

I didn't think much of that when I was up

there; but when I got downstairs where she was, and when, after I had said I felt better and she only said she was glad and went right on with her work, I began to ache again.

I thought, "I'll bet I die of it. I bet I do."

I went out to the front porch and sat down. I was pretty sore at Mother.

"If she really knew the truth, that I have inflammatory rheumatism and I may just drop down dead any time, I'll bet she wouldn't care about that either," I thought.

I was getting more and more angry the more thinking I did.

"I know what I'm going to do," I thought; "I'm going to go fishing."

I thought that, feeling the way I did, I might be sitting on the high bank just above the deep pool where the water went over the dam, and suddenly my heart would stop beating.

And then, of course, I'd pitch forward, over the bank into the pool; and, if I wasn't dead when I hit the water, I'd drown sure.

They would all come home to supper and they'd miss me.

"But where is he?"

Then Mother would remember that I'd come home from school aching.

She'd go upstairs, and I wouldn't be there. One day during the year before, there was a child got drowned in a spring. It was one of the Wyatt children.

Right down at the end of the street there was a spring under a birch tree, and there had been a barrel sunk in the ground.

Everyone had always been saying the spring ought to be kept covered, but it wasn't.

Illustration by David Barnett.

So the Wyatt child went down there, played around alone, and fell in and got drowned.

Mother was the one who had found the drowned child. She had gone to get a pail of water, and there the child was, drowned and dead.

This had been in the evening when we were all at home, and Mother had come running up the street with the dead, dripping child in her arms. She was making for the Wyatt house as hard as she could run, and she was pale.

She had a terrible look on her face, I remembered then.

"So," I thought, "they'll miss me, and there'll be a search made. Very likely there'll be someone who has seen me sitting by the pond fishing, and there'll be a big alarm and all the town will turn out and they'll drag the pond."[1]

What has the boy imagined?

review

I was having a grand time, having died. Maybe, after they found me and had got me out of the deep pool, Mother would grab me up in her arms and run home with me as she had run with the Wyatt child.

I got up from the porch and went around the house. I got my fishing pole and lit out

---

1. drag the pond: pull a net over the bottom to find the body of a drowning victim.

for the pool below the dam. Mother was busy—she always was—and didn't see me go. When I got there, I thought I'd better not sit too near the edge of the high bank.

By this time I didn't ache hardly at all, but I thought,

"With inflammatory rheumatism you can't tell," I thought.

"It probably comes and goes," I thought.

"Walter has it and he goes fishing," I thought.

I had got my line into the pool and suddenly I got a bite. It was a regular whopper; I knew that. I'd never had a bite like that.

I knew what it was. It was one of Mr. Fenn's big carp.

Mr. Fenn was a man who had a big pond of his own. He sold ice in the summer, and the pond was to make the ice. He had bought some big carp and put them into his pond; and then, earlier in the spring when there was a freshet, his dam had gone out.

So the carp had got into our creek, and one or two big ones had been caught—but none of them by a boy like me.

The carp was pulling and I was pulling and I was afraid he'd break my line, so I just tumbled down the high bank, holding onto the line and got right into the pool. We had it out, there in the pool. We struggled. We wrestled. Then I got a hand under his gills and got him out.

He was a big one all right. He was nearly half as big as I was myself. I had him on the bank and I kept one hand under his gills and I ran.

I never ran so hard in my life. He was slippery, and now and then he wriggled out of my arms; once I stumbled and fell on him, but I got him home.

So there it was. I was a big hero that day. Mother got a washtub and filled it with water. She put the fish in it, and all the neighbors came to look. I got into dry clothes and went down to supper—and then I made a break that spoiled my day.

There we were, all of us, at the table, and suddenly Father asked what had been the matter with me at school. He had met the teacher, Sarah Suggett, on the street, and she told him how I had become ill.

"What was the matter with you?" Father asked; and before I thought what I was saying, I let it out.

"I had the inflammatory rheumatism," I said—and a shout went up. It made me sick to hear them, the way they all laughed.

It brought back all the aching again, and like a fool I began to cry.

"Well, I *have* got it—I *have*," I cried, and I got up from the table and ran upstairs.

I stayed there until Mother came up. I knew it would be a long time before I heard the last of the inflammatory rheumatism. I was sick all right, but the aching I now had wasn't in my legs or in my back. ❧

EXPLAIN

Responding to Reading

First Impressions

1. What do you think of the boy in this story? Share your reactions with your classmates.

Second Thoughts

2. What do you think was really wrong with the boy? Explain, using information from the story.

3. What is your opinion of the way the boy is treated by his family? Find evidence to explain your answer.

4. What advice would you give to either the boy or his family?

Literary Concept: Point of View

When planning a story, the writer must decide who will narrate or tell the story. This is called the story's **point of view.** In first-person point of view, a narrator who is also a character in the story speaks directly to the reader using pronouns such as *I, me,* and *we.* In third-person point of view, the story is told by someone outside the story using pronouns like *he, she,* and *they.* From which point of view is "Stolen Day" written? What other stories have you read that were told from this point of view?

Writing Options

1. Using first-person point of view, write the narrator's **journal entry** at the end of the day, expressing his feelings about what happened. Before you write, skim the story and try to make your writing sound like the narrator's.

2. Which character or characters in this story have tunnel vision? Write an **explanation** to identify your choice and explain the effect of tunnel vision on the character.

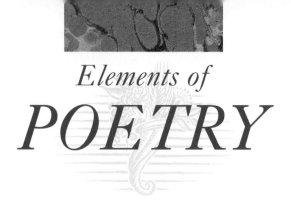

Elements of
POETRY

Poetry is the most compact form of literature. A poem packs all kinds of ideas, feelings, and sounds into a few carefully chosen words. The look, sound, and language of poetry all work together to create a total effect.

Understanding Poetry

Form   The way a poem looks—or its arrangement on the page—is **form.** Poetry is written in **lines,** which may or may not be sentences. Sometimes the lines are separated into groups called **stanzas.** Remember that poets choose the arrangements of words and lines deliberately. The form of a poem can add to its meaning.

Sound   Poems are meant to be read aloud. Therefore, poets choose and arrange words to create the sounds they want the listener to hear. There are many techniques that poets can use to achieve different sounds. Three of these are described below.

• **Rhyme**   When words end with the same sounds, the words rhyme. In Western cultures, traditional poems such as "The Charge of the Light Brigade" on page 86, often contain rhyming words at the ends of the lines:

> Theirs not to reason *why,*
> Theirs but to do and *die.*

• **Rhythm**   The rhythm is sometimes called the "beat" of the poem. It is the pattern of stressed (́) and unstressed (‿) sylla-

bles, or those word parts that are read with more and less emphasis, in a line of poetry. In these lines from "The Charge of the Light Brigade," listen for a beat that sounds like the pounding of horses' hooves.

> Cánnŏn tŏ rīght ŏf thĕm,
>
> Cánnŏn tŏ lĕft ŏf thĕm,

Poems that do not have a regular rhythm and sound more like conversation are called **free verse.** "For My Father" on page 90 is written in free verse.

• **Repetition**   Poets often choose to repeat sounds, words, phrases, or whole lines in a poem. Repetition helps the poet emphasize an idea or create a certain feeling.

Imagery   Imagery involves words and phrases that appeal to the five senses. Poets use imagery to create a picture in the reader's mind, or to remind the reader of a familiar sensation. Notice how these lines from "in the inner city" on page 33 give you a visual picture as well as a sound picture. They help bring the poem "inside" of you.

> we think a lot about uptown
> and the silent nights
> and the houses straight as
> dead men

Figurative Language   Poets use figurative language when they choose words and phrases that help the reader to picture ordinary things in new ways. These special descriptions are called **figures of speech.** Three figures of speech are explained below.

- **Simile** A comparison that uses the words *like* or *as* is called a simile. This simile from "Dream Deferred" on page 268 compares a raisin to a dream that has not come true:

  > What happens to a dream deferred:
  > Does it dry up
  > like a raisin in the sun?

- **Metaphor** A comparison that does *not* use the words *like* or *as* is called a metaphor. To what is the road compared in this line from "The Highwayman" on page 408?

  > The road was a ribbon of moonlight
  >   over the purple moor

- **Personification** When a poet describes an animal or object as if it were human or had human qualities, he or she is using personification. In these lines from "Formula" on page 268, the poet gives human characteristics to the night and the fish.

  > Perhaps the night dreams
  > that it is no longer night;
  > the fish, that they are boats;

Theme All the poetic elements you have read about help the poet establish the theme. Just as in fiction, the message about life that the poem conveys is the poem's theme.

*S*trategies for Reading Poetry

1. **Preview the poem.** Notice the poem's form on the page: its shape, its length, the length of the lines, and whether or not it has stanzas.

2. **Read the poem aloud.** Pause at the ends of complete thoughts, not necessarily at the ends of lines. Look for end punctuation to help you find the end of a complete thought. As you read, see if there is rhyme and listen for rhythm as well as the overall sound of the words in the poem.

3. **Visualize the images.** In your mind's eye, picture the images and comparisons the poem makes. Do the images remind you of feelings or experiences you have had?

4. **Think about the words and phrases.** Allow yourself to wonder about any phrases or words that seem to stand out. Think about what that choice of words adds to the poem.

5. **Try to figure out the theme.** Ask yourself, What's the point of the poem? What message is the poet trying to send or help you create?

6. **Let your understanding grow.** When you finish reading, you are left with first impressions of the poem. Over time, you will add to your understanding based on the poem, your discussions in class, and other poetry you read.

7. **Allow yourself to enjoy poetry.** Remember that poetry is about feelings. You may connect with a particular poem because it expresses feelings that you yourself have felt.

Poetry

The Charge of the Light Brigade

ALFRED, LORD TENNYSON

Examine What You Know

The following poem is based on a tragedy that took place because of orders given during wartime. What do you know about the military and the giving and taking of orders? Must all orders be obeyed? As a class, discuss what you know about military orders.

Expand Your Knowledge

The real Charge of the Light Brigade came during the Crimean War, 1853–1856, a war between Russia and a group of nations that included Great Britain. Russia eventually lost the war. On October 25, 1854, a British brigade was mistakenly ordered to attack a Russian artillery post. The Light Brigade, so called because it was lightly armed with swords, made a suicidal charge and actually overran the Russian guns and gunners. That victory came at a tragic cost, however. Of the 673 soldiers who made the charge, 247 were wounded or killed.

Enrich Your Reading

Sound Effects   Poetry is meant to be read aloud. Often the sounds of the words add to the poem's meaning and overall effect. In the poem you are about to read, the poet has created short lines of carefully chosen words that suggest the sounds of battle. Read the poem once silently to yourself. Then read it again aloud. Notice the **repetition** of short words and phrases that suggest the **rhythm,** or regular beat, of soldiers riding into battle. Listen for the rhyme and for other sound effects that suggest a wild and desperate struggle.

■ *Author biography in Reader's Handbook*

The Charge of the Light Brigade

ALFRED, LORD TENNYSON

Half a league,[1] half a league,
Half a league onward,
All in the valley of death
    Rode the six hundred.
5 "Forward, the Light Brigade!
Charge for the guns!" he said:
Into the valley of death
    Rode the six hundred.

"Forward, the Light Brigade!"
10 Was there a man dismayed?
Not though the soldier knew
    Someone had blundered;
Theirs not to make reply,
Theirs not to reason why,
15 Theirs but to do and die;
Into the valley of death
    Rode the six hundred.

Cannon to right of them,
Cannon to left of them,
20 Cannon in front of them
    Volleyed and thundered;
Stormed at with shot and shell,
Boldly they rode and well,
Into the jaws of death,
25 Into the mouth of hell
    Rode the six hundred.

---

1. league: distance of about three miles

THE CHARGE OF THE LIGHT BRIGADE   (detail)   early 20th century   Christopher Clark
Historical Pictures/Stock Montage.

Flashed all their sabers bare,
Flashed as they turned in air
Sab'ring the gunners there,
30 Charging an army, while
    All the world wondered.
Plunged in the battery smoke,
Right through the line they broke;
Cossack and Russian
35 Reeled from the saber-stroke,
    Shattered and sundered.[2]
Then they rode back, but not,
    Not the six hundred.

Cannon to right of them,
40 Cannon to left of them,
Cannon behind them
    Volleyed and thundered;
Stormed at with shot and shell,
While horse and hero fell,
45 They that had fought so well
Came through the jaws of death,
Back from the mouth of hell,
All that was left of them,
    Left of six hundred.

50 When can their glory fade?
Oh, the wild charge they made!
    All the world wondered.
Honor the charge they made,
Honor the Light Brigade,
55   Noble six hundred! 🌢

---

2. sundered: split; broken apart

Responding to Reading

First Impressions

1. What images went through your mind as you read this poem? Discuss them with your classmates.

Second Thoughts

2. Do you consider the soldiers of the Light Brigade to be heroes? Why or why not?

   Think about
   - lines 11–12 of the poem
   - the outcome of the soldiers' decision

3. How do you think the speaker of the poem feels about the Light Brigade? Why do you think so?

4. Do you think an incident like this suicidal charge could happen today? Why or why not?

Literary Concept: Rhythm

Rhythm is the pattern of stressed and unstressed syllables in a line of poetry. You can understand the rhythm of a poem more clearly if you mark the stressed and unstressed syllables. The words or word parts you read with more emphasis (stress) are marked with ´. The weaker-sounding syllables (unstressed) are marked with ˘.

Example "Fórwărd, thĕ Líght Brĭgáde!
Chárge fŏr thĕ gúns!" hĕ sáid:

Working in pairs, copy the first stanza on a separate piece of paper. Then chart the rhythmic pattern as shown in the example.

Writing Options

1. Research and write a short **research report** on the causes and outcome of the Crimean War. Share your information with the class.

2. Imagine that you are a reporter on the field of battle. Write a **news report** describing what you see.

Poetry

For My Father

JANICE MIRIKITANI (mi′ ri ki tän′ ē)

Examine What You Know

Very often the conflicts we have with others are caused by communication gaps. Sometimes people are unable to express their feelings. Think about times when you have had a problem with someone else. In your journal, draw and fill in a chart like the one below.

Conflict between	Problem about	Who couldn't communicate?
Jill & me	borrowing clothes	both of us

Expand Your Knowledge

The father in the poem you are about to read is a Japanese immigrant. Although the Japanese people who moved to the United States were good citizens and hard workers, they faced a great deal of prejudice. Resentment against them grew so strong that in 1924 a law was passed that excluded any more Japanese and other nonwhite people from entering the country. In 1941, during World War II, Pearl Harbor was bombed by Japan, and Japanese Americans faced even worse discrimination. Although 20,000 Japanese Americans served in the U.S. military during World War II, Japanese Americans on the West Coast were forced to give up their homes and belongings and go to special camps that were like prisons. One of these camps, Tule Lake, is mentioned in the poem.

Enrich Your Reading

Visualizing   Poets often select words that put a mental picture in the mind of the reader. As you read this poem, try to visualize, or picture in your mind, the images described by the writer. Take time to try to picture each thing that is described. Not only will visualizing help you remember details, it will also help you enjoy the poem more.

■ *Author biography in Reader's Handbook*

For My Father

JANICE MIRIKITANI

He came over the ocean
carrying Mt. Fuji[1] on
his back / Tule Lake on his chest
hacked through the brush
5   of deserts
and made them grow
strawberries

      we stole berries
      from the stem
10   we could not afford them
      for breakfast

his eyes held
nothing
as he whipped us
15   for stealing.

the desert had dried
his soul.

wordless
he sold
20   the rich,
full berries
to hakujin[2]
whose children
pointed at our eyes

25   they ate fresh
      strawberries
      on corn flakes.

Father,
i wanted to scream
30   at your silence.
Your strength
was a stranger
i could never touch.

iron
35   in your eyes
to shield
the pain
to shield desert-like wind
from patches
40   of strawberries
grown
from
tears.

---

1. **Mt. Fuji** (fōō′ jē): the highest mountain in Japan.
2. **hakujin** (hä kōō jən): a Japanese term for Caucasians.

*R*esponding to Reading

First Impressions

1. Choose one word to describe your feelings about this poem. Then explain your choice to the class.

Second Thoughts

2. Do you feel that the father's treatment of his child was fair? Why or why not?

3. How do you think the father would explain his side of the issue?
   Think about
   • the reference to Tule Lake
   • the tears mentioned in the last stanza

4. How do you think the speaker feels about the father? Why do you think so?

*L*iterary Concept: Figurative Language

The creative use of words to extend ideas beyond their literal or dictionary meanings is called **figurative language.** The words in a figurative expression are not literally true but instead paint vivid images in the minds of readers. For example, the speaker begins this poem by saying the father carried Mount Fuji on his back. What do you think this might mean? What other examples of figurative language can you find in this poem?

*W*riting Options

1. Think back to "The Charge of the Light Brigade." Write your **opinion** about whether both Tennyson's poem and "For My Father" were good choices for a subunit called "Tunnel Vision."

2. Imagine you are either the father or the child in this poem. Write a **letter** to the other person fully describing how you feel about him or her and about the events in the poem. Try to include some figurative language.

Nonfiction   *from* # Exploring the Titanic

ROBERT BALLARD

Examine What You Know

You probably know something about the sinking of the great ship *Titanic,* but what else would you like to learn about it? Copy the following chart on the board. As a class, fill in the first two columns now, and the last column when you finish reading the piece.

What We Know	What We Want to Learn	What We Learned

Expand Your Knowledge

As with most specialized fields, the shipping industry has its own special vocabulary, or **jargon.** To understand this selection more clearly, review the definitions of the terms below and refer to them as you read.

bow: front of a ship
stern: rear of a ship
hull: outside frame of a ship
deck: any floor on a ship
funnel: smokestack
mooring rope: rope that ties ship to dock

mast: tall pole that holds a sail or radio equipment
crow's nest: small platform on the mast for the lookout
hold: cargo compartment below deck
keel: beam along the bottom of a ship

Enrich Your Reading

Literary Nonfiction   If you read about the *Titanic* in an encyclopedia, you could learn the facts about the sinking in a few minutes. Giving facts is the purpose of informational nonfiction.

Literary nonfiction such as the selection you will read next also provides factual information. However, this type of nonfiction is often written in narrative form. Like a story, it might introduce characters—real people—and allow you to live through an event with them. As you read the following account, compare it to the informational nonfiction you read in encyclopedias. Think about when you might use each type.

■ *Author biography on Extend page*

from *Exploring the Titanic*

ROBERT D. BALLARD

The story of the *Titanic* began before anyone had even thought about building the great ship. In 1898, fourteen years before the *Titanic* sank, an American writer named Morgan Robertson wrote a book called *The Wreck of the Titan.* In his story, the *Titan,* a passenger ship almost identical to the *Titanic,* and labeled "unsinkable," sails from England headed for New York. With many rich and famous passengers on board, the *Titan* hits an iceberg in the North Atlantic and sinks. Because there are not enough lifeboats, many lives are lost.

The story of the *Titan* predicted exactly what would happen to the *Titanic* fourteen years later. It was an eerie prophecy of terrible things to come.

In 1907, nearly ten years after *The Wreck of the Titan* was written, two men began making plans to build a real titanic ship. At a London dinner party, as they relaxed over coffee and cigars, J. Bruce Ismay, president of the White Star Line of passenger ships, and Lord Pirrie, chairman of Harland & Wolff shipbuilders, discussed a plan to build three enormous ocean liners. Their goal was to give the White Star Line a competitive edge in the Atlantic passenger trade with several gigantic ships whose accommodations would be the last word in comfort and elegance.

The two men certainly dreamed on a grand scale. When these floating palaces were finally built, they were so much bigger than other ships that new docks had to be built on each side of the Atlantic to service them. Four years after that London dinner party, the first of these huge liners, the *Olympic,* safely completed her maiden voyage.

On May 31, 1911, the hull of the *Titanic* was launched at the Harland & Wolff shipyards in Belfast, Ireland, before a cheering crowd of 100,000. Bands played, and people came from miles around to see this great wonder of the sea. Twenty-two tons of soap, grease, and train oil were used to slide her

Words to Know and Use

prophecy (präf′ ə sē) *n.* a prediction; foretelling of future events
competitive (kəm pet′ ə tiv) *adj.* relating to rivalry among businesses, groups, or individuals
accommodation (ə käm′ ə dā′ shən) *n.* a room and food in hotels, ships, trains, and so on

into the water. In the words of one eyewitness, she had "a rudder as big as an elm tree . . . propellers as big as a windmill. Everything was on a nightmare scale."

For the next ten months the *Titanic* was outfitted and carefully prepared down to the last detail. The final size and richness of this new ship was astounding. She was 882 feet long, almost the length of four city blocks. With nine decks, she was as high as an eleven-story building.

Among her gigantic features, she had four huge funnels, each one big enough to drive two trains through. During construction an astonishing three million rivets[1] had been hammered into her hull. Her three enormous anchors weighed a total of thirty-one tons—the weight of twenty cars. And for her maiden voyage, she carried enough food to feed a small town for several months.

As her name boasted, the *Titanic* was indeed the biggest ship in the world. Nicknamed "the Millionaires' Special," she was also called "the Wonder Ship," "the Unsinkable Ship," and "the Last Word in Luxury" by newspapers around the world.

The command of this great ocean liner was given to the senior captain of the White Star Line, Captain Edward J. Smith. This proud, white-bearded man was a natural leader and was popular with both crew members and passengers. Most important, after thirty-eight years' service with the White Star Line, he had an excellent safety record. At the age of fifty-nine, Captain Smith was going to retire after this last trip, a perfect final <u>tribute</u> to a long and successful career.

The Grand Staircase was five stories high and covered by a glass dome.

On Wednesday, April 10, 1912, the *Titanic*'s passengers began to arrive in Southampton for the trip to New York. Ruth Becker was dazzled as she boarded the ship with her mother, her younger sister, and two-year-old brother, Richard. Ruth's father was a missionary in India. The rest of the family was sailing to New York to find medical help for young Richard, who had developed a serious illness in India. They had booked second-class tickets on the *Titanic*.

Twelve-year-old Ruth was delighted with the ship. As she pushed her little brother about the decks in a stroller, she was impressed with what she saw. "Everything was new. New!" she recalled. "Our cabin was just like a hotel room, it was so big. The dining room was beautiful—the linens, all the bright, polished silver you can imagine."

---

1. rivets: metal bolts used to fasten beams.

Words to Know and Use | **tribute** (trib' yo͞ot) *n.* an action or gift that honors a deserving individual

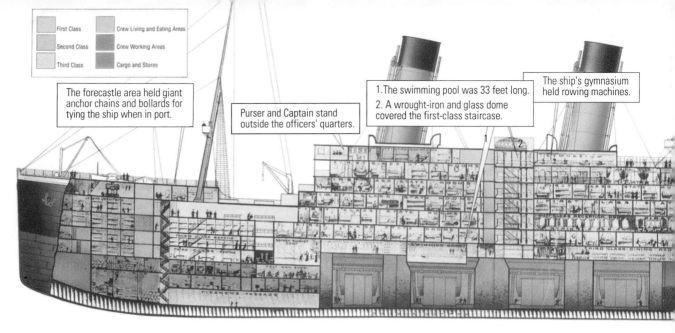

The forecastle area held giant anchor chains and bollards for tying the ship when in port.

Purser and Captain stand outside the officers' quarters.

1. The swimming pool was 33 feet long.
2. A wrought-iron and glass dome covered the first-class staircase.

The ship's gymnasium held rowing machines.

First Class

Second Class

Third Class

Crew Living and Eating Areas

Crew Working Areas

Cargo and Stores

Meanwhile, seventeen-year-old Jack Thayer from Philadelphia was trying out the soft mattress on the large bed in his cabin. The first-class rooms his family had reserved for themselves and their maid had thick carpets, carved wooden panels on the walls, and marble sinks. As his parents were getting settled in their adjoining stateroom, Jack decided to explore this fantastic ship.

On A Deck, he stepped into the Verandah and Palm Court and admired the white wicker furniture and the ivy growing up the trellised walls. On the lower decks, Jack discovered the squash court,[2] the swimming pool, and the Turkish bath decorated like a room in a sultan's palace. In the gymnasium, the instructor was showing passengers the latest in exercise equipment, which included a mechanical camel you could ride on, stationary bicycles, and rowing machines.

Daylight shone through the huge glass dome over the Grand Staircase as Jack went down to join his parents in the first-class reception room.

There, with the ship's band playing in the background, his father pointed out some of the other first-class passengers. "He's supposed to be the world's richest man," said his father of Colonel John Jacob Astor, who was escorting the young Mrs. Astor. He also identified Mr. and Mrs. Straus, founders of Macy's of New York, the world's largest department store. Millionaire Benjamin Guggenheim was aboard, as were Jack's parents' friends from Philadelphia, Mr. and Mrs. George Widener and their son, Harry. Mr. Widener had made a fortune building streetcars. Mr. and Mrs. William Carter were also friends of the Thayers. Stowed in one of the holds below was a new Renault car that they were bringing back from England.

There was absolutely nothing to worry about.

J. Bruce Ismay, president of the White Star Line, moved about the room saying hello to people. He wanted to make sure

---

2. **squash court:** a walled court for playing squash, a racquet game in which a rubber ball is hit off walls.

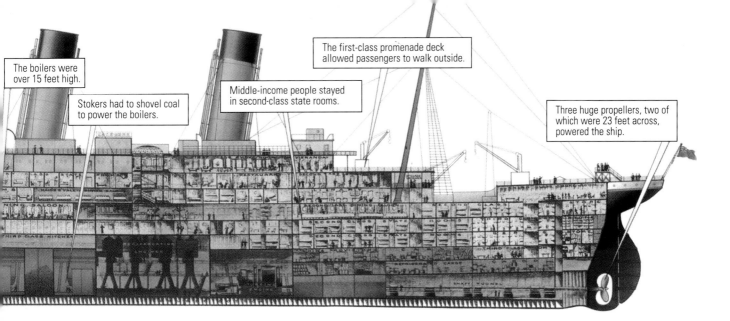

The boilers were over 15 feet high.

Stokers had to shovel coal to power the boilers.

Middle-income people stayed in second-class state rooms.

The first-class promenade deck allowed passengers to walk outside.

Three huge propellers, two of which were 23 feet across, powered the ship.

that his wealthy passengers were comfortable, that they would feel relaxed and safe aboard his floating palace.

Indeed, when Ruth Becker's mother had asked one of the second-class staff about the safety of the ship, she had been told that there was absolutely nothing to worry about. The ship had watertight compartments that would allow her to float indefinitely. There was much talk among the passengers about the *Titanic* being unsinkable.

In 1912, people were divided into social classes according to background, wealth, and education. Because of these class lines, the *Titanic* was rather like a big floating layer cake. The bottom layer consisted of the lowly manual workers sweating away in the heat and grime of the boiler rooms and engine rooms. The next layer was the third-class passengers, people of many nationalities hoping to make a new start in America. After that came the second class—teachers, merchants, and professionals of moderate means like Ruth's family. Then, finally,

there was the icing on the cake in first class: the rich and the aristocratic. The differences between these groups were enormous. While the wealthy brought their maids and valets and mountains of luggage, most members of the crew earned such tiny salaries that it would have taken them years to save the money for a single first-class ticket.

At noon on Wednesday, April 10, the *Titanic* cast off. The whistles on her huge funnels were the biggest ever made. As she began her journey to the sea, they were heard for miles around.

Moving majestically down the River Test, and watched by a crowd that had turned out for the occasion, the *Titanic* slowly passed two ships tied up to a dock. All of a sudden, the mooring ropes holding the passenger liner *New York* snapped with a series of sharp cracks like fireworks going off. The enormous pull created by the *Titanic* moving past her had broken the *New York*'s ropes and was now drawing her stern toward the *Titanic*.

| *Words to Know and Use* | **indefinitely** (in def′ ə nit lē) *adv.* for an unlimited length of time
aristocratic (ə ris′ tə krat′ ik) *n.* wealthy, privileged people | 97 |

Jack Thayer watched in horror as the two ships came closer and closer. "It looked as though there surely would be a collision," he later wrote. "Her stern could not have been more than a yard or two from our side. It almost hit us." At the last moment, some quick action by Captain Smith and a tugboat captain nearby allowed the *Titanic* to slide past with only inches to spare.

It was not a good sign. Did it mean that the *Titanic* might be too big a ship to handle safely? Those who knew about the sea thought that such a close call at the beginning of a maiden voyage was a very bad <u>omen</u>.

Jack Phillips, the first wireless operator[3] on the *Titanic* quickly jotted down the message coming in over his headphones. "It's another iceberg warning," he said wearily to his young assistant, Harold Bride. "You'd better take it up to the bridge." Both men had been at work for hours in the *Titanic*'s radio room, trying to get caught up in sending out a large number of personal messages. In 1912, passengers on ocean liners thought it was a real <u>novelty</u> to send postcard-style messages to friends at home from the middle of the Atlantic.

Bride picked up the iceberg message and stepped out onto the Boat Deck. It was a sunny but cold Sunday morning, the fourth day of the *Titanic*'s maiden voyage. The ship was steaming at full speed across a calm sea. Harold Bride was quite pleased with himself at having landed a job on such a magnificent new ship. After all, he was only twenty-two

years old and had just nine months' experience at operating a "wireless set," as a ship's radio was then called. As he entered the bridge area, he could see one of the crewmen standing behind the ship's wheel steering her course toward New York.

What danger could a few pieces of ice present?

Captain Smith was on duty in the bridge, so Bride handed the message to him. "It's from the *Caronia,* sir. She's reporting icebergs and pack ice ahead." The captain thanked him, read the message, and then posted it on the bulletin board for other officers on watch to read. On his way back to the radio room, Bride thought the captain had seemed quite unconcerned by the message. But then again, he had been told that it was not unusual to have ice floating in the sea lanes during an April crossing. Besides, what danger could a few pieces of ice present to an unsinkable ship?

Elsewhere on board, passengers relaxed on deck chairs, reading or taking naps. Some played cards, some wrote letters, while others chatted with friends. As it was Sunday, church services had been held in the morning, the first-class service led by Captain Smith. Jack Thayer spent most of the day walking about the decks getting

---

3. **wireless operator:** a person who works a telegraph transmitter.

Words to Know and Use | **omen** (ō′ mən) *n.* an event or sign believed to point toward a future happening
novelty (näv′ əl tē) *n.* something new, original, or unusual

some fresh air with his parents.

Two more ice warnings were received from nearby ships around lunch time. In the chaos of the radio room, Harold Bride only had time to take one of them to the bridge. The rest of the day passed quietly. Then, in the late afternoon, the temperature began to drop rapidly. Darkness approached as the bugle call announced dinner.

Jack Thayer's parents had been invited to a special dinner for Captain Smith, so Jack ate alone in the first-class dining room. After dinner, as he was having a cup of coffee, he was joined by Milton Long, another passenger going home to the States. Long was older than Jack, but in the easy-going atmosphere of shipboard travel, they struck up a conversation and talked together for an hour or so.

At 7:30 P.M., the radio room received three more warnings of ice about fifty miles ahead. One of them was from the steamer *Californian* reporting three large icebergs. Harold Bride took this message up to the bridge, and it was again politely received. Captain Smith was attending the dinner party being held for him when the warning was delivered. He never got to see it. Then, around 9:00 P.M., the captain excused himself and went up to the bridge. He and his officers talked about how difficult it was to spot icebergs on a calm, clear, moonless night like this with no wind to kick up white surf around them. Before going to bed, the captain ordered the lookouts to keep a sharp watch for ice.

After trading travel stories with Milton Long, Jack Thayer put on his coat and walked around the deck. "It had become

Jack Thayer at age sixteen.

very much colder," he said later. "It was a brilliant, starry night. There was no moon, and I have never seen the stars shine brighter . . . sparkling like diamonds. . . . It was the kind of night that made one feel glad to be alive." At eleven o'clock, he went below to his cabin, put on his pajamas, and got ready for bed.

In the radio room, Harold Bride was exhausted. The two operators were expected to keep the radio working twenty-four hours a day, and Bride lay down to take a much-needed nap. Phillips was so busy with the passenger messages that he actually brushed off the final ice warning of the night. It was from the *Californian*. Trapped in a field of ice, she had stopped for the night about nineteen miles north of the *Titanic*. She was so close that the message literally blasted in Phillips's ears. Annoyed by the loud interruption, he cut off the *Californian's* radio operator with the words, "Shut up, shut up. I'm busy."

The radio room had received a total of seven ice warning messages in one day. It was quite clear that floating icebergs lay ahead of the *Titanic*.

The *Titanic* collides with the iceberg, most of which lay hidden under water.

High up in the crow's nest on the forward mast, Fred Fleet had passed a quiet watch. It was now 11:40 P.M., and he and his fellow lookout were waiting to be relieved so they could head below, perhaps for a hot drink before hopping into their warm bunks. The sea was dead calm. The air was bitterly cold.

Suddenly, Fleet saw something. A huge, dark shape loomed out of the night directly ahead of the *Titanic*. An iceberg! He quickly sounded the alarm bell three times and picked up the telephone.

"What did you see?" asked the duty officer.

"Iceberg right ahead," replied Fleet.

Immediately, the officer on the bridge ordered the wheel turned as far as it would go. The engine room was told to reverse the engines, while a button was pushed to close the doors to the watertight compartments in the bottom of the ship.

The lookouts in the crow's nest braced themselves for a collision. Slowly the ship started to turn. It looked as though they would miss it. But it was too late. They had avoided a head-on crash, but the iceberg had struck a glancing blow along the *Titanic*'s starboard bow. Several tons of ice fell on the ship's decks as the iceberg brushed along the side of the ship and passed into the night. A few minutes later, the *Titanic* came to a stop.

Many of the passengers didn't know the ship had hit anything. Because it was so cold, almost everyone was inside, and most people had already gone to bed. Ruth Becker and her mother were awakened by the dead silence. They could no longer hear the soothing hum of the vibrating engines from below. Jack Thayer was about to step into bed when he felt himself sway ever so slightly. The engines stopped. He was startled by the sudden quiet.

Something was very wrong.

Sensing trouble, Ruth's mother looked out of the door of their second-class cabin and asked a steward[4] what had happened. He told her that nothing was the matter, so Mrs. Becker went back to bed. But as she lay there, she couldn't help feeling that something was very wrong.

Jack heard running feet and voices in the hallway outside his first-class cabin. "I hurried into my heavy overcoat and drew on my slippers. All excited, but not thinking anything serious had occurred, I called in to

---

4. **steward:** a worker on a ship who attends to the needs of passengers.

my father and mother that I was going up on deck to see the fun."

On deck, Jack watched some third-class passengers playing with the ice that had landed on the forward deck as the iceberg had brushed by. Some people were throwing chunks at each other, while a few skidded about playing football with pieces of ice.

Down in the very bottom of the ship, things were very different. When the iceberg had struck, there had been a noise like a big gun going off in one of the boiler rooms. A couple of stokers[5] had been immediately hit by a jet of icy water. The noise and the shock of cold water had sent them running for safety.

Twenty minutes after the crash, things looked very bad indeed to Captain Smith. He and the ship's builder, Thomas Andrews, had made a rapid tour below decks to inspect the damage. The mail room was filling up with water, and sacks of mail were floating about. Water was also pouring into some of the forward holds and two of the boiler rooms.

Captain Smith knew that the *Titanic*'s hull was divided into a number of watertight compartments. She had been designed so that she could still float if only the first four compartments were flooded, but not any more than that. But water was pouring into the first five compartments. And when the water filled them, it would spill over into the next compartment. One by one all the remaining compartments would flood, and the ship would eventually sink. Andrews told the captain that the ship could last an hour, an hour and a half at the most.

Harold Bride had just awakened in the radio room when Captain Smith stuck his head in the door. "Send the call for assistance," he ordered.

"What call should I send?" Phillips asked.

"The regulation international call for help. Just that." Then the captain was gone. Phillips began to send the Morse code "CQD" distress call, flashing away and joking as he did it. After all, they knew the ship was unsinkable.

Five minutes later, the captain was back. "What are you sending?" he asked.

"CQD," Phillips answered. Then Bride cut in and suggested that they try the new SOS signal that was just coming into use. They began to send out the new international call for help—it was one of the first SOS calls ever sent out from a ship in distress.

Ruth and her family had stayed in their bunks for a good fifteen minutes or so after the room steward had told them nothing was wrong. But Ruth's mother couldn't stop worrying as she heard the sound of running feet and shouting voices in the hallway. Poking her head out of the cabin, she found a steward and asked what the matter was.

"Put on your things and come at once," said the steward.

"Do we have time to dress?" she asked.

"No, madam. You have time for nothing. Put on your life jackets and come up to the top deck."

Ruth helped her mother dress the children quickly. But they only had time to throw their coats over their nightgowns and put on their shoes and stockings. In their

---

5. **stokers:** people who tended the boilers that powered steamships.

rush, they forgot to put on their life jackets.

Just after midnight, Captain Smith ordered the lifeboats uncovered. The ship's squash court, which was thirty-two feet above the keel, was now completely flooded. Jack Thayer and his father came into the first-class lounge to try to find out exactly what the matter was. When Thomas Andrews, the ship's builder, passed by, Mr. Thayer asked him what was going on. He replied in a low voice that the ship had not much more than an hour to live. Jack and his father couldn't believe their ears.

From the bridge of the *Titanic,* a ship's lights were observed not far away, possibly the *Californian's.* Captain Smith then ordered white distress rockets fired to get the attention of the nearby ship. They burst high in the air with a loud boom and a shower of stars. But the rockets made no difference. The mystery ship in the distance never answered.

In the radio room, Bride and Phillips now knew how serious the accident was and were feverishly sending out calls for help. A number of ships heard and responded to their calls, but most were too far away to come to the rescue in time. The closest ship they had been able to reach was the *Carpathia* about fifty-eight miles away. Immediately, the *Carpathia* reported that she was racing full steam to the rescue. But could she get there in time?

Not far away, the radio operator of the *Californian* had gone to bed for the night and turned off his radio. Several officers and crewmen on the deck of the *Californian* saw rockets in the distance and reported them to their captain. The captain told them to try to contact the ship with a Morse lamp. But they received no answer to their flashed calls. No one thought to wake up the radio operator.

On board the *Titanic,* almost an hour after the crash, most of the passengers still did not realize the seriousness of the situation. But Captain Smith was a very worried man. He knew that the *Titanic* only carried lifeboats for barely half the estimated twenty-two hundred people on board. He would have to make sure his officers kept order to avoid any panic among the passengers. At 12:30 A.M. Captain Smith gave the orders to start loading the lifeboats—women and children first. Even though the *Titanic* was by now quite noticeably down at the bow and listing slightly to one side, many passengers still didn't want to leave the huge, brightly lit ship. The ship's band added to a kind of party feeling as the musicians played lively tunes.

About 12:45 A.M. the first lifeboat was lowered. It could carry sixty-five people, but left with only twenty-eight aboard. Indeed, many of the first boats to leave were half empty. Ruth Becker noticed that there was no panic among the crowds of passengers milling about on the decks. "Everything was calm, everybody was orderly." But the night air was now biting cold. Ruth's mother told her to go back to their cabin to get some blankets. Ruth hurried down to the cabin

Words to Know and Use | **feverishly** (fē′ vər ish lē) *adv.* in a highly emotional or nervous way

As he hit the water, Jack Thayer was sucked down. "The cold was terrific. The shock of the water took the breath out of my lungs. Down and down I went, spinning in all directions." When he finally surfaced, gasping for air and numbed by the water, the ship was about forty feet away from him. His friend Milton Long was nowhere to be seen. Jack would never see him again.

Jack Thayer was lucky. As he struggled in the water, his hand came to rest on an overturned lifeboat. He grabbed hold and hung on, barely managing to pull himself up out of the water. Harold Bride had been washed overboard and now also clung to this same boat.

Both Jack and Harold witnessed the mighty ship's last desperate moments. "We could see groups of . . . people aboard, clinging in clusters or bunches, like swarming bees; only to fall in masses, pairs, or singly, as the great part of the ship . . . rose into the sky. . . ." said Thayer. "I looked upwards—we were right under the three enormous propellers. For an instant, I thought they were sure to come right down on top of us.

Then . . . she slid quietly away from us into the sea."

Out in the safety of her lifeboat, Ruth Becker also witnessed the end of the *Titanic*. "I could look back and see this ship, and the decks were just lined with people looking over. Finally, as the *Titanic* sank faster, the lights died out. You could just see the stern remaining in an upright position for a couple of minutes. Then . . . it disappeared."

Then, as Ruth recalled, "there fell upon the ear the most terrible noise that human beings ever listened to—the cries of hundreds of people struggling in the icy cold water, crying for help with a cry we knew could not be answered." In Thayer's words, they became "a long continuous wailing chant." Before long this ghastly wailing stopped, as the freezing water took its toll.

Jack Thayer and Harold Bride and a number of other survivors clung to their overturned lifeboat, inches away from an icy death in the North Atlantic. Numb from the cold and not daring to move in case the boat sank under their weight, they prayed and waited for help. Then, as the first light of dawn crept on the horizon, a rocket was seen in the distance. The *Carpathia* had come to their rescue. ❧

*R*esponding to Reading

First Impressions

1. What were you thinking about as you finished this selection? Jot down some notes and be prepared to share them with your classmates.

Second Thoughts

2. Based on the description of the *Titanic* early in the selection, would you have wanted to travel on it? Would you have felt safe? Explain why, citing evidence from the passage in your explanation.

3. Was anyone to blame for the sinking of the ship? Cite details from the story to support your judgment.

   Think about
   - the advance publicity about the *Titanic*
   - the safety record of the captain

4. Evaluate the behavior of passengers and crew as the *Titanic* was sinking.

5. How might this account differ from an article on the same topic written as informational nonfiction?

Broader Connections

6. Are people more or less cautious about new technology than they used to be? Give some examples to support your opinion.

*L*iterary Concept: Informational Writing

Writers of nonfiction material use whatever organization works best for their topic and purpose. In this selection, Ballard describes the *Titanic* using paragraphs organized by topic sentence. When the ship is sinking, he uses chronological order. Find an example of each kind of organization in the article. Why do you think he changed the type of organization he used?

Writing Options

1. The *Titanic* was evacuated tradition-ally, "women and children first." Write an **essay** on whether you agree or disagree with this principle.

2. Write an **advertisement** for the *Titanic*. Before you begin, skim the description of the *Titanic* to find details and features that you could use to entice customers.

3. Write a **message in a bottle** you might have thrown overboard if you had been one of the passengers in a crowded lifeboat.

4. Imagine that you are the captain of the *Carpathia*. Write the ship's **log entry** describing what you see when you arrive, too late, at the scene.

Vocabulary Practice

Exercise   On a separate sheet of paper, write the word from the list that best completes the sentence.

1. The passenger ship business in 1907 was just as __?__ as the airline industry is now.

2. Even today, people pay __?__ to the courage of the *Titanic's* captain and crew.

3. Given a choice, most people would choose first class rooms over a third class __?__.

4. The rich and __?__, like the Astors, were physically separated from the lower classes.

5. The swimming pool on board was a real __?__; it was the first to be built on a steamship.

6. A near collision at the *Titanic's* launching seemed to be an __?__ of bad things to come.

7. Even though it was called "unsinkable," the *Titanic* did not stay afloat __?__.

8. In fearful haste, grim sailors __?__ lowered lifeboats into the cold water.

9. With no lifeboats left, some passengers leaped __?__ into the icy waters.

10. No one would have believed a __?__ that predicted the *Titanic's* sinking.

> *Words to Know and Use*
>
> **accommodation**
> **aristocratic**
> **competitive**
> **desperately**
> **feverishly**
> **indefinitely**
> **novelty**
> **omen**
> **prophecy**
> **tribute**

Options for Learning

1 • Facts to Fathom Read the rest of *Exploring the Titanic*, or use other resources, to find out how the sunken ship was finally discovered. Report on your findings to the class.

2 • See the Movie! Rent either *The Titanic* (1953) or *A Night to Remember* (1958). Screen it for your class and lead a discussion on the differences between the movie version and Ballard's written account.

3 • Dramatic Drawing Based on what you've learned, illustrate a dramatic scene from the sinking of the *Titanic*.

4 • On the Rocks Using articles from magazines such as *National Geographic*, report to the class on modern technologies that now help prevent disasters like the sinking of the *Titanic*.

FACT FINDER SCIENCE

What percentage of an iceberg lies under water?

Robert D. Ballard
1942-

Robert Ballard has been fascinated by the sea since childhood, when he explored beaches and read about famous sailors such as Captain Cook and Admiral Byrd. As an adult, Ballard helped pay for his education in oceanography by training dolphins at a marine park. Eventually, Ballard joined the staff at Woods Hole Oceanographic Institute in Massachusetts. There he began his search for and eventual discovery of the *Titanic*, using remote-control underwater robots. Among the first things the robot cameras saw were the empty lifeboat racks— "the last thing many of the people saw as they were looking for a lifeboat," Ballard says.

The explorer has now set his sights on inspiring children to learn. "We need to declare war on ignorance, and the only way is through education. I want to recruit people to study science, just as a coach recruits basketball players."

WRITER'S WORKSHOP

DESCRIPTIVE WRITING

What's one food that you know you'll never forget? In the subunit you've just read, a poem describes the taste of stolen strawberries, freshly picked. A short story describes a mysterious dessert called swoodies. What are your own best or worst—or strangest— experiences with food? This workshop will let you share some of them as you write a restaurant review. You may review an eating place you love, one you hate, or one you have mixed feelings about. You'll use **observation** and **description** as you put your impressions into words.

USE DESCRIPTIVE WRITING FOR

character sketches
letters
stories
poems
reports
reviews
advertisements
travel guides

GUIDED ASSIGNMENT: RESTAURANT REVIEW

Write a review describing a restaurant or another eating place you know well. In your review make your opinion clear.

Here is one writer's PASSkey to this assignment.

P URPOSE: To observe and describe

A UDIENCE: People in your community

S UBJECT: A local restaurant or eating place

S TRUCTURE: Review

The Real Thing
by Lee Granville

Buck, buck, ba-gawk! I can almost hear clucking as we step through the door. Inside, the walls are covered with pictures of chickens and a cartoon mural of two puzzled chickens looking at an ax and a chopping block. This is the Chicken Pie Shop, my favorite restaurant.

My mother and I find an empty booth. The clatter of dishes and silverware being dumped into bus trays rings in my ears. Under the fluorescent lights, the yellow plastic seats look greenish, and the Formica tables look old. A waitress in a yellow uniform zooms up,

STUDENT MODEL

◄ A surprising first line catches readers' interest.

◄ The writer sets a positive focus.

◄ Sensory details describe sights and sounds.

An unusual comparison describes the waitress. ▶

takes our order without smiling, and zooms off again like a taxi. However, the tacky atmosphere and grouchy service don't bother us. We're about to eat the world's tastiest chicken pies.

Here they are, steaming on the plates that the waitress has just slapped down in front of us. The only problem with eating here is the danger of burning your mouth. This happens when you can't wait to dig in to the moist chunks of chicken and the creamy gravy you see through the hole in the crust. The crust is not thin or greasy like the crusts of frozen chicken pies. It's smooth and sort of floury and smells like warm pie crust fresh from the oven.

Specific adjectives and adverbs describe the food. ▶

As you carefully begin eating, you discover that this pie is the real thing. It has huge pieces of chicken, thick gravy, and no peas or carrots to get in your way. Next to the pie is an ice-cream scoop of real, not fake, mashed potatoes, covered in spicy gravy.

My mother and I don't talk—we're too busy shoveling in the food. As soon as we finish, the waitress is back. All in one swoop she clears the table, gives us the bill, and asks if we want dessert. She can't wait to be rid of us. Another load of dishes crashes into a bus tray as we pass the chicken mural on our way out. This place is definitely not elegant—but it does serve really good chicken pie.

The writer clearly states an opinion. ▶

Now that you've read Lee's review, start your own.

Prewrite and Explore

1 **Let your taste buds talk**   Imagine your taste buds brainstorming about eating places they especially like and hate. Try jotting down the places they'd probably put in each category. Think of places you visit often, like fast-food shops or the school cafeteria, as well as places you've visited only once or twice.

When you've listed several places, you can take a quick mental tour of them. Any place you remember well or have strong feelings about will make a good subject.

2 **Set your focus**   In a restaurant review you explain your opinion of the restaurant. Your opinion may be positive or negative. It may be based on the way the food tastes, looks, and is prepared or on the service or the atmosphere. It may be based on several of these factors. Freewrite briefly to focus on your opinion. In **freewriting** you write whatever comes to your mind about the subject for three to five minutes. Don't worry about using complete sentences or proper spelling or punctuation. When you finish, see if you know yet which factors your opinion is based on.

GATHERING INFORMATION

Now you have time to recall details about the place you've chosen. Your freewriting can guide your memory. Using a chart like the one below can help you think of details. Fill in the sections you can. Notice what Lee filled in about the Chicken Pie Shop.

Hear	Smell	Touch
dishes clanking not much talk	oven-fresh	hot!

See	Taste
chicken pictures old Formica tables faded yellow seats steaming pies	smooth, floury crust moist chicken rich gravy real mashed potatoes

◀ TIP . . . .
Use "tunnel vision" to zero in on one sense at a time.

◀ STUDENT MODEL . . . .

Draft and Discover

1 **Begin drafting**   As you draft, go into as much detail as possible. Your prewriting chart will help. You might start by describing the first thing you notice when you walk into the restaurant, then move on to other things you notice. If you prefer, you may start by stating your opinion, then describe the factors that support it.

2 **Use comparisons**   One way to help a reader imagine what you are describing is by comparing it to something else. Look at the following example. Which two things are compared?

LITERARY MODEL
from "Lose Now, Pay Later," by Carol Farley

▶ Do you know that wonderful spurt of air that rushes out when you first open an expensive box of candy? The inside of that store smelled just like the inside of one of those boxes.

COMPUTER TIP
A search feature can find all the places you've used a certain word. Try searching for vague adjectives like *nice* and *gross,* then replace them with a more specific modifier.

▶ **3** **Be specific**   Go for specific adjectives and adverbs. Describing a hamburger as *bad, gross, fine,* or *delicious* is vague. Specific modifiers—like *greasy, dry,* or *tender*—convey stronger sensory details. General terms like *good* and *bad* weaken description, but you may need them to sum up your opinion. Ask a friend whether you're using them effectively.

Revise Your Writing

1 **Showcase your reasons and opinion**   As you read your draft, look again for the reasons that support your opinion. They will be clearer now, and you can revise to spotlight them. For example, you may decide that the food is only average but you love the atmosphere. Then you might write a paragraph about each, or you might add more details about food and atmosphere to each body paragraph.

2 **Get a strong start**   After you have a draft you like, try adding a catchy first sentence: a vivid description, an unusual comparison, or a surprising statement. When you are satisfied with your introduction, use the questions below to help you polish your work.

Revision Questions

For You	For a Peer Reader
1. How do I use sensory details to support my opinion?	1. What would you expect to find if you ate at this place?
2. Where might I use a comparison or a more specific modifier?	2. How would you sum up my opinion? On which factors do you think I based it?
3. Does my first sentence catch the readers' interest?	3. Which part of my review was most vivid or surprising?

Proofread

Correct errors in grammar and mechanics. Look carefully at your use of adjectives and adverbs. If you wish, ask a peer to help.

THE EDITOR'S EYE: CONFUSING ADJECTIVES AND ADVERBS

Choose adjectives to modify nouns and pronouns. Choose adverbs to modify verbs, adjectives, and other adverbs.

Sometimes you may not be sure whether to choose an adjective or an adverb. Ask yourself which kind of word the modifier describes.

Problem   But it does serve *real* good chicken pie.

The modifier *real* describes *good,* an adjective. Only adverbs describe adjectives, so the adverb form is needed.

Revised   But it does serve *really* good chicken pie.

NEED MORE HELP?

See the Language Workshop on pages 114–116 and pages 752–753 of the Language Handbook.

Publish and Present

Here is a suggestion for sharing your work with others.

A Restaurant Guide   Gather the class's reviews, grouping together reviews of similar places. Create a table of contents, design a cover, and distribute copies to class members and friends.

Reflect on Your Writing

Write answers to the following questions. Then attach them to your review and add it to your portfolio.

◀ FOR YOUR PORTFOLIO

1. Which part of this review was most fun to write? Why?
2. As I worked, what did I discover about my writing process?

LANGUAGE
WORKSHOP

USING ADJECTIVES AND ADVERBS

> Use **adjectives** to describe nouns and pronouns. Use **adverbs** to describe verbs, adjectives, and other adverbs.

The more specific and vivid your adjectives and adverbs are, the stronger your descriptions will be.

Adjectives

Adjectives modify, or describe, nouns and pronouns. In the sentences below, the words in italics are adjectives.

LITERARY MODEL

from *Exploring the Titanic,* by Robert D. Ballard

▶

> The ship was about *forty* feet away. . . .

> "I could look back and see *this* ship, and the decks were just lined with people looking over. . . .

> Before long this *ghastly* wailing stopped, as the *freezing* water took its toll.

Adjectives tell *which one* (this ship), *how much* or *how many* (forty feet), or *what kind* (freezing water). Specific adjectives are as exact as possible. For example, *forty* is more specific than *several,* and *ghastly* is a vivid way to describe *wailing.*

Adverbs

Adverbs modify verbs, adjectives, and other adverbs. In the sentences below, the words in italics are adverbs.

SPELLING TIP

When you form an adverb by adding *-ly* to an adjective that ends in *l,* keep both *l*'s: *painful + -ly = painfully*

▶

> I limped *painfully away.* . . .

> They did laugh at me *pretty often.* . . .

Adverbs answer the question *how* (I limped painfully), *where* (I limped away), *when* (they laughed often), or *to what extent* (pretty often). Many adverbs are formed by adding *-ly* to adjectives (painful/painfully). Specific, vivid adverbs bring your writing to life.

Common Errors in Using Adjectives and Adverbs

This, These, That,* and *Those   *This, these, that*, and *those* can be **demonstrative adjectives,** or adjectives that point out *which one* or *which ones. This* and *that* are singular and modify singular nouns and pronouns. *These* and *those* are plural and modify plural nouns and pronouns. In addition, the nouns *kind* and *sort* are singular; *kinds* and *sorts* are plural. Use the correct demonstrative adjectives with them.

Singular	Plural
this shoe	these shoes
that shoe	those shoes
this kind	these kinds
that sort	those sorts

Never use the words *here* or *there* with demonstrative adjectives.

Incorrect	Correct
Look at that there cabin.	Look at that cabin.

Never use the pronoun *them* in place of a demonstrative adjective.

Incorrect	Correct
Who sent them messages?	Who sent those messages?

Exercise 1   Concept Check   Write the correct adjective.

1. I wonder if (this, these) life jacket is the right size.
2. You may not enter (that, those) lifeboats without permission.
3. Have you ever seen (this, these) type of flare before?
4. Quickly, grab (that, that there) rope and pull!
5. (Them, Those) radio operators stayed on the job all night.

Good/Well, Real/Really, Bad/Badly

Because the adjectives *good, real,* and *bad* and their adverb partners *well, really,* and *badly* are used in similar situations, writers sometimes confuse them. To make the correct choice, first decide which part of speech the modifier is describing.

Sherwood Anderson writes (good, well).

The modifier tells how Anderson *writes;* it describes a verb. So you would choose the adverb, *well.*

His story is (real, really) funny.

The modifier tells how *funny* the story is; it describes an adjective. So you would choose the adverb, *really.*

At school, the boy's legs hurt (bad, badly).

The modifier tells how the boy's legs *hurt;* it describes a verb. So you would choose the adverb, *badly.*

Watch for modifiers that follow linking verbs (*is, seems, looks, smells, tastes, sounds, feels,* and so forth). These modifiers are not adverbs but predicate adjectives.

He feels (bad, badly) when his family laughs at him.

The modifier describes a pronoun, *he.* So you would choose the adjective, *bad.*

Exercise 2   Concept Check   Write the correct modifier.

1. The pond sparkles (bright, brightly) in the sun.
2. (Sudden, Suddenly) the boy decides to go fishing.
3. To his bare toes the water feels (cool, coolly).
4. He wants (bad, badly) to catch the giant carp.
5. The carp is (heavy, heavily) in his arms, but he gets it home.
6. He (proud, proudly) shows the carp to his family.
7. The boy feels (good, well) about his accomplishment.
8. His family is (real, really) surprised at the size of the fish.
9. His brothers and sisters shout (happy, happily).
10. (Tired, Tiredly) after a long day, the boy finally goes to bed.

Exercise 3   Revision Skill   Copy the paragraph correctly.

Have you tried this new desserts called swoodies? Those shops offering them are everywhere now. The scent of them swoodies is irresistible. My favorite flavor is that there chocolate almond. I enjoy this kind of treat as often as I want. Since I've gained a few pounds, my clothes fit tight, but if I use the slimmer, they'll look well again. The slimmer seems real eerie at first. It's a tall plain booth without windows. Still, it works real good.

LANGUAGE HANDBOOK
. . . .
For review and practice: Section 7, Using Adjectives and Adverbs, pages 749–752, 756–758.

Exercise 4   Revising Your Writing

1. Reread the descriptive writing you did for the Writer's Workshop.
2. Correct any errors in your use of adjectives and adverbs.
3. Add five specific, vivid modifiers to your writing.

VOCABULARY
WORKSHOP

CONTEXT CLUES

Part of reading is discovering new words. Often, you can figure out the meanings of unfamiliar words by using context clues. A word's **context** is the sentences and paragraphs surrounding it. If you didn't know the meaning of *saber,* which clues in the sentence below could help you figure it out?

> The men of the Light Brigade charged, their sharp sabers flashing in the air, slashing at the enemy.

When you read that a saber is sharp, can flash in the air, and is used to slash at an enemy, you can guess that it is a kind of sword.

A **definition,** one kind of context clue, directly states the meaning of a word. Definition clues may be set off with commas, dashes, or parentheses. They may follow the key terms *or, is, that is, who is, which is,* or *in other words.*

> The enemy forces were shattered, *or* completely broken.

An **example,** another kind of context clue, may follow the key terms *like, such as, for example, for instance,* or *other.*

> Did no soldiers feel misgivings, *such as* the uneasy sense that the order was a mistake or the fear that they were outnumbered?

◀ NOTE
. . . .
Use inference to help you guess what an example clue reveals about a word's meaning.

Exercise   Using Context Clues   With the help of context clues, explain the meaning of each italicized word as it is used below.

1. The men rode a *league,* or three miles, into the valley and back.
2. Of the entire *brigade*—a group of hundreds of soldiers—only a few survived.
3. None of the soldiers showed signs of *dismay,* such as trembling or running away.
4. Like other famous mistakes, the order to charge was a *blunder.*
5. The unexpected charge of the Light Brigade *sundered,* or divided, the enemy forces.
6. Tennyson's poem praises the soldiers' *fortitude;* for example, the soldiers attacked bravely, though they knew they couldn't win.

Reading on Your Own

Suggested Novels for Unit One

The novels introduced on these pages allow you to explore the unit theme, "A Matter of Perspective," in more depth and in different ways.

MONKEY ISLAND

PAULA FOX ©1991

After his father and his mother both leave him, eleven-year-old Clay becomes a homeless person living on the streets of New York City. Clay's new life is a sad and frightening change from his former life. His father has lost his job and is gone; his mother is unable to bear life in a welfare hotel and disappears. Clay's new circumstances completely change his perspective. While he searches for his mother, Clay makes friends with two homeless men, who become his family. Clay now must survive cold, hunger, and vicious street gangs that prey on homeless people. Throughout this exciting urban survival story, Clay discovers that although homelessness can happen to anyone, only the strong survive. Read to find out . . .

- whether Clay can survive on his own in this nightmarish environment

- whether Clay will find his mother

- whether Clay and his mother will be able to make a decent life together

THE WITCH OF BLACKBIRD POND

ELIZABETH GEORGE SPEARE ©1958

How would you feel if you were accused of witchcraft and put on trial because of your actions and beliefs? In this exciting historical novel set in New England in the late 1600s, a girl named Kit faces persecution by the entire community when she moves to a Puritan village. Read to find out how she tries to overcome the tunnel vision of people who are suspicious of everyone. As you read, consider the following questions:

• What if everything you normally do were suddenly seen as unnatural?

• How would you have responded to the fear and persecution common during this time of witch hunts?

• How would it feel to suddenly become the target of a whole community's suspicions?

AGAINST THE STORM

GAYE HICYILMAZ ©1992

From the perspective of twelve-year-old Mahmet, life in his Turkish village is wonderful—he has friends, flowers, and plenty of space. When his family decides to improve their lives by moving to the large, unfamiliar city of Ankara, Mahmet finds himself living in a shantytown, surrounded by poverty. Based on a real-life incident, this modern survival story shows how a false impression—the idea that city life will be better—can almost ruin a family. Read to discover . . .

• what has become of Mahmet's best friend, who has moved to the city

• what Mahmet can do when he sees his family changing

• whether Mahmet can survive and help his family

Other Recommended Books

Commodore Perry in the Land of the Shogun by Rhoda Blumberg (©1985). In this nonfictional book, the author describes how Commodore Perry helped to open Japan to world trade in the 1850s.

Reflections on a Gift of Watermelon Pickle . . . and other Modern Verse edited by Stephen Dunning, Edward Lueders, and Hugh Smith (©1967). This classic collection of poetry contains engaging poems by many well-known poets.

The Wright Brothers: How They Invented the Airplane by Russell Freedman (©1991). The fascinating activities of the Wright brothers as they develop the airplane are related and illustrated with numerous original photographs by Wilbur and Orville Wright.

A Solitary Blue by Cynthia Voigt (©1983). In a contemporary realistic novel, a boy discovers that he may have false impressions of family members and friends. As he develops new insights, he also makes valuable discoveries about himself.

SCALES
OF
JUSTICE

It does not require many

words to speak the truth.

Chief Joseph

DAKOTA PIPE CLAN MAGIC
Oscar Howe
Courtesy, Mr. and Mrs. Peter A. Hassrick.

$\mathcal{V}$ICTIMS OR VICTORS ?

Have you ever seen justice portrayed as a blindfolded woman holding a pair of scales in her hand? The scales show the importance of fairness when making a decision. Before a just decision can be made, both sides of a conflict must be studied. In this unit you will be reading about issues of justice. Like the blindfolded woman, you must weigh the evidence and come to your own decisions.

In "Victims or Victors?" you will meet some characters who are defeated by injustice and others who rise in triumph. You will need to decide who really is the victor and who is the victim.

Fiction

All Summer in a Day

RAY BRADBURY

Examine What You Know

Think of times when a group has excluded or picked on a person who was somehow different from the members of the group. Why do you think groups feel the need to exclude people unlike themselves? Discuss your ideas with the class.

Expand Your Knowledge

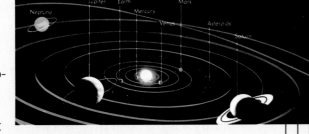

One source of differences among people is their reaction to the environment. The **setting** of the following science fiction story is a classroom on the planet Venus—an imaginary Venus unlike the real planet—in the future. The author has created a world without sunshine. Although most of us feel slightly depressed when deprived of sunlight for a long time, some people develop serious cases of depression. One treatment for such depression involves the use of special lights that give off ultraviolet rays similar to those found in sunlight. Patients are exposed to the lights for limited periods, and their depression is usually relieved.

Enrich Your Reading

Finding Contrasts   When two things are examined together, the differences between them are called **contrasts.** Writers use contrasts to help readers get a clear picture of a character, an event, a place, or an idea. As you read, think about the differences between Margot (the main character) and her classmates. As soon as you finish reading, jot down some of those differences in a chart like the one below. Share your ideas when you finish.

Margot	Her Classmates
would not sing or play games	played and sang happily

■ *Author biography in Reader's Handbook*

All Summer in a Day

RAY BRADBURY

"Ready?"

"Ready."

"Now?"

"Soon."

"Do the scientists really know? Will it happen today, will it?"

"Look, look; see for yourself!"

The children pressed to each other like so many roses, so many weeds, intermixed, peering out for a look at the hidden sun.

It rained.

It had been raining for seven years; thousands upon thousands of days compounded and filled from one end to the other with rain, with the drum and gush of water, with the sweet crystal fall of showers and the con<u>cussion</u> of storms so heavy they were <u>tidal</u> waves come over the islands. A thousand forests had been crushed under the rain and grown up a thousand times to be crushed again. And this was the way life was forever on the planet Venus, and this was the schoolroom of the children of the rocket men and women who had come to a raining world to set up civilization and live out their lives.

"It's stopping, it's stopping!"

"Yes, yes!"

Margot stood apart from them, from these children who could never remember a time when there wasn't rain and rain and rain. They were all nine years old, and if there had been a day, seven years ago, when the sun came out for an hour and showed its face to the stunned world, they could not recall. Sometimes, at night, she heard them stir, in remembrance, and she knew they were dreaming and remembering gold or a yellow crayon or a coin large enough to buy the world with. She knew that they thought they remembered a warmness, like a blushing in the face, in the body, in the arms and legs and trembling hands. But then they always awoke to the tatting drum, the endless shaking down of clear bead necklaces upon the roof, the walk, the gardens, the forest, and their dreams were gone.

All day yesterday they had read in class about the sun. About how like a lemon it was, and how hot. And they had written small stories or essays or poems about it:

I think the sun is a flower
That blooms for just one hour.

Words to Know and Use | **concussion** (kən kush′ ən) *n.* a strong shaking

PORTRAIT OF A SICK GIRL
1901 Paula Modersohn-Becker
Courtesy, Westfälisches Landesmuseum
für Kunst und Kulturgeschichte,
Münster, Germany.

That was Margot's poem, read in a quiet voice in the still classroom while the rain was falling outside.

"Aw, you didn't write that!" protested one of the boys.

"I did," said Margot. "I *did*."

"William!" said the teacher.

But that was yesterday. Now, the rain was slackening, and the children were crushed to the great thick windows.

"Where's teacher?"

"She'll be back."

"She'd better hurry; we'll miss it!"

They turned on themselves, like a feverish wheel, all tumbling spokes.

Margot stood alone. She was a very frail girl who looked as if she had been lost in the rain for years and the rain had washed out the blue from her eyes and the red from her mouth and the yellow from her hair. She was an old photograph dusted from an album, whitened away, and if she spoke at all, her voice would be a ghost. Now she stood, separate, staring at the rain and the loud, wet world beyond the huge glass.

"What're *you* looking at?" said William.

Margot said nothing.

"Speak when you're spoken to." He gave her a shove. But she did not move; rather, she let herself be moved only by him and nothing else.

They edged away from her; they would not look at her. She felt them go away. And this was because she would play no games with them in the echoing tunnels of the underground city. If they tagged her and ran, she stood blinking after them and did not follow. When the class sang songs about happiness and life and games, her lips barely moved. Only when they sang about the sun and the summer did her lips move, as she watched the drenched windows.

She was different, and they knew her difference and kept away.

And then, of course, the biggest crime of all was that she had come here only five years ago from Earth, and she remembered the sun and the way the sun was and the sky was when she was four, in Ohio. And they, they had been on Venus all their lives, and they had been only two years old when last the sun came out and had long since forgotten the color and heat of it and the way that it really was. But Margot remembered.

"It's like a penny," she said, once, eyes closed.

"No, it's not!" the children cried.

"It's like a fire," she said, "in the stove."

"You're lying; you don't remember!" cried the children.

But she remembered and stood quietly apart from all of them and watched the patterning windows. And once, a month ago, she had refused to shower in the school shower rooms, had clutched her hands to her ears and over her head, screaming that the water mustn't touch her head. So after that, dimly, dimly, she sensed it; she was different, and they knew her difference and kept away.

There was talk that her father and mother were taking her back to Earth next year; it seemed vital to her that they do so, though it would mean the loss of thousands of dollars to her family. And so the children hated her for all these reasons, of big and little consequence. They hated her pale, snow face, her waiting silence, her thinness, and her possible future.

"Get away!" The boy gave her another push. "What're you waiting for?"

Then, for the first time, she turned and looked at him. And what she was waiting for was in her eyes.

"Well, don't wait around here!" cried the boy, savagely. "You won't see nothing!"

Her lips moved.

"Nothing!" he cried. "It was all a joke, wasn't it?" He turned to the other children. "Nothing's happening today. *Is* it?"

They all blinked at him and then, understanding, laughed and shook their heads. "Nothing, nothing!"

"Oh, but," Margot whispered, her eyes helpless. "But, this is the day, the scientists predict, they say, they *know*, the sun . . ."

"All a joke!" said the boy, and seized her roughly. "Hey, everyone, let's put her in a closet before teacher comes!"

"No," said Margot, falling back.

They surged about her, caught her up and bore her, protesting and then pleading and then crying, back into a tunnel, a room, a closet, where they slammed and locked

Words to Know and Use | **surge** (sɐrj) *v.* to suddenly push forward in a violent way

the door. They stood looking at the door and saw it tremble from her beating and throwing herself against it. They heard her muffled cries. Then, smiling, they turned and went out and back down the tunnel, just as the teacher arrived.

"Ready, children?" She glanced at her watch.

"Yes!" said everyone.

"Are we all here?"

"Yes!"

The rain slackened still more.

They crowded to the huge door.

The rain stopped.

It was as if, in the midst of a film concerning an avalanche, a tornado, a hurricane, a volcanic eruption, something had, first, gone wrong with the sound apparatus, thus muffling and finally cutting off all noise, all of the blasts and repercussions and thunders, and then, secondly, ripped the film from the projector and inserted in its place a peaceful tropical slide which did not move or tremor. The world ground to a standstill. The silence was so <u>immense</u> and unbelievable that you felt that your ears had been stuffed or you had lost your hearing altogether. The children put their hands to their ears. They stood apart. The door slid back, and the smell of the silent, waiting world came in to them.

The sun came out.

It was the color of flaming bronze, and it was very large. And the sky around it was a blazing blue tile color. And the jungle burned with sunlight as the children, released from their spell, rushed out, yelling, into the summertime.

"Now, don't go too far," called the teacher after them. "You've got only one hour, you know. You wouldn't want to get caught out!"

But they were running and turning their faces up to the sky and feeling the sun on their cheeks like a warm iron; they were taking off their jackets and letting the sun burn their arms.

"Oh, it's better than the sunlamps, isn't it?"

"Much, much better!"

They stopped running and stood in the great jungle that covered Venus, that grew and never stopped growing, <u>tumultuously</u>, even as you watched it. It was a nest of octopuses, clustering up great arms of flesh-like weed, wavering, flowering in this brief spring. It was the color of rubber and ash, this jungle, from the many years without sun. It was the color of stones and white cheeses and ink.

The children lay out, laughing, on the jungle mattress and heard it sigh and squeak under them, <u>resilient</u> and alive. They ran among the trees, they slipped and fell, they pushed each other, they played hide-and-seek and tag; but most of all they squinted at the sun until tears ran down their faces, they put their hands up at that yellowness and that amazing blueness, and they breathed of the fresh air and listened and listened to the silence which suspended them in a blessed sea of no sound and no motion. They looked at everything and <u>savored</u> everything. Then, wildly, like animals

Words to Know and Use
| **immense** (im mens') *adj.* very large; enormous
tumultuously (tōō mul' chōō əs lē) *adv.* in a wild and disorderly way
resilient (ri zil' yənt) *adj.* flexible and springy
savor (sā' vər) *v.* to take great pleasure in

127

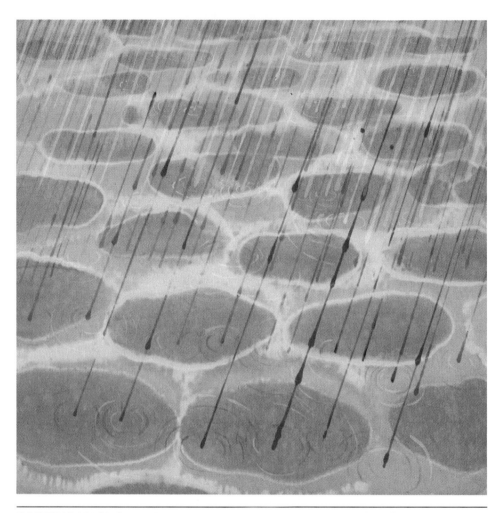

JAPANESE RAIN ON CANVAS   1972   David Hockney   Acrylic on canvas, 48" x 48".
© David Hockney 1972.

escaped from their caves, they ran and ran in shouting circles. They ran for an hour and did not stop running.

And then—

In the midst of their running, one of the girls wailed.

Everyone stopped.

The girl, standing in the open, held out her hand.

"Oh, look, look," she said, trembling.

They came slowly to look at her opened palm.

In the center of it, cupped and huge, was a single raindrop.

She began to cry, looking at it.

They glanced quickly at the sky.

"Oh. Oh."

A few cold drops fell on their noses and their cheeks and their mouths. The sun faded behind a stir of mist. A wind blew cool around them. They turned and started to walk back toward the underground house, their hands at their sides, their smiles vanishing away.

A boom of thunder startled them, and like leaves before a new hurricane, they tumbled upon each other and ran. Lightning struck ten miles away, five miles away, a mile, a half mile. The sky darkened into midnight in a flash.

They stood in the doorway of the underground for a moment until it was raining hard. Then they closed the door and heard the gigantic sound of the rain falling in tons and avalanches everywhere and forever.

"Will it be seven more years?"

"Yes. Seven."

Then one of them gave a little cry.

"Margot!"

"What?"

"She's still in the closet where we locked her."

"Margot."

They stood as if someone had driven them, like so many stakes, into the floor. They looked at each other and then looked away. They glanced out at the world that was raining now and raining and raining steadily. They could not meet each other's glances. Their faces were solemn and pale. They looked at their hands and feet, their faces down.

"Margot."

One of the girls said, "Well . . . ?"

No one moved.

"Go on," whispered the girl.

They walked slowly down the hall in the sound of cold rain. They turned through the doorway to the room, in the sound of the storm and thunder, lightning on their faces, blue and terrible. They walked over to the closet door slowly and stood by it.

Behind the closet door was only silence.

They unlocked the door, even more slowly, and let Margot out. ❧

I N S I G H T

What Do We Do with a Variation?

JAMES BERRY

What do we do with a difference?
Do we stand and discuss its oddity
or do we ignore it?

Do we shut our eyes to it
or poke it with a stick?
Do we clobber it to death?

Do we move around it in rage
and enlist the rage of others?
Do we will it to go away?

Do we look at it in awe
or purely in wonderment?
Do we work for it to disappear?

Do we pass it stealthily
or change route away from it?
Do we will it to become like ourselves?

What do we do with a difference?
Do we communicate to it,
let application acknowledge it
for barriers to fall down?

Responding to Reading

First Impressions

1. What feeling do you have at the end of the story? Why?

Second Thoughts

2. How do you think Margot's classmates feel about what they've done? Support your answer with evidence from the story.

3. Why do you think the class picks on Margot?

   Think about
   - your discussion about why groups exclude those who are different
   - the ways in which the writer contrasts Margot with the group

4. Margot is a victim in this story. In your opinion, are her classmates victims or victors? Explain your answer.

Literary Concepts: Simile and Metaphor

Similes and metaphors help create images and make a story more vivid. A **simile** compares two things using words such as *like, as, than,* or *resembles: The sun is like a lemon.* Find two similes in the story.

A **metaphor** is also a comparison of two things, but a metaphor does not contain the words *like* or *as.* Metaphors are sometimes harder to find than similes. "She was an old photograph dusted from an album, whitened away" is a metaphor describing Margot. In pairs or small groups, use your ideas about the story to make up metaphors that begin with the phrases *The rain was _____, Margot's classmates were _____; The classroom was _____.* Share your best metaphors with the rest of the class.

Writing Options

1. Do you think Margot's classmates are entirely at fault, or did some of her actions encourage their behavior? Write your **opinion** about the responsibility of both Margot and the class in the incident.

2. Write your own **story** or **poem** about how you or your friends might deal with someone who is different. Include three *Words to Know and Use.*

Fiction

Upon the Waters

JOANNE GREENBERG

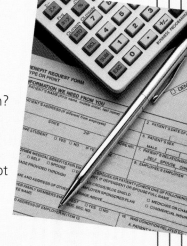

Examine What You Know

Have you ever felt frustrated filling out a complicated form? Have you ever tried to sign up for an activity at a park or school, only to find yourself in an endless line? If so, you have encountered a **bureaucracy**—an organization having numerous rules and complicated procedures. Make a concept map of *bureaucracy.* Copy the model below on a sheet of paper. Use the dictionary to define *bureaucracy,* and then fill in the other boxes with examples and descriptions.

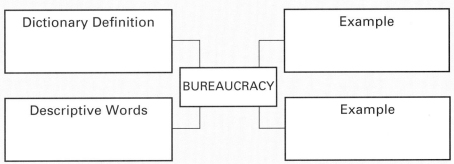

Expand Your Knowledge

Today, the welfare system in the United States is a giant bureaucracy. It started out, however, as a response to the Great Depression. Between 1929 and 1932, the U.S. economy nearly collapsed, and almost a third of the nation's workers lost their jobs. Franklin Roosevelt, elected president in 1932, created the New Deal to get the country back on track. The New Deal programs provided food and clothing, jobs, and other forms of relief.

Enrich Your Reading

Appreciating Humor   This story pokes fun at the bureaucracy of the welfare system. As you read, think about the humor that arises from the different perceptions of the main character and the office workers.

■ *Author biography on Extend page*

Upon the Waters

JOANNE GREENBERG

It was a bright green day. Big trees on the side streets were raining seeds, and the wind stirred in its second sleep. A long flatbed truck came rattling down one of the streets and stopped by the new steel, chrome, and glass building. The building's lines were so "functional" it made Cephas wonder if anyone actually worked in it. Then he saw some women going in. Good.

He checked his appearance by hitching up to the rearview mirror. He was wearing a clean white shirt and a bow tie, and his thin gray hair had been slicked down with water. When he was sure he was presentable, he got down out of the cab of the truck, dusted himself off, and began to walk slowly toward the building.

It had been many years . . . perhaps they had moved. No, there was the sign: BOONE COUNTY DEPARTMENT OF PUBLIC WELFARE. The last time he had been here the building had been a temporary shed, and people had been lined up outside waiting for the relief trucks to come. That had been in 1934, in the winter. His father had been proud of holding out until '34.

Cephas stopped and looked at the building again. Some secretaries came out, laughing and talking. They didn't look at him, being used to seeing people who came hesitantly to their offices to acknowledge failure in life.

Cephas checked himself again in the big glass door and then went in. There was a large booth with a woman behind it and eight or nine rows of benches facing it. People were sitting quietly, staring at nothing, waiting. To the right there were a series of chutes with numbers over them. Cephas went up to the booth.

"Take a number," the woman said without looking at him.

"Ma'am?"

"You take a number and wait your turn. We'll call you."

He took one of the plastic number cards. It said 15. He sat down and waited.

"Five," the woman called. A heavy woman got up slowly and went to the booth and then to one of the chutes.

Cephas waited. Minutes were born, ripened, aged, and died without issue.

"Number six." Around him the springtime asthmatics[1] whistled and gasped in their season. He looked at the cracks in his fingers.

"Number seven." An hour went by; another. He was afraid to go out and check his truck lest the line speed up and he lose his place.

"Number thirteen," the woman called. . . .

They came to his number at last, and he

---

1. **springtime asthmatics:** people who wheeze and have difficulty breathing in the spring season.

STATION   1980-1982   Billy Morrow Jackson   Courtesy, Jane Haslem Gallery, Washington, D.C.

went up to the desk, gave back the plastic card, and was directed to his chute. Another woman was there at another desk. She took his name, Cephas Ribble, and his age, sixty-eight.

Had he been given aid before?

Yes.

Had he been on General Assistance, Aid to the Needy, <u>Disabled</u> or Tuberculosis Aid?

"It was what they called Relief."

"But under what category was it?"

"It was for people that was off their farms or else didn't have nothin' to eat. They called it 'goin' on the county.' It was back in nineteen and thirty-four. We held out till thirty-four."

"I see. . . . Now you are applying for the old-age pension?"

He said he wasn't.

"Are you married, Mr. Ribble?" She sighed.

"Never had the pleasure," he said.

"Are you without funds, in emergency status?"

He said he wasn't.

"Then take this card and go to Room Eleven, to your left." She pressed a little light or something, and he felt the people shifting their weight behind him, Number Sixteen, he supposed. He made his way to Room Eleven.

The lady there was nice; he could see it right off. She told him about the different requirements for what they called Aid, and then she had him sign some forms: permission to inquire into his bank account, accep-

<table>
<tr><td>Words
to Know
and Use</td><td>disabled (dis ā′ bəld) n. people with an illness or physical handicap that limits their
activities</td></tr>
</table>

tance of surplus or donated food, release of medical information, and several others. Then she said sympathetically, "In what way are you disabled?"

He thought about all the ways a man might be disabled and checked each one off. It was a proud moment, a man sixty-eight without one thing in the world to complain of in his health.

"I ain't disabled no way. I am pleased you asked me, though. A man don't take time to be grateful for things like his health. If the shoe don't pinch, you don't take notice, do you?" He sat back, contented. Then he realized that the sun was getting hotter, and what with everything in the truck, he'd better get on.

The woman had put down her ballpoint pen. "Mr. Ribble, if you aren't disabled or without funds, what kind of aid do you want?" A shadow of irritation crossed her face.

"No aid at all," he said. "It's about somethin' different." He tried to hold down his excitement. This was his special day, a day for which he had waited for over a decade, but it was no use bragging and playing the boy, so he said no more.

question

Why is Cephas at the Welfare Office if he doesn't need aid?

The woman was very annoyed. "Then why didn't you tell the worker at the desk?"

"She didn't give me no chance, ma'am, an' neither did that other lady. I bet you don't have many repairmen comin' in here

to fix things—not above once, anyway, except them gets paid by the hour."

"Well, Mr. Ribble, what is it you want?" She heard the noise of co-workers leaving or returning on their coffee breaks. She sighed and began to drum her fingers, but Cephas wasn't aware of her impatience. He was beginning back in 1934. Good God, she thought, he's senile. She knew that she would have to listen to all of it. In his time, in his way.

"'Thirty-four cleaned us out—cleaned us bare. You wonder how *farmers* could go hungry. I don't know, but we did. After the drought hit, there was nothin' to do but come in town an' sign up on the County. Twice a month my pa would come in an' bring back food. Sometimes I came with him. I seen them lines of hungry men just standin' out there like they was poleaxed[2] an' hadn't fallen yet. I tell you, them days was pitiful, *pitiful*." He glanced at her and then smiled. "I'm glad to see *you* done good since—a new buildin' an' all. Yes, you come right up." He looked around with approval at the progress they had made.

"Mr. Ribble . . . ?"

He returned. "See, we taken the Relief, but we never got to tell nobody the good it done for us. After that year, things got a little better, and soon we was on toward bein' a payin' farm again. In 'forty-six we built us a new house—every convenience—an' in 'fifty-two we got some of them automated units for cattle care. Two years ago we dug out of debt, an' last year, I knew it was time

---

2. **poleaxed**: attacked with a long-handled spiked tool.

Words to Know and Use

surplus (sur′ plus′) *adj.* extra
senile (sē′ nīl′) *adj.* showing the mental confusion sometimes found in old people

134

to think about my plan for real. It was time to thank the Welfare."

"Mr. Ribble, thanks are not necessary—"

"Don't you mind, ma'am; you just get your men an' come with me."

"I beg your pardon. . . ."

"I don't just talk, ma'am; I act. You just bring your men."

Mr. Morrissey had come back from his coffee break and was standing in the hall.

The woman signaled him with her eyes as she followed Cephas Ribble, now walking proud and sure out the door to his truck. Mr. Morrissey sighed and followed, wondering why he was always around when somebody needed to make a madness plain. Why did it never happen to McFarland?

Cephas reached into his pocket, and both of the Welfare people thought, *Gun.* He took out a piece of paper and turned to them as they stood transfixed and pale, thinking of death. "I got it all here, all of what's in the truck. Get your men, ma'am, no use wastin' time. It's all in the truck, and if it don't get unloaded soon, it's gonna spoil."

"What is this *about,* Mr. Ribble?"

"My gift, ma'am; my donation. I'm giving the Relief four hundred chickens, thirty barrels of tomatoes, thirty barrels of apricots—I figured, for variety. Don't you think the apricots was a good idea—ten barrels Eyetalian beans, six firkins of butter. . . . Ma'am, you better get the chickens out—it don't do to keep 'em in the sun. I thought about milk, so I give two cans—that's a hundred gallons of milk in case there's hungry babies."

They were dumbfounded. Cephas could see that. He wanted to tell them that it wasn't a case of trying to be big. He'd figured that everybody gave when they could. He'd even signed a form right there in the office about promising to accept donated food and clothing. Their amazement at his gift embarrassed him. Then he realized that it was probably the only way they could thank him—by making a fuss. People on the State payroll must have to walk a pretty narrow line. They'd have to be on the lookout for people taking advantage. That was it. It was deep work, that Welfare—mighty deep work.

What is Cephas trying to do? *review*

"What are we supposed to do with all that food?" Mr. Morrissey asked.

Cephas knew that the man was just making sure that it wasn't a bribe. "Why, give it to the poor. Call 'em in an' let 'em get it. You can have your men unload it right now, an' I'd do it quick if I was you. Like I said, it won't be long till it starts to turn in all this heat."

Mr. Morrissey tried to explain that modern welfare methods were different than those in 1934. Even then, the food had been U. S. surplus, not privately donated. It had come from government warehouses.

Cephas spoke of the stupidity and waste of Government in Farming and rained invective on the Soil Bank.[3]

Mr. Morrissey tried again to make his point. "We don't *give* out any food. There hasn't been any food *donated* since nineteen sixteen!"

---

3. **rained ... Soil Bank:** Cephas complained about a government program in the late 1950s that paid farmers not to grow crops.

No doubt of it, these Welfare people had to be awful careful. Cephas nodded. "The others do what they can—don't blame 'em if it don't seem like much," he said sympathetically. "I signed that slip in there about the donated food, so there must *be* a lot of donated food."

"It's an old law," Morrissey argued tiredly. "It's one of the old Poor Laws[4] that never got taken off the books."

"An' here you folks are followin' it, right today," Cephas mused. "It must make you mighty proud."

"Mr. Ribble, *we have no place to store all this!*"

Cephas found his throat tightening with happiness. He had come in humility, waited all morning just so he could show his small gratitude and be gone, and everyone was thunderstruck at the plenty. "Mister," he said, "I pay my taxes without complainin', but I never knowed how hard you people was workin' for your money. You got to guard against every kind of bribes an' invitations to break the law; you got to find ways to get this food to the poor people so fast you can't even store it! By God, Mister, you make me proud to be an American!"

review

What is the misunderstanding between Cephas and Mr. Morrissey?

A policeman had stopped by the truck and was tranquilly writing a ticket. Cephas excused himself modestly and strode off to defend his situation. The two Welfare workers stood staring after him as he engaged the officer.

It was, after all, State law that food could be donated. Were there no loading ramps, no men attending them? Had the department no parking place for donors? The policeman began to look at the two stunned bearers of the State's trust. He had stopped writing.

"Could that truck fit in the workers' parking lot?" Morrissey murmured.

"What are we going to *do* with it all?" Mrs. Traphagen whimpered.

"All those chickens—four hundred chickens!"

Mrs. Traphagen sighed. "The poor will never stand for it."

"First things first," Mr. Morrissey decided, and he went to confront the policeman.

Cephas's truck in the workers' parking lot blocked all their cars. As a consequence, the aid applications of eight families were held pending investigation. Six discharged[5] inmates of the State hospital remained incarcerated[6] for a week longer pending home checkups. Thirty-seven women washed floors and children's faces in the expectation of home visits which did not come about. A meeting at the Midtown Hotel was one speaker short, and high school students who had been scheduled to hear a lecture entitled "Social Work, Career of Tomorrow"

---

4. **Poor Laws:** rules that allow a government to give money or food to the needy.
5. **discharged:** legally released.
6. **incarcerated:** confined or imprisoned.

Words to Know and Use

humility (hyo͞o mil′ ə tē) *n.* lack of pride
pending (pen′ diŋ) *prep.* while waiting for; until

remained unedified[7]. Applicants who came to apply for aid that afternoon were turned away. There was no trade in little plastic cards, and the hive of offices were empty. But the people of the Boone County Department of Public Welfare were not idle. It was only that the action had moved from the desks and files and chutes to the workers' parking lot and into the hands of its glad tyrant, Cephas Ribble.

All afternoon Cephas lifted huge baskets of apricots and tomatoes into the arms of the Welfare workers. All afternoon they went from his truck to their cars, carrying baskets, or with chickens festooned limply over their arms. When they complained to Mr. Unger, the head of the department, he waved them off. Were they to go to every home and deliver the food? He said he didn't care—they were to get rid of it. Were big families to get the same amount as small families? He said that the stuff was political dynamite and that all he wanted was to be rid of it before anybody noticed.

Cephas, from the back of his flatbed, was a titan[8]. He lifted, smiling, and loaded with a strong hand. He never stopped to rest or take a drink. The truck steamed in the hot spring light, but he was living at height, unbothered by the heat, or the closeness, or the increasing rankness of his chickens. Of course he saw that the Welfare people weren't dressed for loading food. They were dressed for church, looked like. It was deep work, very deep, working for the State. You had to set a good example. You had to dress up and talk very educated so as to give the poor a moral uplift. You had to be honest. A poor man could lie; Cephas had been poor himself, so he knew; but it must be a torment to deal with people free to lie and not be able to do it yourself.

By three-thirty the truck had been unloaded, and Cephas was free to go home and take up his daily life again. He shook hands with the director and the casework supervisor, the head bookkeeper and the statistician. To them he presented his itemized list, with weights carefully noted and items given the market value as of yesterday, in case they needed it for their records. Then he carefully turned the truck out of the parking lot, waved goodbye to the sweating group, nosed into the sluggish mass of afternoon traffic, and began to head home.

A cacophony[9] of high-pitched voices erupted in the lot behind him:

"I've got three mothers of dropouts to visit!"

"What am I going to *do* with all this stuff?"

"Who do we give this to? . . . My people won't take the Lady Bountiful[10] bit!"

"Does it count on their food allowance? Do we go down Vandalia and hand out apricots to every kid we see?"

"I don't have the time!"

"Which families get it?"

---

7. **unedified:** uneducated; not taught.

8. **titan:** person of great power.

9. **cacophony:** harsh sound.

10. **Lady Bountiful:** a person who gives away money or other things in a showy way; originally from George Farquhar's 1707 comedy, *The Beaux' Strategem*.

Words to Know and Use | **tyrant** (tī′ rənt) *n.* a ruler with unlimited power
sluggish (slug′ ish) *adj.* moving at a slow pace

137

"Do we take the value off next month's check?"

"It's hopeless to try to distribute this fairly," the supervisor said.

"It will cost us close to a thousand dollars to distribute it at all," the statistician said.

"It would cost us close to two thousand dollars to alter next month's checks," the bookkeeper said, "and the law specifies that we have to take extra income-in-kind off the monthly allowance."

"If I were you," the director said, "I would take all this home and eat it and not let anyone know about it."

"Mr. Morrissey!" Mrs. Traphagen's face paled away the red of her exertion. "That is fraud! You know as well as I do what would happen if it got out that we had <u>diverted</u> Welfare commodities to our own use! Can you imagine what the Mayor would say? The Governor? The State Department of Health? The HEW, The National Association of Social Workers?!" She had begun to tremble, and the two chickens that were hanging limply over her arm nodded to each other with slow decorum, their eyes closed righteously against the thought.

Cars began to clot the exit of the parking lot. The air was redolent[11].

But many of the workers didn't take the food home. The wolf of hunger was patient in shadowing the poor, even in summer, even on Welfare. As the afternoon wore on, apricots began to appear in the hands of children from Sixteenth and Vandalia Street all the way to the Boulevard. Tomatoes flamed

ANONYMOUS MAN   Emily Steadman   Courtesy of the artist.

briefly on the windowsills of the Negro ghetto between Fourteenth and Kirk, and on one block there was a chicken in every pot.

The complaints began early the next day. Sixteen Negroes called the Mayor's Committee on Racial Harmony, claiming that chickens, fruit, and vegetables had been given to the White Disadvantaged, while they had received tomatoes, half of them rotten. . . .

There were eighteen calls at the Department of Welfare protesting a tomato fight which had taken place on Fourteenth and

---

11. **redolent:** sweet-smelling.

Words to Know and Use | **divert** (də vʉrt′) *v.* to shift; to turn aside

Vandalia, in which passersby had been pelted with tomatoes. The callers demanded that the families of those involved be stricken from the Welfare rolls as Relief cheaters, encouraging waste and damaging the moral fiber of working people.

review How is the community responding to Cephas's gift?

Eighteen mothers on the Aid to Dependent Children program picketed the Governor's mansion, carrying placards that read HOPE, NOT HANDOUTS and JOBS NOT CHARITY.

Sixty-eight welfare clients called to say that they had received no food at all and demanded equal service. When they heard that the Vandalia Street mothers were picketing, a group of them went down as counter-pickets. Words were exchanged between the two groups, and a riot ensued in which sixteen people were hospitalized for injuries, including six members of the city's riot squad. Seven of the leaders were arrested and jailed pending investigation. The FBI was called in to the case in the evening to ascertain if the riot was Communist-inspired.

At ten o'clock the Mayor appeared on TV with a plea for reason and patience. He stated that the riot was a reflection of the general decline in American morals and a lack of respect for the law. He ordered a six-man commission to be set up to hear testimony and make recommendations. A political opponent demanded a thorough investigation of the county Welfare system, the War on Poverty, and the local university's radicals.

The following day, Mrs. Traphagen was unable to go to work at the Welfare Office, having been badly scalded on the hand while canning a bushel of apricots.

Cephas Ribble remembered everyone at the Welfare Office in his prayers. After work, he would think about the day he had spent in the city, and of his various triumphs: the surprise and wonder on the faces of the workers, the open awe of the lady who had said, "You don't need to thank us." How everyone had dropped the work they were doing and run to unload the truck. It had been a wonderful day. He had given his plenty unto the poor, the plenty and nourishment of his own farm. He rose refreshed to do his work, marveling at the meaning and grandeur with which his chores were suddenly invested.

"By God," he said, as he checked the chickens and noted their need for more calcium in the feed, "a man has his good to do. I'm gonna do it every year. I'm gonna have a day for the poor. Yessir, every year." And he smiled genially on the chickens, the outbuildings, and the ripening fields of a generous land. ❧

Words to Know and Use

ascertain (as′ ər tān) *v.* to find out
genially (jēn′ yəl lē) *adv.* in a friendly way

Responding to Reading

First Impressions

1. What are your impressions of Cephas? Jot down your thoughts on a sheet of paper.

Second Thoughts

2. Why is the bureaucratic welfare system unable to deal with Cephas's simple act of gratitude?

> **Think about**
> - the differences between Cephas's view of welfare and that of the office workers
> - the problems Cephas's gift might cause
> - the concept map you made for *bureaucracy*

3. Why do you think Cephas's donation causes so much trouble in the community? Is the community's reaction reasonable?

4. Do you think Cephas does the right thing by thanking the government in the manner that he does? Explain why or why not.

Broader Connections

5. In 1934, Cephas's family sought temporary relief to help them through hard times. Compare the welfare system then with the welfare system now.

Literary Concept: Satire

To criticize someone or something in a humorous way is to use **satire.** Satire exposes foolishness, stupidity, or wrongdoing in people or institutions. In your opinion, what are the targets of Greenberg's satire? Whom or what is she criticizing?

Concept Review: Characterization   Work with a partner to identify details in the story that show the kind of person Cephas is. Share your findings with the class.

Writing Options

1. Write Mr. Morrissey's official **report** about Cephas's gift and its results. Remember that officials, or bureaucrats, can usually find an excuse when things go wrong.

2. Write a **letter** to Cephas, telling him what you think of his actions at the Welfare Office.

3. This story is in a subunit called "Victims or Victors?" Identify the victims and the victors in "Upon the Waters" and write an **essay** explaining your opinion.

4. Write an **anecdote,** or very short true story, about a time when you tried to help someone and got unexpected results.

Vocabulary Practice

Exercise   Refer to the word list to answer the questions below. Use each word once.

1. What word could be used for Cephas when he acted like a tough boss?

2. Instead of being boastful, Cephas showed what quality?

3. If Cephas had many more apricots than he needed, what did he have?

4. If Cephas had been forgetful and weak in the mind because of old age, what word would describe him?

5. What word should *not* be applied to Cephas as he energetically unloaded his truck?

6. What word describes the friendly manner in which Cephas gave away his chickens?

7. What verb describes how the welfare workers make sure a statement is true?

8. If Cephas were handicapped in some way, what word would describe him?

9. What word is associated with waiting?

10. What word would the police use to ask for traffic to be directed to a different street?

> *Words to Know and Use*
>
> ---
>
> **ascertain**
> **disabled**
> **divert**
> **genially**
> **humility**
> **pending**
> **senile**
> **sluggish**
> **surplus**
> **tyrant**

Options for Learning

1 • Live at Five Present a "live" news report that shows Cephas unloading his truck in the middle of the confusion at the Welfare Office. Some students can play the roles of Cephas and various bureaucrats, while another student can be an "on the scene" reporter who interviews them.

2 • Feed the Poor Work in small groups to devise fair plans for dealing with Cephas's donation. Take into account each item he brought. Report the plans to the whole class. Then, as a class, vote on which plan is the best.

3 • Oral History Interview someone who lived during the Great Depression. Before the interview, draw up a list of questions that will prompt your source to give vivid descriptions of the times. Tape record the interview, and play the most interesting part for your class.

4 • Cephas Comics Reduce the plot of this story to five important scenes. Then draw these scenes as a panel cartoon showing the events of the day. Add dialogue balloons with humorous comments by the characters.

 FACT FINDER HISTORY

Why were Roosevelt's new government agencies called alphabet soup?

Joanne Greenberg
1932-

Joanne Greenberg, who lives in the Colorado mountains, drew the inspiration for "Upon the Waters" from an incident related by her husband, who worked in a welfare office. She says that she "started laughing" from the time she invented Cephas Ribble and has "not stopped since."

Greenberg, a native of Brooklyn, New York, has written nine novels and four collections of short stories. Her most famous novel is *I Never Promised You a Rose Garden,* published in 1964 under the pseudonym, or pen name, Hannah Green. This novel, which was made into a movie in 1977, deals with schizophrenia, a type of mental disorder. Greenberg herself suffered from this disease and courageously overcame it. More recently, Greenberg wrote *In This Sign,* about communication between deaf people, which was later dramatized for television.

Nonfiction

The Noble Experiment
from I Never Had It Made
JACKIE ROBINSON *as told to* **ALFRED DUCKETT**

Examine What You Know

Prejudice is the result of *prejudging,* or judging before all the facts are known. It often consists of judging a whole group of people by their appearance or by the actions of a few members of the group. Usually it results in negative and unfair treatment of individuals. Share with your classmates some examples of prejudice you have experienced or seen, and the effects on the people involved.

Expand Your Knowledge

In the 1940s, African Americans faced many barriers created by prejudice. In the South, "Jim Crow" laws kept African Americans from mixing with whites in schools, restaurants, hospitals, and parks. African Americans were forced to use separate restrooms and water fountains.

Athletic competition did not escape this segregation. Even in baseball, blacks played in separate "Negro leagues"; they were barred from the major leagues. In 1947, Jackie Robinson became the first African American to break the major-league "color barrier." A superb athlete, he helped the Brooklyn Dodgers win six league championships and was named the league's most valuable player in 1949. He was voted into the Baseball Hall of Fame in 1962.

Enrich Your Reading

Problem Solving   In this selection, Branch Rickey, the owner of the Brooklyn Dodgers, faces a difficult problem. Create a chart like that below to track the steps in Rickey's problem-solving strategy.

Problem	Problem-Solving Strategy
No blacks are allowed in baseball.	1. Identify best black player.
	2.

■ *Author biography on Extend page*

The *Noble Experiment*

from I Never Had It Made

JACKIE ROBINSON
as told to Alfred Duckett

In 1910 Branch Rickey was a coach for Ohio Wesleyan. The team went to South Bend, Indiana, for a game. The hotel management registered the coach and team but refused to assign a room to a black player named Charley Thomas. In those days college ball had a few black players. Mr. Rickey took the manager aside and said he would move the entire team to another hotel unless the black athlete was accepted. The threat was a bluff because he knew the other hotels also would have refused accommodations to a black man. While the hotel manager was thinking about the threat, Mr. Rickey came up with a compromise. He suggested a cot be put in his own room, which he would share with the unwanted guest. The hotel manager wasn't happy about the idea, but he gave in.

Years later Branch Rickey told the story of the misery of that black player to whom he had given a place to sleep. He remembered that Thomas couldn't sleep.

"He sat on that cot," Mr. Rickey said, "and was silent for a long time. Then he began to cry, tears he couldn't hold back. His whole body shook with emotion. I sat and watched him, not knowing what to do until he began tearing at one hand with the other—just as if he were trying to scratch the skin off his hands with his fingernails. I was alarmed. I asked him what he was trying to do to himself.

"'It's my hands,' he sobbed. 'They're black. If only they were white, I'd be as good as anybody then, wouldn't I, Mr. Rickey? If only they were white.'"

"Charley," Mr. Rickey said, "the day will come when they won't have to be white."

Thirty-five years later, while I was lying awake nights, frustrated, unable to see a future, Mr. Rickey, by now the president of the Dodgers, was also lying awake at night, trying to make up his mind about a new experiment.

He had never forgotten the agony of that black athlete. When he became a front-office executive in St. Louis, he had fought, behind the scenes, against the custom that consigned black spectators to the Jim Crow section of the Sportsman's Park, later to become Busch Memorial Stadium. His pleas to change the rules were in vain. Those in power argued that if blacks were allowed a free choice of seating, white business would suffer.

Branch Rickey lost that fight, but when he became the boss of the Brooklyn Dodgers in 1943, he felt the time for equality in baseball had come. He knew that achieving it would be terribly difficult. There would be deep resentment, determined opposition, and perhaps even racial violence. He was convinced he was morally right, and he shrewdly sensed that making the game a truly national one would have healthy financial results. He took his case before the startled directors of the club, and using persuasive eloquence, he won the first battle in what would be a long and bitter campaign. He was voted permission to make the Brooklyn club the pioneer in bringing blacks into baseball.

Winning his directors' approval was almost insignificant in contrast to the task which now lay ahead of the Dodger president. He made certain that word of his plans did not leak out, particularly to the press. Next, he had to find the ideal player for his project, which came to be called "Rickey's noble experiment." This player had to be one who could take abuse, name-calling, rejection by fans and sportswriters and by fellow players not only on opposing teams but on his own. He had to be able to stand up in the face of merciless persecution and not retaliate. On the other hand, he had to be a contradiction in human terms; he still had to have spirit. He could not be an Uncle Tom.[1] His ability to turn the other cheek had to be predicated[2] on his determination to gain acceptance. Once having proven his ability as player, teammate, and man, he had to be able to cast off humbleness and stand up as a full-fledged participant whose triumph did not carry the poison of bitterness.

Unknown to most people and certainly to me, after launching a major scouting program, Branch Rickey had picked me as that player. The Rickey talent hunt went beyond national borders. Cuba, Mexico, Puerto Rico, Venezuela, and other countries where dark-skinned people lived had been checked out. Mr. Rickey had learned that there were a number of black players, war veterans mainly, who had gone to these countries, despairing of finding an opportunity in their own country. The manhunt had to be camouflaged. If it became known he was looking for a black recruit for the Dodgers, there would have been all kinds of trouble. The gimmick he used as a coverup was to make the world believe that he was about to establish a new Negro league. In the spring of 1945 he called a press conference and announced that the Dodgers were organizing the United States League, composed of all black teams. This, of course, made blacks and prointegration whites indignant. He was accused of trying to uphold the existing segregation and, at the same time, capitalize on black players. Cleverly, Mr. Rickey replied that his league would be better organized than the current ones. He said its main purpose, eventually, was to be absorbed into the majors. It is ironic that by coming very close to telling the truth, he was able to conceal that truth from the enemies of integrated baseball. Most people assumed that when he

---

1. **Uncle Tom:** a black person who tries overly hard to please white people; originally from the novel *Uncle Tom's Cabin* written by Harriet Beecher Stowe in 1852.

2. **predicated:** based

Words to Know and Use

shrewdly (shrōōd' lē) *adv.* wisely; in a clever way
eloquence (el' ə kwəns) *n.* forceful, convincing speech
retaliate (ri tal' ē āt') *v.* to get revenge; get even
indignant (in dig' nənt) *adj.* angry because of an action that seems wrong

145

spoke of some distant goal of integration, Mr. Rickey was being a hypocrite on this issue as so many of baseball's leaders had been.

Black players were familiar with this kind of hypocrisy. When I was with the Monarchs, shortly before I met Mr. Rickey, Wendell Smith, then sports editor of the black, weekly Pittsburgh *Courier*, had arranged for me and two other players from the Negro league to go to a tryout with the Boston Red Sox. The tryout had been brought about because a Boston city councilman had frightened the Red Sox management. Councilman Isadore Muchneck threatened to push a bill through banning Sunday baseball unless the Red Sox hired black players. Sam Jethroe of the Cleveland Buckeyes, Marvin Williams of the Philadelphia Stars, and I had been grateful to Wendell for getting us a chance in the Red Sox tryout, and we put our best efforts into it. However, not for one minute did we believe the tryout was sincere. The Boston club officials praised our performance, let us fill out application cards, and said "So long." We were fairly certain they wouldn't call us, and we had no intention of calling them.

Incidents like this made Wendell Smith as cynical as we were. He didn't accept Branch Rickey's new league as a genuine project, and he frankly told him so. During this conversation, the Dodger boss asked Wendell whether any of the three of us who had gone to Boston was really good major league material. Wendell said I was. I will be forever indebted to Wendell because, without his even knowing it, his recommendation was in the end partly responsible for my career. At the time, it started a thorough investigation of my background.

In August 1945, at Comiskey Park in Chicago, I was approached by Clyde Sukeforth, the Dodger scout. Blacks have had to learn to protect themselves by being cynical but not cynical enough to slam the door on potential opportunities. We go through life walking a tightrope to prevent too much disillusionment. I was out on the field when Sukeforth called my name and beckoned. He told me the Brown Dodgers were looking for top ballplayers, that Branch Rickey had heard about me and sent him to watch me throw from the hole.[3] He had come at an unfortunate time. I had hurt my shoulder a couple of days before that, and I wouldn't be doing any throwing for at least a week.

Sukeforth said he'd like to talk with me anyhow. He asked me to come to see him after the game at the Stevens Hotel.

Here we go again, I thought. Another time-wasting experience. But Sukeforth looked like a sincere person, and I thought I might as well listen. I agreed to meet him that night. When we met, Sukeforth got right to the point. Mr. Rickey wanted to talk to me about the possibility of becoming a Brown Dodger. If I could get a few days off and go to Brooklyn, my fare and expenses would be paid. At first I said that I couldn't leave my team and go to Brooklyn just like that.

---

3. throw from the hole: ability to throw from deep in the infield to first base.

Words to Know and Use | **cynical** (sin′ i kəl) *adj.* mistrustful of others' sincerity

Jackie Robinson stealing home during a Braves–Dodgers game at Ebbets Field in Brooklyn, 1948.
UPI/Bettmann, New York.

Sukeforth wouldn't take no for an answer. He pointed out that I couldn't play for a few days anyhow because of my bum arm. Why should my team object?

I continued to hold out and demanded to know what would happen if the Monarchs fired me. The Dodger scout replied quietly that he didn't believe that would happen.

I shrugged and said I'd make the trip. I figured I had nothing to lose.

Branch Rickey was an impressive-looking man. He had a classic face, an air of command, a deep, booming voice, and a way of cutting through red tape and getting down to basics. He shook my hand vigorously and, after a brief conversation, sprang the first question.

"You got a girl?" he demanded.

It was a heck of a question. I had two reactions: why should he be concerned about my relationship with a girl; and, second, while I thought, hoped, and prayed I had a girl, the way things had been going, I was afraid she might have begun to consider me a hopeless case. I explained this to Mr. Rickey and Clyde.

Mr. Rickey wanted to know all about Rachel. I told him of our hopes and plans.

"You know, you *have* a girl," he said heartily. "When we get through today, you may want to call her up because there are times when a man needs a woman by his side."

My heart began racing a little faster again as I sat there speculating. First he asked me if I really understood why he had sent for me. I told him what Clyde Sukeforth had told me.

"That's what he was supposed to tell you," Mr. Rickey said. "The truth is you are not a candidate for the Brooklyn Brown Dodgers. I've sent for you because I'm interested in you as a candidate for the Brooklyn National League Club. I think you can play in the major leagues. How do you feel about it?"

My reactions seemed like some kind of weird mixture churning in a blender. I was thrilled, scared, and excited. I was incredulous. Most of all, I was speechless.

Robinson after signing his contract with the Brooklyn Dodgers.   AP/Wide World Photos, New York.

"You think you can play for Montreal?" he demanded.

I got my tongue back. "Yes," I answered.

Montreal was the Brooklyn Dodgers' top farm club. The players who went there and made it had an excellent chance at the big time.

I was busy reorganizing my thoughts while Mr. Rickey and Clyde Sukeforth discussed me briefly, almost as if I weren't there. Mr. Rickey was questioning Clyde. Could I make the grade?

Abruptly, Mr. Rickey swung his swivel chair in my direction. He was a man who conducted himself with great drama. He pointed a finger at me.

"I know you're a good ballplayer," he barked. "What I don't know is whether you have the guts."

I knew it was all too good to be true. Here was a guy questioning my courage. That virtually amounted to him asking me if I was a coward. Mr. Rickey or no Mr. Rickey, that was an insinuation hard to take. I felt the heat coming up into my cheeks.

Before I could react to what he had said, he leaned forward in his chair and explained.

I wasn't just another athlete being hired by a ball club. We were playing for big stakes. This was the reason Branch Rickey's search had been so exhaustive. The search had spanned the globe and narrowed down to a few candidates, then finally to me. When it looked as though I might be the number-one choice, the investigation of my life, my habits, my reputation, and my character had become an intensified study.

"I've investigated you thoroughly,

Words to Know and Use

speculating (spek' yōō lāt' iŋ) *adj.* thinking about different possibilities; guessing what might happen **speculate** *v.*
incredulous (in krej' ōō ləs) *adj.* unable or unwilling to believe something
insinuation (in sin' yōō ā' shən) *n.* a suggestion or hint intended to insult

148

Robinson," Mr. Rickey said.

One of the results of this thorough screening were reports from California athletic circles that I had been a "racial agitator"[4] at UCLA. Mr. Rickey had not accepted these criticisms on face value. He had demanded and received more information and came to the conclusion that if I had been white, people would have said, "Here's a guy who's a contender, a competitor."

After that he had some grim words of warning. "We can't fight our way through this, Robinson. We've got no army. There's virtually nobody on our side. No owners, no umpires, very few newspapermen. And I'm afraid that many fans will be hostile. We'll be in a tough position. We can win only if we can convince the world that I'm doing this because you're a great ballplayer and a fine gentleman."

He had me transfixed as he spoke. I could feel his sincerity, and I began to get a sense of how much this major step meant to him. Because of his nature and his passion for justice, he had to do what he was doing. He continued. The rumbling voice, the theatrical gestures, were gone. He was speaking from a deep, quiet strength.

"So there's more than just playing," he said. "I wish it meant only hits, runs, and errors—only the things they put in the box score. Because you know—yes, you would know, Robinson, that a baseball box score is a democratic thing. It doesn't tell how big you are, what church you attend, what color you are, or how your father voted in the last election. It just tells what kind of baseball player you were on that particular day."

I interrupted. "But it's the box score that really counts—that and that alone, isn't it?"

"It's all that *ought* to count," he replied.

(From left) Gil Hodges, Gene Hermanski, Branch Rickey, and Jackie Robinson in Yankee Stadium, 1949.
The Bettmann Archive, New York.

"But it isn't. Maybe one of these days it *will* be all that counts. That is one of the reasons I've got you here, Robinson. If you're a good enough man, we can make this a start in the right direction. But let me tell you, it's going to take an awful lot of courage."

He was back to the crossroads question that made me start to get angry minutes earlier. He asked it slowly and with great care.

"Have you got the guts to play the game no matter what happens?"

"I think I can play the game, Mr. Rickey," I said.

The next few minutes were tough. Branch Rickey had to make absolutely sure that I knew what I would face. Beanballs[5] would be

---

4. racial agitator (rā shəl aj′ i tāt′ ər): a negative term used for someone who tried to stir up trouble between the races.

5. beanballs: pitches thrown purposefully at a batter's head.

The Brooklyn Dodgers in 1949. Robinson is second from the right in the third row.   UPI/Bettmann, New York.

thrown at me. I would be called the kind of names which would hurt and infuriate any man. I would be physically attacked. Could I take all of this and control my temper, remain steadfastly loyal to our <u>ultimate</u> aim?

He knew I would have terrible problems and wanted me to know the extent of them before I agreed to the plan. I was twenty-six years old, and all my life—back to the age of eight when a little neighbor girl called me a nigger[6]—I had believed in payback, retaliation. The most luxurious possession, the richest treasure anybody has, is his personal dignity. I looked at Mr. Rickey guardedly, and in that second I was looking at him not as a partner in a great experiment, but as the enemy—a white man. I had a question, and it was the age-old one about whether or not you sell your birthright.

"Mr. Rickey," I asked, "are you looking for a Negro who is afraid to fight back?"

I never will forget the way he exploded.

"Robinson," he said, "I'm looking for a ballplayer with guts enough not to fight back."

After that, Mr. Rickey continued his lecture on the kind of thing I'd be facing.

He not only told me about it, but he acted out the part of a white player charging into me, blaming me for the "accident" and calling me all kinds of foul racial names. He talked about my race, my parents, in language that was almost unendurable.

"They'll <u>taunt</u> and goad you," Mr. Rickey said. "They'll do anything to make you react.

---

6. **nigger:** *slang,* a derogatory name for an African American. The word is offensive and insulting.

Words to Know and Use | **ultimate** (ul′ tə mit) *adj.* final; most important
taunt (tônt) *v.* to make fun of; jeer

They'll try to provoke a race riot in the ballpark. This is the way to prove to the public that a Negro should not be allowed in the major league. This is the way to frighten the fans and make them afraid to attend the games."

If hundreds of black people wanted to come to the ballpark to watch me play and Mr. Rickey tried to discourage them, would I understand that he was doing it because the emotional enthusiasm of my people could harm the experiment? That kind of enthusiasm would be as bad as the emotional opposition of prejudiced white fans.

Suppose I was at shortstop. Another player comes down from first, stealing, flying in with spikes high, and cuts me on the leg. As I feel the blood running down my leg, the white player laughs in my face.

"How do you like that, nigger boy?" he sneers.

Could I turn the other cheek? I didn't know how I would do it. Yet I knew that I must. I had to do it for so many reasons. For black youth, for my mother, for Rae, for myself. I had already begun to feel I had to do it for Branch Rickey.

I was offered, and agreed to sign later, a contract with a $3,500 bonus and $600-a-month salary. I was officially a Montreal Royal. I must not tell anyone except Rae and my mother. ❧

I N S I G H T

I'll Walk the Tightrope

MARGARET DANNER

I'll walk the tightrope that's been stretched for me,
and though a wrinkled forehead, perplexed why,
will accompany me, I'll delicately
step along. For if I stop to sigh
at the earth-propped stride
of others, I will fall. I must balance high
without a parasol to tide
a faltering step, without a net below,
without a balance stick to guide.

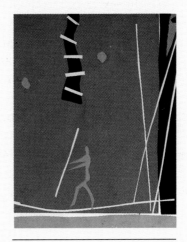

THE CIRCUS (detail)   1961   Romare Bearden   Courtesy, The Estate of Romare Bearden and ACA Galleries, New York.

Responding to Reading

First Impressions

1. What was your reaction to Branch Rickey as you finished reading? Jot down words and phrases to describe your thoughts about him.

Second Thoughts

2. In your opinion, what were the most ingenious parts of Rickey's plan to integrate major-league baseball?

> **Think about**
> - his search for "a great ballplayer and a fine gentleman"
> - how and why he kept his plan secret
> - his meeting with Jackie Robinson

3. Consider the difficulties both men faced in fighting prejudice. How do you think both Rickey and Robinson showed courage? Explain.

4. If you had been in Robinson's shoes, would you have agreed to play for the Dodgers? Give your reasons.

> **Think about**
> - your discussion of prejudice and its effects
> - Rickey's predictions of what Robinson would face

5. Reread the poem "I'll Walk the Tightrope" on page 151. What lines of this poem apply to Robinson's life? Explain why you think so.

Broader Connections

6. Many saw Jackie Robinson as a role model for young people. Should we expect professional athletes to be role models, or should they be judged only on their athletic performance?

Literary Concept: Motivation

The reasons for a person's action are known as **motivation.** What motivated Branch Rickey and Jackie Robinson? Were their motivations the same or different? Explain.

Concept Review: Autobiography   An **autobiography** usually focuses on events that shape or change a person's life. How did the meeting with Branch Rickey change Jackie Robinson's life?

Writing Options

1. Jackie Robinson had to become a victim in order to become a victor. Can you think of any other real or fictional characters who have had to do the same thing? Write a **comparison** of Robinson with someone else in a similar situation.

2. Baseball programs include profiles of each player, noting the player's strengths and special qualities. Write a **profile** of Jackie Robinson for a Brooklyn Dodgers program.

3. Branch Rickey said that he was "looking for a ballplayer with guts enough not to fight back." Write a **definition** of *courage* with which Rickey would agree.

4. A **rap** is a spoken song with a strong rhythm. Some raps tell a story. Write a rap that tells the story of "The Noble Experiment." Practice speaking it, and then share it with your classmates.

Vocabulary Practice

Exercise   On a separate sheet of paper, write the word from the list that is the best substitute for each word or phrase in dark type.

1. Rickey **cleverly** devised a cover story for the press.

2. Some **unbelieving** fans gasped when Robinson walked onto the field for his first major-league game.

3. The majority of fans were wrong about Rickey's plans as they sat home, **guessing.**

4. Many African Americans felt very **mistrustful** about promises made by whites.

5. Some ballplayers on other teams would **mock** Robinson and try to anger him.

6. Robinson was not allowed to **fight back.**

7. The **final** goal of the experiment was to integrate the major leagues.

8. Sportswriters filled their columns with many a **sly negative comment** about Robinson's character.

9. Several ministers spoke with **great speaking skill** about the evils of prejudice.

10. Many people were **upset** about the treatment of the rookie Robinson.

Words to Know and Use

cynical
eloquence
incredulous
indignant
insinuation
retaliate
shrewdly
speculating
taunt
ultimate

Options for Learning

1 • A League of Their Own Research the various Negro leagues that existed earlier in this century. Then make a display featuring interesting facts, such as team nicknames, locations of teams, names of star players, and uniform designs.

2 • Now and Then Research the progress that African Americans have made in baseball since Robinson's time. Gather information about blacks in major-league baseball. Find out about stars, the percentage of black players today, and the numbers of black managers, umpires, and owners. Share your statistics by making a chart to display in class.

3 • A Telling Moment Write the dialogue that might have taken place between Jackie and his girlfriend, Rachel, when he told her that he planned to join the Brooklyn Dodgers. Have him explain his decision, and have Rachel voice her concerns. Then act out the scene for your classmates.

4 • Robinson Report Read the rest of Robinson's autobiography, *I Never Had It Made*. Give a report on his experiences in baseball and his other achievements.

 FACT FINDER SPORTS

What was Jackie Robinson's lifetime batting average?

Alfred A. Duckett
1917–1984

It seems natural that Alfred Duckett would want to tell Jackie Robinson's story, since he was born in Brooklyn and was a baseball fan as well as a journalist. Robinson and Duckett worked together to produce *I Never Had It Made: The Autobiography of Jackie Robinson.*

Besides writing books, Duckett also wrote poetry, magazine articles, and speeches.

Perhaps his most famous speech was written with Martin Luther King, Jr. Dr. King delivered this "I Have a Dream" speech in Washington, D.C., in 1963.

Duckett also cofounded *Equal Opportunities* magazine and was the director of Associated Negro Press International, Inc. He appeared on national television programs and lectured in many schools, churches, and universities. Duckett ran a public relations firm in Chicago until his death in 1984.

Elements of
DRAMA

A **drama,** or **play,** is a form of literature that is performed for an audience, either on stage or before a camera.

The elements of drama are similar to the elements of fiction. Like fiction, drama usually tells a story with characters, plot, and setting. Unlike fiction, drama is written to be performed for an audience. For this reason, drama is written in a special form called a **script,** in which lines are written out for the characters to speak. The script has various parts, which are described below.

Understanding Drama

Cast of Characters   A script usually begins with a list of the characters in the play. Often a short description appears next to a character's name.

Dialogue   A play consists almost entirely of dialogue—conversation between the characters. Both the plot of the play and the characters' personalities are revealed through dialogue. The dialogue appears in lines next to the characters' names, as in this example from *The Monsters Are Due on Maple Street,* page 157:

Steve. What was that? A meteor?

Don. That's what it looked like. I didn't hear any crash though, did you?

Stage Directions   A play includes instructions for the director, the performers, and the stage crew. These are called stage directions and are printed in italics in this book; often they are also enclosed in parentheses. Many stage directions tell actors how to speak or move. Stage directions also describe the **scenery**—all the decorations on stage that help create the setting. Some stage directions describe **props**—the objects that actors need during the play. Many scripts also include suggestions for lighting and sound. Notice how these stage directions from *Funny Boy,* in Unit 5, tell the actor what to do and what props to use.

Kaufman. Thank you. *(He sits down, eyes the trayful of food, sighs, picks up his glass of juice, and starts to take a sip of it.)*

The stage directions in dramas that are meant to be filmed must also include camera directions. Through the medium of the camera, the audience might see a close-up of a character, a look between characters while someone else is speaking, or a quick shot of the outside of a high school. These types of camera shots are carefully planned by the playwright and are an important element in the play.

Acts and Scenes   The action of a play is divided into scenes. A scene changes whenever the setting—time, place, or both time and place—changes. Sometimes scenes are grouped into acts. In *The Monsters Are Due on Maple Street,* four scenes are grouped into two acts.

In a movie or television script, the scenes

might not be labeled by number. In *Driving Miss Daisy,* in Unit 4, scene changes are simply marked with extra space, followed by the location of the next scene in capital letters. Here is an example:

Daisy. No, thank you.

FRONT HALL. Daisy puts on her hat and gathers her gloves and purse.

Strategies for Reading Drama

1. **Read the play silently.** Before you try to read the play aloud with others, read it to yourself. You need to know the entire plot and understand the characters before you perform the play.

2. **Figure out what is happening.** When you watch a movie, it takes you a while to understand exactly what the movie is about. The same is true when you read a play. Be patient and read several pages to understand what is happening.

3. **Read the stage directions carefully.** If you were watching a drama on stage or on television, you would see the action and the scenery. When you read a drama, you have to imagine both. The stage directions tell exactly where and when each scene is happening and help you visualize the action. If you skip over the stage directions, you will miss important information.

4. **Get to know the characters.** In drama, you get to know the characters through dialogue. Just as if you were reading fiction, analyze the characters'

words carefully and try to discover the feelings behind the words.

5. **Keep track of the plot.** As in fiction, the plot of a drama centers on a main conflict that the characters try to resolve. Look for the conflict and let yourself become involved in the story. Watch for the action to build to a climax, and evaluate how the conflict is resolved.

6. **Read the play aloud with others.** When drama is performed, it takes on a whole new aspect; it becomes almost like real life. When you read the part of a character, you become an actor. You will play the part differently from anyone else because you bring your own interpretation to the role. Let yourself become that character for a while. React to what other characters say and do to you. Be ready with your character's lines and read only the words your character says. Do not read the stage directions aloud. You may find that you really enjoy playing the part of someone totally different from yourself.

Drama

The Monsters Are Due on Maple Street

ROD SERLING

Examine What You Know

How do you react to fear of the unknown? What happens to you when danger lurks around the corner? How does your body react? What goes through your mind? As a class, brainstorm the ways people react to fear using a chart like the one below.

Individuals		Groups
dry mouth	FEAR	cling together

Expand Your Knowledge

The Twilight Zone was a television series created by Rod Serling that ran from 1959 through 1965. It was an eerie and very suspenseful series that became one of the most popular shows in television history. The action often took place in suburbs typical of the late 1950s, and the characters were ordinary people. The events, however, were far from ordinary because they involved an imaginary world beyond ours—the twilight zone. The characters faced the unknown—and reacted in both typical and unexpected ways.

Enrich Your Reading

Reading a Teleplay   The script for a television show is called a teleplay. Like all drama scripts, a teleplay includes stage directions. These directions provide suggestions for the actors and the director, explain the setting, and describe the lighting, sound effects, and props. A teleplay also includes camera instructions. Pay careful attention to these directions, printed in italic type.

■ *Author biography on Extend page*

The Monsters Are Due on Maple Street

ROD SERLING

CHARACTERS

Narrator

Tommy

Steve Brand

Don Martin

Myra Brand, *Steve's wife*

Woman

Voice One

Voice Two

Voice Three

Voice Four

Voice Five

Pete Van Horn

Charlie

Sally, *Tommy's mother*

Man One

Les Goodman

Ethel Goodman,
Les's wife

Man Two

Figure One

Figure Two

Ice-cream vendor

Second Boy buying
ice cream

Charlie's wife

Other Residents of Maple
Street

ACT ONE

(Fade in on a shot of the night sky. The various heavenly bodies stand out in sharp, sparkling relief. The camera moves slowly across the heavens until it passes the horizon and stops on a sign that reads "Maple Street." It is daytime. Then we see the street below. It is a quiet, tree-lined, small-town American street. The houses have front porches on which people sit and swing on gliders, talking across from house to house. Steve Brand is polishing his car, which is parked in front of his house. His neighbor, Don Martin, leans against the fender watching him. An ice-cream vendor riding a bicycle is just in the process of stopping to sell some ice cream to a couple of kids. Two women gossip on the front lawn. Another man is watering his lawn with a garden hose.

As we see these various activities, we hear the Narrator's *voice.)*

Narrator. Maple Street, U.S.A., late summer. A tree-lined little world of front-porch gliders, hopscotch, the laughter of children, and the bell of an ice-cream vendor.

(There is a pause, and the camera moves over to a shot of the ice-cream vendor and two small boys who are standing alongside just buying ice cream.)

Narrator. At the sound of the roar and the flash of the light, it will be precisely six-forty-three P.M. on Maple Street.

(At this moment Tommy, *one of the two boys buying ice cream from the vendor, looks up to listen to a tremendous screeching roar from overhead. A flash of light plays on the faces of both boys and then moves down the street and disappears.*

Various people leave their porches or stop what they are doing to stare up at the sky.

Steve Brand, *the man who has been polishing his car, stands there transfixed, staring upwards. He looks at* Don Martin, *his neighbor from across the street.)*

Steve. What was that? A meteor?

Don. That's what it looked like. I didn't hear any crash though, did you?

Steve. Nope. I didn't hear anything except a roar.

Myra *(from her porch).* What was that?

Steve *(raising his voice and looking toward the porch).* Guess it was a meteor, honey. Came awful close, didn't it?

Myra. Too close for my money! Much too close.

(The camera moves slowly across the various porches to people who stand there watching and talking in low conversing tones.)

Narrator. Maple Street. Six-forty-four P.M. on a late September evening. *(He pauses.)* Maple Street in the last calm and reflective moment *(pause)* before the monsters came!

(The camera takes us across the porches again. A man is replacing a light bulb on a front porch. He gets off his stool to flick the switch and finds that nothing happens.

Another man is working on an electric power mower. He plugs in the plug, flicks the switch of the mower off and on, but nothing happens.

Through a window we see a woman pushing her finger up and down on the dial hook of a telephone. Her voice sounds far away.)

Woman. Operator, operator, something's wrong on the phone, operator! (Myra Brand *comes out on the porch and calls to* Steve.)

Myra *(calling).* Steve, the power's off. I had the soup on the stove, and the stove just stopped working.

Woman. Same thing over here. I can't get anybody on the phone either. The phone seems to be dead.

(We look down again on the street. Small, mildly disturbed voices are heard coming from below.)

Voice One. Electricity's off.

Voice Two. Phone won't work.

Voice Three. Can't get a thing on the radio.

Voice Four. My power mower won't move, won't work at all.

Voice Five. Radio's gone dead!

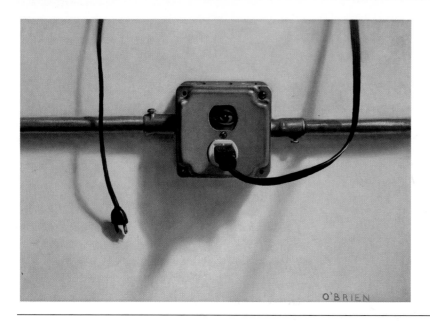

O'BRIEN

Illustration by Tim O'Brien.

(Pete Van Horn, *a tall, thin man, is seen standing in front of his house.*)

Pete. I'll cut through the back yard to see if the power's still on, on Floral Street. I'll be right back!

(*He walks past the side of his house and disappears into the back yard.*

The camera pans down slowly until we are looking at ten or eleven people standing around the street and overflowing to the curb and sidewalk. In the background is Steve Brand's car.).

Steve. Doesn't make sense. Why should the power go off all of a sudden and the phone line?

Don. Maybe some kind of an electrical storm or something.

Charlie. That don't seem likely. Sky's just as blue as anything. Not a cloud. No lightning. No thunder. No nothing. How could it be a storm?

Woman. I can't get a thing on the radio. Not even the portable.

(*The people again begin to murmur softly in wonderment.*)

Charlie. Well, why don't you go downtown and check with the police, though they'll probably think we're crazy or something. A little power failure and right away we get all <u>flustered</u> and everything–

Steve. It isn't just the power failure, Charlie. If it was, we'd still be able to get a broadcast on the portable.

(*There is a murmur of reaction to this. Steve looks from face to face and then at his car.*)

Steve. I'll run downtown. We'll get this all straightened out.

(*He gets in the car and turns the key.*

Looking through the open car door, we see the crowd watching Steve from the other

Words to Know and Use

flustered (flus′ tərd) *adj.* nervous or confused **fluster** *v.*

160

side. He starts the engine. It turns over sluggishly and then stops dead. He tries it again, and this time he can't get it to turn over. Then very slowly he turns the key back to "off" and gets out of the car.

The people stare at Steve. *He stands for a moment by the car and then walks toward them.)*

Steve. I don't understand it. It was working fine before—

Don. Out of gas?

Steve *(shakes his head)*. I just had it filled.

Woman. What's it mean?

Charlie. It's just as if *(pause)* as if everything had stopped. *(Then he turns toward* Steve.) We'd better walk downtown.

(Another murmur of assent to this.)

Steve. The two of us can go, Charlie. *(He turns to look back at the car.)* It couldn't be the meteor. A meteor couldn't do this.

(He and Charlie *exchange a look. Then they start to walk away from the group.*

Tommy *comes into view. He is a serious-faced young boy in spectacles. He stands halfway between the group and the two men, who start to walk down the sidewalk.)*

Tommy. Mr. Brand—you'd better not!

Steve. Why not?

Tommy. They don't want you to.

(Steve and Charlie *exchange a grin, and* Steve *looks back toward the boy.)*

Steve. *Who* doesn't want us to?

Tommy *(jerks his head in the general direction of the distant horizon)*. Them!

Steve. Them?

Charlie. Who are them?

Tommy *(intently)*. Whoever was in that thing that came by overhead.

(Steve knits his brows for a moment, cocking his head questioningly. His voice is intense.)

Steve. What?

Tommy. Whoever was in that thing that came over. I don't think they want us to leave here.

(Steve leaves Charlie, *walks over to the boy, and puts his hand on the boy's shoulder. He forces his voice to remain gentle.)*

Steve. What do you mean? What are you talking about?

Tommy. They don't want us to leave. That's why they shut everything off.

Steve. What makes you say that? Whatever gave you that idea?

Woman *(from the crowd)*. Now isn't that the craziest thing you ever heard?

Tommy *(persistent but a little frightened)*. It's always that way, in every story I ever read about a ship landing from outer space.

Woman *(to the boy's mother,* Sally, *who stands on the fringe of the crowd)*. From outer space yet! Sally, you better get that boy of yours up to bed. He's been read-

---

Words to Know and Use

intense (in tens′) *adj.* firm; very serious
persistent (pər sist′ ənt) *adj.* refusing to stop; continuing stubbornly

ing too many comic books or seeing too many movies or something!

Sally. Tommy, come over here and stop that kind of talk.

Steve. Go ahead, Tommy. We'll be right back. And you'll see. That wasn't any ship or anything like it. That was just a . . . a meteor or something. Likely as not—*(He turns to the group, now trying very hard to sound more optimistic than he feels.)* No doubt it did have something to do with all this power failure and the rest of it. Meteors can do some crazy things. Like sunspots.

Don *(picking up the cue).* Sure. That's the kind of thing—like sunspots. They raise Cain[1] with radio reception all over the world. And this thing being so close— why, there's no telling the sort of stuff it can do. *(He wets his lips and smiles nervously.)* Go ahead, Charlie. You and Steve go into town and see if that isn't what's causing it all.

(Steve and Charlie walk away from the group down the sidewalk as the people watch silently.

Tommy *stares at them, biting his lips, and finally calls out again.)*

Tommy. Mr. Brand!

(The two men stop. Tommy *takes a step toward them.)*

Tommy. Mr. Brand . . . please don't leave here.

(Steve and Charlie stop once again and turn toward the boy. In the crowd there is a murmur of irritation and concern, as if the boy's words—even though they didn't make sense—were bringing up fears that shouldn't be brought up.

Tommy *is both frightened and defiant.)*

Tommy. You might not even be able to get to town. It was that way in the story. Nobody could leave. Nobody except—

Steve. Except who?

Tommy. Except the people they sent down ahead of them. They looked just like humans. And it wasn't until the ship landed that—*(The boy suddenly stops, conscious of the people staring at him and his mother and of the sudden hush of the crowd.)*

Sally *(in a whisper, sensing the antagonism of the crowd).* Tommy, please son . . . honey, don't talk that way—

Man One. That kid shouldn't talk that way . . . and we shouldn't stand here listening to him. Why this is the craziest thing I ever heard of. The kid tells us a comic book plot, and here we stand listening—

(Steve walks toward the camera and stops beside the boy.)

Steve. Go ahead, Tommy. What kind of story was this? What about the people they sent out ahead?

---

1. **raise Cain:** cause problems. As told in the Bible, Adam and Eve's son Cain killed his brother Abel.

Words to Know and Use

optimistic (äp′ tə mis′ tik) *adj.* hopeful about the future; confident
defiant (dē fī′ ənt) *adj.* refusing to obey or act in a way acceptable to others
antagonism (an tag′ ə niz′ əm) *n.* hostility; unfriendliness

Tommy. That was the way they prepared things for the landing. They sent four people. A mother and a father and two kids who looked just like humans . . . but they weren't.

(There is another silence as Steve *looks toward the crowd and then toward* Tommy. *He wears a tight grin.)*

Steve. Well, I guess what we'd better do then is to run a check on the neighborhood and see which ones of us are really human.

AMERICAN STREET 1983 Roger Brown
Courtesy, Phyllis Kind Gallery, Chicago and New York.

(There is laughter at this, but it's a laughter that comes from a desperate attempt to lighten the atmosphere. The people look at one another in the middle of their laughter.)

Charlie *(rubs his jaw nervously).* I wonder if Floral Street's got the same deal we got. *(He looks past the houses.)* Where is Pete Van Horn anyway? Isn't he back yet?

(Suddenly there is the sound of a car's engine starting to turn over.
We look across the street toward the driveway of Les Goodman's *house. He is at the wheel trying to start the car.)*

Sally. Can you get started, Les?

(Les Goodman gets out of the car, shaking his head.)

Les. No dice.

(He walks toward the group. He stops suddenly as, behind him, the car engine starts up all by itself. Les whirls around to stare at the car.
The car idles roughly, smoke coming from the exhaust, the frame shaking gently.
Les's eyes go wide, and he runs over to his car.
The people stare at the car.)

Man One. He got the car started somehow. He got *his* car started!

(The people continue to stare, caught up by this revelation and wildly frightened.)

Woman. How come his car just up and started like that?

Sally. All by itself. He wasn't anywheres near it. It started all by itself.

(Don Martin *approaches the group and stops a few feet away to look toward* Les's *car.*)

Don. And he never did come out to look at that thing that flew overhead. He wasn't even interested. *(He turns to the group, his face taut and serious.)* Why? Why didn't he come out with the rest of us to look?

Charlie. He always was an oddball. Him and his whole family. Real oddball.

Don. What do you say we ask him?

(The group starts toward the house. In this brief fraction of a moment, it takes the first step toward changing from a group into a mob. The group members begin to head purposefully across the street toward the house. Steve stands in front of them. For a moment their fear almost turns their walk into a wild stampede, but Steve's voice, loud, incisive, and commanding, makes them stop.)

Steve. Wait a minute . . . wait a minute! Let's not be a mob!

(The people stop, pause for a moment, and then, much more quietly and slowly, start to walk across the street.
Les stands alone facing the people.)

Les. I just don't understand it. I tried to start it, and it wouldn't start. You saw me. All of you saw me.

(And now, just as suddenly as the engine started, it stops, and there is a long silence that is gradually intruded upon by the frightened murmuring of the people.)

Les. I don't understand. I swear . . . I don't understand. What's happening?

Don. Maybe you better tell us. Nothing's working on this street. Nothing. No lights, no power, no radio, *(then meaningfully)* nothing except one car—yours!

(The people's murmuring becomes a loud chant filling the air with accusations and demands for action. Two of the men pass Don *and head toward* Les, *who backs away from them against his car. He is cornered.)*

Les. Wait a minute now. You keep your distance—all of you. So I've got a car that starts by itself—well, that's a freak thing—I admit it. But does that make me a criminal or something? I don't know why the car works—it just does!

(This stops the crowd momentarily, and Les, *still backing away, goes toward his front porch. He goes up the steps and then stops, facing the mob.)*

Les. What's it all about, Steve?

Steve *(quietly).* We're all on a monster kick, Les. Seems that the general impression holds that maybe one family isn't what we think they are. Monsters from outer space or something. Different from us. Aliens from the vast beyond. *(He chuckles.)* You know anybody that might fit that description around here on Maple Street?

Les. What is this, a gag? *(He looks around the group again.)* This a practical joke or something?

(Suddenly the car engine starts all by itself, runs for a moment, and stops. One

woman begins to cry. The eyes of the crowd are cold and accusing.)

Les. Now that's supposed to <u>incriminate</u> me, huh? The car engine goes on and off, and that really does it, doesn't it? *(He looks around at the faces of the people.)* I just don't understand it . . . any more than any of you do! *(He wets his lips, looking from face to face.)* Look, you all know me. We've lived here five years. Right in this house. We're no different from any of the rest of you! We're no different at all. . . . Really . . . this whole thing is just . . . just weird—

Woman. Well, if that's the case, Les Goodman, explain why—*(She stops suddenly, clamping her mouth shut.)*

Les *(softly)*. Explain what?

Steve *(interjecting)*. Look, let's forget this—

Charlie *(overlapping him)*. Go ahead, let her talk. What about it? Explain what?

Woman *(a little reluctantly)*. Well . . . sometimes I go to bed late at night. A couple of times . . . a couple of times I'd come out here on the porch, and I'd see Mr. Goodman here in the wee hours of the morning standing out in front of his house . . . looking up at the sky. *(She looks around the circle of faces.)* That's right, looking up at the sky as if . . . as if he were waiting for something, *(pauses)* as if he were looking for something.

(There's a murmur of reaction from the crowd again as Les backs away.)

Les. She's crazy. Look, I can explain that. Please . . . I can really explain that . . . . She's making it up anyway. *(Then he shouts.)* I tell you she's making it up!

(He takes a step toward the crowd, and they back away from him. He walks down the steps after them, and they continue to back away. Suddenly he is left completely alone, and he looks like a man caught in the middle of a menacing circle as the scene slowly fades to black.)

ACT TWO

Scene 1.

(Fade in on Maple Street at night. On the sidewalk, little knots of people stand around talking in low voices. At the end of each conversation they look toward Les Goodman's *house. From the various houses, we can see candlelight but no electricity. The quiet that blankets the whole area is disturbed only by the almost whispered voices of the people standing around. In one group* Charlie *stands staring across at the* Goodmans' *house. Two men stand across the street from it in almost sentrylike poses.)*

Sally *(in a small, hesitant voice)*. It just doesn't seem right, though, keeping watch on them. Why . . . he was right when he said he was one of our neighbors. Why, I've known Ethel Goodman ever since they moved in. We've been good friends—

Charlie. That don't prove a thing. Any guy who'd spend his time lookin' up at the sky early in the morning—well, there's something wrong with that kind of person. There's something that ain't legiti-mate. Maybe under normal circumstances we could let it go by, but these aren't normal circumstances. Why, look at this street! Nothin' but candles. Why, it's like goin' back into the Dark Ages or somethin'!

(Steve *walks down the steps of his porch, down the street to the* Goodmans' *house, and then stops at the foot of the steps.* Les *is standing there;* Ethel Goodman *behind him is very frightened.*)

Les. Just stay right where you are, Steve. We don't want any trouble, but this time if anybody sets foot on my porch—that's what they're going to get—trouble!

Steve. Look, Les—

Les. I've already explained to you people. I don't sleep very well at night sometimes. I get up and I take a walk and I look up at the sky. I look at the stars!

Ethel. That's exactly what he does. Why, this whole thing, it's . . . it's some kind of madness or something.

Steve (*nods grimly*). That's exactly what it is—some kind of madness.

Charlie's Voice (*shrill, from across the street*). You best watch who you're seen with, Steve! Until we get this all straightened out, you ain't exactly above suspicion yourself.

Steve (*whirling around toward him*). Or you, Charlie. Or any of us, it seems. From age eight on up!

Woman. What I'd like to know is—what are we gonna do? Just stand around here all night?

Charlie. There's nothin' else we *can* do! (*He turns back, looking toward* Steve *and* Les *again.*) One of 'em'll tip their hand. They got to.

Steve (*raising his voice*). There's something you can do, Charlie. You can go home and keep your mouth shut. You can quit strutting around like a self-appointed judge and climb into bed and forget it.

Charlie. You sound real anxious to have that happen, Steve. I think we better keep our eye on you, too!

Don (*as if he were taking the bit in his teeth, takes a hesitant step to the front*). I think everything might as well come out now. (*He turns toward* Steve.) Your wife's done plenty of talking, Steve, about how odd you are!

Charlie (*picking this up, his eyes widening*). Go ahead, tell us what she's said.

(Steve *walks toward them from across the street.*)

Steve. Go ahead, what's my wife said? Let's get it all out. Let's pick out every idiosyncrasy of every single man, woman, and child on the street. And then we might as well set up some kind of citizens' court. How about a firing squad at dawn,

Words to Know and Use

legitimate (lə jit′ ə mət) *adj.* normal; according to the rules
idiosyncrasy (id′ ē ō′ siŋ′ krə sē) *n.* a personal way of acting; odd mannerism

Charlie, so we can get rid of all the suspects. Narrow them down. Make it easier for you.

Don. There's no need gettin' so upset, Steve. It's just that . . . well . . . Myra's talked about how there's been plenty of nights you spent hours down in your basement workin' on some kind of radio or something. Well, none of us have ever seen that radio—

(By this time Steve *has reached the group. He stands there defiantly.)*

Charlie. Go ahead, Steve. What kind of "radio set" you workin' on? I never seen it. Neither has anyone else. Who do you talk to on that radio set? And who talks to you?

Steve. I'm surprised at you, Charlie. How come you're so dense all of a sudden? *(He pauses.)* Who do I talk to? I talk to monsters from outer space. I talk to three-headed green men who fly over here in what look like meteors.

*(*Myra Brand *steps down from the porch, bites her lip, calls out.)*

Myra. Steve! Steve, please. *(Then looking around, frightened, she walks toward the group.)* It's just a ham radio set, that's all. I bought him a book on it myself. It's just a ham radio set. A lot of people have them. I can show it to you. It's right down in the basement.

Steve *(whirls around toward her)*. Show them nothing! If they want to look inside our house—let them go and get a search warrant.

Charlie. Look, buddy, you can't afford to—

Steve *(interrupting him)*. Charlie, don't start telling me who's dangerous and who isn't and who's safe and who's a menace. *(He turns to the group and shouts.)* And you're with him, too—all of you! You're standing here all set to crucify—all set to find a scapegoat—all desperate to point some kind of a finger at a neighbor! Well now, look, friends, the only thing that's gonna happen is that we'll eat each other up alive—

(He stops abruptly as Charlie *suddenly grabs his arm.)*

Charlie *(in a hushed voice)*. That's not the only thing that can happen to us.

(Down the street, a figure has suddenly materialized in the gloom. In the silence we hear the clickety-clack of slow, measured footsteps on concrete as the figure walks slowly toward them. One of the women lets out a stifled cry. Sally grabs her boy, as do a couple of other mothers.)

Tommy *(shouting, frightened)*. It's the monster! It's the monster!

(Another woman lets out a wail, and the people fall back in a group staring toward the darkness and the approaching figure.

The people stand in the shadows watching. Don Martin joins them, carrying a shotgun. He holds it up.)

Don. We may need this.

Steve. A shotgun? *(He pulls it out of* Don's *hand.)* No! Will anybody think a thought around here! Will you people wise up. What good would a shotgun do against—

(The dark figure continues to walk toward them as the people stand there, fearful, mothers clutching children, men standing in front of their wives.)

Charlie *(pulling the gun from* Steve's *hands)*. No more talk, Steve. You're going to talk us into a grave! You'd let whatever's out there walk right over us, wouldn't yuh? Well, some of us won't!

(Charlie swings around, raises the gun, and suddenly pulls the trigger. The sound of the shot explodes in the stillness.

The figure suddenly lets out a small cry, stumbles forward onto his knees, and then falls forward on his face. Don, Charlie, and Steve race forward to him. Steve is there first and turns the man over. The crowd gathers around them.)

Steve *(slowly looks up)*. It's Pete Van Horn.

Don *(in a hushed voice)*. Pete Van Horn! He was just gonna go over to the next block to see if the power was on—

Woman. You killed him, Charlie. You shot him dead!

Charlie *(looks around at the circle of faces, his eyes frightened, his face contorted)*. But . . . but I didn't know who he was. I certainly didn't know who he was. He comes walkin' out of the darkness—how am I supposed to know who he was? *(He grabs* Steve.) Steve—you know why I shot! How was I supposed to know he wasn't a monster or something? *(He grabs* Don.) We're all scared of the same thing. I was just tryin' to . . . tryin' to protect my

RUSH HOUR   1983   George Segal
Courtesy, Sidney Janis Gallery, New York.

home, that's all! Look, all of you, that's all I was tryin' to do. *(He looks down wildly at the body.)* I didn't know it was somebody we knew! I didn't know—

(There's a sudden hush and then an intake of breath in the group. Across the street all the lights go on in one of the houses.)

Woman *(in a hushed voice)*. Charlie . . . Charlie . . . the lights just went on in your house. Why did the lights just go on?

Don. What about it, Charlie? How come you're the only one with lights now?

Les. That's what I'd like to know.

(Pausing, they all stare toward Charlie.)

Les. You were so quick to kill, Charlie, and you were so quick to tell us who we had to be careful of. Well, maybe you had to

Words to Know and Use | **contorted** (kən tôrt' əd) *adj.* twisted or pulled out of shape   **contort** *v.*

kill. Maybe Pete there was trying to tell us something. Maybe he'd found out something and came back to tell us who there was amongst us we should watch out for—

(Charlie *backs away from the group, his eyes wide with fright.*)

Charlie. No . . . no . . . it's nothing of the sort! I don't know why the lights are on. I swear I don't. Somebody's pulling a gag or something.

(*He bumps against* Steve, *who grabs him and whirls him around.*)

Steve. A gag? A gag? Charlie, there's a dead man on the sidewalk, and you killed him! Does this thing look like a gag to you?

(Charlie *breaks away and screams as he runs toward his house.*)

Charlie. No! No! Please!

(*A man breaks away from the crowd to chase* Charlie.

As the man tackles him and lands on top of him, the other people start to run toward them. Charlie *gets up, breaks away from the other man's grasp, and lands a couple of desperate punches that push the man aside. Then he forces his way, fighting, through the crowd and jumps up on his front porch.*

Charlie *is on his porch as a rock thrown from the group smashes a window beside him, the broken glass flying past him. A couple of pieces cut him. He stands there perspiring, rumpled, blood running down from a cut on the cheek. His wife breaks away from the group to throw herself into his arms. He buries his face against her. We can see the crowd converging on the porch.*)

Voice One. It must have been him.

Voice Two. He's the one.

Voice Three. We got to get Charlie.

(*Another rock lands on the porch.* Charlie *pushes his wife behind him, facing the group.*)

Charlie. Look, look I swear to you…it isn't me . . . but I do know who it is . . . I swear to you, I do know who it is. I know who the monster is here. I know who it is that doesn't belong. I swear to you I know.

Don (*pushing his way to the front of the crowd*). All right, Charlie, let's hear it!

(Charlie's *eyes dart around wildly.*)

Charlie. It's . . . it's . . .

Man Two (*screaming*). Go ahead, Charlie.

Charlie. It's . . . it's the kid. It's Tommy. He's the one!

(*There's a gasp from the crowd as we see* Sally *holding the boy.* Tommy *at first doesn't understand and then, realizing the eyes are all on him, buries his face against his mother.*)

Sally (*backs away*). That's crazy! He's only a boy.

Woman. But he knew! He was the only one! He told us all about it. Well, how did he know? How could he have known?

(*Various people take this up and repeat the question.*)

Voice One. How could he know?

Voice Two. Who told him?

Voice Three. Make the kid answer.

(The crowd starts to converge around the mother, who grabs Tommy *and starts to run with him. The crowd starts to follow, at first walking fast, and then running after him.*

Suddenly Charlie's *lights go off and the lights in other houses go on, then off.)*

Man One *(shouting)*. It isn't the kid . . . it's Bob Weaver's house.

Woman. It isn't Bob Weaver's house, it's Don Martin's place.

Charlie. I tell you it's the kid.

Don. It's Charlie. He's the one.

(People shout, accuse, and scream as the lights go on and off. Then, slowly, in the middle of this nightmarish confusion of sight and sound, the camera starts to pull away until, once again, we have reached the opening shot looking at the Maple Street sign from high above.)

Scene 2.

(The camera continues to move away while gradually bringing into focus a field. We see the metal side of a spacecraft that sits shrouded in darkness. An open door throws out a beam of light from the illuminated interior. Two figures appear, silhouetted against the bright lights. We get only a vague feeling of form.)

Figure One. Understand the procedure now? Just stop a few of their machines and radios and telephones and lawn mowers . . . . Throw them into darkness for a few hours, and then just sit back and watch the pattern.

Figure Two. And this pattern is always the same?

Figure One. With few variations. They pick the most dangerous enemy they can find . . . and it's themselves. And all we need do is sit back . . . and watch.

Figure Two. Then I take it this place . . . this Maple Street . . . is not unique.

Figure One *(shaking his head)*. By no means. Their world is full of Maple Streets. And we'll go from one to the other and let them destroy themselves. One to the other . . . one to the other . . . one to the other—

Scene 3.

(The camera slowly moves up for a shot of the starry sky, and over this we hear the Narrator's *voice.)*

Narrator. The tools of conquest do not necessarily come with bombs and explosions and fallout.[2] There are weapons that are simply thoughts, attitudes, prejudices—to be found only in the minds of men. For the record, prejudices can kill and suspicion can destroy. A thoughtless, frightened search for a scapegoat has a fallout all its own for the children . . . and the children yet unborn, *(a pause)* and the pity of it is . . . that these things cannot be confined to . . . The Twilight Zone!

(Fade to black.) ❧

---

2. fallout: radioactive particles that fall to earth after a nuclear explosion.

Responding to Reading

First Impressions

1. In your notebook or journal, jot down words and phrases to describe your reaction to the end of the play.

Second Thoughts

2. Do you think the aliens were correct in their judgment of human behavior? Why?

3. In your opinion, who are the monsters on Maple Street? Why?

   Think about
   - who shares responsibility for the death of Pete Van Horn
   - what the aliens and the narrator say at the end

4. Consider your earlier discussion of how people react to fear. Is the crowd's reaction of searching for someone to blame a common reaction? Explain your opinion.

5. Why do you think the author chose Maple Street as the **setting?**

Broader Connections

6. This play shows what can happen when a crowd becomes a mob. How does being in a crowd change the way people act? What other examples of "mob mentality" can you name?

Literary Concepts: Dialogue and Theme

In drama, the story is told mostly through the conversations, or **dialogue,** between the characters. The dialogue also reveals the beliefs and values of the characters. According to the dialogue in this play, which characters are most eager to find a scapegoat for the unusual events?

The **theme** of a literature selection is the main message about life or human nature that an author presents. Often, the theme is not stated directly. A selection might have more than one theme, and different readers might find different themes. For example, one theme from "The War of the Wall" might be, "Don't jump to conclusions." What do you think is the theme of *The Monsters Are Due on Maple Street*?

*W*riting Options

1. Write a short **summary** of the play as it might appear in the coming-attractions section of a video catalog. Remember to tempt the readers to watch the show.

2. Write **stage directions** to describe what a visitor would find on Maple Street if he or she arrived the next day.

3. Imagine that the aliens have targeted your school next. With classmates, write a **teleplay** that presents your version of the events.

4. Choose one victim from the selections in this subunit. Write an angry **letter to the editor** of a local newspaper, blasting those who mistreated the victim.

*V*ocabulary Practice

Exercise Use your understanding of the meanings of the boldfaced words to complete the following sentences. Write the letter of each correct answer on your paper.

1. A student who is **flustered** is probably (a) confused (b) happy (c) asleep (d) mean.

2. **Intense** fans might (a) clap softly (b) show boredom (c) scream (d) leave early.

3. **Optimistic** students expect (a) punishment (b) failure (c) homework (d) success.

4. A **legitimate** answer to a question is (a) silly (b) correct (c) false (d) dishonest.

5. If one's face is **contorted,** it is (a) clean (b) red (c) pale (d) twisted.

6. A child who is **defiant** answers (a) boldly (b) promptly (c) cautiously (d) timidly.

7. A **persistent** talker would be (a) shy (b) seldom quiet (c) dishonest (d) bragging.

8. If the police found evidence to **incriminate** you, you would be (a) relieved (b) in trouble (c) thankful (d) released.

9. A nurse may feel **antagonism** toward a patient who (a) is insulting (b) is considerate (c) arrives on time (d) feels feverish.

10. An **idiosyncrasy** is (a) a persistent drip (b) a repeated sound (c) an annoying habit (d) a stupid person.

*Words
to Know
and Use*

antagonism
contorted
defiant
flustered
idiosyncrasy
incriminate
intense
legitimate
optimistic
persistent

Options for Learning

1 • **Map Maple**   Using details from the play, draw a diagram of what you think Maple Street looks like. Include houses, cars, and other objects mentioned in the teleplay.

2 • **Day in Court**   Put Charlie on trial for the unlawful killing of Pete Van Horn. Have class members play the parts of judge, jury, trial lawyers, and witnesses from the neighborhood. The jury should decide whether Charlie killed Pete in self-defense or he is guilty of manslaughter.

3 • **Shoot the Monsters**   Using the stage directions as a guide, videotape one act or both acts of the play. Assign class members to play the characters and to work on the production crew, for which you will need a director, a camera operator, and a sound crew.

4 • **What Saucer?**   Research the controversy about the existence of UFO's (unidentified flying objects). Find out what the U. S. Air Force and others have to say about whether or not aliens have visited the earth. Present your findings to the class.

 FACT FINDER VOCABULARY

What is the origin of the word scapegoat?

Rod Serling
1924–1975

Though the public knew Rod Serling as the creator of exciting television shows, those in the entertainment business knew him as "the angry young man of television." Serling began his career by writing for radio and television in Cincinnati. In 1955, he scored his first big hit with his television drama *Patterns,* which won an Emmy Award. He hoped to write meaningful plays about important social issues. However, television sponsors and executives often found his topics too controversial. Thus began his long battle with those who controlled the networks.

Serling turned to writing science fiction and fantasy with series such as *The Twilight Zone* and *Night Gallery.* Because these shows were not realistic, he had more freedom to deal with issues such as prejudice and intolerance. Serling eventually won six Emmy Awards and many other honors for the extraordinary quality of his work.

WRITER'S WORKSHOP

NARRATIVE WRITING

USE NARRATIVE WRITING FOR

stories
narrative poems
oral histories
plays
skits
biographies

Like the characters in this subunit, each of us has experienced unfair treatment at one time or another. We have been victims, seen victims, and maybe even victimized someone else. In this workshop you will write the true story of such an experience. The victim might be you or someone you know. When you write a story, true or imagined, you are using **narrative** writing. In a **personal narrative,** you base your story on the experiences of someone you know better than anyone else—you.

Here is one writer's PASSkey to this assignment.

GUIDED ASSIGNMENT: PERSONAL NARRATIVE

Write about a time when you were a victim, saw someone being victimized, or helped make someone else a victim.

P URPOSE: To tell a true story
A UDIENCE: Classmates, friends
S UBJECT: A victim
S TRUCTURE: Personal narrative

STUDENT MODEL

Before you write, read how one student responded to the assignment.

Signal words such as *when* make the order of events clear.

> The Perfect Victim
> by Chris Nelson
>
> Mrs. King, the new math teacher, smiled her odd smile and moved clumsily back and forth as she erased the board. It was between classes, and as kids passed Mrs. King, they grinned and giggled. She probably thought they were finally beginning to like her. Peering through her thick glasses at those friendly faces, she didn't realize that they were laughing at her.
>
> Class started. "Today," she began, "I have a brain teaser for you." The kids giggled again, and Mrs. King smiled again. When she turned back to the board, however, the reason for the giggles was clear. On the back of her skirt was a sign saying "I need a face lift."

You might think the author of this nasty trick was the class clown or some other troublemaker. You'd be wrong. The person who did it was always polite, got good grades, and was probably Mrs. King's favorite student. I know a lot about this person because I did it.

Before class I had my friend Lon go up to Mrs. King. He had trouble with math, and she knew it. "I didn't understand the third homework problem," he complained, as I had told him to.

"Just remember our four steps, Lon," she began patiently. While she talked, I went behind her and hung the sign from her belt loop. I felt like I was going to throw up. I was nervous, excited, and scared, all at once.

When I think back, it's hard to figure out why I did such a mean thing. I know I wanted to be popular—part of the "in" group. I thought doing something really crazy might make me an instant member. Mrs. King was my way in. She was the perfect victim.

Mrs. King didn't return this year. I hope my stupid trick didn't have anything to do with it. At the time I was thinking only about myself. I never thought about Mrs. King at all. Now I think about her a lot.

◀ Notice that the writer began her story in the middle. Now a **flashback,** a jump back in time, tells how it all started.

◀ **Dialogue**— conversation between characters—gives readers insights into characters and adds life to your writing.

◀ The writer tells what the incident meant to her.

Prewrite and Explore

1 Search your memory If you can't think of anything to write about, try listing times when you, or someone you know, felt like a victim. Think of recent experiences as well as experiences from the past. Remember times when you have felt guilty or felt sorry for yourself or someone else.

◀ WRITER'S CHOICE
Another way to find ideas is to brainstorm aloud while a partner takes notes. Then take notes for your partner.

2 Choose your topic and gather information Be sure to choose an experience you will feel comfortable sharing with others. Once you've made a choice, you can begin to gather information.

Begin by visualizing the experience you've chosen. Use your mind as a camera, zooming in for close-ups. Next, make a **story map**—a set of notes that breaks the story into its literary elements—to focus your thoughts. Jot notes as you search through your memories. To see how this works, look at the story map and notes Chris made.

STUDENT MODEL ▶

Plot—what happened?	Characters—who was involved and what were they like?
I played a practical joke on a teacher. I got Lon to distract her. I hung a sign on her back. Everyone cracked up. This year she's gone.	Me: a goody-goody—felt excited, scared, guilty Mrs. King: new math teacher—strange and sad Lon: my friend—no good at math Other kids: the "in" kids—laughing
Setting—where and when? November, sixth grade Between classes	Motivation—why did it happen? I wanted to be liked.

Draft and Discover

1 **Begin drafting** You may want to start with the part of the story you remember most clearly. Your story map will remind you what else to put in. Remember to write more than just the facts—include your feelings and impressions too.

2 **Bring it to life**   To make your narrative vivid, you can include **dialogue**—words that the characters say. As you learned on page 155, writers use dialogue to reveal characters' personalities. Look at this example and decide what it shows about Margot and the boy. Then try putting a few lines of dialogue in your own writing.

"Oh, but," Margot whispered, her eyes helpless. "But, this is the day, the scientists predict, they say, they *know*, the sun. . . ."
"All a joke!" said the boy, and seized her roughly. "Hey, everyone, let's put her in a closet before teacher comes!"

◀ **LITERARY MODEL**
. . . .
from "All Summer in a Day" by Ray Bradbury

Revise Your Writing

ASK FOR HELP
. . . .
Need more details? Try telling your story to a classmate. See if any new ideas come out as
◀ you talk.

1 **Find your angle**   As you read your draft, decide what the event you're narrating meant to you. Try to sum up its meaning in one sentence. Then you can add details that will make the meaning clearer to readers.

2 **Shape your draft**   Narratives are usually organized in chronological order. You might devote one paragraph to each major part of the story. You could also begin your story in the middle, as Chris did. In such a case, you can use a flashback to help readers understand how the beginning of the story came about. A **flashback** explains the events that happened before the story begins. Since Chris's story begins with the kids laughing at the sign on the teacher, a flashback is needed to explain how the sign got there.
Use the following questions to review your work.

◀ **COMPUTER TIP**
. . . .
Will it work best to narrate events from the beginning, to start in the middle, or even to start at the end? Try moving sections of your story around on the computer.

Revision Questions

For You	For a Peer Reader
1. Should I add details or dialogue to make the important parts stand out?	**1.** Which parts of my story could you imagine most clearly?
2. Should I add signal words to make the order of events clearer?	**2.** Were there any parts that you had to reread to understand?
3. Would a flashback help explain events more clearly?	**3.** How do you think I felt about the events in the story?

◀ **SIGNAL WORDS**
. . . .
Signal words such as *first, then, before, when, after,* and *while* help keep the events clear for readers.

Proofread

Review your work for errors in grammar, spelling, capitalization, and punctuation. If possible, ask a peer editor to review your work. Check dialogue carefully for correct punctuation.

THE EDITOR'S EYE: PUNCTUATING DIALOGUE

Enclose dialogue in quotation marks. Start a new paragraph each time the speaker changes.

When you write a character's exact words, put quotation marks around them. Each time a different character begins speaking, indent the sentence to start a new paragraph.

Problem	I didn't understand the third homework problem, he complained, as I had told him to. Just remember our four steps, Lon, she began patiently.
Revised	"I didn't understand the third homework problem," he complained, as I had told him to. "Just remember our four steps, Lon," she began patiently.

NEED MORE HELP?

See the Language Workshop on pages 179–181 and pages 784–785 of the Language Handbook.

Publish and Present

Here is a suggestion for sharing your work with others.

A Memory Album   Put all the stories into an album that can be borrowed by class members. Add photographs or drawings if you wish.

Reflect on Your Writing

FOR YOUR PORTFOLIO ▶ Write answers to the following questions. Attach your answers to your paper, and add it to your writing portfolio.

1. Which part of your story do you like best now? Why?
2. Which part of the writing process was most difficult for you this time? Why?

LANGUAGE WORKSHOP

PUNCTUATING DIALOGUE

> A **dialogue** is a conversation between two or more people.

Using Dialogue in Writing

When you write a story, you can use indirect quotations, in which you report secondhand what characters say, as in this sentence:

Cephas explained that the chickens wouldn't keep long in the sun.

However, if you use direct quotations instead, your characters speak for themselves. Then your stories come alive.

"Ma'am, you better get the chickens out—it don't do to keep 'em in the sun."

Direct quotations need careful punctuation. Careless punctuation can leave your readers wondering who said what and when. The following rules can help you keep the speakers and their words clear.

1. Use quotation marks to enclose direct quotations.

A direct quotation gives a speaker's exact words. Use quotation marks to show where this speech begins and ends.

"Take a number," the woman said without looking at him.

2. Use quotation marks to enclose both parts of a divided quotation.

"The food might spoil," said Mr. Ribble, "if you don't hurry."
"In 1934 we came here for help," he remembered. "Today I'm here for a different reason."

Notice that when the words in quotation marks are a complete sentence, the quotation begins with a capital letter.

◀ **GRAMMAR TIP**
· · · · · · · · · · · · · · ·
The word *that* often signals an indirect quotation.

LITERARY MODELS
· · · · · · · · · · · · · · ·
from "Upon the Waters" by Joanne Greenberg

MEMORY TIP

Here's an easy way to
remember rule 3:
Commas and periods
always go inside
quotation marks—
they're too little to stay
outside.

3. Put commas and periods inside quotation marks.

Cephas Ribble said, "I didn't come for aid**.**"
"I'm grateful**,**" he added, "and I want to show it**.**"

4. If an exclamation point or a question mark is part of a quotation, put it inside the quotation marks. Otherwise, put it outside.

The woman asked**,** "Are you married, Mr. Ribble**?**"
Did she look up as she said**,** "Go to Room Eleven"**?**

Notice that commas set off **explanatory words**—the words that
come before, after, or in the middle of a quotation and tell who is
speaking. In the examples above, *The woman asked* and *she said* are
explanatory words.

5. Begin a new paragraph every time the speaker changes.

The woman was very annoyed. "Then why didn't you tell the
worker at the desk?"
"She didn't give me no chance, ma'am. . . ."

Exercise 1   Concept Check   Rewrite the following
sentences. Add quotation marks and commas in the correct places.

1. Exactly why are you here? the woman asked impatiently.
2. Cephas announced I have a whole truckload of food outside.
3. It's for the poor. There are even apricots he added with pride.
4. But the woman sputtered We have no way to handle this!
5. Why didn't the director say Just take it back home?
6. Mrs. Traphagen exclaimed The poor won't stand for it!
7. I put in some milk confided Cephas in case there are hungry babies.
8. As Cephas spoke to the police officer, Mr. Morrissey asked Can the truck fit into the parking lot?
9. Mrs. Traphagen told a friend I'll never know how we got rid of it all.
10. Imagine how happy they'll be when they see me coming back with more next year! Cephas said to himself.

Exercise 2   Proofreading Skill   Work in small groups to
punctuate the following dialogue. Decide together how each sentence
should be punctuated, and have one person write the dialogue according
to your decisions. Remember to start a new paragraph each time the
speaker changes.

There's nothing as good as fresh-picked apricots Gram began brightly. Why do you mention that? my cousin inquired as we edged toward the door. We had a pretty good idea what was coming. Well, that tree out in back is getting loaded down Gram said sweetly, and I'd hate to see the birds get all the fruit. Besides, I've been wanting to make some jam. But Gram I protested we were just going to go Rollerblading with our friends. Can't the apricots wait? You can go Rollerblading another time Gram stated firmly. Right now there's work to be done, and you're just the two I need to do it!

Exercise 3   Looking at Style   Work with a partner to find a passage containing dialogue in one of the selections in Unit 1. Together, rewrite the passage to make it a narrative without dialogue, using indirect quotations if necessary. When you finish, decide which passage you prefer—the original, written in dialogue, or the one you rewrote without dialogue. Share your rewritten passage with others.

Exercise 4   Revising Your Writing   Reread your personal narrative. Where you have used dialogue, check your punctuation and paragraphing. Correct any errors you find.

LANGUAGE HANDBOOK
For review and practice:
Section 10, Punctuation, pages 784–785.

READER'S WORKSHOP

CAUSE AND EFFECT

Events in stories are often linked as **cause and effect.** In other words, one event is the reason why another event happens. The event that happens first in time is called the **cause.** What follows is the **effect.** Try to identify the cause and the effect in the following excerpt:

LITERARY MODEL
from "All Summer in a Day" by Ray Bradbury

> A boom of thunder startled them, and like leaves before a new hurricane, they tumbled upon each other and ran.

The thunder booms first; this is the cause. The effect is that the children tumble upon each other and run.

Effects do not always come after causes in a story. A story or incident might begin with an effect. Then the events in the plot explain the causes. For example, in the student model in the Writer's Workshop, the writer states first that the students were laughing at Mrs. King. The reader learns the cause of this laughter later in the piece—that the laughter was the effect of the prank the writer played on her teacher.

As you read, look for the ways events are connected. Picture the order of events in your mind. Look for signal words such as *because, therefore, since, in order that, so that,* and *if . . . then,* which point out causes and their effects.

Exercise 1   Look back at the play *The Monsters Are Due on Maple Street.* On a chart like the one below, note examples of cause and effect in the play. One example has been filled in for you.

Cause	Effect
1. The power goes off on Maple Street.	Steve decides to drive downtown.
2.	

Exercise 2   In the personal narrative you wrote for the Writer's Workshop on pages 174–178, identify at least one example of cause and effect.

TURNING THE TABLES

....

The phrase "turning the tables" comes from backgammon, a game that was originally called Tables and often involves dramatic reversals of fortune.

Today, we turn the tables on someone when we put that person in a situation we have been in ourselves. When a doctor becomes a patient, when a thief's wallet is stolen, or when a losing sports team wins a game, the tables are turned.

Putting another person in your position can sometimes lead to a well-earned reward. However, when turning the tables is motivated by revenge, people may go beyond what is right or legal. In the following selections you will discover rewards, revenge, and satisfaction as the tables are turned.

Fiction

The *Revolt of the Evil Fairies*

TED POSTON

Examine What You Know

What do you know about rebels and revolts? You have probably read about group rebellions in your history class, but what individual rebels have you known? Perhaps you know someone who has rebelled against unfair treatment. What caused the rebellion? What were the results? Discuss your ideas with your classmates.

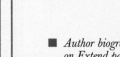

Expand Your Knowledge

The **setting** of this story is a small town in the South during the early 1900s, long before the "rebellion" of the civil rights movement. At that time, segregated schools, or schools for one race only, were legal. Although all African Americans experienced discrimination to some degree, those with lighter complexions fared better than those with darker skin. Even within the black community, certain prejudices existed. Lighter-skinned blacks were considered superior to those who were darker, and those with lighter skins were often the wealthiest and most favored members of African-American society.

Enrich Your Reading

Cause and Effect   Events in a story are often related as causes and effects. One event causes another event, the effect, to occur. For example, mistreatment (the cause) might lead to rebellion (the effect). Sometimes clue words or phrases, such as *because, since,* and *so that* signal cause-and-effect relationships. When you finish reading, create a cause-and-effect chart like the one started below. As you write, notice how some effects become the causes of other effects.

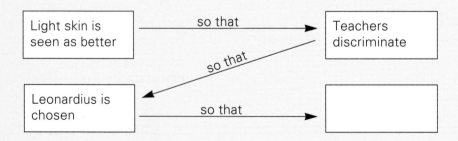

■ *Author biography on Extend page*

The Revolt of the Evil Fairies

TED POSTON

The grand dramatic offering of the Booker T. Washington Colored Grammar School was the biggest event of the year in our social life in Hopkinsville, Kentucky. It was the one occasion on which they let us use the old Cooper Opera House, and even some of the white folks came out yearly to applaud our presentation. The first two rows of the orchestra were always reserved for our white friends, and our leading colored citizens sat right behind them—with an empty row intervening, of course.

Mr. Ed Smith, our local undertaker, invariably occupied a box to the left of the house and wore his cutaway coat and striped breeches. This distinctive garb was usually reserved for those rare occasions when he officiated at the funerals of our most prominent colored citizens. Mr. Thaddeus Long, our colored mailman, once rented a tuxedo and bought a box too. But nobody paid him much mind. We knew he was just showing off.

The title of our play never varied. It was always Prince Charming and the Sleeping Beauty, but no two presentations were ever the same. Miss H. Belle LaPrade, our sixth-grade teacher, rewrote the script every season, and it was never like anything you read in the storybooks.

Miss LaPrade called it "a modern morality play[1] of conflict between the forces of good and evil." And the forces of evil, of course, always came off second best.

The Booker T. Washington Colored Grammar School was in a state of ferment from Christmas until February, for this was the period when parts were assigned. First there was the selection of the Good Fairies and the Evil Fairies. This was very important, because the Good Fairies wore white costumes and the Evil Fairies black. And strangely enough most of the Good Fairies usually turned out to be extremely light in complexion, with straight hair and white folks' features. On rare occasions a dark-skinned girl might be lucky enough to be a Good Fairy, but not one with a speaking part.

There never was any doubt about Prince

---

1. **morality play:** a drama intended to teach people right from wrong.

*Words
to Know
and Use*

intervening (in′ tər vēn′ iŋ) *adj.* coming between **intervene** *v.*
distinctive (di stiŋk′ tiv) *adj.* different from others; characteristic

PORCH NO. 2   1947   Philip Guston
Munson-Williams-Proctor Institute, Utica, New York.

Charming and the Sleeping Beauty. They were always light-skinned. And though nobody ever discussed those things openly, it was an accepted fact that a lack of pigmentation was a decided advantage in the Prince Charming and Sleeping Beauty sweepstakes.

And therein lay my personal tragedy. I made the best grades in my class; I was the leading debater and the scion[2] of a respected family in the community. But I could never be Prince Charming, because I was black.

In fact, every year when they started casting our grand dramatic offering, my family started pricing black cheesecloth at Franklin's Department Store. For they knew that I would be leading the forces of darkness and skulking back in the shadows—waiting to be vanquished in the third act.

Mamma had experience with this sort of thing. All my brothers had finished Booker T. before me.

Not that I was alone in my disappointment. Many of my classmates felt it too. I probably just took it more to heart. Rat Joiner, for instance, could rationalize the situation. Rat was not only black; he lived on Billy Goat Hill.[3] But Rat summed it up like this:

"If you black, you black."

I should have been able to regard the matter calmly too. For our grand dramatic offering was only a reflection of our daily community life in Hopkinsville. The yallers[4] had the best of everything. They held most of the teaching jobs in Booker T. Washington Colored Grammar School. They were the Negro doctors, the lawyers, the insurance men. They even had a "Blue Vein Society,"[5] and if your dark skin obscured your throbbing pulse, you were hardly a member of the elite.

Yet I was inconsolable the first time they turned me down for Prince Charming. That was the year they picked Roger Jackson. Roger was not only dumb; he stuttered. But he was light enough to pass for white, and that was apparently sufficient.

In all fairness, however, it must be admitted that Roger had other qualifications. His

---

2. **scion** (sī′ ən): a descendant.
3. **Billy Goat Hill:** the name of a very poor section of town.
4. **yallers:** *dialect,* black people with light brown, tan, or yellowish skin.
5. **Blue Vein Society:** the upper class, sometimes called blue bloods.

Words to Know and Use	**pigmentation** (pig mən tā′ shən) *n.* a skin color
	vanquish (vaŋ′ kwish) *v.* to conquer, defeat
	rationalize (rash′ ən əl īz′) *v.* to explain or make excuses for
	elite (ā lēt′) *n.* a group regarded as the best
	inconsolable (in′ kən sōl′ ə bəl) *adj.* brokenhearted; not able to be comforted

father owned the only colored saloon in town and was quite a power in local politics. In fact, Mr. Clinton Jackson had a lot to say about just who taught in the Booker T. Washington Colored Grammar School. So it was understandable that Roger should have been picked for Prince Charming.

My real heartbreak, however, came the year they picked Sarah Williams for Sleeping Beauty. I had been in love with Sarah since kindergarten. She had soft light hair, bluish-gray eyes, and a dimple which stayed in her left cheek whether she was smiling or not.

Of course Sarah never encouraged me much. She never answered any of my fervent love letters, and Rat was very scornful of my one-sided love affairs. "As long as she don't call you a black baboon," he sneered, "you'll keep on hanging around."

After Sarah was chosen for Sleeping Beauty, I went out for the Prince Charming role with all my heart. If I had declaimed boldly in previous contests, I was matchless now. If I had bothered Mamma with rehearsals at home before, I pestered her to death this time. Yes, and I purloined[6] my sister's can of Palmer's Skin Success.[7]

I knew the Prince's role from start to finish, having played the Head Evil Fairy opposite it for two seasons. And Prince Charming was one character whose lines Miss LaPrade never varied much in her many versions. But although I never admitted it, even to myself, I knew I was doomed from the start. They gave the part to Leonardius Wright. Leonardius, of course, was yaller.

The teachers sensed my resentment. They were almost apologetic. They pointed out that I had been such a splendid Head Evil Fairy for two seasons that it would be a crime to let anybody else try the role. They reminded me that Mamma wouldn't have to buy any more cheesecloth because I could use my same old costume. They insisted that the Head Evil Fairy was even more important than Prince Charming because he was the one who cast the spell on Sleeping Beauty. So what could I do but accept?

I had never liked Leonardius Wright. He was a goody-goody, and even Mamma was always throwing him up to me. But, above all, he too was in love with Sarah Williams. And now he got a chance to kiss Sarah every day in rehearsing the awakening scene.

Well, the show must go on, even for little black boys. So I threw my soul into my part and made the Head Evil Fairy a character to be remembered. When I drew back from the couch of Sleeping Beauty and slunk away into the shadows at the approach of Prince Charming, my facial expression was indeed something to behold. When I was vanquished by the shining sword of Prince Charming in the last act, I was a little hammy perhaps—but terrific!

The attendance at our grand dramatic offering that year was the best in its history. Even the white folks overflowed the two rows reserved for them, and a few were forced to sit in the intervening one. This created a delicate situation, but everybody tactfully ignored it.

When the curtain went up on the last act, the audience was in fine fettle. Everything

---

6. **purloined:** stole.

7. **Palmer's Skin Success:** a product that is supposed to lighten the skin of black people.

had gone well for me too—except for one spot in the second act. That was where Leonardius unexpectedly rapped me over the head with his sword as I slunk off into the shadows. That was not in the script, but Miss LaPrade quieted me down by saying it made a nice touch anyway. Rat said Leonardius did it on purpose.

The third act went on smoothly, though, until we came to the vanquishing scene. That was where I slunk from the shadows for the last time and challenged Prince Charming to mortal combat. The hero reached for his shining sword—a bit unsportsmanlike, I always thought, since Miss LaPrade consistently left the Head Evil Fairy unarmed—and then it happened!

Later I protested loudly—but in vain—that it was a case of self-defense. I pointed out that Leonardius had a mean look in his eye. I cited the impromptu rapping he had given my head in the second act. But nobody would listen. They just wouldn't believe that Leonardius really intended to brain me when he reached for his sword.

Anyway, he didn't succeed. For the minute I saw that evil gleam in his eye—or was it my own?—I cut loose with a right to the chin, and Prince Charming dropped his shining sword and staggered back. His astonishment lasted only a minute, though, for he lowered his head and came charging in, fists flailing. There was nothing yellow about Leonardius but his skin.

The audience thought the scrap was something new Miss LaPrade had written in. They might have kept on thinking so if

SHIFTING EMBRACE 1990 Philemona Williamson Collection of Mr. and Mrs. Clarence Otis. Photo by Manu Sassoonian. Courtesy, June Kelly Gallery, New York .

Miss LaPrade hadn't been screaming so hysterically from the sidelines. And if Rat Joiner hadn't decided that this was as good a time as any to settle old scores. So he turned around and took a sock at the male Good Fairy nearest him.

When the curtain rang down, the forces of Good and Evil were locked in combat. And Sleeping Beauty was wide awake and streaking for the wings.

They rang the curtain back up fifteen minutes later, and we finished the play. I lay down and expired according to specifications, but Prince Charming will probably remember my sneering corpse to his dying day. They wouldn't let me appear in the grand dramatic offering at all the next year. But I didn't care. I couldn't have been Prince Charming anyway. ❧

Words to Know and Use

impromptu (im prämp′ to͞o′) *adj.* without preparation; on the spur of the moment
expire (ek spīr′) *v.* to die
sneering (snir′ iŋ) *adj.* having a mocking smile **sneer** *v.*

188

*R*esponding to Reading

First Impressions

1. What event in this story affected you the most? Jot down your thoughts in a notebook or journal.

Second Thoughts

2. Do you think the narrator is justified in his rebellion during the third act? Give reasons for your answer.

3. Name all the causes of the chain of events in this story. Was any one cause more important than the others? Explain.

> **Think about**
> • Leonardius's actions
> • the attitudes of the teachers and townspeople

4. The narrator and his friend Rat Joiner have different attitudes about their situation. Which character would you resemble if you were in the story? Why?

5. Do you think the author intended the story to be funny? Explain your opinion.

Broader Connections

6. Were you surprised about the discrimination within the African-American community in the story? Do you think that attitude still exists? Share your opinion.

*L*iterary Concept: Conflict

Conflict is a struggle between opposing forces that forms the basis for the plot of a story. **External conflict** is a struggle between a character and an outside force, such as another character, society, or nature. **Internal conflict** occurs when a character has to struggle within himself or herself, as when making a decision or resolving a problem. With whom or what does the narrator of this story have conflict? Are his conflicts internal, external, or both?

Concept Review: Climax What is the climax, or turning point, of this story?

Writing Options

1. This story is told from one character's point of view. Rewrite the **climax** of the story from Leonardius's point of view.

2. What if Sarah, Leonardius, and the narrator had met after the play? Write the **conversation** they might have had among themselves.

3. Skim "The Noble Experiment," on page 143. Then compare and contrast the personalities of Jackie Robinson and the narrator of this story. Would the narrator of this story have ever been chosen for the "noble experiment"? Write your **opinion** and give reasons.

4. The school play in this story did not go quite according to the script. Write an **account** of a performance in which you participated that, like the one in the story, unexpectedly changed from what was planned.

Vocabulary Practice

Exercise On your paper, write the word from the list that best completes the meaning of each sentence below.

1. The narrator's __?__ expression showed contempt, not respect, for Leonardius.

2. Those children of lighter __?__ were chosen to be Good Fairies.

3. In the __?__ years since this episode, schools have become integrated.

4. In most "Sleeping Beauty" productions, Prince Charming is able to __?__ the Evil Fairies.

5. The __?__ nature of this performance could not be denied; it was unique.

6. Rat Joiner would have happily joined in any __?__ fight; he was always ready.

7. Sobbing, Sarah was __?__ about her ruined acting debut.

8. The teacher tried to __?__ the narrator's role by saying that he already had the costume.

9. In the last scene, the Head Evil Fairy is supposed to __?__.

10. Many of the town's most important citizens, the __?__, attended the annual play.

> *Words to Know and Use*
>
> ---
>
> **distinctive**
> **elite**
> **expire**
> **impromptu**
> **inconsolable**
> **intervening**
> **pigmentation**
> **rationalize**
> **sneering**
> **vanquish**

*O*ptions for Learning

1 • **Speak from the Heart**
Suppose you were the narrator of this story. Plan, practice, and give a speech to your class, explaining how you feel about being discriminated against because of your dark skin color.

2 • **Plays for Little Folks** Write your own stage play for young children based on "Sleeping Beauty" or another fairy tale. Make the dialogue and the stage directions easy enough for third or fourth graders to follow.

3 • **Booker T. and W. E. B.** In a small group, divide yourselves into two research teams. One team should research Booker T. Washington to learn about his accomplishments and what he stood for. The other team should research W. E. B. Du Bois. Find out how the two men differed in their outlooks. Both teams can share their information with the rest of the class.

 FACT FINDER HISTORY
What Supreme Court case abolished segregation in public schools?

*T*ed Poston
1906–1974

Theodore Roosevelt was President when Ted Poston was born in Hopkinsville, Kentucky, and named Theodore Roosevelt Augustus Major Poston. Poston began his writing career as a teenager working on his family's newspaper, which was forced to close when it became too controversial. After college, Poston worked for black-owned newspapers in Pittsburgh and New York City. When he applied for a job with the *New York Post* in 1937, only two black journalists had ever worked for a white-owned daily newspaper in New York.

Poston was told that the job was his if he could find a front-page story for the next day's paper. He did, and he stayed at the *Post* until 1972.

Poston faced danger reporting events concerning race relations in the South. During the 1955 bus boycotts in Montgomery, Alabama, his boss in New York asked him to call every night to prove that he was alive. He won the Heywood Broun Award of the American Newspaper Guild and several other awards in the 1950s for those reports. Poston also wrote short stories, some autobiographical, about barriers faced by African Americans.

Fiction

*A*unt *M*illicent

MARY STEELE

*E*xamine What You Know

A character in this story says, "The most interesting characters in the world are usually the made-up ones." Think about adventurous characters in movies and books and compare them with real people you know or know about. Do you agree or disagree with the statement? Discuss your thoughts with your class, giving examples to support your opinion.

*E*xpand Your Knowledge

Although the **setting** of this story is Australia, the mysterious character of Aunt Millicent finds adventure almost halfway around the world in Cameroon, on the west coast of Africa. Originally Cameroon was called the Cameroons, because one part was ruled by France and the other by Great Britain. The Cameroons became independent in the early 1960s, and in 1972 the two countries united to become the United Republic of Cameroon. Lake Chad, at the northern tip of Cameroon, is a lake that grows and shrinks in the rainy and dry seasons.

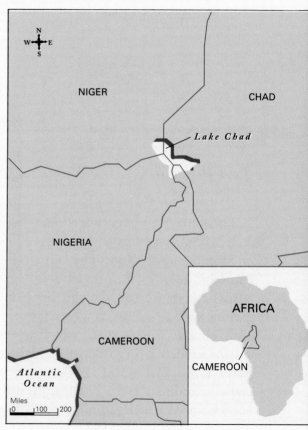

*W*rite Before You Read

If you were able to choose an exciting adventure for yourself, what would you do? Where would you go? Whom would you take with you? In your journal or notebook, write notes to describe the most exciting adventure that you personally would enjoy.

■ *Author biography on Extend page*

Aunt Millicent

MARY STEELE

I, said Angelica Tonks, grandly, "have eight uncles and eleven aunts."

Angelica Tonks had more of most things than anyone else. She held the class record for pairs of fashion sneakers and Derwent pencil sets, and her pocket-money supply was endless. Now, it seemed, she also had the largest uncle-and-aunt collection in town. Her classmates squirmed and made faces at each other. *Awful* Angelica Tonks.

Mr. Wilfred Starling dusted the chalk from his bony hands and sighed. "Well, Angelica, aren't you a lucky one to have nineteen uncles and aunts. You'll just have to choose the most interesting one to write about, won't you?"

"But they're *all* interesting," objected Angelica. "The Tonks family is a wonderfully interesting family, you know. It will be terribly hard to choose just one."

There were more squirms. The class was fed up with the wonderfully interesting Tonks family. In fact, Mr. Wilfred Starling nearly screamed. He just managed to swallow his exasperation, which sank down to form a hard bubble in his stomach. Straightening his thin shoulders, he said, "Right; everyone, copy down this week's homework assignment from the board. And remember, Angelica, a pen portrait of just one aunt or uncle is all I want. Just *one*." *Please not a whole gallery of tedious and terrible Tonkses,* he thought to himself.

The class began to write. Jamie Nutbeam, sitting behind Angelica, leaned forward and hissed, "If the rest of your family is so *wonderfully interesting,* they must be a big improvement on you, Honky![1] And, anyway, I bet the aunt I write about will beat any of yours!"

"I bet she won't," Angelica hissed back. "She'll be so *boring*. What's her name, this boring aunt?"

Jamie finished copying and put down his pen. "Aunt Millicent, and she's pretty special."

"Millicent!" scoffed Angelica. "What a name! No one's called Millicent these days!"

"QUIET, you two!" barked Mr. Starling, massaging his stomach, "and start tidying up, everyone—it's time for the bell." *Oh bliss,* he thought.

As the classroom emptied, Jamie lingered behind.

---

1. **Honky:** a nickname which when combined with her last name, *Tonks,* makes *Honky Tonks,* a term for noisy nightclubs.

"What is it, Jamie?" asked Mr. Starling wearily, piling his books and papers together and trying not to burp.

"Well, the trouble is I haven't any aunts or uncles to do a portrait of," said Jamie, turning rather red, "so is it all right if I make one up? An aunt?"

Oh, I see! Well, in that case . . . yes, perfectly all right," replied Mr. Starling. He gazed rather sadly out the window. "The most interesting characters in the world are usually the made-up ones, you know, Jamie. Think of Sherlock Holmes and Alice and Dr. Who and Indiana Jones . . ."

Jamie interrupted. "Does anyone need to know I've made her up? This aunt?"

"Well, *I* won't say anything," promised Mr. Starling. "It's for you to make her seem real so we all believe in her. You go home and see what you can dream up."

"She has a name already," Jamie called back as he left the room. "She's Aunt Millicent."

Aunt Millicent Nutbeam! The hard bubble in Mr. Starling's stomach began to melt away.

That evening, Jamie Nutbeam said to his family at large, "Did you know that awful Angelica Tonks has eight uncles and eleven aunts?"

"Well, everybody knows that they're a big family," replied his mother.

"Prolific, I'd call it," grunted Jamie's father from behind his newspaper.

"Yes, dear—prolific. Now, Mrs. Tonks was a Miss Blizzard," continued Mrs. Nutbeam,

"and there are lots of Blizzards around here as well as Tonkses, all related, no doubt. But fancy nineteen! Who told you there were nineteen, Jamie?"

"She did—old Honky Tonks herself. She told the whole class *and* Mr. Starling—boasting away as usual. She's a *pill*." Jamie was jotting things on paper as he talked. "We have to write a pen portrait of an aunt or uncle for homework, and Honky can't decide which one to do because they're all so *wonderfully interesting,* she says. Urk!" He paused and then added, "I'm doing Aunt Millicent."

Jamie's father peered over the top of his newspaper. "Aunt who?"

"Who's Aunt Millicent?" demanded Jamie's sister, Nerissa.

"You haven't got an Aunt Millicent," said his mother. "You haven't any aunts at all, or uncles, for that matter."

"I *know* I haven't," Jamie snapped. "It's *hopeless* belonging to a nuclear family![2] It's unfair—I mean, awful Honky has nineteen aunts and uncles, and Nerissa and I haven't got any, not one." Jamie ground the pencil between his teeth.

"You won't have any teeth either, if you munch pencils like that," remarked his father, who was a dentist.

Jamie glowered, spitting out wet splinters.

"Anyway, he's right," announced Nerissa. "It would be great to have even one aunt or

---

2. **nuclear family:** a mother, a father, and their children living together in one house.

Words to Know and Use | **prolific** (prō lif′ ik) *adj.* producing many children

uncle. Then we might have some cousins, too. Everyone else has cousins. Angelica Tonks probably has about a hundred and twenty-seven."

"Well, I'm sorry," sighed Mrs. Nutbeam, "but your father and I are both 'onlys,' and there's nothing we can do about that, is there? Not a thing! Now, what's all this about an Aunt Millicent?"

"Oh, it's OK," grumbled her son. "Mr. Starling said to write about *an* aunt or uncle, not exactly *my* aunt or uncle. He says I can invent one."

"Will you explain that she's not real?" asked Nerissa, doubtfully.

"Mr. Starling says I don't have to, and he's not going to tell. He says I have to make people believe that she *is* real. Anyway, I don't want Honky Tonks to know that she's made-up, because Aunt Millicent is going to be amazing—much better than any of those boring Tonkses. It's time Honky was taken down a peg or two."

predict How will Jamie's Aunt Millicent project turn out?

Dr. Nutbeam quite understood how Jamie felt. From time to time Angelica Tonks visited his dentist's chair. She would brag about her "perfect" teeth if there was nothing to be fixed, but if she needed a filling, her shrieks of "agony" would upset everyone in the waiting room, and Mrs. Tonks would call Dr. Nutbeam a *brute*. He was often tempted to give Angelica a general anesthetic[3] and post her home in a large jiffy bag.

Now he folded his newspaper; Jamie's project sounded rather fun. "Right, Jamie," he said, "tell us about Aunt Millicent and let us get some facts straight. Is she my sister, or Mum's? We must get that settled to start with."

"I can't decide," frowned Jamie. "What do you think?"

"She'd better be your sister, dear," said Mrs. Nutbeam calmly to her husband. "I grew up here and everyone knows I was an only child, but you came from another town. You're more mysterious."

D r. Nutbeam looked pleased. "Mm . . . mm. That's nice . . . having a sister, I mean. Is she younger than me?"

"No, older," said Jamie.

"Where does she live?" asked Nerissa. "Has she a family of her own? Lots of cousins for us?"

"No way—she hasn't time for all that sort of thing. And she doesn't live anywhere in particular."

Mrs. Nutbeam looked puzzled. "What *do* you mean, dear? What does Auntie Millicent do, exactly?"

"She's an explorer," said Jamie, proudly. "She works for foreign governments, and she's terribly busy—flat out."

There was something of a pause. Then Dr. Nutbeam said, "Ah," and stroked his bald patch. "That explains why we haven't seen her for so long."

"What does she explore?" demanded Nerissa. "Is there anything left in the world to look for?"

Jamie was beginning to feel a bit rushed.

---

3. **general anesthetic** (an´ es thet´ ik): a drug or gas used to cause a person to fall into a deep sleep.

EXOTIC LANDSCAPE   1910   Henri Rousseau (1844-1910) Oil on canvas, 51 3/4 x 64 inches.
Norton Simon Foundation, Pasadena, California.

"Well, I'm not sure yet, but foreign governments need people like her to search for water in deserts and rich mineral deposits and endangered species and things . . . you know."

Nerissa lay on the floor with her eyes closed and began to imagine her new aunt slashing a path through tangled jungle vines, searching for a rare species of dark blue frog. The mosquitoes were savage. The leeches were huge and bloated. Aunt Millicent's machete was razor sharp . . .

"This is all very unexpected," murmured Mrs. Nutbeam, "to have a sister-in-law who is an explorer, I mean. I wonder how you get started in that sort of career?" Her own job as an assistant in an antique and curio shop suddenly seemed rather drab.

Dr. Nutbeam was staring at the wall. In his mind's eye he clearly saw his sister on a swaying rope suspension bridge above a terrifying ravine. She was leading a band of native bearers to the other side. How much more adventurous, he thought, than drilling little holes in people's teeth. He wrenched his gaze back to Jamie and asked, "Do we know what Millie is actually exploring at present?"

Jamie munched his pencil for a moment and then said, "She's in Africa, somewhere near the middle, but I'm not sure where, exactly."

"In the middle of Africa, is she?" echoed Dr. Nutbeam. "Mm . . . then it wouldn't surprise me if she were in the Cameroons. There's a lot of dense forest in the Cameroons, you know."

"I thought Cameroons were things to eat," frowned Nerissa. "Sort of coconut biscuits."

"No, no, dear, those are macaroons," said her mother.

"*They're* bad for your teeth, too," remarked her father, absently, "like eating pencils."

Jamie fetched the atlas and found a map of Africa. His father stood behind him, peering at it. "There it is, in the middle on the left-hand side, just under the bump."

"It's called Cameroon here," Jamie said. "Just one of them."

"Well, there's East Cameroon and West Cameroon, see," pointed his father, "and sometimes you lump them together and call them Cameroons. Look—here's the equator just to the south, so it must be pretty hot and steamy at sea level."

"Poor Millicent," sighed Mrs. Nutbeam. "I do hope her feet don't swell in the heat, with all that walking."

Jamie examined the map closely. "That's peculiar—the north border of the Cameroons seems to be floating in a big lake . . . um, Lake Chad . . . it looks all swampy, with funny dotted lines and things. I bet that bit needs exploring. They've probably lost their border in the mud, and Aunt Millicent could be on an expedition to find it."

"Is she all by herself?" asked Nerissa. "I'd be scared in a place like that."

"Of course she's not by herself," snorted Jamie. "She works for a foreign government, don't forget, and she'd have a whole support team of porters and cooks and scientists and things."

"She must be an expert at something herself, don't you think?" suggested Mrs. Nutbeam. "I would imagine that she's a surveyor."

"Yes, she'd use one of those instruments

you look through, on legs," added Nerissa.

"You mean a theodolite, dimwit," answered her brother.

"She'd certainly need one of those if she's measuring angles and distances and drawing maps," agreed Dr. Nutbeam. "My word, what a clever old sister I have!"

"I wonder if she was good at geography at school?" said Nerissa.

"Well, you'll be able to ask Grandma tomorrow. She's coming for her winter visit, remember?"

"Oh help! What'll Grandma *say?*" gasped Jamie. "Do you think she'll mind? I mean— we've invented a daughter for her without asking!"

"I shouldn't think she'd mind," said his mother. "We'll break the news to her carefully and see how she takes it."

Grandma Nutbeam, as it turned out, was delighted.

"How exciting!" she exclaimed. "I always wanted a daughter, and it's been very lonely since Grandpa died. Now I'll have a new interest! Just show me on the map where Millicent is at the moment, please, dear."

Jamie pointed to the dotted lines in swampy Lake Chad near the top end of the Cameroons, and Grandma stared in astonishment.

"Gracious heaven! What an extraordinary place to go to, the silly girl! I hope she's remembered her quinine tablets.[4] Millicent was never very good at looking after herself, you know. Let me see—I think I'll get some wool tomorrow and knit her some good stout hiking socks."

Jamie blinked. "There's no need to do that, Grandma. She's not really real, you know."

"Well, she'll be more real to me if I make

her some socks," Grandma declared.

"Wouldn't they be rather hot in the Cameroons?" objected Nerissa. "It's awfully near the equator, don't forget."

"Woolen socks are best in any climate," said Grandma firmly. "They breathe."

"Now, Mother," interrupted Dr. Nutbeam, "you can tell us what Millicent was like as a girl. I can't remember her very well, as she was so much older than me, but I have a feeling that she ran away from home a lot."

Grandma pondered a moment. "Now that you mention it, she did. She did indeed. I thought we'd have to chain her up sometimes! We lived near the edge of town, you'll remember, and Millie would look out toward the paddocks[5] and hills and say that she wanted to know what was over the horizon, or where the birds were flying to, or where the clouds came from behind the hills. We never knew where she'd be off to next—but she certainly ended up in the right job! I'm so glad she became an explorer. If I were a bit younger and had better feet, I might even go and join her. It would be most interesting to see the Cameroons. It's full of monkeys, I believe."

"Was Aunt Millicent good at geography at school?" Nerissa remembered to ask.

"Let me think—yes, she must have been because one year she won a prize for it, and the prize was a book called *Lives of the Great Explorers.*"

"Well, there you are," remarked Mrs.

---

4. **quinine** (kwī′ nīn′) **tablets:** pills taken to treat malaria.

5. **paddocks:** in Australia, fields surrounded by a fence.

Nutbeam. "That's probably how it all started."

Next day, Grandma Nutbeam began to knit a pair of explorer's socks. She decided on khaki with dark blue stripes around the top.

evaluate | How do you like Jamie's family?

Angelica Tonks had found it so difficult to select one of the nineteen aunts and uncles that her pen portrait was left until the very last minute and then scrawled out in a great hurry. She had finally chosen Aunt Daisy Blizzard, Mrs. Tonks's eldest sister.

Mr. Wilfred Starling asked Angelica to read her portrait to the class first, to get it over with. As he had expected and as Jamie Nutbeam had hoped, Angelica's aunt sounded anything but wonderfully interesting. She had always lived on the same street, her favorite color was deep purple and she grew African violets on the bathroom shelf, but that was about all.

Many of the other portraits weren't much better, although there was one uncle who had fallen into Lake Burley Griffin and been rescued by a passing Member of Parliament. Someone else's aunt had competed in a penny-farthing bicycle race in northern Tasmania, only to capsize and sprain both her knees; and there was a great-uncle who had been present at the opening of the Sydney Harbor Bridge in 1932 but couldn't remember it at all as he'd been asleep in his pram[6] at the time.

Mr. Starling saved Jamie's portrait until last, hoping for the best. Jamie cleared his throat nervously and began:

"I have never met Aunt Millicent, and no one in my family knows her very well as she hasn't been in Australia for a long time. This is because Aunt Millicent is an explorer . . . "

Mr. Wilfred Starling had been hoping for a bright spot in his day, and Aunt Millicent Nutbeam was it. He smiled happily when Jamie explained how Millicent had gained her early training as an explorer by regularly running away from home. He sighed with pleasure as Jamie described the swampy region of Lake Chad, where Millicent was searching through the mud and papyrus[7] for the northern border of the Cameroons. He positively beamed when he heard that Grandma Nutbeam was knitting explorer's socks for her daughter.

The rest of the class sat spellbound as Jamie read on, except for Angelica Tonks, whose scowl grew darker by the minute. Jamie had barely finished his portrait when her hand was waving furiously.

Mr. Starling's beam faded. "What *is* it, Angelica?"

"I don't believe it. Women don't go exploring! I think Jamie's made it all up! He's a cheat!"

Mr. Starling's stomach lurched, but before he had time to say anything, the

---

6. **pram:** a British term for a baby carriage.
7. **papyrus** (pə pī′ rəs): tall water plant.

Illustration by David Tamura.

other girls in the class rose up in a passion and rounded on Angelica.

"Who *says* women don't go exploring?"

"Women can do anything they want to these days, Angelica Tonks! Don't you know that?"

"I'd really like to be an explorer or something–maybe a test pilot."

Who says women don't go exploring?

"Well, *I'd* like to be a diver and explore the ocean floor and have a good look at the *Titanic*."

"What does your aunt wear when she's at work?"

"What color are her new socks?"

The boys began to join in.

"Can your aunt really use a machete?"

"How many languages can she speak?"

"Does she always carry a gun? I bet she's a crack shot!"

"How does a theodolite work?"

The clamor was so great that hardly anyone heard the bell. Angelica Tonks heard it and vanished in a sulk. Mr. Starling heard it and happily gathered up his books. He gave Jamie a secret wink as he left the room.

The end of the assignment was not the end of Aunt Millicent. At school, the careers teacher ran some special sessions on "Challenging Occupations for Women" after he had been stormed by the girls from Jamie's class for information about becoming test pilots, mobile-crane drivers, buffalo hunters and ocean-floor mappers. The science teacher was asked to explain the workings of a theodolite to the class.

At home, Aunt Millicent settled happily into the Nutbeam family, who all followed her adventures with great interest. Dr. Nutbeam brought home library books about the Cameroons and Central Africa. Jamie roared his way through one called *The Bafut Beagles*. Mrs. Nutbeam rummaged through an old storeroom at the curio shop and began to collect exotic objects. She brought home a brace of hunting spears from Kenya, which she hung on the family-room wall.

"Just the sort of souvenir Millicent could have sent us," she explained. "See—those marks on the blades are very probably dried bloodstains."

Another time she unwrapped a stuffed mongoose, announcing that Auntie had sent this from India on one of her earlier trips.

Jamie and Nerissa stroked it. "What a funny animal," said Nerissa. "Like a weasel."

Grandma was knitting her way down the second sock leg. "That funny animal is a very brave creature," she admonished, tapping the mongoose with her knitting needle. "I'll always remember Kipling's story of Rikki-tikki-tavi and how he fought that dreadful king cobra. Brrr!"

"Who won?" asked Jamie.

"You could read it yourself and find out, young man," said Grandma, starting to knit a new row. "I expect Millicent has met a few cobras in her time."

Nerissa had splendid dreams nearly every night. Aunt Millicent strode through most of them, wielding her machete or shouldering her theodolite. Sometimes Nerissa found herself wading through swirling rivers or swinging on jungle vines like a gibbon.[8] Jamie was often there, too, or some of her school friends, or Grandma followed by a mongoose on a lead. Once, Mrs. Nutbeam speared a giant toad, which exploded and woke Nerissa up. In another dream, Nerissa's father was polishing the fangs of a grinning crocodile, which lay back in the dentist's chair with its long tail tucked neatly under the sterilizer. It looked slightly like Mrs. Tonks.

Mrs. Nutbeam brought home still more curios: a bamboo flute and a small tom-tom, which Jamie and Nerissa soon learned to play. Mysterious drumbeats and thin flutey tunes drifted along the street from the Nutbeams' house. School friends came to beat the tom-tom and to stroke the mongoose and to see how the explorer's socks were growing.

"Will you be sending them off soon, to the Cameroons?" they asked Grandma, who was turning the heel of the second sock.

"I think I'll make another pair, perhaps even three pairs," replied Grandma. "I might just as well send a large parcel as a small one."

"Yes, and then Aunt Millie will have spare pairs of socks she can wash," said Nerissa. "Socks must get very smelly near the equator."

Word of Millicent Nutbeam, intrepid explorer, began to spread through the town. Children told their families about the spears, the tom-tom, the mongoose and the khaki socks. Not every small town could claim to be connected to a famous international explorer—it was exciting news.

---

8. **gibbon:** a small ape.

Words to Know and Use

exotic (eg zät′ ik) *adj.* strange; unusual
wielding (wēld′ in) *adj.* handling and using **wield** *v.*
intrepid (in trep′ id) *adj.* very brave

201

Angelica Tonks, however, told her mother that she didn't believe Jamie's aunt was an explorer at all. "I bet he just invented that to make his aunt seem more interesting than all the rest," she scoffed.

Mrs. Tonks sniffed a good deal and then decided it was time to have a dental checkup. "I'll get to the bottom of that Millicent Nutbeam, you mark my words," she told Angelica, as she telephoned Dr. Nutbeam's surgery for an appointment.

"Well, well–good morning, Mrs. Tonks," said Dr. Nutbeam, a few days later. "We haven't seen you for a while! Just lie right back in the chair, please, and relax!"

Mrs. Tonks lay back, but she didn't relax one bit. Her eyes were sharp and suspicious. "Good morning, Dr. Nutbeam. How is the family?" she inquired. "And how is your sister?"

Dr. Nutbeam pulled on his rubber gloves. "My sister? Which one? . . . Er, probe, please, nurse."

Before he could say "Open wide," Mrs. Tonks snapped, "Your sister the so-called explorer. Huh! The one in the Cameroons."

"Ah, *that* sister. You mean Millicent . . . now, just open wider and turn this way a little. Yes, our Millie, she does work so hard . . . oops, there's a beaut cavity! A real crater!" He crammed six plugs of cotton wool around Mrs. Tonks's gums. "My word, what a lot of saliva! We'll have some suction, please, nurse, and just wipe that dribble from the patient's chin." He continued to poke and scrape Mrs. Tonks's molars, none too gently. "Ah, here's another trouble spot. Mm . . . have you ever been to the Cameroons, Mrs. Tonks?"

Mrs. Tonks's eyes glared. She tried to shake her head, but could only gurgle, "Arggg . . ."

"No, I didn't think you had. Such a fascinating place!" Dr. Nutbeam turned on the squealing high-speed drill and bored into her decaying tooth, spraying water all over her chin.

When he had told his family about this encounter with Mrs. Tonks, his wife complained, "It's all very well for you. *You* can just cram people's mouths full of wadding and metal contraptions and suction tubes if they start asking awkward questions, but what am I supposed to do?"

People are asking to see photos of Millicent.

The truth was that increasing numbers of townsfolk were calling at the antique shop where Mrs. Nutbeam worked. They were eager to know more about Millicent Nutbeam and her adventurous life. They felt proud of her.

"It's getting quite tricky," Mrs. Nutbeam explained. "People are asking to see photos of Millicent and wanting us to talk at the elderly citizens' club about her. This aunt is becoming an embarrassment. I wish people weren't so curious. Sometimes I don't know what to say!"

Grandma found herself on slippery ground, too, when she met the postman at the gate.

"Morning," he said, sorting through his mailbag. "You must be Jamie's grandmother, then."

PORTRAIT OF MADAME BÉNARD 1930 Edouard Vuillard
Musée National d'Art Moderne, Paris. Giraudon/Art Resource, New York.

"Yes, I am," Grandma replied, rather surprised.

"Mother of the explorer, eh?"

"Gracious!" exclaimed Grandma. "Fancy you knowing about that!"

"Oh, my girl Julie has told us all about it. She's in Jamie's class at school. Funny thing—Julie's gone round the twist since she heard about all that exploring business. Says she wants to buy a camel and ride it around Australia, and one of her friends is going to apply for a job on an oil rig. I ask you!"

"Well, that's nice," said Grandma, soothingly. "Girls are so enterprising these days."

"Huh! Mad, I call it." The postman held out a bundle of letters. "Here you are. Now, that's *another* funny thing—the Nutbeams don't get much foreign mail, come to think of it. You'd think the explorer would write to them more often, her being in the traveling line."

Grandma breathed deeply. "Oh, it's not easy, you know, writing letters when you're exploring. For one thing, there's never a decent light in the tent at night—and besides, there's hardly ever a post office to hand when you need it. She glanced through the letters. "Goodness! There's one from South America . . . Peru."

"That's what made me wonder. Is it from her?" asked the postman, eagerly.

Her? Ah . . . Millicent. I don't know. It's for Dr. Nutbeam, my son, and it's typed. Anyway, as far as we know, Millicent is still in the Cameroons, although we've not had word for some time."

"She could have moved on, couldn't she?" suggested the postman. "Peru, eh? Oh well, I'd better move on, too. G'day to you!"

At school, Julie, the postman's daughter, said to Jamie, "Why has your auntie gone to South America? What's she exploring now?"

"Who said she's gone to South America?" demanded Jamie. He felt he was losing control of Aunt Millicent.

"My dad said there was a letter from her in Peru," replied Julie.

"Well, no one told *me,*" growled Jamie.

At home he announced, "Julie is telling everybody that our Aunt Millicent is in Peru! What's she talking about? What's happening?"

Grandma stopped knitting. "Julie. Is that the name of the postman's girl?"

"Yes—her dad said there was a letter for us from Auntie in Peru, or somewhere mad."

"Oh, I remember—he asked me about it," said Grandma.

"Well . . . what did you *say?*" wailed Jamie.

"I just said I didn't know who the letter was from and that I thought Millicent was still in the Cameroons, but that we hadn't heard for a while where she was. That's all."

"The letter from Peru," chuckled Dr. Nutbeam, "is about the World Dental Conference on plaque, which is being held next year in Lima. It has nothing to do with Millicent."

"Well of *course* it hasn't," spluttered Jamie. "She doesn't exist!"

"But Jamie, in a funny sort of way she *does* exist," said Mrs. Nutbeam.

His father grinned. "My sister is quite a girl! She's begun to live a life of her own!"

"That's the trouble," said Jamie. "She seems to be doing things we don't know about."

While they were talking, the telephone rang. Dr. Nutbeam was no longer grinning when he came back from answering it. "That was Frank Figgis from the local paper."

"Frank, the editor?" asked Mrs. Nutbeam. "What did he want?"

"He wants to do a full-page feature on our Millicent," groaned her husband. "He's heard that she's about to set out on a climbing expedition in the Andes! Up some peak that has never yet been conquered!"

"What nonsense!" snapped Grandma. "She's too old for that sort of thing."

"It's just a rumor!" shouted Jamie. "Who said she's going to the Andes? *I* didn't say she was going there. She's still in the Cameroons!"

"Calm down, dear," said his mother, "and

let's hear what Dad said to Frank Figgis."

Dr. Nutbeam was rubbing his head. "I stalled for time—I said we'd not heard she was in the Andes but that we'd make inquiries and let him know. Whatever happens, Millicent mustn't get into print. We'll all be up on a charge of false pretenses[9] or something!"

Jamie snorted. "Well, if she's climbing an Ande, it might be best if she fell off and was never seen again."

review Is Jamie's Aunt Millicent getting out of control?

Nerissa shrieked, *"No!* She mustn't—she's our only aunt, and we've only just got her!"

Mrs. Nutbeam sighed. "Listen, Jamie, perhaps the time has come to own up that Aunt Millicent is not real."

"We can't do that!" wailed Jamie. "Everyone would think we're loony . . . and that Grandma's absolutely bonkers, knitting socks for an aunt who isn't there. And what about the mongoose? Anyway, I *can't* let Honky Tonks find out now—she'd never stop crowing, and she'd be more awful than ever."

Jamie decided to lay the whole problem of Aunt Millicent Nutbeam before Mr. Starling, right up to her unexpected expedition to the Andes and Mr. Figgis's plan to write a full-page feature about her for the local paper. He finished by saying, "I think I might have to kill her off."

"That'd be a shame," sighed Mr. Starling. "She's quite a lady, your aunt!"

"It would be pretty easy to get rid of her," Jamie went on. "In her sort of job she could sink into a quicksand, or be trampled by a herd of elephants, or something."

Mr. Starling shook his head violently. "No, no—it would only make things worse if she died a bloodcurdling death like that. No one would be likely to forget her if she was squashed flat by a stampeding elephant. She'd become more interesting than ever!"

"Well, she could die of something boring, like pneumonia," said Jamie. "Or . . . will I have to own up that she isn't real?"

"Do you want to own up?"

"Not really. I'd feel stupid, and I specially don't want Angelica Tonks to know I invented an aunt."

Mr. Starling quite understood. "I see! Anyway, a lot of people would be sad to discover that Millicent Nutbeam was a <u>hoax</u>. The girls in your class, for example—she means a lot to them."

"What'll I do then?"

"If you want people to lose interest in her, you'll just have to make her less interesting. I think she should retire from exploring, for a start."

"Aw, gee!" Jamie felt very disappointed. "I suppose so. I'll see what they think at home."

"What he means," said Dr. Nutbeam, when Jamie had repeated Mr. Starling's

---

9. **false pretenses:** a legal term that means to lie or purposely mislead.

advice, "is that it's time my dear sister Millicent settled down."

"I quite agree with that," remarked Grandma, who was up to the sixth sock foot. "She's not as young as she was, and it's high time she had some normal home life. I think she should get married, even though she's getting on a bit. Perhaps to a widower."

"That sounds terribly boring," yawned Nerissa.

"Well, that's what we need," said Jamie, "something terribly boring to make people lose interest."

Grandma sniffed. "In my day it would have been called a happy ending."

"Well, I suppose it's a happier ending than being squashed by an elephant," conceded Jamie.

"How about marrying her to a retired accountant who used to work for a cardboard-box company?" suggested his father. "That sounds pretty dull."

"Good heavens, it's all rather sudden!" said Mrs. Nutbeam. "Last time we heard of her she was climbing the Andes!"

"No, she *wasn't*." At last Jamie felt he had hold of Aunt Millicent again. "That South American stuff was just a rumor. The postman started it because of the letter from Peru, and then the story just grew!"

Dr. Nutbeam nodded. "Stories seem to have a habit of doing that, and so do rumors! But we can easily squash this one about the Andes. I'll just explain about the World Dental Conference on plaque. I even have the letter to prove it."

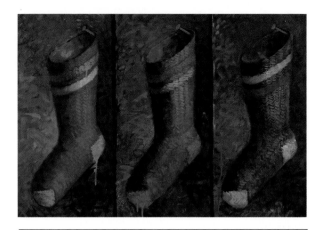

Illustration by Steve Johnson with Lou Fancher.

Dr. Nutbeam called Frank Figgis on the phone. He explained about the letter from Peru and about the ridiculous rumor which the postman had started. "In your profession, Frank," he added sternly, "you should be much more careful than to listen to baseless rumor. It could get you into all sorts of trouble! In any case, Millicent is giving up exploring to marry a retired accountant. She's had enough."

Frank Figgis was fast losing interest. "I see—well, sometime when she's in Australia, we could do an interview about her former life . . . maybe."

"Maybe, although she has no immediate plans to return here. I believe she and her husband are going to settle down in England—somewhere on the seafront, like Bognor."

Jamie passed on the same information to

Words to Know and Use | **baseless** (bās′ lis) *adj.* having no foundation in fact his classmates. The girls were shocked.

"She's what?"

"Getting married to an *accountant?*"

"She can't be!"

"How boring for her!"

"Where in the world is Bognor? Is there really such a place?"

Angelica Tonks smiled like a smug pussycat. "See! Your Aunt Millicent is just like any other old aunt, after all!"

Jamie caught Mr. Starling's eye. It winked.

Aunt Millicent Nutbeam retired, not to Bognor but to live quietly with her family. Nerissa still had wonderful dreams. Dr. Nutbeam still brought home books about far-off places. The bloodstained spears remained on the wall and the mongoose on the shelf. Jamie and Nerissa still played the tom-tom and the bamboo flute.

Grandma Nutbeam's holiday came to an end, and she packed up to return home. She left a parcel for Jamie. When he opened it, he found three pairs of khaki socks with dark blue stripes and a card which said:

Dear Jamie,

Aunt Millicent won't have any use for these now that she has settled down, so you might as well have them for school camps. Isn't it lucky that they are just your size!

With love from Grandma.

Responding to Reading

First Impressions

1. Who is your favorite character in this story? Why? Jot down your thoughts in your journal.

Second Thoughts

2. Why do you think the imaginary Aunt Millicent becomes so popular with Jamie's family and with the people in the town?

3. What good and bad results does Jamie's story have?

4. What do you think of Jamie's family? Are they a typical family? Explain your opinion.

Broader Connections

5. Even though they know she is imaginary, Jamie's family enjoys Aunt Millicent and her adventures. In small groups, discuss your favorite fictional characters from books or movies. Why do you think these kinds of characters are popular with so many people?

Literary Concept: Humor

One of the techniques that writers use to create humor is **exaggeration,** or an extreme overstating of an idea. Dr. Nutbeam exaggerates when he thinks that he would like to anesthetize Angelica and send her home in a jiffy bag.

Another way to create humor is by using **sarcasm,** which is criticism hidden by humor. A sarcastic remark seems complimentary but is really meant to criticize. Mr. Starling uses sarcasm when he says, "Well, Angelica, aren't you a lucky one to have nineteen uncles and aunts." Actually, the teacher finds the Tonkses "tedious and terrible."

Skim the story to find other examples of exaggeration and sarcasm. Then see if you can find others ways in which humor is created in this selection.

Writing Options

1. How might Aunt Millicent feel if she knew that her amazing adventures were a topic of town gossip? Use your imagination and what you know from the story to write a **letter** from her to one of the townspeople.

2. Write an **article** for the full-page feature Frank Figgis planned about Aunt Millicent. It may be about her childhood, her work in Cameroon, or her travels.

3. Both Jamie and the narrator of "The Revolt of the Evil Fairies" faced a problem. **Compare and contrast** how each deals with his problem.

4. Write your own **pen-portrait** of a real or imaginary aunt or uncle. If your relative is imaginary, use the notes about the adventure you described in your journal to spice up the character's life.

Vocabulary Practice

Exercise   Decide whether the boldfaced word in each sentence below is used correctly or incorrectly. Write *Correct* or *Incorrect* on your paper, and give your reason for each answer.

1. The townspeople took pride in Aunt Millicent's **intrepid** adventures in far-off parts of the world.

2. When Jamie tried the **hoax,** he wondered if it would taste as good as his last piece.

3. Girls in Jamie's school hoped for the excitement of a **tedious** career like Aunt Millicent's.

4. Jamie might have felt **exasperation** when his good idea got out of hand.

5. Jamie created Aunt Millicent because his real family was so **exotic.**

6. It was easy to picture Millicent **wielding** her long, sharp knife in the jungle.

7. Aunt Millicent would hate to have her boat **capsize** in the swampy waters of Lake Chad.

8. Grandma Nutbeam was not **prolific** because she had only one son.

9. Grandma Nutbeam called only the most easily embarrassed girls **enterprising.**

10. The story about Millicent's going to Peru was **baseless.**

Words to Know and Use

baseless
capsize
enterprising
exasperation
exotic
hoax
intrepid
prolific
tedious
wielding

*O*ptions for Learning

1 • Your Turn   In small groups or as a class, compose the further adventures of Aunt Millicent. Try brainstorming before you start, as Jamie's family did. One student can begin with a sentence or episode, then each student can add a new part to the story.

2 • Fabulous Females   As Jamie's grandmother says, "Girls are so enterprising these days." Women work far out in space, deep in the ocean, and most places in between. Research a woman who has an unusual, exciting career. Share your findings with your class.

3 • A Cartography Career?   Try your hand as a cartographer. Draw a topographical map of Cameroon, indicating wetlands, dry areas, jungles, and rivers. Include the countries and bodies of water that border Cameroon. Show on your map where Aunt Millicent worked.

4 • Play Time   Rewrite an episode of the story as a play. Include dialogue and stage directions. Then invite classmates to join you in performing the play for the rest of your class.

FACT FINDER SOCIAL STUDIES

What is the population of Cameroon?

*M*ary Steele
1930–

Mary Steele has lived in Australia all of her life. She grew up surrounded by pets: a flock of ducks, canaries, finches, a peacock, a cockatoo, and a parakeet. Two of her favorite authors are E. B. White and Roald Dahl.

Steele likes to write for young people "because they are curious and full of fun, and their imaginations still work." She rewrites stories several times before she is satisfied. "By the time I've finished," she says, "the characters seem like old friends or part of the family."

In 1986, her book *Arkwright* was named the Australian Junior Book of the Year. In 1989 she was asked, as one of Australia's sixteen leading children's writers, to write a story on the theme of "dream time." She wrote "Aunt Millicent."

Fiction

Gentleman of Río en Medio

JUAN A. A. SEDILLO (hwän, se dĕ' yô)

Examine What You Know

Owning a piece of property gives people certain rights. Do property owners have responsibilities as well, or may they do anything they want to with what is theirs? As a class, discuss these rights and responsibilities. Have one class member take notes, separating your ideas into two categories. One should list the rights of property owners. The other should list their responsibilities.

Expand Your Knowledge

Land ownership is an important issue in this story. Although the story is fictional, the setting—a small Hispanic farming community called Río en Medio—actually exists. Located in the mountains above

Santa Fe, New Mexico, Río en Medio consists of a few scattered adobe (sunbaked-brick) ranch houses along a river that is often dry. Since there is little good land, only a few crops and fruit trees grow on terraced mountainsides. Río en Medio is a close-knit community where members of extended families depend on one another for survival. Hispanic people have lived there for generations, and some families even trace their origins to the Spanish settlers of the sixteenth and seventeenth centuries.

Write Before You Read

Imagine that you owned a piece of land. Would you allow people in the community to use it? Would the way people used it affect your decision? Write your responses in your journal. As you read, compare your ideas with those of the characters in this story.

■ *Author biography in Reader's Handbook*

Gentleman of Río en Medio

JUAN A. A. SEDILLO

It took months of negotiation to come to an understanding with the old man. He was in no hurry. What he had the most of was time. He lived up in Río en Medio[1], where his people had been for hundreds of years. He tilled the same land they had tilled. His house was small and wretched, but quaint. The little creek ran through his land. His orchard was gnarled and beautiful.

The day of the sale he came into the office. His coat was old, green and faded. I thought of Senator Catron,[2] who had been such a power with these people up there in the mountains. Perhaps it was one of his old Prince Alberts.[3] He also wore gloves. They were old and torn, and his fingertips showed through them. He carried a cane, but it was only the skeleton of a worn-out umbrella. Behind him walked one of his innumerable kin—a dark young man with eyes like a gazelle.

The old man bowed to all of us in the room. Then he removed his hat and gloves, slowly and carefully. Chaplin[4] once did that in a picture, in a bank—he was the janitor. Then he handed his things to the boy, who stood obediently behind the old man's chair.

There was a great deal of conversation, about rain and about his family. He was very proud of his large family. Finally we got down to business. Yes, he would sell, as he had agreed, for twelve hundred dollars, in cash. We would buy, and the money was ready. "Don[5] Anselmo," I said to him in Spanish, "we have made a discovery. You remember that we sent that surveyor, that engineer, up there to survey your land so as to make the deed. Well, he finds that you own more than eight acres. He tells us that your land extends across the river and that you own almost twice as much as you thought." He didn't know that. "And now, Don Anselmo," I added, "these Americans are *buena gente*,[6] they are good people, and they are willing to pay you for the additional land as well, at the same rate per acre, so that instead of twelve hundred dollars you will get almost twice as much, and the money is here for you."

---

1. Río en Medio: (rē′ ô en mā′ dyô) *Spanish.*

2. Senator Catron (ka′ trən): Thomas Benton Catron, U.S. senator from New Mexico, 1912–1917.

3. Prince Alberts: long, double-breasted dress coats.

4. Chaplin: Charlie Chaplin, a famous comedian and star of silent films.

5. Don (dôn) *Spanish:* a title of respect, much like *Sir* in English.

6. *buena gente* (bwe′ nä hen′ tā) *Spanish*: good people.

SPRINGTIME   W. Victor Higgins   Courtesy, Gerald Peters Gallery, Santa Fe, New Mexico.

The old man hung his head for a moment in thought. Then he stood up and stared at me. "Friend," he said, "I do not like to have you speak to me in that manner." I kept still and let him have his say. "I know these Americans are good people, and that is why I have agreed to sell to them. But I do not care to be insulted. I have agreed to sell my house and land for twelve hundred dollars and that is the price."

I argued with him, but it was useless.

Finally he signed the deed and took the money but refused to take more than the amount agreed upon. Then he shook hands all around, put on his ragged gloves, took his stick, and walked out with the boy behind him.

A month later my friends had moved into Río en Medio. They had replastered the old adobe house, pruned the trees, patched the fence, and moved in for the summer. One day they came back to the office to complain. The children of the village were over-running their property. They came every day and played under the trees, built little play fences around them, and took blossoms. When they were spoken to, they only laughed and talked back good-naturedly in Spanish.

I sent a messenger up to the mountains for Don Anselmo. It took a week to arrange another meeting. When he arrived, he repeated his previous preliminary performance. He wore the same faded cutaway,[7] carried the same stick, and was accompanied by the boy again. He shook hands all around, sat down with the boy behind his chair, and talked about the weather. Finally I broached the subject. "Don Anselmo, about the ranch you sold to these people. They are good people and want to be your friends and neighbors always. When you sold to them, you signed a document, a deed, and in that deed you agreed to several things. One thing was that they were to have the complete possession of the property. Now, Don Anselmo, it seems that every day the children of the village overrun the orchard and spend most of their time there. We would like to know if you, as the most respected man in the village, could not stop them from doing so in order that these people may enjoy their new home more in peace."

Don Anselmo stood up. "We have all learned to love these Americans," he said, "because they are good people and good neighbors. I sold them my property because I knew they were good people, but I did not sell them the trees in the orchard."

This was bad. "Don Anselmo," I pleaded, "when one signs a deed and sells real property, one sells also everything that grows on the land, and those trees, every one of them, are on the land and inside the boundaries of what you sold."

"Yes, I admit that," he said. "You know," he added, "I am the oldest man in the village. Almost everyone there is my relative, and all the children of Río en Medio are my *sobrinos* and *nietos*,[8] my descendants. Every time a child has been born in Río en Medio since I took possession of that house from my mother, I have planted a tree for that child. The trees in that orchard are not mine, *Señor*; they belong to the children of the village. Every person in Río en Medio born since the railroad came to Santa Fe owns a tree in that orchard. I did not sell the trees because I could not. They are not mine."

There was nothing we could do. Legally we owned the trees, but the old man had been so generous, refusing what amounted to a fortune for him. It took most of the following winter to buy the trees, individually, from the descendants of Don Anselmo in the valley of Río en Medio. ❧

---

7. **cutaway**: man's formal daytime coat.
8. ***sobrinos* and *nietos*** (sō brē′ nôs; nyā′ tôs) *Spanish*: nephews and nieces; grandchildren.

Bums in the Attic

from The House on Mango Street

SANDRA CISNEROS

I want a house on a hill like the ones with the gardens where Papa works. We go on Sundays, Papa's day off. I used to go. I don't anymore. You don't like to go out with us, Papa says. Getting too old? Getting too stuck-up, says Nenny. I don't tell them I am ashamed—all of us staring out the window like the hungry. I am tired of looking at what we can't have. When we win the lottery . . . Mama begins, and then I stop listening.

People who live on hills sleep so close to the stars they forget those of us who live too much on earth. They don't look down at all except to be content to live on hills. They have nothing to do with last week's garbage or fear of rats. Night comes. Nothing wakes them but the wind.

One day I'll own my own house, but I won't forget who I am or where I came from. Passing bums will ask, Can I come in? I'll offer them the attic, ask them to stay, because I know how it is to be without a house.

Some days after dinner, guests and I will sit in front of a fire. Floorboards will squeak upstairs. The attic grumble.

Rats? they'll ask.

Bums, I'll say, and I'll be happy.

HODGKIN'S HOUSE, CAPE ANN, MASSACHUSETTS 1928 Edward Hopper
Private collection. Courtesy, Hirschl and Adler Galleries, New York.

EXPLAIN

Responding to Reading

First Impressions

1. Jot down words and phrases to describe Don Anselmo.

Second Thoughts

2. In your opinion, who turned the tables on whom in this story? Explain.

3. Do you agree with Don Anselmo's understanding of his rights and responsibilities as a landowner?

> **Think about**
> • why he refuses to accept more money for his land
> • why he feels the trees belong to the children
> • the ideas you wrote about earlier concerning land ownership

4. Read "Bums in the Attic," on page 215. How does the narrator's attitude toward ownership compare with Don Anselmo's?

Broader Connections

5. Do you think people such as Don Anselmo exist in the real world? Give examples of people you know to explain your opinion.

Literary Concept: Narrator

A **narrator** is a person who tells a story. A first-person narrator is usually a character in the story. He or she uses the pronoun I or we in telling the story. How would you describe the narrator of this story? How do you think he feels about Don Anselmo? Use evidence from the story to support your answer.

Writing Options

1. If you owned a tree in Don Anselmo's orchard, would you sell it to the Americans? Write your **opinion** and explain your reasoning.

2. Suppose the Americans were really angry about the children's use of their orchard. Write an angry **letter** to the citizens of Río en Medio, informing them that they have no right to be on the property.

Poetry

old age sticks

E. E. CUMMINGS

The Rebel

MARI EVANS

Examine What You Know

Do you know someone who is controversial—someone who argues or says things that cause a dispute? With classmates, brainstorm a list of reasons that might explain why some people "cause so much trouble." Then list examples of people who might be labeled controversial.

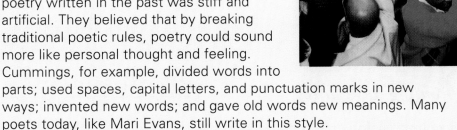

Expand Your Knowledge

Early in this century, many well-known U.S. poets (including E. E. Cummings) rebelled against using traditional forms of poetry to express their images and ideas. These controversial new poets felt that the poetry written in the past was stiff and artificial. They believed that by breaking traditional poetic rules, poetry could sound more like personal thought and feeling. Cummings, for example, divided words into parts; used spaces, capital letters, and punctuation marks in new ways; invented new words; and gave old words new meanings. Many poets today, like Mari Evans, still write in this style.

Enrich Your Reading

Reading Modern Poetry   Because modern poets often break lines or words into unfamiliar patterns, some modern poetry may seem confusing at first glance. Read and reread the poems slowly. In "old age sticks," decide whose words are *inside* the parentheses, and whose words are *outside* them. In "The Rebel," look for differences between the speaker and other people.

■ *Author biographies on Extend page*

old age sticks

E. E. CUMMINGS

old age sticks
up Keep
Off
signs)&

5 youth yanks them
down(old
age
cries No

Tres)&(pas)
10 youth laughs
(sing
old age

scolds Forbid
den Stop
15 Must
n't Don't

&)youth goes
right on
gr
20 owing old

Responding to Reading

First Impressions of "old age sticks"

1. What words and phrases from the poem stand out in your mind? Jot these down in your journal.

Second Thoughts on "old age sticks"

2. What do you think the last stanza means?

3. Do you agree with the ideas the poet expresses about old age and youth? Explain.

4. If you had been a critic in the 1920s reviewing Cummings's controversial new poetry, would you have criticized or praised him? Why?

The Rebel

MARI EVANS

When I
die
I'm sure
I will have a
5 Big Funeral . . .
Curiosity
seekers . . .
coming to see
if I
10 am really
Dead . . .
or just
trying to make
Trouble . . .

NEW ORLEANS FAREWELL 1974   Romare Bearden
Courtesy, The Estate of Romare Bearden and
George and Joyce Wein Collection.

Responding to Reading

First Impressions of "The Rebel"

1. What is your impression of the speaker? Jot down your thoughts in your notebook or journal.

Second Thoughts on "The Rebel"

2. What do you learn about the speaker from this poem? Give evidence from the poem for your answer.

   Think about
   - why the speaker believes she will have a "Big Funeral"
   - what kind of person attracts "Curiosity seekers"

3. Note which words are capitalized in the poem. Why do you think Evans did this?

Comparing the Poems

4. Who causes controversy in the two poems? Explain how those people are alike and how they are different.

5. In what way do you think the tables are turned in these poems?

Literary Concept: Free Verse

Poetry without regular rhyme, rhythm, or line length is called **free verse.** When you read these two poems aloud, you will notice the absence of regular rhyme and rhythm. What other differences do you notice between these poems and more traditional poems, like "The Charge of the Light Brigade" on page 86?

Writing Options

1. Look at your list of controversial people. Write a **free-verse poem** about a person from your list or a controversial event. You may want to experiment with a variety of nontraditional forms as Evans and Cummings do.

2. As a youth, what would you say to old age? Write a **letter** stating your complaints, praise, or other feelings you might have about old people in general or about the process of aging.

Options for Learning

1 • Oral Interpretation Choose either poem to read aloud. Try emphasizing different words and varying your voice tones. Read the poem to your classmates, and let them compare your interpretation with the interpretations of other readers.

2 • Free-Thinking Poets Look through poetry books for other poems that have forms different from those of traditional poems. Share the most interesting with your class.

Mari Evans

Mari Evans writes poetry, political articles, theater pieces, literary criticism, and short stories. She has received many honors, including a National Endowment for the Arts Creative Writing Award.

After college, Evans wrote for a weekly paper owned by African Americans. She has also worked as a research associate, a director of publications, and an editor. She has taught at Indiana, Northwestern, Purdue, and Cornell Universities and produced and directed a TV series, *The Black Experience.*

Evans learned, from Langston Hughes among others, that writing is a craft that "one learns by doing." She revises endlessly, and even regards a printed poem as still in process.

E. E. Cummings   1894-1962

E. E. Cummings wrote a poem every day from the time he was eight until he was twenty-two. Critics either loved or hated his poetry from the time his first book, *Tulips and Chimneys,* was published in 1923. Cummings won many honors and prizes for poetry. At Harvard University he helped start a poetry society.

During World War I, Cummings volunteered as an ambulance driver in France. Later, however, he was imprisoned in a French prisoner-of-war camp, mainly because he refused to say he hated the Germans. He wrote a novel about his experiences and then joined the U.S. Army. After World War I, Cummings studied painting in Paris. There he established a routine he followed most of his life: painting in the afternoon and writing poetry and plays at night. In 1930 he was drawn to the lively artistic and intellectual life of New York's Greenwich Village, where he settled.

Nonfiction

from **Boy**

Tales of Childhood

ROALD DAHL (rōō' äl däl)

*E*xamine What You Know

Childhood pranks take many forms—funny or not so funny, harmless or harmful. In small groups, describe your own pranks or ones you have heard about, and explain what the results of the pranks were.

*E*xpand Your Knowledge

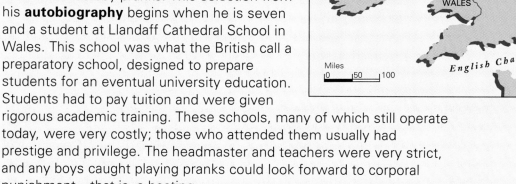

Roald Dahl, a well-known author of books for young people, was also the author of many real-life schoolboy pranks. This selection from his **autobiography** begins when he is seven and a student at Llandaff Cathedral School in Wales. This school was what the British call a preparatory school, designed to prepare students for an eventual university education. Students had to pay tuition and were given rigorous academic training. These schools, many of which still operate today, were very costly; those who attended them usually had prestige and privilege. The headmaster and teachers were very strict, and any boys caught playing pranks could look forward to corporal punishment—that is, a beating.

*W*rite Before You Read

Below are ten terms that relate to this selection. Use these clues and your imagination to predict, in one or two paragraphs, what might happen in the selection. After you read, compare your predictions with the actual events.

1. boys
2. sweet jars
3. small treasures
4. Mrs. Pratchett
5. filthy fingers
6. dead mouse
7. loose floorboard
8. prank
9. glory
10. headmaster

■ *Author biography on Extend page*

from *Boy*
Tales of Childhood

ROALD DAHL

The Bicycle and the Sweetshop

When I was seven my mother decided I should leave kindergarten and go to a proper boy's school. By good fortune, there existed a well-known preparatory school for boys about a mile from our house. It was called Llandaff Cathedral School, and it stood right under the shadow of Llandaff cathedral. Like the cathedral, the school is still there and still flourishing.

But here again, I can remember very little about the two years I attended Llandaff Cathedral School, between the ages of seven and nine. Only two moments remain clearly in my mind. The first lasted not more than five seconds, but I will never forget it.

It was my first term, and I was walking home alone across the village green after school when suddenly one of the senior twelve-year-old boys came riding full speed down the road on his bicycle about twenty yards away from me. The road was on a hill and the boy was going down the slope; and as he flashed by, he started backpedaling very quickly so that the freewheeling mechanism of his bike made a loud whirring sound. At the same time, he took his hands off the handlebars and folded them casually across his chest. I stopped dead and stared after him. How wonderful he was! How swift and brave and graceful in his long trousers with bicycle clips around them and his scarlet schoolcap at a jaunty angle on his head! One day, I told myself, one glorious day I will have a bike like that, and I will wear long trousers with bicycle clips, and my school cap will sit jaunty on my head, and I will go whizzing down the hill pedaling backwards with no hands on the handlebars!

I promise you that if somebody had caught me by the shoulder at that moment and said to me, "What is your greatest wish in life little boy? What is your absolute ambition? To be a doctor? A fine musician? A painter? A writer? Or the Lord Chancellor?" I would have answered without hesitation that my only ambition, my hope, my longing was to have a bike like that and to go whizzing down the hill with no hands on the handlebars. It would be fabulous. It made me tremble just to think about it.

My second and only other memory of Llandaff Cathedral School is extremely

---

Words to Know and Use | **flourish** (flʉr′ ish) *v.* to thrive; grow vigorously

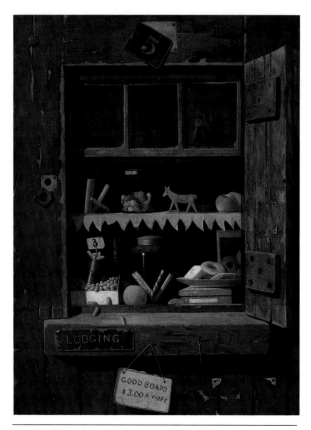

THE POOR MAN'S STORE   1885   John Frederick Peto
Museum of Fine Arts, Boston. Gift of Maxim Karolik to the M. and
M. Karolik Collection of American Paintings, 1815-1865.

bizarre. It happened a little over a year later, when I was just nine. By then I had made some friends, and when I walked to school in the mornings, I would start out alone but would pick up four other boys of my own age along the way. After school was over, the same four boys and I would set out together across the village green and through the village itself, heading for home. On the way to school and on the way back, we always passed the sweetshop. No we

didn't; we never passed it. We always stopped. We lingered outside its rather small window, gazing in at the big glass jars full of Bull's-eyes and Old-fashioned Humbugs and Strawberry Bonbons and Glacier Mints and Acid Drops and Pear Drops and Lemon Drops and all the rest of them. Each of us received sixpence[1] a week for pocket money, and whenever there was any money in our pockets, we would all troop in together to buy a pennyworth of this or that. My own favorites were Sherbet Suckers and Licorice Bootlaces.

One of the other boys, whose name was Thwaites, told me I should never eat Licorice Bootlaces. Thwaites's father, who was a doctor, had said that they were made from rats' blood. The father had given his young son a lecture about Licorice Bootlaces when he had caught him eating one in bed. "Every rat catcher in the country," the father had said, "takes his rats to the Licorice Bootlace Factory, and the manager pays tuppence[2] for each rat. Many a rat catcher has become a millionaire by selling his dead rats to the factory."

"But how do they turn the rats into licorice?" the young Thwaites had asked his father.

"They wait until they've got ten thousand rats," the father had answered, "then they dump them all into a huge shiny steel <u>cauldron</u> and boil them up for several hours. Two men stir the bubbling cauldron with

---

1. **sixpence** (siks′ pəns): in England, six pennies.
2. **tuppence** (tup′ əns): in England, two pennies.

Words to Know and Use | **cauldron** (kôl′ drən) *n.* a large kettle

long poles, and in the end they have a thick, steaming rat stew. After that, a cruncher is lowered into the cauldron to crunch the bones, and what's left is a pulpy substance called rat mash."

"Yes, but how do they turn that into Licorice Bootlaces, Daddy?" the young Thwaites had asked, and this question, according to Thwaites, had caused his father to pause and think for a few moments before he answered it. At last he had said, "The two men who were doing the stirring with the long poles now put on their Wellington boots[3] and climb into the cauldron and shovel the hot rat mash out onto a concrete floor. Then they run a steamroller over it several times to flatten it out. What is left looks rather like a gigantic black pancake, and all they have to do after that is to wait for it to cool and to harden so they can cut it up into strips to make the Bootlaces. Don't ever eat them," the father had said. "If you do, you'll get ratitis."

"What is ratitis, Daddy?" young Thwaites had asked.

"All the rats that the rat catchers catch are poisoned with rat poison," the father had said. "It's the rat poison that gives you ratitis."

"Yes, but what happens to you when you catch it?" young Thwaites had asked.

"Your teeth become very sharp and pointed," the father had answered. "And a short stumpy tail grows out of your back just above your bottom. There is no cure for ratitis. I ought to know. I'm a doctor."

We all enjoyed Thwaites's story, and we made him tell it to us many times on our walks to and from school. But it didn't stop any of us except Thwaites from buying Licorice Bootlaces. At two for a penny they were the best value in the shop. A Bootlace, in case you haven't had the pleasure of handling one, is not round. It's like a flat black tape about half an inch wide. You buy it rolled up in a coil, and in those days it used to be so long that when you unrolled it and held one end at arm's length above your head, the other end touched the ground.

Sherbet Suckers were also two a penny. Each Sucker consisted of a yellow cardboard tube filled with sherbet powder, and there was a hollow licorice straw sticking out of it. (Rat's blood again, young Thwaites would warn us, pointing at the licorice straw.) You sucked the sherbet up through the straw, and when it was finished, you ate the licorice. They were delicious, those Sherbet Suckers. The sherbet fizzed in your mouth, and if you knew how to do it, you could make white froth come out of your nostrils and pretend you were throwing a fit.

Gobstoppers, costing a penny each, were enormous hard, round balls the size of small tomatoes. One Gobstopper would provide about an hour's worth of nonstop sucking, and if you took it out of your mouth and inspected it every five minutes or so, you would find it had changed color. There was something fascinating about the way it went from pink to blue to green to yellow. We used to wonder how in the world the Gobstopper Factory managed to achieve this magic. "How *does* it happen?" we would ask each other. "How *can* they make it keep changing color?"

---

3. **Wellington boots:** high, rubber boots.

"It's your spit that does it," young Thwaites proclaimed. As the son of a doctor, he considered himself to be an authority on all things that had to do with the body. He could tell us about scabs and when they were ready to be picked off. He knew why a black eye was blue and why blood was red. "It's your spit that makes a Gobstopper change color," he kept insisting. When we asked him to elaborate on this theory, he answered, "You wouldn't understand it if I did tell you."

Pear Drops were exciting because they had a dangerous taste. They smelled of nail varnish, and they froze the back of your throat. All of us were warned against eating them, and the result was that we ate them more than ever.

Then there was a hard brown lozenge called the Tonsil Tickler. The Tonsil Tickler tasted and smelled very strongly of chloroform. We had not the slightest doubt that these things were saturated in the dreaded anesthetic which, as Thwaites had many times pointed out to us, could put you to sleep for hours at a stretch. "If my father has to saw off somebody's leg," he said, "he pours chloroform onto a pad, and the person sniffs it and goes to sleep, and my father saws his leg off without him even feeling it."

"But why do they put it into sweets and sell them to us?" we asked him.

You might think a question like this would have baffled Thwaites. But Thwaites was never baffled. "My father says Tonsil Ticklers were invented for dangerous prisoners in jail," he said. "They give them one with each meal, and the chloroform makes them sleepy and stops them rioting."

"Yes," we said, "but why sell them to children?"

"It's a plot," Thwaites said. "A grown-up plot to keep us quiet."

The sweetshop in Llandaff in the year 1923 was the very center of our lives. To us, it was what a bar is to a drunk or a church is to a bishop. Without it, there would have been little to live for. But it had one terrible drawback, this sweetshop. The woman who owned it was a horror. We hated her, and we had good reason for doing so.

*W*e hated her, and we had good reason for doing so.

Her name was Mrs. Pratchett. She was a small skinny old hag with a moustache on her upper lip and a mouth as sour as a green gooseberry. She never smiled. She never welcomed us when we went in, and the only times she spoke were when she said things like, "I'm watchin' you, so keep yer thievin' fingers off them chocolates!" Or "I don't want you in 'ere just to look around! Either you *forks* out or you *gets* out!"

But by far the most loathsome thing about Mrs. Pratchett was the filth that clung around her. Her apron was gray and greasy. Her blouse had bits of breakfast all over it, toast crumbs and tea stains and splotches of dried egg yolk. It was her hands, however, that disturbed us most. They were disgust-

Words to Know and Use

loathsome (lōth′ səm) *adj.* deserving of hate; disgusting

ing. They were black with dirt and grime. They looked as though they had been putting lumps of coal on the fire all day long. And do not forget, please, that it was these very hands and fingers that she plunged into the sweet-jars when we asked for a pennyworth of Treacle Toffee or Wine Gums or Nut Clusters or whatever. There were precious few health laws in those days, and nobody, least of all Mrs. Pratchett, ever thought of using a little shovel for getting out the sweets as they do today. The mere sight of her grimy right hand with its black fingernails digging an ounce of Chocolate Fudge out of a jar would have caused a starving tramp to go running from the shop. But not us. Sweets were our lifeblood. We would have put up with far worse than that to get them. So we simply stood and watched in <u>sullen</u> silence while this disgusting old woman stirred around inside the jars with her foul fingers.

The other thing we hated Mrs. Pratchett for was her meanness. Unless you spent a whole sixpence all in one go, she wouldn't give you a bag. Instead you got your sweets twisted up in a small piece of newspaper which she tore off a pile of old *Daily Mirrors* lying on the counter.

So you can well understand that we had it in for Mrs. Pratchett in a big way, but we didn't quite know what to do about it. Many schemes were put forward, but none of them was any good. None of them, that is, until suddenly, one memorable afternoon, we found the dead mouse.

The Great Mouse Plot

My four friends and I had come across a loose floorboard at the back of the classroom, and when we prized it up with the blade of a pocketknife, we discovered a big hollow space underneath. This, we decided, would be our secret hiding place for sweets and other small treasures such as conkers[4] and monkey nuts and birds' eggs. Every afternoon, when the last lesson was over, the five of us would wait until the classroom had emptied, then we would lift up the floorboard and examine our secret hoard, perhaps adding to it or taking something away.

One day, when we lifted it up, we found a dead mouse lying among our treasures. It was an exciting discovery. Thwaites took it out by its tail and waved it in front of our faces. "What shall we do with it?" he cried.

"It stinks!" someone shouted. "Throw it out of the window quick!"

"Hold on a tick," I said. "Don't throw it away."

Thwaites hesitated. They all looked at me.

When writing about oneself, one must strive to be truthful. Truth is more important than modesty. I must tell you, therefore, that it was I and I alone who had the idea for the great and daring Mouse Plot. We all have our moments of brilliance and glory, and this was mine.

"Why don't we," I said, "slip it into one of

---

4. **conkers:** horse chestnuts threaded on a string used in a boys' game in England.

Mrs. Pratchett's jars of sweets? Then when she puts her dirty hand in to grab a handful, she'll grab a stinky dead mouse instead."

The other four stared at me in wonder. Then, as the sheer genius of the plot began to sink in, they all started grinning. They slapped me on the back. They cheered me and danced around the classroom. "We'll do it today!" they cried. "We'll do it on the way home! *You* had the idea," they said to me, "so *you* can be the one to put the mouse in the jar."

Thwaites handed me the mouse. I put it into my trouser pocket. Then the five of us left the school, crossed the village green and headed for the sweetshop. We were tremendously jazzed up. We felt like a gang of desperados setting out to rob a train or blow up the sheriff's office.

"Make sure you put it into a jar which is used often," somebody said.

"I'm putting it in Gobstoppers," I said. "The Gobstopper jar is never behind the counter."

"I've got a penny," Thwaites said, "so I'll ask for one Sherbet Sucker and one Bootlace. And while she turns away to get them, you slip the mouse in quickly with the Gobstoppers."

Thus everything was arranged. We were strutting a little as we entered the shop. We were the victors now, and Mrs. Pratchett was the victim. She stood behind the counter, and her small malignant pig-eyes watched us suspiciously as we came forward.

"One Sherbet Sucker, please," Thwaites said to her, holding out his penny.

I kept to the rear of the group, and when I saw Mrs. Pratchett turn her head away for a couple of seconds to fish a Sherbet Sucker out of the box, I lifted the heavy glass lid of the Gobstopper jar and dropped the mouse in. Then I replaced the lid as silently as possible. My heart was thumping like mad, and my hands had gone all sweaty.

"And one Bootlace, please," I heard Thwaites saying. When I turned around, I saw Mrs. Pratchett holding out the Bootlace in her filthy fingers.

"I don't want all the lot of you troopin' in 'ere if only one of you is buyin'," she screamed at us. "Now beat it! Go on, get out!"

As soon as we were outside, we broke into a run. "Did you do it?" they shouted at me.

"Of course I did!" I said.

"Well done you!" they cried. "What a super show!"

I felt like a hero. I *was* a hero. It was marvelous to be so popular.

Mr. Coombes

The flush of triumph over the dead mouse was carried forward to the next morning as we all met again to walk to school.

"Let's go in and see if it's still in the jar," somebody said as we approached the sweetshop.

"Don't," Thwaites said firmly. "It's too

Words to Know and Use | **malignant** (mə lig′ nənt) *adj.* wishing or causing evil; very harmful dangerous. Walk past as though nothing has happened."

As we came level with the shop, we saw a cardboard notice hanging on the door.

We stopped and stared. We had never known the sweetshop to be closed at this time in the morning, even on Sundays.

"What's happened?" we asked each other. "What's going on?"

We pressed our faces against the window and looked inside. Mrs. Pratchett was nowhere to be seen.

"Look!" I cried. "The Gobstopper jar's gone! It's not on the shelf! There's a gap where it used to be!"

"It's on the floor!" someone said. "It's smashed to bits, and there's Gobstoppers everywhere!"

"There's the mouse!" someone else shouted.

We could see it all, the huge glass jar smashed to smithereens with the dead mouse lying in the wreckage and hundreds of many-colored Gobstoppers littering the floor.

"She got such a shock when she grabbed hold of the mouse that she dropped everything," somebody was saying.

"But why didn't she sweep it all up and open the shop?" I asked.

Nobody answered me.

We turned away and walked toward the school. All of a sudden we had begun to feel slightly uncomfortable. There was something not quite right about the shop being closed. Even Thwaites was unable to offer a reasonable explanation. We became silent. There was a faint scent of danger in the air now. Each one of us had caught a whiff of it. Alarm bells were beginning to ring faintly in our ears.

After a while, Thwaites broke the silence. "She must have got one heck of a shock," he said. He paused. We all looked at him, wondering what wisdom the great medical authority was going to come out with next.

"After all," he went on, "to catch hold of a dead mouse when you're expecting to catch hold of a Gobstopper must be a pretty frightening experience. Don't you agree?"

Nobody answered him.

"Well now," Thwaites went on, "when an old person like Mrs. Pratchett suddenly gets a very big shock, I suppose you know what happens next?"

"What?" we said. "What happens?"

"You ask my father," Thwaites said. "He'll tell you."

"You tell us," we said.

"It gives her a heart attack," Thwaites announced. "Her heart stops beating, and

she's dead in five seconds."

For a moment or two my own heart stopped beating. Thwaites pointed a finger at me and said darkly, "I'm afraid you've killed her."

I'm afraid you've killed her.

"*Me?*" I cried. "Why just *me?*"

"It was *your* idea," he said. "And what's more, *you* put the mouse in."

All of a sudden, I was a murderer.

At exactly that point, we heard the school bell ringing in the distance, and we had to gallop the rest of the way so as not to be late for prayers.

Prayers were held in the Assembly Hall. We all perched in rows on wooden benches, while the teachers sat up on the platform in armchairs, facing us. The five of us scrambled into our places just as the Headmaster marched in, followed by the rest of the staff.

The Headmaster is the only teacher at Llandaff Cathedral School that I can remember, and for a reason you will soon discover, I can remember him very clearly indeed. His name was Mr. Coombes, and I have a picture in my mind of a giant of a man with a face like a ham and a mass of rusty-colored hair that sprouted in a tangle all over the top of his head. All grown-ups appear as giants to small children. But Headmasters (and policemen) are the biggest giants of all and acquire a marvelously exaggerated stature. It is possible that Mr. Coombes was a perfectly normal being, but in my memory he was a giant, a tweed-suited giant who always wore a black gown[5] over his tweeds and a waistcoat under his jacket.

Mr. Coombes now proceeded to mumble through the same old prayers we had every day, but this morning, when the last amen had been spoken, he did not turn and lead his group rapidly out of the hall as usual. He remained standing before us, and it was clear he had an announcement to make.

"The whole school is to go out and line up around the playground immediately," he said. "Leave your books behind. And no talking."

Mr. Coombes was looking grim. His hammy pink face had taken on that dangerous scowl which only appeared when he was extremely cross and somebody was for the high jump. I sat there small and frightened among the rows and rows of other boys, and to me at that moment the Headmaster, with his black gown draped over his shoulders, was like a judge at a murder trial.

"He's after the killer," Thwaites whispered to me.

I began to shiver.

"I'll bet the police are here already," Thwaites went on. "And the Black Maria's[6] waiting outside."

As we made our way out to the playground, my whole stomach began to feel as though it was slowly filling up with swirling water. *I am only eight years old,* I told myself. *No little boy of eight has ever murdered anyone. It's not possible.*

Out in the playground on this warm,

---

5. black gown: a robe much like those worn by graduating students.

6. Black Maria: a police patrol wagon.

© Superstock.

cloudy September morning, the Deputy Headmaster was shouting, "Line up in forms! Sixth Form over there! Fifth Form next to them! Spread out! Spread out! Get on with it! Stop talking all of you!"

Thwaites and I and my other three friends were in the Second Form, the lowest but one, and we lined up against the red-brick wall of the playground shoulder to shoulder. I can remember that when every boy in the school was in his place, the line stretched right around the four sides of the playground—about one hundred small boys altogether, aged between six and twelve, all of us wearing identical gray shorts and gray blazers and gray stockings and black shoes.

"Stop that *talking!*" shouted the Deputy Head. "I want absolute silence!"

But why for heaven's sake were we in the playground at all? I wondered. And why were we lined up like this? It had never happened before.

I half expected to see two policemen come bounding out of the school to grab me by the arms and put handcuffs on my wrists.

A single door led out from the school onto the playground. Suddenly it swung open and through it, like the angel of death, strode Mr. Coombes, huge and bulky in his tweed suit and black gown, and beside him, believe it or not, right beside him trotted the tiny figure of Mrs. Pratchett herself!

Mrs. Pratchett was alive!

The relief was tremendous.

"She's alive!" I whispered to Thwaites standing next to me. "I didn't kill her!" Thwaites ignored me.

"We'll start over here," Mr. Coombes was

saying to Mrs. Pratchett. He grasped her by one of her skinny arms and led her over to where the Sixth Form was standing. Then, still keeping hold of her arm, he proceeded to lead her at a brisk walk down the line of boys. It was like someone inspecting the troops.

"What on earth are they doing?" I whispered.

Thwaites didn't answer me. I glanced at him. He had gone rather pale.

"Too big," I heard Mrs. Pratchett saying. "Much too big. It's none of this lot. Let's 'ave a look at some of them titchy ones."

Mr. Coombes increased his pace. "We'd better go all the way around," he said. He seemed in a hurry to get it over with now, and I could see Mrs. Pratchett's skinny goat's legs trotting to keep up with him. They had already inspected one side of the playground where the Sixth Form and half the Fifth Form were standing. We watched them moving down the second side . . . then the third side.

"Still too big," I heard Mrs. Pratchett croaking. "Much too big! Smaller than these! Much smaller! Where's them nasty little ones?"

They were coming closer to us now . . . closer and closer.

They were starting on the fourth side . . .

Every boy in our form was watching Mr. Coombes and Mrs. Pratchett as they came walking down the line toward us.

"Nasty, cheeky lot, these little'uns!" I heard Mrs. Pratchett muttering. "They comes into my shop, and they thinks they can do whatever they well likes!"

Mr. Coombes made no reply to this.

"They nick things when I ain't lookin'," she went on. "They put their grubby 'ands all over everything, and they've got no manners. I don't mind girls. I never 'ave no trouble with girls, but boys is 'ideous and 'orrible! I don't 'ave to tell *you* that, 'Eadmaster, do I?"

"These are the smaller ones," Mr. Coombes said.

I could see Mrs. Pratchett's piggy little eyes staring hard at the face of each boy she passed.

Suddenly she let out a high-pitched yell and pointed a dirty finger straight at Thwaites. "That's 'im!" she yelled. "That's one of 'em! I'd know 'im a mile away, the scummy little bounder!"

The entire school turned to look at Thwaites. "W-what have *I* done?" he stuttered, appealing to Mr. Coombes.

"Shut up," Mr. Coombes said.

Mrs. Pratchett's eyes flicked over and settled on my own face. I looked down and studied the black asphalt surface of the playground.

"'Ere's another of 'em!" I heard her yelling. "That one there!" She was pointing at me now.

"You're quite sure?" Mr. Coombes said.

"Of course I'm sure!" she cried. "I never forgets a face, least of all when it's as sly as that! 'Ee's one of 'em all right! There was five altogether! Now where's them other three?"

The other three, as I knew very well, were coming up next.

Mrs. Pratchett's face was glimmering with venom as her eyes traveled beyond me down the line.

"There they are!" she cried out, stabbing the air with her finger. "'Im . . . and 'im . . . and 'im! That's the five of 'em all right! We don't need to look no farther than this, 'Eadmaster! They're all 'ere, the nasty, dirty little pigs! You've got their names, 'ave you?"

"I've got their names, Mrs. Pratchett," Mr. Coombes told her. "I'm much obliged to you."

"And I'm much obliged to you, 'Eadmaster," she answered.

As Mr. Coombes led her away across the playground, we heard her saying, "Right in the jar of Gobstoppers it was! A stinkin' dead mouse which I will never forget as long as I live!"

"You have my deepest sympathy," Mr. Coombes was muttering.

"Talk about shocks!" she went on "When my fingers caught 'old of that nasty, soggy, stinkin' dead mouse, . . . " Her voice trailed away as Mr. Coombes led her quickly through the door into the school building. ❧

Editor's Note: After being identified by Mrs. Pratchett in the schoolyard lineup, Roald and his friends were ordered into the headmaster's office. There they received a caning (beating) from Mr. Coombes, while Mrs. Pratchett watched. When Roald's mother saw her son's bruises, she promised to send him to school in England. The following year, Roald went to boarding school.

*R*esponding to Reading

First Impressions

1. What part of this selection did you enjoy most? Write your reaction in your journal or on a sheet of paper.

Second Thoughts

2. Was the boys' revenge worth their punishment?

3. What do you think of Mrs. Pratchett?

> **Think about**
> * how she treats the boys
> * the problems of owning a shop in which many customers are children

4. What parts of this selection remind you of experiences you had when you were younger?

> **Think about**
> * the terror Dahl felt when he thought he'd killed Mrs Pratchett
> * feelings about the candy or the store
> * stories you heard that were similar to the rat-mash story
> * pranks you discussed before reading

5. How do you think the grown-up Dahl feels about the prank he played in order to get even with Mrs. Pratchett? Why?

Broader Connections

6. Is a prank like the one in this story acceptable or not? In other words, how far is too far?

*L*iterary Concept: Dialect

You remember that **dialect** is the type of language spoken by a group of people in a particular region. Dialect includes both expressions and pronunciation. In our country, a southern drawl and a western twang are both dialects. Writers sometimes try to record these special accents on paper so that the reader will have a better idea of how the characters might sound. In *Boy,* Roald Dahl imitates Mrs. Pratchett's British working-class accent by dropping the beginning *h* from words like *here: 'ere.* Find other ways he represents her dialect. Then read some of her speeches aloud.

Writing Options

1. A **ballad** is a song or poem that tells a story. Use the events of this selection to write "The Ballad of the Dead Mouse."

2. From the selections in this subunit, choose a character who you think would fit in with Roald Dahl's gang of friends. Write a **persuasive essay** convincing Dahl to accept this person as part of his group.

3. Imagine that you are the local health inspector. Write a **memo** to the Board of Health after you inspect Mrs. Pratchett's sweetshop.

4. In rat-mash style, create a gruesome **story** about how your favorite kind of candy is made. Include a description of the candy, using Dahl's description on pages 224–225 as a model.

Vocabulary Practice

Exercise A On your paper write the word from the list that best completes the meaning of the sentence.

1. The hatred that Mrs. Pratchett feels toward the boys is like _____.

2. The boys think Mrs. Pratchett is _____ because of her disgusting clothes and filthy hands.

3. The huge container for cooking rat-mash is called a _____.

4. Children help candy stores _____ even when the shopkeepers are disagreeable.

5. When Mrs. Pratchett screams at them, the boys become quiet and _____.

6. A flickering _____ of hope shines from Dahl's eyes when he sees that Mrs. Pratchett is alive.

7. It is obvious from the _____ look in Mrs. Pratchett's eyes that she wants a severe punishment for the boys.

Exercise B Find the three adjectives in the list of words. Write a synonym for each.

> *Words to Know and Use*
>
> **cauldron**
> **flourish**
> **glimmer**
> **loathsome**
> **malignant**
> **sullen**
> **venom**

*O*ptions for Learning

1 • Jawbreakers and Licorice Gobstoppers and Licorice Bootlaces are British names for candy that is also sold in the United States. From a candy manufacturer or another source, find out how jawbreakers or licorice is really made. Share your information with the class.

2 • Clean Up Pratchett Find out about health codes in your area that would have forced Mrs. Pratchett to clean up her store. You might interview a candy store owner to find out what the government requires in the way of cleanliness and packaging.

3 • British Public Schools How do British public schools differ from U.S. public schools? Do research in a library, or ask someone who attended a British public school to describe his or her school days. List differences on a chart to display in class.

4 • Meet Roald Read *Boy: Tales of Childhood*, from which this piece was taken, to enjoy more tales of Dahl's youth. Share some of his adventures with the class.

 FACT FINDER SOCIAL STUDIES

In Great Britain, how many tuppence were in a crown?

*R*oald Dahl
1916–1990

Roald Dahl became a writer even though his school reports said, "I have never met a boy who so persistently writes the exact opposite of what he means. He seems incapable of marshaling his thoughts on paper," and "Vocabulary negligible, sentences malconstructed. He reminds me of a camel."

He is most famous for his twenty children's books, which some critics complain are too violent. Children love them. His first children's book was *The Gremlins* (a word he invented), about tiny people who cause mysterious malfunctions in airplanes. Two of his best known children's books are *James and the Giant Peach* and *Charlie and the Chocolate Factory*. Dahl once said, "Had I not had children of my own, I would have never written books for children, nor would I have been capable of doing so."

WRITER'S WORKSHOP

NARRATIVE WRITING

Think about a television show or a movie you really like. Why does it hook you and keep your interest? Chances are that it involves a dramatic twist like the ones in the selections in this subunit; for example, a change of fortune, an unexpected reversal of power, or a "loser" managing to come out on top. Since people enjoy these kinds of plots, such stories—whether fiction or nonfiction—are often turned into dramas. Plays, films, and television shows are all types of drama. A drama, like a story, is a kind of narrative writing. In this workshop you'll choose a story and rewrite it as a drama.

USE NARRATIVE WRITING FOR

stories
ballads
plays
skits
biographies

GUIDED ASSIGNMENT: FROM STORY TO DRAMA

Choose a selection you have read and rewrite it as a drama for the stage.

Here is one writer's PASSkey to this assignment.

PURPOSE: To dramatize a narrative
AUDIENCE: Other students
SUBJECT: Selection from this book
STRUCTURE: Stage drama

```
                The Painter
                by Denny Fox

based on "The War of the Wall" by Toni Cade Bambara

                  Characters

Tina .........cousins, age    Frieda .......twins, age
Lou           thirteen        Hattie          eight
Painter .....muralist         Mama .........Tina's mom
Side Pocket ..pool shark       Daddy ........Tina's dad
Mr. Eubanks ..barber          Mrs. Morris ..twins' mom

  Scene 1: A spring morning in the 1970s. On a
  street in a Southern town are a barber shop, a
  stretch of high, marked-up wall, and a pool
```

◀ **STUDENT MODEL**

Before you write, read the first scene of one student's drama.

◀ A brief description of characters and setting is provided before the play begins.

hall with a gumball machine in front. A ladder leans against the wall. Nearby, a woman in overalls stirs a bucket of paint. Her car sits at the curb. Tina and Lou approach.

TINA (noticing the painter). What's she doing?

LOU. Hey, she can't paint that wall! It's ours!

TINA. Yeah! We've been pitching pennies there since we were kids. And we've got important stuff carved on it.

LOU. Yeah—even Jimmy Lyons's name. That's all we've got to remember him by now. Remember how he used to take us fishing?

TINA. You think I'm ever going to forget him? I wish he'd never had to go fight in Vietnam.

LOU. I still can't believe he's dead. (The cousins have reached the painter.)

TINA (angrily). Quit messing with our wall!

PAINTER (absent-mindedly, not looking at the children). The barber gave me permission.

LOU (exchanging a look with Tina and slouching against the painter's car). Listen. If you lean close, you'll get a whiff of bubble gum and kids' sweat. And that'll tell you something—that this wall belongs to the kids of Taliaferro Street.

TINA (moving toward the ladder as the painter climbs it). You think you can just ignore us? And climb on up with your paint bucket? You're not even from around here—you've got New York plates on your old clunky car! (Tina grabs the ladder, about to shake it.)

LOU (alarmed, pulling Tina away). Hey, don't! Come on—we're already late for school. (Tina and Lou walk away.)

Stage directions (underlined and in parentheses) guide the actors.

Dialogue replaces the short story's description and narration.

A direct quotation is taken from the story.

The dialogue leads into more action, which is described in stage directions.

The first scene draws viewers in by setting up a conflict.

Prewrite and Explore

1 **Choose your material** To choose a piece to dramatize, skim the selections you have already read. You need a piece that you like and that means something to you. You also need a piece that tells a story. You may use fiction, nonfiction, or poetry. The strongest dramas will come from stories with action that you can see in your mind and with characters you can relate to.

2 **Get the big picture** Plays are divided into scenes, which change when the time or place of the action changes. To plan the scenes in your play, you can start with a list of the main events in the story you've chosen. Each event can become a scene. You may later choose to leave out a scene or invent a new one, to tell the story clearly in play form.

After you've listed the events, you're ready to gather information.

◄ **WORK TOGETHER**
. . . .
Does your favorite story seem too long or complicated? Try asking others to join you in a group effort.

◄ **WORK TOGETHER**
. . . .
Try working as a group to list scenes. Then each member might plan and write one scene.

GATHERING INFORMATION

Each scene you write must reflect the setting, the characters' personalities, and the action. Therefore, you'll need to start with a detailed plan for each scene. Scene charts like the one Denny Fox used can help you gather details.

SCENE 1
Summary: The cousins notice the painter.

Setting	Characters	Action
Small-town business district, quiet morning, kids walking to school past a marked-up wall	Tina—impulsive, bossy Lou—quiet, thoughtful Painter— artsy-looking, focusing on her task, ignoring surroundings	Painter prepares to do a mural on wall. Cousins recall the wall's importance to them, then heckle the painter.

◄ **STUDENT MODEL** . . . .

Draft and Discover

1 Set the format   When you follow standard drama format, starting your draft is easy. First, list your cast of characters, perhaps with a brief description of each. Next, for each scene, write a short paragraph that describes the setting. To guide actors, include stage directions, underlined and in parentheses, with your dialogue. You can look at *The Monsters Are Due on Maple Street* or the stage directions in *Funny Boy* (Unit 5) to see how this format works. Review the Elements of Drama on pages 155–156 for additional help.

STAGE DIRECTIONS

Use stage directions to (1) show the action, (2) describe facial expressions, tone of voice, or movements, and (3) describe setting and props.

2 Get into character   In a short story, the author narrates the action and describes the characters. For your drama, you will invent dialogue to replace narration and description. Try imagining what each character might say in the scenes you have set up. Your scene charts will help. You can use—or ignore—any dialogue in the original story. Make sure your dialogue sounds like real speech and is not artificial. Use it to show characters' personalities and concerns. If you think a character might say something that's not in the original story, go ahead and write it. It may help bring the character to life.

WORKING TOGETHER

For help with dialogue, try improvising your scene with a small group. One group member can take notes.

Revise Your Writing

1 Focus on action   Your scene charts show the action you planned for each scene. Now you need to make sure that your dialogue clearly explains the action as well as the reasons for the action. If it does not, revise to include references to the action. For example, you might have characters anticipate an action, discuss it, or respond to it. You can also use your stage directions to specify the action.

COMPUTER TIP

Save, then copy your drama. As you tinker with scenes, try out changes on the copy.

2 Adjust the scenes   Now that you have a draft, you should also have a firmer sense of what your play is about. Review each scene, asking yourself what it contributes to your play's message. Adding, changing, or even cutting scenes can help you focus your drama. You might even decide to add a narrator, as in *The Monsters Are Due on Maple Street.*

3 Talk through it   Try reading your draft aloud with friends, each taking one or more parts. Afterwards, you can use the revision questions on the next page.

Revision Questions

For You

1. Does each scene help the story move forward?
2. Does the dialogue reflect each character's personality?
3. Is the action clear?

For a Peer Reader

1. Which lines of dialogue do you like best? Why?
2. Which parts of the action are most vivid to you?
3. Do I need a narrator?

Proofread

Proofread for errors in grammar, spelling, capitalization, and punctuation. Pay special attention to subject-verb agreement.

THE EDITOR'S EYE: AGREEMENT

A verb must agree with its subject in number.

Singular subjects need singular verbs. Plural subjects need plural verbs.

Problem   One of the cousins <u>talk</u> angrily to the painter.

Revised   One of the cousins <u>talks</u> angrily to the painter.

NEED MORE HELP?

See the Language Workshop on pages 242–244 and pages 759–761 of the Language Handbook.

Publish and Present

On with the Show   With the help of friends, present your drama as a dramatic reading. If time permits, have the group present your drama as a stage play, with props, costumes, and so on.

◀ **DRAMATIC READING TIPS**

See the Speaking and Listening Workshop on page 245.

Reflect on Your Writing

Briefly answer the following questions. Put the answers with your drama, and add it to your portfolio.

1. What new things did you discover about the story as you dramatized it?
2. Is drama easy or hard for you to write?

◀ **FOR YOUR PORTFOLIO**

LANGUAGE WORKSHOP

SUBJECT—VERB AGREEMENT

A verb and its subject must agree in number.

In drama, every word counts, and audiences listen carefully. Errors in subject-verb agreement can make dialogue sound jarring and unreal. Such errors can distract an audience.

Nouns and verbs have **number**—that is, they can be **singular** (one thing or action) or **plural** (two or more things or actions). When we say ▶ that a subject and verb **agree** in number, we mean that they are both singular or both plural.

GRAMMAR TIP
An *s* at the end of a verb shows that the verb is singular—just the opposite of what it shows for nouns!

The <u>phone</u> (singular) <u>is</u> (singular) dead.
The <u>phones</u> (plural) <u>are</u> (plural) dead.

You can usually decide whether a subject and verb agree by saying the sentence to yourself.

The <u>boy</u> (singular) <u>talks</u> (singular) about space creatures.
The <u>boys</u> (plural) <u>talk</u> (plural) about space creatures.

Often a phrase appears between the subject and the verb. The simple subject is never part of such a phrase. Don't mistake the noun ▶ in the phrase for the subject. Make the verb agree with the simple subject.

REMINDER
The **simple subject** is the key word in the subject that tells whom or what the sentence is about.

One (of the neighbors) <u>is</u> afraid.
The <u>men</u> (on the block) <u>discuss</u> their lawns.

Exercise 1   Concept Check   Write the simple subject of each sentence. Then write the verb form that agrees with the subject.

1. A bright object with strange markings (zooms, zoom) over Maple Street.
2. A group of neighbors (comes, come) out to watch.
3. Gradually, people (discovers, discover) mysterious problems.
4. Even their cars (is, are) not working.

5. In the confusion, a boy carrying comic books (mentions, mention) space invaders.
6. Then one man's car (starts, start) by itself.
7. His neighbors from Maple Street quickly (grows, grow) suspicious of him.
8. One of the people (accuses, accuse) him of being an alien.
9. I (was, were) fascinated by this play.
10. By reading it, you (gets, get) insights into the way mobs act.

Compound Subjects

Compound subjects are two or more subjects sharing the same verb. Compound subjects joined with *and* take a plural verb.

<u>Steve</u> and his <u>friend</u> <u>stay</u> calm.

When compound subjects are joined with *or* or *nor,* the verb agrees in number with the subject that is closer to the verb.

Either <u>Tommy</u> or his <u>mother</u> <u>buys</u> comic books.
A <u>meteor</u> or <u>sunspots</u> <u>cause</u> power failure.

Verbs in Questions

In most sentences, the subject comes before the verb. However, in questions, part or all of the verb comes first. The subject and verb must still agree in number.

<u>Does</u> <u>Les</u> <u>stare</u> at the sky every night?
Why <u>is</u> <u>he</u> so different?
Where <u>does</u> <u>Les</u> really <u>live</u>?

Verbs in Sentences that Start with There and Here

When *there* or *here* begins a sentence, look for the subject later in the sentence. Then check for agreement with the verb.

There <u>are</u> <u>clues</u> in Tommy's comic book.
There <u>is</u> a <u>moral</u> to this story.
Here <u>is</u> one <u>explanation</u> for the disaster.

CAUTION
. . . .
Don't be fooled by the contractions *there's, here's,* and *where's.* All three are singular and agree only with singular subjects. There <u>are</u> (not *there's*) no <u>batteries</u> left. Here <u>are</u> (not *here's*) some <u>suggestions</u>. Where <u>are</u> (not *where's*) Tommy's <u>parents</u>?

Exercise 2   Concept Check   Write the simple or compound subject in each sentence. Then write the verb that agrees in number.

1. Even lawn mowers and transistor radios (refuses, refuse) to work.
2. A man and his friend (tries, try) to quiet the crowd.
3. Neither Sally nor Steve (feels, feel) right about watching Les.
4. There (is, are) good reasons why Les scans the sky at night.
5. (Doesn't, Don't) anyone believe him?
6. (Is, Are) the neighbors desperate enough to attack Les?
7. Myra and Ethel (defends, defend) their husbands.
8. Either Tommy or another child (screams, scream).
9. (There's, There are) two shadowy forms watching from a distance.
10. Where (does, do) the aliens go next?

Exercise 3   Revision Skill   Rewrite the following portion of a drama, correcting errors in subject-verb agreement.

Scene 2: Sunday evening, April 14, 1912. In the radio room of the *Titanic,* in the North Atlantic, two radio operators talk. Jack, in his headphones, sit at the radio; Harold stretch out on a sofa.

Harold. I'm beat. Those rich passengers from first class sure doesn't give us much rest, do they?

Jack. Well, to them, the radio is a new toy. Passengers wants to play with it by sending messages. That lady with the diamonds come in here every two hours. She and her father in New York seems worried about each other. *(New messages comes in over the headphones.)*

Harold. We're doing a good job, anyway. The captain and the first mate says so. *(as Jack writes a message)* What's the news?

Jack *(sounding bored)*. There's more icebergs ahead. Either the captain or the helmsman need to know. Can you take the messages up?

Harold *(tiredly)*. Sure. I'll bring back coffee and doughnuts.

LANGUAGE HANDBOOK

For review and practice: Section 8, Subject-Verb Agreement, pages 259–261.

Exercise 4   Revising Your Writing   Reread the drama you wrote for the Writer's Workshop on pages 237–241. Lightly underline the subject and verb of each sentence and check to be sure that subjects and verbs agree in number. Correct any errors you find.

SPEAKING AND LISTENING
WORKSHOP

DRAMATIC READING SKILLS

Dramas, like the one you wrote in the Writer's Workshop, are created to be performed. A **dramatic reading** is one kind of performance. In a dramatic reading, actors sit or stand on a bare stage and hold scripts. They must keep the audience's attention without props, scenery, or costumes. The techniques they use can help you when you read your own drama aloud.

1. Prepare   Read your material—aloud, if possible—several times beforehand. Know the high points: the flashes of humor, excitement, or tension.

2. Project   Speak up! Hold your head, and the script, *up* as you read. Don't shout, but aim your voice outward, to the very back of the room. To emphasize humor, try a slight increase in the volume of your voice. To show tension, try raising the volume, then dropping it.

3. Create   You may be able to come up with a special tone of voice, or a special way of pronouncing words, that fits your character. Match this voice to the character's personality.

4. Pause   Nothing shouts like silence. At the exciting points in the drama, you may tend to rush through your lines. Pause instead. The people in the audience will hold their breath with you.

5. Think   Don't drone along on automatic pilot. Think about what other characters say, and react as if you were really the character. Also think about what you're saying. How does your character feel? How can you show it?

6. Move   Use your whole body. Your hands and face can express your emotions. Body language, including your posture and movements, also express emotions. For example, a quick double take can convey humor. Your posture also affects your voice—both its tone and its volume.

Exercise 1   Choose a sentence you like from one of the works in this unit. Read it aloud several times, practicing the six tips above.

Exercise 2   With a small group, participate in a reading of the drama you wrote for the Writer's Workshop on page 237. Try out various interpretations of key dialogue before you begin.

◀ REMINDER
There's only one time *not* to pause: when another character has just stopped speaking and it's your turn to begin. Then, don't let it drag—jump right in.

Reading on Your Own

Suggested Novels for Unit Two

The novels introduced on these pages allow you to explore the unit theme, "Scales of Justice," in more depth and in different ways.

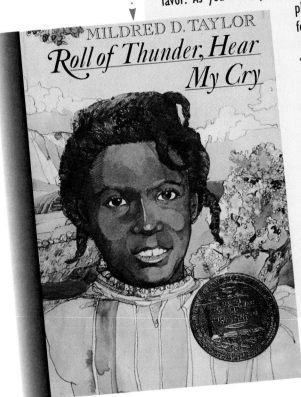

ROLL OF THUNDER, HEAR MY CRY

MILDRED D. TAYLOR ©1976

During the Depression, when many people lost their jobs, life was especially difficult for African Americans. *Roll of Thunder, Hear My Cry* is a historical novel about a family who must struggle to overcome both prejudice and poverty in rural Mississippi. The story contains both terrifying and humorous incidents. As you draw close to the Logan family, you will watch them keep their spirits up in the face of discrimination. You may become angry at the injustice of the poor treatment received by the black school that the Logan children attend. However, you will enjoy the Logan children's occasional tipping of the scales of justice in their favor. As you read, put yourself in the children's place and ask yourself the following questions:

- How would you react if a school bus deliberately splashed dirty water on you?

- How would you feel if your whole school were treated as second-class?

- What might you do to turn the tables on mean-spirited people without getting in trouble?

BROTHER EAGLE, SISTER SKY: A MESSAGE FROM CHIEF SEATTLE

SUSAN JEFFERS ©1991

Based on a letter that Chief Seattle supposedly wrote to the President of the United States around 1855, *Brother Eagle, Sister Sky: A Message From Chief Seattle* explains Native American beliefs about the earth and the way people should treat it. Chief Seattle clearly explains his belief that the earth does not belong to people but people belong to the earth and must care for it and cherish it. His letter will make you think hard about how we modern Americans treat our environment. As you read, you might consider the following questions:

- Do you agree with Chief Seattle's view of people's relationship with nature?

- If you had a conversation with Chief Seattle, what concerns would you talk about?

- How would Chief Seattle make himself heard today?

MANIAC MAGEE

JERRY SPINELLI ©1990

Enjoy the humorous adventures of Maniac Magee, a very different sort of boy hero. Besides being able to run faster and hit more home runs than anybody else, Maniac can also settle problems between angry gangs of kids. In fact, his exploits are so unbelievable that other kids write jump-rope rhymes about them. Maniac Magee acts according to his own scales of justice—with humorous and positive results. As you smile over his strange ways of dealing with problems, think about the following questions:

- What would it be like to be better at all sports than anyone you know?

- If you were a superhero, what real problems would you solve?

- Would you be happy if everyone shared Maniac Magee's unusual way of thinking?

Other Recommended Books

Jack Tales by Richard Chase (©1943). This enjoyable collection of folk tales from the southern Appalachians is filled with stories about justice, turning the tables, and victims and victors.

Stepping on the Cracks by Mary Downing Hahn (©1991). This historical novel, set in Maryland during World War II, deals with a deserter from the army and a group of young friends who decide to take care of him. In this story courage of all kinds is tested.

The Black Americans: A History in Their Own Words, 1619-1983 by Milton Meltzer (©1984). This fascinating book is a collection of letters, speeches, articles, and other documents written by African Americans. It includes testimonies from slaves and free men and women, both famous and unknown.

Sing Down the Moon by Scott O'Dell (©1970). In this historical novel, a Navaho girl is involved in the three-hundred-mile journey known as the Long Walk, from Canyon de Chelly to Fort Sumner. The heroine escapes from the fort and returns to her canyon, where she discovers that survival of the spirit is just as important as physical survival.

REACHING FOR THE STARS

If there is no

struggle, there

is no progress.

Frederick Douglass

THE STARRY NIGHT   1889   Vincent van Gogh
Oil on canvas, 29 x 35 1/4 inches (73.3 x 92.1 cm).
Collection of The Museum of Modern Art, New
York. Acquired through the Lillie B. Bliss Bequest.
Photograph © 1992 The Museum of Modern Art,
New York.

Driven by Dreams

Stars have always inspired people to dream, to stretch beyond themselves. We "reach for a star" when we set a high goal or fight a good fight, when we let our imagination soar or tap hidden strengths. There are billions of real stars, but none are as bright as the stars we create for ourselves with our dreams and goals.

In *Driven by Dreams,* you will read about dreamers of all kinds, from a boy fighting for glory to a woman who worked for people who had no one else to speak for them. Their struggles to achieve their dreams may inspire you to work hard to achieve your own dreams.

Fiction

The Smallest Dragonboy

ANNE McCAFFREY

Examine What You Know

Think about a time when you wanted something so much that you could hardly think about anything else. What did you desire? What obstacles were in your way? In your journal or notebook, describe the situation.

Expand Your Knowledge

The main character of this story, which takes place on the imaginary planet Pern, has his heart set on becoming a dragonrider. The dragonriders of Pern are brave warriors who ride fire-breathing dragons to protect their planet from deadly plant spores. These spores, called Thread because of their shape, fall from the sky on regular occasions. If Thread are allowed to reach Pern's soil, they will destroy all living things.

Newborn dragons, hatched from huge eggs, choose their young riders through a silent communication known as Impression. An Impression allows a dragon and its rider to read each other's mind, thus creating a lifelong partnership based on trust and love.

The people of Pern live in cave colonies called *weyrs*. This particular story takes place in Benden Weyr, a colony of dragonriders located in the Benden Mountains of Pern.

Enrich Your Reading

Fantasy This story is a **fantasy**, a story set in an imaginary world in which characters wish for things that are impossible in the real world. As you read, you will be presented with detailed information about life on Pern. At various places, you will find questions to help you review this information. Keep in mind that you do not have to understand all the details to enjoy the story.

■ *Author biography on Extend page*

The Smallest Dragonboy

ANNE McCAFFREY

Although Keevan lengthened his walking stride as far as his legs would stretch, he couldn't quite keep up with the other candidates. He knew he would be teased again.

Just as he knew many other things that his foster mother told him he ought not to know, Keevan knew that Beterli, the most senior of the boys, set that spanking pace just to embarrass him, the smallest dragonboy. Keevan would arrive, tail fork-end of the group, breathless, chest heaving, and maybe get a stern look from the instructing wingsecond.

Dragonriders, even if they were still only hopeful candidates for the glowing eggs which were hardening on the hot sands of the Hatching Ground cavern, were expected to be punctual and prepared. Sloth was not tolerated by the weyrleader of Benden Weyr. A good record was especially important now. It was very near hatching time, when the baby dragons would crack their mottled[1] shells and stagger forth to choose their lifetime companions. The very thought of that glorious moment made Keevan's breath catch in his throat. To be chosen—to be a dragonrider! To sit astride the neck of the winged beast with the jeweled eyes; to

be his friend in telepathic communion[2] with him for life; to be his companion in good times and fighting extremes; to fly effortlessly over the lands of Pern! Or, thrillingly, *between* to any point anywhere on the world! Flying *between* was done on dragonback or not at all, and it was dangerous.

Keevan glanced upward, past the black mouths of the weyr caves in which grown dragons and their chosen riders lived, toward the Star Stones that crowned the ridge of the old volcano that was Benden Weyr. On the height, the blue watch-dragon, his rider mounted on his neck, stretched the great transparent pinions[3] that carried him on the winds of Pern to fight the evil Thread that fell at certain times from the sky. The many-faceted rainbow jewels of his eyes glistened momentarily in the greeny sun. He folded his great wings to his back, and the watch-pair resumed their statuesque pose of alertness.

Then the enticing view was obscured as Keevan passed into the Hatching Ground

---

1. mottled (mät′ 'ld): spotted or streaked with different colors.
2. telepathic communion: a close relationship in which ideas and feelings are communicated between two minds without talking.
3. pinions (pin′ yənz): wings.

Words to Know and Use

sloth (slōth) *n.* laziness
obscured (əb skyoord′) *adj.* hidden from view   **obscure** *v.*

PANORAMA OF MACHU PICCHU   1978   Susan Shatter   Private collection, Courtesy, Fischbach Gallery, New York.

cavern. The sands underfoot were hot, even through heavy wher-hide boots. How the boot maker had protested having to sew so small! Keevan was forced to wonder again why being small was reprehensible.[4] People were always calling him "babe" and shooing him away as being "too small" or "too young" for this or that. Keevan was constantly working, twice as hard as any other boy his age, to prove himself capable. What if his muscles weren't as big as Beterli's? They were just as hard. And if he couldn't overpower anyone in a wrestling match, he could outdistance everyone in a footrace.

"Maybe if you run fast enough," Beterli had jeered on the occasion when Keevan had been goaded to boast of his swiftness, "you could catch a dragon. That's the only way you'll make a dragonrider!"

"You just wait and see, Beterli, you just wait," Keevan had replied. He would have liked to wipe the contemptuous smile from Beterli's face, but the guy didn't fight fair even when the wingsecond was watching. "No one knows what Impresses a dragon!"

"They've got to be able to *find* you first, babe!"

Yes, being the smallest candidate was not an enviable position. It was therefore imperative that Keevan Impress a dragon in his first hatching. That would wipe the smile off every face in the cavern and accord him the respect due any dragonrider, even the smallest one.

Besides, no one knew exactly what Impressed the baby dragons as they struggled from their shells in search of their lifetime partners.

---

4. **reprehensible:** deserving of blame; bad.

Words to Know and Use

contemptuous (kən temp′ cho͞o əs) *adj.* lacking respect; scornful
imperative (im per′ ə tiv) *adj.* absolutely necessary

253

"I like to believe that dragons see into a man's heart," Keevan's foster mother, Mende, told him. "If they find goodness, honesty, a flexible mind, patience, courage—and you've that in quantity, dear Keevan—that's what dragons look for. I've seen many a well-grown lad left standing on the sands, Hatching Day, in favor of someone not so strong or tall or handsome. And if my memory serves me" (which it usually did—Mende knew every word of every Harper's tale worth telling, although Keevan did not interrupt her to say so), "I don't believe that F'lar, our weyrleader, was all that tall when bronze Mnementh chose him. And Mnementh was the only bronze dragon of that hatching."

Dreams of Impressing a bronze were beyond Keevan's boldest reflections, although that goal dominated the thoughts of every other hopeful candidate. Green dragons were small and fast and more numerous. There was more prestige to Impressing a blue or a brown than a green. Being practical, Keevan seldom dreamed as high as a big fighting brown, like Canth, F'nor's fine fellow, the biggest brown on all Pern. But to fly a bronze? Bronzes were almost as big as the queen, and only they took the air when a queen flew at mating time. A bronze rider could aspire to become weyrleader! Well, Keevan would console himself, brown riders could aspire to become wingseconds, and that wasn't bad. He'd even settle for a green dragon; they were small, but so was he. No matter! He simply had to Impress a dragon his first time in the Hatching Ground. Then no one in the weyr would taunt him anymore for being so small.

"Shells," thought Keevan now, "but the sands are hot!"

"Impression time is imminent,[5] candidates," the wingsecond was saying as everyone crowded respectfully close to him. "See the extent of the striations on this promising egg." The stretch marks *were* larger than yesterday.

Everyone leaned forward and nodded thoughtfully. That particular egg was the one Beterli had marked as his own, and no other candidate dared, on pain of being beaten by Beterli on the first opportunity, to approach it. The egg was marked by a large yellowish splotch in the shape of a dragon backwinging to land, talons outstretched to grasp rock. Everyone knew that bronze eggs bore distinctive markings. And naturally, Beterli, who'd been presented at eight Impressions already and was the biggest of the candidates, had chosen it.

Some of you may be disappointed on the great day.

"I'd say that the great opening day is almost upon us," the wingsecond went on, and then his face assumed a grave expression. "As we well know, there are only forty eggs and seventy-two candidates. Some of you may be disappointed on the great day. That doesn't necessarily mean you aren't dragonrider material, just that *the* dragon for

---

5. **imminent:** about to happen.

you hasn't been shelled. You'll have other hatchings, and it's no disgrace to be left behind an Impression or two. Or more."

Keevan was positive that the wing-second's eyes rested on Beterli, who'd been stood off at so many Impressions already. Keevan tried to squinch down so the wingsecond wouldn't notice him. Keevan had been reminded too often that he was eligible to be a candidate by one day only. He, of all the hopefuls, was most likely to be left standing on the great day. One more reason why he simply had to Impress at his first hatching.

review

Why is Keevan afraid that he won't Impress a dragon?

"Now move about among the eggs," the wingsecond said. "Touch them. We don't know that it does any good, but it certainly doesn't do any harm."

Some of the boys laughed nervously, but everyone immediately began to circulate among the eggs. Beterli stepped up officiously to "his" egg, daring anyone to come near it. Keevan smiled, because he had already touched it . . . every inspection day . . . as the others were leaving the Hatching Ground, when no one could see him crouch and stroke it.

Keevan had an egg he concentrated on, too, one drawn slightly to the far side of the others. The shell bore a soft greenish-blue tinge with a faint creamy swirl design. The consensus was that this egg contained a mere green, so Keevan was rarely bothered by rivals. He was somewhat perturbed then to see Beterli wandering over to him.

"I don't know why you're allowed in this Impression, Keevan. There are enough of us without a babe," Beterli said, shaking his head.

"I'm of age." Keevan kept his voice level, telling himself not to be bothered by mere words.

"Yah!" Beterli made a show of standing on his toe tips. "You can't even see over an egg. Hatching Day, you better get in front or the dragons won't see you at all. 'Course, you could get run down that way in the mad scramble. Oh, I forget, you can run fast, can't you?"

"You'd better make sure a dragon sees *you* this time, Beterli," Keevan replied. "You're almost overage, aren't you?"

Beterli flushed and took a step forward, hand half raised. Keevan stood his ground, but if Beterli advanced one more step, he would call the wingsecond. No one fought on the Hatching Ground. Surely Beterli knew that much.

Fortunately, at that moment the wingsecond called the boys together and led them from the Hatching Ground to start on evening chores.

There were "glows" to be replenished in the main kitchen caverns and sleeping cubicles, the major hallways, and the queen's apartment. Firestone sacks had to be filled against Thread attack, and black rock brought to the kitchen hearths. The boys fell to their chores, tantalized by the odors

Words to Know and Use

consensus (kən sen′ səs) *n.* an opinion shared by most; general agreement
replenished (ri plen′ ishd) *adj.* added to; resupplied **replenish** *v.*

255

THE WHITE DRAGON ©1992 Michael Whelan.

of roasting meat. The population of the weyr began to assemble for the evening meal, and the dragonriders came in from the Feeding Ground or their sweep checks.

It was the time of day Keevan liked best. Once the chores were done, before dinner was served, a fellow could often get close to the dragonriders and listen to their talk. Tonight Keevan's father, K'last, was at the main dragonrider table. It puzzled Keevan how his father, a brown rider and a tall man, could *be* his father—because he, Keevan, was

so small. It obviously never puzzled K'last when he deigned[6] to notice his small son: "In a few more turns, you'll be as tall as I am—or taller!"

K'last was pouring Benden drink all around the table. The dragonriders were relaxing. There'd be no Thread attack for three more days, and they'd be in the mood

---

6. deigned (dānd): lowered oneself to do something beneath one's dignity.

to tell tall tales, better than Harper yarns, about impossible maneuvers they'd done a-dragonback. When Thread attack was closer, their talk would change to a discussion of tactics of <u>evasion</u>, of going *between,* how long to suspend there until the burning but fragile Thread would freeze and crack and fall harmlessly off dragon and man. They would dispute the exact moment to feed firestone to the dragon so he'd have the best flame ready to sear Thread midair and render it harmless to ground—and man—below. There was such a lot to know and understand about being a dragonrider that sometimes Keevan was overwhelmed. How would he ever be able to remember everything he ought to know at the right moment? He couldn't dare ask such a question; this would only have given additional weight to the notion that he was too young yet to be a dragonrider.

"Having older candidates makes good sense," L'vel was saying, as Keevan settled down near the table. "Why waste four to five years of a dragon's fighting prime until his rider grows up enough to stand the rigors?" L'vel had Impressed a blue of Ramoth's first clutch. Most of the candidates thought L'vel was marvelous because he spoke up in front of the older riders, who awed them. "That was well enough in the Interval when you didn't need to mount the full weyr complement[7] to fight Thread. But not now. Not with more eligible candidates than ever. Let the babes wait."

"Any boy who is over twelve turns has the right to stand in the Hatching Ground," K'last replied, a slight smile on his face. He never argued or got angry. Keevan wished he were more like his father. And oh, how he wished he were a brown rider! "Only a dragon . . . each particular dragon . . . knows what he wants in a rider. We certainly can't tell. Time and again the theorists"—and K'last's smile deepened as his eyes swept those at the table—"are surprised by dragon choice. *They* never seem to make mistakes, however."

Now, K'last, just look at the roster of this Impression. Seventy-two boys and only forty eggs. Drop off the twelve youngest, and there's still a good field for the hatchlings to choose from. Shells! There are a couple of weyrlings unable to see over a wher egg, much less a dragon! And years before they can ride Thread."

"True enough, but the weyr is scarcely under fighting strength, and if the youngest Impress, they'll be old enough to fight when the oldest of our current dragons go *between* from senility."

"Half the weyrbred lads have already been through several Impressions," one of the bronze riders said then. "I'd say drop some of *them* off this time. Give the untried a chance."

"There's nothing wrong in presenting a clutch with as wide a choice as possible," said the weyrleader, who had joined the table with Lessa, the weyrwoman.

---

7. **complement:** the entire group.

Words to Know and Use | **evasion** (ē vā′ zhən) *n.* the act of avoiding or escaping from

"Has there ever been a case," she said, smiling in her odd way at the riders, "where a hatchling didn't choose?"

Her suggestion was almost heretical and drew astonished gasps from everyone, including the boys.

F'lar laughed. "You say the most outrageous things, Lessa."

"Well, *has* there ever been a case where a dragon didn't choose?"

"Can't say as I recall one," K'last replied.

"Then we continue in this tradition," Lessa said firmly, as if that ended the matter.

But it didn't. The argument ranged from one table to the other all through dinner, with some favoring a weeding out of the candidates to the most likely, lopping off those who were very young or who had had multiple opportunities to Impress. All the candidates were in a swivet,[8] though such a departure from tradition would be to the advantage of many. As the evening progressed, more riders were favoring eliminating the youngest and those who'd passed four or more Impressions unchosen. Keevan felt he could bear such a dictum[9] only if Beterli was also eliminated. But this seemed less likely than that Keevan would be tuffed out, since the weyr's need was for fighting dragons and riders.

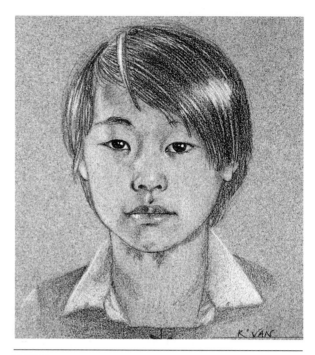

KEEVAN. Illustration by Robin Wood.

review   What are the adults arguing about?

By the time the evening meal was over, no decision had been reached, although the weyrleader had promised to give the matter due consideration.

He might have slept on the problem, but few of the candidates did. Tempers were uncertain in the sleeping caverns next morning as the boys were routed out of their beds to carry water and black rock and cover the "glows." Mende had to call Keevan to order twice for clumsiness.

"Whatever is the matter with you, boy?" she demanded in exasperation when he tipped black rock short of the bin and sooted up the hearth.

"They're going to keep me from this Impression."

"What?" Mende stared at him. "Who?"

"You heard them talking at dinner last night. They're going to tuff the babes from the hatching."

---

8. **swivet:** a state of annoyance.

9. **dictum:** a pronouncement made with authority.

Mende regarded him a moment longer before touching his arm gently. "There's lots of talk around a supper table, Keevan. And it cools as soon as the supper. I've heard the same nonsense before every hatching, but nothing is ever changed."

"There's always a first time," Keevan answered, copying one of her own phrases.

"That'll be enough of that, Keevan. Finish your job. If the clutch does hatch today, we'll need full rock bins for the feast, and you won't be around to do the filling. All my fosterlings make dragonriders."

"The first time?" Keevan was bold enough to ask as he scooted off with the rockbarrow.

Perhaps, Keevan thought later, if he hadn't been on that chore just when Beterli was also fetching black rock, things might have turned out differently. But he had dutifully trundled the barrow to the outdoor bunker for another load just as Beterli arrived on a similar errand.

"Heard the news, babe?" asked Beterli. He was grinning from ear to ear, and he put an unnecessary emphasis on the final insulting word.

"The eggs are cracking?" Keevan all but dropped the loaded shovel. Several anxieties flicked through his mind then: He was black with rock dust—would he have time to wash before donning the white tunic of candidacy? And if the eggs were hatching, why hadn't the candidates been recalled by the wingsecond?

"Naw! Guess again!" Beterli was much too pleased with himself.

With a sinking heart Keevan knew what the news must be, and he could only stare with intense desolation at the older boy.

"C'mon! Guess, babe!"

"I've no time for guessing games," Keevan managed to say with indifference. He began to shovel black rock into his barrow as fast as he could.

"I said, 'Guess.'" Beterli grabbed the shovel.

"And I said I'd no time for guessing games."

Beterli wrenched the shovel from Keevan's hands. "Guess!"

"I'll have the shovel back, Beterli." Keevan straightened up, but he didn't come up to Beterli's bulky shoulder. From somewhere, other boys appeared, some with barrows, some mysteriously alerted to the prospect of a confrontation among their numbers.

He must've been dropped from the candidacy.

"Babes don't give orders to candidates around here, babe!"

Someone sniggered, and Keevan knew, incredibly, that he must've been dropped from the candidacy.

He yanked the shovel from Beterli's loosened grasp. Snarling, the older boy tried to regain possession, but Keevan clung with all his strength to the handle, dragged back and forth as the stronger boy jerked the shovel about.

With a sudden, unexpected movement,

Words
to Know
and Use

desolation (des′ ə lā′ shən) *n.* feeling of loneliness and misery
indifference (in dif′ ər əns) *n.* a lack of interest or concern

Beterli rammed the handle into Keevan's chest, knocking him over the barrow handles. Keevan felt a sharp, painful jab behind his left ear, an unbearable pain in his right shin, and then a painless nothingness.

Mende's angry voice roused him, and startled, he tried to throw back the covers, thinking he'd overslept. But he couldn't move, so firmly was he tucked into his bed. And then the constriction of a bandage on his head and the dull sickishness in his leg brought back recent occurrences.

"Hatching?" he cried.

N o, lovey," said Mende, and her voice was suddenly very kind, her hand cool and gentle on his forehead. "Though there's some as won't be at any hatching again." Her voice took on a stern edge.

Keevan looked beyond her to see the weyrwoman, who was frowning with irritation.

"Keevan, will you tell me what occurred at the black-rock bunker?" Lessa asked, but her voice wasn't angry.

He remembered Beterli now and the quarrel over the shovel and . . . what had Mende said about some not being at any hatching? Much as he hated Beterli, he couldn't bring himself to tattle on Beterli and force him out of candidacy.

"Come, lad," and a note of impatience crept into the weyrwoman's voice. "I merely want to know what happened from you, too. Mende said she sent you for black rock. Beterli—and every weyrling in the cavern—seems to have been on the same errand. What happened?"

"Beterli took the shovel. I hadn't finished with it."

"There's more than one shovel. What did he *say* to you?"

"He'd heard the news."

"What news?" The weyrwoman was suddenly amused.

"That . . . that . . . there'd been changes."

"Is that what he said?"

"Not exactly."

"What did he say? C'mon, lad. I've heard from everyone else, you know."

"He said for me to guess the news."

"And you fell for that old gag?" The weyrwoman's irritation returned.

"Consider all the talk last night at supper, Lessa," said Mende. "Of course the boy would think he'd been eliminated."

"In effect, he is, with a broken skull and leg." She touched his arm, a rare gesture of sympathy in her. "Be that as it may, Keevan, you'll have other Impressions. Beterli will not. There are certain rules that must be observed by all candidates, and his conduct proves him unacceptable to the weyr."

She smiled at Mende and then left.

How will what happened to Keevan affect his candidacy?

"I'm still a candidate?" Keevan asked urgently.

"Well, you are and you aren't, lovey," his foster mother said. "Is the numb weed working?" she asked, and when he nodded, she said, "You just rest. I'll bring you some nice broth."

At any other time in his life, Keevan would have relished such cosseting,[10] but he lay there worrying. Beterli had been dismissed. Would the others think it was his

_____

10. **cosseting:** pampering.

fault? But everyone was there! Beterli provoked the fight. His worry increased, because although he heard excited comings and goings in the passageway, no one tweaked back the curtain across the sleeping alcove he shared with five other boys. Surely one of them would have to come in sometime. No, they were all avoiding him. And something else was wrong. Only he didn't know what.

Mende returned with broth and beachberry bread.

"Why doesn't anyone come see me, Mende? I haven't done anything wrong, have I? I didn't ask to have Beterli tuffed out."

Mende soothed him, saying everyone was busy with noontime chores and no one was mad at him. They were giving him a chance to rest in quiet. The numb weed made him drowsy, and her words were fair enough. He permitted his fears to dissipate. Until he heard the humming. It started low, too low to be heard. Rather he felt it in the broken shinbone and his sore head. And thought, at first, it was an effect of the numb weed. Then the hum grew, augmented by additional sources. Two things registered suddenly in Keevan's groggy mind: The only white candidate's robe still on the pegs in the chamber was his; and dragons hummed when a clutch was being laid or being hatched. Impression! And he was flat abed.

Bitter, bitter disappointment turned the warm broth sour in his belly. Even the small voice telling him that he'd have other opportunities failed to alleviate[11] his crushing depression. *This* was the Impression that mattered! This was his chance to show *everyone* from Mende to K'last to L'vel and even the weyrleaders that he, Keevan, was worthy of being a dragonrider.

He twisted in bed, fighting against the tears that threatened to choke him. Dragonmen don't cry! Dragonmen learn to live with pain. . . .

Pain? The leg didn't actually pain him as he rolled about on his bedding. His head felt sort of stiff from the tightness of the bandage. He sat up, an effort in itself since the numb weed made exertion difficult. He touched the splinted leg, but the knee was unhampered. He had no feeling in his bone, really. He swung himself carefully to the side of his bed and slowly stood. The room wanted to swim about him. He closed his eyes, which made the dizziness worse, and he had to clutch the bedpost.

Gingerly he took a step. The broken leg dragged. It hurt in spite of the numb weed, but what was pain to a dragonman?

No one had said he couldn't go to the Impression. "You are and you aren't," were Mende's exact words.

Clinging to the bedpost, he jerked off his bed shirt. Stretching his arm to the utmost, he jerked his white candidate's tunic from the peg. Jamming first one arm and then the other into the holes, he pulled it over his head. Too bad about the belt. He couldn't wait. He hobbled to the door, hung on to

---

11. **alleviate:** to lessen; decrease.

the curtain to steady himself. The weight on his leg was unwieldy. He'd not get very far without something to lean on. Down by the bathing pool was one of the long crook-necked poles used to retrieve clothes from the hot washing troughs. But it was down there, and he was on the level above. And there was no one nearby to come to his aid. Everyone would be in the Hatching Ground right now, eagerly waiting for the first egg to crack.

The humming increased in volume and tempo, an urgency to which Keevan responded, knowing that his time was all too limited if he was to join the ranks of the hopeful boys standing about the cracking eggs. But if he hurried down the ramp, he'd fall flat on his face.

He could, of course, go flat on his rear end, the way crawling children did. He sat down, the jar sending a stab of pain through his leg and up to the wound on the back of his head. Gritting his teeth and blinking away the tears, Keevan scrabbled down the ramp. He had to wait a moment at the bottom to catch his breath. He got to one knee, the injured leg straight out in front of him. Somehow he managed to push himself erect, though the room wanted to tip over his ears. It wasn't far to the crooked stick, but it seemed an age before he had it in his hand.

*T*hen the humming stopped!

Then the humming stopped!
Keevan cried out and began to hobble frantically across the cavern, out to the bowl of the weyr. Never had the distance between the living caverns and the Hatching Ground seemed so great. Never had the weyr been so silent, breathless. As if the multitude of people and dragons watching the hatching held every breath in suspense. Not even the wind muttered down the steep sides of the bowl. The only sounds to break the stillness were Keevan's ragged breathing and the thump-thud of his stick on the hard-packed ground. Sometimes he had to hop twice on his good leg to maintain his balance. Twice he fell into the sand and had to pull himself up on the stick, his white tunic no longer spotless. Once he jarred himself so badly he couldn't get up immediately.

Then he heard the first exhalation of the crowd, the ooohs, the muted cheer, the susurrus[12] of excited whispers. An egg had cracked, and the dragon had chosen his rider. Desperation increased Keevan's hobble. Would he never reach the arching mouth of the Hatching Ground?

Another cheer and an excited spate of applause spurred Keevan to greater effort. If he didn't get there in moments, there'd be no unpaired hatchling left. Then he was actually staggering into the Hatching Ground, the sands hot on his bare feet.

No one noticed his entrance or his halting progress. And Keevan could see nothing but the backs of the white-robed candidates, seventy of them ringing the area around the eggs. Then one side would surge forward or back, and there'd be a cheer. Another dragon had been Impressed. Suddenly a large gap appeared in the white human wall, and Keevan had his first sight of the eggs. There didn't seem to be *any* left uncracked, and he

---

12. susurrus (sə sŭr′ əs): a murmuring or rustling sound.

could see the lucky boys standing beside wobble-legged dragons. He could hear the unmistakable plaintive crooning of hatchlings and their squawks of protest as they'd fall awkwardly in the sand.

Suddenly he wished that he hadn't left his bed, that he'd stayed away from the Hatching Ground. Now everyone would see his ignominious[13] failure. He scrambled now as desperately to reach the shadowy walls of the Hatching Ground as he had struggled to cross the bowl. He mustn't be seen.

He didn't notice, therefore, that the shifting group of boys remaining had begun to drift in his direction. The hard pace he had set himself and his cruel disappointment took their double toll on Keevan. He tripped and collapsed sobbing to the warm sands. He didn't see the consternation[14] in the watching weyrfolk above the Hatching Ground, nor did he hear the excited whispers of speculation. He didn't know that the weyrleader and weyrwoman had dropped to the arena and were making their way toward the knot of boys slowly moving in the direction of the archway.

"Never seen anything like it," the weyrleader was saying. "Only thirty-nine riders chosen. And the bronze trying to leave the Hatching Ground without making Impression!"

"A case in point of what I said last night," the weyrwoman replied, "where a hatch-

Photograph used with permission of Windstone Editions © 1988,1992. No copying permitted.

ling makes no choice because the right boy isn't there."

"There's only Beterli and K'last's young one missing. And there's a full wing of likely boys to choose from. . . ."

"None acceptable, apparently. Where is the creature going? He's not heading for the entrance after all. Oh, what have we there, in the shadows?"

Keevan heard with dismay the sound of voices nearing him. He tried to burrow into the sand. The mere thought of how he would be teased and taunted now was unbearable.

Don't worry! Please don't worry! The thought was urgent, but not his own.

Someone kicked sand over Keevan and butted roughly against him.

"Go away. Leave me alone!" he cried.

Why? was the injured-sounding question inserted into his mind. There was no voice, no tone, but the question was there, perfectly clear, in his head.

Incredulous, Keevan lifted his head and stared into the glowing jeweled eyes of a small bronze dragon. His wings were wet; the tips hung drooping to the sand. And he sagged in the middle on his unsteady legs, although he was making a great effort to keep erect.

Keevan dragged himself to his knees, oblivious[15] to the pain of his leg. He wasn't

---

13. **ignominious** (ig′ nə min′ ē əs): shameful; disgraceful.
14. **consternation:** concern; fear.
15. **oblivious:** unaware of; not paying attention to.

even aware that he was ringed by the boys passed over, while thirty-one pairs of resentful eyes watched him Impress the dragon. The weyrleaders looked on, amused and surprised at the draconic choice, which could not be forced. Could not be questioned. Could not be changed.

Why? asked the dragon again. *Don't you like me?* His eyes whirled with anxiety, and his tone was so piteous that Keevan staggered forward and threw his arms around the dragon's neck, stroking his eye ridges, patting the damp, soft hide, opening the fragile-looking wings to dry them, and assuring the hatchling wordlessly over and over again that he was the most perfect, most beautiful, most beloved dragon in the entire weyr, in all the weyrs of Pern.

"What's his name, K'van?" asked Lessa, smiling warmly at the new dragonrider. K'van stared up at her for a long moment. Lessa would know as soon as he did. Lessa was the only person who could "receive" from all dragons, not only her own Ramoth.

Then he gave her a radiant smile, recognizing the traditional shortening of his name that raised him forever to the rank of dragonrider.

My name is Heath, thought the dragon mildly and hiccuped in sudden urgency. *I'm hungry.*

"Dragons are born hungry," said Lessa, laughing. "F'lar, give the boy a hand. He can barely manage his own legs, much less a dragon's."

K'van remembered his stick and drew himself up. "We'll be just fine, thank you."

"You may be the smallest dragonrider ever, young K'van, but you're the bravest," said F'lar.

And Heath agreed! Pride and joy so leaped in both chests that K'van wondered if his heart would burst right out of his body. He looped an arm around Heath's neck, and the pair—the smallest dragonboy and the hatchling who wouldn't choose anybody else—walked out of the Hatching Ground together forever. ❧

Responding to Reading

First Impressions

1. What were your feelings during the Impression? Jot down your response in your journal or notebook.

Second Thoughts

2. How does Keevan prove himself worthy of the bronze dragon?

3. Why do you think Beterli and Keevan have such a powerful effect on each other?

4. What human qualities seem to be most valued by the people of Pern?

Think about
- what dragons look for in humans
- why Beterli is disqualified
- the difficulties and dangers of life on Pern

5. Would you like to live on Pern? Why or why not?

Broader Connections

6. People often cheer for underdogs, competitors like Keevan who are not expected to win. What other underdogs do you know about? What makes their success satisfying? How are they like Keevan?

Literary Concept: Suspense

Suspense is the excitement or tension that readers feel as they become involved in a story. Suspense is usually caused by uncertainty about what will happen next. One way writers achieve suspense is by adding complications. For example, the dinner discussion adds the complication that Keevan might be too young to be a candidate.

Work with a partner to see how McCaffrey creates suspense. Create a line graph to track the suspense. On the horizontal line, list important events in the plot, such as *"Beterli fights Keevan."* On the vertical line, make a suspense scale by listing the numbers 1 (least suspenseful) to 10 (most suspenseful). Then place a dot on the graph above each event and across from the number that shows your level of suspense. After finishing, draw a line that connects the dots. Compare your graph to others in the class.

Writing Options

1. Review the story to find rules and instructions for dragonrider candidates. Use what you find to write a **handbook** for candidates.

2. Write a **dialogue** of a talk show that has Keevan, you, and one other literary character as guests. The topic: Overcoming the obstacles to your dreams. Be sure to include your own dreams and the obstacles standing in your way.

3. Write **notes** that a reporter at the hatching ground might have made. Describe the sights and sounds of the hatching.

4. Lessa is the only character who can "receive" from all dragons. Review the story and write a **character sketch** of her. Include information about her job, her powers, and her personality.

Vocabulary Practice

Exercise   On your paper, write the vocabulary word that most closely matches the meaning of the boldfaced word or phrase in each sentence.

1. To **renew** the food supply of the dragons takes hard work.

2. It is **essential** that Thread be stopped from destroying Pern.

3. **Avoidance** is difficult when Thread falls from the sky.

4. Dragonrider candidates must avoid **laziness.**

5. The dragonriders did not reach an **agreement** during their dinner discussion.

6. Beterli showed a **disrespectful** attitude toward Keevan.

7. Keevan tried to show his **lack of concern** about the dinner discussion.

8. The morning mist could **hide** the view of the Hatching Ground.

9. The crowd of candidates will **scatter** after the last hatching.

10. Beterli probably felt **great sadness** when he realized he would not be a candidate.

Words to Know and Use

consensus
contemptuous
desolation
dissipate
evasion
imperative
indifference
obscure
replenish
sloth

Options for Learning

1 • A Book by Its Cover Design an eye-catching bookcover for "The Smallest Dragonboy." Your cover should include a front and back side, as well as inside flaps that summarize the story and the author's life.

2 • Pern Tour Guide Create a glossary of Pern terms from the story to help first-time visitors. You might use one of the many reference books about Pern, such as *The Dragonlover's Guide to Pern,* by Jody Lynn Nye with Anne McCaffrey, to help you. Make up definitions and create illustrations to help visitors.

3 • Thread Alert Scan some of McCaffrey's Pern novels to find a description of a Thread attack. Then draw an illustration or give an oral report to describe the event.

4 • Dragon, Dragon Find a myth, folk tale, or legend from another country about dragons, and retell the story to your class. Describe the dragons so that your classmates can compare them to the dragons in Pern.

 FACT FINDER MATHEMATICS

In the hatching described in the story, what percentage of the candidates Impressed dragons?

Anne McCaffrey
1926—

The inspiration for "The Smallest Dragonboy" came from Anne McCaffrey's brother, Kevin. When Kevin was twelve, a bone disease forced him to keep his arm in a painful cast. His bravery inspired his sister to write about a boy who overcomes pain.

McCaffrey writes her novels and short stories at Dragonhold, her name for her home in County Wicklow, Ireland. Born in Cambridge, Massachusetts, McCaffrey's writing career began in the United States, where she has spent most of her life.

Nicknamed "the Dragon Lady" by fans, her best-known books are *Dragonflight, Dragonsong,* and *Dragonsinger.* These stories are set in Pern, a world with its own history, geography, and culture.

McCaffrey tries to give all her books a scientific basis. While writing, she talks to experts in many areas. McCaffrey is the first woman to have won a Hugo Award for science fiction.

She encourages "anyone to write—to dream up their own special world—as an escape or an exercise in imagination."

Poetry

Wishes

GEORGIA DOUGLAS
JOHNSON

Dream Deferred

LANGSTON HUGHES

Formula

ANA MARIA IZA

Examine What You Know

Daydreams can be pleasant fantasies, wishes for a better life, or ways of setting goals. What types of daydreams do you have? Complete a spider word web like the one below. Name some of your daydreams on the spider's "legs." On the lines coming out of the legs, write details about your dreams.

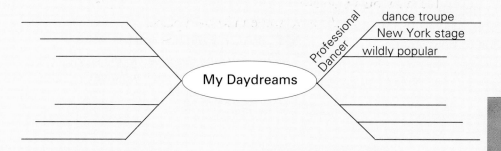

dance troupe
New York stage
wildly popular

Professional Dancer

My Daydreams

Expand Your Knowledge

Daydreams are the key to the three poems you will read next. Psychologists say that daydreams are important for mental health. Daydreams offer harmless ways of expressing wishes, fears, and hopes. They release tension and relieve boredom. They are also a way of rehearsing for the future.

Enrich Your Reading

Understanding Poetry You may not understand everything in these poems all at once. The meanings are hinted at, not stated directly. Your imagination will help you follow those hints. As you read, let ideas and images freely surface in your mind. Look for **imagery,** or language that appeals to the senses, and **figurative language,** or language that describes things in new ways. Be ready to see, hear, and feel things the way the poet wants you to imagine them.

■ *Author biographies in Reader's Handbook*

Wishes

GEORGIA DOUGLAS JOHNSON

I'm tired of pacing the petty round of the ring of the thing I know—
I want to stand on the daylight's edge and see where the sunsets go.

I want to sail on a swallow's tail and peep through the sky's blue glass.
I want to see if the dreams in me shall perish or come to pass.

5 I want to look through the moon's pale crook and gaze on the moon-man's face.
I want to keep all the tears I weep and sail to some unknown place.

*R*esponding to Reading

First Impressions of "Wishes"

1. What images came to mind as you read this poem? Describe them briefly in your journal or notebook.

Second Thoughts on "Wishes"

2. What do the wishes in the poem reveal about the speaker and her dreams?

3. Are the wishes expressed in the poem anything like your own daydreams? Explain.

4. The **mood** of a poem is the feeling it creates in the reader. How would you describe the mood of this poem? Cite lines or phrases that help establish the mood.

Dream Deferred

LANGSTON HUGHES

What happens to a dream deferred:
Does it dry up
like a raisin in the sun?
Or fester like a sore—
5 And then run?
Does it stink like rotten meat?
Or crust and sugar over—
like a syrupy sweet?

Maybe it just sags
10 like a heavy load.

Or does it explode?

*R*esponding to Reading

First Impressions of "Dream Deferred"

1. What are you left thinking about at the end of this poem?

Second Thoughts on "Dream Deferred"

2. What does the phrase "dream deferred" mean to you? Give examples of your own or someone else's deferred dreams.

3. What do you think is the **theme** of the poem?

   Think about
   • the kinds of comparisons that are made throughout the poem
   • the emphasis given to the last line

Formula

ANA MARIA IZA
Translated by Ron Connally

To dream,
you don't have to ask permission,
nor cry out,
nor humble yourself,
5   nor put on lipstick;
it's enough to close your eyes halfway
and feel distant.
Perhaps the night dreams
that it is no longer night;
10   the fish, that they are boats;
the boats, fish;
the water, crystal.
To dream . . .
is a simple thing;
15   it doesn't cost a cent,
you need only to turn your back
on the hours that pass
and cover over pain,
your ears,
20   your eyes
and stay so,
stay . . .
until we are awakened
by a blow upon the soul.

RECLINING WOMAN   1978   Will Barnet © 1992
Will Barnet/VAGA New York.

Responding to Reading

First Impressions of "Formula"

1. How did this poem affect you? Jot down your thoughts.

Second Thoughts on "Formula"

2. Do you think the ending of the poem is hopeful, sad, or something else? Explain.

3. What is your opinion of the speaker's formula for dreaming?

Comparing the Poems

4. Which poem meant the most to you or came the closest to describing your own dreams? Explain.

5. How do the moods of the three poems differ? Give evidence from each poem to support your answer.

Literary Concept: Imagery

You know that **imagery** is language that appeals to the senses. Most images are visual; they create mental pictures in the reader's mind. "Wishes," for example, describes a desire "to sail on a swallow's tail," causing readers to picture a swallow in flight. Other images appeal to senses of touch, smell, taste, or sound. In order to see how poets use imagery, create a chart listing the five senses. Then find images in the three poems to fill in as much of the chart as you can. Some images may appeal to two senses.

Concept Review: Simile   Find two similes in "Dream Deferred."

Writing Options

1. You described some of your dreams before you read. Now write a **poem** about your dreams. Choose a form that best fits your ideas and feelings.

2. Find a poem that fits the theme of "Driven by Dreams." Copy it and write a **thematic connection,** or an explanation of why the poem fits the theme.

Nonfiction

Eleanor Roosevelt

WILLIAM JAY JACOBS

Examine What You Know

You may know that Eleanor Roosevelt was the wife of the United States' thirty-second President, Franklin Delano Roosevelt. She was also one of the most famous American women of this century. What do you know about these two famous people? Share your knowledge in a class discussion.

Expand Your Knowledge

As you will learn, Eleanor Roosevelt was much more than the wife of a president. Her life spanned a period of dramatic changes in the United States and the world. The time line below shows some events that occurred during her lifetime.

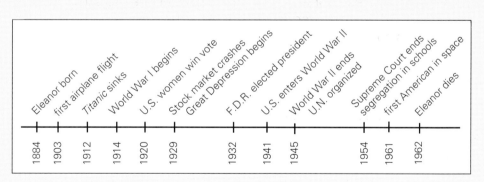

Eleanor born — 1884
first airplane flight — 1903
Titanic sinks — 1912
World War I begins — 1914
U.S. women win vote — 1920
Stock market crashes / Great Depression begins — 1929
F.D.R. elected president — 1932
U.S. enters World War II — 1941
World War II ends / U.N. organized — 1945
Supreme Court ends segregation in schools — 1954
first American in space — 1961
Eleanor dies — 1962

Write Before You Read

Many people become involved in political and social issues because, like Eleanor Roosevelt, they dream of a better world. What issues do you care about? What dreams do you have for your community, your nation, or the world? List these issues and dreams in your notebook or journal.

■ *Author biography on Extend page*

Eleanor Roosevelt

WILLIAM JAY JACOBS

Eleanor Roosevelt was the wife of President Franklin Delano Roosevelt. But Eleanor was much more than just a president's wife, an echo of her husband's career.

Sad and lonely as a child, Eleanor was called "Granny" by her mother because of her seriousness. People teased her about her looks and called her the "ugly duckling." . . .

Yet despite all of the disappointments, the bitterness, the misery she experienced, Eleanor Roosevelt refused to give up. Instead she turned her unhappiness and pain to strength. She devoted her life to helping others. Today she is remembered as one of America's greatest women.

Eleanor was born in a fine townhouse in Manhattan. Her family also owned an elegant mansion along the Hudson River, where they spent weekends and summers. As a child Eleanor went to fashionable parties. A servant took care of her and taught her to speak French. Her mother, the beautiful Anna Hall Roosevelt, wore magnificent jewels and fine clothing. Her father, Elliott Roosevelt, had his own hunting lodge and liked to sail and to play tennis and polo. Elliott, who loved Eleanor dearly, was the younger brother of Theodore Roosevelt, who in 1901 became President of the United States. The Roosevelt family, one of America's oldest, wealthiest families, was respected and admired.

To the outside world it might have seemed that Eleanor had everything that any child could want—everything that could make her happy. But she was not happy. Instead her childhood was very sad.

Almost from the day of her birth, October 11, 1884, people noticed that she was an unattractive child. As she grew older, she could not help but notice her mother's extraordinary beauty, as well as the beauty of her aunts and cousins. Eleanor

Photo of Eleanor Roosevelt's family: *left*, brothers Elliott and Hall; *center*, Eleanor's father; *right*, Eleanor at age six.
UPI/Bettmann.

was plain looking, ordinary, even, as some called her, homely. For a time she had to wear a bulky brace on her back to straighten her crooked spine.

Her parents had wanted a boy.

When Eleanor was born, her parents had wanted a boy. They were scarcely able to hide their disappointment. Later, with the arrival of two boys, Elliott and Hall, Eleanor watched her mother hold the boys on her lap and lovingly stroke their hair, while for Eleanor there seemed only coolness, distance.

Feeling unwanted, Eleanor became shy and withdrawn. She also developed many fears. She was afraid of the dark, afraid of animals, afraid of other children, afraid of being scolded, afraid of strangers, afraid that people would not like her. She was a frightened, lonely little girl.

The one joy in the early years of her life was her father, who always seemed to care for her, love her. He used to dance with her, to pick her up and throw her into the air while she laughed and laughed. He called her "little golden hair" or "darling little Nell."

Then, when she was six, her father left. An alcoholic, he went to live in a sanitarium[1] in Virginia in an attempt to deal with his drinking problem. Eleanor missed him greatly.

Next her mother became ill with painful headaches. Sometimes for hours at a time, Eleanor would sit holding her mother's head in her lap and stroking her forehead. Nothing else seemed to relieve the pain. At those times Eleanor often remembered how her mother had teased her about her looks and called her "Granny." But even at the age of seven, Eleanor was glad to be helping someone, glad to be needed—and noticed.

The next year, when Eleanor was eight, her mother, the beautiful Anna, died. Afterward her brother Elliott suddenly caught diphtheria[2] and he, too, died. Eleanor and her baby brother, Hall, were taken to live with their grandmother in Manhattan.

A few months later another tragedy struck. Elliott Roosevelt, Eleanor's father, also died. Within eighteen months Eleanor had lost her mother, a brother, and her dear father. . . .

Few things in life came easily for Eleanor, but the first few years after her father's death proved exceptionally hard. Grandmother Hall's dark and gloomy townhouse had no place for children to play. The family ate meals in silence. Every morning Eleanor and Hall were expected to take cold baths for their health. Eleanor had to work at better posture by walking with her arms behind her back, clamped over a walking stick.

Instead of making new friends, Eleanor often sat alone in her room and read. For many months after her father's death, she pretended that he was still alive. She made him the hero of stories she wrote for school. Sometimes, alone and unhappy, she just cried.

Some of her few moments of happiness came from visiting her uncle, Theodore

---

1. **sanitarium:** an institution for the care of people with a specific disease or other health problem.
2. **diphtheria** (dif thir′ ē ə): a serious infectious disease.

Roosevelt, in Oyster Bay, Long Island. A visit with Uncle Ted meant playing games and romping outdoors with the many Roosevelt children.

Once Uncle Ted threw her into the water to teach her how to swim, but when she started to sink, he had to rescue her. Often he would read to the children old Norse tales and poetry. It was at Sagamore Hill, Uncle Ted's home, that Eleanor first learned how much fun it could be to read books aloud.

For most of the time, Eleanor's life was grim. Although her parents had left plenty of money for her upbringing, she had only two dresses to wear to school. Once she spilled ink on one of them, and since the other was in the wash, she had to wear the dress with large ink stains on it to school the next day. It was not that Grandmother Hall was stingy. Rather, she was old and often confused. Nor did she show much warmth or love for Eleanor and her brother. Usually she just neglected them.

Just before Eleanor turned fifteen, Grandmother Hall decided to send her to boarding school in England. The school she chose was Allenswood, a private academy for girls located on the outskirts of London.

It was at Allenswood that Eleanor, still thinking of herself as an "ugly duckling," first dared to believe that one day she might be able to become a swan.

At Allenswood she worked to toughen herself physically. Every day she did exercises in the morning and took a cold shower. Although she did not like competitive team sports, as a matter of self-discipline she tried out for field hockey. Not only did she make the team but, because she played so hard, also won the respect of her teammates.

They called her by her family nickname, "Totty," and showed their affection for her by putting books and flowers in her room, as was the custom at Allenswood. Never before had she experienced the pleasure of having schoolmates actually admire her rather than tease her.

At Allenswood, too, she began to look after her health. She finally broke the habit of chewing her fingernails. She learned to eat nutritious foods, to get plenty of sleep, and to take a brisk walk every morning, no matter how miserable the weather. . . .

Eleanor was growing up, and the joy of young womanhood had begun to transform her personality.

In 1902, nearly eighteen years old, she left Allenswood, not returning for her fourth year there. Grandmother Hall insisted that, instead, she must be introduced to society as a debutante—to go to dances and parties and begin to take her place in the social world with other wealthy young women.

Away from Allenswood, Eleanor's old uncertainty about her looks came back again. She saw herself as too tall, too thin, too plain. She worried about her buckteeth, which she thought made her look horselike. The old teasing began again, especially on the part of Uncle Ted's daughter, "Princess" Alice Roosevelt, who seemed to take pleasure in making Eleanor feel uncomfortable.

Eleanor, as always, did as she was told. She went to all of the parties and dances. But she also began working with poor children at the Rivington Street Settlement House on New York's Lower East Side. She taught the girls gymnastic exercises. She took children to museums and to musical performances. She tried to get the parents interested in politics in order to get better schools and cleaner, safer streets.

Meanwhile, Eleanor's life reached a turning point. She fell in love! The young man was her fifth cousin, Franklin Delano Roosevelt.

Eleanor and Franklin had known each other since childhood. Franklin recalled how once he had carried her piggyback in the nursery. When she was fourteen, he had danced with her at a party. Then, shortly after her return from Allenswood, they had met by chance on a train. They talked and almost at once realized how much they liked each other.

For a time they met secretly. Then they attended parties together. Franklin—tall, strong, handsome—saw her as a person he could trust. He knew that she would not try to dominate him.

But did he really love her? Would he always? She wrote to him, quoting a poem she knew: "'Unless you can swear, *For life, for death!*' Oh, never call it loving!'"

Franklin promised that his love was indeed "for life," and Eleanor agreed to marry him. It was the autumn of 1903. He was twenty-one. She was nineteen.

On March 17, 1905, Eleanor and Franklin were married. "Uncle Ted," by then President of the United States, was there to "give the bride away."...

In May 1906 the couple's first child was born. During the next nine years Eleanor gave birth to five more babies, one of whom died in infancy. Still timid, shy, afraid of making mistakes, she found herself so busy that there was little time to think of her own drawbacks.

Still, looking back later on the early years of her marriage, Eleanor knew that she should have been a stronger person, especially in the handling of Franklin's mother, or, as they both called her, "Mamma." Too often Mamma made the decisions about such things as where they would live, how their home would be furnished, how the children would be disciplined. Eleanor and Franklin let her pay for things they could not afford—extra servants, vacations, doctor bills, clothing. She offered, and they accepted.

Before long, trouble developed in the relationship between Eleanor and Franklin. Serious, shy, easily embarrassed, Eleanor could not share Franklin's interests in golf and tennis. He enjoyed light talk and flirting with women. She could not be lighthearted. So she stayed on the sidelines. Instead of losing her temper, she bottled up her anger and did not talk to him at all. As he used to say, she "clammed up." Her silence only made things worse, because it puzzled him. Faced with her coldness, her brooding silence, he only grew angrier and more distant.

Meanwhile, Franklin's career in politics advanced rapidly. In 1910 he was elected to the New York State Senate. In 1913 President Wilson appointed him Assistant Secretary of the Navy—a powerful position in the national government, which required the Roosevelts to move to Washington, D.C.

In 1917 the United States entered World War I as an active combatant. Like many socially prominent women, Eleanor threw

---

Words to Know and Use

brooding (brōod′ iŋ) *adj.* full of worry; troubled **brood** *v.*
combatant (kəm bat′ 'nt) *n.* fighter
prominent (präm′ ə nənt) *adj.* well-known; widely recognized

277

herself into the war effort. Sometimes she worked fifteen or sixteen hours a day. She made sandwiches for soldiers passing through the nation's capital. She knitted sweaters. She used Franklin's influence to get the Red Cross to build a recreation room for soldiers who had been shell-shocked in combat. . . .

In 1920 the Democratic Party chose Franklin as its candidate for Vice-President of the United States. Even though the Republicans won the election, Roosevelt became a well-known figure in national politics. All the time, Eleanor stood by his side, smiling, doing what was expected of her as a candidate's wife.

She did what was expected—and much more—in the summer of 1921 when disaster struck the Roosevelt family. While on vacation Franklin suddenly fell ill with infantile paralysis—polio—the horrible disease that each year used to kill or cripple thousands of children, and many adults as well. When Franklin became a victim of polio, nobody knew what caused the disease or how to cure it.

Franklin lived, but the lower part of his body remained paralyzed. For the rest of his life, he never again had the use of his legs. He had to be lifted and carried from place to place. He had to wear heavy steel braces from his waist to the heels of his shoes.

His mother, as well as many of his advisers, urged him to give up politics, to live the life of a country gentleman on the Roosevelt estate at Hyde Park, New York. This time, Eleanor, calm and strong, stood up for her ideas. She argued that he should not be treated like a sick person, tucked away in

Franklin Delano Roosevelt reading victory telegram on election night, November 1932. © N.Y. Daily News, used by permission.

the country, inactive, just waiting for death to come.

Franklin agreed. Slowly he recovered his health. His energy returned. In 1928 he was elected governor of New York. Then, just four years later, he was elected President of the United States.

Meanwhile, Eleanor had changed. To keep Franklin in the public eye while he was recovering, she had gotten involved in politics herself. It was, she thought, her "duty." From childhood she had been taught "to do the thing that has to be done, the way it has to be done, when it has to be done."

With the help of Franklin's adviser Louis Howe, she made fund-raising speeches for the Democratic Party all around New York State. She helped in the work of the League of Women Voters, the Consumer's League, and the Foreign Policy Association. After becoming interested in the problems of working women, she gave time to the Women's Trade Union League (WTUL).

It was through the WTUL that she met a group of remarkable women—women doing exciting work that made a difference in the world. They taught Eleanor about life in the slums. They awakened her hopes that something could be done to improve the condition of the poor. She dropped out of the "fashionable" society of her wealthy friends and joined the world of reform—social change.

For hours at a time, Eleanor and her reformer friends talked with Franklin. They showed him the need for new laws: laws to get children out of the factories and into schools; laws to cut down the long hours that women worked; laws to get fair wages for all workers.

By the time that Franklin was sworn in as president, the nation was facing its deepest depression. One out of every four Americans was out of work, out of hope. At mealtimes people stood in lines in front of soup kitchens for something to eat. . . .

Eleanor worked in the charity kitchens, ladling out soup. She visited slums. She crisscrossed the country learning about the suffering of coal miners, shipyard workers, migrant farm workers, students, housewives—Americans caught up in the paralysis of the Great Depression. Since Franklin himself remained crippled, she became his eyes and ears, informing him of what the American people were really thinking and feeling.

Eleanor also was the president's conscience, personally urging on him some of the most compassionate, forward-looking laws of his presidency, including, for example, the National Youth Administration (NYA), which provided money to allow impoverished young people to stay in school.

She lectured widely, wrote a regularly syndicated[3] newspaper column, "My Day," and spoke frequently on the radio. She fought for equal pay for women in industry. Like no other First Lady up to that time, she became a link between the president and the American public.

Above all she fought against racial and religious prejudice. When Eleanor learned that the DAR (Daughters of the American Revolution) would not allow the great black singer Marian Anderson to perform in their auditorium in Washington, D.C., she resigned from the organization. Then she arranged to have Miss Anderson sing in front of the Lincoln Memorial.

Similarly, when she entered a hall where, as often happened in those days, blacks and whites were seated in separate sections, she made it a point to sit with the blacks. Her example marked an important step in making the rights of blacks a matter of national priority.

---

3. **syndicated:** sold to many newspapers for publication.

Words to Know and Use	**compassionate** (kəm pash′ ən it) *adj.* showing concern or sympathy **priority** (prī ôr′ ə tē) *n.* something that must receive attention first

On December 7, 1941, Japanese forces launched a surprise attack on the American naval base at Pearl Harbor, Hawaii, as well as on other American installations in the Pacific. The United States entered World War II, fighting not only against Japan but against the brutal dictators who then controlled Germany and Italy.

Eleanor helped the Red Cross raise money. She gave blood, sold war bonds. But she also did the unexpected. In 1943, for example, she visited barracks and hospitals on islands throughout the South Pacific. When she visited a hospital, she stopped at every bed. To each soldier she said something special, something that a mother might say. Often, after she left, even battle-hardened men had tears in their eyes. Admiral Nimitz, who originally thought such visits would be a nuisance, became one of her strongest admirers. Nobody else, he said, had done so much to help raise the spirits of the men.

By spring 1945 the end of the war in Europe seemed near. Then, on April 12, a phone call brought Eleanor the news that Franklin Roosevelt, who had gone to Warm Springs, Georgia, for a rest, was dead. . . .

After Franklin's funeral, every day that Eleanor was home at Hyde Park, without fail, she placed flowers on his grave. Then she would stand very still beside him there.

With Franklin dead, Eleanor Roosevelt might have dropped out of the public eye, might have been remembered in the history books only as a footnote to the president's program of social reforms. Instead she found new strengths within herself, new ways to live a useful, interesting life—and to help others. Now, moreover, her successes were her own, not the result of being the president's wife.

In December 1945 President Harry S Truman invited her to be one of the American delegates going to London to begin the work of the United Nations. Eleanor hesitated, but the president insisted. He said that the nation needed her; it was her duty. After that, Eleanor agreed.

In the beginning some of her fellow delegates from the United States considered her unqualified for the position, but after seeing her in action, they changed their minds.

It was Eleanor Roosevelt who, almost single-handedly, pushed through the United Nations General Assembly a resolution giving refugees from World War II the right *not* to return to their native lands if they did not wish to. . . .

Next Mrs. Roosevelt helped draft the United Nations Declaration of Human Rights. The Soviets wanted the declaration to list the duties people owed to their countries. Again Eleanor insisted that the United Nations should stand for individual freedom—the rights of people to free speech, freedom of religion, and such human needs as health care and education. In December 1948, with the Soviet Union and its allies refusing to vote, the Declaration of Human Rights won approval of the UN General Assembly by a vote of forty-eight to zero.

Even after retiring from her post at the UN, Mrs. Roosevelt continued to travel. In places around the world she dined with presidents and kings. But she also visited tenement slums[4] in Bombay, India; factories

---

4. **tenement slums:** parts of a city where poor people live in crowded, shabby buildings.

Eleanor Roosevelt reading to children during a picnic at Hyde Park, New York, July 1952. AP/Wide World Photos.

in Yugoslavia; farms in Lebanon and Israel.

Everywhere, she met people who were eager to greet her. Although as a child she had been brought up to be formal and distant, she had grown to feel at ease with people. They wanted to touch her, to hug her, to kiss her.

Eleanor's doctor had been telling her to slow down, but that was hard for her. She continued to write her newspaper column, "My Day," and to appear on television. She still began working at seven-thirty in the morning and often continued until well past midnight. . . .

Gradually, however, she was forced to withdraw from some of her activities, to spend more time at home.

On November 7, 1962, at the age of seventy-eight, Eleanor died in her sleep. She was buried in the rose garden at Hyde Park, alongside her husband.

Adlai Stevenson, the American ambassador to the United Nations, remembered her as "the First Lady of the World," as the person—male or female—most effective in working for the cause of human rights. As Stevenson declared, "She would rather light a candle than curse the darkness."

And perhaps, in sum, that is what the struggle for human rights is all about. 🕊

from The Autobiography of Eleanor Roosevelt

ELEANOR ROOSEVELT

In the beginning, because I felt, as only a young girl can feel it, all the pain of being an ugly duckling, I was not only timid, I was afraid. Afraid of almost everything, I think: of mice, of the dark, of imaginary dangers, of my own inadequacy. My chief objective, as a girl, was to do my duty. This had been drilled into me as far back as I could remember. Not my duty as I saw it, but my duty as laid down for me by other people. It never occurred to me to revolt. Anyhow, my one overwhelming need in those days was to be approved, to be loved, and I did whatever was required of me, hoping it would bring me nearer to the approval and love I so much wanted.

As a young woman, my sense of duty remained as strict and rigid as it had been when I was a girl, but it had changed its focus. My husband and my children became the center of my life, and their needs were my new duty. I am afraid now that I approached this new obligation much as I had my childhood duties. I was still timid, still afraid of doing something wrong, of making mistakes, of not living up to the standards required by my mother-in-law, of failing to do what was expected of me.

As a result, I was so hidebound by duty that I became too critical, too much of a disciplinarian. I was so concerned with bringing up my children properly that I was not wise enough just to love them. Now, looking back, I think I would rather spoil a child a little and have more fun out of it.

It was not until I reached middle age that I had the courage to develop interests of my own, outside of my duties to my family. In the beginning, it seems to me now, I had no goal beyond the interests themselves, in learning about people and conditions and the world outside our own United States. Almost at once I began to discover that interest leads to interest, knowledge leads to more knowledge, the capacity for understanding grows with the effort to understand.

From that time on, though I have had many problems, though I have known the grief and the loneliness that are the lot of most human beings, though I have had to make and still have to make endless adjustments, I have never been bored, never found the days long enough for the range of activities with which I wanted to fill them. And, having learned to stare down fear, I long ago reached the point where there is no living person whom I fear, and few challenges that I am not willing to face.

Responding to Reading

First Impressions

1. What words and phrases would you use to describe Eleanor Roosevelt? Record them in your journal or notebook.

Second Thoughts

2. Which feelings or experiences from Eleanor's childhood are similar to your own?

3. Which of Eleanor Roosevelt's accomplishments do you find most impressive? Why?

4. Why do you think Eleanor was able to overcome her fears?

> **Think about**
> * her feelings about herself
> * her goals and values
> * what she says in her autobiography

5. Do you think Eleanor's strong sense of duty helped or hurt her? Explain.

Broader Connections

6. Think about the organizations and issues Eleanor Roosevelt worked for during her lifetime. If she were alive today, which national and world issues would concern her? Explain your answer.

Literary Concept: Biography

A **biography** is the story of a person's life, written by another person. Biographies can vary in style. Some biographies are carefully balanced, showing both the strengths and the weaknesses of the subject. Other biographies are more one-sided, either praising the subject or finding fault. How would you describe the style of Jacobs's biography? What details in the selection support your ideas?

Concept Review: Conflict   Name the most important conflicts Eleanor faced, both external and internal.

Writing Options

1. Write an **advice column** from Eleanor Roosevelt to a teenager who wants to overcome a lack of self-confidence. Use examples from her own life in your letter.

2. Write a **summary** of what you learned about Eleanor Roosevelt in this selection. At the end of your summary, list three things you would like to know more about.

3. Eleanor called herself "the President's conscience." Look back at the list you made of your own dreams for a better world. Decide which issue Eleanor would care about most, and then write the **conversation** she might have with her husband about solving that problem.

4. Write a **job description** of Eleanor's role as First Lady. Describe her activities and responsibilities.

Vocabulary Practice

Exercise   On your paper, respond to each of the following questions.

1. Would Eleanor have preferred to be called **compassionate** or **prominent?** Why?

2. Were comfort and relaxation a main **priority** in Eleanor's life? How can you tell?

3. Can Eleanor be considered a **combatant** for social justice? Why or why not?

4. Would wounded soldiers enjoy talking to a **brooding** visitor? Why or why not?

5. Which two adjectives from the vocabulary list describe personality traits?

*Words
to Know
and Use*

**brooding
combatant
compassionate
priority
prominent**

*O*ptions for Learning

1 • The Time of Her Life Make a collage to create a visual impression of Eleanor Roosevelt's life. Look through biographies of Eleanor and through newspapers and magazines of her time. Pick out photographs, drawings, cartoons, advertisements, and other visual items. Make copies of what you find and use them for your collage. Display your work in your classroom.

2 • In Her Footsteps Eleanor Roosevelt has been a role model for many women. Conduct a panel discussion about whether or not she should be a role model for women today. The panelists should represent a variety of viewpoints.

3 • Battle of the First Ladies Research the wife of a president who served after Franklin Roosevelt. Compare and contrast this First Lady with Eleanor Roosevelt. Make a poster that shows similarities and differences to share with your class.

4 • The Hot Seat Eleanor Roosevelt was extremely controversial in her day. With a classmate, act out an interview with her. Prepare questions ahead of time that reflect the split in public opinion about her actions. If needed, research the answers. The interview should capture Eleanor's personality and beliefs.

 FACT FINDER HISTORY

During what years was Eleanor Roosevelt a delegate to the United Nations General Assembly?

*W*illiam Jay Jacobs
1933

Jacobs's admiration for Eleanor Roosevelt goes back a long way. "As a child, Franklin Roosevelt was my hero, my model of personal courage. Like Roosevelt, I had polio. . . . The more I learned about Eleanor Roosevelt, the more I saw her as a woman of courage. She turned her pain to strength." Jacobs believes young people need historical role models who faced tests and persisted.

Jacobs has written many biographies for young people, including biographies of Hernando Cortes, Edgar Allan Poe, Abraham Lincoln, and Winston Churchill. His book *Mother, Aunt Susan and Me: The First Fight for Women's Rights* won several awards.

In addition to being a writer, Jacobs has taught history and social studies since 1975 in the Darien, Connecticut, public schools. Before then, he taught at several colleges and universities.

WORKSHOP

INFORMATIVE WRITING

USE INFORMATIVE
WRITING FOR

news articles
magazine articles
summaries
job descriptions
reports
comparison-contrast
 papers
essays

This subunit is full of dreamers, both imaginary and real. Your own experience tells you how powerful dreams can be. In this workshop you'll write a magazine article about a real person who has pursued a dream. You'll use **informative writing,** or writing that explains facts. Yet you'll also use your creativity to help you choose facts that create the impression you want. With creative choices, you can show how well you understand a person driven by dreams.

Here is one writer's PASSkey
to this assignment.

GUIDED ASSIGNMENT:
MAGAZINE ARTICLE

Write a magazine article about a person who has pursued a dream.

PURPOSE: To inform

AUDIENCE: Classmates and other students

SUBJECT: A person who pursued a dream

STRUCTURE: A magazine article

STUDENT MODEL

The opening hooks readers' curiosity.

> ### A Winner
> ### by Liz Herrera
>
>   At school track meets, you can always pick out Irene Grainge. She's the one who sets her starting blocks by bending down so low that her nose touches the track. She's not goofing around. She's trying to find the right distance from the starting line to set the blocks. "I'm not blind," Irene jokes. "I just can't see."
>   Irene was born with an incurable eye disease. Her vision was almost gone by the time she was ten. On eye charts, she can read only the big E. She can see colors and shapes, but she can't make out details unless they're right in front of her nose. Still, she's dreamed of competing as a runner since she was five and watched her first Olympics on television.

The writer clearly states Irene's dream.

When Irene wanted to go out for track, the gym teachers thought she shouldn't. Irene didn't argue. Instead, she had her brother walk her around the track so that she could get her bearings. Then she started running laps. Every lunch period, before she ate, she ran. Sometimes a friend ran with her. Often Irene ran alone. She didn't miss a day. After two months the coach gave in and let her enter a meet.

Now Irene competes in the fifty-yard dash, the hundred-yard dash, and the four-hundred-meter relay. She's also practicing for the hurdles. Each day, repeating "Step, step, step, jump" to herself, she clears a row of barriers she can hardly see.

So far, Irene has never placed first in an event. However, she's never placed below third either. Her personal best gets a little better at each meet. People sometimes make fun of her when she puts her face against the blocks. She doesn't mind. "I'm doing what I love," she says. "I just feel lucky." To those who don't know her, Irene's actions may look weird. To those who know her, she looks like a winner.

◄ Irene's story is told in chronological order.

◄ Facts and figures help readers understand.

◄ The writer includes a quote from Irene.

◄ The writer's opinion appears only briefly, at the end.

Prewrite and Explore

1 **Find the dreamers** Try brainstorming about dreamers you've known. For example, you may know someone who has started a wildlife shelter or helped a troubled child. You might also ask an older relative to tell you about dreamers in your family. You may know of politicians, entertainers, or sports figures who have been inspired by dreams. List as many names as you can think of. Remember, your article need not be about someone famous—or even about someone who succeeds. With dreams, it's the trying that matters most.

2 **Get ready to roll** Scan your list of dreamers for the one you'd like to focus on. Then you can use the ideas on the next page to gather facts for your article.

NEED MORE IDEAS?
Try flipping through magazines and newspapers. Look for stories about people you admire.

◄ **ASK FOR HELP**
Want a good source of facts about famous people? Ask a librarian to help you find a biographical dictionary.

IN OTHER CLASSES
A similar list of
questions based on
what you know can
help you gather
information for reports
in science and social
studies.

STUDENT MODEL

GATHERING INFORMATION

You might review your own memories, ask to look through your subject's scrapbooks, or interview your subject or someone close to him or her. Using a list of questions will help. (If your subject is a famous person you can't contact, a list of questions can guide your research in magazines and books.) What questions you use will depend on what you already know and what you think will interest your readers. Notice how Liz used a list to develop her questions for an interview.

<u>Who is my subject? What is he or she like?</u>
Irene: upbeat, fast runner, determined. Vision problems—not sure what they are. Ask Irene for details.

<u>What is the dream? How did it start?</u>
Dream: to run track. Don't know how it started. Ask Irene.

<u>How has the person pursued it?</u>
On track team, but joined late. Why? Ask.

<u>What obstacles have come up, and how has the person handled them?</u>
Obstacle: can't see how far to set starting blocks, so she scrunches down so close her nose touches. Others? Ask.

<u>What has the dream meant to the subject?</u>
<u>What does it mean to me?</u>
To me: I admire her. She works a lot, doesn't get much glory. I think she's a hero for trying. To her? Ask how she feels about it.

TIPS FOR INTERVIEWS
• Ask permission
beforehand to tape or
take notes.
• Tell the person what
you know—but listen
more than you talk.
• Share your responses
as you listen.
• If the person starts a
new topic, follow it.
You can always come
back to your list.

3 Get the scoop You might use written notes, audiotape, or videotape to record an interview. Be sure to record the date and the place of the interview too. If you use written sources, take notes. Include titles, authors, and page numbers in your notes so that you can check back easily if you need to.

Draft and Discover

1 Jump in Don't worry yet about an introduction. It's fine to start in the middle. You'll find a lot to say if you start with the part of the person's story that impresses you most. For example, you might start by describing the person's response to a tough obstacle. Then see where your writing leads. Be sure to write in the third person (*she, he,* or *they*), not in the first person (*I* or *we*).

2 Use your notes When you run out of words, go back to your notes or tapes. Use them to fill in details you forgot and to remind you of other areas you want to cover. Because this is informative writing, you need to downplay your opinions and focus on facts. Load your draft with details, figures, and specifics. To make your writing even more authentic, use quotes from your subject.

◀ **GRAMMAR TIP**
Use pronouns carefully. Word your sentences so that it's always clear who's being discussed.

Revise Your Writing

1 Shape and smooth it At this point your draft is probably in sections. Now you can choose a means of organization. You might tell the person's story in chronological order or start at the present and work backward. You might describe the dream, then explain how the person pursued it, and finally explain what the pursuit has meant to the dreamer. Transitions like *at first, now, later,* and *in 1990* can help you join sections smoothly.

2 Add a hook After your article has taken shape, look again at the beginning. Try adding an unusual statement, a catchy quote, or a vivid description. Then use the revision questions below.

Revision Questions

For You	For a Peer Reader
1. Have I made the dream as clear as possible?	**1.** Which part of my article holds your attention best?
2. Would more facts or figures make my article more specific?	**2.** Were you ever unsure who was being talked about?
3. Does my opinion appear only at the end if at all?	**3.** How would you sum up this person's dream?

Proofread

Proofread carefully, and correct any errors in grammar, spelling, capitalization, and punctuation. Watch for run-ons.

COMPUTER TIP

To catch run-ons in your writing, scroll backwards. Read each sentence aloud, starting at the bottom of the screen and working up.

NEED MORE HELP?

See the Language Workshop on pages 291–293 and pages 718–720 of the Language Handbook.

THE EDITOR'S EYE: RUN-ON SENTENCES

Avoid run-on sentences—two or more sentences written incorrectly as one.

Two complete sentences must be separated with a period. When you forget the period, the result is a run-on sentence. You can catch run-ons easily when you proofread. To repair them, end each sentence with a period, and begin each with a capital letter.

Problem	Often Irene ran alone she didn't miss a day.
Revised	Often Irene ran alone. She didn't miss a day.

Publish and Present

Here is a class project that will let you share your work with others.

A Magazine of Dreamers   Combine the class's articles into a magazine. Choose a title, and design a cover that indicates what's inside. Each student might be responsible for supplying photos or drawings for his or her article and for choosing one or two lines of the article to highlight in large type, as in published magazines.

Reflect on Your Writing

Write brief answers to the questions below. Put your answers in your portfolio with your article.

FOR YOUR PORTFOLIO ▶

1. Now that you have written this article, do you admire the person more or less? Why?
2. As you wrote about someone else's dream, what insights did you gain about your own dreams?

LANGUAGE WORKSHOP

AVOIDING FRAGMENTS AND RUN-ONS

A group of words that is only part of a sentence is a **sentence fragment**. A **run-on sentence** is two or more sentences written incorrectly as one.

Sentence Fragments

When you're deeply involved in *what* you're writing, you may pay less attention to *how* you're writing. You may not notice that you're writing fragments instead of sentences.

When we talk, sentence fragments are natural, so in written dialogue or drama, fragments are fine. Fragments are also acceptable in journals, since personal writing is like talking. In other kinds of writing, however, fragments leave readers guessing.

You know that a complete sentence has two main parts: a subject and a predicate. To repair a fragment, first decide what's missing. Then add the missing part.

Fragment	Elliott Roosevelt's only daughter. (What about his only daughter? The predicate is missing.)
Sentence	Elliott Roosevelt's only daughter was born in 1884.
Fragment	Had many fears. (Who had many fears? The subject is missing.)
Sentence	Young Eleanor Roosevelt had many fears.
Fragment	Feeling homely and shy. (Who did what while feeling homely and shy? Both subject and predicate are missing.)
Sentence	Feeling homely and shy, Eleanor became withdrawn.

Notice that words ending in *-ing* are not necessarily verbs. An *-ing* word is part of a verb only when used with a form of *to be* (*is, was, has been, could be*, and so forth).

PROOFREADING TIP ....

The proofreading stage is a good time to catch fragments. A peer editor may be able to spot them more easily than you can.

REMINDER ....

The **predicate** tells what the subject *does* or *is*.

Exercise 1 Concept Check   Write *S* for each complete sentence. Write *F* for each fragment. Then add words to make each fragment a sentence.

1. The article about Eleanor Roosevelt.
2. Was born into a wealthy family.
3. Noticing her mother's coldness toward her.
4. She feared the dark.
5. Was married at nineteen and raised five children.
6. An illness paralyzed her husband's legs.
7. Learning about human rights.
8. Eleanor blossomed.
9. A powerful public speaker.
10. Continued to help the world's needy people.

BREAKING THE RULES

Exercise 2 Looking at Style   Professional writers sometimes use fragments on purpose. For example, in "The Smallest Dragonboy" (page 251), Anne McCaffrey writes that leaders were surprised at one baby dragon's choice, which could not be forced. Then she adds, "Could not be questioned. Could not be changed."

1. Explain why the two word groups quoted are fragments. Which part is missing? How would you make each a complete sentence?
2. How would McCaffrey's paragraph sound if the two fragments were complete sentences?
3. Find two other examples of fragments in "The Smallest Dragonboy." Why do you think a professional like McCaffrey would choose to use these fragments?

Run-on Sentences

   Like fragments, run-on sentences can occur when you're more involved with ideas than with form. In one kind of run-on, sentences are strung together with no punctuation. In another kind, sentences are joined with only a comma; this error is called a **comma splice.** To repair run-ons, end each complete sentence with a period. Then start the next sentence with a capital letter.

SAY IT ALOUD

Reading your work aloud may help you spot run-on sentences. Notice where you pause to end each complete thought. Have you placed a period there?

Run-on	Eleanor had to wear a back brace her mother teased her by calling her Granny.
Run-on	Eleanor had to wear a back brace, her mother teased her by calling her Granny.
Correct	Eleanor had to wear a back brace. Her mother teased her by calling her Granny.

Exercise 3   Concept Check   On your paper, correct these run-ons.

1. Elliott Roosevelt was the younger brother of Theodore Roosevelt, Elliott loved his daughter Eleanor dearly.

2. As a child, Eleanor lived in luxury she was taught French and cared for by servants.

3. When Eleanor was only eight her mother died then within eighteen months her father and brother died too.

4. Eleanor made her first real friends at an English boarding school, they called her Totty and admired her spirit.

5. At eighteen Eleanor began working to help children in New York slums about this time she and Franklin Roosevelt fell in love.

6. Franklin entered politics, in 1920 he ran for vice-president.

7. After several years an illness left Franklin unable to walk, then Eleanor entered politics herself.

8. Franklin was elected president in 1932, Eleanor traveled around the country seeing the effects of poverty and prejudice.

9. She learned of the need for social change she also convinced Franklin to work for change.

10. In 1945 Eleanor Roosevelt was made a delegate to the United Nations there she continued to fight for human rights.

Exercise 4   Proofreading Skill   Working in small groups, correct each fragment and each run-on in the following paragraph.

◀ HINT
. . . .
Try having one group member read the paragraph aloud.

Eleanor Roosevelt saw the world change in amazing ways during her lifetime. Born just over a hundred years ago. She was nineteen when the Wright brothers flew the first airplane at Kitty Hawk, she was seventy-six when Alan Shepard became the first American in space. She saw the beginning and the end of both world wars. The tragedies of the Great Depression. The victory of the Supreme Court decision against segregation. Eleanor's own life was another kind of victory. She overcame her own sorrows and fears she became a tireless fighter for human rights.

LANGUAGE HANDBOOK
. . . .
For review and practice: Section 2, Understanding Sentences, pages 717–720.

Exercise 5   Revising Your Writing   Proofread the article you wrote for the Writer's Workshop on pages 286–290. Correct any fragments and run-ons you find. Then do the same with the other pieces in your portfolio.

SKIMMING AND SCANNING

When you read to find information, skimming and scanning can help. These techniques make both research and studying easier.

Skimming is reading quickly to find the main idea or to get an overview. When you skim, you read only the title, the headings, the words in special type, and the first sentence of each paragraph. You also take time to read charts, graphs, and time lines.

Scanning is searching for a particular fact or definition. When you scan, your eyes sweep across a page, looking for key words that may lead you to the information you want.

You can use a folded piece of paper to train yourself to scan. Choose a textbook page you've already read. Put the edge of the folded paper below the first line of the page. Then move the paper quickly down the page. Look for a fact you know is there. When you come to key words about the fact, remove the paper. Read that section more slowly to find what you need.

Exercise   Follow these directions step by step.

Step 1   Try skimming the first two pages of "The Noble Experiment" (pages 144–145). What are three things that especially stand out? Write your answers on your paper.

Step 2   Using a folded piece of paper, scan the excerpt from Eleanor Roosevelt's autobiography on page 282. Search for an answer to the following question:

How did Eleanor Roosevelt feel about spoiling children?

Write your answer.

Step 3   Skim the excerpt from Eleanor Roosevelt's autobiography, reading the first sentence of each paragraph. Then write a sentence summing up the main idea of the excerpt.

IN OTHER CLASSES

Before you start reading a science or social studies chapter, skim it to get the big picture.

TEST-TAKING TIP

In open-book tests, scan your book for specific facts or figures.

TEST-TAKING TIP

Take a minute to skim a test before you start it. The overview will help you decide how much time to spend on each part.

FIGHT TO THE FINISH

An Olympic runner refuses to give up, despite her twisted ankle, and she hobbles to the finish line. A child fighting a deadly disease greets visitors with a smile. An old soldier boldly leads a charge from which he may never return.

Some people never quit. When the challenge is greatest, they dig deep within themselves for courage or grit. They stretch their powers, whether mental or physical, to the limit. They put everything on the line.

As you read these selections, look for the qualities that enable these characters to fight to the finish. Think about how you would handle the dangers and difficulties they face.

Fiction

Old Sly Eye
RUSSELL GORDON CARTER

Examine What You Know

Have you ever been in a situation where you had nothing to count on but your own resources? Perhaps it was some sort of emergency or danger. Maybe you had to face someone or something at school. In a class discussion, describe a time when you or someone you've heard of or read about faced a great difficulty all alone. How did you or the other person react? What lessons might have been learned from the experience?

Expand Your Knowledge

Self-reliance was a necessary quality for the early settlers of the American colonies. They, like the main **character** in the following story, struggled to gather or grow enough to eat and to survive the killing cold of New England winters. Because they faced the constant threat of Indian raids, wild animals, and war with the French, most settlers, including young boys, kept their guns close at hand, even while eating or attending church.

Enrich Your Reading

Problem Solving   The conflict in a story is usually a problem or a set of related problems that the characters must solve. The main character of this story, Alben, must face a very dangerous series of problems all by himself. As you read or when you finish, identify Alben's problems and solutions by making a chart like the one started below. You can then evaluate Alben's problem-solving abilities and understand how the conflict is resolved.

Problem	Solution
Alben hears loud noises in the barn.	He goes to investigate.

■ *Author biography in Reader's Handbook*

Old Sly Eye

RUSSELL GORDON CARTER

It was a May evening in the year 1675. Alone in his father's log house on the northern edge of Dover township in the province of New Hampshire, Alben Hastings lit the lantern and opened his worn copy of *The Pilgrim's Progress*. Suddenly a loud commotion sounded in the direction of the barn—mad squeals and frightened bellowings and the hollow thudding of hoofs. Leaping erect, he seized his musket and, lantern in hand, went racing outside.

He was within a dozen yards of the barn, the wind singing in his ears, when the moon rolled from beneath a formation of ragged clouds, and he checked himself abruptly. There beside the shed lay the recently born calf, and over it crouched a big catlike creature, its solitary eye gleaming, its great round tufted tail weaving savagely to and fro—a panther.

Dropping the lantern, Alben raised the musket and fired, only to see the creature leap sidewise, apparently unhurt. The next instant it swept past him and vanished in the deep shadows.

The boy clenched his teeth. "Old Sly Eye!" he muttered angrily, and his thoughts went swiftly back to the morning two weeks earlier when his father had set forth with Mr. Stephen Wainright on a prolonged trapping expedition beyond the Piscataqua.

"Yes, my lad," John Hastings had said then, "I know how much you would like to come along, but 'tis your duty to stay behind and look after your mother and sister. And mind ye keep a good watch over the livestock! I wouldn't want to come home and find Old Sly Eye had done to us what he's done to others."

Alben strode to where the calf was lying. It wasn't his fault that Old Sly Eye had somehow managed to break into the barn, for his father himself had said the barn was reasonably secure against varmints. The calf lay motionless—there was no question that it was dead. Within the barn the cow and the two oxen were still stamping about and letting out occasional bellows, but the boy was not so much concerned with them; they were safe and unhurt.

As Alben continued to stare at the calf, he thought of other plunderings within the township—cattle and swine slain by the big one-eyed panther that often killed for the mere sake of killing. Ever since the previous autumn, Old Sly Eye had eluded the bullets and traps of the angry settlers—and tonight

Words to Know and Use

abruptly (ə brupt′ lē) *adv.* suddenly
elude (ē lōōd′) *v.* to avoid or get away from by being sly or quick

297

BLACK HOUSE   1984   Jennifer Bartlett   The St. Louis Art Museum, Purchase: Eliza McMillan Purchase Fund.

he, Alben Hastings, had had an easy shot at close range and had failed to bring the beast down!

Well, regrets wouldn't help. Since the calf was dead, it would serve as food, and therefore the thing for him to do was to hang it on a tree or against the barn, high enough so that nothing could get at it. At the cabin—up in the loft where he and his father were accustomed to sleep—there was a coil of rope he could use. Returning to the lantern, which had gone out, he picked it up and started at a slow walk for the house.

In the south, silver-edged clouds were racing past the moon. He wondered what the hour might be. Perhaps his mother and Rebecca would soon be coming home from the Wainright cabin, a mile or so to the west. They had gone over to help care for old Mrs. Wainright, who had fallen and broken a leg.

The door to the log house was swinging and creaking on its hinges, and as he shouldered his way inside, the wind caught it and thrust it shut behind him. Striding to the fireplace, he groped for the powder horn and bag of shot on the high mantel and reloaded the musket.

On the frontier a loaded musket sometimes meant the difference between life and

death. After he had set it down, resting the muzzle against the wall, he crossed the hard-packed earthen floor to the ladder leading to the loft. It would be as black as midnight up there, but there was no need to bother with flint and steel.[1] He knew exactly where the rope was hanging.

With quick, sure steps he started up the ladder, but as his hands closed on the top rung, he felt his heart tighten and his throat go suddenly dry. Something was in the loft—something heavy enough to cause the boards to creak! He was about to back downward when there was a snarl and a rush of padded feet, and the next instant a heavy body thudded against his shoulder and then hurtled past him, knocking the ladder violently sidewise. With a desperate lunge Alben clutched at the edge of the loft, and for several seconds after the ladder had crashed to the floor, he clung there, his legs dangling. Then he succeeded in swinging himself upward.

Old Sly Eye! Crouching on the edge of the high platform, Alben felt the tumultuous pounding of his heart as he stared downward into blackness. The panther was over near the door; he could hear it crooning and snarling. He could hear the occasional thump and swish of its long, heavy tail against the wall. Presently it moved, and he had a partial glimpse of it in a narrow band of moonlight slanting through the opening in the shutter across the south window. He saw its solitary gleaming eye, the other lost perhaps in an encounter with another panther. Then it vanished again in the blackness, and now he could hear it going around and around the room, hissing and muttering, and making other catlike sounds deep within its throat.

Why had Old Sly Eye entered the house? Alben asked himself the question while he was groping about for something with which to defend himself. Was it in hope of finding another victim? Panthers as a rule kept away from humans, yet Old Sly Eye was no ordinary panther. Or was it perhaps curiosity that had prompted the creature to enter the partly open door? The boy could not be sure. He knew only that the panther was down there, unable to get out, and that he himself was in danger.

The loft held no weapon or heavy object that could be used as a weapon. In his two hands he held the rope. It was a stout new half-inch Portsmouth rope, more than a score of feet long—but what good was it? As he finally tossed it aside, he thought longingly of his loaded musket down near the fireplace.

The panther continued to move here and there, now and again passing through the band of moonlight. Every little while it would snarl in a way that made Alben shiver, and once he thought he heard it sharpening its claws on one of the logs. Or was it trying to reach the loft? The logs that formed the walls were unevenly placed—it might come slithering upward. And he was utterly defenseless, lacking even a knife.

---

1. flint and steel: tools used to start a fire. Flint is a hard rock that when struck on steel produces a spark.

Words to Know and Use | **grope** (grōp) *v.* to touch or feel about in search of something

Suddenly, with a feeling of icy water cascading down his spine, he remembered his mother and sister. Why had he not thought of them before? They, perhaps more than himself, were the ones who were in danger! Even at that moment they might be approaching the house. They would open the door and then . . .

Perspiration bathed his face and neck and armpits. With cold hands clutching one of the posts, he stared downward, lips drawn tightly across his teeth. What could he do to warn them? Of course, if he should hear them coming he would shout; yet even so, Rebecca might think he was joking. He remembered with regret some of the jokes he had played in the past. But it was possible that they might reach the door before he heard them. The thought of the two of them unsuspectingly entering the cabin sent a chill through him. "I must do something!" he said to himself.

Yes, but what? He was a virtual prisoner in the loft. There were no windows, and the only way to get down was either to jump or slide down the rope secured to a post. In either case the panther would be waiting for him. Again he thought of his musket. Was there any way he could reach it, perhaps with the aid of the rope? No, the weapon was too far away.

The more he pondered, the more he became convinced that the only thing to do would be to go down the rope and then make a rush for the door. It would perhaps take three seconds to go down the rope and another three seconds to reach the door—but during that time Old Sly Eye was not likely to be sitting quietly on his haunches! Alben drew his sleeve across his moist forehead. He was strong and active, but what chance would he have in a barehanded struggle with a powerful panther? Nevertheless, there seemed no other way.

Knotting an end of the rope securely round a post, he gathered up the rest of it, ready to toss it downward. His eyes had by now grown more accustomed to the darkness, and he thought he could make out the panther directly below him. He let the rope drop, and an instant later the house resounded to a frightful scream that set his teeth to chattering. He saw the creature bound like a ghost through the band of moonlight, and then heard it snarling over near the door.

While he waited, listening, he fancied he heard distant voices, as if his mother and sister coming through the forest might be talking to each other—or was it merely the sound of the wind? Raising his own voice, he shouted, "Mother! Rebecca! Keep away, there's a panther in the house!" There was no response. He waited a minute or two and then shouted again. Still there was no response. He had the sudden unhappy feeling that perhaps no one could hear him outside the stout log house—that no matter how much he might shout, it would do no good.

The night was silent now save for occasional gusts of wind and the snarling of the panther and the thumping of its tail against the door. Supposing the door should suddenly open and Rebecca should call, "Alben,

Words to Know and Use | **ponder** (pän′ dər) *v.* to think deeply; carefully consider

are you asleep?" Then the panther would leap and strike—and then . . .

It was more than he could <u>endure</u>! He must risk his life. He mustn't remain idle another moment. But if only he had a weapon of some sort—anything, even a short stick with which he could thrust! Maybe he could find a stick. He would make another search. It would take only a few seconds.

As he was feeling about in the darkness, his hands encountered the blankets that on cold nights he and his father used for sleeping. There they were, neatly folded against the wall. With a quick exclamation he seized one and shook it out. Here was something perhaps better than a stick! The blanket was thick and heavy—at least it would protect his face.

Holding it loosely over his left arm, he seated himself on the edge of the loft, ready to descend. The panther was still over by the door, and he imagined it waiting for him, teeth bared, claws prepared to strike and to rip. Again he thought of the musket. If only he could get his hands on it!

Still holding the blanket loosely over his left arm, he started downward. His feet had hardly touched the floor when a nerve-shattering scream filled the house and a glistening body flashed toward him through the band of moonlight. Crouching, he flung the blanket out protectingly almost at the same instant the snarling panther was upon him.

Perhaps for half a minute it seemed that he and the panther and the blanket were all hopelessly entangled. He could feel the

LORD OF THE RIMROCK 1988 Leon Parson Print from National Wildlife Galleries, Fort Myers, Florida.

rough wool against his face. He could feel the weight of the creature upon him and smell the strong unpleasant odor of it. Then needlelike claws, caught in the folds of wool, were raking his back and shoulders. Lashing out with hands and feet, Alben tried desperately to free himself. A corner of the blanket covered his head. He reached upward, tore it loose, then rolled sidewise, all the while kicking and struggling.

Suddenly he was free! Rolling twice over, he sprang to his feet. The musket over there by the fireplace! Darting across the room, he snatched it up.

At that moment, above the snarls of the panther still with claws entangled in the blanket, he heard voices outside. It was not the wind; it was not his fancy—the voices

Words to Know and Use

endure (en door´) *v.* to withstand; put up with; tolerate

301

were real. With musket raised, he hesitated. Should he risk a shot in the darkness? If he were to miss, it might be fatal, not merely to himself but also to his mother and sister. No, he must not miss! Racing to the door, he flung it wide and leaped outside into the night.

His mother and Rebecca were crossing the clearing from the western edge of the woods. Catching sight of him in the moonlight, the girl shouted, "Alben, what are you doing?"

He paid no heed to her. He was half a score of yards now from the open door of the cabin, musket raised, jaws set. The seconds passed while he waited, listening to the thumping of his heart.

"Alben!" This time it was his mother. "What's wrong?"

At that moment a great tawny, glistening shape appeared in the doorway, its solitary eye gleaming. It swung its head first to the right and then to the left. It raised its voice in a prolonged scream. Then spying the boy, it came bounding forward.

A tongue of flame flashed from the musket, and the crash sent the echoes flying.

They continued to tremble across the moonlit clearing while the panther lay twitching on the grass.

Alben strode to where it was lying. Dead, he said to himself. As dead as the calf! But there were two bullet marks on the panther, one on the throat and the other on the side of the small narrow head, close to one of the rounded ears! Suddenly he understood. His first shot had not missed, after all! Probably it was that first bullet, momentarily bewildering the creature, which had caused it to seek shelter in the house.

"Alben, Alben! Oh, Alben!"

He turned to confront the others. Both were talking to him at once. "Your shirt, 'tis torn to shreds! And you are bleeding! Oh, Alben, are you badly hurt? Tell us what happened!"

He took a deep breath and then smiled. It was easy enough to smile now! "Not so very much happened," he replied slowly. "Yes, I know I'm a bit scratched an' torn, but after all, nobody could expect to fight Old Sly Eye barehanded and not get himself hurt a little!" And then while they gazed at him, wide-eyed, he told them the whole story. ❧

E X P L A I N

Responding to Reading

First Impressions

1. Do you think this story would make a good television program or movie? Share your opinion with your classmates.

Second Thoughts

2. Why do you think Alben is able to win the fight with Old Sly Eye?

Think about
- his motivation for killing the panther
- his previous training in self-reliance
- his personal qualities

3. Look back at your chart describing how Alben solves his problems. Think of other solutions he could have tried.

4. Do you think this story could have really happened? Explain.

Writing Options

1. Write a **new ending** for the story. Begin with Alben in the loft. What might he discover instead of a blanket that would change the story?

2. Write a **notice** (that might begin "Be it known to all that . . . "), to be posted in the territory, describing Alben's heroic achievement.

Vocabulary Practice

Exercise   Analogies   An **analogy** contains two pairs of related words. The second pair is related in the same way as the first pair, as in this example: TALL : SHORT; pretty : ugly. *Tall* and *short* are opposites; *pretty* and *ugly* are also opposites. In each item below, determine how the words in the first pair are related. Then decide which vocabulary word best completes the second pair.

1. QUIETLY : SILENTLY; _____ : suddenly

2. TRY : SUCCEED; _____ : seize

3. SEARCH : FIND; _____ : decide

4. NICE : PLEASANT; _____ : tolerate

5. WHISPER : SHOUT; _____ : confront

> *Words to Know and Use*
>
> **abruptly**
> **elude**
> **endure**
> **grope**
> **ponder**

Nonfiction

from Nadja on My Way

NADJA SALERNO-SONNENBERG

Examine What You Know

Competition plays a big part in almost everyone's life. With a partner, brainstorm the types of competition you and your friends experience. Then, on a chart like the one below, list the "highs" or good things about competition and also the "lows" or things you don't like.

	_____	
_____		_____
_____	Highs	_____
_____	Lows	_____
	_____	
	_____	

Expand Your Knowledge

From the time they are little, thousands of talented young people struggle to succeed in the highly competitive field of classical music. The very best of them gain acceptance to schools that specialize in the performing arts, such as the Juilliard School in New York City. There, young musicians spend years of dedication and hard work perfecting their skills. Older students audition for the right to participate in national and international competitions. Those students talented enough to win a major competition are almost guaranteed a successful international career as a concert musician.

Enrich Your Reading

Making Connections   Every reader connects with a literary work in a different way. What you like or don't like depends a great deal on how much you already know and care about a particular subject. Nadja Salerno-Sonnenberg describes her competitive spirit in this selection. As you read, think about how your feelings about competition connect with Nadja's.

■ *Author biography on Extend page*

from *Nadja on My Way*

NADJA SALERNO-SONNENBERG

Back when my mother first put the violin under my chin, I didn't just accept it because I was a wimp . . . I never listened to authority easily.

I fought my mother and I fought my teachers a lot. But I did listen to logic easily. Why would Mama want me to play the violin if it were bad for me? I trusted her love, so playing the violin must be good. . . .

Nadja holding violin. © Janette Beckman.

I never questioned why I was playing the violin. At the age of twelve, I wasn't thinking about my life. At the age of sixteen, I cared about the Yankees. I was falling in love and wondering what I should do with my hair.

A life as a musician didn't seem particularly noble at that age, but playing violin was something I could do, so I did it. The older I got, the better I got. And the better I got, the harder it would be to quit and become something useful.

During my first year of college at Juilliard, I resolved to work out my technical problems with Miss DeLay [Nadja's violin teacher]. I just took it for granted that I would keep getting better. I never thought I might reach the limit of my talent or end up not good enough to make it.

But I began to see that I hadn't even begun to work. There were college players my age and younger who could blow me out of the room. All of them were intensely ambitious about making a career, and I finally realized a career is what I wanted too. At the same time, though, I began to feel I'd come to that realization too late. . . . The big question wouldn't go away. Would I be good enough to make it? Could I make a living as a violinist? The more I thought about it, the worse things got.

A piece such as the *Carmen Fantasy* (a violin transcription[1] of Bizet's opera by Sarasate) is very hard technically. I played it easily when I didn't know how hard it was. Then I turned eighteen and thought, "My God, that piece is really difficult! How did I ever play it?"

And as I realized it was hard, I couldn't play it at all. Never mind that I played it just fine yesterday.

I started realizing how difficult it was to play thirds.[2] The lower my self-confidence sunk, the more I thought, "How did I ever do any of this before?"

By the time I was halfway through being nineteen, I couldn't play a G-major scale in tune. I was a cripple on the instrument. It got to the point where I didn't even want to hear myself play because I sounded so bad. It was torture. I stopped playing the violin for seven long months: the worst period of my life.

I couldn't play anymore, and my life was over.

I was used to success, to the prodigy label in newspapers, and now I felt like a failure. A has-been. I couldn't play anymore, and my life was over. I felt like a bum, that I should go hang out on the Bowery.[3]

I started showing up for my lesson without my fiddle. Thank God, Miss DeLay understood, and we spent the lesson time talking about music, life, and my problems.

Everything I was going through boiled down to fear. Fear of trying and failing. To measure up against all those wonderfully talented players at Juilliard, I would have to commit myself as never before. And if I disciplined myself to really work, and gave the violin my all, and *failed* . . . I would have to deal with it forever.

If you go to an audition and don't really try, if you're not really prepared, if you didn't work as hard as you could have and you don't win, you have an excuse.

"Honest," you can say, "if I had worked harder, I would have won." But nothing is harder than saying, "I gave it my all and it wasn't good enough."

Even having nothing to do with music, that's a really hard thing for anybody to face. It's very hard to give everything you have and then hear someone say, "Sorry. Do something else." . . .

Not long after I turned twenty, one week, like every week, I went to see Miss DeLay.

This time, Miss DeLay looked at me and said, "Listen, if you don't bring your violin next week, I'm throwing you out of my class."

And I laughed. I thought she and I were such good friends she would never do that.

Miss DeLay rose from the couch and, in a very calm way, said, "I'm not kidding. If

---

1. **transcription:** a musical arrangement made so a musical piece can be played on a particular instrument.
2. **thirds:** chords composed of three notes, each two degrees apart on a musical scale.
3. **Bowery:** a run-down area of New York City.

Words to Know and Use

prodigy (präd′ ə jē) *adj.* of a child with extraordinary talent or genius
audition (ô dish′ ən) *n.* a test of skill or ability, usually of a musician or actor; a tryout

you're going to waste your talent, I don't want to be part of it. This has gone on long enough."

Then she walked out of the room.

I went home in deep shock. I was petrified. Should I quit? Could I lose Miss DeLay as a teacher and friend? There was one person I could talk to, my oldest friend, Cecile Licad.

Cecile had stayed at Curtis after I left and then moved on to the Institute for Young Musicians in Vermont. But we had stayed best buddies and, over the years, had played many recitals together—from New Rochelle to Manila. Thankfully, Cecile was living nearby in New York just then, and I called her immediately.

"Cecile," I said, "what am I going to do?"

Cecile hardly ever speaks, but when she does, it's usually wise for you to listen.

There was a pause, and then she said in her wonderful gruff voice, "Don't give up."

Three words. That was it.

"Okay, Cecile. I won't."

Now I just needed to prove it.

The 1981 Walter W. Naumburg International Violin Competition was coming up in two months. I was in no shape for a competition. I hadn't touched the violin for more than half a year. I had no idea if I could touch the violin now without feeling sick. If I could even manage to get into the finals of the competition, it would be a miracle.

The winner would receive three thousand dollars and solo recitals at the Library of Congress, Lincoln Center's Alice Tully Hall, and the Ambassador Auditorium in Pasadena. There would also be performances with the Chicago Symphony, the American Symphony Orchestra in Carnegie Hall, and with orchestras in Detroit, Buffalo, Aspen, and Los Angeles.

I put my name down for the audition.

Despite all the fear, all the self-doubt, I needed to take a shot. I needed to see what I was made of.

I wanted to live. Even as an honest failure.

I wanted to live. Even as an honest failure.

From the day I signed up for the Naumburg competition, everything changed. I had made a decision to start again, to save my life, and that meant a 360-degree turnaround.

I immersed myself in practicing. An enormous amount of work had to be done in two months. I went from not practicing at all to thirteen hours a day.

My fingers were like linguine.[4] I spent two weeks just playing scales. If I thought I sounded bad before, now I sounded worse than awful.

At the time, I lived on 72nd Street, close to West End Avenue. I had an efficiency apartment with a window the size of a shoebox. I didn't do my laundry; I left my apartment only to walk to Juilliard—and not on Broadway like everyone else. I walked

---

4. **linguine** (liŋ gwē′ nē): thin, flat noodles.

*Words
to Know
and Use*

gruff (gruf) *adj.* rough and husky
immerse (im murs′) *v.* to involve oneself completely

307

up Amsterdam Avenue because I didn't want to see anybody, didn't want to bump into anybody, didn't want anyone to ask what I was doing.

I stopped going to classes and became a hermit. I even talked Miss DeLay into giving my lesson at night.

My eating habits were awful. I lived on fried sausages, a pint of peanut butter/chocolate ice cream, and a gallon of Coca-Cola every day. That's all I ate for eight weeks.

I was nuts. I was completely obsessed with getting back into shape, with doing well in this competition. If I could, people would know I was still on earth. Not to count me out; to stop asking, "Whatever happened to Nadja?"

The last week before the Naumburg auditions, I couldn't touch the violin. I had worked and worked and worked and worked, and then I just couldn't work anymore.

I certainly could have used it. I wasn't as prepared as I should have been. But I simply had to say, "Nadja, you've dedicated yourself to this thing. Ready or not, do your best."

Fifty violinists from around the world auditioned for the competition on May 25, 26, and 27, 1981. Those that made it past the preliminaries would go on to the semifinals. Those that passed that stage would go to the finals. In years past, one violinist was chosen as winner and two received second and third place.

On May 26, the day of my audition, I went to the Merkin Concert Hall at 67th Street and Broadway. I waited, played for twenty minutes, and went home. I couldn't tell whether the preliminary judges were impressed or not. I'd find out the next evening.

Maybe subconsciously I was trying to keep busy; that night, when I fried the sausages, I accidentally set my apartment on fire. I grabbed my cat and my violin and ran out the door. The fire was put out, but everything in my place was wrecked.

Fortunately, the phone was OK, and on the evening of May 27, I had the news from Lucy Rowan Mann of Naumburg. Thirteen of us had made it.

Talk about mixed emotions. I was thrilled to be among the thirteen, a group that

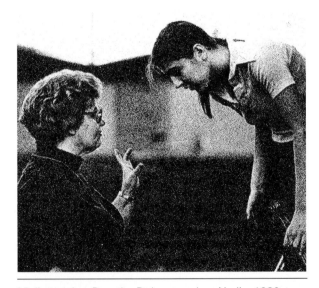

Violin teacher Dorothy DeLay coaches Nadja, 1980.
Photograph by Charles Abbott.

Words to Know and Use | **obsessed** (əb sest′) *adj.* greatly preoccupied with something **obsess** *v.*
preliminary (prē lim′ ə ner′ ē) *n.* a match or competition before the main contest; *plural*—**preliminaries**
subconsciously (sub kän′ shəs lē) *adv.* without being fully aware

included established violinists, some of whom had already made records. But it also meant I had to play the next day in the semifinals of the competition.

Everyone entering the competition had been given two lists of concertos.[5] One was a list of standard repertory[6] pieces. The other list was twentieth-century repertory. For our big competition piece, we were to choose from each list and play a movement from one in the semifinals and a movement from the other in the finals—if we made it that far.

From the standard repertory list, I chose the Tchaikovsky[7] Concerto. I had been playing the Tchaik for three years, so it was a good piece for me.

From the twentieth-century list, I chose the Prokofiev[8] G-minor Concerto. I had never played it onstage before.

My goal had been just passing the auditions, but now my thought pattern began to change. If I wanted a sliver of a chance of advancing again, my brain said, "Play your strong piece first."

Logically, I should play the Tchaikovsky in the semifinals just to make it to the next stage. Who cared if that left me with a piece I probably wouldn't play as well in the finals of the competition? It'd be a miracle to get that far.

There wouldn't be more than seven violinists chosen for the final round, and if I were in the top seven of an international group, that was plenty good enough.

The semifinals were held on May 28 in Merkin Concert Hall. You were to play for thirty minutes: your big piece first, then the judges would ask to hear another.

There was a panel of eight judges. They had a piece of paper with my choices of the Tchaikovsky and the Prokofiev in front of them. "Which would you like to play?" they asked.

I said meekly, "Prokofiev."

My brain and all the logic in the world had said play your strong piece. My heart said, "Go for it all. Play your weak piece now, save Tchaikovsky for the finals."

Maybe I don't listen to logic so easily after all.

I was so tense, I was beyond shaking.

My good friend, the pianist Sandra Rivers, had been chosen as accompanist for the competition. She knew I was nervous. There had been a very short time to prepare; I was sure there'd be memory slips, that I'd blank out in the middle and the judges would throw me out. My hands were like ice.

The first eight measures of the Prokofiev don't have accompaniment. The violin starts the piece alone. So I started playing.

I got through the first movement, and Sandra said later my face was white as snow. She said I was so tense, I was beyond shaking. Just a solid brick.

It was the best I'd ever played it. No memory slips at all. Technically, musically, it was there.

---

5. **concertos** (kən cher′ tōz): musical compositions for one or more solo instruments and an orchestra.

6. **repertory** (rep′ ər tôr′ ē): a group of musical works a musician is expected to know how to play.

7. **Tchaikovsky** (chī kôf′ skē): Peter Ilich Tchaikovsky (1840–1893), a famous Russian composer.

8. **Prokofiev** (prō kôf′ ē ef′): Sergey Prokofiev (1891–1953), a noted modern Russian composer.

I finished it thinking, "Have I sold my soul for this? Is the devil going to visit me at midnight? How come it went so well?"

I didn't know why, but often I do my best under the worst of circumstances. I don't know if it's guts or a determination not to disappoint people. Who knows what it is, but it came through for me, and I thank God for that.

As the first movement ended, the judges said, "Thank you." Then they asked for the *Carmen Fantasy.*

I turned and asked Sandy for an A, to retune, and later she said the blood was just rushing back into my face.

I whispered, "Sandy, I made it. I did it."

"Yeah," she whispered back, kiddingly, "too bad you didn't screw up. Maybe next time."

At that point I didn't care if I did make the finals because I had played the Prokofiev so well. I was so proud of myself for coming through.

I needed a shot in the arm; that afternoon I got evicted. While I was at Merkin, my moped[9] had blown up. For my landlord, that was the last straw.

What good news. I was completely broke and didn't have the next month's rent anyway. The landlord wanted me out that day. I said, "Please, can I have two days? I might get into the finals; can I please go through this first?"

I talked him into it and got back to my place in time for the phone call. "Congratulations, Nadja," they said. "You have made the finals."

I had achieved the ridiculously unlikely,

and I had saved my best piece. Yet part of me was sorry. I wanted it to be over already. In the three days from the preliminaries to the semifinals, I lost eight pounds. I was so tired of the pressure.

There was a fellow who advanced to the finals with me, an old, good friend since pre-college. Competition against friends is inevitable in music, but I never saw competition push a friendship out the window so quickly. By the day of the finals, I hated him and he hated me. Pressure was that intense.

The finals were held on May 29 at Carnegie Hall and open to the public. I was the fourth violinist of the morning, then there was a lunch break, and three more violinists in the afternoon.

I played my Tchaikovsky, Saint-Saëns's *Havanaise,* and Ravel's *Tzigane* for the judges: managers, famous violinists, teachers, and critics. I went on stage at five past eleven and finished at noon. Those fifty-five minutes seemed like three days.

I was so relieved when I finished playing; I was finished! It's impossible to say how happy I was to see the dressing room. I destroyed my gown tearing it off, changed, and went out for lunch with my friends.

It was like coming back from the grave. We laughed and joked, and I got caught up on *General Hospital.* I was calm but thrilled it was over. I made it to the finals, that's it, I'm done.

---

9. **moped** (mō′ ped′): a motorized bicycle.

Words to Know and Use	**evicted** (ē vikt′ ′d) *v.* to be forced to move from a rented house or apartment **inevitable** (in ev′ i tə bəl) *adj.* sure to happen; unavoidable

As I returned to Carnegie Hall to hear the other violinists, I realized I'd made a big mistake: they might ask for recalls. A recall is when they can't decide between two people and they want you to play again. It's been done; it's done all the time in competitions. No way was I in shape to go onstage and play again.

In the late afternoon, the competition was over. Everybody had finished playing. Quite luckily—no recalls.

The judges <u>deliberated</u> for an hour. The tension in the air was unbelievable. All the violinists were sitting with their little circle of friends. I had my few friends around me, but no one was saying much now.

Finally, the Naumburg Foundation president—founder and first violinist of the Juilliard String Quartet and that year's presenter—Robert Mann came on stage.

"It's always so difficult to choose . . ." he began.

E very year we hold this competition," Robert Mann said. "And in the past, we've awarded three prizes. This year we've elected to only have one prize, the first prize."

My heart sank. Nothing for me. Not even Miss Congeniality.

"We have found," Mann went on, "that second place usually brings great dismay to the artist because he or she feels like a loser. We don't want anyone here to feel like a loser. Every finalist will receive five hundred dollars except the winner, who will receive three thousand dollars."

And then he repeated how difficult it was to choose, how well everyone had played . . . dah, dah, dah.

I was looking down at the floor.

"The winner is . . ."

And he said my name.

A friend next to me said, "Nadja, I think you won!"

I went numb. My friends pulled me up and pointed me toward the stage. It was a long walk because I had slipped into a seat in the back.

Sitting up in front was my old friend. I would have to walk right past him and I was dreading it, but before I could, he got up and stopped me.

He threw his arms around me, and I threw my arms around him. I kept telling him how sorry I was. I was holding him and started to cry, saying, "I'm sorry, I'm sorry, I'm sorry." I didn't want to lose, but I really didn't want him to lose either. And he was holding me and saying, "Don't be sorry. I'm so proud of you." It was over, and we would be friends again.

I took my bow, then ran to Juilliard. Ten blocks uptown, one block west, to give Miss DeLay the news. She could be proud of me now, too.

Suddenly, everything was clear. Playing the violin is what I'd do with my life. Heaven handed me a prize: "You've been through a lot, kid. Here's an international competition."

Everything had changed when I prepared for the Naumburg, and now everything changed again. I bought a gown at Saks that cost as much as a season ticket at Yankee Stadium (I kept thinking I could find some-

---

Words to Know and Use | **deliberate** (di lib' ər āt') v. to carefully consider

Nadja rehearsing with conductor James Levine for a performance at The Ravinia Festival, Highland Park, Illinois, 1987.

thing as good for five dollars at a garage sale). I made my first recording—Fauré and Prokofiev sonatas with Sandra Rivers on the Musicmasters label. Between September 1981 and May 1982, I played a hundred concerts in America, made one trip to Europe, then two months of summer festivals. And people asked me back.

There was a great deal of anxiety playing in Europe for the first time. American musicians have their nationality to overcome. When you play Beethoven in Germany, no matter what, they're going to hate you. The audience has come to hear the American violinist who dares to play Beethoven.

My first time in Germany, walking onstage and feeling the vibes, I would rather have been a fire hydrant on Broadway. But I was able to rely on my self-confidence to pull me through.

Self-confidence onstage doesn't mean a lack of nerves backstage. The stakes had increased. This wasn't practice anymore; this was my life. I'd stare into a dressing-room mirror and say, "Nadja, people have bought tickets, hired baby sitters; you've got to calm down; go out there and prove yourself."

Every night I'd prove myself again. My life work had truly begun. ❧

*R*esponding to Reading

First Impressions

1. As you think about Nadja, what words or phrases come to mind? Jot them down in your journal.

Second Thoughts

2. How well does Nadja fit your image of a classical musician? Explain.

3. What were the "highs" and "lows" of Nadja's decision to compete in the Naumburg International Violin Competition?

> **Think about**
> • her lifestyle when she decided to resume playing
> • how she felt before, during, and after the competition

4. Think about how Miss DeLay handled Nadja. Would you have dealt with Nadja in the same way? Why or why not?

5. What do you think Nadja would have done if she had fought to the finish but lost the competition?

Broader Connections

6. In some middle schools, competition has been made much less important. Tryouts for teams, bands, and other activities have been eliminated. Anyone who wants to join a team or club may do so and can participate as much as anyone else. Based on Nadja's experiences and your own, do you think this is a good idea? Explain your opinion.

*L*iterary Concept: *Style*

The **style** of a piece of literature refers to the way it is written. Style does not describe *what* is said, but rather *how* it is said. Style includes sentence length, word choice, tone, use of dialogue, and imagery. Nadja's writing style is informal and conversational, as if she were talking directly to the reader. How does her style differ from that in the selections "Eleanor Roosevelt" or "Homeless"?

Concept Review: Internal Conflict Remember that internal conflict involves struggles or problems that a character faces within herself or himself. Describe Nadja's internal conflicts.

Writing Options

1. Write a short **essay** about whether you would you be willing to go through what Nadja did in order to succeed.

2. Using Nadja's experiences as a guide, compose a pep club **chant** that the Juilliard cheerleaders could shout to boost the competitive spirit of the students.

3. Imagine you are Nadja and write a **letter** to your mother explaining why you haven't picked up your violin for seven months.

4. Listen to a recording of classical violin music. Then listen to your favorite rock music recording. Write a **comparison** of the two pieces of music, including a description of the feelings both recordings give you.

Vocabulary Practice

Exercise   On your paper, write the word from the list that best completes the meaning of each sentence.

1. Because the violinist was __?__ with winning, she practiced thirteen hours a day.

2. She did not want to lose the __?__ reputation that she earned at the age of four.

3. She could play her music almost __?__, neither thinking nor looking at the notes.

4. The landlord wanted to __?__ her because of her constant practicing.

5. She was nervous before the __?__ for a position with the local symphony.

6. Before making a decision, the judges had to __?__ over her performance for an hour.

7. Finally the oldest judge, in a raspy, __?__ voice, announced that the young woman had made the finals.

8. Having passed the __?__ with flying colors, she prepared herself for the semifinals.

9. For the next week she would __?__ herself in her music.

10. Because of her talent and hard work, it seemed __?__ that she would become a violinist for a major orchestra.

Words to Know and Use

audition
deliberate
evict
gruff
immerse
inevitable
obsessed
preliminaries
prodigy
subconsciously

Options for Learning

1 • Listen to Nadja Find a recording of Nadja's music or one of the pieces she mentions in the selection. Play the recording in class, and discuss your feelings about the music with classmates.

2 • Emotional Performance When Nadja performs, she throws herself completely into her work; her face mirrors what she feels as she plays. Look through magazines for pictures of performers, whether they are in music, sports, chess, or other fields. Find pictures that show extreme emotions. Copy the pictures and create a collage, which you can title and share with your class.

3 • Competitor Talk Interview artists, athletes, or others who compete regularly. Before the interview, prepare a list of questions for the competitors. Tape your interviews, summarize your findings, and play interesting segments as part of an oral report on the subject of competition.

4 • Make a Mandala In art, a mandala is a circular design containing images that are intended to be a symbol for a person, idea, or place. Make a mandala showing Nadja's personality. You may make the mandala flat, using paints and other colors, or three-dimensional, by gluing on objects that represent Nadja's personality.

 FACT FINDER MUSIC

Who was Antonio Stradivari and what was his biggest contribution to music?

Nadja Salerno-Sonnenberg
1961–

Although Nadja was born in Rome, her family moved to New Jersey when she was eight so that she could study at the nearby Curtis Institute of Music in Philadelphia. Although she and her mother were abandoned by both her natural father and stepfather, Nadja says that her mother kept prodding her to play the violin. "I studied the violin because I was forced to. I'm naturally lazy—not disciplined at all. So my mother made me practice." Since winning the Naumburg Competition in 1981, she has played with many of the major orchestras of the world including the Chicago, New York, and London symphonies.

Nadja is known as a rebel with an unusual style. When she plays, instead of a traditional black dress, she wears purple or electric blue pants, a blouse, and boots. During her performances she makes faces and moans. This has no effect on her playing, however. Nadja gives about one hundred performances a year.

Poetry

The *Women's 400 Meters*

LILLIAN MORRISON

To James

FRANK HORNE

Examine What You Know

Think about the running events that you have seen or that you have run yourself. Then, visualize the emotions on the runners' faces as they cross the finish line. What motivates people to make such an effort? What are the rewards for running a race? With your class, discuss why people might choose to participate in races, and whether or not you think the activity is worth the hours of practice and stress, both physical and mental, that it requires.

Expand Your Knowledge

The runners described in the following poems are competing in a track meet. Older tracks were covered with cinders—black bits of burnt wood or coal ashes that gave traction to a runner's feet. At the starting line, runners dug starting holes in the cinders to give their feet something to push off from when they leaped forward at the start. Newer tracks have a rubberized asphalt or other synthetic surface. Sprinters now may use metal starting blocks. Whether old or new, most tracks are 400 meters around and a pistol is still fired to signal the start.

Enrich Your Reading

Recognizing the Speaker   In poetry, the voice that "talks" to the reader is called the **speaker.** The speaker in a poem is similar to the narrator in a work of fiction. The speaker may reflect the thoughts and feelings of the poet, but sometimes a poet creates a speaker with a separate identity. As you read the next two poems, ask yourself what you know or might guess about the speaker.

■ *Author biographies on Extend page*

The *Women's* *400 Meters*

LILLIAN MORRISON

Skittish,
they flex knees, drum heels and
shiver at the starting line

waiting the gun
5   to pour them over the stretch
like a breaking wave.

Bang! they're off
careening down the lanes,
each chased by her own bright tiger.

---

*R*esponding to Reading

First Impressions of "The Women's 400 Meters"

1. Write a few words or phrases that describe your impressions of the runners in the poem.

Second Thoughts on "The Women's 400 Meters"

2. Why do you think the poem describes only the beginning of the race?

3. Based on the poem and your own experience, what might the runners be thinking as they await the start?

4. What do you think the last line of the poem means?

To James

FRANK HORNE

© 1979   Robert M. Cunningham from U.S. Postal Service Olympic stamp album.

Do you remember
How you won
That last race . . . ?
How you flung your body
5 At the start . . .
How your spikes
Ripped the cinders
In the stretch . . .
How you catapulted
10 Through the tape . . .
Do you remember . . . ?
Don't you think
I lurched with you
Out of those starting holes . . . ?
15 Don't you think
My sinews tightened
At those first
Few strides . . .
And when you flew into the stretch
20 Was not all my thrill
Of a thousand races
In your blood . . . ?
At your final drive
Through the finish line
25 Did not my shout

Tell of the
Triumphant ecstasy
Of victory . . . ?
Live
30 As I have taught you
To run, Boy—
It's a short dash
Dig your starting holes
Deep and firm
35 Lurch out of them
Into the straightaway
With all the power
That is in you
Look straight ahead
40 To the finish line
Think only of the goal
Run straight
Run high
Run hard
45 Save nothing
And finish
With an ecstatic burst
That carries you
Hurtling
50 Through the tape
To victory. . . .

Responding to Reading

First Impressions of "To James"

1. What do you think of the speaker of this poem? Jot down your ideas in your journal or notebook.

Second Thoughts on "To James"

2. What do you think is the speaker's relationship to James? Explain your reasoning, based on details from the poem.

3. In your opinion, what is the **theme** of this poem?

4. Do you think the author of *Nadja on My Way* would agree with the speaker's advice? Explain.

Comparing the Poems

5. Do you think the speakers of the two poems would agree or disagree about the subject of winning? Explain.

6. Which poem comes closer to your idea of what runners might think and experience during a race?

Broader Connections

7. Both poems are told from the point of view of a spectator. What effect do you think spectators have on athletes or performers?

Writing Options

1. Based on your own feelings about running, as you wrote them in your journal, write your **response** to the advice given by the speaker in "To James."

2. Think of a time when you were a spectator at an event. Write a **poem** that describes the scene and expresses what you felt while watching the event.

Options for Learning

1 • **Art of Racing** Try making a textured picture to depict the race in either poem. Glue fabric or any other materials you wish on cardboard or heavy paper to illustrate the scene. Incorporate details from the poem in your artwork, and try to convey the emotions that either the runners or the spectators feel.

2 • **Road to Victory** Interview a track coach or a high school runner to find out how runners prepare for meets. Find out how much practice is required, what kinds of training procedures are used, and how much time is spent in training. Share your findings with your class.

Lillian Morrison 1917–

Lillian Morrison has made a career of writing books for young people. Born in New Jersey, she graduated from Columbia University with a degree in library science. Morrison then began work with the New York Public Library. She served as the young-adult librarian and later as the coordinator of young-adult services.

Morrison's love of sports is so great that she wrote an entire collection of poems about sports, called *Sprints and Distances*. As Morrison says, "I am drawn to athletes, dancers, drummers, jazz musicians, who . . . symbolize for us something joyous, ordered, and possible in life." Morrison's poetry has appeared in a number of books and in such magazines as *Prairie Schooner, Sports Illustrated,* and *Atlantic Monthly.*

Frank S. Horne 1899–1974

Born and raised in Brooklyn, New York, Frank Horne graduated from the City College of New York. While there, he became an outstanding track star.

Horne then left New York to earn a master's degree and a doctorate in optometry. A few years later he was struck by what he called a "mean illness" that caused some loss of the use of his legs. Moving to a warmer climate, Horne began teaching at a high school in Georgia. As the track coach, he led his runners to several championships. Horne's poem "To James" is based on these experiences. The poem appeared as part of a collection of poems written as "letters" to others. In 1936 Horne stopped teaching and became a public housing specialist for the federal government in Washington, D.C.

Fiction

Rikki-tikki-tavi

RUDYARD KIPLING

Examine What You Know

Natural enemies fight or fear each other by instinct. What natural enemies can you name from the animal kingdom? Think about common enemies such as dogs and cats as well as more exotic animals you may have heard or read about. With a partner, brainstorm a list of natural enemies. Combine your ideas with those of your classmates.

Expand Your Knowledge

If you lived in India, you would almost certainly mention the mongoose and the cobra as a pair of natural enemies—a pair that will fight to the death. The mongoose, growing only as long as sixteen inches, seems hardly a match for the poisonous cobra, a snake that averages six feet in length and six inches in diameter. You will learn more about these animals in this story, which is set in India during the late 1800s. At that time the British ruled India. British families lived in open, airy houses called bungalows—one-story homes with big windows and large shaded porches to pro-

tect the inhabitants from the hot sun. Because of the heavy seasonal rains, vines and creepers covered every outside wall, and bushes could grow to be as big as an average-sized American garage. The jungle grew so close to the bungalows that it was not uncommon to find snakes, insects, or wild animals near or even in these homes.

Enrich Your Reading

Personification In the story, you will see what Kipling imagines that animals think, feel, and say about each other. Kipling creates in each animal a distinct human personality. Giving human qualities to an object, animal, or idea is called **personification.** As you read, think of people you know who have personalities similar to the ones Kipling gives his animal characters.

■ *Author biography on Extend page*

Rikki-tikki-tavi

RUDYARD KIPLING

This is the story of the great war that Rikki-tikki-tavi fought single-handed, through the bathrooms of the big bungalow in Segowlee cantonment.[1] Darzee the Tailorbird helped him, and Chuchundra the Muskrat, who never comes out into the middle of the floor, but always creeps around by the wall, gave him advice, but Rikki-tikki did the real fighting.

He was a mongoose, rather like a little cat in his fur and his tail, but quite like a weasel in his head and his habits. His eyes and the end of his restless nose were pink. He could scratch himself anywhere he pleased with any leg, front or back, that he chose to use. He could fluff up his tail till it looked like a bottle brush, and his war cry as he scuttled through the long grass was *Rikk-tikk-tikki-tikki-tchk!*

One day, a high summer flood washed him out of the burrow where he lived with his father and mother, and carried him, kicking and clucking, down a roadside ditch. He found a little wisp of grass floating there, and clung to it till he lost his senses. When he revived, he was lying in the hot sun on the middle of a garden path, very draggled indeed, and a small boy was saying, "Here's a dead mongoose. Let's have a funeral."

"No," said his mother, "let's take him in and dry him. Perhaps he isn't really dead."

They took him into the house, and a big man picked him up between his finger and thumb and said he was not dead but half choked. So they wrapped him in cotton wool, and warmed him over a little fire, and he opened his eyes and sneezed.

"Now," said the big man (he was an Englishman who had just moved into the bungalow), "don't frighten him, and we'll see what he'll do."

It is the hardest thing in the world to frighten a

Bronze cobra about 1919 Jean Dunand The Metropolitan Museum of Art, Rogers Fund, 1970.

1. **cantonment:** a place where soldiers are lodged.

Words to Know and Use | **revive** (ri vīv′) *v.* to regain consciousness; wake up

mongoose, because he is eaten up from nose to tail with curiosity. The motto of all the mongoose family is "Run and find out," and Rikki-tikki was a true mongoose. He looked at the cotton wool, decided that it was not good to eat, ran all around the table, sat up and put his fur in order, scratched himself, and jumped on the small boy's shoulder.

The motto of all the mongoose family is "Run and find out."

"Don't be frightened, Teddy," said his father. "That's his way of making friends."

"Ouch! He's tickling under my chin," said Teddy.

Rikki-tikki looked down between the boy's collar and neck, snuffed at his ear, and climbed down to the floor, where he sat rubbing his nose.

"Good gracious," said Teddy's mother, "and that's a wild creature! I suppose he's so tame because we've been kind to him."

"All mongooses are like that," said her husband. "If Teddy doesn't pick him up by the tail, or try to put him in a cage, he'll run in and out of the house all day long. Let's give him something to eat."

They gave him a little piece of raw meat. Rikki-tikki liked it immensely; and when it was finished, he went out into the veranda and sat in the sunshine and fluffed up his fur to make it dry to the roots. Then he felt better.

"There are more things to find out about in this house," he said to himself, "than all my family could find out in all their lives. I shall certainly stay and find out."

He spent all that day roaming over the house. He nearly drowned himself in the bathtubs, put his nose into the ink on a writing table, and burned it on the end of the big man's cigar, for he climbed up in the big man's lap to see how writing was done. At nightfall he ran into Teddy's nursery to watch how kerosene lamps were lighted, and when Teddy went to bed, Rikki-tikki climbed up too. But he was a restless companion, because he had to get up and attend to every noise all through the night, and find out what made it. Teddy's mother and father came in, the last thing, to look at their boy, and Rikki-tikki was awake on the pillow.

"I don't like that," said Teddy's mother. "He may bite the child."

"He'll do no such thing," said the father. "Teddy is safer with that little beast than if he had a bloodhound to watch him. If a snake came into the nursery now—"

But Teddy's mother wouldn't think of anything so awful.

Early in the morning Rikki-tikki came to early breakfast in the veranda, riding on Teddy's shoulder, and they gave him banana and some boiled egg. He sat on all their laps one after the other, because every well-brought-up mongoose always hopes to be a house mongoose some day and have rooms to run about in; and Rikki-tikki's mother (she used to live in the general's house at Segowlee) had carefully told Rikki what to

Words to Know and Use

immensely (im mens′ lē) *adv.* very much; enormously
veranda (və ran′ də) *n.* a long open porch, usually with a roof

do if ever he came across white men.

Then Rikki-tikki went out into the garden to see what was to be seen. It was a large garden, only half <u>cultivated</u>, with bushes, as big as summerhouses, of Marshal Niel roses, lime and orange trees, clumps of bamboos, and thickets of high grass. Rikki-tikki licked his lips. "This is a splendid hunting ground," he said, and his tail grew bottle-brushy at the thought of it; and he scuttled up and down the garden, snuffing here and there till he heard very sorrowful voices in a thornbush. It was Darzee the Tailorbird and his wife. They had made a beautiful nest by pulling two big leaves together and stitching them up the edges with fibers, and had filled the hollow with cotton and downy fluff. The nest swayed to and fro, as they sat on the rim and cried.

"What is the matter?" asked Rikki-tikki.

"We are very miserable," said Darzee. "One of our babies fell out of the nest yesterday and Nag ate him."

"H'm," said Rikki-tikki, "that is very sad—but I am a stranger here. Who is Nag?"

Darzee and his wife only <u>cowered</u> down in the nest without answering, for from the thick grass at the foot of the bush there came a low hiss—a horrid cold sound that made Rikki-tikki jump back two clear feet. Then inch by inch out of the grass rose up the head and spread hood of Nag, the big black cobra, and he was five feet long from tongue to tail. When he had lifted one-third of himself clear of the ground, he stayed balancing to and fro exactly as a dandelion tuft balances in the wind, and he looked at Rikki-tikki with the wicked snake's eyes that never change their expression, whatever the snake may be thinking of.

"Who is Nag?" said he. "*I* am Nag. The great God Brahm[2] put his mark upon all our people, when the first cobra spread his hood to keep the sun off Brahm as he slept. Look, and be afraid!"

He spread out his hood more than ever, and Rikki-tikki saw the spectacle mark on the back of it that looks exactly like the eye part of a hook-and-eye fastening. He was afraid for the minute, but it is impossible for a mongoose to stay frightened for any length of time; and though Rikki-tikki had never met a live cobra before, his mother had fed him on dead ones, and he knew that all a grown mongoose's business in life was to fight and eat snakes. Nag knew that too and, at the bottom of his cold heart, he was afraid.

"Well," said Rikki-tikki, and his tail began to fluff up again, "marks or no marks, do you think it is right for you to eat fledglings out of a nest?"

Nag was thinking to himself, and watching the least little movement in the grass behind Rikki-tikki. He knew that mongooses in the garden meant death sooner or later for him and his family, but he wanted to get Rikki-tikki off his guard. So he dropped his head a little, and put it on one side.

"Let us talk," he said. "You eat eggs. Why

---

2. Brahm: another name for *Brahma,* creator of the universe in the Hindu religion.

Words
to Know
and Use

cultivated (kul′ tə vāt′ id) *adj* . planted or prepared for planting, as opposed to wild
cultivate *v.*
cower (kou′ ər) *v.* to crouch or shrink down in fear

should not I eat birds?"

"Behind you! Look behind you!" sang Darzee.

Rikki-tikki knew better than to waste time in staring. He jumped up in the air as high as he could go, and just under him whizzed by the head of Nagaina, Nag's wicked wife. She had crept up behind him as he was talking, to make an end of him. He heard her savage hiss as the stroke missed. He came down almost across her back, and if he had been an old mongoose, he would have known that then was the time to break her back with one bite; but he was afraid of the terrible lashing return stroke of the cobra. He bit, indeed, but did not bite long enough; and he jumped clear of the whisking tail, leaving Nagaina torn and angry.

"Wicked, wicked Darzee!" said Nag, lashing up as high as he could reach toward the nest in the thornbush. But Darzee had built it out of reach of snakes, and it only swayed to and fro.

Rikki-tikki felt his eyes growing red and hot (when a mongoose's eyes grow red, he is angry); and he sat back on his tail and hind legs like a little kangaroo, and looked all around him, and chattered with rage. But Nag and Nagaina had disappeared into the grass. When a snake misses its stroke, it never says anything or gives any sign of what it means to do next. Rikki-tikki did not care to follow them, for he did not feel sure that he could manage two snakes at once. So he trotted off to the gravel path near the house, and sat down to think. It was a serious matter for him.

review   What problems does Rikki face?

If you read the old books of natural history, you will find they say that when the mongoose fights the snake and happens to get bitten, he runs off and eats some herb that cures him. That is not true. The victory is only a matter of quickness of eye and quickness of foot—snake's blow against mongoose's jump—and as no eye can follow the motion of a snake's head when it strikes, this makes things much more wonderful than any magic herb. Rikki-tikki knew he was a young mongoose, and it made him all the more pleased to think that he had managed to escape a blow from behind.

It gave him confidence in himself, and when Teddy came running down the path, Rikki-tikki was ready to be petted. But just as Teddy was stopping, something wriggled a little in the dust, and a tiny voice said: "Be careful. I am Death!" It was Karait, the dusty brown snakeling that lies for choice on the dusty earth; and his bite is as dangerous as the cobra's. But he is so small that nobody thinks of him, and so he does the more harm to people.

Rikki-tikki's eyes grew red again, and he danced up to Karait with the peculiar rocking, swaying motion that he had inherited from his family. It looks very funny, but it is so perfectly balanced a gait that you can fly off from it at any angle you please, and in dealing with snakes this is an advantage.

If Rikki-tikki had only known, he was doing a much more dangerous thing than fighting Nag; for Karait is so small, and can turn so quickly, that unless Rikki bit him close to the back of the head, he would get the return stroke in his eye or his lip. But Rikki did not know. His eyes were all red,

DEBER DHOORA DEE, KUMAON, INDIA, WITH ITS WELL AND DEODARS (CEDRUS DEODARA)   Marianne North   © 1992
The Trustees of the Royal Botanic Gardens, Kew, U.K.

and he rocked back and forth, looking for a good place to hold. Karait struck out. Rikki jumped sideways and tried to run in, but the wicked little dusty gray head lashed within a fraction of his shoulder, and he had to jump over the body, and the head followed his heels close.

Teddy shouted to the house, "Oh, look here! Our mongoose is killing a snake." And Rikki-tikki heard a scream from Teddy's mother. His father ran out with a stick, but by the time he came up, Karait had lunged out once too far, and Rikki-tikki had sprung, jumped on the snake's back, dropped his head far between his forelegs, bitten as high up the back as he could get hold, and rolled away.

That bite paralyzed Karait, and Rikki-tikki was just going to eat him up from the tail, after the custom of his family at dinner, when he remembered that a full meal makes a slow mongoose; and if he wanted all his strength and quickness ready, he must keep himself thin. He went away for a dust bath under the castor-oil bushes, while Teddy's father beat the dead Karait.

"What is the use of that?" thought Rikki-tikki. "I have settled it all."

And then Teddy's mother picked him up from the dust and hugged him, crying that he had saved Teddy from death; and Teddy's father said that he was a providence,[3] and Teddy looked on with big scared eyes. Rikki-tikki was rather amused at all the fuss, which, of course, he did not understand. Teddy's mother might just as well have petted Teddy for playing in the dust. Rikki was thoroughly enjoying himself.

review   Why is Rikki amused by the fuss?

That night at dinner, walking to and fro among the wineglasses on the table, he might have stuffed himself three times over with nice things. But he remembered Nag and Nagaina, and though it was very pleasant to be patted and petted by Teddy's mother, and to sit on Teddy's shoulder, his eyes would get red from time to time, and he would go off into his long war cry of *"Rikk-tikk-tikki-tikki-tchk!"*

Teddy carried him off to bed and insisted on Rikki-tikki sleeping under his chin. Rikki-tikki was too well bred to bite or scratch, but as soon as Teddy was asleep, he went off for his nightly walk around the house; and in the dark he ran up against Chuchundra the Muskrat, creeping around by the wall. Chuchundra is a brokenhearted little beast. He whimpers and cheeps all the night, trying to make up his mind to run into the middle of the room. But he never gets there.

"Don't kill me," said Chuchundra, almost weeping. "Rikki-tikki, don't kill me!"

"Do you think a snake-killer kills muskrats?" said Rikki-tikki scornfully.

"Those who kill snakes get killed by snakes," said Chuchundra, more sorrowfully than ever. "And how am I to be sure that Nag won't mistake me for you some dark night?"

"There's not the least danger," said Rikki-tikki. "But Nag is in the garden, and I know you don't go there."

"My cousin Chua the Rat told me—" said Chuchundra, and then stopped.

"Told you what?"

"H'sh! Nag is everywhere, Rikki-tikki. You should have talked to Chua in the garden."

"I didn't—so you must tell me. Quick, Chuchundra, or I'll bite you!"

Chuchundra sat down and cried till the tears rolled off his whiskers. "I am a very poor man," he sobbed. "I never had spirit enough to run out into the middle of the room. H'sh! I mustn't tell you anything. Can't you *hear*, Rikki-tikki?"

Rikki-tikki listened. The house was as still as still, but he thought he could just catch the faintest *scratch-scratch* in the world—a noise as faint as that of a wasp walking on a windowpane—the dry scratch of a snake's scales on brickwork.

"That's Nag or Nagaina," he said to himself, "and he is crawling into the bathroom sluice.[4] You're right, Chuchundra; I should have talked to Chua."

---

3. providence: a blessing; something good given by God.

4. bathroom sluice: a passageway fitted with a gate or other device that controls the water flow out of a bathtub.

He stole off to Teddy's bathroom, but there was nothing there, and then to Teddy's mother's bathroom. At the bottom of the smooth plaster wall there was a brick pulled out to make a sluice for the bath water, and as Rikki-tikki stole in by the masonry curb where the bath is put, he heard Nag and Nagaina whispering together outside in the moonlight.

"When the house is emptied of people," said Nagaina to her husband, "*he* will have to go away, and then the garden will be our own again. Go in quietly, and remember that the big man who killed Karait is the first one to bite. Then come out and tell me, and we will hunt for Rikki-tikki together."

"But are you sure that there is anything to be gained by killing the people?" said Nag.

"Everything. When there were no people in the bungalow, did we have any mongoose in the garden? So long as the bungalow is empty, we are king and queen of the garden; and remember that as soon as our eggs in the melon bed hatch (as they may tomorrow), our children will need room and quiet."

"I had not thought of that," said Nag. "I will go, but there is no need that we should hunt for Rikki-tikki afterward. I will kill the big man and his wife, and the child if I can, and come away quietly. Then the bungalow will be empty, and Rikki-tikki will go."

Rikki-tikki tingled all over with rage and hatred at this, and then Nag's head came through the sluice, and his five feet of cold body followed it. Angry as he was, Rikki-tikki was very frightened as he saw the size of the big cobra. Nag coiled himself up, raised his head, and looked into the bathroom in the dark, and Rikki could see his eyes glitter.

"Now, if I kill him here, Nagaina will know; and if I fight him on the open floor, the odds are in his favor. What am I to do?" said Rikki-tikki-tavi.

Nag waved to and fro, and then Rikki-tikki heard him drinking from the biggest water jar that was used to fill the bath. "That is good," said the snake. "Now, when Karait was killed, the big man had a stick. He may have that stick still, but when he comes in to bathe in the morning, he will not have a stick. I shall wait here till he comes. Nagaina—do you hear me?—I shall wait here in the cool till daytime."

There was no answer from outside, so Rikki-tikki knew Nagaina had gone away. Nag coiled himself down, coil by coil, around the bulge at the bottom of the water jar, and Rikki-tikki stayed still as death. After an hour he began to move, muscle by muscle, toward the jar. Nag was asleep, and Rikki-tikki looked at his big back, wondering which would be the best place for a good hold. "If I don't break his back at the first jump," said Rikki, "he can still fight. And if he fights—O Rikki!" He looked at the thickness of the neck below the hood, but that was too much for him; and a bite near the tail would only make Nag savage.

"It must be the head," he said at last; "the head above the hood. And, when I am once there, I must not let go."

Then he jumped. The head was lying a little clear of the water jar, under the curve of it; and, as his teeth met, Rikki braced his back against the bulge of the red earthenware to hold down the head. This gave him just one second's purchase, and he made the most of it. Then he was battered to and fro as a rat is shaken by a dog—to and fro on the floor, up and down, and around in great circles; but his eyes were red, and he held on as the body cart-whipped over the floor, upsetting the tin dipper and the soap dish and the flesh brush, and banged against the tin side of the bath.

As he held, he closed his jaws tighter and tighter, for he made sure he would be banged to death; and, for the honor of his family, he preferred to be found with his teeth locked. He was dizzy, aching, and felt shaken to pieces when something went off like a thunderclap just behind him. A hot wind knocked him senseless, and red fire singed his fur. The big man had been awakened by the noise, and had fired both barrels of a shotgun into Nag just behind the hood.

review   What happened in the fight?

Rikki-tikki held on with his eyes shut, for now he was quite sure he was dead. But the head did not move, and the big man picked him up and said, "It's the mongoose again, Alice. The little chap has saved *our* lives now."

Then Teddy's mother came in with a very white face, and saw what was left of Nag, and Rikki-tikki dragged himself to Teddy's bedroom and spent half the rest of the night shaking himself tenderly to find out whether he really was broken into forty pieces, as he fancied.

When morning came, he was very stiff, but well pleased with his doings. "Now I have Nagaina to settle with, and she will be worse than five Nags; and there's no know-ing when the eggs she spoke of will hatch. Goodness! I must go and see Darzee," he said.

Without waiting for breakfast, Rikki-tikki ran to the thornbush where Darzee was singing a song of triumph at the top of his voice. The news of Nag's death was all over the garden, for the sweeper had thrown the body on the rubbish heap.

"Oh, you stupid tuft of feathers!" said Rikki-tikki angrily. "Is this the time to sing?"

"Nag is dead—is dead—is dead!" sang Darzee. "The valiant Rikki-tikki caught him by the head and held fast. The big man brought the bang stick, and Nag fell in two pieces! He will never eat my babies again."

"All that's true enough. But where's Nagaina?" said Rikki-tikki, looking carefully around him.

"Nagaina came to the bathroom sluice and called for Nag," Darzee went on, "and Nag came out on the end of a stick—the sweeper picked him up on the end of a stick and threw him upon the rubbish heap. Let us sing about the great, the red-eyed Rikki-tikki!" And Darzee filled his throat and sang.

"If I could get up to your nest, I'd roll your babies out!" said Rikki-tikki. "You don't know when to do the right thing at the right time. You're safe enough in your nest there, but it's war for me down here. Stop singing a minute, Darzee."

What danger does Rikki still face?   *review*

"For the great, the beautiful Rikki-tikki's sake I will stop," said Darzee. "What is it, O Killer of the terrible Nag?"

"Where is Nagaina, for the third time?"

"On the rubbish heap by the stables,

mourning for Nag. Great is Rikki-tikki with the white teeth."

"Bother my white teeth! Have you ever heard where she keeps her eggs?"

"In the melon bed, on the end nearest the wall, where the sun strikes nearly all day. She hid them there weeks ago."

"And you never thought it worthwhile to tell me? The end nearest the wall, you said?"

"Rikki-tikki, you are not going to eat her eggs?"

"Not eat exactly, no. Darzee, if you have a grain of sense you will fly off to the stables and pretend that your wing is broken, and let Nagaina chase you away to this bush. I must get to the melon bed, and if I went there now, she'd see me."

Darzee was a feather-brained little fellow who could never hold more than one idea at a time in his head. And just because he knew that Nagaina's children were born in eggs like his own, he didn't think at first that it was fair to kill them. But his wife was a sensible bird, and she knew that cobra's eggs meant young cobras later on. So she flew off from the nest, and left Darzee to keep the babies warm, and continue his song about the death of Nag. Darzee was very like a man in some ways.

She fluttered in front of Nagaina by the rubbish heap and cried out, "Oh, my wing is broken! The boy in the house threw a stone at me and broke it." Then she fluttered more desperately than ever.

Nagaina lifted up her head and hissed. "You warned Rikki-tikki when I would have killed him. Indeed and truly, you've chosen a bad place to be lame in." And she moved toward Darzee's wife, slipping along over the dust.

"The boy broke it with a stone!" shrieked Darzee's wife.

"Well! It may be some consolation to you when you're dead to know that I shall settle accounts with the boy. My husband lies on the rubbish heap this morning, but before night the boy in the house will lie very still. What is the use of running away? I am sure to catch you. Little fool, look at me!"

Darzee's wife knew better than to do *that*, for a bird who looks at a snake's eyes gets so frightened that she cannot move. Darzee's wife fluttered on, piping sorrowfully, and never leaving the ground, and Nagaina quickened her pace.

Rikki-tikki heard them going up the path from the stables, and he raced for the end of the melon patch near the wall. There, in the warm litter above the melons, very cunningly hidden, he found twenty-five eggs, about the size of a bantam's[5] eggs, but with whitish skins instead of shells.

"I was not a day too soon," he said, for he could see the baby cobras curled up inside the skin, and he knew that the minute they were hatched they could each kill a man or a mongoose. He bit off the tops of the eggs as fast as he could, taking care to crush the young cobras, and turned over the litter from time to time to see whether he had missed any. At last there were only three eggs left, and Rikki-tikki began to chuckle to himself, when he heard Darzee's wife screaming.

"Rikki-tikki, I led Nagaina toward the house, and she has gone into the veranda

---

5. **bantam's:** of a breed of small hen.

CORNER OF AN APARTMENT   1875   Claude Monet   Musée d'Orsay, Paris. Giraudon/Art Resource, New York.

and—oh, come quickly—she means killing!"

Rikki-tikki smashed two eggs, and tumbled backward down the melon bed with the third egg in his mouth, and scuttled to the veranda as hard as he could put foot to the ground. Teddy and his mother and father were there at early breakfast, but Rikki-tikki saw that they were not eating anything. They sat stone-still, and their faces were white. Nagaina was coiled up on the matting by Teddy's chair, within easy striking distance of Teddy's bare leg; and she was swaying to and fro, singing a song of triumph.

"Son of the big man that killed Nag," she hissed, "stay still. I am not ready yet. Wait a little. Keep very still, all you three! If you move, I strike; and if you do not move, I strike. Oh, foolish people, who killed my Nag!"

Teddy's eyes were fixed on his father, and all his father could do was to whisper, "Sit still, Teddy. You mustn't move. Teddy, keep still."

Then Rikki-tikki came up and cried, "Turn around, Nagaina. Turn and fight!"

"All in good time," she said, without moving her eyes. "I will settle my account with you presently. Look at your friends, Rikki-tikki. They are still and white. They are afraid. They dare not move, and if you come a step nearer, I strike."

"Look at your eggs," said Rikki-tikki, "in the melon bed near the wall. Go and look, Nagaina!"

The big snake turned half around, and saw the egg on the veranda. "Ah-h! Give it to me," she said.

Rikki-tikki put his paws on each side of the egg, and his eyes were blood-red. "What price for a snake's egg? For a young cobra? For a young king cobra? For the last—the very last of the brood? The ants are eating all the others down by the melon bed."

What price for a snake's egg? For a young cobra?

Nagaina spun clear around, forgetting everything for the sake of the one egg. Rikki-tikki saw Teddy's father shoot out a big hand, catch Teddy by the shoulder, and drag him across the little table with the teacups, safe and out of reach of Nagaina.

"Tricked! Tricked! Tricked! *Rikk-tck-tck!*" chuckled Rikki-tikki. "The boy is safe, and it was I—I—I that caught Nag by the hood last night in the bathroom." Then he began to jump up and down, all four feet together, his head close to the floor. "He threw me to and fro, but he could not shake me off. He was dead before the big man blew him in two. I did it! *Rikki-tikki-tck-tck!* Come then, Nagaina. Come and fight with me. You shall not be a widow long."

Nagaina saw that she had lost her chance of killing Teddy, and the egg lay between Rikki-tikki's paws. "Give me the egg, Rikki-tikki. Give me the last of my eggs, and I will go away and never come back," she said, lowering her hood.

"Yes, you will go away, and you will never come back. For you will go to the rubbish heap with Nag. Fight, widow! The big man has gone for his gun. Fight!"

Rikki-tikki was bounding all round Nagaina, keeping just out of reach of her stroke, his little eyes like hot coals. Nagaina gathered herself together and flung out at him. Rikki-tikki jumped up and backward. Again and again and again she struck, and each time her head came with a whack on the matting of the veranda, and she gathered herself together like a watch spring. Then Rikki-tikki danced in a circle to get behind her, and Nagaina spun around to keep her head to his head, so that the rustle of her tail on the matting sounded like dry leaves blown along by the wind.

He had forgotten the egg. It still lay on the veranda, and Nagaina came nearer and nearer to it, till at last, while Rikki-tikki was drawing breath, she caught it in her mouth, turned to the veranda steps, and flew like an arrow down the path, with Rikki-tikki behind her. When the cobra runs for her life, she goes like a whiplash flicked across a horse's neck. Rikki-tikki knew that he must catch her, or all the trouble would begin again.

She headed straight for the long grass by the thornbush, and as he was running, Rikki-tikki heard Darzee still singing his foolish little song of triumph. But Darzee's wife was wiser. She flew off her nest as Nagaina came along, and flapped her wings about Nagaina's head. If Darzee had helped her, they might have turned her, but Nagaina only lowered her hood and went on. Still, the instant's delay brought Rikki-tikki up to her, and as she plunged into the rat hole where she and Nag used to live, his little white teeth were clenched on her tail, and he went down with her—and very few mongooses, however wise and old they may be, care to follow a cobra into its hole.

It was dark in the hole; and Rikki-tikki never knew when it might open out and give Nagaina room to turn and strike at him. He held on savagely, and stuck out his feet to act as brakes on the dark slope of the hot, moist earth.

Very few mongooses . . . care to follow a cobra into its hole.

Then the grass by the mouth of the hole stopped waving, and Darzee said, "It is all over with Rikki-tikki! We must sing his death song. Valiant Rikki-tikki is dead! For Nagaina will surely kill him underground."

So he sang a very mournful song that he made up on the spur of the minute; and just as he got to the most touching part, the grass quivered again, and Rikki-tikki, covered with dirt, dragged himself out of the hole leg by leg, licking his whiskers. Darzee stopped with a little shout. Rikki-tikki shook some of the dust out of his fur and sneezed. "It is all over," he said. "The widow will never come out again." And the red ants that live between the grass stems heard him, and began to troop down one after another to see if he had spoken the truth.

Rikki-tikki curled himself up in the grass and slept where he was—slept and slept till it was late in the afternoon, for he had done a hard day's work.

"Now," he said, when he awoke, "I will go back to the house. Tell the Coppersmith, Darzee, and he will tell the garden that Nagaina is dead."

The Coppersmith is a bird who makes a

noise exactly like the beating of a little hammer on a copper pot. The reason he is always making it is that he is the town crier to every Indian garden, and tells all the news to everybody who cares to listen. As Rikki-tikki went up the path, he heard his "attention" notes like a tiny dinner gong, and then the steady *"Ding-dong-tock!* Nag is dead*—dong!* Nagaina is dead! *Ding-dong-tock!"* That set all the birds in the garden singing, and the frogs croaking, for Nag and Nagaina used to eat frogs as well as little birds.

When Rikki got to the house, Teddy and Teddy's mother (she looked very white still, for she had been fainting) and Teddy's father came out and almost cried over him; and that night he ate all that was given him till he could eat no more, and went to bed on Teddy's shoulder, where Teddy's mother saw him when she came to look late at night.

"He saved our lives and Teddy's life," she said to her husband. "Just think, he saved all our lives."

Rikki-tikki woke up with a jump, for the mongooses are light sleepers.

"Oh, it's you," said he. "What are you bothering for? All the cobras are dead. And if they weren't, I'm here."

Rikki-tikki had a right to be proud of himself. But he did not grow too proud, and he kept that garden as a mongoose should keep it, with tooth and jump and spring and bite, till never a cobra dared show its head inside the walls. 🦢

*R*esponding to Reading

First Impressions

1. How did you feel about Rikki by the end of the story? Jot down your reaction in your notebook or journal.

Second Thoughts

2. What abilities or qualities enable Rikki to fight the cobras to the finish?

   Think about
   - the battle with Nag in the bathroom
   - Nagaina's threatened attack on the family at breakfast

3. Do you think Rikki fights Nag and Nagaina to protect Teddy and his parents, or does he act only from instinct? Explain your answer.

4. What human weaknesses are shown in the animal characters?

5. What do you think the use of **personification** adds to the story?

Broader Connections

6. "Rikki-tikki-tavi" is considered by many to be a **classic** story—one that is read and enjoyed by many generations. Why do you think this story is a classic?

*L*iterary Concept: *Minor Characters*

Characters that play a small role in the plot are called **minor characters.** An author often uses them to keep the plot moving, or to provide a contrast to a main character. For example, Chuchundra advances the plot (when he tells Rikki where Nag is) and contrasts with Rikki (Chuchundra is a coward). How do other minor characters function in the story?

Concept Review: Setting   Compile a list of details that Kipling uses in the story to establish the setting.

Writing Options

1. In the story, Darzee sings a song about Rikki killing Nag. Write the **lyrics** of that song, beginning with the words quoted in the story.

2. Most, but not all, of the characters in the story consider Rikki to be a hero. Write a **summary** of the story from Nagaina's point of view.

3. Choosing a pair from the list you prepared earlier, write a **battle scene** between natural enemies. Use details, as Kipling did, to make the battle exciting and easy to follow.

4. Skim the story for details about the habits of a mongoose. Check in an encyclopedia for additional information. Combine them to write an **informative report** about mongooses.

Vocabulary Practice

Exercise   On a separate sheet of paper, write the letter of the situation that best demonstrates the meaning of the boldfaced word.

1. **revive**
   a. a package sent to a faraway country
   b. a drowning victim brought back to life
   c. a teacher writing a lesson on the board

2. **veranda**
   a. a couple having tea on the porch
   b. a young lady reading in the park
   c. a child sitting quietly in a classroom

3. **cower**
   a. an animal trembling in fear
   b. a bird singing a song
   c. a snake slithering through the grass

4. **cultivated**
   a. a table covered with breakfast dishes
   b. a garden planted with flowers
   c. a bungalow filled with people

5. **immensely**
   a. an extremely happy lottery winner
   b. a slightly bored audience
   c. a contented, sleepy young boy

> *Words to Know and Use*
>
> cower
> cultivated
> immensely
> revive
> veranda

*O*ptions for Learning

1 • The Deadly Cobra   Create a display about cobras. Do research to find out about their habitat and habits. Include such facts as how many people are killed by cobras in an average year, whether there is an antidote for cobra venom, and whether cobras can really be hypnotized by snake charmers.

2 • Comic Creation   Make a comic-book version of part of this story. Reread the story to determine the important scenes you want to use. Select dialogue for the talk balloons in your comic. Illustrate your scenes and then share your book with younger audiences.

3 • Radio Rikki   Stage a radio reading of the story. Assign students to perform the parts of the characters and the narrator and to supply sound effects. Rehearse, then tape your performance for other classes.

4 • Disney's Version   Disney cartoons and movies also personify animals. In fact, the Disney studios have animated several of Kipling's stories. Watch one of the animated versions. Then have a panel discussion analyzing the Disney version and comparing how Kipling and the Disney studios personify animals.

 FACT FINDER SCIENCE

To what animal family do mongooses belong?

*J*oseph *Rudyard Kipling*
1865–1936

Though educated in England, Kipling was born in India, where his father was a school principal. Kipling loved to read as a child, and his first job was as a journalist on a British newspaper in India. His stories about his Indian travels made him wildly popular, and when he returned to London in 1889 he was already famous.

When he had children of his own, Kipling turned to writing children's stories. His first collection, *The Jungle Books,* was about an Indian boy who was raised by wolves. Between chapters about the boy, Kipling inserted other stories. "Rikki-tikki-tavi" is one of these.

Kipling received numerous honors and awards for his work. In 1907 he became the first Englishman to win the Nobel Prize for Literature. He is buried in London in Poet's Corner of Westminster Abbey, near Shakespeare.

WRITER'S WORKSHOP

INFORMATIVE AND PERSUASIVE WRITING

In this subunit, you've met fighters—characters who stood up to difficult problems, even life-and-death struggles, and found solutions. In this workshop, you will propose your own solution to a real-life problem. You will also stand up for your ideas, convincing readers that your solution is worthwhile. You will write a **guest editorial.** Newspapers, newsmagazines, and television news programs often include guest editorials, which offer the views of people who are not on the regular staff. For this assignment, you will combine two types of writing. You will use **informative** writing to explain your ideas, and you will use **persuasive** writing to convince readers to accept those ideas.

COMBINE
INFORMATIVE AND
PERSUASIVE WRITING
FOR
. . . .
advertisements
editorials
campaign pamphlets
letters to lawmakers
speeches
fund-raising appeals
letters of complaint

Here is one writer's PASSkey to this assignment.

GUIDED ASSIGNMENT: PROBLEM-SOLUTION

Write an editorial that explains a problem, proposes a solution for the problem, and persuades readers to accept that solution.

P URPOSE: To inform and persuade

A UDIENCE: Readers of the school newspaper

S UBJECT: A problem

S TRUCTURE: Guest editorial

STUDENT MODEL

```
         Solving the Money Blues
            by Jason Harkness

   Doug is in seventh grade. His brother Darrell
is in tenth. Both boys need money for things
like clothes, sports equipment, after-school
treats, and entertainment. Both get allowances,
but Darrell gets more because he's older. Also,
Darrell has a part-time job at a taco shop.
What does Doug have? He has a money problem.
   Many middle school students are like Doug.
We need money as much as high school students
do. Yet we have fewer ways to earn it.
Legally, most of us are too young to hold
```

An anecdote grabs readers' attention.

The second paragraph explains the problem, using facts and details.

jobs. The only ways a seventh grader can earn money are paper routes, odd jobs, and babysitting. There aren't enough paper routes for everyone. Odd jobs don't provide steady money. Babysitting is our best chance, and some of us do get regular babysitting jobs. However, we risk losing them if we ever say no because of illness or other plans.

The third paragraph offers a solution.

We probably can't change the employment laws any time soon. But there is a simple thing we can do to ease our money problems. We can start working in groups. Imagine five friends forming a group that does babysitting, pet care, or yardwork. They would have more customers than any of them had alone. They could back each other up too. If one of them was sick or had plans, another could fill in.

The writer anticipates a possible objection and answers it.

Facts and an example stress the benefits of the solution.

Some people might think that sharing work means less money for individuals. However, the opposite is true. For example, my cousins and their friends have had a successful babysitting group for over a year. Their customers never have to make more than one call to get a sitter. They know all the students are reliable, charge the same rate, and go by the same rules. My cousins earn the money they need and still have free time.

Persuasive language makes the conclusion strong.

Their success shows how well a group can work. Isn't the idea worth a try? We have nothing to lose—except our money problems.

Prewrite and Explore

WRITER'S CHOICE

Try finishing this sentence: *If I ruled the world, I'd* . . . What would you change? What would you fix?

1 **Look for problems** What really makes you mad? What bugs you in small ways, day after day? Try freewriting to recall all the things that have bothered you recently. You may recall large or small things from home or school. Newspapers, magazines, or television may have alerted you to issues in your community, the country, or the world. After freewriting, underline each problem you came up with.

2 **Collect your thoughts**   Any problem that matters to you and that you have ideas about will make a good topic. A focused **freewriting** is a good way to explore a problem. In this freewriting, you can concentrate on one problem, its causes and effects, and your questions and feelings about it.

3 **Shape a solution**   Once you've explored a problem, you can focus on your solution. Brainstorming with friends can help now. As you work, think about your audience. Are you aiming at readers of a school newspaper, readers of a national magazine, or viewers of local or national television? What do they already know, and what will you need to explain to them? You might research facts and figures about the problem and your solution. Filling out a box chart like the one Jason used, below, is one way to shape your ideas.

◀ REMINDER . . . .

Freewriting is continuous writing for a short time—writing whatever comes into your head. It is brainstorming on paper.

GATHERING INFORMATION

Problem		Solution	
Middle school kids have a hard time earning money		Work in groups	
Causes	**Effects**	**How it works**	**Advantages**
Need money for extras	Stuck with odd jobs	Share customers and jobs	More customers and jobs
Low allowances	No steady income	Fill in for each other	Free time when needed

◀ STUDENT MODEL . . . .

◀ COMPUTER TIP . . . .

Above your draft, make four headings, one for each of your four sections. As you get new ideas or find new facts, file them under the appropriate headings.

Draft and Discover

1 **Write in sections**   A problem-solution paper can have four main sections: an introduction that identifies the problem, a part that examines the problem in detail, a part that explains your solution, and a conclusion that tells why your solution is the right one. You can start with whichever section you're most interested in. You might try developing each section as one paragraph.

2 **Deal with objections**   To "sell" your solution to readers, you can't ignore objections they might have. Mention one or two objections. Then explain why your solution is good in spite of them.

Revise Your Writing

1 Review the problem First, try focusing on the sections of your draft that deal with the problem. Your main goal here is to explain the problem clearly, and in detail. You might want to open with an anecdote or a surprising statistic to introduce the problem and get readers interested. Then, be sure to show readers why the problem is important. You also might explain the causes of the problem. This knowledge will help readers see why your solution would be effective.

2 Adjust the solution Your view of the problem may have changed as you wrote. Make sure the solution still fits. You also can make sure you've dealt with readers' possible objections.

3 End strongly As you "sell" your solution, you'll need to be persuasive. This means choosing facts that show the strengths of your solution and explaining logically why your solution will work. Your conclusion may include a call to action, urging readers to do something or to change their ways of thinking.

4 Build bridges As you rework your draft, notice how the four sections of your paper are connected. Ask yourself which thoughts lead from one section to the next. Then look for words and phrases that could make these thought-bridges clearer to your readers. Words and phrases that help readers make connections from one paragraph to the next are called **transitions.** You might ask a peer to read your final draft for sense and smoothness.

THINKING SKILLS
For more about using logic and persuasion, see the Reader's Workshop on page 347.

IN OTHER CLASSES
In social studies, try looking at current or historical events as solutions to problems. Ask yourself which problems an event solved, and how it solved them.

Revision Questions

For You

1. Have I shown why the problem is important to me?
2. Have I included enough facts to help readers understand the problem and the solution?
3. Have I used clear logic to convince readers?

For a Peer Reader

1. Have I given enough information to clearly explain the problem?
2. What is your opinion of my solution?
3. How could I make my conclusion more persuasive?

Proofread

Read your paper carefully, repairing any grammar, capitalization, punctuation, or spelling errors you find. Pay special attention to words that are easily confused.

THE EDITOR'S EYE: WORDS OFTEN CONFUSED

Homonyms are words that sound alike, but have different spellings and different meanings. Double-check these words when you write.

Be careful with *there*, *they're*, and *their*.

The word *there* is an adverb: Put the books *there*.

The word *they're* is a contraction of *they are*: *They're* late again.

The word *their* is a possessive pronoun: They brought *their* books.

Problem *There* success shows how well a group can work.

Revised *Their* success shows how well a group can work.

NEED MORE HELP?
. . . .
See the Language Workshop on pages 344–346.

Publish and Present

Mail It Off   With your teacher's help, find the address of a local or national newspaper, magazine, or television news program. Submit a copy of your editorial and include a short cover letter.

Reflect on Your Writing

Write short answers to the following questions. Attach your answers to your editorial, and add it to your portfolio.

◀ FOR YOUR PORTFOLIO
. . . .

1. Now that you've finished your editorial, how has your view of the problem changed?
2. What did you enjoy about working with persuasion? What was hardest for you?

LANGUAGE WORKSHOP

WORDS OFTEN CONFUSED OR MISSPELLED

> Do not confuse words that are homonyms or that are similar in sound or appearance.

Misspelled and misused words make your writing less convincing. Oddly, simple words can be the trickiest. **Homonyms** are words that have the same sound but have different spellings and different meanings, such as *here* and *hear*. Other word pairs are confused because they are similar in sound or appearance, such as *lose* and *loose*.

capital means "excellent, very serious, or most important." It also means "a seat of government."

The word **capitol** means "a building in which a state legislature meets."

The **Capitol** is the building in Washington, D.C., in which the U.S. Congress meets.

> The *capital* of New Hampshire is Concord.
> New Hampshire's legislature meets in the *capitol* building.
> The Senate meets in the *Capitol* building in Washington, D.C.

SPELLING TIP
Remember—you h*ear* with your *ear*.

▶ **hear** means "to listen to" or "to take notice of."
here means "in this place."

> Alben could *hear* the panther snarling in the darkness.
> "Why did Old Sly Eye come in *here?*" he wondered.

SPELLING TIP
Possessive forms of pronouns (*yours, his, hers, its, theirs, ours, whose*) NEVER have apostrophes.

its is a possessive pronoun meaning "belonging to it."
▶ **it's** is a contraction for *it is* or *it has.*

> The panther had lost one of *its* eyes years before.
> "*It's* killed the calf," Alben thought. "Will it kill me?"

lose means "to mislay" or "to suffer the loss of something."
loose means "unfastened, slack, or free."

> Alben tried not to *lose* his composure.
> He remembered the *loose* rope hanging in the corner.

344   UNIT THREE   FIGHT TO THE FINISH

our means "belonging to us."

are is a form of the verb *to be.*

"I couldn't save *our* calf," he thought grimly.

"Now my mother and sister *are* in danger as well."

peace means "quiet" or "freedom from disagreements."

piece means "a section or part of something."

Wishing for *peace* and safety, Alben tried to decide what to do.

He didn't even have a *piece* of wood to use as a weapon.

◀ SPELLING TIP

Remember—you can take a *pie*ce of *pie.*

principle means "a standard, a rule of behavior, or a basic truth."

principal means "of central importance" or "the head of a school."

Alben's family made it a *principle* to help their neighbors.

Protecting his mother and sister was Alben's *principal* goal.

◀ SPELLING TIP

Remember—it's smart to make the princi*pal* your *pal.*

quite means "really or truly" or "to a considerable degree."

quiet means "noiseless, peaceful, or motionless" or "silence or stillness."

Alben knew that Old Sly Eye was *quite* dangerous.

In the *quiet* darkness, he heard the panther moving about.

there means "in that place."

their means "belonging to them."

they're is a contraction for *they are.*

"Old Sly Eye is *there* by the door," he thought.

"My mother and sister are probably on *their* way home."

"*They're* going to be here soon. I must act," he decided.

to means "toward" or "in the direction of." It also can be joined to the base form of a verb, as in *to sing* or *to become.*

too means "also." It can also mean "excessively," as in *too hot.*

two is the number 2.

He would jump from the loft *to* the floor.

"Will Old Sly Eye kill me *too?*" he asked himself.

He heard the voices of *two* people approaching the cabin.

weather means "atmospheric conditions, such as temperature and cloudiness."

whether is a word that helps to express choice or alternative.

The blankets were folded when the *weather* grew warmer.

Alben wasn't sure *whether* or not a blanket would protect him.

whose means "belonging to whom." It is the possessive form of *who*.

who's is a contraction for *who is* or *who has.*

▶   Alben knew a lot of men *whose* shots had missed the cat.

       "Now I'm another one *who's* missed Old Sly Eye," he thought.

SPELLING TIP

A lot is always two words! This overused phrase is NEVER written as one word.

Exercise 1   Concept Check   Write the correct word from the choices in parentheses.

1. "Where (our, are) my mother and sister?" Alben wondered.
2. In the cabin, it was (to, too, two) dark (to, too, two) see.
3. Then Alben knew (who's, whose) voices he had heard outside.
4. He had to decide (weather, whether) to risk a shot.
5. The panther had torn a (piece, peace) out of his shirt.
6. "Don't come over (hear, here)—stay back!" he shouted.
7. If Alben missed, he might (lose, loose) his life.
8. Now he could see (there, their, they're) frightened faces in the moonlight.
9. The roar of the musket shattered the (quite, quiet) night.
10. "Oh, Alben! (Your, You're) hurt!" his mother cried.

Exercise 2   Proofreading Skill   Rewrite the following paragraph, correcting the ten misspelled or misused words.

    Have you ever had a chance to here Nadja Salerno-Sonnenberg perform? Its an experience I'll never forget. Wearing a big, lose shirt and tight pants, she looks alot like a punk whose wandered into a classical concert. She takes up her violin, and the hall becomes absolutely quite. As she plays, she twists and bends so much that I wonder weather she'll fall. Yet her playing is smooth as water. "It sounds to good to be real," my friend whispers. After Nadja finishes, my friend and I clap until our hands get sore. Around us, people jump to they're feet, shouting, "Encore, encore!" Nadja grins and does a little strut-dance, then begins playing one final peace.

PROOFREADING TIP

Use scanning (see page 294) to spot tricky words in proofreading. Try scanning backwards, starting with the last word in your paper.

Exercise 3   Revising Your Writing   Reread the problem-solution paper you wrote for the Writer's Workshop on pages 339–343. When you find any of the commonly confused words covered in this lesson, check their spelling. Then do the same for the other papers in your portfolio.

THE LANGUAGE OF PERSUASION

As a writer, you have two main ways to persuade. You can use emotion, and you can use logic. **Logic** is correct reasoning. Incorrect, or **faulty,** reasoning weakens persuasive writing. Learn to recognize and avoid the kinds of faulty reasoning listed below.

Incorrect Generalization   A **generalization** is a broad statement about a number of people or things, such as "Cobras are venomous." Some generalizations are true. However, words like *none, all, every, always,* or *never* can make some generalizations too broad to be true. "None of today's kids are physically fit" is an example of a generalization that is too broad. Data aren't available on *every* young person's physical fitness. Also, the terms *kids* and *physically fit* don't refer to measurable things like ages or specific physical abilities. Help keep your generalizations accurate with words like *few, most, many, sometimes, often,* or *seldom* and with specific facts that can be proved.

Either/Or   Sometimes a writer suggests that there are only two choices, when actually there are many. "If we don't give seventh-graders more homework, they'll do badly on state tests" illustrates either/or reasoning. There's more than one way to raise test scores.

Bandwagon   A statement like "Join the crowd! Support my plan!" appeals to people's desire to belong—to jump on the bandwagon. This is an indirect and unfair use of emotion, and it is not logical.

Snob Appeal   This technique appeals indirectly to another emotion—the desire to be special. Statements like "Only the brightest people see the wisdom of this idea" rely on snob appeal.

Exercise 1   Concept Check   Identify each of the four types of faulty reasoning used in the paragraph below.

> (1) Everyone would be better off if we used my recycling plan. (2) So don't be left out—join the effort. (3) Those who truly have foresight will appreciate this plan most of all. (4) If we don't start doing as I suggest, we'll soon be buried in our own litter.

Exercise 2   Revising Your Writing   Reread your problem-solution paper, checking for faulty reasoning. Make any needed revisions.

Reading on Your Own

Suggested Novels for Unit Three

The novels introduced on these pages allow you to explore the unit theme, "Reaching for the Stars," in more depth and in different ways.

THE HOBBIT

J.R.R. TOLKIEN ©1938

This exciting fantasy is the story of a hero's struggle to win a dragon's treasure. As you follow the adventures of Bilbo, the wizard Gandalf, and twelve dwarfs, you will be plunged into a different world—the world of Middle Earth. Follow Bilbo as he leaves the safety of his home, crosses the Misty Mountains, proceeds through Mirkwood, and finally reaches the Lonely Mountain, home of the terrible Smaug. Find out how Bilbo and his friends battle the forces of evil, fight a dragon, and make personal sacrifices for the good of the community. As you are drawn into their quest, see if you can . . .

- become involved with the characters of a whole new land, called Middle Earth

- imagine the frightening and unfamiliar setting of the Lonely Mountain

- recognize how the heroes of this fantasy are like heroes in real life

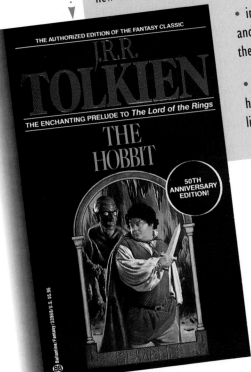

THE AUTHORIZED EDITION OF THE FANTASY CLASSIC

J.R.R. TOLKIEN

THE ENCHANTING PRELUDE TO *The Lord of the Rings*

THE HOBBIT

50TH ANNIVERSARY EDITION!

Ballantine/Fantasy/32968/U.S. $5.95

THE GIFT OF THE GIRL WHO COULDN'T HEAR

SUSAN SHREVE ©1991

This novel is about dreams and the courage it takes to make those dreams come true. It is the story of a seventh grader who changes from a smart, friendly, self-confident teenager to someone who is insecure and bad-tempered. Thirteen-year-old Eliza has had a dream that has focused her life since she was in the third grade. She is an excellent singer and has dreamed of singing the lead in the seventh-grade musical. Now, all of a sudden, she loses her confidence and self-esteem. Consequently, she refuses to try out for the musical. It is her best friend, Lucy—a deaf girl—who teaches Eliza a valuable lesson and shows her the meaning of true courage. As you read, ask yourself the following questions:

• How can a girl who cannot hear teach Eliza a lesson about music?

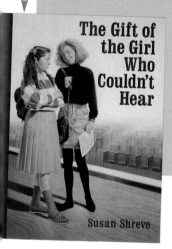

The Gift of the Girl Who Couldn't Hear

Susan Shreve

• Who do you believe has more courage, Eliza or Lucy?

• How can people find the courage required to achieve their dreams?

ANPAO: AN AMERICAN INDIAN ODYSSEY

JAMAKE HIGHWATER ©1977

In this novel a number of Native American tales are combined as the hero, Anpao, goes on a quest to learn about his heritage. Driven by his dream, Anpao experiences terrible struggles and battles as he travels through the past in search of his destiny. Along the way he meets remarkable beings and becomes a participant in many of the myths and legends handed down in Native American oral history. His journey through the cultures and customs of many different tribes allows him to understand the great diversity of Native American lifestyles and experiences. As you read, think about the following questions:

• Which of the Native American beliefs and customs appeal most to you?

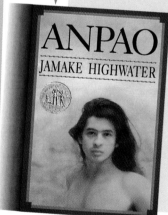
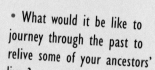

ANPAO
JAMAKE HIGHWATER

• What would it be like to journey through the past to relive some of your ancestors' lives?

• Will Anpao be able to succeed in spite of the dangers he faces?

Other Recommended Books

The Dream Catcher by Monica Hughes (©1987). In this science fiction novel a fifteen-year-old girl in a futuristic society is involved in a political rescue as she strives to free people from the control of a giant computer that has taken over their minds.

The Hero and the Crown by Robin McKinley (©1984). In this fantasy a girl goes on a difficult quest for the magical objects that will restore power to her kingdom. Along the way she must battle dragons and an evil magician.

The Mouse Rap by Walter Dean Myers (©1990). In this contemporary realistic novel a group of fourteen-year-old friends from Harlem have numerous adventures, including a search for a treasure hidden in the days of Al Capone.

Park's Quest by Katherine Paterson (©1988). An eleven-year-old boy has a dream and a quest in this realistic novel. He wants to learn about his father, who died in Vietnam. As he travels and meets various people, he makes discoveries about both his family and himself.

PERSON

TO

PERSON

Can I ever know you

Or you know me?

Sara Teasdale

THE BOATING PARTY   1893–94
Mary Cassatt   National Gallery of Art,
Washington, D.C. Chester Dale Collection.

TESTS OF CONSCIENCE

People are social—we live together and need each other. The ties that join one person to another—whether based on love, friendship, necessity, or duty—are strong and, at times, demanding. These ties require us to give and receive, to make decisions, to be unselfish, sometimes even to make sacrifices.

Our personal relationships often depend on treating each other fairly and with compassion. Our consciences tell us what is right and fair. Daily, we are confronted with situations in which we have to decide if we will do the *right* thing or do the thing that will please us personally, which is often the more selfish, easier path to follow.

This group of selections presents situations that offer choices. The characters must decide whether or not to listen to their consciences. As you imagine yourself in each situation, decide which path you would choose.

Fiction

The *Christmas Hunt*

BORDEN DEAL

Examine What You Know

In many places in the United States, hunting is a common pastime, and for some people it is an occupation. What do you know about hunting? For what reasons do people hunt? What are your feelings about hunting? Write your ideas about hunting in your journal or notebook.

Expand Your Knowledge

The following story is about hunting quail, small game birds that can legally be shot. Bird hunters frequently have trained bird dogs. These dogs instinctively stop quartering, or searching, a field when they smell the birds' scent on the ground. The dogs freeze, lift a front paw, and point their nose toward the birds. On command they flush the quail, or scare the birds into the air, and then the hunters fire. The dogs, which are trained not to eat the fallen birds, find and bring the birds back to the hunters. Bird dogs are sometimes entered in competitive field trials, in which they are judged on their ability to obey orders, search a field, smell out game birds, and retrieve the birds without damaging them.

Enrich Your Reading

Predicting   Based on the material on this page, the title, large blue quotes, and pictures, what do you predict this story will be about? As you read, look for clues in the main character's behavior and speech to predict what will happen next and how the story will end. Be aware that your expectations will probably change as you are reading. Copy the chart below onto a separate sheet of paper and track your changing expectations.

Event in the story	Prediction
1. Tom asks father to take him on hunt	Father will refuse
2.	

■ *Author biography on Extend page*

The *Christmas Hunt*

BORDEN DEAL

It should have been the best Christmas of them all, that year at Dog Run. It started out to be, anyway. I was so excited, watching my father talking on the telephone, that I couldn't stand still. For I was ten years old, and I had never been on a quail shoot in my whole life. I wanted to go on the big Christmas Day hunt even more than I wanted that bicycle I was supposed to get. And I really needed the bicycle to cover with speed and ease the two miles I had to walk to school.

The Christmas Day hunt was always the biggest and best of the season. It was almost like a field trial; only the best hunters and the finest dogs were invited by my father. All my life I had been hearing tales of past Christmas Day hunts. And now I knew with a great ten-year-old certainty that I was old enough to go.

My father hung up the phone and turned around, grinning. "That was Walter," he said. "There'll be ten of them this year. And Walter is bringing his new dog. If all he claims for that dog is true—"

"Papa," I said.

"Lord," my mother said. "That'll be a houseful to feed."

My father put his arm around her shoulders, hugging her. "Oh, you know you like it," he said. "They come as much for your cooking as they do for the hunting, I think."

My mother pursed her lips in the way she had and then smiled. "Wild turkey," she said. "You think you could shoot me four or five nice fat wild turkeys?"

I wanted to jump up and down to attract attention. But that was kid stuff, a <u>tactic</u> for the five-year-olds, though I had to admit it was effective. But I was ten. So I said, "Papa."

My father laughed. "I think I can," he said. "I'll put in a couple of mornings trying."

"Papa," I said desperately.

"Wild turkey stuffed with wild rice," my mother said quickly, thoughtfully, in her planning voice. "Giblet gravy, mashed potatoes, maybe a nice potato salad—"

"If I don't fail on the turkeys," my father said.

"Papa!" I said.

My father turned to me. "Come on, Tom," he said. "We've got to feed those dogs."

That's the way parents are, even when you're ten years old. They can talk right on

Words to Know and Use | **tactic** (tak′ tik) *n.* a method used to accomplish something; a strategy

and never hear a word you say. I ran after my father as he left the kitchen, hoping for a chance to get my words in edgewise. But my father was walking fast, and already the <u>clamor</u> of the bird dogs was rising up to cover any speech I might want to make.

Already the clamor of the bird dogs was rising.

The dogs were standing on the wire fence in long, dappled rows, their voices lifted in greeting. Even in my urgent need I had to stop and admire them. There's nothing prettier in the whole world than a good bird dog. There's a nobleness to its head, an intelligence in its eyes, that no other animal has. Just looking at them sent a shiver down my backbone, and the thought of shooting birds over them—well, the shiver just wasn't in my backbone now; I was shaking all over.

All of the dogs except one were in the same big run. But my father kept Calypso Baby in her own regal pen. I went to her and looked into her soft brown eyes. She stood up tall on the fence, her strong, lithe body stretched to its full height, as tall as I was.

"Hello, Baby," I whispered, and she wagged her tail. "You gonna find me some birds this Christmas, Baby? You gonna hunt for me like you do for Papa?"

She lolled her tongue, laughing at me. We were old friends. Calypso Baby was the finest bird dog in that part of the country. My father owned a number of dogs and kept and trained others for his town friends. But Calypso Baby was his personal dog, the one that he took to the field trials, the one he shot over in the big Christmas Day hunt held at Dog Run.

My father was bringing the sack of feed from the shed. I put out my hand, holding it against the wire so Calypso Baby could lick my fingers.

"This year," I whispered to her. "This year I'm going." I left Calypso Baby, went with determination toward my father. "Papa," I said, in a voice not to be denied this time.

My father was busy opening the sack of dog food.

"Papa," I said firmly, "I want to talk to you." It was the tone and the words my father used often toward me, so much of <u>mimicry</u> that my father looked down at me in surprise, at last giving me his attention.

"What is it?" he said. "What do you want?"

"Papa, I'm ten years old," I said.

My father laughed. "Well, what of it?" he said. "Next year you'll be eleven. And the next year twelve."

"I'm old enough to go on the Christmas hunt," I said.

Incredibly, my father laughed. "At ten?" he said. "I'm afraid not."

I stood, <u>stricken</u>. "But—" I said.

"No," my father said, in the voice that meant No, and no more talking about it. He hoisted the sack of feed and took it into the wire dog pen, the bird dogs crowding around him, rearing up on him in their eagerness.

Words to Know and Use

clamor (klam′ ər) *n.* a loud noise; uproar
mimicry (mim′ ik rē) *n.* an act of imitation
stricken (strik′ ən) *adj.* suddenly affected by pain; wounded

"Well, come on and help me," my father said impatiently. "I've got a lot of things to do."

Usually I enjoyed the daily feeding of the dogs. But not today; I went through the motions dumbly, silently, not paying any attention to the fine bird dogs crowding around me. I cleaned the watering troughs with my usual care, but my heart was not in it.

After the feeding was over, I scuffed stubbornly about my other tasks and then went up to my room, not even coming down when my father came home at dusk excited with the two wild turkeys he had shot. I could hear him talking to my mother in the kitchen, and the ring of their voices had already the feel of Christmas, a hunting cheer that made them brighter, livelier, than usual. But none of the cheer and the pleasure came into me, even though Christmas was almost upon us and yesterday had been the last day of school.

That night I hunted. In my dreams I was out ahead of all the other men and dogs, Calypso Baby quartering the field in her busy way, doing it so beautifully I ached inside to watch her. All the men and dogs stopped their own hunting to watch us, as though it were a field trial. When Calypso Baby pointed, I raised the twelve-gauge[1] shotgun, moved in on her on the ready, and Calypso Baby flushed the birds in her fine, steady way. They came up in an explosive whir, and I had the gun to my shoulder, squeezing off the shot just the way I'd been told to do. Three quail dropped like stones out of the covey,[2] and I swung the gun, following a single. I brought down the single with the second barrel, and Calypso Baby was already bringing the first bird to me in her soft, unbruising mouth. I knelt to pat her for a moment, and Baby whipped her tail to tell me how fine a shot I was, how much she liked for me to be the one shooting over her today.

Soon there was another covey, and I did even better on this one, and then another and another, and nobody was hunting at all, not even my father, who was laughing and grinning at the other men, knowing this was his boy, Tom, and his dog, Calypso Baby, and just full of pride with it all. When it was over, the men crowded around and patted me on the shoulder, hefting the full game

THE EYES HAVE IT   Andrew Chapman   Courtesy of the artist.

---

1. **twelve-gauge** (gāj): having the widest barrel in common use.
2. **covey** (kuv′ ē): a small flock.

Words
to Know
and Use

heft (heft) *v.* to lift something to see how heavy it is

356

bag in admiration, and then there was my father's face close before me, saying, "I was wrong, son, when I said a ten-year-old boy isn't old enough to go bird hunting with the best of us."

Then I was awake, and my father, dressed in his hunting clothes, was shaking me, and it was morning. I looked up dazedly into his face, unable to shake off the dream, and I knew what it was I had to do. I had to show my father. Only then would he believe.

"Are you awake?" my father said. "You'll have to change the water for the dogs. I'm going to see if I can get some more turkeys this morning."

"All right," I said. "I'm awake now."

My father left. I got up and ate breakfast in the kitchen, close to the warm stove. I didn't say anything to my mother about my plans. I went out and watered the dogs as soon as the sun was up, but I didn't take the time, as I usually did, to play with them.

"Me and you are going hunting," I told Calypso Baby as I changed her water. She jumped and quivered all over, knowing the word as well as I did.

I went back into the house, listening for my mother. She was upstairs, making the beds. I went into the spare room where my father kept all the hunting gear. I was trembling, remembering the dream, as I went to the gun rack and touched the cold steel of the double-barreled twelve-gauge. But I knew it would be very heavy for me. I took the single-barrel instead, though I knew that pretty near ruined my chances for a second shot unless I could reload very quickly.

I picked up a full shell[3] bag and hung it under my left arm. I found a game bag and hung it under my right arm. The strap was too long, and the bag dangled emptily to my knees, banging against me as I walked. I tied a knot in the strap so the bag would rest comfortably on my right hip. The gun was heavy in my hands as I walked into the hallway, listening for my mother. She was still upstairs.

"Mamma, I'm gone," I shouted up to her. "I'll be back in a little while." That was so she wouldn't be looking for me.

"All right," she called. "Don't wander far off. Your father will be back in an hour or two and might have something for you to do."

I hurried out of the house, straight to Calypso Baby's pen. I did not look up, afraid that my mother might be watching out of the window. That was a danger I could do nothing about, so I just ignored it. I opened the gate to Baby's pen, and she came out, circling and cavorting.

"Come on, Baby," I whispered. "Find me some birds now. Find me a whole lot of birds."

We started off, circling the barn so we would not be seen from the house and going straight away in its shadow as far as we could. Beyond the pasture we crossed a cornfield, Calypso Baby arrowing straight for the patch of sedge grass beyond. Her tail was whiplike in its thrash, her head high as she plunged toward her work, and I had to hurry to keep up. The gun was clumsy in

---

3. **shell:** a shotgun cartridge.

my hands, and the two bags banged against my hips. But I remembered not to run with the gun, remembered to keep the breech[4] open until I was ready to shoot. I knew all about hunting; I just hadn't had a chance to practice what I knew. When I came home with a bag full of fine birds, my father would have to admit that I knew how to hunt, that I was old enough for the big Christmas Day hunt when all the great hunters came out from town for the biggest day of the season.

When I ducked through the barbed-wire fence, Calypso Baby was waiting for me, standing a few steps into the sedge grass, her head up watching me alertly. Her whole body quivered with her eagerness to be off. I swept my arm in the gesture I had seen my father use so many times, and Calypso Baby plunged instantly into the grass. She was a fast worker, quartering back and forth with an economical use of her energy. She could cover a field in half the time it took any other dog. The first field was empty, and we passed on to the second one. Somehow Calypso Baby knew that birds were here. She steadied down, hunting slowly, more thoroughly.

Then, startling me though I had been expecting it, she froze into a point, one foot up, her tail straight back, her head flat with the line of her backbone. I froze too. I couldn't move; I couldn't even remember to breech the gun and raise it to my shoulder. I stood as still as the dog, all of my knowledge flown out of my head, and yet far back under the panic, I knew that the birds weren't going to hold. They were going to

rise in just a moment. Calypso Baby, surprised at my inaction, broke her point to look at me in inquiry. Her head turned toward me, and she asked the question as plain as my father's voice: *Well, what are you going to do about these fine birds I found for you?*

I could move then. I took a step or two, fumblingly breeched the gun, raised it to my shoulder. The birds rose of their own accord in a sudden wild drum of sound. I yanked at the trigger, unconsciously bracing myself against the blast and the recoil. Nothing happened. Nothing at all happened. I tugged at the trigger wildly, furiously, but it was too late and the birds were gone.

I lowered the gun, looking down at it in bewilderment. I had forgotten to release the safety. I wanted to cry at my own stupidity. I could feel the tears standing in my eyes. This was not at all like my dream of last night, when I and the dog and the birds had all been so perfect.

Calypso Baby walked back to me and looked up into my face. I could read the puzzled contempt in her eyes. She lay down at my feet, putting her muzzle on her paws. I looked down at her, ashamed of myself and knowing that she was ashamed. She demanded perfection, just as my father did.

"It was my fault, Baby," I told her. I leaned over and patted her on the head. "You didn't do anything wrong. It was me."

I started off then, looking back at the bird dog. She did not follow me. "Come on," I told her. "Hunt."

She got up slowly and went out ahead of me again. But she worked in a puzzled manner, checking back to me frequently.

---

4. **breech:** the back part of a gun barrel.

She no longer had the joy, the confidence, with which she had started out.

"Come on, Baby," I coaxed her. "Hunt, Baby. Hunt."

We crossed into another field, low grass this time, and when we found the covey, there was very little time for setting myself. Calypso Baby pointed suddenly. I jerked the gun to my shoulder, remembering the safety this time, and then Calypso Baby flushed the birds. They rose up before me, and I pulled the trigger, hearing the blast of the gun, feeling the shock of it into my shoulder knocking me back a step.

But not even one bird dropped like a fateful stone out of the covey. The covey had gone off low and hard on an angle to the left, and I had completely missed the shot, aiming straight ahead instead of swinging with the birds. Calypso Baby did not even attempt to point singles. She dropped her head and her tail and started away from me, going back toward the house.

I ran after her, calling her, crying now but with anger rather than hurt. Baby would never like me again. She would hold me in the indifference she felt toward any person who was not a bird hunter. She would tolerate me as she tolerated my mother and the men who came out with shiny new hunting clothes and walked all over the land talking about how the dogs didn't hold the birds properly so you could get a decent shot.

I couldn't be one of those. I ran after the dog, calling her, until at last she suffered me to come near. I knelt, fondling her head, talking to her, begging her for another chance.

"I'll get some birds next time," I told her. "You just watch. You hear?"

At last, reluctantly, she consented to hunt again. I followed her, my hands gripping the heavy gun, determined this time. I knew it was my last chance; she would not give me another. I could not miss this time.

We hunted for an hour before we found another covey of birds. I was tired, the gun and the frustration heavier with every step. But, holding only last night's dream in my mind, I refused to quit. At last Calypso Baby froze into a beautiful point. I could feel myself sweating, my teeth gritted hard. I had to bring down a bird this time.

I had to bring down a bird this time.

It seemed to be perfect. I had plenty of time, but I hurried anyway, just to be sure. Then the birds were rising in a tight cluster, and I was pulling the trigger before I had the heavy gun lined up—and in the midst of the thundering blast, I heard Calypso Baby yell with pain as the random shot tore into her hip.

I threw down the gun and ran toward her, seeing the blood streaking down her leg as she staggered away from me, whimpering. I knelt, trying to coax her to me, but she was afraid. I was crying, feeling the full weight of the disaster. I had committed the worst crime of any bird hunter; I had shot my own dog.

Calypso Baby was trying to hide in a clump of bushes. She snapped at me in her fear when I reached in after her, but I did not feel the pain in my hand. I knelt over her, looking at the shredded hip. It was a terrible wound. I could see only blood and raw flesh. I snatched off the empty hunting bag I had donned so optimistically, the shell bag, and took off my coat. I wrapped her in the coat and picked her up in my arms. She was very heavy, hurting, whining with each jolting step as I ran toward the house.

I came into the yard doubled over with the catch in my side from the running, and my legs were trembling. My father was sitting on the back porch with three wild turkeys beside him, cleaning his gun. He jumped to his feet when he saw the wounded dog.

"What happened?" he said. "Did some fool hunter shoot her?"

I stopped, standing before my father and holding the wounded dog. I looked into his angry face. They were the most terrible words I had ever had to say. "I shot her, Papa," I said.

My father stood very still. I did not know what would happen. I had never done anything so bad in my whole life, and I could not even guess how my father would react. The only thing justified would be to wipe me off the face of the earth with one irate gesture of his hand.

I gulped, trying to move the pain in my throat out of the way of the words. "I took her out bird hunting," I said. "I wanted to show you—if I got a full bag of birds, I thought you'd let me go on the Christmas Day hunt—"

"I'll talk to you later," my father said grimly, taking the dog from me and starting into the kitchen. "I've got to try to save this dog's life now."

I started into the kitchen behind my father. He turned. "Where's the gun you shot her with?" he said.

"I—left it."

"Don't leave it lying out there in the field," my father said in a stern voice.

I wanted very badly to go into the kitchen, find out that the dog would live. But I turned, instead, and went back the way I had come, walking with my head down, feeling shrunken inside myself. I had overreached. I had risen up today full of pride beyond my ability, and in the stubbornness of the pride, I had been blind until the terrible accident had opened my eyes so that I could see myself clearly—too clearly. I found the gun, the two bags, where I had dropped them. I picked them up without looking at the smear of blood where Calypso had lain. I went back to the house slowly, not wanting to face it, reluctant to see the damage I had wrought.

When I came into the kitchen, my father had the dog stretched out on the kitchen table. My mother stood by his side with bandages and ointment in her hands. The wound was cleaned of the bird shot and dirt and blood. Calypso Baby whined when she saw me, and I felt my heart cringe with the rejection.

My father looked at me across the dog. The anger was gone out of him; his voice was slow and searching and not to be denied. "Now I want to know why you took my gun and my dog without permission," he said.

"David," my mother said to him.

Words to Know and Use

irate (ī rāt') *adj.* angry
cringe (krinj) *v.* to shrink back from something unpleasant

360

My father ignored her, kept his eyes hard on my face. I knew it wouldn't do any good to look toward my mother. This was between me and my father, and there was no refuge for me anywhere in the world. I didn't want a refuge. I knew I had to face not only my father but myself.

"I–I wanted to go on the Christmas Day hunt," I said again. "I thought if I–" I stopped. It was all that I had to say. It seemed pretty flimsy to me now.

You understand what you've done?

My father looked down at the dog. I was surprised at the lack of anger in him. I could read only sadness in his voice. "She may be ruined for hunting," he said. "Even if the wound heals good, if she doesn't lose the use of her leg, she may be gun-shy for the rest of her life. At best, I'll never be able to show her in field trials again. You understand what you've done?"

"Yes, sir," I said. I wanted to cry. But that would not help, any more than anger from my father would help.

"You see now why I said you weren't old enough?" my father said. "You've got to be trained for hunting, just like a dog is trained. Suppose other men had been out there; suppose you had shot a human being?"

"David!" my mother said.

My father turned angrily toward her. "He's got to learn!" he said. "There's too many people in this world trying to do things without learning how to do them first. I don't want my boy to be one of them."

"Papa," I said. "I'm–I'm sorry. I wouldn't have hurt Calypso Baby for anything in the world."

I'm not going to punish you," my father said. He looked down at the dog. "This is too bad for a whipping to settle. But I want you to think about today. I don't want you to put it out of your mind. You knew that when the time came ripe for it, I intended to teach you, take you out like I'd take a puppy, and hunt with you. After a while, you could hunt by yourself. Then if you were good enough–and only if you were good enough–you could go on the Christmas Day hunt. The Christmas Day hunt is the place you come to, not the place you start out from. Do you understand?"

"Yes, sir," I said. I would have been glad to settle for a whipping. But I knew that a mere dusting of the breeches would be inadequate for my brashness, my overconfidence, for the hurt I had given not only to the fine bird dog but also to my father–and to myself.

"You've got to take special care of Calypso Baby," my father said. "Maybe if you take care of her yourself while she's hurt, she'll decide to be your friend again."

I looked at the dog, and I could feel the need of her confidence and trust. "Yes, sir," I said. Then I said humbly, "I hope she will be friends with me again."

Words to Know and Use | **refuge** (ref′ yo͞oj) *n.* a safe place
inadequate (in ad′ i kwət) *adj.* not enough
brashness (brash′ nəs) *n.* recklessness; foolish daring

WOODLAND WALK © 1989 Burt Silverman.

I went toward the hall, needing to be alone in my room. I stopped at the kitchen doorway, looking back at my father and mother watching me. I had to say it in a hurry if I was going to say it at all.

"Papa," I said, the words rushing softly in my throat, threatening to gag there before I could get them out. "I—I don't think I deserve that bicycle this Christmas. I don't deserve it at all."

My father nodded his head. "All right, son," he said gravely. "This is your own punishment for yourself."

"Yes," I said, forcing the word, the loss empty inside me, and yet feeling better too. I turned and ran out of the room and up the stairs.

Christmas came, but without any help from me at all. I went to bed on Christmas Eve heavy with the knowledge that tomorrow morning there would be no shiny new bicycle under the tree; there would be no

Christmas Day hunt for me. I couldn't prevent myself from waking up at the usual excited time, but I made myself turn over and go back to sleep. When I did, reluctantly, go downstairs, the Christmas tree did not excite me, nor the usual gifts I received every year: the heavy sweater, the gloves, the scarf, the two new pairs of blue jeans. I just wouldn't let myself think about the bicycle.

After my father had gone outside, my mother hugged me to her in a sudden rush of affection. "He would have given you the bicycle anyway," she said, "if you hadn't told him you didn't want it."

I looked up at her. "I didn't deserve it," I said. "Maybe next year I will."

She surprised me then by holding me and crying. I heard the first car arrive outside, the voices of the men excited with the promise of hunting. My mother stood up and said briskly, "Well, this is not getting that big dinner cooked," and went into the kitchen without looking back.

I went out on the front porch. It was perfect quail-hunting weather, cold but not too cold, with a smoky haze lying over the earth. The dogs knew that today was for hunting. I could hear them from around behind the house, standing on the wire fence in broad-shouldered rows, their voices yelping and calling. All except Calypso Baby. All except me.

I stood aside, watching the men arrive in their cars, my father greeting them. Their breaths hung cloudy in the air, and they moved with a sharp movement to their bodies. These were the best hunters in the whole countryside, and today would be a great comradeship and competition. Any man invited on this hunt could be proud of the invitation alone.

I felt almost remote as I watched, as I went with them around the side of the house to the dogs. They all went to examine Calypso Baby, and I felt a freezing inside; but my father only said, "She got shot by accident," and did not tell the whole terrible story.

Then my father looked at his watch and said, "Let's wait for a few more minutes. Walter ought to be here soon. Hate to start without him."

One of the men called, "Here he comes now," and Walter drove up in his battered car.

"Come here, son," my father said, speaking to me for the first time this morning, and I went reluctantly to his side. I was afraid it was coming now, the whole story, and all the men would look at me in the same way that Calypso Baby had after I had shot her.

My father drew me to the side of Walter's car, reached in, and brought out a basket. "You wanted a bicycle," he said. "Then you decided yourself you should wait. Because you made the decision yourself, I decided you were old enough for this."

I looked at the bird-dog puppy in the basket. All of a sudden Christmas burst inside me like a skyrocket, out of the place where I had kept it suppressed all this time.

"Papa," I said. "Papa—"

"Take him," my father said.

I reached into the basket and took out the puppy. The puppy licked my chin with his harsh, warm tongue. He was long, gangly, his feet and head too big for his body—but absolutely beautiful.

My father knelt beside me, one hand on the puppy. "I told Walter to bring me the finest bird-dog puppy he could find," he said. "He's kin to Calypso Baby. He's got good blood."

"Thank you, Papa," I said in a choking voice. "I—I'd rather have him than the bicycle. I'll name him Calypso Boy, I'll—"

"When this puppy is ready for birds, we'll train him," my father said. "While we train the puppy, we'll train you too. When the time comes, you can both go on the Christmas Day hunt—if you're good enough."

"We'll be good enough," I said. "Both of us will be good enough."

"I hope so," my father said. He stood up and looked at the men standing around us, all of them smiling down at me and Calypso Boy. "Let's go," he said. "Those birds are going to get tired of waiting on us."

They laughed and hollered, and the dogs moiled and sounded[5] in the excitement as they were let out of the pen. They fanned out across the pasture, each man or two men taking a dog. I stood watching, holding the puppy warm in my arms. I looked at Calypso Baby, standing crippled in her pen looking longingly after the hunters. I went over and spoke to her. She whined; then for the first time since the accident, she wagged her tail at me.

I looked down at the puppy in my arms. "We'll be going," I told him, as he licked at my chin. "One of these days, when you're a dog and I'm a man, we'll be right out there with the best of them."

It was three years more before I got to go on my first Christmas hunt. Papa had been right, of course. In the time between, I had learned a great deal myself while training Calypso Boy to hunt. With the good blood in him, he turned out to be a great bird dog—second only, I guess, to Calypso Baby, who recovered well from her wound and was Papa's dog the day Calypso Boy and I made our first Christmas hunt.

But of all the Christmases, before and since, I guess I remember best the one when Calypso Baby was hurt—and Calypso Boy first came to me. ❧

---

5. **moiled and sounded:** ran about and howled.

Responding to Reading

First Impressions

1. What were your feelings at the end of the story? Jot them down in your notebook or journal.

Second Thoughts

2. Do you think Tom should have received a puppy at the end of the story? Explain your opinion.

3. How would you evaluate the way Tom's father treated him?

   Think about
   - the father's behavior before the accident
   - his reaction when he learned Tom had shot Calypso Baby
   - his actions on Christmas Day

4. Why is the Christmas Day hunt so important to Tom?

5. How do you think this experience has changed Tom? Base your answer on the story and your own experiences.

Broader Connections

6. Alben, the hero of "Old Sly Eye," and Tom both use guns. How are the two boys different? What might Alben say to Tom?

Literary Concept: Foreshadowing

When writers hint at a future event in a story, they are using a technique called **foreshadowing.** Deal uses foreshadowing in the first two sentences of this story. When Tom says "It should have been the best Christmas of them all. . . . It started out to be, anyway," you get a clue that this Christmas did not turn out the way Tom had expected. Review the story to find two more clues that foreshadow what happened. Then look back at your prediction chart and see if your predictions reflected any of those clues.

Writing Options

1. Did you ever do something that bothered your conscience? Write about a **personal experience** that might be compared to Tom's. Include your feelings at the time and the outcome of your actions.

2. Imagine that you are a psychologist analyzing Tom's hunting dream. Write a **summary** of the dream, describe what it shows about Tom, and indicate why it's in the story.

3. Tom's father says, "The Christmas Day hunt is the place you come to, not the place you start out from." Write an **explanation** of what he means.

4. Look at the journal entry you wrote about hunting. Use these notes, as well as what you learned from the story, to write a **persuasive essay** arguing for or against hunting.

Vocabulary Practice

Exercise On your paper write the letter of the word or phrase that best completes the sentences below.

> *Words to Know and Use*
> ———
> **brashness**
> **clamor**
> **cringe**
> **heft**
> **inadequate**
> **irate**
> **mimicry**
> **refuge**
> **stricken**
> **tactic**

1. If Tom heard a **clamor,** the noise would be   (a) musical   (b) loud   (c) soothing   (d) soft.

2. If Tom's father had been **irate,** he might have   (a) praised   (b) laughed at   (c) cried with   (d) shouted at   Tom.

3. Since Tom was **stricken** by his father's refusal, he looked   (a) excited   (b) eager   (c) dejected   (d) confident.

4. When Tom used **mimicry** in his talk with his father, he was   (a) questioning   (b) imitating   (c) yelling   (d) explaining.

5. If the men were to **heft** the bag, they could determine its   (a) weight   (b) odor   (c) age   (d) color.

6. If quail are in a **refuge,** they are probably   (a) dead   (b) frightened   (c) safe   (d) exposed.

7. If Tom has learned a lesson about **brashness,** he will avoid   (a) fear   (b) cowardliness   (c) anticipation   (d) recklessness.

8. If Tom's punishment was **inadequate,** it was   (a) just right   (b) too quick   (c) appropriate   (d) not sufficient.

9. To persuade his father, Tom developed a **tactic,** or   (a) strategy   (b) question   (c) gift   (d) game.

10. Calypso Baby's rejection of Tom made Tom **cringe,** or   (a) cry   (b) fight   (c) reach out   (d) draw back.

Options for Learning

1 • Fifty Lashes? Whether you agree or disagree with the way Tom's father handled him, what punishment might he have used? Discuss the father's actions with your parents, counselor, or classmates. Then describe another way he could have dealt with the situation.

2 • History's Canine Hunters Dogs have helped humans hunt for many centuries. Research the history of hunting dogs in books about dogs and in encyclopedias. Give an oral presentation with visual aids.

3 • Feelings in Art Think about the setting, sounds, and colors, as well as Tom's feelings, when he shoots Calypso Baby. Then choose an art form to express his feelings. Share your art with your classmates.

4 • Nobody Heard Mother Tom's mother twice started to say something while Tom's father spoke to Tom about the shooting, but she never finished her sentences. With another student, role-play the conversation that might have occurred between Tom's parents after Tom left the kitchen.

 FACT FINDER SCIENCE
How large are most adult quail?

Borden Deal
1922–1985

Borden Deal once said that his characters "live and work in real time in real places." Much of his work is set in the South, which Deal knew well. Born in Pontotoc, Mississippi, Deal worked on his father's cotton farm during the Great Depression. After graduating from the University of Alabama, he wrote advertisements before beginning his own full-time writing career.

Deal's novels and short stories have been translated into more than twenty languages and adapted for the stage, movies, radio, and television. More than one hundred of Deal's stories, poems, and reviews have been published in magazines. Several stories were included in *Best American Short Stories*, *Best Detective Stories of the Year*, and *The Wonderful World of Dogs*.

Poetry

If I Can Stop One Heart from Breaking

EMILY DICKINSON

Bitter Cold, Living in the Village

PO CHÜ-I (bô′ chü′ ē′)

Examine What You Know

Compassion means both a feeling of sorrow for the suffering of others and the urge to help them. You probably know people who are very sensitive to the suffering of others—you may be such a person yourself. Do you think most people feel compassion, or do most not care about others? Can people switch their feelings of compassion on and off? Do enough people act on their compassion to help relieve the suffering of others? Discuss your ideas with a small group of students. Then compare your group's conclusions with the speakers' feelings in these poems.

Expand Your Knowledge

Eleven hundred years and twelve thousand miles separated Po Chü-i and Emily Dickinson. Po lived in China from 772 to 846. Dickinson lived in Massachusetts during the mid-1800s. Their personalities were as different as the times they lived in. Po was a popular and sought-after officer of the imperial court, a man who worked in large cities and traveled widely. Dickinson was a shy girl from a small town, who after a failed romance retired to her father's home and lived there for the rest of her life. Yet both wrote about the same universal ideas that have fascinated poets over the centuries and across cultures: love, grief, compassion, and death.

Write Before You Read

■ *Author biographies on Extend page*

In your journal, write about a person or persons for whom you have felt compassion. What caused your feelings? Did you help the person?

If I Can Stop One Heart from Breaking

EMILY DICKINSON

If I can stop one Heart from breaking
I shall not live in vain
If I can ease one Life the Aching
Or cool one Pain

5   Or help one fainting Robin
Unto his Nest again
I shall not live in Vain.

Responding to Reading

First Impressions of "If I Can Stop One Heart from Breaking"

1. What is your reaction to the speaker in this poem? Explain your answer.

Second Thoughts on "If I Can Stop One Heart from Breaking"

2. Why do you think the speaker says it is enough to help only one heart or one robin?

3. What effect does Dickinson's unusual capitalization have on the poem?

Bitter Cold, Living in the Village

PO CHÜ-I

In the twelfth month of this Eighth Year,
On the fifth day, a heavy snow fell.
Bamboos and cypress all perished from the freeze.
How much worse for people without warm clothes!

5 As I looked around the village,
Of ten families, eight or nine were in need.
The north wind was sharper than the sword,
And homespun cloth could hardly cover one's body.
Only brambles were burnt for firewood,
10 And sadly people sat at night to wait for dawn.

From this I know that when winter is harsh,
The farmers suffer most.
Looking at myself, during these days—
How I'd shut tight the gate of my thatched hall,
15 Cover myself with fur, wool, and silk,
Sitting or lying down, I had ample warmth.
I was lucky to be spared cold or hunger,
Neither did I have to labor in the field.

Thinking of that, how can I not feel ashamed?
20 I ask myself what kind of man am I.

HERDSMEN IN SNOW STORM Zeng Shanqing
Courtesy, The Chinese Cultural Institute, San Francisco.

Responding to Reading

First Impressions of "Bitter Cold, Living in the Village"

1. What might you say to the speaker if you met him? Jot down your thoughts on a sheet of paper.

Second Thoughts on "Bitter Cold, Living in the Village"

2. In your opinion, should the speaker feel ashamed? Why or why not?

3. Which image showing the contrast between the speaker and the villagers is the most memorable?

4. Do you think the speaker's twinge of conscience has changed him permanently? Explain your answer, using your earlier discussion about compassion, as well as evidence from the poem.

Comparing the Poems

5. Do you think one speaker is more or less compassionate than the other one? Explain.

6. If only one of these poems about compassion could be in this text, which one would you choose? Why?

Broader Connections

7. Dickinson focuses her compassion on individuals; Po focuses his compassion on a group. Do you think it is more useful to help an individual, or is it more efficient to work with a group or organization that helps many people?

Writing Options

1. Imagine that you need help. Which speaker would you ask? Write a short **essay** explaining your choice.

2. Write a **poem** about feeling compassion for other people. You might use the example you wrote about in Write Before You Read to express your ideas about compassion. Before writing, consider whether a poem with rhyme and rhythm or a poem with free verse will best suit your ideas.

E X T E N D

Options for Learning

1 • **How People Help** Research charities that help the unfortunate. Find out the total amount of money that is donated each year to charities. How much time is volunteered? What charities operate in your town? Share your discoveries with the class in an oral report.

2 • **Poetry Festival** At the library or bookstore, locate more poetry by Emily Dickinson, Po Chü-i, or your favorite poet. In a class poetry reading, read your favorite poem. You might choose appropriate music to accompany your reading.

Emily Dickinson   1830–1886

Emily Dickinson was born in Amherst, Massachusetts, the daughter of a U.S. Congressman. After a happy childhood, she attended college for a year. Back home in Amherst, she filled her days with domestic chores, while at night she wrote poems about nature, life, and death. After a failed love affair, she lived a solitary life, visiting only close friends and relatives, and frequently writing love poetry.

Whenever Dickinson completed a poem, she sewed it into a small booklet and put it in her bottom bureau drawer. Though she sometimes shared a poem with her family or close friends, no one knew until her death that 1,755 poems were hidden in her room. In 1955, sixty-nine years after her death, all of her poems were published in one volume. Unknown during her lifetime, Emily Dickinson is now famous worldwide.

Po Chü-i   772–846

Po Chü-i was China's earliest popular poet. He wrote more than 2,800 poems, some of which were copied on inn and monastery walls by those who appreciated his work. Po Chü-i took his craft and his audience seriously; it is said that he continually revised and simplified his poems until even an unschooled peasant woman could enjoy them.

Although Po is now most famous for his long narrative poetry, he had hoped to be remembered for a group of fifty poems about social evils.

Writing poetry was only part of Po's life. He passed the imperial government's civil service exam when he was only eighteen, and he held many important posts in his career as a loyal and responsible servant of the Emperor.

Nonfiction

America the Not-so-Beautiful

ANDREW A. ROONEY

Examine What You Know

What have you thrown away in the last twenty-four hours—cereal boxes, paper napkins, plastic yogurt cups, pop cans, lunch bags, shampoo bottles, school papers, ballpoint pens? Make a list. Combine your list with those of your classmates to get a class total. What does the class trash-o-meter tell you?

Expand Your Knowledge

Every day, people in the United States throw out 438,000 tons of garbage, which would fill 63,000 trucks. Of this amount, 150,000 tons consists of packaging material, 43,000 tons is food, and the remainder consists of every other imaginable waste. Yearly, we throw away 350 million plastic cigarette lighters, 1½ billion ballpoint pens, 200 million tires, 13 million tons of newspaper, and 34 million Christmas trees.

Where does our trash go? Most of it goes into landfills, which are filling up as waste increases. The world's largest landfill, Fresh Kills, on New York's Staten Island, is the size of 16,000 baseball diamonds. It is so large that astronauts reported seeing only two man-made objects from space with their naked eyes: the Great Wall of China and the Fresh Kills dump.

Enrich Your Reading

Fact and Opinion   Writers use facts and opinions to persuade readers to accept their point of view. A **fact** is a statement that can be proved to be true, such as "The Fresh Kills landfill in New York is the world's largest landfill." You can check an almanac or a book of statistics to prove or disprove this statement. In contrast, an **opinion** is a person's belief and cannot be proved. "Most New Yorkers don't care enough about the environment" is an opinion. There are no statistics to prove this statement. As you read this essay, decide which statements are facts and which are opinions.

■ *Author biography in Reader's Handbook*

America the Not-so-Beautiful

ANDREW A. ROONEY

Next to saving stuff I don't need, the thing I like to do best is throw it away. My idea of a good time is to load up the back of the car with junk on a Saturday morning and take it to the dump. There's something satisfying about discarding almost anything.

Throwing things out is the American way. We don't know how to fix anything, and anyone who does know how is too busy to come, so we throw it away and buy a new one. Our economy depends on us doing that. The trouble with throwing things away is, there is no "away" left.

Sometime around the year 500 B.C., the Greeks in Athens passed a law prohibiting people from throwing their garbage in the street. This Greek law was the first recognition by civilized people that throwing things away was a problem. Now, as the population explodes and people take up more room on Earth, there's less room for everything else.

The more civilized a country is, the worse the trash problem is. Poor countries don't have the same problem because they don't have much to discard. Prosperity in the United States is based on using things up as fast as we can, throwing away what's left, and buying new ones.

We've been doing that for so many years that (1) we've run out of places to throw things because houses have been built where the dump was and (2) some of the things we're throwing away are poisoning the Earth and will eventually poison all of us and all living things.

Ten years ago most people thought nothing of dumping an old bottle of weed or insect killer in a pile of dirt in the back yard or down the drain in the street, just to get rid of it. The big companies in America had the same feeling, on a bigger scale. For years the chemical companies dumped their poisonous wastes in the rivers behind the mills, or they put it in fifty-gallon drums in the vacant lots, with all the old, rusting machinery in it, up behind the plants. The drums rusted out in ten years and dumped their poison into the ground. It rained, the poisons seeped into the underground streams and poisoned everything for miles around. Some of the manufacturers who did this weren't even evil. They were dumb and irresponsible. Others were evil because they knew how dangerous it was but didn't want to spend the money to do it right.

The problem is staggering. I often think of it when I go in a hardware store or a Sears, Roebuck and see shelves full of poison. You know that, one way or another, it's all going to end up in the Earth or in our rivers and lakes.

I have two pint bottles of insecticide with 5 percent DDT in them in my own garage that I don't know what to do with. I bought them years ago when I didn't realize how bad they were. Now I'm stuck with them.

The people of the city of New York throw away nine times their weight in garbage and junk every year. Assuming other cities come close to that, how long will it be before we trash the whole Earth?

Of all household waste, 30 percent of the weight and 50 percent of the volume is the packaging that stuff comes in.

Not only that, but Americans spend more for the packaging of food than all our farmers together make in income growing it. That's some statistic.

Trash collectors are a lot more independent than they used to be because we've got more trash than they've got places to put it. They have their own schedules and their own holidays. Some cities try to get in good with their trash collectors or garbage men by calling them "sanitation engineers." Anything just so long as they pick it up and take it away.

We often call the dump "the landfill" now, too. I never understood why land has to be filled, but that's what it's called. If you're a little valley just outside town, you have to be careful or first thing you know you'll be getting "filled."

If 5 billion people had been living on Earth for the past thousand years as they have been in the past year, the planet would be nothing but one giant landfill, and we'd have turned America the beautiful into one huge landfill.

The best solution may be for all of us to pack up, board a spaceship, and move out. If Mars is habitable, everyone on Earth can abandon this planet we've trashed, move to Mars, and start trashing that. It'll buy us some time. ❧

Responding to Reading

First Impressions

1. What feelings does Rooney's article trigger in you? Describe them briefly in your journal.

Second Thoughts

2. In your opinion, which of the problems Rooney discusses is the most serious? Why?

3. Rooney says, "Prosperity in the United States is based on using things up as fast as we can, throwing away what's left, and buying new ones." Explain what he means by this and give your opinion.

4. Rooney's article was published in 1989. Based on your observations, is our trash crisis now better, the same, or worse than he reports?

Literary Concept: Persuasive Writing

In a persuasive essay such as "America the Not-so-Beautiful," writers use **facts** and **opinions** to convince readers to accept their viewpoint. Another persuasive writing technique is **exaggeration,** or making an extreme statement that startles the reader. For example, Rooney suggests that a solution to Earth's trash problem is to "move to Mars and start trashing that." A third technique is the use of **personal examples.** These make the issue real, as in Rooney's anecdote about the insecticide in his garage. Work with a partner to find other examples of these persuasive techniques in the article.

Writing Options

1. Review the list you created earlier of "thrown-away" articles. How many of the articles could have been reused or recycled? Could you have used permanent articles such as glasses instead of disposable ones such as paper cups? Write an **analysis** of your trash habits.

2. With his article, Rooney is trying to awaken the conscience of the nation, and he blames companies as well as individuals. Think of one group that you blame for the trash problem. Write a **letter** to that group with a specific suggestion that will help solve the problem.

Nonfiction

from The Endless Steppe
Growing Up in Siberia

ESTHER RUDOMIN HAUTZIG

Examine What You Know

In many places around the world, people are being forced out of their homelands for political or economic reasons. Imagine what it would be like to suddenly be sent against your will to somewhere far away. How would you cope with the shock and the adjustments you would have to make to a totally unfamiliar location? In your journal or notebook, describe the kinds of feelings you think you might have in such a situation.

Expand Your Knowledge

In 1941, the family in this selection was sent from their home in Poland to Siberia, 2,500 miles away. Banishing criminals and political prisoners, such as this family, to the harsh, barren plains, or steppes, of Siberia was a common practice of the Russian government from the time of the czars. The vast, empty landscape and the long, brutal winters made Siberia the perfect natural prison. There was no way to escape and nowhere to escape to. In the 1930s and 1940s during Josef Stalin's leadership, ten million Soviet peasants, in addition to millions of others who opposed Soviet government policies, were sent to Siberia and forced to do manual labor. Many never returned.

Enrich Your Reading

Historical Setting   You know that the setting is the time and place in which the action happens. In nonfiction pieces set in the past, however, the setting includes more than just a physical description of the location. It also involves the customs and beliefs of the times. As you read, notice how the physical setting, as well as the values and customs, influences the people in the selection.

■ *Author biography on Extend page*

from *The Endless Steppe*

Growing Up in Siberia

ESTHER RUDOMIN HAUTZIG

The spring came, the rather thin spring of the Siberian steppe.

But it is impossible to have any thoughts of the thin Siberian spring without first recalling the thick mud. What with the spring rains and the thaw, the steppe became an ocean of mud, and to walk through it was like walking through knee-deep molasses. If one was not lucky enough to own a pair of *sapogy,* the handsome knee-high leather boots that the well-to-do wore, if one had nothing but the same old pair of school oxfords, or even *pimy* boots, along with the energy needed to pull a foot up from the bottom of this mud, one also more often than not had to stop to hunt for the shoe left behind. Whatever one wore, the object developed a crust of mud that had to be broken off after each excursion. While I may have found some of this fun, my mother did not; her trips to and from the bakery in the mud required more energy than she had. She said that time and again, exhausted, she would stand still, with both legs buried in the mud, thinking that only a derrick would be able to hoist her out.

Mud or no mud, Siberia notwithstanding, with the spring I was happy. I had a friend to whisper and gossip with; I played tag and hopscotch—which a less muddy patch in the schoolyard permitted—and along with the other girls, I watched the boys' preoccupation with their pigeons. Raising pigeons was one of their favorite pastimes, and luring the birds away from each other apparently its major objective.

Svetlana and I studied together and complemented[1] each other: she helped me with my Russian grammar and spelling, and I helped her with ideas for themes. Although I always enjoyed school, going to school in Siberia became for me a daily trip to paradise. The return trip to the hut was not. The last day of school for me was a sad day.

As soon as school was over, we began to work on our potato crop for the coming winter.

The government had allotted individual plots of land on the outskirts of the village, and one bought tiny potatoes to sow, with the expectation that they would produce a new crop.

This was not a foregone conclusion[2] with

---

1. **complemented:** worked together to make a complete whole
2. **foregone conclusion:** something sure to occur

Words to Know and Use

preoccupation (prē äk′ yoo pā′ shən) *n.* a state of being wrapped up or engrossed in something
allot (ə lät′) *v.* to give out as a share or portion

that unyielding earth. Very early in the morning, we would go out with shovels and sacks of potatoes to fight, cajole[3], and work this land. Whatever was produced here would belong to us, which was worth remembering as our backs ached and our skin blistered in the sun. And what was produced, what little, *did* belong to us. There was no pilfering in the unprotected, unguarded potato plots. Considering the empty bellies, this degree of honesty was astonishing.

With summer upon us, the hut became unbearably stifling, the vermin[4] unbearably populous, and all tempers reacted accordingly—our landladies', the little boy's, and ours. After all, ten human beings were inhabiting this wretched little oven.

Father decided to investigate the possibility of finding us new quarters.

On the north side of the village, there were some dilapidated[5] and unoccupied huts. Unoccupied with reason: there was no heating of any kind, no floors, and no glass in the windows. But they were empty. Father went to the village housing chief and asked if we might enjoy the privilege of occupying one of these huts.

About this time, factories were beginning to be built in Rubtsovsk—among them a huge tractor factory—and with them came a large migration from European Russia of engineers, technicians of all sorts, and workers. In order to house these people, large

Esther Hautzig in Siberia at age thirteen. Photo copy by Peter Schaaf.

new buildings were erected near the factories and alongside the huts. The district where they existed became known as the *novostroyka*, meaning new buildings. To me, these buildings were the ultimate in beauty and comfort. They were painted white and yellow and light green, and there were floors in them; and some apartments even had bathrooms, but these were only for the chiefs of the factories.

Miraculously, we were permitted to move into one of the empty huts, and we were to be alone at last!

The Kaftals elected to stay on with the sisters. Inevitably, seven people who had been virtually[6] bedfellows ended up getting on one another's nerves.

As for me, the wretched little hut became my dream house. Every day, after working in the potato patch, I went there and cleaned it as best I could. We also picked up manure, mixed it with clay, and either replaced some of the old square blocks in the walls or repaired others. Father got some whitewash at the construction job, and we covered the walls with it. And someplace or other we found glass for the windows.

Before we could cover the floor with fresh clay, we had to dig a cold cellar. Since it

---

3. **cajole** (kə jōl'): to coax, usually by flattering.
4. **vermin:** bugs or small animals that are pests.
5. **dilapidated:** run down; shabby; falling apart.
6. **virtually:** practically; in effect.

would be impossible to keep the potatoes from freezing in an outdoor cellar, we dug one in the middle of our room. Father found some split logs lying around the *novostroyka* and covered the hole with them. Since the rounded logs were also still covered with bark, they gave our floor an odd look, but no matter: we had our own home and our own stove, an outdoor summer one that Father had constructed of bricks, where we could cook our own little flour cakes and our own soup without lining up to do so—and without any helpful and unhelpful, welcome and unwelcome, hints as to their preparation.

That spring Mother had learned that there was such a marvelous thing as a public bath, a *bania,* in the village, and to get there became her dearest wish. What if we did eat a little less for a week or two to save up for such a treat? Wouldn't it be heavenly to feel *clean* before we moved to our own home?

The *bania* was in a small building with two entrances, one for men and one for women. We found that Mother was not the only woman with a passion for cleanliness: the line was long; the wait would be a couple of hours at least. We waited.

There were two rooms in the *bania;* one had stone benches and faucets along the walls, the other was a steam room, a rather crude sauna where one used twigs in the Finnish fashion to clean oneself and stir up one's circulation.

We were assigned a cubbyhole for our clothes, and since we were to use the room with the faucets, we were given a basin and a piece of pumice.[7] We filled our basins at a faucet, sat down on a stone bench, and

scrubbed away. The water was *hot.* Mother was entranced. Now we were quite ready to move.

Outside the hut, there was a small piece of land that no one seemed to be using. With our potatoes and some tomato plants and corn seed given to us by Svetlana, we would turn it into a vegetable patch.

The plans Grandmother and I were making for this garden inevitably recalled Grandfather and our garden in Vilna. As her eyes filled with tears, Grandmother tested my memory. Did I remember what Grandfather had said about the irises? and the pansies? Did I remember the lilac tree?

Yes, I remembered everything. I remembered exactly where Grandfather had said to plant each flower. I remembered the prize of fifty groshes[8] that each week was given to the child whose flowers looked best. Yes, I remembered.

"Good!" Grandmother raised her head; she was proud of me. I had passed the test. "And you will never forget?" No, I would never forget. "Good!" Now my memory was to be honored, she seemed to say; it was to become the <u>archive</u> of her beloved past.

Why is Esther's memory of the flowers so important to Grandmother?

review

Could we plant some flowers? I wanted to know. Grandmother was a realist who lived in the future as well as the past; no, we could not; we needed every inch for growing food.

In this world of scarcity, the <u>acquisition</u> of

---

7. pumice (pum′ is): light volcanic rock used for rubbing away dirt.

8. groshes (grôsh′ əz): a form of *groszy,* Polish coins of small value.

Words to Know and Use

archive (är′ kīv) *n.* a storehouse for records of the past
acquisition (ak′ wə zish′ ən) *n.* the act of getting something

the most trivial or seemingly useless object was a topic for conversation. So Svetlana told me that her father had gotten a large quantity of hospital gauze.[9] (How and why I did not know or care to ask.) She asked me if I wanted some. I assured her I did; I would use it for curtains.

"White hospital gauze for curtains, Esther?"

"You will see," I said mysteriously.

I began to save onion peelings and asked Svetlana to do the same. In school, we had learned that onion peelings when boiled in water exuded a yellow pigment which could be used as dye. Svetlana had either forgotten this or else had no need to remember such things. She wondered what I was up to, but I told her it was a secret.

When I had gathered a big pile of onion peel, I boiled it until the water was a pot of pale yellow dye. I dunked the gauze in this, let it stay for several hours, and to my delight it worked. The gauze was now a pretty yellow. I stretched it out and dried it in the sun, and then I made our curtains. There were no curtain rods to be had, so we tacked them on with little nails, and my pride in the result was very great. Everyone agreed that the curtains were very pretty and just what this hut needed.

The hut was heaven. We ate when we wanted to, slept when we wanted to; at night we would sit outside and gaze at the Siberian sky where there was always something to see; we would sit there quietly, quietly. Even Mother seemed to regain some of her old zest for life.

It was too good to be true to last.

One day the village housing chief came to our hut when I was alone and told me that the next day we were to have a tenant, whether we wanted one or not.

"Who is it going to be?" I asked.

"Vanya, the bum."

"Vanya, the bum? . . . " I was horrified.

---

9. **gauze** (gôz): a thin open-weaved fabric used as bandages.

A typical Siberian mud hut (1929). Sovfoto.

I had been taught never to call anyone names, but everyone called this one-legged man "Vanya the bum." He was the village beggar, and people said he stole. Now this bum was going to live with us? In Vilna, there had been many beggars. Whenever I saw them, I was morbidly affected. Where did they eat? Did they ever bathe at all? And, most important, where did they go at night? Where did they sleep? Thinking about them, I used to shudder.

Now one was going to live with us.

connect How would it feel to have a beggar move in with you?

When I gave the news to my parents, they were no less stunned than I was.

"Vanya, the bum? . . ." Father asked.

I assured him that I had heard correctly.

Mother coughed. A signal to father that she disapproved of his language. Vanya was not to be called a bum. The lecture that followed seemed to me—and perhaps to Father too—untimely, like correcting the grammar of someone who is trying to tell you the house is on fire. The lecture continued: Vanya was not to be called Vanya either. He must have a proper name. We were to introduce ourselves as usual, etc. Perhaps this man has a *worthy* reason for begging? Don't you *agree,* Samuel?

Father not only agreed but, having been rebuked,[10] went on to remind me that we must not judge people by their appearance, etc., etc.

Fidgeting from foot to foot, I listened to everything they had to say; but as far as I was concerned, Vanya the bum was coming to live with us, and I was not only terrified but revolted.

Perhaps the village housing chief would have a change of heart, I thought to myself.

The next evening, Vanya the bum stood at our open door.

"May I come in?"

"Of course you may." Mother stood up.

"Good evening." Father went toward Vanya.

"Good . . . evening." Vanya's response was tentative.

Regardless of all these amenities,[11] this tall, bone-thin specter in filthy clothes, with dark bushy hair and a matted beard, was still a bum to me. But I felt Mother's eyes on me.

"Good evening," I said, going forward but keeping my hands rigidly at my sides. "My name is Esther Rudomin. What's yours?"

"Vanya."

His deeply sunken eyes darted from Mother to Father and back to me.

"My name is Ivan Petrovich, my child," he amended, and there was a tiny spark in his eyes.

"Welcome to our house, Ivan Petrovich," my father said.

For the first time, Grandmother, who had been watching this scene more or less huddled in her bed, spoke up. "Welcome," she murmured.

---

10. **rebuked:** blamed; scolded in a sharp way.
11. **amenities:** courteous acts and pleasant manners of polite social behavior.

Words to Know and Use | **morbidly** (môr′ bid lē) *adv.* in a gloomy, depressed way

"Thank you, thank you. Where may I put down my stick? And this bag?" The bag was a tattered, dusty bundle.

No one had given this matter a thought.

In a tiny room with a hole in its center and three of its corners already occupied by beds, the obvious answer was the fourth corner. But the intention had been to build the winter stove in that corner.

*T**he transformation from village bum to Ivan Petrovich did not take place overnight—*

"So we will make the stove smaller," Mother said, answering our unspoken words, and pointed to the corner. "Maybe we can get some wood for a *nari,* like ours."

"Oh, please—don't worry about me. I'll be very comfortable just as it is." He smiled a little sardonically.[12] "I beg your pardon for this intrusion. Your privacy—"

I could see that my parents and my grandmother were as impressed as I was at his language and his accent: this was no illiterate.

Using his stick <u>dexterously</u>, he hobbled off to his corner on his one leg. There, he stretched out on the floor with his head on his bundle and said that he would rest.

It was an awkward moment. It was still early; what were we to do now? Just sit and watch this stranger rest?

"Please," he said with his eyes closed, "the child can sing and play and do anything she likes. When I am tired, I sleep; and when I sleep, I sleep the sleep of the dead."

"Thank you," I said.

And I meant it. Living with a bum was going to be more agreeable than living with our former landladies, who were forever hushing me and the little boy.

The <u>transformation</u> from village bum to Ivan Petrovich did not take place overnight—either in my mind or in reality. At first he remained a shadowy figure from the dark world of the homeless, the friendless, the outcast. He left very early each morning, and when he came home at night, he went directly to his corner—not that there was anyplace else to go. He talked very little, munched on bits of food he had picked up, and went to sleep. But before he ate, he always offered me anything he had brought—a fresh carrot, perhaps, or a beet. My parents always offered food in return, but he always refused. I, on the other hand, used to accept a bit of carrot or beet because I didn't want to hurt his feelings. Recently, Mother had amended her view of the <u>etiquette</u> for accepting precious food: When some was offered, you took a tiny bit if you thought they did not have enough, but that you took; it was only polite to do so.

After a few weeks had gone by, the transformation began: he started to eat with us, sharing whatever he had brought. If we cooked potatoes, we added his carrot to it

---

12. **sardonically:** in a mocking or bitter way.

Words to Know and Use | **dexterously** (deks′ tər əs lē) *adv.* skillfully
transformation (trans′ fər mā′ shən) *n.* a change
etiquette (et′ i kit) *n.* the proper way to behave toward others; good manners

and called it a vegetable stew. If it was a white beet, we boiled it until we could spread it on bread instead of jam.

Then he began to talk. Ivan Petrovich was a shoemaker from the Ukraine, a man who knew his craft and who had read many books. But once he had talked too much or too carelessly or had been misunderstood. He never did know why he had been sent to prison in Siberia; such a piece of information had been considered superfluous. And when he had been released, he had only one leg left and made his way from village to village begging.

Soon he began to wash himself, which pleased us more than it is polite to say. And to comb his beard. And to carry himself with dignity. He became Ivan Petrovich—for the time being at least.

When he first came to our house, we were the object of much curiosity: What is it like to have a bum in your house? Does he steal? How do you talk to a bum? How does he talk to you? Doesn't it make you shudder?

But as Ivan Petrovich came to regard himself differently, so did the villagers: he became much less a bum and much more just another human being cast off on the great Siberian steppe.

One day he disappeared. He left as usual early one morning, and that was the last that any of us ever saw of Ivan Petrovich, formerly known as Vanya the bum. ❧

Words to Know and Use | **superfluous** (sə pʉr′ flo͞o əs) *adj.* unnecessary; not important

Responding to Reading

First Impressions

1. What were your thoughts as you finished reading this piece? Jot them down in your journal or notebook.

Second Thoughts

2. How do you think the family felt when Ivan Petrovich left?

3. Why did the family's treatment of Vanya help transform him into Ivan?

4. How were Esther and her family able to keep their dignity in such a terrible setting?

5. Of the hardships Esther and her family faced, which would be the most difficult for you? Explain.

Broader Connections

6. If each family in the United States took in a "bum" like Ivan, do you think the homeless problem would be solved?

Literary Concept: Description

Writers use **description** to help readers get a mental picture of a scene, an event, or a character. Skim the second paragraph of the selection in which Hautzig describes the mud of Siberia. How does this description explain the kinds of things that became important to Esther and her mother later in the selection?

Concept Review: External Conflict   With what external forces do Esther and her family struggle in this account?

*W*riting Options

1. Write a **comparison** of this selection and "Homeless" (page 44). Consider the behavior of Ann and Vanya, as well as the beliefs of Quindlen and the Rudomins.

2. Esther and her family adjusted as best they could to their new environment. Based on what they did, write a Siberian **survival guidebook.** Give tips on how to make a home, decorate, find food, cook, and even entertain. You may invent details and descriptions.

3. Imagine that Ivan left the village to become a wandering preacher. Write his **sermon** telling people how one family's treatment of him helped change his life.

4. Suppose the Rudomins decided to sell the hut. Write the **house listing** (real estate ad) describing the house. Begin with a summarizing phrase such as "Home for sale, cheap," and include important details about the house and grounds.

*V*ocabulary Practice

Exercise On a separate sheet of paper, write *Synonyms* or *Antonyms* to show whether each pair of words mean the same thing or the opposite.

1. morbidly : cheerfully
2. superfluous : necessary
3. transformation : change
4. allot : distribute
5. pilfering : donation
6. acquisition : loss
7. etiquette : manners
8. dexterously : clumsily
9. preoccupation : concentration
10. archive : storehouse

Words to Know and Use

acquisition
allot
archive
dexterously
etiquette
morbidly
pilfering
preoccupation
superfluous
transformation

Options for Learning

1 • **Treacherous Times** Research the dictatorship of Joseph Stalin during the 1930s and 1940s in the Soviet Union. Why did Stalin banish so many people? What happened to those he banished? Share your findings with the class.

2 • **Not Just History** In many places in the world today, people are being banished from their homelands for various reasons—race or ethnic background, religion, political beliefs, and so on. Research one area from which refugees are streaming today, and, in an oral report, compare the lives of the exiles to that of the Rudomins.

3 • **Passport to Siberia** Design and write a travel brochure for modern Siberia. Find pictures and information in *National Geographic* or other magazines. Recommend places to go and sights to see. Include a brief history of Siberia.

4 • **Model Maker** Build a diorama of the Rudomins' hut after their makeover. Use details from the story and your imagination. Display your model in class.

 FACT FINDER SOCIAL STUDIES

What is the population of Siberia today?

Esther Rudomin Hautzig
1930–

Esther Hautzig and her family traveled six weeks in a cattle car to Siberia, where her mother was assigned to work in a mine, and her father was drafted into the Soviet army. Her grandfather died in a slave labor camp.

After World War II, Esther immigrated to America. She lived with an uncle in Brooklyn, finished high school, and attended college. "I had always dreamt of becoming a writer," Hautzig says, "though that didn't necessarily mean becoming a published author!" Her first three books were how-to books about cooking without a stove, making inexpensive gifts, and home decorating with little money, skills she learned in Siberia. "I think I'm frugal because I didn't have (anything). I don't believe in waste, and I believed in recycling maybe before the word had been invented."

The Endless Steppe was rejected by several publishers as an adult book. Published as a children's book, it won seven awards and was translated into eight languages.

Hautzig says, "I never pass street people without remembering Vanya the bum. I have to look them in the eye, wish them a good day, and treat them as human beings who are down on their luck."

WRITER'S WORKSHOP

PERSUASIVE WRITING

USE PERSUASIVE WRITING FOR

advertisements
letters to the editor
persuasive speeches
debates
personal requests
editorials

The pieces in this subunit stir our consciences. They make us think about the way things ought to be. When you write to persuade, you start with something that is bothering you and think of a way it can be fixed. You express your opinions, and you try to get others to agree. In many cases, persuasive writing is also meant to move people to action. In this workshop, you'll use persuasion as you write a speech.

Here is one writer's PASSkey to this assignment.

GUIDED ASSIGNMENT: SPEECH TO PERSUADE

Write a speech that persuades listeners to take some kind of action on an issue you care about.

PURPOSE: To persuade
AUDIENCE: Classmates
SUBJECT: A shelter for the homeless
STRUCTURE: Speech

STUDENT MODEL

The writer starts by stating the issue and her position.

Facts and statistics back up the writer's reasons.

Support the Shelter
by Margo Bachman

Next month, our city will vote on creating a shelter for the homeless. The plan calls for the city to lease the old Fitzroy Hotel building downtown. Homeless people could have rooms and bathrooms and share the kitchens that will be installed on each floor. People could stay up to one month. I think everyone should do his or her best to help this plan succeed.

I support the shelter for several reasons. First, the plan is practical. The building was a hotel, so it's already set up to house a lot of people. It has seventy-five rooms. Second, the plan is low-cost. The owner would lease the Fitzroy to the city for only a thousand dollars a month. The city would pay the rent with the money it makes on restaurant taxes. The cost of adding kitchens would also be low because the Rotary Club has offered free materials.

Most importantly, setting up a shelter just seems like the right thing to do. Our city has hundreds of homeless families today. So many new families are homeless because the whole country is having money problems. Last year, over fifty thousand businesses closed, and hundreds of thousands of people lost their jobs. Families could no longer afford their homes. Many moved in with relatives, but when the relatives could no longer afford to help them, they became homeless. I think it's our duty to help people who have experienced this bad luck.

Some people think a shelter will encourage the homeless to stay homeless. I think the short stays allowed in the shelter would prevent that problem. During that worry-free month, people can look for jobs and figure out what they will do next.

As kids, we won't vote on the shelter, but we still have voices. We can talk to adults and hand out leaflets. There's a lot of unhappiness in the world, and we can't do much about it. Here's something we <u>can</u> do. Let's do it.

The writer stresses her most important reason.

The writer uses logic to answer an opposing argument.

The writer states what she wants listeners to do, ending with a strong appeal.

Now you can start on your own speech.

Prewrite and Explore

1 **Take your pick** To find a topic, try brainstorming with a few classmates. Your group might use headings like *world, country, community, school, parents,* and *friends.* Under each heading, group members can list things that upset them or that need fixing. Your friends' ideas may spark new ideas in you. Afterwards, scan the lists for the issues you care most about. Any issue that has two sides will make a good speech topic.

2 **Set your direction**   Before you go any further, try writing one sentence that sums up your position or opinion. If you can list reasons for your position, jot them down too. When you know your position, you can start gathering information.

GATHERING INFORMATION

The more accurate and current your facts and statistics, the stronger your speech. Magazines provide current facts. You can use the *Readers' Guide to Periodical Literature* in your public library to find out which magazines have the information you need. Usually the *Readers' Guide* is in the reference section of the library.

USING THE *READERS' GUIDE*

Start by looking up your subject. For example, Margo looked up "Homeless." She found quite a few articles within subtitles under "Homeless." Here is what she saw under the subtitle "Housing":

HOMELESS

Housing

Gimme shelter [Los Angeles Mission] B. Streisand. il *U.S. News & World Report* 112:17 F 3 '92

Homelessness is a housing problem [New York City study by Marybeth Shinn] *Health* (San Francisco, Calif.: l992) 6:15 F/Mr '92

The Wright shelter [housing for the homeless in Mari County, Calif. originally designed by F. L. Wright] M. M. Soviero. il *Popular Science* 240:58+ Ja '92

The many abbreviations in the *Readers' Guide* are explained in the front of the guide. The diagram below shows one entry.

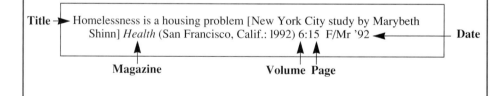

Title ➤ Homelessness is a housing problem [New York City study by Marybeth Shinn] *Health* (San Francisco, Calif.: l992) 6:15 F/Mr '92 ◄── Date

Magazine   **Volume Page**

NOTETAKING

For help in taking notes, see the Research and Report Writing Section in the Writer's Handbook.

▶ Once you have found the listing for an article that might be useful to you, copy the name and date of the magazine and the page numbers. Go to the magazine room, and ask the librarian for the issue of the magazine you want. Often, magazines are bound in large volumes, so keep your date and page numbers with you. When you find the article, skim it to see if it will help you. If so, take notes, including bibliography notes.

3 Target your audience Persuasion works best when it's geared to a specific audience. Make notes about your audience: their ages, their main concerns, their knowledge and viewpoint about your issue. Think of opposing views they might have. Try to guess which kinds of evidence might convince them.

Draft and Discover

1 Start drafting You might start with a paragraph that sums up the issue and states your position. If your audience isn't familiar with the issue, explain it as clearly and briefly as possible.

2 Speak your mind Write about the reasons for your position. Check your notes for facts and statistics that back up your reasons. As you write, bear in mind the main arguments your listeners might raise. You can mention and then counter these arguments.

3 Talk action Come right out and say what you want your listeners to do. For example, you may want them to write letters, volunteer, or give money. Decide exactly what you want, and express it in one or more sentences. This is your call to action.

◀ **WRITER'S CHOICE**
Keep an open mind as you research your issue. You may change your mind! It's OK to switch sides before— or after—you start to draft.

Revise Your Writing

1 Sort it out As you reread your draft, think about organization. You might try this type of plan:

Paragraph 1: Summary of issue and your position statement
Paragraph 2: Reasons and supporting evidence
Paragraph 3: Opposing arguments and your answer to them
Paragraph 4: Your call to action

◀ **PARAGRAPHING**
You might choose to write a new paragraph for each reason.

2 Use strategy Three strategies can help you convince your listeners. First, back up each point with facts and statistics. Second, appeal to logic: use reasoning that makes sense. Third, appeal to emotion: choose words that create the feelings you want.

◀ **VOCABULARY TIP**
How can you use words to create feelings? See the Denotation and Connotation Workshop on page 465.

3 Practice out loud Try reading your speech to a partner, who can help you revise the weaker areas.

Revision Questions

For You	For a Peer Reader
1. Do I state the issue clearly and show its importance?	**1.** What main message does my speech leave you with?
2. Is my reasoning logical? Do I offer enough evidence?	**2.** Which part works best to persuade you?
3. What words would help me strengthen my persuasion?	**3.** Can you think of important arguments I ignored?

Proofread

Check your grammar and mechanics carefully, and correct any errors you find. Pay special attention to indefinite pronouns.

THE EDITOR'S EYE: INDEFINITE PRONOUNS

An indefinite pronoun is a pronoun that does not refer to a particular person, place, or thing.

Words like *everyone* and *anybody* are indefinite pronouns. Personal pronouns used with them must agree in number.

Problem   I think *everyone* should do *their* best.

Correct   I think *everyone* should do *his or her* best.

NEED MORE HELP?
See the Language Workshop on pages 393–395.

SPEAKING AND LISTENING TIP
Practice reading your speech aloud several times in advance. If you stumble at the same places each time, try changing your wording.

Publish and Present

▶ **Classroom Soapbox**   Deliver your speech to your class. Use effective speaking skills: make eye contact with your listeners, speak at a normal rate, and project your voice toward the back wall of the room.

Reflect on Your Writing

FOR YOUR PORTFOLIO ▶   Add your answers to the questions below to your portfolio.

1. When you first read your speech aloud, what surprised you most?

2. Did you find it harder to appeal to logic or to emotion? Why?

LANGUAGE WORKSHOP

PRONOUN PROBLEMS

Indefinite Pronouns

You remember that a pronoun takes the place of a noun or another pronoun. You probably also remember that personal pronouns, such as *he, she,* or *they,* refer to specific people, places, or things. Indefinite pronouns are different. An indefinite pronoun does not refer to any specific person, place, or thing. Study the indefinite pronouns below. Notice which are singular and which are plural.

INDEFINITE PRONOUNS				
Singular another	anybody	anyone	anything	each
either	everybody	everyone	everything	one
neither	nobody	somebody	someone	no one
Plural both	few	many	several	

With singular indefinite pronouns, use singular personal pronouns. With plural indefinite pronouns, use plural personal pronouns.

Singular

In Siberia, the girls waded through mud so deep that *one* lost *her* shoe.

Each of the boys hoped *he* could raise a champion racing pigeon.

Nobody neglected *his or her* potato plot during the brief summer.

Plural

In the hot, flea-infested huts, *few* could control *their* tempers.

Many knew Vanya the bum, but *they* didn't know his story.

Don't be confused if a phrase appears between the indefinite pronoun and the personal pronoun.

◀ **HIS OR HER?**
When the person referred to could be either male or female, use "he or she," "him or her," or "his or her(s)."

Incorrect   Each of the girls studied *their* lessons. (The personal pronoun should agree with *each,* not with *girls.*)

Correct   Each of the girls studied *her* lessons.

Exercise 1   Concept Check   For each indefinite pronoun, choose the correct personal pronoun. Write your choices on your paper.

1. In Esther's hut, everyone shared what (he or she, they) had.
2. No one wanted Vanya the bum to live with (him or her, them).
3. Couldn't anybody have a home of (his or her, their) own?
4. Many of the villagers had (his or her, their) own reasons for not trusting Vanya.
5. Several told (his or her, their) friends that Vanya was a thief.
6. Could anyone hide (his or her, their) surprise at Vanya's story?
7. He endured many hardships, and each left (its, their) mark.
8. Long ago, one of Vanya's neighbors had spread (his or her, their) opinion that this honest, well-educated man was a traitor.
9. Soon, as everybody watched from (his or her, their) window, Vanya was removed and sent to prison in Siberia.
10. Esther liked and respected Vanya; both enjoyed (his or her, their) time together.

Who and Whom

When *who* and *whom* are used to ask questions, they are called interrogative pronouns. *Who* is used for the subject form and *whom* is the object form.

> *Who* found the ruined hut? (*Who* is the subject of *found.*)

> *Whom* did you invite to dinner? (*Whom* is the direct object. The subject is *you,* and the verb is *did invite.*)

> From *whom* did you hear the news? (*Whom* is the object of the preposition *from.*)

REMINDER
To find the subject and verb of a question more easily, change the question into a statement: *You did hear the news from whom.*

Exercise 2   Concept Check   In each sentence below, choose the correct interrogative pronoun.

1. (Who, Whom) told Esther how to make dye from onion peels?
2. From (who, whom) did she get the material for her curtains?
3. In school, (who, whom) did Esther like best?

4. (Who, Whom) reminded Esther of her grandmother's flower garden?
5. (Who, Whom) did Mrs. Rudomin tell about the public baths?
6. With (who, whom) did the Rudomins sit and watch the stars?
7. To (who, whom) did Esther tell the news about Vanya?
8. (Who, Whom) decided how the family would treat Vanya?
9. (Who, Whom) did Vanya blame for his misfortunes?
10. (Who, Whom) knows why Vanya left the Rudomins?

Exercise 3   Proofreading Skill   Correct the pronoun problems in the following paragraph. Look for problems with indefinite pronouns and personal pronouns, and with the use of *who* and *whom.*

Growing up on the Siberian steppe was hard. No one had enough room for their belongings, or even enough food. Everyone had to find ways to keep their self-respect. Esther's family noticed a ruined hut and moved in. Each of the family members used their talents to make the hut a home. Whom would have expected Esther to make bright curtains in such a place? Few could believe his or her eyes when Mr. Rudomin found glass for the windows. Who did the village leader send to live with the family then? He sent someone with almost nothing to call their own. It seemed that all of the family were being punished for his or her pride.

Exercise 4   Revise Your Writing   Reread the persuasive speech you wrote for the Writer's Workshop on pages 388–392. Then follow the steps below.

1. Lightly underline each indefinite pronoun you have used. Label each **S** (singular) or **P** (plural).
2. Correct any agreement problems involving indefinite pronouns and personal pronouns.
3. Lightly circle the words *who* and *whom* each time you find them.
4. Correct any problems involving the use of *who* and *whom.*

LANGUAGE HANDBOOK
. . . .
For review and practice: Section 5, Using Pronouns, pages 736–737, 738–739; Section 8, Subject-Verb Agreement, page 762.

SPEAKING AND LISTENING
WORKSHOP

CRITICAL LISTENING

Critical listening doesn't mean finding fault. Instead, it means listening carefully and thinking about what you hear. You use critical listening skills before, during, and after any presentation, speech, class lecture, and even when watching television.

Before You Listen

1. Keep an open mind   Don't prejudge the speaker. Instead, think about the speaker's purpose. Try to predict what he or she might focus on.

2. Prepare yourself   Go over what you already know about the speaker's topic. Then think of some questions or areas you'd like to see discussed.

While You Listen

3. Look interested   Be kind to the speaker. Return his or her eye contact, and make it clear that you're paying attention. If you chat with neighbors, the speaker may get thrown off track.

4. Concentrate   Don't just let the words flow over you—pick up on the speaker's strategies. Is he or she relying on logic, emotion, or both? Does the speaker's reasoning make sense? Does he or she supply enough facts and statistics, or does he or she use mostly opinions?

5. Process key ideas   Catch the speaker's key words and ideas, perhaps jotting them down. Then, mentally, put them in your own words. Do they still make sense? Do they have the same impact?

After You Listen

6. Ask questions   Repeat the speaker's words in your questions, so that you check your understanding as you get answers.

7. Sum up and evaluate   What does the speaker want you to do, and why? Are you convinced? Why or why not?

Exercise   Follow Steps 1–6 above as you listen to a classmate give his or her persuasive speech. Then write answers to the questions in Step 7. Finally, write an evaluation of your own listening.

HELP!
For tips on spotting faulty reasoning, see the Reader's Workshop on page 347.

IN OTHER CLASSES
In math class, try mentally putting key ideas and instructions into your own words to check your understanding and remember what you hear.

BONDS OF THE HEART

When people form close relationships, anything may happen. The bonds they establish may bring unexpected joy, comic irritation, heartfelt love, or even heroic sacrifice. Sometimes, their bonds can endure all hardships, even surviving separation or death. At other times, bonds strain to the breaking point.

In the following selections you will read about very different links between people. The characters range from a man who falls instantly in love to an old woman who takes years to let down her guard. As you read, think about how these relationships compare to your own.

Fiction

A *Crush*

CYNTHIA RYLANT

Examine What You Know

How do you react toward people who are mentally retarded? Are you uncomfortable or frightened? Do you feel pity or curiosity or compassion? Or do you just see them as human beings? Discuss with your classmates how people of normal intelligence often react to mentally retarded people, and whether you think such reactions are justified.

Expand Your Knowledge

The most common standard by which people's intelligence is compared is a number called IQ, or intelligence quotient. IQ is measured by tests. While the average person has an IQ of 90 to 109, people with an IQ below 70 are considered mentally retarded. Retarded people, such as one of the characters you will meet in this story, are classified by the degree of their retardation as mildly, moderately, severely, or profoundly retarded. Today, about three percent of the people in the United States are considered retarded. In the past, many of the retarded were put into institutions. Today, however, most mentally handicapped people live within the community, either in group homes or with their families.

Enrich Your Reading

Character Development   In the following story, some characters change and grow while others remain the same. A **static character** is one who changes little, if at all, from the beginning of a story to the end. A **dynamic character** changes significantly. As you read the next story, decide which characters are static and which are dynamic.

■ *Author biography on Extend page*

A *Crush*

CYNTHIA RYLANT

When the windows of Stan's Hardware started filling up with flowers, everyone in town knew something had happened. Excess flowers usually mean death, but since these were all real flowers bearing the aroma of nature instead of floral preservative, and since they stood bunched in clear Mason jars instead of impaled on Styrofoam crosses, everyone knew nobody had died. So they all figured somebody had a crush and kept quiet.

There wasn't really a Stan of Stan's Hardware. Dick Wilcox was the owner, and since he'd never liked his own name, he gave his store half the name of his child-hood hero, Stan Laurel in the movies. Dick had been married for twenty-seven years. Once, his wife Helen had dropped a German chocolate cake on his head at a Lion's Club dance, so Dick and Helen were not likely candidates for the honest expres-sion of the flowers in those clear Mason jars lining the windows of Stan's Hardware, and speculation had to move on to Dolores.

Dolores was the assistant manager at Stan's and had worked there for twenty years, since high school. She knew the store like a mother knows her baby, so Dick—who had trouble keeping up with things like prices and new brands of drywall com-pound—tried to keep himself busy in the back and give Dolores the run of the floor. This worked fine because the carpenters and plumbers and painters in town trusted Dolores and took her advice to heart. They also liked her tattoo.

Dolores was the only woman in town with a tattoo.

Dolores was the only woman in town with a tattoo. On the days she went sleeve-less, one could see it on the taut brown skin of her upper arm: "Howl at the Moon." The picture was of a baying coyote, which must have been a dark gray in its early days but which had faded to the color of the spack-ling paste Dolores stocked in the third aisle. Nobody had gotten out of Dolores the true story behind the tattoo. Some of the men who came in liked to show off their own, and they'd roll up their sleeves or pull open their shirts, exhibiting bald eagles and rat-tlesnakes and Confederate flags, and they'd

---

Words to Know and Use

impaled (im pāld') *adj.* pierced through **impale** *v.*

try to coax out of Dolores the history of her coyote. All of the men had gotten their tattoos when they were in the service, drunk on weekend leave and full of the spitfire of young soldiers. Dolores had never been in the service, and she'd never seen weekend leave, and there wasn't a tattoo parlor anywhere near. They couldn't figure why or where any half-sober woman would have a howling coyote ground into the soft skin of her upper arm. But Dolores wasn't telling.

That the flowers in Stan's front window had anything to do with Dolores seemed completely improbable. As far as anyone knew, Dolores had never been in love, nor had anyone ever been in love with her. Some believed it was the tattoo, of course, or the fine, dark hair coating Dolores's upper lip which kept <u>suitors</u> away. Some felt it was because Dolores was just more of a man than most of the men in town, and fellows couldn't figure out how to court someone who knew more about the carburetor of a car or the backside of a washing machine than they did. Others thought Dolores simply didn't want love. This was a popular theory among the women in town who sold Avon and Mary Kay cosmetics. Whenever one of them ran into the hardware for a package of light bulbs or some batteries, she would mentally pluck every one of

the black hairs above Dolores's lip. Then she'd wash that grease out of Dolores's hair, give her a good blunt cut, dress her in a decent silk-blend blouse with a nice Liz Claiborne skirt from the Sports line, and, finally, tone down that <u>swarthy</u>, longshoreman look of Dolores's with a concealing beige foundation,[1] some frosted peach lipstick, and a good gray liner for the eyes.

Dolores simply didn't want love, the Avon lady would think as she walked back to her car carrying her little bag of batteries. If she did, she'd fix herself up.

The man who was in love with Dolores and who brought her zinnias and cornflowers and nasturtiums and marigolds and asters and four-o'clocks in clear Mason jars did not know any of this. He did not know that men showed Dolores their tattoos. He did not know that Dolores understood how to use and to sell a belt sander. He did not know that Dolores needed some concealing beige foundation so she could get someone to love her. The man who brought flowers to Dolores on Wednesdays when the hardware opened its doors at 7:00 A.M. didn't care who Dolores had ever been or what anyone had ever thought of her. He loved her, and he wanted to bring her flowers.

Ernie had lived in this town all of his life and had never before met Dolores. He was thirty-three years old, and for thirty-one of those years he had lived at home with his mother in a small dark house on the edge of

---

1. **concealing beige foundation:** a cosmetic that covers skin flaws.

Words to Know and Use

suitor (sōot′ ər) *n.* a man seeking a woman's love
swarthy (swôr*th*′ ē) *adj.* having darkish skin

town near Beckwith's Orchards. Ernie had been a beautiful baby, with a shock of shining black hair and large blue eyes and a round, wise face. But as he had grown, it had become clearer and clearer that though he was indeed a perfectly beautiful child, his mind had not developed with the same perfection. Ernie would not be able to speak in sentences until he was six years old. He would not be able to count the apples in a bowl until he was eight. By the time he was ten, he could sing a simple song. At age twelve, he understood what a joke was. And when he was twenty, something he saw on television made him cry.

Ernie's mother kept him in the house with her because it was easier, so Ernie knew nothing of the world except this house. They lived, the two of them, in tiny dark rooms always illuminated by the glow of a television set, Ernie's bags of Oreos and Nutter Butters littering the floor, his baseball cards scattered across the sofa, his heavy winter coat thrown over the arm of a chair so he could wear it whenever he wanted, and his box of Burpee seed packages sitting in the middle of the kitchen table.

These Ernie <u>cherished</u>. The seeds had been delivered to his home by mistake. One day a woman wearing a brown uniform had pulled up in a brown truck, walked quickly to the front porch of Ernie's house, set a box down, and with a couple of toots of her horn, driven off again. Ernie had watched her through the curtains and, when she was gone, had ventured onto the porch and shyly, cautiously, picked up the box. His mother checked it when he carried it inside.

The box didn't have their name on it, but the brown truck was gone, so whatever was in the box was theirs to keep. Ernie pulled off the heavy tape, his fingers trembling, and found inside the box more little packages of seeds than he could count. He lifted them out, one by one, and examined the beautiful photographs of flowers on each. His mother was not interested, had returned to the television, but Ernie sat down at the kitchen table and quietly looked at each package for a long time, his fingers running across the slick paper and outlining the shapes of zinnias and cornflowers and nasturtiums and marigolds and asters and four-o'clocks, his eyes drawing up their colors.

Two months later Ernie's mother died. A neighbor found her at the mailbox beside the road. People from the county courthouse came out to get Ernie, and as they ushered him from the home he would never see again, he picked up the box of seed packages from his kitchen table and passed through the doorway.

Eventually Ernie was moved to a large white house near the main street of town. This house was called a group home, because in it lived a group of people who, like Ernie, could not live on their own. There were six of them. Each had his own room. When Ernie was shown the room that would be his, he put the box of Burpee seeds—which he had kept with him since his mother's death—on the little table beside the bed, and then he sat down on the bed and cried.

Ernie cried every day for nearly a month. And then he stopped. He dried his tears, and he learned how to bake refrigerator biscuits and how to dust mop and what to do if the indoor plants looked brown.

Ernie loved watering the indoor plants, and it was this pleasure which finally drew him outside. One of the young men who worked at the group home—a college student named Jack—grew a large garden in the back of the house. It was full of tomato vines and the large yellow blossoms of healthy squash. During his first summer at the house, Ernie would stand at the kitchen window, watching Jack and sometimes a resident of the home move among the vegetables. Ernie was curious, but too afraid to go into the garden.

Then one day when Ernie was watching through the window, he noticed that Jack was ripping open several slick little packages and emptying them into the ground. Ernie panicked and ran to his room. But the box of Burpee seeds was still there on his table, untouched. He grabbed it, slid it under his bed, then went back through the house and out into the garden as if he had done this every day of his life.

He stood beside Jack, watching him empty seed packages into the soft black soil, and as the packages were emptied, Ernie asked for them, holding out his hand, his eyes on the photographs of red radishes and purple eggplant. Jack handed the empty packages over with a smile and with that gesture became Ernie's first friend.

Jack tried to explain to Ernie that the seeds would grow into vegetables, but Ernie could not believe this until he saw it come true. And when it did, he looked all the more intently at the packages of zinnias and cornflowers and the rest hidden beneath his bed. He thought more deeply about them, but he could not carry them to the garden. He could not let the garden have his seeds.

That was the first year in the large white house.

The second year, Ernie saw Dolores, and after that he thought of nothing else but her and of the photographs of flowers beneath his bed.

Love is such a mystery.

Jack had decided to take Ernie downtown for breakfast every Wednesday morning to ease him into the world outside that of the group home. They left very early, at 5:45 A.M., so there would be few people and almost no traffic to frighten Ernie and make him beg for his room. Jack and Ernie drove to the Big Boy restaurant which sat across the street from Stan's Hardware. There they ate eggs and bacon and French toast among those whose work demanded rising before the sun: bus drivers, policemen, nurses, millworkers. Their first time in the Big Boy,

Ernie was too nervous to eat. The second time, he could eat, but he couldn't look up. The third time, he not only ate everything on his plate, but he lifted his head and he looked out the window of the Big Boy restaurant toward Stan's Hardware across the street. There he saw a dark-haired woman in jeans and a black T-shirt unlocking the front door of the building, and that was the moment Ernie started loving Dolores and thinking about giving up his seeds to the soft black soil of Jack's garden.

Love is such a mystery, and when it strikes the heart of one as mysterious as Ernie himself, it can hardly be spoken of. Ernie could not explain to Jack why he went directly to his room later that morning, pulled the box of Burpee seeds from under his bed, then grabbed Jack's hand in the kitchen and walked with him to the garden, where Ernie had come to believe things would grow. Ernie handed the packets of seeds one by one to Jack, who stood in silent admiration of the lovely photographs before asking Ernie several times, "Are you sure you want to plant these?" Ernie was sure. It didn't take him very long, and when the seeds all lay under the moist black earth, Ernie carried his empty packages inside the house and spent the rest of the day spreading them across his bed in different arrangements.

That was in June. For the next several Wednesdays at 7:00 A.M., Ernie watched every movement of the dark-haired woman behind the lighted windows of Stan's Hardware. Jack watched Ernie watch Dolores and discreetly said nothing.

When Ernie's flowers began growing in

Illustration by Patty Dryden.

July, Ernie spent most of his time in the garden. He would watch the garden for hours, as if he expected it suddenly to move or to impress him with a quick trick. The fragile green stems of his flowers stood uncertainly in the soil, like baby colts on their first legs, but the young plants performed no magic for Ernie's eyes. They saved their shows for the middle of the night and next day surprised Ernie with tender small blooms in all the colors the photographs had promised.

The flowers grew fast and hardy, and one early Wednesday morning, when they looked as big and bright as their pictures on the empty packages, Ernie pulled a glass canning jar off a dusty shelf in the basement of his house. He washed the jar, half filled it with water, then carried it to the garden where he placed in it one of every kind of flower he had grown. He met Jack at the car and rode off to the Big Boy with the jar of flowers held tight between his small hands. Jack told him it was a beautiful bouquet.

When they reached the door of the Big Boy, Ernie stopped and pulled at Jack's arm, pointing to the building across the street. "OK," Jack said, and he led Ernie to the front door of Stan's Hardware. It was 6:00 A.M., and the building was still dark. Ernie set the clear Mason jar full of flowers under the sign that read "Closed," then he smiled at Jack and followed him back across the street to get breakfast.

When Dolores arrived at seven and picked up the jar of zinnias and cornflowers and nasturtiums and marigolds and asters and four-o'clocks, Ernie and Jack were watching her from a booth in the Big Boy. Each had a wide smile on his face as Dolores put her nose to the flowers. Ernie giggled. They watched the lights of the hardware store come up and saw Dolores place the clear Mason jar on the ledge of the front window. They drove home still smiling.

All the rest of that summer, Ernie left a jar of flowers every Wednesday morning at the front door of Stan's Hardware. Neither Dick Wilcox nor Dolores could figure out why the flowers kept coming, and each of them assumed somebody had a crush on the other. But the flowers had an effect on them anyway. Dick started spending more time out on the floor making conversation with the customers, while Dolores stopped wearing T-shirts to work and instead wore crisp white blouses with the sleeves rolled back off her wrists. Occasionally she put on a bracelet.

By summer's end Jack and Ernie had become very good friends, and when the flowers in the garden behind their house began to wither, and Ernie's face began to grow gray as he watched them, Jack brought home one bright day in late September a great long box. Ernie followed Jack as he carried it down to the basement and watched as Jack pulled a long glass tube from the box and attached this tube to the wall above a table. When Jack plugged in the tube's electric cord, a soft lavender light washed the room.

"Sunshine," said Jack.

Then he went back to his car for a smaller box. He carried this down to the basement where Ernie still stood staring at the strange light. Jack handed Ernie the small box, and when Ernie opened it, he found more little packages of seeds than he could count, with new kinds of photographs on the slick paper.

"Violets," Jack said, pointing to one of them.

Then he and Ernie went outside to get some dirt. ❧

Responding to Reading

First Impressions

1. How did the story make you feel? Describe your reaction in your journal or notebook.

Second Thoughts

2. What are the effects of Ernie's crush?

   Think about
   - the changes in Ernie
   - the changes in other characters

3. How do you think Dolores would react if she found out who was sending her flowers? Explain your opinion.

   Think about
   - what you know about her personality
   - the differences between Dolores and Ernie

4. Think about your previous discussion about retarded people. Have your feelings changed after reading the story? Why or why not?

Broader Connections

5. Do you have a friend, neighbor, or relative who is mentally disabled? How does the character of Ernie compare with the retarded person you know? How does the care received by Ernie compare with the care received by the person you know?

Literary Concept: Third-Person Point of View

In a story told from a **third-person point of view,** the narrator is outside of the action, not one of the characters. This kind of narrator uses pronouns such as *he* and *she* to tell the story. A third-person narrative can be either omniscient or limited. If the story is told from an **omniscient,** or all-knowing, point of view, the narrator reports the thoughts of more than one character. In the **limited** point of view, the narrator tells what only one character thinks and feels. Is the third-person point of view in "A Crush" omniscient or limited? Why?

Concept Review: Minor Character Jack is a minor character in this story. What does he contribute to the plot? Is he dynamic or static?

Writing Options

1. Assume that Jack is working in the group home as part of his college studies. Write an entry from his **learning log**—his personal learning diary—in which he discusses what he has learned from and about Ernie.

2. Write a **personal narrative** about a time when you had a crush on someone. Your narrative can be humorous or serious.

3. Everyone in town is curious about Dolores's tattoo. Write a **story** that explains how, when, where, and why she got her coyote tattoo.

4. How would you feel if in your neighborhood someone wanted to build a group home for retarded people? Write a **speech** you might deliver at a town meeting that explains your opinion.

Vocabulary Practice

Exercise   On a separate sheet of paper, write the word from the list that best completes the meaning of the sentence.

1. While eating breakfast, Ernie __?__ watched the hardware store so that other people would not notice his interest.

2. Dolores had dark eyes and a __?__ complexion.

3. To love someone without reservation is to __?__ him or her.

4. If Ernie decided to try to convince Dolores to marry him, he would have been her __?__.

5. Empty seed packets, __?__ on sticks in the garden, showed which flowers were planted in each row.

Words to Know and Use

———

**cherish
discreetly
impaled
suitor
swarthy**

Options for Learning

1 • Avon Calling Imagine that some women in town take it upon themselves to change Dolores's appearance. Draw or paint before-and-after pictures of Dolores, similar to those sometimes found in popular women's magazines.

2 • A Tale of Tattoo Research the history of tattoos. How are they created? What countries or cultures are known for tattoos? Why are they worn? What are unusual examples? Present your findings, with pictures if possible. In addition, you may want to design a tattoo for Ernie and Jack.

3 • Mood Music Imagine that you are making a movie version of this story. Choose a piece of music, either classical or popular, to use as the movie's musical theme. Explain your choice to the class.

4 • Special Olympics The Special Olympics was created not only to allow mentally handicapped people to participate in athletic activities, but also to help change the general public's attitude toward retarded people. Find out who started these games and when and how they work, both in the United States and internationally.

 FACT FINDER HEALTH

At what age would Ernie have spoken in sentences if he had been a normal child?

Cynthia Rylant
1954–

In the town of Kent, Ohio, where Cynthia Rylant lives, a strange small man sometimes brings flowers in Mason jars to waitresses at a little diner. He became the inspiration for Ernie. Beside the diner is a hardware store. "That's where my imagination found Dolores," reports Rylant.

Rylant grew up in the mountains of West Virginia. She lived with her grandparents for four years while her mother studied nursing. Later, she shared an apartment with her mother. She wrote her first book, *When I Was Young in the Mountains,* in one night. Nevertheless, she says, "It took me about seven years to feel like a writer."

Rylant has achieved success in many forms of writing: picture books for children, young-adult novels, short stories, and poetry. One of her recent books, *A Fine White Dust,* was named a Newbery Honor Book. Her award-winning book of poetry is called *Waiting to Waltz: A Childhood.*

Poetry

The *Highwayman*

ALFRED NOYES

Examine What You Know

What kinds of sacrifices would you be willing to make for someone you love? Rate each of the items below on a scale of 1 to 5. Discuss your responses with your classmates.

What would you sacrifice for love?					
	Completely unwilling				Very willing
	1	2	3	4	5
Money					
Personal property					
Personal goals					
Safety					
Freedom					
Life					

Expand Your Knowledge

This poem about two lovers is set in eighteenth-century England. One of the lovers is a highwayman—a thief on horseback. Highwaymen were usually young and daring men who streaked through the night, skillfully racing their horses down dark and lonely country roads. They stole jewels and money from the rich who traveled by stagecoach. Some of them, like Robin Hood, gave what they stole to the poor. Redcoats—the same English soldiers who fought against American colonists—defended citizens from these raiders of the night.

Enrich Your Reading

Narrative Poetry   Like fiction, narrative poetry tells a story. Unlike fiction, however, narrative poems are written in lines and stanzas. They rely on sound devices such as rhyme and rhythm and are meant to be read aloud. As you read, think about why the writer told the story of "The Highwayman" in the form of a poem.

■ *Author biography in Reader's Handbook*

The *Highwayman*

ALFRED NOYES

Part 1

The wind was a torrent of darkness among the gusty trees,
The moon was a ghostly galleon[1] tossed upon cloudy seas,
The road was a ribbon of moonlight over the purple moor,[2]
And the highwayman came riding—
5   Riding—riding—
The highwayman came riding, up to the old inn door.

He'd a French cocked hat on his forehead, a bunch of lace at his chin,
A coat of the claret[3] velvet, and breeches of brown doeskin.
They fitted with never a wrinkle. His boots were up to the thigh.
10 And he rode with a jeweled twinkle.
    His pistol butts a-twinkle.
His rapier hilt[4] a-twinkle, under the jeweled sky.

Over the cobbles[5] he clattered and clashed in the dark innyard
He tapped with his whip on the shutters, but all was locked and barred.
15 He whistled a tune to the window, and who should be waiting there
But the landlord's black-eyed daughter,
    Bess, the landlord's daughter,
Plaiting[6] a dark red love knot into her long black hair.

---

1. **galleon** (gal′ ē ən): a large sailing ship.
2. **moor:** a stretch of open, rolling wasteland, usually covered with heather.
3. **claret:** dark red, like the color of red wine.
4. **rapier** (rā′ pē ər) **hilt:** sword handle.
5. **cobbles:** rounded stones used for paving roads.
6. **plaiting:** braiding.

Original illustration by Charles Mikolaycak for "The Highwayman." Courtesy of the Kerlan Collection at the University of Minnesota. Used with permission of the illustrator and Lothrop, Lee and Shepard Publishers.

And dark in the dark old innyard a stable wicket[7] creaked
20   Where Tim the ostler[8] listened. His face was white and peaked.
His eyes were hollows of madness, his hair like moldy hay,
But he loved the landlord's daughter,
      The landlord's red-lipped daughter,
Dumb as a dog he listened, and he heard the robber say—

25   "One kiss, my bonny sweetheart, I'm after a prize tonight,
But I shall be back with the yellow gold before the morning light;
Yet, if they press me sharply, and harry me through the day,
Then look for me by moonlight,
      Watch for me by moonlight,
30   I'll come to thee by moonlight, though hell should bar the way."

---

7. **wicket:** a small door or gate.
8. **ostler** (äs′ ler): an inn employee who cares for guests' horses.

He rose upright in the stirrups. He scarce could reach her hand,
But she loosened her hair in the casement.[9] His face burnt like a brand
As the black cascade of perfume came tumbling over his breast;
And he kissed its waves in the moonlight,
35   (Oh, sweet black waves in the moonlight!)
Then he tugged at his rein in the moonlight, and galloped away to the west.

Part 2

He did not come in the dawning. He did not come at noon;
And out of the tawny sunset, before the rise of the moon,
When the road was a gypsy's ribbon, looping the purple moor,
40 A redcoat troop came marching—
   Marching—marching—
King George's men came marching, up to the old inn door.

They said no word to the landlord. They drank his ale instead.
But they gagged his daughter, and bound her, to the foot of her narrow bed.
45 Two of them knelt at her casement, with muskets at their side!
There was death at every window;
   And hell at one dark window;
For Bess could see, through her casement, the road that *he* would ride.

They had tied her up to attention, with many a sniggering jest.
50 They had bound a musket beside her, with the muzzle beneath her breast!
"Now keep good watch!" and they kissed her. She heard the doomed man
   say—
Look for me by moonlight;
   Watch for me by moonlight;
I'll come to thee by moonlight, though hell should bar the way!

55 She twisted her hands behind her; but all the knots held good!
She writhed her hands till her fingers were wet with sweat or blood!
They stretched and strained in the darkness, and the hours crawled by like
   years,
Till, now, on the stroke of midnight,
   Cold, on the stroke of midnight,
60 The tip of one finger touched it! The trigger at least was hers!

---

9. **casement:** a window frame with side hinges.

The tip of one finger touched it. She strove no more for the rest.
Up, she stood to attention, with the muzzle beneath her breast.
She would not risk their hearing; she would not strive again;
For the road lay bare in the moonlight;
65 Blank and bare in the moonlight;
And the blood in her veins, in the moonlight, throbbed to her love's refrain.

Tlot-tlot; tlot-tlot! Had they heard it? The horse hoofs ringing clear;
Tlot-tlot, tlot-tlot, in the distance? Were they deaf that they did not hear?
Down the ribbon of moonlight, over the brow of the hill.
70 The highwayman came riding—
   Riding—riding—
The redcoats looked to their priming![10] She stood up, straight and still.

---

10. priming: the explosive used to set off a firearm.

Original illustration by Charles Mikolaycak for "The Highwayman." Courtesy of the Kerlan Collection at the University of Minnesota. Used with permission of the illustrator and Lothrop, Lee and Shepard Publishers.

Tlot-tlot, in the frosty silence! *Tlot-tlot,* in the echoing night!
Nearer he came and nearer. Her face was like a light.
75 Her eyes grew wide for a moment; she drew one last deep breath,
Then her finger moved in the moonlight,
    Her musket shattered the moonlight,
Shattered her breast in the moonlight and warned him—with her death.

He turned. He spurred to the west; he did not know who stood
80 Bowed, with her head o'er the musket, drenched with her own blood!
Not till the dawn he heard it, his face grew gray to hear
How Bess, the landlord's daughter,
    The landlord's black-eyed daughter,
Had watched for her love in the moonlight, and died in the darkness there.

85 Back, he spurred like a madman, shouting a curse to the sky,
With the white road smoking behind him and his rapier brandished high.
Blood-red were his spurs in the golden noon; wine-red his velvet coat;
When they shot him down on the highway,
    Down like a dog on the highway,
90 And he lay in his blood on the highway, with a bunch of lace at his throat.

And still of a winter's night, they say, when the wind is in the trees,
When the moon is a ghostly galleon tossed upon cloudy seas,
When the road is a ribbon of moonlight over the purple moor,
A highwayman comes riding—
95   *Riding—riding—*
A highwayman comes riding, up to the old inn door.

Over the cobbles he clatters and clangs in the dark innyard;
He taps with his whip on the shutters, but all is locked and barred.
He whistles a tune to the window, and who should be waiting there
100 *But the landlord's black-eyed daughter,*
    Bess, the landlord's daughter,
Plaiting a dark red love knot into her long black hair.

Responding to Reading

First Impressions

1. What images will you remember from this poem? Describe them briefly in your journal or notebook.

Second Thoughts

2. Do you think either Bess or the highwayman is heroic? Explain.

Think about
- the sacrifice each made
- your own views about love and sacrifice
- the reasons for their entrapment and death

3. What is your opinion of the actions of the redcoats?

Think about
- their duty to capture outlaws
- the trap that they set up
- their treatment of Bess

Literary Concept: Onomatopoeia

The use of words that imitate sounds is called **onomatopoeia.** *Tick-tock,* for example, imitates the sound of a clock. What examples of onomatopoeia can you find in the poem? What do these sound effects add to the poem?

Concept Review: Rhyme and Rhythm Read aloud the last two stanzas. Then make a copy of the stanzas, marking the beats, or the syllables that receive emphasis. Draw lines that connect rhyming words at the ends of lines. Discuss how the rhythm and rhyme affect your enjoyment of the poem. How would the effect be different if the poem had been written in free verse?

Writing Options

1. Write a **summary** of the story from the viewpoint of the landlord, the ostler, or a redcoat soldier.

2. An **epitaph** is a written tribute to a dead person. Write an epitaph for either the highwayman or Bess.

Poetry

Graduation Morning
PAT MORA

There Is No Word for Goodbye
MARY TALLMOUNTAIN

Examine What You Know

Think about the crossroads in your life—times when one part of your life ends and a new part begins. For example, the transition from elementary to middle school would be a crossroad, as would saying goodbye to a best friend who is moving. What feelings and thoughts do such situations bring about? Why is it sometimes so hard to say goodbye to the old and hello to the new? In your journal, describe your thoughts at such times.

Expand Your Knowledge

The following poems portray two young people who are moving on to new chapters in their lives. The first poem is set near the Rio Grande, the boundary between Texas and Mexico. In this border area, customs and traditions from the United States and Mexico blend together. Many residents on both sides of the river speak two languages, English and Spanish. A number of Mexican citizens, like the woman in this poem, work in Texas and return at night to their homes in Mexico.

The second poem describes a farewell scene between two Native Americans. They are Athabaskans, the name given to various tribes in northern Canada—including the Sarsis, the Beavers, and the Chipewyans—who speak the Athabaskan language. Though their numbers are now small, the Athabaskans have a long, proud history.

Enrich Your Reading

Understanding Cultural Contexts The scenes presented in these two poems reflect how crossroads or passages are experienced in different cultures. As you read, look for details about each culture. Then think about the ways in which the poems are similar, despite the differences in the cultures.

■ *Author biographies in Reader's Handbook*

Graduation Morning

PAT MORA

for Anthony

She called him *Lucero,*[1] morning star,
snared him with sweet coffee, pennies,
Mexican milk candy, brown bony hugs.

Through the years she'd cross the Rio
5 Grande to clean his mother's home. "*Lucero,
mi*[2] *lucero,*" she'd cry, when she'd see him
running toward her in the morning,
when she pulled stubborn cactus thorns
from his small hands, when she found him
10 hiding in the creosote.[3]

Though she's small and thin,
black sweater, black scarf,
the boy in the white graduation robe
easily finds her at the back of the cathedral,
15 finds her amid the swirl of sparkling clothes,
finds her eyes.

Tears slide down her wrinkled cheeks.
Her eyes, *luceros,* stroke his face.

---

1. lucero (lo͞o se′ rô) *Spanish.*
2. mi (mē) *Spanish:* my.
3. creosote (krē′ ə sōt′): short for *creosote bush,* a bush
found in the Southwest.

R*esponding to Reading*

First Impression of "Graduation Morning"

1. What images do you form of the woman and the boy in this poem?
Briefly describe them in your journal or notebook.

Second Thoughts on "Graduation Morning"

2. Why do you think the housekeeper and the boy feel such a strong
bond between them?

3. What feelings do you think the housekeeper has at this crossroads in
the boy's life?

4. Why do you think the poem focuses on the housekeeper rather than
the boy's parents?

There Is No Word for Goodbye

MARY TALLMOUNTAIN

Sokoya,[1] I said, looking through
    the net of wrinkles into
    wise black pools
    of her eyes.

5 What do you say in Athabaskan
    when you leave each other?
    What is the word
    for goodbye?

A shade of feeling rippled
10   the wind-tanned skin.
    Ah, nothing, she said,
    watching the river flash.

She looked at me close.
    We just say, Tlaa.[2] That means,
15   See you.
    We never leave each other.
    When does your mouth
    say goodbye to your heart?

---

1. sokoya (sə koi′ yə): aunt on mother's side.
2. tlaa (tlä).

SHUGNAK, ALASKA   1974   Alex Harris   Courtesy of the photographer.

She touched me light
20   as a bluebell.
            You forget when you leave us,
            You're so small then.
            We don't use that word.

We always think you're coming back,
25   but if you don't,
            we'll see you some place else.
            You understand,
                There is no word for goodbye.

EXPLAIN

*R*esponding to Reading

First Impressions of "There Is No Word for Goodbye"

1. How do you feel about the aunt's response to her niece's question? Describe your feelings in your journal or notebook.

Second Thoughts on "There Is No Word for Goodbye"

2. What can you infer about the bonds between the aunt and the niece?

3. In this poem, what do you learn about the Athabaskans and how they view one another?

> **Think about**
> * why they have "no word for goodbye"
> * what the aunt means by saying, "we'll see you some place else"

Comparing the Poems

4. Which poem comes closer to expressing your own feelings about crossroads in your life? Explain.

5. What similarities do you see between the two poems?

*L*iterary Concept: Repetition

Repetition is the technique of using a sound, a word, a phrase, or a sentence over and over again for emphasis. In "Graduation Morning," the Spanish word *lucero,* or its plural form, appears four times. Why do you think the word is repeated so often? How is it used differently at the end of the poem?

*W*riting Options

1. Create a **thesaurus entry** for *goodbye.* A thesaurus entry lists words or phrases that can be used as synonyms for a given word. In your entry, include expressions that suggest meeting one another again. You may include foreign phrases or slang terms.

2. Write a **poem** or **character sketch** that describes an older person who has influenced your life.

Drama

Driving Miss Daisy

ALFRED UHRY

Examine What You Know

This drama, which takes place in the South between 1948 and 1973, is about a wealthy Jewish widow and the African-American chauffeur who works for her. Based on what you know, how do you think these characters would view one another? What problems might they encounter in their relationship? Share your ideas in a class discussion.

Expand Your Knowledge

Few people would have expected this gentle drama about a relationship between two people to become such a success. *Driving Miss Daisy* opened in 1987 as a small production in New York City. It soon moved to Broadway and won the Pulitzer Prize in drama. You are about to read the original screenplay of the 1989 movie version of the play. The movie won four Academy Awards (Oscars), including the award for Best Picture.

Enrich Your Reading

Reading a Screenplay   If you were to see the movie *Driving Miss Daisy,* you would understand where the action occurs just by watching. In the screenplay, changes in time and location are written. Each new scene is marked by a word or phrase in capital letters that tells where it takes place. Since the play spans many years, the year, if it has changed from the previous scene, is named next. Read all stage directions carefully so that you can keep track of when and where the action occurs.

If you were listening to the movie, you would have no trouble understanding the dialect spoken by the actors. In the script, the author shows dialect by omitting letters and respelling words. If you come to dialect that seems confusing, try reading it aloud. For example, Hoke says, "You doan' mean! Oscar say you need a driver for yo' family. What I be doin'?" Read the lines aloud and you will "hear" the meaning.

■ *Author biography on Extend page*

Driving Miss Daisy

ALFRED UHRY

CHARACTERS

Daisy Werthan

Boolie, her son

Florine, his wife

Hoke Colburn, chauffeur

Beulah, friend

Nonie, friend

Miriam, friend

Miss McClatchey, secretary

Oscar, porter

Idella, housekeeper

Katie Bell, cook

State Trooper

Second Trooper

Produce Man

PART 1

DAISY'S KITCHEN, August 1948. Daisy, *who is seventy-two and energetic, enters.* Idella, *who is* Daisy's *age, is polishing silver.*

Daisy. I'm gone to the market, Idella.

Idella. Mmmmm.

BACK YARD. Daisy *is backing her car out of the garage. It suddenly shoots backward and stops, hanging over the edge of the neighbor's stone wall.* Daisy *gets out and slams the door, and the car drops into the neighbor's garden.*

KITCHEN, later. Idella *and* Boolie *are eating fried chicken.*

Boolie. Mama!

Daisy *(off camera).* No!

Boolie. Mama!

Daisy *(off camera).* No!

Boolie. It's a miracle you're not laying in Emory Hospital—or decked out at the funeral parlor.

(Boolie *goes into the pantry, where* Daisy *is transferring pickles from a large crock into jars.)*

Daisy. The cucumbers are pretty this summer.

Boolie. Look at you! You didn't even break your glasses.

Daisy. It was the car's fault.

Boolie. Mama, you had the car in the wrong gear.

Daisy. I did not. *(calls to* Idella) Idella, you want a pickle with your lunch?

Idella *(off camera).* Not me.

Daisy. Well, I'm putting up a jar for you to take home to William, you hear?

Idella *(off camera).* Yassum. Thank you. He love your pickles.

Daisy. That's because he has more sense than you do.

Boolie. You backed the car right into the Pollocks' yard!

Daisy. You should have let me keep my LaSalle. It never would have behaved this way.

Boolie. Mama, cars don't behave. They are behaved upon. The fact is that you, all by yourself, <u>demolished</u> that Packard.[1]

Daisy. Think what you want. I know the truth.

Boolie. The truth is you just cost the insurance company twenty-seven hundred dollars. You are a terrible risk. Nobody is going to issue you a policy after this.

Daisy. You're just saying that to be hateful.

Boolie. OK. Yes. I'm making it all up. Every insurance company in America is lined up out there in the driveway, falling all over themselves to get you to sign up.

Daisy. If you're going to stand in my pantry and lie like a rug, well, I think it's time for you to go somewhere else.

Boolie. OK. I'd better get back to the office. Florine'll have a fit if I don't come home on time tonight.

Daisy. Y'all must have plans tonight.

Boolie. Going to the Ansleys for a dinner party.

Daisy. I see.

Boolie. You see what?

Daisy. This is her idea of heaven on earth, isn't it?

Boolie. What?

Daisy. Socializing with Episcopalians.

Boolie. You're a doodle, Mama. I'll stop by tomorrow evening.

Daisy. How do you know I'll be here? I'm certainly not dependent on you for company.

Boolie. Fine. I'll call first. But you know that we have got some real serious talking to do.

Daisy. No.

Boolie. Mama! (Daisy *starts singing and goes upstairs.)*

HALLWAY, next day. Daisy *is on the phone.*

---

1. **Packard:** name of a luxury American automobile, 1899–1958.

Words to Know and Use

422

demolish (di mäl′ ish) *v.* to wreck; destroy

Daisy. Well, I need you now! I have to be at the beauty shop in half an hour! . . . No, I most certainly did not know you had to call a minimum of two hours ahead. I don't know why you call yourselves a taxi company if you can't provide taxicabs! *(She hangs up.* Idella *is nearby, dusting rag in hand.)*

Idella. You call your son at the mill, he send somebody to carry you.

Daisy. That won't be necessary. I'll fix my own hair.

Idella. Sometimes I think you ain't got the sense God gave a lemon! *(Daisy glares at her;* Idella *returns the glare.)*

LIVING ROOM. Daisy *and three friends are finishing a game of mah-jongg.*

Beulah. Well, it's not my day for mah-jongg. That's easy to see.

Daisy. I have to thank y'all for coming here again. I'm a real pariah[2] without my car.

Nonie. When are you getting your new one?

Daisy. I don't know. Boolie's being real pokey.

Miriam. Don't worry, sugar. I'll come after you for temple tomorrow. *(Idella enters with dishes of ice cream.)*

Beulah. Oh, it's your peach, Daisy. That's my favorite.

Daisy. Well then, try not to get your cigarette dirt in it.

FRONT HALL, later. Boolie *and* Florine *enter. He is wearing jeans and a plaid shirt. She is wearing a denim skirt and a plaid blouse.*

Boolie *(calling).* Mama? You there?

Florine *(calling).* Hey, Mother Werthan! It's just us! *(Daisy comes downstairs, a book in her hand.)*

Daisy. Why didn't you call?

Florine. We can't stay.

Daisy *(sizing up both of their outfits).* So I gather.

Boolie. The Millers are giving a hayride for their anniversary.

Florine. I had these made. Doesn't your baby look cute?

Daisy. That's not exactly the word I'd pick.

Boolie *(seeing her book).* Oh, I've been meaning to read that!

Daisy. Well, I'm sorry. I can't lend it to you. It's due back at the library tomorrow.

Boolie. You want me to return it for you?

Daisy. No, thank you. I will go to the library on the streetcar.

Boolie. Mama! Quit being so stubborn! You know perfectly well that we are going to have to—*(Florine puts a hand on his arm to hush him up.)*

Daisy. Go on now. You don't want to keep the horses waiting. *(Boolie looks exasperated.)*

LIBRARY. Daisy *leaves the library holding two slim books and her purse. Miss Jensen, the librarian, hurries outside, carrying a hefty book.*

Miss Jensen. Miz Werthan! Miz Werthan! Just a minute!

Daisy. Miss Jensen! What in the world?

---

2. **pariah** (pə rī′ ə): a person rejected by others; social outcast.

Miss Jensen. You forgot to ask for the Lincoln biography you reserved. I checked it out for you.

Daisy *(eyeing the book dubiously).* Well! Aren't you the sweet thing!

Miss Jensen. Why, you're just about my best customer! *(She hands* Daisy *the book.)*

Daisy. Thank you. *(She heads off.)*

PIGGLY WIGGLY MARKET. Daisy's *shopping cart contains her three books, her purse, a bar of soap, one lamb chop, and a can of peas.*

Produce Man. How many peaches for you today, Miz Werthan?

Daisy. Three, thank you.

Produce Man. You're not gonna be gettin' any better ones the rest of the summer. Lemme give you a few more.

Daisy. Just the three.

Produce Man. How about a nice watermelon? *(*Daisy *shakes her head no and walks to the checkout counter.)*

DAISY'S DRIVEWAY. Daisy *lugs her parcels slowly up the driveway.*

BOOLIE'S OFFICE. Boolie's *on the phone.*

Boolie. Well, I. W., you know as well as I do that Werthan Bag and Cotton isn't the only textile mill in Atlanta. If you want to get other bids . . . Oh, you did. . . . That's what Ideal bid, huh? . . . Okay. You ever do business with Ideal before? *(*Miss

Photographs from the Zanuck production of *Driving Miss Daisy,* starring Jessica Tandy, Morgan Freeman, and Dan Aykroyd. Warner Brothers, 1989.

McClatchey *appears at the door. He raises his hand, telling her to wait.)*

Miss McClatchey. It's important, Mr. Werthan.

Boolie *(on the phone).* Can you have lunch with me tomorrow? . . . Herrens all right? . . . Yes. Twelve-thirty. Love to Peggy and the children. *(He hangs up. To* Miss McClatchey.) What's wrong?

Words to Know and Use | **dubiously** (dōo′ bē əs lē) *adv.* in a doubtful way; skeptically

Miss McClatchey. Oscar's stuck in the freight elevator.

FREIGHT ELEVATOR. The elevator is well above floor level, revealing only a pair of legs up to the knees. Boolie arrives.

Boolie. Oscar?

Oscar *(from inside the elevator).* Yassuh. Here I am.

Boolie. You all right?

Oscar. Nawsuh. I'm stuck.

Boolie. I know. Fiddle with the lever.

Oscar. It all fiddled out. I done everythin' I know how.

Boolie *(angry).* Call Bell Elevator, Miss McClatchey.

Miss McClatchey. I already did. They're backed up. But they'll be here around one.

Boolie. One! Did you tell them it's an emergency?

Miss McClatchey. You don't have to holler at me, Mr. Werthan. I didn't break the elevator. *(A crowd of workers has gathered.)*

Boolie. You got that stuff for Davison Paxon in there, Oscar?

Oscar. Wrapped and ready to go.

Boolie. I told them they'd have it yesterday. Call Bell back! *(Miss McClatchey goes off. We hear a voice from the crowd.)*

Hoke. Oscar! *(Boolie turns and sees Hoke, who is about sixty.)* You hear me, Oscar?

Oscar. I hear you.

Hoke. Is there a little doohickey up yonder where the gate suppose to close? Stickin' down a little?

Oscar. Wait a minute. Yeah. It right here.

Hoke. Well, reach up and mash on it. Mash it up till it catch.

Oscar. I done it. Now what?

Hoke. Well, just work the lever. *(The elevator comes down, and Oscar comes into view. The workers applaud.)*

Boolie *(to Hoke).* Excuse me, do you work here?

Oscar. Nawsuh, this Hoke.

Hoke. Pleased to see you, suh.

Boolie. Oh. Well, thank you. How did you know about the elevator?

Hoke. I used to drive for the Avondale Dairy, and they have a sorry old elevator worse then disheah.

Oscar. Don't you remember? Hoke the one I told you about.

Boolie. Oh, of course. *(He heads back to his office, and Hoke follows.)*

Hoke. Mist' Werthan. Y'all people Jewish, ain't you?

Boolie. Yes, we are. Why do you ask?

Hoke. Well, suh, I'd druther work for Jews. People always talkin' 'bout they stingy and they cheap, but don' say none of that 'round me.

Boolie. Good to know you feel that way.

Hoke. Yassuh. One time I workin' for this woman over near Little Five Points. What was that woman's name? I forget. Anyway, one day, she have all these old shirts and collars be on the bed, and she say, "They b'long to my daddy, and we fixin' to sell 'em to you for twenty-five cents apiece." *(pause)* Any fool can see the whole bunch together ain't worth a nickel.

Anyway, them the people callin' Jews cheap. So I say, "Yassum, I think about it," and I get me another job as fast as I can. So then I go to work for Judge Harold Stone, another Jewish gentleman jes' like you.

Boolie. You drove for Judge Stone?

Hoke. Seven years to the day, nearabout. An' I be there still if he din' up and die. Miz Stone say, "Move on down to Savannah with me, Hoke," 'cause my wife dead by then, but I say, "No, thank you." I din' want to leave my granbabies.

Boolie. Judge Stone was a friend of my father's.

Hoke. You doan' mean! Oscar say you need a driver for yo' family. What I be doin'? Runnin' yo' children to school and yo' wife to the beauty parlor and like that?

Boolie. I don't have any children, but tell me—

Hoke. Thass a shame. My daughter bes' thing ever happen to me. But you a young man yet. I wouldn't worry none.

Boolie. I won't. Thank you. Hoke, what I'm looking for is somebody to drive my mother around.

Hoke. Excuse me for askin', suh, but how come she ain' hiring for herself?

Boolie. Well, it's a difficult situation.

Hoke. Mmmm hmmm. She done gone 'round the bend[3] a little? That'll happen when they get on.

Boolie. Oh, no. She's all there. Too much there is the problem. It just isn't safe for her to drive anymore. She knows it, but she won't admit it.

Hoke. Cahill! That woman in Little Five Points name Miz Frances Cahill! I leave her and go right to Judge Stone, and he the reason I happy to hear y'all Jews.

Boolie. Hoke, I want you to understand— my mother is a little high-strung. But the fact is you'd be working for me. She can say anything she likes, but she can't fire you. You understand?

Hoke. Doan' you worry none about it. I hold on no matter what way she run me. When I nothin' but a little boy down there on the farm above Macon where I come from, I used to wrastle hogs to the ground at killin' time. And ain' no hog got away from me yet.

Boolie. How does twenty dollars a week sound?

Hoke. Soun' like you done hire yo' mama a chauffeur.

Boolie *smiles with relief.*

DAISY'S FRONT HALL. Idella *is using a carpet sweeper.* Boolie *and* Hoke *enter.*

Boolie. How are you, Idella?

Idella. Livin'.

Boolie. Where's that vacuum cleaner I brought over here?

Idella. In the closet.

Boolie *(to* Hoke*).* She won't touch it.

Idella. I would if it didn' give me a shock every time I go near it.

---

3. **gone 'round the bend:** a phrase suggesting that someone has lost mental alertness or become senile.

Boolie. It works for me.

Idella. Good. You clean up. I go down and run yo' office. (Hoke *laughs*. Idella *shoots him a look*.)

Boolie. Where's Mama?

Idella. Up yonder.

Boolie. I guess you know who this is.

Idella. Mmmm hmmm.

Boolie. I'll be right back, Hoke. (*He heads upstairs*.)

Idella (*to* Hoke). I wouldn't be in your shoes if the Sweet Lawd Jesus come down and ask me hisself!

DAISY'S BEDROOM. Daisy *is at a desk, paying bills*. Boolie *enters*.

Boolie. Good morning, Mama. (*She ignores him*.) All I'm asking is for you to come and say hello.

Daisy. Now you listen here. Unless they rewrote the Constitution and didn't tell me, I still have rights.

Boolie. Well, of course, Mama, but—

Daisy. What I do not want—and absolutely will not have—is some chauffeur sitting in my kitchen, gobbling up my food, running up my phone bill. Oh, I hate all that in my house.

Boolie. You have Idella.

Daisy. Idella is different. She's been coming to me since you were in the eighth grade, and we know how to stay out of each other's way. And even so, there are nicks and chips in my wedding china.

Boolie. Do you think Idella has a vendetta[4] against your wedding china?

Daisy. Stop being sassy. I was brought up to do for myself. On Forsythe Street we couldn't afford them. That's still the best way if you ask me!

Boolie. Them? Afford them? You sound like Governor Talmadge.

Daisy. Why, Boolie! What a thing to say! I'm not prejudiced! Aren't you ashamed?

Boolie. I got to get back to the mill. You might as well try to make the best of this, Mama. (*He leaves*.)

KITCHEN. Idella *is rolling out biscuit dough*. Hoke *is sitting nearby*.

Hoke. I knew a Miss Idella once, down there in Macon.

Idella. Doan' say.

Hoke. You talkin' about sing! I mean that woman had lungs! She'd a been a whole church choir by herself if they'd a let her. And fat, too! She about the size of that stove yonder. (Idella *laughs*. Daisy *enters*.)

Daisy. Don't talk to Idella. She's got work to do.

Hoke. Yassum.

GARDEN. Hoke, *a trowel in hand, is kneeling by a bed of flowers*. Daisy *appears at a window*. Hoke *looks up*.

Hoke. Looks like yo' zinnias could use a little tendin' to.

Daisy. You leave my flower bed alone.

---

4. **vendetta:** a bitter quarrel; effort to take revenge.

Hoke. Yassum. You know, Miz Daisy, you got a nice place back beyond the garage ain't doin' nothin' but sittin' there. I could put you some butter beans and some Irish potatoes—

Daisy. If I want a vegetable garden, I'll plant it for myself.

Hoke. Well, anything else I kin do for you?

Daisy. Go back where you belong. *(She closes the window.)*

HALLWAY. Hoke *is studying the pictures on the wall.* Daisy *appears.*

Daisy. What are you doing there?

Hoke. I love a house with pictures. Make a home. Disheah you, ain't it?

Daisy. Yes.

Hoke. Look like you been a teacher or something.

Daisy. I don't like you nosing through my things. *(She leaves.)*

GARAGE. Hoke *gets into the new car.* Daisy *enters the garage.*

Daisy. What are you doing?

Hoke. Fixin' to back de car out.

Daisy. Why? I'm not going anywhere.

Hoke. I know that, but I brung disheah from home. *(He pulls a cloth from his coat.)* Give the car a good wipe off.

Daisy. What for? It's never been out of the garage.

Hoke. You tellin' me!

Daisy. I don't want you touching my car. You understand? *(He reluctantly gets out of the car.)*

Hoke. Yassum. I reckon I jes' set in the kitchen till five o'clock.

Daisy. That's your affair. *(Hoke goes toward the back door. Then Daisy attacks her flower bed.)*

SCREEN PORCH. Daisy *is reading the morning paper.* Hoke *enters.*

Hoke. Mornin', Miz Daisy.

Daisy. Good morning.

Hoke. Right cool in the night, wasn't it?

Daisy. I wouldn't know. I was asleep.

Hoke. Idella says we runnin' outta coffee and Dutch Cleanser.

Daisy. We are?

Idella *is in the living room, working.*

Idella. Yassum, and we low on silver polish, too.

Daisy. I know . . . and I'm fixin' to go to the Piggly Wiggly on the trolley. *(She gets up and walks toward the front hall.)*

Hoke. Now, Miz Daisy, how come you doan' let me drive you?

Daisy. No, thank you.

FRONT HALL. Daisy *puts on her hat and gathers her gloves and purse.*

Hoke. Ain' that what Mist' Werthan done hire me for?

Daisy. That's his problem.

Hoke. All right den. I find somethin' to do.

Daisy. You leave my things alone! *(She marches outside;* Hoke *follows.)*

Hoke. You know, that Oldsmobile ain't moved an inch from where Mist' Werthan rode it over here from Century Motors.

Seem like that insurance company done give you a whole new car for nothin'.

Daisy. That's your opinion.

Hoke. Yassum. And my other opinion is a fine rich Jewish lady like you doan' b'long draggin' up the steps of no bus luggin' no grocery bags. I come along and carry them fo' you.

Daisy. I don't need you. I don't want you. And I don't like you saying I'm rich.

Hoke. I won' say it no more then.

Daisy. Is that what you and Idella talk about in the kitchen? I hate being discussed behind my back in my own house! I was born on Forsythe Street, and, believe you me, I know the value of a penny. My brother Manny brought home a white cat one day, and Papa said we couldn't keep it because we couldn't afford to feed it. My sisters saved up money so I could go to school and be a teacher. We didn't have anything!

Hoke. Yassum, but look like you doin' all right now. (Daisy g*lares at him, and he retreats to the house.*)

STREET. Daisy *is walking along the sidewalk. She notices that* Hoke *is driving slowly behind her.*

Daisy (*horrified*). What are you doing?

Hoke. Tryin' to take you to the sto'. (*A neighbor, who is gardening in her front yard, looks surprised at this unusual spectacle.*)

Daisy (*to Hoke*). Go away! I've ridden the trolley with groceries plenty of times.

Hoke. Yassum, but I feel bad takin' Mist' Werthan's money for doin' nothin'.

Daisy. How much does he pay you?

Hoke. That between him and me, Miz Daisy.

Daisy. Anything over seven dollars a week is robbery. Highway robbery.

Hoke. Specially when I doan' do nothin' but set on a stool in the kitchen all day long. (Daisy *notices another neighbor watching her through a window.*)

Daisy. All right, the Piggly Wiggly. And then home. Nowhere else.

Hoke. Yassum. (*He stops the car and hops out, but she quickly gets in before he can help her.* Hoke *gets back in.*)

Daisy. Wait. You don't know how to run this car.

Hoke. Ain' you jes' seen me do it? Anyway, disheah automatic. Any fool can run it.

Daisy. Any fool but me, apparently.

Hoke. Ain' no need to be so hard on yoseff now. You cain' drive, but you probably do alotta things I cain' do. It all work out.

Daisy. The idea! (Hoke *starts driving.*)

Hoke. I love the smell of a new car. Doan' you, Miz Daisy? (*no answer*)

Daisy. I'm nobody's fool, Hoke.

Hoke. Nome.

Daisy. I can see that speedometer as well as you can.

Hoke. I see dat.

Daisy. My husband taught me how to run a car.

Hoke. Yassum.

Daisy. So don't think for even a minute that you can—wait! You're speeding! I see it!

Hoke. We ain' goin' but nineteen miles an hour.

Daisy. I like to go under the speed limit.

Hoke. Yassum, but the speed limit thirty-five here.

Daisy. The slower you go, the more you save on gas.

Hoke. We barely moving. Might as well walk to the Piggly Wiggly.

Daisy. Is this your car?

Hoke. Nome.

Daisy. Do you pay for the gas?

Hoke. Nome.

Daisy. All right then. My son may think I'm losing my abilities, but I am still in control of what goes on in my car. Where are you going?

Hoke. To the grocery sto'.

Daisy. Then why didn't you turn on Highland Avenue?

Hoke. Piggly Wiggly ain't on Highland Avenue. It on Euclid.

Daisy. I know where it is, and I want to go to it the way I always go. On Highland Avenue.

Hoke. That three blocks out of the way, Miz Daisy.

Daisy. Go back! Go back this minute!

Hoke. We in the wrong lane. I cain' jes'—

Daisy. If you don't go back, I'll get out of this car and walk.

Hoke. We movin'! You cain' open the do'!

Daisy. This is wrong. Where are you taking me?

Hoke. The sto'.

Daisy. This is wrong. You have to go back to Highland Avenue.

Hoke. Mmmm. Hmmm.

Daisy. I have been driving to the Piggly Wiggly since they put it up and opened it for business! This isn't the way! Go back! Go back this minute!

Hoke. Yonder the Piggly Wiggly, Miz Daisy.

Daisy. Get ready to turn.

Hoke. Yassum.

Daisy. Look out! There's a little boy behind that shopping cart!

Hoke. I see dat.

Daisy. Pull in next to the blue car.

Hoke. We closer to the do' right here.

Daisy. I don't park in the sun! It fades the upholstery.

Hoke. Yassum. *(He parks the car as directed.* Daisy *quickly gets out, heads for the store, then stops.)*

Daisy. Wait a minute. Give me the keys.

Hoke. Yassum.

Daisy. Stay right here by the car. And you don't have to tell everybody my business.

Hoke. Nome. Don't forget the Dutch Cleanser now. *(She glares at him and enters the store.* Hoke *goes to a pay phone and dials a number.)*

Hoke. Hello? Miz McClatchey? Hoke Colburn here. Can I speak to him? . . . Mornin', Mist' Werthan. Guess where I'm at. . . . I jes' drove yo' mama to the sto'. . . . Oh, she flap around a little on the way. But she all right. She in the sto'. *(He sees* Daisy *in the store through the front window. She suddenly sees him.)*

Uh oh. She done see me on the phone. She liable to throw a fit right there by the checkout. . . . Yassuh. Only took me six days. Same time it take the Lawd to make the worl'.

DAISY'S HOUSE, autumn. A Werthan Company truck is parked outside.

LIVING ROOM. Oscar and his assistant, Junior, *are removing slipcovers and rolling up rugs.* Hoke, *jacket off, is helping them.*

Oscar. How the old lady been treating you, Hoke?

Hoke. She know how to pitch a fit. I tell you that. (Oscar *and* Junior *laugh.* Daisy *enters, wearing a fur piece, a hat, and gloves.)*

Daisy. What's so funny?

Hoke. Nothin', Miz Daisy. We jes' carryin' on.

Daisy. Oscar and Junior have been doing my fall cleaning for fifteen years, and they never carried on before. Leave them alone.

Hoke. Yassum.

Daisy. And put your coat on. We're late.

Hoke. I be right there.

Daisy *(off camera).* Idella! I'm gone to temple!

Hoke *(as he leaves).* And I right behind her, Idella.

THE TEMPLE. The service is over, and people are leaving. Daisy, *who is with friends, sees* Hoke *standing beside her car, which is parked right in front of the temple. Two other chauffeur-driven sedans are behind it. She hurries to the car and gets in by herself.*

Daisy. I can get myself in. Just go. Hurry up out of here!

Hoke. Yassum. (*Bewildered, he gets in the car and starts driving.*)

Daisy. I didn't say speed. I said get me away from here.

Hoke. Somethin' wrong back yonder?

Daisy. No.

Hoke. Somethin' I done?

Daisy. No. (*a beat*) Yes.

Hoke. I ain' done nothin'!

Daisy. You had the car parked right in front of the temple! Like I was the queen of Romania! Everybody saw you! Didn't I tell you to wait for me in the back?

Hoke. I jes' tryin' to be nice. They two other chauffeurs right behind me.

Daisy. You made me look like a fool.

Hoke. You ain' no fool, Miz Daisy.

Daisy. Slow down. Miriam and Beulah and them, I could see what they were thinking.

Hoke. What that?

Daisy. That I'm trying to pretend I'm rich.

Hoke. You is rich, Miz Daisy!

Daisy. No, I'm not. And nobody can ever say I put on airs. On Forsythe Street we made many a meal off of grits[5] and gravy. I did without plenty of times, I can tell you.

Hoke. And now you doin' with. What so terrible in that?

Daisy. You! Why do I talk to you? You don't understand me.

Hoke. Nome, I don't. I truly don't. 'Cause if I ever was to get ahold of what you got, I be shakin' it around for everybody in the worl' to see.

Daisy. That's vulgar! Don't talk to me! (Hoke *mutters something under his breath.*) What? What did you say? I heard that!

Hoke. Miz Daisy, you needs a chauffeur, and I needs a job. Let's jes' leave it at dat. (*They eye each other warily in the rearview mirror.*)

BOOLIE'S FRONT HALL, early morning, winter. The phone rings. Boolie answers it.

Boolie. Good morning, Mama. What's the matter? . . . No, I don't always think something's the matter when you call. It's just that when you call so early in the morning. . . . What? . . . All right. I'll be there as soon as I can. (*He hangs up and enters the breakfast room.*) I better go on over there.

Florine. It's not healthy for you to rush like this in the morning.

Boolie. I eat too much anyway. And it sounds like she needs me.

Florine. When doesn't it? (*She smiles at him.*) Give Mother Werthan my love. (*He hurries out.*)

DAISY'S KITCHEN. Daisy, in a warm bathrobe, is pacing. Boolie enters.

Boolie. I didn't expect to find you in one piece.

Daisy. I wanted you to be here when he comes. I wanted you to hear it for yourself.

---

5. **grits:** short for *hominy grits,* a Southern dish made of coarsely ground dry corn.

Boolie. Hear what? What is going on?

Daisy. He's stealing from me.

Boolie. Hoke? Are you sure?

Daisy. I don't make empty accusations. I have proof!

Boolie. What proof?

Daisy. This! (*She pulls an empty can of salmon from her robe pocket.*) I found this hidden in the garbage pail under some coffee grounds.

Boolie. You mean he stole a can of salmon?

Daisy. I knew something was funny. They all take things, you know. So I counted.

Boolie. You counted?

Daisy. The silverware first and then the linen napkins, and then I went into the pantry. The first thing that caught my eye was a hole behind the corned beef. And I knew right away. There were only eight cans of salmon. I had nine. Three for a dollar on sale.

Boolie. Very clever, Mama. You made me miss my breakfast and be late for a meeting at the bank for a thirty-three-cent can of salmon. (*He pulls some bills from his pocket.*) Here. You want thirty-three cents? Here's a dollar! Here's ten dollars! Buy a pantry full of salmon.

Daisy. Why, Boolie! The idea! Waving money at me like I don't know what! I don't want the money. I want my things.

Boolie. One can of salmon?

Daisy. Well, it was mine! I leave him plenty of food every day, and I always tell him exactly what it is. They want something, they just take it. He'll never admit this. "Nome," he'll say. "I doan' know nothin'

'bout that." And I don't like it! I don't like living this way! I have no privacy!

Boolie. All right. I give up. You want to drive yourself again, you just go ahead and arrange it with the insurance company. Take your blessed trolley. Buy yourself a taxicab. Anything you want. Just leave me out of it.

Daisy. Boolie. . . . (Hoke *and* Idella *enter by the back door, and* Idella *goes off to the pantry.*)

Hoke. Mornin', Miz Daisy. I b'lieve it fixin' to clear up. 'Scuse me, Mist' Werthan. Y'all busy?

Boolie. Hoke, I think we have to have a talk.

Hoke. All right. Jes' lemme put my coat away. I be right back. (*He pulls a small paper bag from his pocket.*) Oh, Miz Daisy. Yestiddy when you out visitin', I ate a can o' your salmon. I know you say eat de leffover pork chops, but they stiff. Here, I done buy you another can. You want me to put it in the pantry?

Daisy. Yes, thank you, Hoke.

Hoke. I be right with you, Mist' Werthan. (*He goes off to the pantry.*)

Daisy (*trying for dignity*). Well, I got to get dressed now. 'Bye, son. (*She heads for the stairs.*)

CEMETERY, May 1951. Daisy *is planting verbena beside a headstone that reads "Sigmund Werthan." Hoke ambles over.*

Hoke. I jes' thinkin', Miz Daisy. We bin out heah to the cemetery three times dis month already.

Daisy. It's good to come in nice weather.

Hoke. Yassum. Mist' Sig's grave mighty well tended. I b'lieve you the best widow in the state of Georgia.

Daisy. Boolie's always pestering me to let the staff out here tend to this plot. Perpetual care they call it.

Hoke. Well, doan' do it. It right to have somebody from the family looking after you.

Daisy. I'll certainly never have that. Boolie will have me in perpetual care before I'm cold.

Hoke. Go on 'way from here!

Daisy. Hoke, put that pot of azaleas on Leo Bauer's grave.

Hoke. Miz Rose Bauer's husband?

Daisy. That's right. She asked me to bring it out here for her.

Hoke. Yassum. Where the grave at?

Daisy. I'm not exactly sure. But I know it's over that way. *(points)* You'll see the headstone. Bauer.

Hoke *(vaguely).* Yassum.

Daisy. What's the matter?

Hoke. Nothin' the matter. *(He goes to the car, gets the azaleas, and comes back.)* Miz Daisy . . .

Daisy. I told you, it's over there. It says Bauer on the headstone.

Hoke. Now, how do that look?

Daisy. What are you talking about?

Hoke. I'm talkin' 'bout I cain' read.

Daisy. What?

Hoke. I cain' read.

Daisy. That's ridiculous. Anybody can read.

Hoke. Nome. Not me.

Daisy. Then how come I see you looking at the paper all the time?

Hoke. Thass it. Jes' lookin'. I dope out what's happenin' from the pictures best I can.

Daisy. You know your letters, don't you?

Hoke. My ABC's? Yassum, pretty good. I jes' cain' read.

Daisy. Stop saying that. It's making me mad. If you know your letters, you can read. You just don't know you can read. I taught some of the stupidest children God ever put on the face of the earth, and all of them could read enough to find a name on a tombstone. The name is Bauer. Buh buh buh buh buh Bauer. What does that buh letter sound like?

Hoke. Sound like a B.

Daisy. Of course. Buh Bauer. Er er er er. BauER. That's the last part. What letter sounds like er?

Hoke. An R?

Daisy. So the first letter is a . . .

Hoke. B.

Daisy. And the last letter is an . . .

Hoke. R.

Daisy. B-R. B-R. B-R. Buh-err. Buh-err. It even sounds like Bauer.

Hoke. Thass it?

Words to Know and Use

perpetual (pər pech′ o͞o əl) *adj.* endless; lasting forever

Daisy. That's it. Now go on over there and look for a headstone with a B at the beginning and an R at the end, and that will be Bauer.

Hoke. We ain' goin' worry 'bout what come in the middle?

Daisy. Not right now. This will be enough for you to find it. Go on now.

Hoke. Yassum.

Daisy. And don't come back here telling me you can't do it. Because you can. (*Hoke carries the potted azaleas past a number of* headstones. Then, there it is—BAUER. *He silently mouths the Buh and the Er and places the azaleas gently by the headstone. Then he returns to* Daisy.)

Hoke. Miz Daisy . . .

Daisy. Yes?

Hoke. I sure 'preciate this, Miz Daisy.

Daisy. Don't be ridiculous! I didn't do anything. Now, let's get all this back to the car. I'm burning up out here. (*He gathers up her digging tools and takes her elbow as they walk to the car.*)

Responding to Reading

First Impressions of Part 1

1. What are your impressions of Daisy and Hoke so far? Write your thoughts in your journal or notebook.

Second Thoughts on Part 1

2. How would you describe Daisy's attitude toward Hoke in the first part of the play?

3. What is your opinion of how Hoke handles Miss Daisy?

Think about
- Daisy's reactions to Hoke and the other characters
- what Boolie expects from Hoke

4. Daisy often reacts to situations with anger and impatience. Why do you think she does this?

5. Why do you think Daisy and Hoke have different attitudes about Daisy's being rich?

Reading On

In the next section of the play, watch to see how Hoke and Daisy's relationship grows. Also take note of Boolie and Florine. What kind of people are they?

PART 2

BOOLIE'S DEN, Christmas morning, 1953. Boolie is going through a pile of long-playing Christmas records, none of them particularly religious. Through the open door we see a huge Christmas tree.

Florine *(off camera)*. Of course I told you! *(We hear a muffled voice rising in protest.)* Now, how can I be expected to buy it if you don't write it down? *(more of the muffled voice)* Boolie! I need you!

Boolie. Be right there! *(He enters the kitchen. Florine is staring at a large bowl full of sliced oranges and bananas.)*

Florine *(to the new cook)*. I told you. I told you a million times, Katie Bell. Write it down.

Katie Bell. Yassum.

Florine. More I cannot do. *(to Boolie)* We're out of coconut.

Boolie *(the peacemaker)*. I'm sure we can manage, Katie Bell.

Katie Bell. I tole her.

Florine. But you didn't write it down! I don't need to stand around and listen to excuses on Christmas Day. Maybe you can figure out how to serve ambrosia to fifty people without coconut. I give up. *(She leaves.)*

Boolie *(to Katie Bell)*. I'll call Mama. She has the whole Piggly Wiggly in her pantry. *(He goes to the phone and dials.)* Mama? Merry Christmas. Listen, do Florine a favor, all right? . . . You got a package of coconut in your pantry? . . .

Would you bring it when you come? . . . Many thanks. See you anon,[6] Mama. Ho ho ho! *(He hangs up and bounds upstairs.)* Honey! Hey, honey! *(He enters the master bedroom.)* Florine! Florine!

Florine *(from her large closet)*. In here.

Boolie. Your ambrosia's saved. Mama's got the coconut!

Florine. I knew she was good for something.

Boolie. Florine! I told you I don't like all this sniping at Mama. She's an old lady for goodness' sake! *(Florine's eyes flash, and she starts to speak, then changes her mind and kisses Boolie seductively.)*

Florine. I think your mama woulda liked it if you'da married some little old bookworm.

Boolie. Mmmm. Hmmm.

DAISY'S CAR, night, passing suburban houses with outdoor Christmas decorations. Hoke is driving. Daisy is not in a festive mood.

Hoke. Ooooooh, look at them lit-up decorations!

Daisy. Everybody's giving the Georgia Power Company a merry Christmas.

Hoke. Miz Florine's got 'em all beat with the lights. 'Specially now they got that new house.

Daisy. That silly Santa Claus winking on the front door!

---

6. **anon:** soon.

Words to Know and Use | **sniping** (snīp' iŋ) *n.* attacking someone in a sly or deceitful way **snipe** *v.*

Hoke. I bet she have the biggest tree in Atlanta. Where she get 'em so large?

Daisy. Absurd. If I had a nose like Florine's, I wouldn't go around saying "Merry Christmas" to anybody.

Hoke. I enjoy Christmas at they house.

Daisy. I don't wonder. You're the only Christian in the place.

Hoke. 'Cept they got that new cook.

Daisy. Florine never could keep help. Of course, it's none of my affair.

Hoke. Nome.

Daisy. Too much running around, if you ask me. The Garden Club this and the Junior League that! But she'd die before she'd fix a glass of iced tea for the Temple Sisterhood!

Hoke. Yassum. You right.

Daisy. I just hope she doesn't take it in her head to sing this year. *(She imitates.)* Glo-o-o-o-o-o-o-o-o-o-o-o-o-ria! She sounds as if she has a bone stuck in her throat.

Hoke. You done say a mouthful, Miz Daisy.

Daisy. You didn't have to come. Boolie would have run me out.

Hoke. I know dat.

Daisy. Then why did you?

Hoke. That my business. (Hoke *turns the car into* Boolie's *driveway, passing a facsimile of Rudolph the Red-Nosed Reindeer.)* Well, looka there. Look what Miz Florine done.

Daisy. Oh, my Lord! If her grandfather, old man Freitag, could see this! What is it you say? I bet he'd jump up out of his grave and snatch her baldheaded. (Hoke *gets out and goes to open the passenger door.)*

Hoke. Go on 'way from here, Miz Daisy! Jump up and snatch her baldheaded!

Daisy. Wait a minute. *(She takes a small package wrapped in brown paper from her purse.)* This isn't a Christmas present.

Hoke. Nome.

Daisy. You know I don't give Christmas presents.

Hoke. Yassum.

Daisy. I just happened to run across it this morning. Go on. Open it. *(He unwraps the present.)*

Hoke. Ain' nobody never give me no book. *(He reads, not without difficulty.)* "Handwriting Copy Book—Grade Five."

Daisy. I always taught out of these.

Hoke. Yassum.

Daisy. It's faded, but it works. If you practice, you'll write nicely.

Hoke. Yassum.

Daisy. But you have to practice. I taught Mayor Hartsfield out of this same book.

Hoke (*very touched*). Thank you, Miz Daisy.

Daisy. It's not a Christmas present.

Hoke. Nome.

Daisy. Jews haven't any business giving Christmas presents. And you don't have to go yapping about this to Boolie and Florine.

Hoke. This strictly between you and me.

Florine (*off camera*). Merry Christmas, Mother Werthan! (*They turn and see* Boolie *and* Florine *at the doorway.*)

Hoke. They done seen us.

Daisy. I hope I don't spit up. (*He helps her up the steps toward the house.*)

DAISY'S CAR, spring, 1955. Hoke *is driving.* Boolie *is with him.*

Hoke. You know, yo' mama done watch over dis machine like a chicken hawk. One day we park in front of de dry cleaner up yonder at de Plaza, and dis white man—look like some kind of lawyer, banker, dress up real fine—he done lay his satchel up on our hood while he open up his trunk, you know, and what he want to do that for? 'Fore I could stop her, yo' mama jump out de back do' and run that man every which way. She wicked 'bout her paint job. (*He stops the car at Mitchell Motors. He and* Boolie *get out.*)

Boolie. Did Mama tell you this new car has air conditioning?

Hoke. She say she doan' like no air cool. Say it give her the neck ache. (*They walk toward a new 1955 Cadillac.*)

Boolie. You know how Mama fought me, but it's time for a trade. I bet you will miss the old one, though.

Hoke. Not me. Unh unh.

Boolie. Oh, come on. Aren't you a little sorry to see it go?

Hoke. It ain' goin' nowhere. I done bought it.

Boolie. You didn't!

Hoke. Already made the deal with Mist' Red Mitchell inside yonder.

Boolie. For how much?

Hoke. Dat for him and me to know.

Boolie. Why didn't you just buy it from Mama? You'd have saved money.

Hoke. Yo' mama in my business enough as it is. I ain' studyin' makin' no monthly car payments to her. Disheah mine the regular way.

Boolie. It's a good car, all right. I guess nobody knows that better than you.

Hoke. Bes' ever come off the line. And dis new one, Miz Daisy doan' take to it, I let her ride in disheah now an' again.

Boolie. Mighty nice of you.

Hoke. Well, we all doin' what we can.

Boolie. You want to drive the new one home?

Hoke. No, suh.

Boolie. Why not?

Hoke. 'Cause I doan' want you gettin' them nasty ashes all over my upholstery.

DAISY'S KITCHEN, June 1957. Idella, in her eighties and looking worn, is taking fried chicken out of a skillet. Daisy enters.

Daisy. That's not enough chicken.

Idella. How much you an' Hoke plannin' to eat?

Daisy. I like to give them leftovers when I get there.

Idella. You will, 'less you make a pig of yoseff.

Daisy. Did you put mustard in those eggs?

Idella. I always put mustard in my stuffed eggs.

Daisy. Spicy things make me sick.

Idella. You go upstairs and see 'bout your packing. *(Daisy starts out, then stops.)*

Daisy. Don't put the peaches in the icebox. I hate cold peaches.

Idella. Yassum. *(Daisy leaves.)* Act like I ain' never made a picnic in my life.

DAISY'S DRIVEWAY. Daisy drags a heavy suitcase out to the garage and returns to the house. Then she comes out with the picnic lunch and a wrapped gift. Hoke pulls up in his car and gets out.

Daisy *(extremely irritated)*. It's three after seven!

Hoke. Yassum. You say we leavin' at fifteen to eight.

Daisy. At the latest, I said.

Hoke. Now what bizness you got, draggin' disheah out de house by yoseff?

Daisy. Who was here to help me?

Hoke. Miz Daisy, it doan' take me more 'an five minutes to load up de trunk of dis car.

Daisy. I hate doing things at the last minute.

Hoke. What you talkin' 'bout? You ready to go for the las' week and a half! *(He picks up the present.)*

Daisy. Don't touch that.

Hoke. Ain' it wrap pretty! Dat Mist' Walter's present?

Daisy. Yes. It's fragile. I'll hold it on the seat with me. *(As Hoke loads the trunk, Boolie pulls up in his car and gets out.)* Well, you nearly missed us.

Boolie. I thought you were leaving at quarter of.

Hoke. She takin' on.

Daisy. Be still.

Boolie *(holding out a gift)*. Florine sent this for Uncle Walter. *(Daisy recoils from it.)* Well, it's not a snake, Mama. I think it's note paper.

Daisy. How appropriate. Uncle Walter can't see.

Boolie. Maybe it's soap.

Daisy. How nice that you show such an interest in your uncle's ninetieth birthday.

Boolie. Don't start up, Mama. I cannot go to Mobile with you. I have to go to New York tonight for the convention.

Daisy. The convention starts Monday. And I know what else I know.

Words to Know and Use | **upholstery** (up hōl′ stər ē) *n.* the soft fabric covering furniture
recoil (ri koil′) *v.* to draw back from something distasteful or painful

439

Boolie. Just leave Florine out of it. She wrote away for those tickets eight months ago.

Daisy. I'm sure *My Fair Lady* is more important than your own flesh and blood.

Boolie. Mama! I can't talk to you when you're like this. (Daisy *gets into the car.*)

Daisy. They expect us for a late supper in Mobile.

Boolie. You'll be there. (He takes Hoke *out of* Daisy's *hearing.*)

Daisy. I know they'll fix crab. All that trouble.

Boolie (to Hoke). I don't know how you'll stand all day in the car.

Hoke. She doan' mean nothin'. She jes' worked up.

Boolie. Here's fifty dollars in case you run into trouble. Don't show it to Mama. You've got your map?

Hoke. She got it in wid her. Study ever' inch of the way.

Boolie. I'll be at the Ambassador Hotel in New York. On Park Avenue.

Daisy. It's seven-sixteen.

Boolie. You ought to have a job on the radio announcing the time.

Daisy. I want to miss the rush hour.

Boolie. Congratulate Uncle Walter for me. And kiss everybody in Mobile. (Hoke *gets in the car and starts the engine.*)

Daisy. Did you have the air condition checked? I told you to have the air condition checked.

Hoke. Yassum, I had the air condition checked, but I don't know what for. You doan' never allow me to turn it on.

Daisy. Hush up. (The car moves down the driveway.)

COUNTRY ROADSIDE. Daisy *and* Hoke *are eating lunch, relaxed.*

Hoke. Idella stuff eggs good.

Daisy. You stuff yourself good. (They eat in peaceful silence.) I was thinking about the first time I ever went to Mobile. It was Walter's wedding. 1888.

Hoke. 1888! You weren't nothing but a little child!

Daisy. I was twelve. We went on the train. And I was so excited. I'd never been in a wedding party, and I'd never seen the ocean. Papa said it was the Gulf of

Mexico and not the ocean. I asked Papa if it was all right to dip my hand in the water. He laughed because I was so timid. And then I tasted the salt water on my fingers. Isn't it silly to remember that?

Hoke. No sillier than most of what folks remember. *(A state patrol car pulls up. Two troopers are in the front seat.)*

Trooper *(to* Hoke*).* Hey, boy! *(Hoke looks at him evenly.)* What do you think you're doing with this car?

Daisy *(calm, but angry).* This is my car, officer.

Trooper *(gets out and walks over).* Yes, ma'am. Can I see the registration, please? *(to* Hoke*)* And your license, boy. *(Hoke produces the registration and the license. The trooper studies both. To* Daisy.*)* What's this name? Wetheran?

Daisy. Werthan.

Trooper. Werthan. Never heard that one before. What kind of name is that?

Daisy. It's of German <u>derivation</u>.

Trooper. German derivation. Unh hunh. *(He hands the papers back to* Hoke *and waves him on. The Cadillac goes off down the road. The trooper gets back in the patrol car.)* An old nigger and an old Jew[7] woman takin' off down the road together. Now that is one sorry sight.

Second Trooper. I'll tell you one sorrier. They're sittin' in a Cadillac, and I'm sittin' here next to you. *(The first trooper guns the car off in the other direction.)*

DAISY'S CAR, passing cotton fields.

Hoke. You talkin' 'bout first time before. I tell you 'bout the first time I ever leave the state of Georgia?

Daisy. When was that?

Hoke. A few minutes back.

Daisy. Go on!

Hoke. Thass right. First time. My daughter, she married to a Pullman porter, and she all the time goin'—Detroit, New York, St. Louis—and I say, "Well, that very nice, Tommie Lee, but I jes' doan' feel the need." So dis it, Miz Daisy, and I got to tell you, Alabama ain' lookin' like much so far.

Daisy. It's nicer the other side of Montgomery.

Hoke. If you say so. Pass me up one of them peaches, please, ma'am.

Daisy. Oh, no!

Hoke. What happen?

Daisy. That sign said Phenix City—thirty miles. We're not supposed to go to Phenix City. We're going the wrong way!

Hoke. Maybe you done read it wrong.

Daisy. I didn't. Stop the car! Stop the car! *(Hoke swerves off the road. Daisy wrestles with the map.)* Here! You took the wrong turn at Opelika! *(He takes the map.)*

Hoke. You took it wid me. And you readin' the map!

Daisy. I'm such a fool! I didn't have any business coming in the car by myself with just you. I should have come on the train.

---

7. **nigger . . . Jew:** *slang. Nigger* is an insulting name for an African American. *Jew* (as in this case) may also be derogatory, depending on the speaker's intent.

I'd be safe there. I just should have come on the train.

Hoke. Yassum. You sho' shoulda'.

DAISY'S CAR, traveling at night. Daisy *and* Hoke *are tired.*

Daisy. They've fixed crab for me! Minnie always fixes crab! They go to so much trouble! It's all ruined by now!

Hoke. We got to pull over, Miz Daisy.

Daisy. Is something wrong with the car?

Hoke. Nome. I got to be 'scused.

Daisy. What?

Hoke. I got to make water.

Daisy. You should have thought of that back at the Standard Oil station.

Hoke. Colored cain' use the toilet at no Standard Oil. You know dat.

Daisy. Well, there's no time to stop. We'll be in Mobile soon. You can wait.

Hoke. Yassum. *(a beat)* Nome. *(He stops the car.)*

Daisy. I told you to wait!

Hoke. Yassum. I hear you. How you think I feel havin' to ax you when can I make water like I some dog?

Daisy. Why, Hoke! I'd be ashamed!

Hoke. I ain' no dog and I ain' no chile and I ain' just a back of the neck you look at while you going wherever you want to go. I a man, nearly seventy-two years old, and I know when my bladder full, and I gettin' out dis car and goin' off down the road like I got to do. And I'm takin' the car key this time. And that's the end of it! *(He gets out of the car and slams the door.*

Daisy *sits still for a moment, then rolls down the window.)*

Daisy. Hoke! *(silence)* Hoke! *(silence)* Hoke! *(She starts to get out of the car—when a man appears in the shadowy dark. She is frightened.)*

Hoke. You all right in there, Miz Daisy?

Daisy *(relieved, but quickly her old snappish self).* Of course I am!

WALTER'S LIVING ROOM, the next evening. Walter, *old and blind, is in a chair surrounded by relatives.* Daisy *is talking to* Boolie *by phone.*

Daisy *(on the phone).* Uncle Walter appreciates your call. I don't think he can come to the phone. . . .

BOOLIE'S HOTEL ROOM.

Boolie *(on phone).* Fine. How is Hoke?

WALTER'S LIVING ROOM.

Daisy *(on phone).* What do you mean? How should he be? *(Uncle Walter's daughter enters with a birthday cake, and the singing of "Happy Birthday" starts.)* I have to hang up, Boolie. . . . I'll tell him. . . . Yes, we will. . . . All right. You, too. 'Bye. *(Daisy looks at* Walter *with love and pride.* Hoke *and* Katie Bell *enter from the kitchen.* Hoke *nods gravely at* Daisy. *She nods back gratefully.)*

BOOLIE'S OFFICE, 1962. Hoke *enters.*

Boolie *(to* Hoke*).* To what do I owe this honor?

Hoke. We got to talk, Mr. Werthan.

Boolie. What is it?

Hoke. It Mist' Sinclair Harris.

Boolie. My cousin Sinclair?

Hoke. His wife.

Boolie. Jeanette?

Hoke. The one talk funny.

Boolie. She's from Canton, Ohio.

Hoke. Yassuh. She's tryin' to hire me.

Boolie. What?

Hoke. She say, "How are they treating you, Hoke?" You know how she soun', like her nose stuff up. And I say, "Fine, Miz Harris," and she say, "Well, if you was lookin' for a change, you know where to call." I thought you want to know 'bout it.

Boolie. I'll be . . .

Hoke. Ain' she a mess? *(a pause)* She say name yo' sal'ry.

Boolie. I see. And did you?

Hoke. Did I what?

Boolie. Name your salary.

Hoke. Now, what you think I am? I ain' studyin' workin' for no trashy somethin' like her.

Boolie. But she got you thinking, didn't she?

Hoke. You might could say dat.

Boolie. Well, how does sixty-five dollars a week sound?

Hoke. Sounds pretty good. Course, seventy-five sounds better.

Boolie. So it does. Beginning this week.

Hoke. Das mighty nice of you, Mist' Werthan. I 'preciate it. Mist' Werthan, you ever had people fightin' over you?

Boolie. No.

Hoke. Well, I tell you. It feel good. *(He smiles and walks happily out of the office.)*

DAISY'S LIVING ROOM, May 1963. Daisy *is playing mah-jongg with* Beulah, Miriam, *and another woman.*

Miriam *(putting a tile on the table)*. Six bams.

Beulah. Mah-jongg!

Miriam. You are the luckiest thing, Beulah!

Daisy. 'Scuse me a second. *(She goes to the kitchen.* Hoke *and* Idella *are watching a soap opera on a black-and-white TV set.* Idella, *now old and frail, is shelling peas.)*

Daisy. I don't know how y'all can look at that.

Hoke. You see it a few times, you get in it.

Daisy. Both of your brains are fixing to evaporate. You can bring in the cake now, Hoke.

Hoke. Yassum.

Daisy. Don't make a mess with those peas, Idella.

Idella. Do I ever? *(Daisy leaves.* Hoke *puts napkins, forks, and plates on a tray that holds a cake.)*

Hoke *(nodding toward the soap opera)*. Ain't the blonde one got a lotta hair? How do she make it so shiny?

Idella. Washes it in my-naise. *(He looks dubious.)* Yes, she do. It was in *Life* maga-zine.

Hoke. Don' seem human, do it? *(He picks up the tray and goes out. The camera focuses on the soap opera. Then* Hoke *comes back.)* What happen? Linda up to somethin', ain' she? *(no answer)* Idella?

(We hear a bowl hit the floor and see peas rolling on the linoleum.) Idella! Idella!

A BAPTIST CHURCH. The congregation is black, except for Daisy, Boolie, *and* Florine, *who sit in the rear.* Hoke *is sitting with them.*

DAISY'S KITCHEN, two months later. Daisy *is frying chicken.* Hoke *enters and watches her.*

Hoke. You fixin' to ruin it?

Daisy. What are you talking about?

Hoke. You got de skillet turn up too high, and de chicken too close together.

Daisy. Mind your business.

Hoke. It's yo' chicken. *(He leaves the kitchen.* Daisy *turns the flame down.)*

DAISY'S DINING ROOM. Daisy *is seated at the table.* Hoke *enters and puts in front of her a plate of fried chicken, stewed okra, and rice.*

Daisy. Thank you, Hoke. *(He goes into the kitchen and begins to eat the same meal at the kitchen table.)*

DAISY'S YARD, July 1963. Daisy *and* Hoke *are working side by side in a vegetable garden.*

DAISY'S LIVING ROOM, winter, 1964. While an ice storm rages outside, Daisy *tries to read by candlelight. She hears the back door open and close.*

Daisy *(alarmed).* Who is it?

Hoke *(off camera).* Mornin', Miz Daisy.

Daisy. Oh, Hoke. *(Hoke enters, wearing an overcoat and galoshes and carrying a small paper bag.)* What in the world?

Hoke. I learn to drive on ice when I deliver milk for the Avondale Dairy. Ain' much to it. Other folks bangin' into each other like they in the funny papers, though. Oh, I stop at the Krispy Kreme. Lawd knows you got to have yo' coffee in the mornin'.

Daisy *(touched).* How sweet of you, Hoke! *(He hands her a cup of coffee and sips his own.)*

Hoke. We ain' had no good coffee 'roun heah since Idella pass.

Daisy. Mmmm. Hmmm. I can fix her biscuits, and we both know how to make her fried chicken. But nobody can make Idella's coffee. I wonder how she did it.

Hoke. I doan' know. *(They sip silently for a moment, deep in thought.)*

Daisy. Idella was lucky.

Hoke. Yassum. I 'spec she was. *(He starts out of the room.)*

Daisy. Where are you going?

Hoke. Take off my overshoes.

Daisy. I didn't think you'd come today.

Hoke. It ain' my day off, is it?

Daisy. Well, I don't know what you can do around here except keep me company.

Hoke. I can light us a fire. *(He goes into the kitchen.)*

Daisy. Eat anything you want out of the icebox. It'll all spoil anyway.

Hoke *(off camera).* Yassum.

Daisy. And wipe up what you tracked onto the kitchen floor.

Hoke (*off camera*). Now, Miz Daisy, what you think I am? A mess? (*The phone rings.*)

Daisy (*on her way to the phone*). Yes. That's exactly what I think you are.

Hoke (*off camera*). All right den. All right.

HALLWAY. Daisy *answers the phone.*

Daisy. Hello?

BOOLIE'S DEN. Intercut between Daisy *and* Boolie *during this conversation.*

Boolie. I'll be out after you as soon as I can get down the driveway.

Daisy. Stay where you are, Boolie. Hoke is here with me.

Boolie. How did he manage that?

Daisy. He's very handy. I'm fine. I don't need a thing in the world.

Boolie. Hello? (*to* Florine) I must have the wrong number. I never heard Mama saying loving things about Hoke before.

Daisy. I didn't say I love him. I said he was handy.

Boolie. Uh hunh.

Daisy. Honestly, Boolie. Are you trying to irritate me in the middle of an ice storm? (*She hangs up.*)

Responding to Reading

First Impressions of Part 2

1. Have your feelings about Hoke or Daisy changed? Jot down your thoughts in your journal or notebook.

Second Thoughts on Part 2

2. How has Hoke and Daisy's relationship changed?

   Think about
   • Daisy's gift to Hoke
   • their trip to Mobile

3. How would you describe Boolie's relationship with his mother? Use examples from the play to explain your answer.

4. Why do you think Daisy and Florine resent each other?

Reading On

The play has now entered the 1960s, a time when African Americans campaigned for their rights in the face of sometimes violent resistance. As you read, look for signs of how the society is changing and how each character responds to these changes.

PART 3

TRAFFIC JAM, September 1964. Daisy *is in her car.* Hoke, *walking against the halted traffic, reaches the car.*

Daisy. Well, what is it? What took so long?

Hoke. Couldn't help it. Big mess up yonder.

Daisy. What's the matter? I might as well not go to temple at all now!

Hoke. You cain' go to temple today, Miz Daisy.

Daisy. Why not? What in the world is the matter with you?

Hoke. Somebody done bomb the temple.

Daisy. What? Bomb the temple?

Hoke. Yassum. Dat why we stuck here so long.

Daisy. I don't believe it.

Hoke. Dat what the police tell me up yonder. Say it happen about a half hour ago.

Daisy. Oh, no! Well, was anybody there? Were people hurt?

Hoke. Din' say.

Daisy. Who would do such a thing?

Hoke. You know good as me. Always be the same ones.

Daisy. Well, it's a mistake. I'm sure they meant to bomb one of the Conservative synagogues or the Orthodox one. The temple is Reform. Everybody knows that.

Hoke. It doan' matter to them people. A Jew is a Jew to them folks. Jes' like light or dark, we all the same nigger. *(Daisy dabs her eyes with a Kleenex.)* I know jes' how you feel, Miz Daisy. Back down there above Macon on the farm—I 'bout ten or 'leven years old—and one day my

frien' Porter, his daddy hangin' from a tree. And the day befo', he laughin' and pitchin' horseshoes wid us. And den he hangin' up yonder wid his hands tie behind his back an' the flies all over him. I threw up right where I was standin'. You go on and cry.

Daisy. I'm not crying. *(collecting herself)* Why did you tell me that story?

Hoke. I doan' know. Seem like disheah mess put me in mind of it.

Daisy. The temple has nothing to do with that!

Hoke. So you say.

Daisy. You don't even know what happened. How do you know that policeman was telling the truth?

Hoke. Now, why would a policeman go and lie 'bout a thing like dat?

Daisy. Well, you never get things right anyway.

Hoke. Miz Daisy, somebody done bomb dat place, and you know it, too.

Daisy. Go on. Just go on now. I don't want to hear any more about it.

Hoke. You de boss.

Daisy. Stop talking to me!

THE COMMERCE CLUB, summer, 1966. A dozen businessmen are seated at a long table. Boolie *is at one end, flanked by* Florine *and* Daisy. *One man, who is standing and holding a large silver bowl, beckons to* Boolie. Boolie *rises and takes the trophy.*

Boolie. Thank you, Wellborn. And thank you all. I am deeply grateful to be chosen 1966 Man of the Year by the Atlanta Business Council—an honor I've seen bestowed upon some mighty fine fellas and which I certainly never expected to come to me. I'm afraid the loss here *(touching his hair)* and the gain here *(patting his belly)* have given me an air of competence I don't possess. But I'll tell you, I sure wish my father and my grandfather could see this. Seventy-two years ago they leased an old mill out on the Decatur Road with two looms in operation. They managed to grow with Atlanta, and to this day, we of Werthan Industries believe we want what Atlanta wants. This award proves we must be right. Thank you. *(applause)*

DAISY'S FRONT HALL, fall, 1966. Daisy *is dialing the phone.*

Daisy. Hidey, Miss McClatchey. . . . You always recognize my voice. What a shame a wonderful girl like you never married. Miss McClatchey, is my son in? . . . Oh, no, no, no. Please tell him I bought the tickets for the UJA banquet. . . . And don't worry. My cousin Tillie in Chattanooga married for the first time at fifty-seven. 'Bye. *(She hangs up.)*

BEDROOM. Daisy *is at her desk, paying bills.* Boolie *enters.*

Boolie. How are you feeling, Mama?

Daisy. Not a good question to ask somebody nearly ninety.

Boolie. Well, you look fine.

Daisy. It's my ageless appeal.

Boolie. Miss McClatchey gave me your message.

Daisy. Florine's invited, too.

Boolie. Thank you very much.

Daisy. I guess Hoke should drive us. There'll be a crowd.

Boolie. Mama, we have to talk about this. You know, I believe Martin Luther King has done some mighty fine things.

Daisy. Boolie, if you don't want to go, why don't you just come right out and say so?

Boolie. I want to go. You know how I feel about him.

Daisy. Of course, but Florine–

Boolie. Florine has nothing to do with it. I still have to conduct business in this town.

Daisy. I see. You will go out of business if you attend the King dinner.

Boolie. Not exactly. But a lot of men I do business with wouldn't like it. They might snicker a little and call me Martin Luther Werthan behind my back. Maybe I wouldn't hear about certain meetings at the Commerce Club. Jack Raphael, over at Ideal Mills, he's a New York Jew instead of a Georgia Jew, and the really smart ones come from New York, don't they? So some of the boys might start throwing business to Jack instead of to old Martin Luther Werthan. I don't know. Maybe it wouldn't happen, but that's the way it works. If we don't use those seats, somebody else will.

Daisy. I'm not supposed to go, either?

Words to Know and Use | **competence** (käm′ pə təns) *n.* a state of being capable

Boolie. Mama, you can do whatever you want.

Daisy. Thanks for your permission.

Boolie. Can I ask you something? When did you get so fired up about Martin Luther King? Time was, I'd have heard a different story.

Daisy. Why, Boolie! I've never been prejudiced, and you know it!

Boolie. OK. Why didn't you ask Hoke to go to the dinner with you?

Daisy. Hoke? Don't be ridiculous! He wouldn't go!

Boolie. Ask him and see.

KITCHEN. Hoke sits at the table, squinting at the paper through thick glasses. Daisy enters.

Daisy. All right. *(They go out and get in the car.* Hoke *drives down the driveway, almost hitting the mailbox.)* I don't know why you still drive. You can't see.

Hoke. Yassum, I can.

Daisy. You didn't see that mailbox.

Hoke. How do you know what I din' see?

Daisy. It nearly poked through my window. This car is all scratched up.

Hoke. Ain' no sucha thing.

Daisy. How would you know? You can't see. What a shame. It's a brand-new car, too.

Hoke. You done had this car two years come March.

MAIN THOROUGHFARE.

Daisy. You forgot to turn.

Hoke. Ain' this dinner at the Biltmo'?

Daisy. You know it is.

Hoke. Biltmo' this way.

Daisy. You know so much!

Hoke. Yassum. I do.

Daisy. I've lived in Atlanta all my life.

Hoke. And ain' run a car in twenty years.

Daisy. Boolie said the silliest thing the other day.

Hoke. That right? *(a long beat)* Well, what did he say?

Daisy. Well, he was talking about Martin Luther King. *(a beat)* I guess you know him, don't you?

Hoke. Martin Luther King? Nome.

Daisy. I was sure you did. But you've heard him preach?

Hoke. Same way as you, over the TV.

Daisy. I think he's wonderful.

Hoke. Yassum. *(a long beat)* What you getting at, Miz Daisy?

Daisy. Well, it's so silly! Boolie said you wanted to go to this dinner with me. Did you tell him that?

Hoke. Nome.

Daisy. I didn't think so. You can hear him whenever you want.

Hoke. You want the front do' or the side do' to the Biltmo'?

Daisy. You pick. Isn't it wonderful the way things are changing?

BILTMORE HOTEL. Hoke *stops the car by the front entrance. He turns in his seat to face* Daisy.

Hoke. What you think I am, Miz Daisy?

Daisy. What do you mean?

Hoke. You think I some old somethin' sittin' up here doan' know nothin' 'bout how to do?

Daisy. I don't know what you're talking about.

Hoke. Invitation to disheah dinner come in the mail a month ago. Did be you want me to go wid you, how come you wait till we in the car and on the way to ask me?

Daisy. What? All I said was that Boolie said you wanted to go.

Hoke. Mmmm. Hmmm.

Daisy. Well, my stars! Aren't you a big baby!

Hoke. Ne'er mind baby. Next time you ask me someplace, ask me regular.

Daisy. You don't have to carry on so much!

Hoke. Thass all. Less drop it.

Daisy. Honestly!

Hoke. You talkin' 'bout things change. They ain' change all dat much. *(He opens his door.)* I hep you to the do'.

Daisy. Thank you, Hoke. I can help myself. *(Daisy gets out and enters the hotel. Hoke makes no effort to help her.)*

HOTEL BALLROOM. The room is filled with people sitting at tables, listening to Dr. King.

Dr. King *(off camera).* . . . Segregation has placed the whole South socially, educationally, and economically behind the rest of the nation. Yet there are in the white South millions of people of good will whose voices are yet unheard, whose course is yet unclear, and whose courageous acts are yet unseen. . . .

DAISY'S CAR. Hoke *is listening to the speech on the radio.*

Dr. King *(off camera).* These persons are often silent today because of fear—fear of social, political, and economic reprisals. In the name of human dignity, and for the cause of democracy, these millions are called upon to gird their courage, to speak out, to offer leadership that is needed.

HOTEL BALLROOM.

Dr. King *(off camera).* If the people of good will of the white South fail to act now, history will have to record that the greatest tragedy of this period of social transition was not the vitriolic[8] words and the violent actions of the bad people, but the appalling silence and the indifference of the good people.

DAISY'S KITCHEN, March 1970. Hoke *enters the back door.*

Hoke *(calling).* Mornin', Miz Daisy. *(no answer)* Miz Daisy? *(He goes into the dining room, where all the drawers in the sideboard are open. He goes into the front hall.)* Miz Daisy?

Daisy *(off camera).* Hoke! Is that Hoke?

---

8. vitriolic: (vi′ trē äl′ ik) harsh and biting.

Words to Know and Use	**reprisal** (ri prī′ zəl) *n.* an injury done in response to an injury received; retaliation **appalling** (ə pôl′ iŋ) *adj.* horrifying; dreadful **appall** *v.*

449

Hoke. Yassum. You all right? (Daisy *makes her way slowly downstairs. Her hair is in disarray.*)

Daisy. Hoke? Hoke?

Hoke. Yassum.

Daisy. Where did you put my papers?

Hoke. What papers, Miz Daisy?

Daisy. My papers! I had them all corrected last night, and I put them in the front so I wouldn't forget them on my way to school. What did you do with them? (*She goes unsteadily into the den.* Hoke *follows.*)

Hoke. School? What you talkin' 'bout? (Daisy *rifling through drawers.*)

Daisy. The children will be so disappointed if I don't give them their homework back. I always give it back the next day. That's why they like me.

Hoke. You talkin' outta yo' head!

Daisy. Why aren't you helping me?

Hoke. What you want me to do, Miz Daisy?

Daisy. Find those papers! I told you. It's all right if you moved them. I won't be mad with you. But I've got to get to school now. I'll be late, and who will take care of my class? Oh, I do everything wrong. (*She totters into the living room.* Hoke *follows her.*)

Hoke. Set down. You 'bout to fall and hurt yoseff.

Daisy. It doesn't matter. It's all my fault. I didn't do right. It's so awful!

Hoke. Now you lissen heah. Ain' nothin' awful 'cep the way you carryin' on.

Daisy. I'm so sorry. It's all my fault. I can't find the papers, and the children are waiting.

Hoke. No, they ain'. You ain' no teacher no mo'.

Daisy. It doesn't make any difference.

Hoke. Miz Daisy, ain' nothin' the matter wid you.

Daisy. You don't know! You don't know! What's the difference?

Hoke. Your mind done took a turn this mornin'. Thass all. (*She has now worked her way to the front hall.* Hoke *dials a number quickly.*)

Hoke (*into the phone*). Lemme have 'im, Miz McClatchey.

Daisy. Go on. Just go on now.

BOOLIE'S OFFICE.

Boolie (*into the phone*). What can I do for you this morning? (*Intercut between* Boolie *and* Hoke *during this conversation.*)

Hoke. It yo' mama.

Boolie. What's the matter?

Hoke. She worked up.

Boolie. Why should today be different from any other day?

Hoke. No, this ain' the same. (Daisy *pulls a drawer out of the commode,*[9] *and it crashes to the floor.*)

Boolie. I'll be right there.

---

9. **commode:** a chest of drawers; bureau.

STAIRCASE. Daisy *starts upstairs.* Hoke *follows her.*

Hoke. You snap right back if you jes' let yoseff.

Daisy. I can't! I can't!

Hoke. You a lucky ole woman! You know dat?

Daisy. No! No! It's all a mess now. And I can't do anything about it. *(She goes into* Boolie's *old bedroom.* Hoke *settles her in a chair.)*

Hoke. You rich, you well fo' yo' time, and you got people care 'bout what happen to you.

Daisy. I'm being trouble. Oh, I don't want to be trouble to anybody.

Hoke. You want somethin' to cry 'bout, I take you to the state home, show you what layin' out dere in de halls. An' I bet none of them take on as bad as yo' doin'.

Daisy *(less agitated, but still confused).* I'm sorry. I'm so sorry. Those poor children in my class.

Hoke. You keep dis up, I promise, Mist' Werthan call the doctor on you, and dat doctor gon' take you in the insane asylum 'fore you know what hit you. Dat de way you want it to be?

Daisy *(in her normal voice).* Hoke, do you still have that Oldsmobile?

Hoke. From when I firs' come here? Go on, Miz Daisy. Dat thing been in the junkyard fifteen years or mo'. I drivin' yo' next to las' car now; '65 Cadillac, runnin' fine as wine.

Daisy. You ought not to be driving anything, the way you see.

Hoke. How you know the way I see, 'less you lookin' outta my eyes?

Daisy. Hoke?

Hoke. Yassum?

Daisy. You're my best friend.

Hoke. Come on, Miz Daisy. You jes'—

Daisy. No. Really. You are. You are. *(She takes his hand.)*

Hoke. Yassum.

LIVING ROOM, November 1973. The furniture is gone. Boolie, *now sixty-five, is checking a moving carton.* Hoke, *now eighty-five, shuffles into the room.*

Hoke. Mornin', Mist' Werthan.

Boolie. Hey, Hoke! Good to see you! You didn't drive yourself out here?

Hoke. No, suh. I doan' drive no mo'. My granddaughter run me out.

Boolie. Is she old enough to drive?

Hoke. Michelle thirty-seven. Teach biology at Spelman College.

Boolie. I never knew that.

Hoke. Yassuh.

Boolie. I've taken most of what I want out of the house. Is there anything you'd like before the Goodwill comes?

Hoke. My place full to bustin' now.

Boolie. It feels funny to sell the house while Mama's still alive.

Hoke. I 'gree.

Boolie. But she hasn't been inside the door for two years now. I suppose you don't get out to see Mama very much.

Hoke. No, suh, I doan'. It hard—not drivin'. Dat place ain' on no bus line. I goes in a taxicab sometimes.

Boolie. I'm sure she appreciates it.

Hoke. Some days she better than others. Who ain't? (Boolie *takes* Hoke's *arm as they head for the back door.)*

NURSING HOME, sun porch. Daisy *is sitting in a sunny corner, her walker close by. She is* ninety-seven years old and very fragile. Boolie *and* Hoke *appear.*

Boolie. Happy Thanksgiving, Mama. Look who I brought.

Hoke. Mornin', Miz Daisy. (She nods.) You keepin' yoseff busy? (no response)

Boolie. She certainly is. She goes to jewelry making—how many times a week, is it, Mama? She makes all kinds of things. Pins and bracelets. She's a regular Tiffany's.[10]

Hoke. Ain't that somethin'? (Daisy *seems far away.)*

Boolie. Hoke, you know I thought of you the other morning on the expressway. I saw an Avondale milk truck.

Hoke. You doan' say.

Boolie. A big monster of a thing; must've had sixteen wheels. I wonder how you'd have liked driving that around.

Daisy (suddenly). Hoke came to see me, not you.

Hoke. This is one of her good days.

Boolie. Florine says to wish you a happy Thanksgiving. She's in Washington, you know. (no response) You remember, Mama. She's a Republican National Committee woman now.

Daisy. Good Lord! (Hoke *laughs.* Boolie *grins.)* Boolie!

Boolie. What is it, Mama?

Daisy. Go charm the nurses.

---

10. **Tiffany's:** name of a well-known expensive jewelry store.

Boolie *(to* Hoke*).* She wants you all to herself. You're a doodle, Mama. *(He leaves. Daisy dozes for a minute. Then she looks at Hoke.)*

Daisy. Boolie payin' you still?

Hoke. Every week.

Daisy. How much?

Hoke. That between me an' him, Miz Daisy.

Daisy. Highway robbery. *(She closes her eyes, then opens them.)* How are you?

Hoke. Doin' the bes' I can.

Daisy. Me, too.

Hoke. Well, thass all there is to it, then. *(She nods, smiles. He sees an untouched slice of pumpkin pie on the table beside her.)* Looka here. You ain' eat yo' Thanksgiving pie. *(She tries to pick up her fork. He gently takes it from her.)* Lemme help you wid it. *(He cuts a small piece of pie and carefully feeds it to her. She is delighted. It tastes good. He feeds her another. And another. The end.)* 🍂

Responding to Reading

First Impressions of Part 3

1. What are your feelings at the end of the play? Write down your response in your journal or notebook.

Second Thoughts on Part 3

2. Irony occurs when an outcome is the opposite of what might have been expected. What is ironic about the ending of the play?

    Think about
    - how you expected Daisy and Hoke to act before you read the play
    - the contrast between the play's ending and its opening

3. In your opinion, what caused Daisy and Hoke to form a bond of the heart?

4. Do you think Hoke changes during the course of the play? Explain.

5. Daisy says twice in the play, "I'm not prejudiced!" Do you agree with her statements, both at the beginning and at the end of the play? Explain, using examples from the play.

Broader Connections

6. The original Uncle Tom was a character from a famous antislavery novel, *Uncle Tom's Cabin.* As a slave, he humbly obeyed the will of his white masters. Morgan Freeman, the actor who played Hoke in the movie, was concerned that his character not be seen as an Uncle Tom. Does Hoke act like an Uncle Tom? Why or why not?

Literary Concept: Foil

A **foil** is a character who provides a striking contrast to a main character. Foils help to draw attention to certain qualities in the main character. Which characters serve as foils to Daisy? What aspects of her personality do they highlight?

Concept Review: Climax Which scene do you consider to be the climax or turning point of the play?

Writing Options

1. Choose your favorite scene in the play. Write **director's notes** for that scene, advising the actors how they should play it and what qualities they should convey.

2. Imagine that the producer of the film suggested cutting the scene with the speech by Martin Luther King, Jr. As the writer, write a **memo** to the producer to explain the importance of that scene.

3. Choose another African American you have read about in this textbook. How would he or she have gotten along with Miss Daisy? Write a short dramatic **scene,** in play form, in which the two characters meet for the first time.

4. Do you think this play should be taught next year? Write a **persuasive letter** to your teacher, stating your opinion and supporting it with reasons.

Vocabulary Practice

Exercise Choose the word from the list that best completes each sentence. Use each word only once. Write the answers on a separate sheet of paper.

1. The lynching of his friend's father upset Hoke; he found the action __?__ .

2. If someone committed another act of violence to revenge the bombing, it would be a __?__ .

3. Alone with Boolie, Florine showed her feelings toward her mother-in-law by __?__ at her.

4. Boolie was sure that Daisy would __?__ another car if she were allowed to drive.

5. Hoke took good care of the inside of the car, including the __?__ .

6. Boolie felt better knowing that Daisy was in the car with a driver like Hoke who showed __?__ .

7. Boolie responded __?__ to Daisy's claim that Hoke was a thief.

8. Daisy's reaction to any gifts from Florine was to __?__ from them.

9. Daisy could have bought __?__ care for her husband's grave but preferred to provide it herself.

10. Daisy told the state troopers that the __?__ of her name was German.

> *Words to Know and Use*
> ___
> **appalling**
> **competence**
> **demolish**
> **derivation**
> **dubiously**
> **perpetual**
> **recoil**
> **reprisal**
> **sniping**
> **upholstery**

*O*ptions for Learning

1 • **At the Movies**   Obtain a video of the movie *Driving Miss Daisy* to show in class or watch at home. Then have a panel discussion with others who have seen the film. Act as movie critics to discuss how well the movie matched your interpretations of the screenplay. For example, did Jessica Tandy portray Daisy as you had imagined her? Did Dan Aykroyd and Morgan Freeman portray Boolie and Hoke in the way you expected? Discuss all the differences that you noticed between the movie and the screenplay.

2 • **The March of Time**   Research the progress that African Americans made from 1948–1973, the period of this play. On a large sheet of paper, make a time line showing major events in the struggle for racial equality.

3 • **That's Entertainment**   As a class, select your favorite scene from the play. Then hold auditions for the parts by taking turns reading. After the parts are assigned, rehearse your scene and perform for the class.

4 • **Friends and Foes**   Like Daisy and Hoke, Jews and African Americans have had a long and sometimes troubled relationship. Read through history books and current magazines to find out more about this subject. Report your findings to the class.

 FACT FINDER HISTORY

In what year was Martin Luther King, Jr., assassinated?

*A*lfred Uhry
1936–

If Alfred Uhry hadn't returned to his roots when he did, the world might never have known Hoke and Miss Daisy. Born in Atlanta, Georgia, Uhry began his career in drama in New York as a lyricist, or song writer, for musicals. In 1975, Uhry wrote both the script and song lyrics for a hit musical entitled *The Robber Bridegroom*. After this hit, however, success seemed to escape Uhry's grasp, and he returned to teaching at New York University.

In his words, "Something whispered in my ear that it was time to sit down and write a play." He remembered his grandmother, who had become a family legend because of her bad temper. She insisted on driving long after it was safe for her to do so, and eventually the family found her a black chauffeur. Thus, the idea for Miss Daisy was born.

Today, Uhry still writes in New York for both the theater and film industries.

WRITER'S WORKSHOP

WRITING ABOUT LITERATURE

Think of some people you know well. You've probably seen them in many different situations. In *Driving Miss Daisy,* we get to know the characters in the same way. As we watch their relationships change over time, we see deeply into the characters themselves. One way to focus your insights about a character—and about a piece of literature—is to write a character analysis. When you **analyze** something, you break it down into its parts, examining each part separately. In a **character analysis,** you examine a character's traits. You look at the ways those traits work together, and you notice the effects they have.

USE LITERARY
ANALYSIS FOR
book reviews
character analyses
essay exams
learning-log entries
study guides

GUIDED ASSIGNMENT: CHARACTER ANALYSIS

Write an analysis of a character in *Driving Miss Daisy.*

Here is one writer's PASSkey to this assignment.

P URPOSE: To write about literature
A UDIENCE: Classmates
S UBJECT: A character in "Charles"
S TRUCTURE: A character analysis

The Monster
by Greg Chu

When I first read "Charles," by Shirley Jackson, I thought Laurie was a little monster. He disrupts his kindergarten, swears, and hits the teacher. The teacher tries to control him, but nothing works. At home, he's a "swaggering character" who often smarts off. He seems like a problem child. However, Laurie has two strengths. He's fair, and he's determined. His strengths just don't go over very well with his teacher.
On the first day of school, Laurie is "awfully fresh," and the teacher spanks him. After that, Laurie acts worse and worse. I

STUDENT MODEL

Before you analyze a character in *Driving Miss Daisy,* read how one student analyzed a character in a story at the beginning of this book.

◄ The writer makes a generalization about the character.

really don't blame him. A teacher who spanks a
kindergartner the first day she meets him,
just because he mouths off, is pretty mean. On
the second day Laurie hits the teacher. Of
course that's wrong, but it may seem fair to
Laurie. She hit him first, the day before.

The writer explores the character's motives. ▶

As the weeks go by, Laurie's sense of
fairness probably makes him see the teacher as
a bully. She hits children, stands them in the
corner, and washes out their mouths with soap.
Laurie is determined not to be bullied. No
matter how much she punishes him, he keeps

Details from the story show what the writer means. ▶

acting up. His determination earns the
children's respect. When the teacher tells them
not to play with him, they ignore her. When she
keeps him after school, they all stay with him.

The good side of Laurie's fairness comes
out, too. One day, without being asked, Laurie
does some chores for the teacher. The teacher
calls him her "helper" and gives him an apple.
After that he behaves better. In other words,
as soon as the teacher stops being mean,
Laurie tries harder to cooperate. He slips up

The conclusion echoes the introduction, with a twist. ▶

at times, but nobody's perfect. Laurie's no
angel, but he's not a problem child. He just
ran into a problem teacher.

Now that you've read Greg's paper, it's time to begin your own.

Prewrite and Explore

1 **Explore a character**   *Driving Miss Daisy* has three major characters: Daisy, Hoke, and Boolie. Start by choosing the one you understand best. Next, try brainstorming about the character's traits. You might jot down your feelings about the character, then list the traits that make you feel as you do.

2 **Find an angle**   Here are three approaches to analyzing a character: (1) you can examine his or her strengths and weaknesses; (2) you can figure out his or her motives, or reasons for doing things; (3) you can trace how and why the character changes. Try choosing one approach and using it to freewrite about the character you selected. After you finish, underline the parts of your freewriting that seem most important to you.

3 **Search the play** Whichever approach you choose, you'll need details and quotations from the play. Keeping your focus in mind, look back through the play. Look for examples of the ideas you are pointing out.

◀ **WRITER'S CHOICE**
You can mix two approaches. For instance, you might see how a character's strengths and weaknesses affect his or her motives.

GATHERING INFORMATION

Try making a chart based on your approach. For example, Greg focused on his character's motives. He made the chart below, and wrote in his ideas, then filled in details from the story.

Action	page	Possible motives	Details and quotes	page
is "awfully fresh" on first day	7	He's a smart aleck.	"swaggering character," smarts off at home	7 8, 9
hits teacher	8	getting even	She hit him first.	7
refuses to cooperate	8, 9 10, 11	Teacher's too mean.	She tries to turn kids against him. She washes out kids' mouths with soap.	8 10, 11

◀ **STUDENT MODEL**

---

4 **Generalize** Look over the details in your prewriting notes, and sum them up in two or more generalizations—broad statements—about your character. For example, scanning his notes, Greg noticed that Laurie seldom gave up. Greg wrote a generalization: *"Laurie is determined."* Then Greg noticed that Laurie often treated the teacher as she had treated him. Greg wrote *"Laurie is fair."*

◀ **NEED MORE HELP?**
For more about generalizations, see the Reader's Workshop on page 347.

Draft and Discover

1 **Fill in the blanks**   One way to draft a character analysis is to write each of your generalizations at the top of a blank page. Then, beneath each generalization, write as much as you can to explain it. Include details and quotations from the play.

2 **Make connections**   After you've written about each generalization, you need to explain how they're connected. Maybe they show strengths or weaknesses, or shed light on motives. Write a sentence explaining the connections. This serves as your **thesis statement,** a sentence that tells the main idea and goal of your paper. Refer to your thesis statement often to keep your writing focused.

Revise Your Writing

1 **Find your organization**   You can start your analysis by naming your character and stating your thesis. Then you can write one or more paragraphs about each generalization, using details and quotations as support. To end your paper with flair, you might use a quotation from the play that illustrates your thesis. You might find a way to refer to the beginning of your paper, perhaps echoing a phrase.

WRITER'S CHOICE
You might prefer a narrative format, explaining your initial impression of the character, then telling how and why your views changed.

2 **Listen to the rhythm**   If you've ever heard rap music, you know that sentences have rhythm. Read your sentences aloud to hear their rhythm. Which ones sound the way you want? To get more of that sound, try changing or combining other sentences.

NEED MORE HELP?
See the Language Workshop on pages 462–464.

THE EDITOR'S EYE: SENTENCE COMBINING

Join two complete sentences with a comma and an appropriate conjunction.

When your sentences sound choppy, you can combine some of them. If two short sentences express similar ideas, join them with a comma and the conjunction *and*. If they express contrasting ideas, join them with a comma and *but*.

Problem   Laurie's no angel. He's not a problem child.

Combined   Laurie's no angel**, but** he's not a problem child.

3 **Try a peer reader**   When you're ready, you can ask a friend to read your character analysis. Use the question lists below.

Revision Questions	
For You	**For a Peer Reader**
1. Do I express main insights about the character?	**1.** What insights did you get from my paper?
2. Could I add details from the play to make my ideas clearer?	**2.** Can you see which parts of the play gave me my ideas?
3. Do my sentences have the sound that I want?	**3.** Can you suggest a way for me to make my ideas clearer?

Proofread

Reread your paper, correcting errors in grammar and mechanics.

Publish and Present

Here is an idea for sharing your writing with others.

Critics' Forum   Think of movie critics who discuss movies with each other on television. Since some of your classmates have also written about the character you chose, you can hold a similar discussion. First, form a group and read your papers aloud. Then respond to one another's interpretations. Say whether you agree or disagree, and explain why.

Reflect on Your Writing

Write brief answers to the questions below. Add them to your character analysis when you put it in your portfolio.

◀ FOR YOUR PORTFOLIO

1. What insights did you gain about the character you analyzed?
2. Has your opinion of the character changed? Why or why not?

LANGUAGE
WORKSHOP

SENTENCE COMBINING

In writing, as in music, repeating one rhythm can get dull. You can vary your sentence rhythms and avoid too many short, choppy sentences by using the techniques below.

Combining Sentences

You can combine two sentences when their thoughts are related. For example, since the thoughts in these two sentences are related, the sentences can be combined:

Everyone wonders how Dolores got her tattoo. She won't tell.
Everyone wonders how Dolores got her tattoo, **but** she won't tell.

The thoughts in the following two sentences are not closely related, so the sentences should not be combined:

Everyone wonders how Dolores got her tattoo. Tattoos can be removed with lasers.

REMINDER
If ideas are similar, use a comma and the word *and.* If ideas contrast, use a comma and the word *but.* If ideas are alternatives, use a comma and the word *or.*

▶ When two related sentences contain equally important ideas, you can join the sentences with a comma and a conjunction (*and, but,* or *or*).

Dick owns Stan's Hardware. Dolores is the assistant manager.
Dick owns Stan's Hardware, **and** Dolores is the assistant manager.

Someone is bringing them flowers. They don't know who it is.
Someone is bringing them flowers, **but** they don't know who it is.

The flowers might be for Dick. They might be for Dolores.
The flowers might be for Dick, **or** they might be for Dolores.

Combining Sentence Parts

Sometimes, instead of joining two entire sentences, you can combine only their subjects, verbs, or objects. In such cases, use conjunctions and leave out words or ideas that are repeated.

The jars hold marigolds. They also hold zinnias.
The jars hold marigolds **and** zinnias.

Ernie had seeds. He had never planted them, though.
Ernie had seeds **but** had never planted them.

▶ PUNCTUATION NOTE
· · · · · · · · · · · · · · · ·
When only sentence parts are joined, no comma is used before the conjunction.

Exercise 1   Concept Check   Rewrite each pair as one sentence. Use the conjunctions in parentheses. Eliminate italicized words.

1. Dolores understands hardware. The customers trust her. (**, and**)
2. Maybe Dolores hates makeup. Maybe she just doesn't care. (**, or**)
3. Ernie doesn't know Dolores. He has a crush on her. (**, but**)
4. Dolores can't figure out who's bringing the flowers. Dick *can't either.* (**and**)
5. Both are curious. *However, they both* say nothing. (**but**)
6. Each wonders if the other has a new friend. *Each thinks the other might have* a secret lover. (**or**)
7. As the weeks go by, Dolores starts dressing differently. *She also starts* wearing jewelry. (**and**)
8. Dolores never sees Ernie. He makes her happy. (**, but**)
9. Ernie learns to grow flowers outdoors. *He even learns to grow them* indoors. (**and**)
10. Jack is just a college student. *However,* he makes a big difference in Ernie's life. (**, but**)

Adding Words to Sentences

Sometimes the ideas in two sentences are not equally important. When you revise, you see that only one word (or word group) in one of the sentences adds new meaning. Add that part to the other sentence.

▶ PUNCTUATION NOTE
· · · · · · · · · · · · · · · ·
When you add a word or word group, you may need to add one or more commas. For comma rules see Section 10, pages 775-776, of the Language Handbook.

Dolores has a tattoo of a coyote. The coyote is howling.
Dolores has a tattoo of a **howling** coyote.

The flowers appear every Wednesday. They are on the doorstep.
The flowers appear **on the doorstep** every Wednesday.

You may need to change some words slightly. You might add *-ly, -ing, -ed,* or other endings.

In the sun, the zinnias seem to glow. They look bright.
In the sun, the zinnias seem to glow **brightly.**

Dolores picks up the flowers. She looks surprised.
Dolores, **looking surprised,** picks up the flowers.

Exercise 2   Concept Check   To the first sentence of each pair below, add the italicized word or word group. Decide where it fits best. Make needed changes, and write your new sentence.

WRITER'S CHOICE
Some words or word groups can fit in several places in a sentence. You can choose the placement that "feels" best to you.

1. Packets of seeds are Ernie's treasures. The packets are *colorful.*
2. Ernie lives in a group home. He lives *with other retarded people.*
3. One day he sees the hardware store. He is looking *through the restaurant window.*
4. Ernie smiles when he sees Dolores. His smile is *shy.* (Use *-ly.*)
5. Jack shows him how to grow flowers. Jack helps him because he *wants to be Ernie's friend.* (Use *-ing.*)
6. Then Ernie brings the flowers to Dolores. He does this in *secret.* (Use *-ly.*)
7. Ernie blossoms. In this way, he is *just like his flowers.*
8. Cynthia Rylant based the character of Ernie on a real person. The person lived *in her town.*
9. Rylant may have known a woman like Dolores. Dolores was *independent.*
10. The real world is filled with people like Dolores and Ernie. These characters are *imperfect,* like real people.

Exercise 3   Revision Skill   Revise the paragraph below, using techniques from this workshop. Then share your work with classmates.

> Cynthia Rylant grew up in West Virginia. There she lived with her grandparents. They lived in the mountains. Her grandfather worked in the mines. He worked hard. He came home covered with dust. The dust was from coal. Her grandmother cooked fried okra. She also cooked corn bread. Cynthia remembers family evenings on the front porch. She treasures those memories. Most of all, she remembers the stars. They sparkled.

Exercise 4   Looking at Style   Look back at "A Crush" on page 398. Rewrite the first two sentences as several shorter sentences. Compare your sentences with the original. Which style do you prefer?

REVISING TIP
Like a musician, you can work by ear, trying out rhythms and patterns to find the ones you're most comfortable with.

Exercise 5   Revising Your Writing   Read the character analysis you wrote for the Writer's Workshop on pages 457–461. Use techniques from this workshop to vary the rhythms of your sentences and remove repetition.

VOCABULARY
WORKSHOP

DENOTATION AND CONNOTATION

The dictionary gives definitions, or **denotations,** of words. As you know, some words have the same denotation. Words also have **connotations**—the ideas or feelings they suggest. No two words have exactly the same connotations—not even words with the same meaning. Connotations can be generally **positive** (suggesting pleasant feelings) or **negative** (suggesting unpleasant feelings). For example, *determined* has positive connotations, but *stubborn* has negative connotations. Some words are **neutral.** Words like *chair* and *talk* have neither positive nor negative connotations.

Exercise 1 First, write *Positive* or *Negative* to describe each italicized word's connotations. Be ready to discuss your reasons. Then, using a dictionary, write the word's denotation. If a word has multiple meanings, choose the one that fits the sentence best.

1. The *nag* and its rider galloped along the deserted road.
2. In the moonlight the road *glistened* like a band of silver.
3. The *ghostly* cry of an owl echoed over the moor.
4. *Sneering,* the horseman peered ahead.
5. He sat poised and *upright* in the saddle.

Exercise 2 The italicized words have positive connotations. Replace each with a synonym whose connotations are negative. You may use a dictionary or a thesaurus.

On a *cool* evening the *highwayman* enters the courtyard of the inn. There at her window stands the landlord's *slender* daughter. He *murmurs* to her, then *slips* away into the *dusky* night. She will wait *eagerly* for his *promised* return.

Exercise 3 Read the paper you wrote for the Writer's Workshop on pages 457–461. Lightly underline all the words you used to describe the character, and evaluate their connotations. Insert words with more appropriate connotations where needed.

◀ WORD PLAY

Which would you rather have—a sly friend or a clever friend? a celebration or a bash? striking clothes or flashy clothes?

◀ MULTIPLE MEANINGS

Many words have more than one denotation—that is, they have multiple meanings. A word's context can help you figure out which meaning is intended. For more about context clues, see the Vocabulary Workshop on page 117.

Reading on Your Own

Suggested Novels for Unit Four

The novels introduced on these pages all present difficult challenges in personal relationships and reflect the Unit theme "Person to Person."

THE FLAWED GLASS

IAN STRACHAN ©1990

Shona MacLeod has such a severe physical handicap that she can hardly speak and walking is difficult for her. She is very intelligent and understands everything that goes on around her, but she cannot respond. Shona's world is so limited that she thinks of herself as being locked in a tower, waiting for a rescuer. Life on her island off the coast of Scotland is simple, bleak, and backwards. Because she is cut off from personal relationships with others, even her own family does not know what Shona can achieve. When a young American boy comes to the island, Shona learns with joy that he is someone who has the patience and insight to see past her difficulties and set her free. As you read, try to imagine . . .

- the pain and frustration of being unable to communicate

- how a computer might link Shona to other people

- how Shona would feel if she could save her family from disgrace

ONE-EYED CAT
PAULA FOX ©1974

Have you ever been tempted to do something forbidden? This is what Ned faces in *One-Eyed Cat.* When Ned's uncle gives Ned a BB gun, Ned's father forbids him to fire it until he is fourteen—three years away! Because he trusts Ned completely, his father stores the gun in the attic, where it remains an irresistible temptation. Ned grapples with an agonizing test of conscience as his secret and his guilt threaten to become more than he can handle. As you read, consider these questions:

• What are the consequences of Ned's firing the gun?

• What will Ned's silence cost him?

• How can Ned make amends to the victim of his shooting spree?

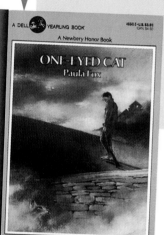

THE CLAY MARBLE
MINFONG HO ©1991

Twelve-year-old Dara and her family flee her peaceful village because there is no food; the land has been destroyed by war. With their belongings in an ox-cart, they head for a refugee camp on the border between Cambodia and Thailand. In this realistic novel, Dara struggles with personal relationships that have been changed by war. She watches her brother Sarun's personality change as he considers joining the army. Read to find answers to these questions:

• Can Dara and her family survive when the shelling begins again?

• Will Sarun join the army?

• Can Dara's family build a new life in a country still at war?

Other Recommended Books

On My Honor by Marion Dane Bauer (©1987). In this contemporary novel, Joel discovers the consequences of disobedience when his best friend drowns in a river. Can Joel tell anyone what really happened?

A Fine White Dust by Cynthia Rylant (©1986). In this realistic novel, a boy struggles to live up to his religious faith in spite of his parents' apathy and his best friend's atheism.

Treasure Island by Robert Louis Stevenson (©1883). This classic adventure tale tests both a boy's courage and his loyalty to a friendly pirate he meets on a search for buried treasure.

So Far from the Bamboo Grove by Yoko Kawashima Watkins (©1986). In this historical novel based on the author's childhood, a Japanese girl and her mother and sister flee Korea in the face of war.

A QUESTION OF IDENTITY

The person portrayed

and the portrait

are two entirely

different things.

José Ortega y Gasset

YO Y MI FUTURO (I and my future)
1951   Jesús Guerrero Galván Collection,
Pascual Gutierrez Roldan.

DECLARATIONS OF INDEPENDENCE

Each of us likes to express our individuality in a different way. For some of us, it may be the clothes we choose to wear or the way we fix our hair. Others express their unique personality through their behavior. Still others express who they are by standing up for their beliefs on important social issues.

No matter how we show our individuality, that expression is a statement of our freedom from the influence of others. In these selections, note the different ways people express their own special beliefs about themselves. See if you can determine each person's unique "declaration of independence."

Nonfiction

from # The Autobiography of Malcolm X

MALCOLM X *with* ALEX HALEY

Examine What You Know

You are about to read a section from the autobiography of the African-American leader Malcolm X. On the diagram below, Malcolm X's life has been divided into four parts. Brainstorm each of these categories to see what you and your classmates already know about Malcolm X. As you read, see if any of your ideas change.

Childhood | **X** | Imprisonment

Civil Rights | | Death

Expand Your Knowledge

Malcolm Little was born in Omaha, Nebraska, in 1925. His father was murdered when Malcolm was only six. Problems throughout his youth reached a climax when Malcolm was arrested in 1942 and sentenced to ten years in prison for burglary.

Prison became a turning point for Malcolm. In prison he joined the Black Muslims, a black religious group. He changed his name to represent what he was leaving behind: "Ex-smoker. Ex-drinker. Ex-Christian. Ex-Slave." His controversial career began upon his release from prison, when he became a Black Muslim minister. A powerful public speaker, Malcolm X preached that in order to achieve independence, African Americans should live and work completely apart from white people. Malcolm X believed that violence was acceptable in the fight for civil rights. Later, he came to believe in the possibility of brotherhood among all people. He was assassinated in 1965.

Write Before You Read

Suppose that, like Malcolm X, you faced ten years of confinement. How would you plan to spend your time? In your journal, describe what your thoughts might be if you faced such a sentence.

■ *Author biography on Extend page*

from The Autobiography of Malcolm X

MALCOLM X
with Alex Haley

It was because of my letters that I happened to stumble upon starting to acquire some kind of a homemade education.

I became increasingly frustrated at not being able to express what I wanted to convey in letters that I wrote, especially those to Mr. Elijah Muhammad.[1] In the street, I had been the most articulate hustler out there—I had commanded attention when I said something. But now, trying to write simple English, I not only wasn't articulate, I wasn't even functional. How would I sound writing in slang, the way I would *say* it, something such as, "Look, daddy, let me pull your coat about a cat, Elijah Muhammad—"

Many who today hear me somewhere in person or on television, or those who read something I've said, will think I went to school far beyond the eighth grade. This impression is due entirely to my prison studies.

It had really begun back in the Charlestown Prison, when Bimbi[2] first made me feel envy of his stock of knowledge.

Bimbi had always taken charge of any conversation he was in, and I had tried to emulate him. But every book I picked up had few sentences which didn't contain anywhere from one to nearly all of the words that might as well have been in Chinese. When I just skipped those words, of course, I really ended up with little idea of what the book said. So I had come to the Norfolk Prison Colony still going through only book-reading motions. Pretty soon, I would have quit even these motions, unless I had received the motivation that I did.

I saw that the best thing I could do was get hold of a dictionary—to study, to learn some words. I was lucky enough to reason also that I should try to improve my penmanship. It was sad. I couldn't even write in a straight line. It was both ideas together that moved me to request a dictionary along with some tablets and pencils from the Norfolk Prison Colony school.

---

1. Elijah Muhammad (e li′ jə moo ham′ əd): 1897–1975; leader of the Black Muslim movement in the United States.

2. Bimbi: a fellow inmate.

Words to Know and Use

articulate (är tik′ yōō lit) *adj.* able to express oneself clearly in words
emulate (em′ yōō lāt′) *v.* to imitate or copy

THE LIBRARIES ARE APPRECIATED 1943 Jacob Lawrence Philadelphia Museum of Art, Louis E. Stern Collection.

I spent two days just riffling uncertainly through the dictionary's pages. I'd never realized so many words existed! I didn't know *which* words I needed to learn. Finally, just to start some kind of action, I began copying.

I'd never realized so many words existed!

In my slow, painstaking, ragged handwriting, I copied into my tablet everything printed on that first page, down to the punctuation marks.

I believe it took me a day. Then, aloud, I read back to myself everything I'd written on the tablet. Over and over, aloud to myself, I read my own handwriting.

I woke up the next morning, thinking about those words—immensely proud to realize that not only had I written so much at one time, but I'd written words that I never knew were in the world. Moreover, with a little effort, I also could remember what many of these words meant. I reviewed the words whose meanings I didn't remember. Funny thing, from the dictionary's first page right now, that *aardvark* springs to my mind. The dictionary had a picture of it, a long-tailed, long-eared,

*Words
to Know
and Use* | **painstaking** (pānz′ tāk′ iŋ) *adj.* very careful

473

burrowing African mammal, which lives off termites caught by sticking out its tongue as an anteater does for ants.

I was so fascinated that I went on—I copied the dictionary's next page. And the same experience came when I studied that. With every succeeding page, I also learned of people and places and events from history. Actually, the dictionary is like a miniature encyclopedia. Finally, the dictionary's A section had filled a whole tablet—and I went on into the B's. That was the way I started copying what eventually became the entire dictionary. It went a lot faster after so much practice helped me to pick up handwriting speed. Between what I wrote in my tablet and writing letters, during the rest of my time in prison, I would guess, I wrote a million words.

I never had been so truly free in my life.

I suppose it was inevitable that as my word base broadened, I could for the first time pick up a book and read and now begin to understand what the book was saying. Anyone who has read a great deal can imagine the new world that opened. Let me tell you something: from then until I left that prison, in every free moment I had, if I was not reading in the library, I was reading on my bunk. You couldn't have gotten me out of books with a wedge.[3] Between Mr. Muhammad's teachings, my correspondence, my visitors—usually Ella and Reginald[4]—and my reading of books, months passed without my even thinking about being imprisoned. In fact, up to then, I never had been so truly free in my life.

The Norfolk Prison Colony's library was in the school building. A variety of classes was taught there by instructors who came from such places as Harvard and Boston universities. The weekly debates between inmate teams were also held in the school building. You would be astonished to know how worked up convict debaters and audiences would get over subjects like "Should Babies Be Fed Milk?"

Available on the prison library's shelves were books on just about every general subject. Much of the big private collection that Parkhurst[5] had willed to the prison was still in crates and boxes in the back of the library—thousands of old books. Some of them looked ancient: covers faded, old-time parchment-looking binding. Parkhurst, I've mentioned, seemed to have been principally interested in history and religion. He had the money and the special interest to have a lot of books that you wouldn't have in general circulation. Any college library would have been lucky to get that collection.

As you can imagine, especially in a prison where there was heavy emphasis on <u>rehabilitation</u>, an inmate was smiled upon if he demonstrated an unusually intense interest in books. There was a sizable number of

---

3. **wedge:** a tapered piece of wood or metal used for splitting wood or rock.
4. **Ella and Reginald:** Malcolm's sister and brother.
5. **Parkhurst:** a millionaire interested in the education and training of prisoners.

Words to Know and Use | **rehabilitation** (rē′ hə bil′ ə tā′ shən) *n.* the restoring of a person's ability to lead a useful life

well-read inmates, especially the popular debaters. Some were said by many to be practically walking encyclopedias. They were almost celebrities. No university would ask any student to devour literature as I did when this new world opened to me, of being able to read and *understand*.

I read more in my room than in the library itself. An inmate who was known to read a lot could check out more than the permitted maximum number of books. I preferred reading in the total isolation of my own room.

When I had progressed to really serious reading, every night at about ten I would be outraged with the "lights out." It always seemed to catch me right in the middle of something engrossing.

Fortunately, right outside my door was a corridor light that cast a glow into my room. The glow was enough to read by, once my eyes adjusted to it. So when "lights out" came, I would sit on the floor where I could continue reading in that glow.

At one-hour intervals the night guards paced past every room. Each time I heard the approaching footsteps, I jumped into bed and feigned sleep. And as soon as the guard passed, I got back out of bed onto the floor area of that light-glow, where I would read for another fifty-eight minutes—until the guard approached again. That went on until three or four every morning. Three or four hours of sleep a night was enough for me. Often in the years in the streets, I had slept less than that. ❧

INSIGHT

Aardvark

JULIA FIELDS

Since
    Malcolm died
    That old aardvark
    has got a sort of fame
    for himself—
    I mean, of late, when I read
    The dictionary the first
    Thing I see
    Is that animal staring at me.
And then
    I think of Malcolm—
    How he read
    in the prisons
    And on the planes
    And everywhere
    And how he wrote
    About old Aardvark.
Looks like Malcolm X helped
Bring attention to a lot of things
We never thought about before.

Words to Know and Use | **feign** (fān) *v.* to pretend

Responding to Reading

First Impressions

1. What are your feelings about Malcolm X's accomplishments? Write your response in your journal.

Second Thoughts

2. Based on this excerpt, how would you describe Malcolm X?

3. What do you think was the most important result of Malcolm X's copying pages from the dictionary? Why?

4. Malcolm X says that when he learned to read he "had never been so truly free" in his life. What do you think he meant by this?

5. Read or reread "Aardvark" on page 475. What do you think the last three lines might mean?

Broader Connections

6. Malcolm X was an eighth-grade dropout. If he had stayed in school, do you think he would have developed the same desire to learn that he did in prison? What steps do you think schools and the community could take to instill in students a greater desire for learning?

Literary Concept: Allusion

An **allusion** is a reference to another work of literature or to a familiar person, place, or event. Usually the reader must understand the allusion in order to understand the work in which it appears. How does the poem "Aardvark" use allusion?

Concept Review: Motivation   Malcolm X states that his original motivation for wanting to improve his reading was envy of his friend Bimbi. Did his motivation for reading change after he completed copying the dictionary?

Writing Options

1. Malcolm X was very frustrated when he could not communicate his ideas and feelings in writing. Write a **personal memoir** about a time when you experienced a similar frustration.

2. Write a **poem** about an instance in your life in which you declared your independence.

3. Consider the actions Malcolm X took in this excerpt and the change he caused in himself. **Compare and contrast** his actions and motivations with those of Jackie Robinson, Jean Little, or Eleanor Roosevelt.

4. Write a **persuasive speech** that Malcolm X might give about literacy—the ability to read and write.

Vocabulary Practice

Exercise Analogies Determine the relationship between the first pair of words. Then decide which vocabulary word best completes the second pair in order to express a similar relationship.

1. FOLLOW : INSTRUCTIONS ::_____: hero
2. GRACEFUL : DANCER ::_____: speaker
3. LOUD : QUIET ::_____: careless
4. RECOVERY : HOSPITAL ::_____: prison
5. WISH : HOPE ::_____: pretend

Words to Know and Use

articulate
emulate
feign
painstaking
rehabilitation

*O*ptions for Learning

1 • Recommended Reading Suppose that you were being sent away for ten years and could select only ten books to take with you. In small groups, decide which books would be the most valuable to have. Compare your lists.

2 • So Many Words, So Little Time Let any dictionary fall open and carefully read one page. Jot down how many entries were on the page, how many were new to you, and how many historical facts were given. Share your results.

3 • Reading Power Write to either a local or national literacy program for information about illiteracy. Find out how many people can't read, how reading is taught to adults, and how learning to read affects them.

4 • Say It Loud Malcolm X urged African Americans to make use of what he called Black Power. Do research to find out what Malcolm believed African Americans should do to improve their lives. Make an oral report on your findings.

 FACT FINDER SOCIAL STUDIES

Find out how much money your state spends per year to jail a criminal and how much the state spends per year to educate a child.

*M*alcolm X
1925–1965

In prison, Malcolm X began to follow the teachings of Elijah Muhammad and the Nation of Islam, also known as the Black Muslims. After his release he became a minister for this group and soon became more famous than Elijah Muhammad. Malcolm X preached in favor of black power and black nationalism, opposing white oppression and integration. However, because of a dispute within the faith, Malcolm was expelled from the group. He then traveled to Africa where he became a follower of traditional Islam.

In 1965 Malcolm X founded the Organization of Afro-American Unity to bring publicity to the plight of African Americans. He and Alex Haley, who later wrote *Roots,* worked together on Malcolm's autobiography. While preparing to speak in Harlem on February 21, 1965, he was assassinated. Three men, two of whom were Black Muslims, were convicted of his murder and sentenced to life in prison. His autobiography was published after his death.

Poetry

Without Commercials

ALICE WALKER

Examine What You Know

The world around us is full of ads for weight-loss programs, hair products, fitness programs, cosmetics, contact lenses, tanning salons, and plastic surgery. It often seems that no one is happy with the way he or she looks. How do you feel about your own appearance? How important are your looks to your view of yourself? In your journal or notebook, write down your feelings.

Expand Your Knowledge

Each year thousands of people are so unhappy about their looks that they decide to change them. Some changes are related to ethnic characteristics. For example, many Caucasians go to tanning salons or spend hours in the sun to darken their skin. Some African Americans bleach their skin to lighten it. Some Asians have surgery to remove the fold in their upper eyelids. Each year over half a million people in the United States have cosmetic surgery of some kind. Cosmetic surgeons flatten ears that stick out. They also perform face lifts, forehead lifts, thigh lifts, hair transplants, nose reshapings, and tummy tucks. The fees for such operations are often high. A nose reshaping alone may cost as much as six thousand dollars.

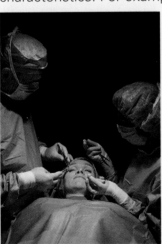

Enrich Your Reading

Reading Stanzas   A group of lines that forms a unit in poetry is called a **stanza.** A stanza is comparable to a paragraph in prose. Like a paragraph, each stanza may present its own unique images. All stanzas in a poem, however, usually relate to a central idea or overall theme. In the following poem, notice how the stanzas help organize the speaker's advice about appearances.

■ *Author biography on Extend page*

Without Commercials

ALICE WALKER

Listen,
stop tanning yourself
and talking about
fishbelly
5   white.
The color white
is not bad at all.
There are white mornings
that bring us days.
10 Or, if you must,
tan only because
it makes you happy
to be brown,
to be able to see
15 for a summer
the whole world's
darker
face
reflected
20 in your own.

*

Stop unfolding
your eyes.
Your eyes are
beautiful.
25 Sometimes
seeing you in the street
the fold zany
and unexpected
I want to kiss
30 them

and usually
it is only
old
gorgeous
35 black people's eyes
I want
to kiss.

* *

Stop trimming
your nose.
40 When you
diminish
your nose
your songs
become little
45 tinny, muted
and snub.
Better you should
have a nose
impertinent
50 as a flower,
sensitive
as a root;
wise, elegant,
serious and deep.

55 A nose that
sniffs
the essence
of Earth. And knows
the message
60 of every
leaf.

* * *

Stop bleaching
your skin
and talking
65 about
so much black
is not beautiful
The color black
is not bad
70 at all.
There are black nights
that rock
us
in dreams.
75 Or, if you must,
bleach only
because it pleases you
to be brown,
to be able to see
80 for as long
as you can bear it
the whole world's
lighter face
reflected
85 in your own.

* * * *

As for me,
I have learned
to worship
the sun
90 again.

To affirm
the adventures
of hair.

For we are all
95 *splendid*
descendants
of Wilderness,
Eden:
needing only
100 to see
each other
without
commercials
to believe.

105 Copied skillfully
as Adam.

Original

as Eve.

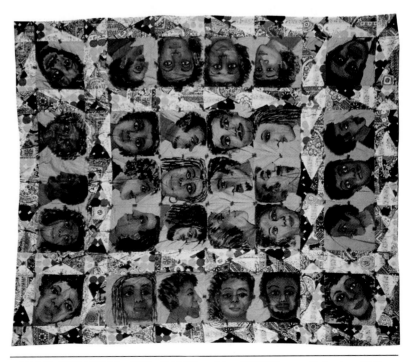

ECHOES OF HARLEM   1980   Faith Ringgold and Willi Posey.   Collection, Philip
Morris Companies.   Courtesy, Bernice Steinbaum Gallery, New York.

Responding to Reading

First Impressions

1. Which part of this poem did you find most meaningful? Why?

Second Thoughts

2. Each of the first four **stanzas** addresses a concern that different people have about their appearance. Do you think the speaker's advice to each group is the same or different? Explain.

3. What do you think it means to see people "without commercials"?

   Think about
   • what the speaker wants people to stop doing
   • why Adam, Eve, and Eden are mentioned

4. Do you agree with the speaker of this poem? Explain.

Literary Concept: Tone

A writer's attitude toward his or her subject is called **tone.** For example, a writer's tone may be angry, bitter, admiring, or humorous, depending on how he or she feels about the subject. You can figure out the tone from the word choice and the kinds of statements the writer makes. How would you describe Walker's tone in this poem?

Concept Review: Theme What theme, or message about life, do you think Walker presents in "Without Commercials"?

Writing Options

1. Write a short **essay** on why you think this poem is in a subunit called Declarations of Independence.

2. Suppose you were a plastic surgeon or you owned a cosmetic company. What would you say to Walker? Write a **rebuttal** in which you defend the right of individuals to change their appearance.

Options for Learning

1 • **A Matter of Looks** Stage a debate on whether people should spend large amounts of time and money on personal appearance. Set up two teams. Each team may do a survey of other students' opinions and do library research. Then hold your debate for your classmates.

2 • **The Old You!** Think of a new product that will immediately undo all the changes people have made in their appearances. Create a television commercial for your product. If possible, add music and videotape your commercial.

3 • **With Commercials** In a week's time period, notice how many television commercials encourage people to change their appearance. Keep a running list of the day, time, product, and appearance change suggested. Post your list on a bulletin board to share with others.

4 • **Cosmetic Surgery** Research one type of cosmetic surgery such as those mentioned on the Explore page. If possible, find out from a plastic surgeon what is involved in the operation and its cost. Share the information with your classmates.

FACT FINDER HISTORY

Who were the first people to use cosmetics?

Alice Walker
1944-

Alice Walker has always been a person with strong beliefs. She was born in Eatonton, Georgia, to sharecropper parents. As one of eight children, Walker felt different from others and spent much time alone reading. She wrote her first poems when she was eight years old.

As an adult, Walker worked in the civil rights movement in the 1960s and then moved to California to begin the most famous of her nine books, *The Color Purple*. The novel won a Pulitzer Prize and the National Book Award, and it was made into a movie.

Walker still acts on her strong opinions. She is now a vegetarian, works for animal rights, and has even been arrested while protesting the development of nuclear weapons.

Fiction

ᴬ *Man Who Had No Eyes*

MacKINLAY KANTOR

Examine What You Know

Blindness is a key element in the selection you are about to read. How do you respond to people who cannot see? What feelings do you have? Do you ever try to help them in any way? Finish the statements below and share your reactions with your classmates.

When I Meet a Blind Person . . .		
I feel . . .	I want to . . .	I never . . .

Expand Your Knowledge

Over twenty million people in the world are partially or totally blind; half a million of these are U.S. citizens. The most common cause of blindness is disease, mainly diabetes. The second leading cause is accidental injury. Approximately one thousand people a day experience eye injuries in the workplace. Such eye injuries cost business and industry over five hundred million dollars a year, yet ninety percent of these injuries could be prevented if workers wore protective eyewear.

Enrich Your Reading

Stereotype A broad and unfair generalization about a particular group of people is called a **stereotype**. People often form stereotypes about racial, religious, political, or social groups. Occasionally people form stereotypes about those with disabilities such as blindness. In any case, stereotypes do not allow for individual differences within a group. As you read the next selection, ask yourself if it presents any stereotypes about blind people.

■ *Author biography in Reader's Handbook*

A Man Who Had No Eyes

MacKinlay Kantor

A beggar was coming down the avenue just as Mr. Parsons emerged from his hotel.

He was a blind beggar, carrying the traditional battered cane and thumping his way before him with the cautious, half-furtive effort of the sightless. He was a shaggy, thick-necked fellow; his coat was greasy about the lapels and pockets, and his hand splayed over the cane's crook with a futile sort of clinging. He wore a black pouch slung over his shoulder. Apparently he had something to sell.

The air was rich with spring; sun was warm and yellowed on the asphalt. Mr. Parsons, standing there in front of his hotel and noting the *clack-clack* approach of the sightless man, felt a sudden and foolish sort of pity for all blind creatures.

And, thought Mr. Parsons, he was very glad to be alive. A few years ago he had been little more than a skilled laborer; now he was successful, respected, admired. . . . Insurance. . . . And he had done it alone, unaided, struggling beneath handicaps. . . . And he was still young. The blue air of spring, fresh from its memories of windy pools and lush shrubbery, could thrill him with eagerness.

He took a step forward just as the tap-tapping blind man passed him by. Quickly the shabby fellow turned.

"Listen, guv'nor. Just a minute of your time."

Mr. Parsons said, "It's late. I have an appointment. Do you want me to give you something?"

"I ain't no beggar, guv'nor. You bet I ain't. I got a handy little article here"—he fumbled until he could press a small object into Mr. Parsons's hand—"that I sell. One buck. Best cigarette lighter made."

Mr. Parsons stood there, somewhat annoyed and embarrassed. He was a handsome figure with his immaculate gray suit and gray hat and Malacca stick. Of course the man with the cigarette lighters could not see him. . . . "But I don't smoke," he said.

"Listen. I bet you know plenty people who smoke. Nice little present," wheedled the man. "And mister, you wouldn't mind helping a poor guy out?" He clung to Mr. Parsons's sleeve.

Mr. Parsons sighed and felt in his vest pocket. He brought out two half dollars and pressed them into the man's hand. "Certainly. I'll help you out. As you say, I can give it to someone. Maybe the elevator boy would—" He hesitated, not wishing to

THE RAGPICKER   about 1865-69
Edouard Manet (1832-1883)   Oil on canvas,
76 3/4 x 51 1/4 inches.   Norton Simon
Foundation, Pasadena, California.

be boorish and inquisitive, even with a blind peddler. "Have you lost your sight entirely?"

The shabby man pocketed the two half dollars. "Fourteen years, guv'nor." Then he added, with an insane sort of pride, "Westbury, sir. I was one of 'em."

"Westbury," repeated Mr. Parsons. "Ah, yes. The chemical explosion. . . . The papers haven't mentioned it for years. But at the time it was supposed to be one of the greatest disasters in—"

"They've all forgot about it." The fellow shifted his feet wearily. "I tell you, guv'nor, a man who was in it don't forget about it. Last thing I ever saw was C shop going up in one grand smudge and gas pouring in at all the busted windows."

Mr. Parsons coughed, but the blind peddler was caught up with the train of his one dramatic reminiscence. And also, he was thinking that there might be more half dollars in Mr. Parsons's pocket.

"Just think about it, guv'nor. There was a hundred and eight people killed, about two hundred injured, and over fifty of them lost their eyes. Blind as bats—" He groped forward until his dirty hand rested against Mr. Parsons's coat. "I tell you, sir, there wasn't nothing worse than that in the war. If I had lost my eyes in the war, OK. I would have been well took care of. But I was just a workman, working for what was in it. And I got it. You're so right I got it, while the capitalists were making their dough! They was insured, don't worry about that. They—"

"Insured," repeated his listener. "Yes. That's what I sell—"

"You want to know how I lost my eyes?" cried the man. "Well, here it is!" His words fell with the bitter and studied drama of a story often told, and told for money. "I was there in C shop, last of all the folks rushing out. Out in the air there was a chance, even with buildings exploding right and left. A lot of guys made it safe out the door and got away. And just when I was about there, crawling along between those big vats, a guy behind me grabs my leg. He says, 'Let me

past, you—!' Maybe he was nuts. I dunno. I try to forgive him in my heart, guv'nor. But he was bigger than me. He hauls me back and climbs right over me! Tramples me into the dirt. And he gets out, and I lie there with all that poison gas pouring down on all sides of me, and flame and stuff. . . ." He swallowed—a studied sob—and stood dumbly expectant. He could imagine the next words: *Tough luck, my man. Awfully tough. Now I want to—*

"That's the story, guv'nor."

The spring wind shrilled past them, damp and quivering.

"Not quite," said Mr. Parsons.

The blind peddler shivered crazily. "Not quite? What do you mean, you—?"

"The story is true," Mr. Parsons said, "except that it was the other way around."

"Other way around?" He croaked unamiably. "Say, guv'nor—"

"I was in C shop," said Mr. Parsons. "It was the other way around. You were the fellow who hauled back on me and climbed over me. You were bigger than I was, Markwardt."

The blind man stood for a long time, swallowing hoarsely. He gulped: "Parsons. I thought you—" And then he screamed fiendishly: "Yes. Maybe so. Maybe so. But I'm blind! I'm blind, and you've been standing here letting me spout to you, and laughing at me every minute! I'm blind!"

People in the street turned to stare at him.

"You got away, but I'm blind! Do you hear! I'm—"

"Well," said Mr. Parsons, "don't make such a row about it, Markwardt. So am I." ❧

E X P L A I N

Responding to Reading

First Impressions

1. What was your reaction to the end of the story? Write your response in your journal or notebook.

Second Thoughts

2. What is your opinion of Mr. Parsons?

   Think about
   - his occupation and outlook on life
   - how his revelation at the end affects your thinking

3. Do you feel sympathy for Markwardt? Why or why not?

4. How does the author use **stereotypes** in this story?

   Think about
   - what the **characters** think about each other
   - the ideas about blind people that you discussed before reading

5. Look back at the story now that you know the end of the plot. What clues might have told you that Mr. Parsons is blind?

Literary Concept: Irony

Irony occurs when there is a big difference between what is expected to happen and what actually happens. For example, when you are certain that you failed a test but receive an A on it, the situation is ironic. What irony exists in "A Man Who Had No Eyes"?

Writing Options

1. The story ends with Mr. Parsons telling Markwardt that he is blind. Write the next few lines of **dialogue** that might take place between the two men.

2. Suppose that Mr. Parsons were honored at an insurance company banquet. Write an **introductory speech** in which you praise him for his accomplishments and independence in spite of his disability.

Drama

Funny Boy
ALLAN BURNS

Examine What You Know

What kinds of jokes or stories does your favorite comedian tell? Does this comedian rely on sarcastic wit, or does he or she use sounds and movement to imitate funny situations? As a class, think of comedians and people you know who use the various kinds of humor described below. Then look for some of these kinds of humor in *Funny Boy*.

sarcastic, dry humor

comic impressions

jokes on current events

daily living, family life stories

FUNNY

pokes fun at self

slapstick comedy

lightning-fast comebacks

language, play on words

Expand Your Knowledge

Funny Boy is from a popular television series entitled *Room 222*. The show, which appeared on ABC from 1969 to 1973, was set in Walt Whitman High School. Each week the half-hour segments explored, with some humor, many situations that real students and teachers faced and continue to face today. For example, the series dealt with racial integration, drug abuse, and teenage pregnancy.

Enrich Your Reading

Stage Directions At the beginning of each scene, this play offers two kinds of stage directions. The directions for the television version include camera directions, like those given in *The Monsters Are Due on Maple Street* (page 157). *Funny Boy* also includes directions labeled *For the stage,* which would be used for a stage version of the play. As you read, notice how the action has been adapted for both kinds of performances.

■ *Author biography on Extend page*

Funny Boy

ALLAN BURNS

CHARACTERS

Pete Dixon, history teacher

Liz McIntyre, guidance counselor

Seymour Kaufman, principal

Alice Johnson, student teacher

Gordon Walters, history teacher

Bill Cruickshank, newspaper advisor

Waiter, in the restaurant

Serving Lady, in the teachers' cafeteria

Carl

Neil Kovack

Boy at Banquet

Marge

Al

Patty

Suzy

Richie's Date

Students

Richie

Harvey Butcher

JoEllen

Nonspeaking Parts

Four girls in Quad

Students on the Newspaper Staff

Exterior of Whitman High School. It is early, before school opens, and there is almost no activity. Interior shot of the teachers' cafeteria. Pete Dixon is eating breakfast and marking papers. Liz McIntyre comes up to the table carrying a tray. On the tray is a small plate containing half a grapefruit.

For the stage: The stage is divided into three acting areas. At the right are several rows of classroom chairs—the kind with a writing surface on the right arm—set diagonally fac- *ing the center of the back wall. There may be three or four chairs to a row. Facing them, also set diagonally, is a teacher's desk and chair. The teacher will be more or less facing the audience, and the students visible mostly in profile. The walls and the door to the classroom are imaginary.*

At left is a group of armchairs, a divan, coffee table and stand with coffee urn and paper cups. This area represents the faculty room.

The center area will be used for various settings, with slight rearrangement of furniture in view of the audience during the play.

There is no opening or closing curtain. At the start of the play, the center area is occupied by a cafeteria table and some chairs. When the play begins, the house lights go down, and Pete Dixon *takes his place at the table. He begins his business of eating breakfast and marking papers and is joined by* Liz McIntyre.

Liz. Good morning, Pete.

Pete. Hi, Liz. Eating light, I see.

Liz. It's my new diet: half a grapefruit every time you're hungry. *(sits down)* You eat about thirty grapefruits a day.

Pete. Is this the Mayo Clinic Diet or the Weight Watchers Diet?

Liz. I think it's the Grapefruit Growers' Diet.

(Suddenly Mr. Kaufman *looms over their table, carrying a tray loaded with food.)*

Kaufman *(sourly).* Good morning, Breakfast Clubbers.

Liz. Hi, Mr. Kaufman . . . join us.

Kaufman. Thank you. *(He sits down, eyes the trayful of food, sighs, picks up his glass of juice, and starts to take a sip of it.)*

Kaufman. I hope you all had a pleasant weekend, because it's going to be a terrible week.

Pete. Why do you say that?

Kaufman. I say that because there's a hair in my orange juice. Any time there's a hair in your orange juice the first thing Monday morning, it's going to be a terrible week. *(Making a face, he sets the glass aside,* picks up a spoon, and starts sugaring his coffee. A highly agitated . . . teacher, Mr. Walters, *comes up to the table.)*

Walters. Mr. Kaufman, I've got to talk to you.

Kaufman. See?

Walters *(nods to* Liz *and* Pete*).* Miss McIntyre . . . Mr. Dixon. *(back to* Kaufman*)* I am *not* going to go through another week trying to teach a history class with Harvey Butcher in it! Either he goes or I do!

*(*Kaufman *looks at him like it's a tough choice.)*

Kaufman *(glumly).* Sit down, Mr. Walters.

*(*Walters *sits, almost quivering with annoyance and agitation. It is obvious that he is not one of* Kaufman's *favorite people.)*

Kaufman. Would you care for a glass of juice? *(He indicates the glass with the hair in it.* Pete *and* Liz *stifle smiles.)*

Walters. Thank you, I've had mine already.

Kaufman. Miss McIntyre, are you familiar with Harvey Butcher?

Liz. I'm afraid I am. I've had him in a dozen times for counseling, but I can't get through to him.

Walters. Nobody can.

Pete. I don't believe that.

Walters. That's because you don't know him. He's not in *your* American history class.

(Alice Johnson comes bouncing up to the table, full of her usual enthusiasm. She is carrying a Coke and a doughnut.)*

Alice. Good morning, everybody!

(Liz *and* Pete *greet her with smiles, and* Mr. Walters *looks annoyed that she is interrupting his business. They shake hands. Alice's is by far the firmer of the two grips.*)

Kaufman. Miss McIntyre, do you think we should consider "Ro-ing" Harvey Butcher?

Liz. Yes, I'm afraid I do.

Walters. So do I!

Alice. What's "Ro-ing"?

Liz. RO is the new term for SA.

Alice. SA?

Pete *(disdainful of the term)*. Social Adjustment.

Liz. RO stands for Readjustment Opportunity.

Pete. Which is just another phony way of saying—

Kaufman. —We're gonna throw him out.

Liz *(to* Alice*)*. *Transfer* him to another school. Sometimes the shock of being uprooted and thrust into a new environment straightens a kid out.

Pete. But most times it doesn't. It's really admitting we've given up on the kid.

Alice. We can't give up on a kid.

Kaufman. Occasionally we *do* give up on a kid.

Walters. And if anybody deserves being given up on, it's Harvey Butcher.

Pete. What's his problem?

Walters. If you knew him, you wouldn't have to ask. He's disruptive, <u>insolent</u>, loud, and rude.

Kaufman. He's going to get a gold pin for perfect attendance in the Detention Room.

Pete. So what's to be accomplished by sending him to another school? What if he doesn't straighten out there? What then?

Liz. He gets expelled permanently.

Walters. Mr. Dixon, you wouldn't be so ready to stand up for him if he was in *your* history class.

Alice *(her back is up)*. We could handle him in our class, couldn't we, Mr. Dixon?

Pete *(embarrassed)*. Alice, I don't think this is any of our business.

Kaufman *(cuts him off)*. Just hold on a second. I think Miss Johnson has the beginnings of an interesting idea here . . .

(Alice *looks pleased.*)

Kaufman. Mr. Walters, you want to get rid of Butcher?

Walters. By all means.

Kaufman. And Mr. Dixon would like to give him one more chance. Is that right, Mr. Dixon?

Alice. Right.

(Pete *gives her a fast dirty look.*)

Kaufman. Well, I'm sure Harvey Butcher's schedule can be rearranged so that he can be in *your* American history class.

Pete *(ironically)*. Don't go to any trouble on my account.

Words to Know and Use | **insolent** (in′ sə lənt) *adj.* boldly showing no respect

Kaufman. No trouble at all.

(Alice gives Pete a triumphant grin.)

Pete *(flat).* Thank you.

Dissolve to: Interior of Room 222, Pete Dixon's classroom. Close shot of the blackboard. Written on the board in chalk are the following questions: (1) How would Benjamin Franklin fit into present-day America? (2) Describe the problems of the opposing factions at the Constitutional Convention.

Camera pulls back to a full shot of the class quietly taking the test. Pete is sitting at his desk, working on some papers. Various shots catching the students in a variety of attitudes as they work on the test: Richie, Jason, and others. Pete glances at his watch.

For the stage: At the end of the last scene, the faculty exit, two stagehands remove the cafeteria table and chairs from the center, and students slide unobtrusively into their seats in the classroom stage right. These actions, and all the others in the play, take place in view of the audience. Pete Dixon, instead of exiting with the other faculty, waits for a moment in the center, possibly puts a pipe in his pocket, then crosses to the classroom, pantomimes opening an imaginary door, and sits at his desk. A moment of silence.

Pete. You have fifteen more minutes.

(They go back to work. Suddenly, the silence is broken by the sound of someone running outside in the hallway. Everyone looks up as the heavy footsteps pass the door, then slow down and come back and slide heavily up to the door. Everyone's attention is riveted on the door, and Pete is beginning to rise from behind his desk when the door is suddenly thrown open and Harvey Butcher bursts in. Harvey is a seventeen-year-old homely, fat boy with a perpetually cherubic expression on his face. He stands in the doorway for a moment, panting exaggeratedly, and the class begins to laugh.)

Pete. Come on in. Don't stand there.

(Harvey nods and starts in, pretending to trip over a nonexistent doorstep, stumbling halfway across the room and dropping his books. The class roars. Harvey smiles pleasantly at Pete, then takes his hand and pumps it.)

Harvey. Hello, there, sir—my name is Harvey Butcher and I want to tell you it's an honor and a pleasure to be in your history class, Mr. Mason.

Pete. *Dixon.*

Harvey *(points at him, as if to say "You're right!").* Dixon. Well, of course. You can see why I made the mistake. Mason—Dixon . . .

(The class laughs. Pete looks annoyed at Harvey, who bends down and starts walking around stiff-legged, picking up his books, to continued laughter.)

Pete *(biting it off).* The class is taking a test.

(Harvey, still bent over, looks up, his face a mask of wide-eyed innocence, and pretends to notice the class for the first time.)

Harvey. Oh. *(pause, then to class)* Best of luck, everyone!

(They laugh again.)

Pete *(to class warningly).* You've got twelve minutes left.

PORTRAIT OF MOISE KISLING   1916
Amedeo Modigliani   Musée d'Art Moderne,
Villeneuve d'Asq, Donation of Genevieve and
Jean Masurel.

(The class quickly resumes taking the test.
Harvey, *with* Pete's *cool assistance, finishes*
picking up his books.)

Harvey *(stage whisper)*. I'm sorry, sir. I did
want to make an impression on you.

Pete. Oh, you have. Now just sit down until
the bell.

(Harvey *nods and heads down the aisle,*
making a funny face that Pete *can't see. There*
are three empty seats, and Harvey *stops, as if*

unable to decide which one to take, then turns to Pete *questioningly as he points to each of the empty desks.)*

Pete. Take any desk you like.

(Harvey nods, then puts down his books and starts to pick a desk up.)

Pete. What do you think you're doing?

Harvey. You said I could take any one I like. I like this one. *(puts it down)* On second thought, I like that one. *(He starts to pick up another desk, but* Pete *stands up and heads down the aisle.)*

Pete. All right, that's enough.

(Harvey, as if expecting this, nods amiably, picks up his books, and heads for the door.)

Pete. Where are you going?

Harvey. To the Detention Room. I thought I'd volunteer and save you the trouble. *(He waves and exits.* Pete *looks after him in amazement, then turns to* Alice.)*

Pete. Miss Johnson, take over.

Alice *(rising).* Right. *(She heads for the door.)*

Pete. I mean take over the class.

Alice. Oh.

(Interior of the corridor. Harvey Butcher *is partway down the hall as* Pete *comes out of Room 222, closing the door behind him.)*

Pete. *Mr.* Butcher.

(Harvey stops and turns.)

Harvey. Sir?

(Pete stands there, his hands on his hips, making Harvey *come back to him.* Harvey *walks slowly back, and we can sense him sizing* Pete *up.)*

Harvey. They'll be expecting me in the Detention Room. If I don't show up, they'll think something's happened to me.

Pete. You can send them a note telling them that you're being held prisoner by Mr. Mason in Room 222.

(Harvey looks at Pete, *bemused.)*

Pete. I want to know why you came to class thirty minutes late. I know you've got a good explanation.

Harvey. I do? I'd sure like to hear it, then.

Pete. I'll tell you what—you go back in the classroom and think up a good excuse that will satisfy both of us. You can make up the test during lunch.

(Pete opens the door and motions him in. Interior shot of Room 222 as the door opens and Harvey *reenters, followed by* Pete. Harvey, *as he enters, grasps his own collar from behind, like he's being carried in by the scruff of the neck, and wears a hangdog expression that gets an immediate laugh from the class.* Pete *just watches, deadpan,[1] as* Harvey, *still holding his collar, goes down the aisle and deposits himself in an empty seat with a large thud. Close-up of* Alice *and* Pete *as she relinquishes the chair behind the desk to him.)*

---

1. **deadpan:** with a face that shows no emotion.

Words to Know and Use

amiably (ā′ mē ə blē) *adv.* agreeably; pleasantly
bemused (bē myo͞ozd′) *adj.* confused; bewildered   **bemuse** *v.*
relinquish (ri liŋ′ kwish) *v.* to give up

Alice (*whispers encouragingly*). I think you're starting to make progress with him!

(Pete *regards her with an expression of disbelief.*)

Exterior of school quadrangle that afternoon. Small knots of students cluster around, lingering after school, chatting, horsing around, laughing. Several couples sit quietly, holding hands, saying little. Harvey Butcher *comes out of the building, looking around, then crosses to a group of girls and, doing a Jackie Gleason "Poor Soul,"[2] walks up to them. He takes a pair of tickets out of his pocket and holds them up.*

For the stage: The quadrangle is suggested by the action center stage, where some boys may be tossing a football; other students are sitting on benches which they have brought in.

Harvey. I've got two tickets for *Hello Dolly* Friday night.

(*No one shows the slightest interest in the fact.*)

Harvey. The reason I've got two tickets is that I take up two seats.

(*The girls laugh.* Harvey *stands there, as if waiting for someone to say something that will include him in their conversation, but no one does.*)

Harvey. Boy, you gotta be fast to keep up with all this fascinating conversation!

(*He turns and does an "away-we-go!" getaway.[3] As soon as he does, the group of girls clusters back together, chattering away. This fact is not lost on* Harvey. *He looks around the quadrangle for a friendly face. A shot of*

JoEllen, *an extremely fresh-faced, pretty girl.* JoEllen *is standing alone, books cradled in her arms, waiting for someone.* Harvey *comes up to her. We are acutely aware of* Harvey's *lack of physical attractiveness when he isn't acting funny—and around* JoEllen *he doesn't act funny.*)

Harvey. Hi, JoEllen.

JoEllen. Hi, Harvey.

Harvey. How did things go in Walters's history class without me today?

JoEllen (*smiles*). It sure was quiet. We missed you.

Harvey. I bet Walters didn't. (*enthusiastically*) Boy, remember the time ole Walters came into class late—

(Carl, *a good-looking boy, joins them. He ignores* Harvey.)

Carl. Let's go, JoEllen. Everybody's waiting.

JoEllen. OK. (*starts off, then stops, remembering* Harvey) So long, Harv. We'll sure miss you in history. (*She runs after* Carl.)

Harvey (*to self*). Sure you will.

(*Close shot of* Harvey. *He's embarrassed, fearing other students may have witnessed the previous scene.* Liz *and* Pete *approach.*)

Liz. Hello, Harvey.

Harvey (*coming on strong*). Hi folks . . . Look, I'd like to stay and spend a little time with you people, but I have to

---

2. Jackie Gleason "Poor Soul": refers to a timid, long-suffering character created by the comedian Jackie Gleason in the 1950s.

3. "away-we-go!" getaway: refers to Jackie Gleason's exaggerated movements when leaving a stage.

spread myself around, you know—I'm very big around here. I'm very big around *everywhere,* here . . . here . . . and here . . . *(indicating his girth)* Oh well, everybody loves a fat boy, right? *(He spins and walks quickly away, doing a stiff-legged funny walk.)*

Liz. Works hard at it, doesn't he?

Pete *(thoughtfully).* He's got energy all right. I'd sure like to do something with it.

(Close shot of Pete *watching* Harvey *go, thinking.)*

Interior of Room 222, next day. Pete *is going around the room, passing out the graded essay tests. The students react typically.* Pete *finishes passing them out and heads back to the front of the room.*

For the stage: At the end of the last scene, the actors exit, taking benches and props with them, and students slide quietly into their classroom seats at right as Pete *enters with the tests.*

Harvey *(raising hand).* Hey, where's *my* test? Did you burn it?

(The class laughs, and Pete *grins.)*

Pete. No, I thought I'd give everybody a treat this morning and read yours aloud. *(picks it up)* On second thought, why don't you read it yourself?

(The class applauds and cheers. Harvey *modestly accedes to their wishes and goes to the head of the class, throwing kisses and bowing. He takes the paper* Pete *is holding out to him.)*

Harvey *(reacts).* What's this—a B minus? This paper is an F if I ever saw one—and I've seen quite a few.

(laughter.)

Pete *(smiles).* Sorry to bring up your average, Harvey, but the grade stands. Read, please. *(to class)* As you recall, the question was to show how Benjamin Franklin would fit into today's society. *(He nods to* Harvey.)

Harvey *(reads).* Fade in The Loan Department of the Liberty Bell Savings and Loan. The vice-president glances up from his desk and sees a man with shoulder-length hair and rectangular glasses standing at the counter. *(pantomimes pushing down intercom button.)* "I thought I said no hippies in here."

(The class laughs.)

Harvey. He's my next appointment? OK, send him in—but have the guard keep an eye on him. *(pantomimes watching Franklin come in, then shakes hands)* Welcome to Liberty Bell, Mr. Franklin. That's a nice kite you're carrying. Is there any particular reason you've got that key tied to the string? *(pause)* You're waiting for the next thunderstorm so you can go out and fly it. *(pantomimes pushing down intercom again)* Have the guard move down this way in case I need him. *(laughter from class)* Well, Mr. Franklin, what can we do for you? *(pause)* You're applying for a loan so you can keep publishing your almanac? May I have your application form, please? *(looks at it)* "Printer,

---

Words to Know and Use | **girth** (gûrth) *n.* the distance around something

writer, inventor, philosopher, statesman, and scientist." *(pause)* Can't you hold a *job,* Mr. Franklin?

(The class roars its appreciation.)

Cut to: Interior of teachers' lounge. Pete *is reading aloud from* Harvey's *paper as* Alice, Liz, Mr. Walters, *and* Bill Cruickshank *listen. Laughter.*

For the stage: The laughter in the classroom scene, stage right, continues as the laughter in the faculty room, stage left, begins. Pete Dixon *leaves the classroom and joins the group in the faculty room. Then the students disappear from the classroom as* Pete *reads from* Harvey's *paper.*

Pete. You say you write wise sayings? Let's see. *(reads)* "A penny saved is a penny earned." *(pause)* Make that "A *dollar* saved is a dollar earned . . . at Liberty Bell Savings and Loan," and we've got a deal.

(They all laugh.)

Liz. That's funny. I like it.

Walters *(smiling)*. Who in the world wrote that? It's very good.

Pete *(pause)*. Harvey Butcher.

(Walters's smile fades. Alice *mugs[4] at him triumphantly. He grabs the paper out of* Pete's *hand and looks at it.)*

Walters *(accusingly)*. You gave him a B minus.

Pete. Why not?

Walters *(sputtering)*. Well, *because . . .* that's not a proper essay! He's ridiculing the assignment.

(Bill Cruickshank reaches out and takes the paper from him and peruses it.)

Pete *(shrugs)*. He's got most of the facts in there. It shows as much thought as some of the essays I gave A's. To write that, he had to know the subject.

Walters *(huffily)*. Well, it's *your* business if you want to encourage that sort of thing.

(Alice looks apoplectic,[5] but Pete *smiles and shakes his head as* Walters *fussily begins correcting papers.* Pete *turns to* Cruickshank, *who is still reading* Harvey's *essay.)*

Pete. What do you think, Bill?

Cruickshank. If I were this kid's creative writing teacher, I'd give him an A.

(Alice wrinkles her nose in Walters's *direction.)*

Pete. I'm glad to hear you say that. I'd like you to offer him a job on the school paper.

Cruickshank *(taken aback)*. Now wait a minute . . .

Pete. Your paper hasn't had a humor column for three years. Harvey Butcher could do one for you.

Cruickshank. Uh uh. I'm having enough problems *without* any humor column.

Liz. What kind of problems?

Cruickshank. Once there was a time when the kids who ran the high school newspaper were cooperative, proadministration types who wrote daring editorials about things like school spirit and litterbugs.

---

4. **mugs:** makes a face at.
5. **apoplectic** (ap′ ə plek′ tik): red-faced and speechless with anger.

PORTRAIT OF HENRI LAURENS   1915   Amedeo Modigliani   Private collection.

But now . . . *now* I've got the rebels, the militants, the free-speechers. I spend most of my time trying to find dirty words they conceal in the backgrounds of the drawings.

Pete *(grinning).* You missed a beauty last week.

Cruickshank. Thanks for reminding me. They crossed me up and made it so big I missed it with my magnifying glass.

Pete *(holding up* Harvey's *paper).* Bill, the kid who wrote this needs help. He's gonna get thrown out of this school unless he shapes up—but he doesn't figure there's anything to shape up *for.* I want to give him something. That column.

Walters *(looks up from his papers).* He isn't worth the trouble, believe me.

Cruickshank *(looks at* Walters, *then at* Pete*).* OK, I'll do it.

Pete *(smiles).* Hey, I must be more persuasive than I thought!

Cruickshank. It wasn't you that sold me. *(nods toward* Walters*)* It was him.

Interior of The Whitman Blue and Gold *office.* Richie *is introducing* Harvey *around. As* Cruickshank *noted, the staffers are, for the most part, an anarchistic-looking[6] bunch.* Neil Kovack, *an intense-looking type with long hair, comes up with some pages of copy. He looks inquiringly at* Harvey.

For the stage: This scene takes place in center stage. The characters, perhaps assisted by one or two stagehands, will bring in their own props—bulletin board, table, chairs, typewriter, painting easel.

Richie. Hey, Neil, this is Harvey Butcher. This here is Neil Kovack, our editor. *(to* Neil*)* Wait'll you read this man's stuff—he's outta sight!

Neil *(nods).* Think of a name for your column. I gotta have a masthead[7] made up.

Harvey. A name. How about "Fred"?

*(*Richie *breaks up.)*

Neil. Take any desk that's empty. I need five hundred words minimum from you by Thursday.

Harvey. I'd better get to work, then—I only *know* four hundred words.

*(*Richie *cracks up again, but* Neil *doesn't.)*

Harvey *(to* Richie*).* Stick around, Baby—I think I'm gonna need your support. *(He crosses to an empty desk with a typewriter on it. A fairly cute girl is standing at a table a few feet away doing paste-up work[8] using rubber cement and a brush.* Harvey *keeps looking at her as he arranges his gear, hoping to catch her eye. He finally does, but she just looks at him blankly.)*

Harvey. I've been watching you work.

Marge. So?

---

6. **anarchistic-looking** (an′ ər kis′ tik): looking like people who rebel against authority and the rules of society.

7. **masthead:** here, the headline that appears above each installment of a newspaper column.

8. **paste-up work:** the arranging and glueing of text, artwork, and photographs onto sheets of paper as a guide for a printer.

Words to Know and Use | **militant** (mil′ i tənt) *n.* a person fighting for a cause

Harvey *(trying to kid her)*. Well, it's a pleasure to watch someone who does their job really well. I mean, the graceful way you dip your brush into that gunk and then . . . *(pantomimes)* . . . stroke it on. It's beautiful.

(The girl stares at him hostilely. This is a person with no sense of humor. Harvey realizes she's not digging him, which makes him try too hard.)

Harvey. Who taught you that backhand? Pancho Gonzales?[9]

Marge. You know, we have a lot of work to do around here. We don't need any clowns. *(She plops her brush angrily into the jar of glue and walks away.)*

Harvey. I wasn't trying–*(He looks after her helplessly, realizing he's <u>alienated</u> her for keeps, a look of misery on his face. Neil strolls over to him.)*

Neil *(notes Harvey's expression)*. For a humor columnist, you certainly don't look very happy.

Harvey. That's the way it is with us funny guys sometimes–all the laughter and gaiety is *inside. (He picks up some typing paper and begins to wind it into his typewriter sadly. Fade out.)*

Fade in: Interior of Mr. Kaufman's *office. Mr. Kaufman is reading* The Whitman Blue and Gold *and wearing a strange expression [for him]: a smile. Not only that, he is chuckling.* Pete Dixon *sticks his head in the open door.*

For the stage: This scene takes place stage left in the faculty lounge.

GIRL WITH PIGTAILS 1918 Amedeo Modigliani
The Nagoya City Art Museum.

Pete. You got a minute for the junior class advisor?

(Kaufman waves him in but continues to read, smiling.)

Kaufman. Did you read this Butcher kid's column in *The Blue and Gold?*

Pete *(nods)*. Pretty funny stuff.

---

9. Pancho Gonzales (pän′ chō gən zä′ ləz) Richard Alonzo Gonzales, a U.S. professional tennis player who dominated the sport in the 1950s.

Words to Know and Use | **alienate** (āl′ yən āt′) *v.* to cause someone to become unfriendly

501

Kaufman. Listen to this. *(reads)* "Dateline: Whitman High School, October third. Militant students took over the school cafeteria today but gave up when the dietician threatened to serve them lunch . . ."

Pete *(smiling)*. Now, that's what I call social satire.

Kaufman. That's what *I* call public service. Pete, I'm happy to report that Harvey's attendance in the Detention Room has dropped off about seventy-five percent.

Pete. I'm glad to hear it. Maybe he just needed a nudge in the right direction. *(pause)* I came in to get your OK to have another Junior Class Achievement Dinner. I want to take the juniors who work on *The Blue and Gold* this time.

Kaufman. I don't know, Pete. Those things are getting expensive.

Pete. Look, you let me take the juniors on the football team . . . the basketball team . . . the class officers and club presidents. The kids on the paper work just as hard.

Kaufman. Maybe you could have it here . . . use the teachers' cafeteria.

Pete. This is supposed to be a reward, not a punishment.

Kaufman. You could tell 'em you're going to have it in the cafeteria and then call it off at the last minute. That would seem like a reward, wouldn't it? *(pause)* Go ahead . . . just don't spend too much.

(Pete grins and exits as Kaufman picks up the issue of the school paper and resumes reading, smiling and chuckling. On the side of the paper facing the camera, there is a large editorial-type drawing, very detailed. Kaufman finishes reading Harvey's column, still smil-
ing, and turns the paper over so that he is looking at the drawing. He stares at it for a minute, then the smile fades from his lips. He picks up a pair of reading glasses and, holding them like a magnifying glass, scans the drawing, prepared for the worst. The expression on his face tells us when he has found it. In fact, it's even worse than he expected.)

Interior of Room 222. Pete *is roaming around the room, throwing questions.*

For the stage: This scene takes place in the classroom, stage right.

Pete. What do you mean President Washington was unpopular? Wasn't he called the father of our country?

Al. Yes, but there sure were a lot of people who didn't agree with him, like what he said in his farewell address.

Pete. Well, what did he say . . . Harvey?

Harvey. Well . . . *(pause)* Mainly he spoke about partisanship[10] in America, sectionalism, we should avoid foreign entanglements.

(The class registers disappointment at Harvey's answer.)

Harvey *(to class at large)*. In case you're all wondering why the straight answer, I don't have time for the funny stuff anymore. I mean, I'm not gonna give you any of my material free when I can use it in my column.

(The bell rings, and the class starts to break.)

Pete. Read Chapter Sixteen tonight.

---

10. partisanship (pärt′ i zən ship′): support of a particular idea or political party.

(As they file out, Harvey *passes* Pete's *desk.)*

Pete. Funny column yesterday. Even Mr. Kaufman liked it.

Harvey. I guess I'm gonna have to aim a little higher, then. *(He starts to go.)*

Pete. Harvey?

(Harvey turns.)

Pete. We're having a dinner Friday for the juniors on *The Blue and Gold* staff. Maybe you can make it.

Harvey *(pleased).* Sure. Sure, I'd like that.

Pete. It's at Emilio's Restaurant. Bring a date if you want.

(Harvey's face suddenly clouds over.)

Harvey *(numbly).* A date . . .

Interior of school cafeteria. Harvey *is sitting alone at a rectangular table for eight. A sort of average-looking girl named* Patty Muller *comes up to the other end of the table carrying a tray.*

For the stage: At the end of the last scene, Pete Dixon *exits, leaving* Harvey *alone in the classroom.* Harvey *remains, absorbed in thought. Meanwhile, stagehands are setting the center stage for the next scene. They bring in a table and chairs and a tray with* Harvey's *lunch. When the stage is ready,* Harvey *moves to the table and begins to eat.* Patty Muller *enters.*

Patty *(indicating chair).* Is this seat taken?

Harvey *(putting her on).* I've been saving it for you.

(Patty nods and takes her lunch off the tray, puts the tray on the stacker, then sits down

and starts to eat. As she eats her lunch at the other end of the table, she takes out a copy of The Blue and Gold *and reads. Close shot of* Harvey, *looking at her furtively. He screws up enough courage to brazen it out.)*

Harvey. You're in Mr. Dixon's first-period history, aren't you?

Patty *(looks up, surprised).* Yes.

Harvey. So am I.

Patty. I know. You're Harvey Butcher.

Harvey *(points at her).* Patty Muller.

Patty *(nods).* You're very funny in class.

(Harvey grins deprecatingly[11] and shrugs. There is a small, awkward silence. Small beads of perspiration appear on Harvey's *forehead.)*

Patty *(indicating newspaper).* Your new column is hysterical. I mean, everybody is talking about how funny it is.

Harvey. Thank you. *(long pause, then haltingly)* Mr. Dixon is having a dinner for the juniors who are on the staff of the paper and I was wondering–

(Another girl, Suzy, *comes up with her tray and plops down next to* Patty.*)*

Suzy. Hi, Patty, did Norman get around to asking you to the party Friday?

Patty. *Finally.* I was sure I was gonna end up sitting home Friday night with nothing to do.

(Harvey quickly resumes eating his lunch.)

---

11. deprecatingly (dep′ rə kāt′ iŋ lē): in a way that mocks himself.

PORTRAIT OF BEATRICE 1916 Amedeo Modigliani
Private collection.

Interior of a phone booth that afternoon.
Harvey *is perspiring profusely as he dials the phone with fear-numbed fingers. After two rings, he nearly hangs up but forces himself not to. After a pause, we hear a phone being answered.*

For the stage: The booth is imaginary, and Harvey *makes his calls in pantomime down right near the footlights. Meanwhile, other actors and stagehands will be changing the set center stage, removing the cafeteria table and replacing the equipment for the newspaper office. The movement behind* Harvey *must be carefully timed so that none of his telephone dialogue will be lost. In pantomime,* Harvey *inserts a coin in the imaginary telephone and dials.*

Harvey. Hello, Connie . . . this is Harvey Butcher. *(pause)* In your third-period English class . . . *(pause)* I'm the funny guy. *(another pause)* . . . Kind of heavy. *(pause)* Uh, Connie . . . I'll tell you why I'm calling. You see, Mr. Dixon is taking the juniors on the staff of *The Blue and Gold* to dinner on Friday and . . . uh . . . well, what I was wondering is . . . if you're not doing anything Friday night—what? *(He listens, then:)* Oh. Well, sure . . . I mean, hair does have to be washed, doesn't it? Bye. (Harvey *is on the phone again.)*

Harvey *(into phone, very fast)*. Hello, Darlene Frank of Claymore Avenue? This is "The Question Man"—answer this question correctly and win a fabulous prize! Ready? All right then, here's the question: Do you have a date Friday night? *(pause)* No? Then you win . . . Miss Frank . . . an all-expenses-paid night on the town with Harvey Butcher, the well-known columnist for *The Whitman Blue and Gold.* How about that? *(pause)* Yeah, this is Harvey. Can you make it? *(listens, nodding)* Your hair . . . I understand. *(faking brightness)* Well, in that case, Darlene, you don't win the big prize, but we're sending you a consolation prize of a bottle of shampoo.

Interior of The Blue and Gold *office. The usual "getting-out-the-paper" activity is in progress as* Harvey *enters. He is very high-*

strung and hypertense and wears some sort of a manic grin.

For the stage: The action takes place center stage in the area prepared during the last scene.

Harvey. Hello, fellow staffers of *The Daily Planet!* Clark Kent here . . . mild-mannered humor columnist . . . who is, in reality . . . *(puffs out chest and holds out arms in Superman pose)* . . . Superfat! *(He lets out his breath, and his stomach swells over his belt. He gets a couple of laughs, but everybody goes back to work. Harvey cannot stop; he goes pacing around the room.)*

Harvey. Has anyone seen Lois Lane? Ah, there you are! *(He crosses to the humorless girl doing paste-up.)*

Harvey. I'm terribly sorry, Lois–I know you've had your heart set on me taking you to that banquet Friday night, but I've got to wash my hair.

(The girl looks at him oddly. Neil Kovack comes up.)

Neil. I need this week's column from you, Harvey.

Harvey. Ah, yes! My column. *(He opens his notebook and hands Neil some pages.)*

Harvey. Here it is, little editor–and I hope you enjoy it, because it's my last one. *(He pats Neil on the shoulder and heads for the door. When he reaches the threshold, he strikes a Superman-taking-off pose.)*

Harvey. Up, up . . . and away! *(His arms extended, he does a flying leap out the door.)*

Interior of Room 222. Pete *is sitting at his desk grading papers when* Harvey *suddenly appears in the open door.* Pete *looks up.*

For the stage: At the end of the last scene, the news staff (except Harvey*) exit, taking their equipment with them and leaving the center stage bare.* Harvey, *after his "Up, up . . . and away!" walks slowly toward the footlights, engrossed in thought. Meanwhile,* Pete Dixon *has taken his place at his desk in the classroom.* Harvey *enters the area. When* Harvey *and* Pete *exit from the classroom later in the scene, they move to center stage.*

Harvey. Brace yourself, Mr. Dixon; your big dinner Friday night is going to be a major bomb.

Pete. Oh?

Harvey. That's right. I'm not going to be there.

Pete. Why not?

Harvey. Because I'm not on *The Blue and Gold* anymore. I just quit. *(He exits.* Pete *gets up and follows him out the door. Interior shot of the corridor. Except for* Harvey, *it is deserted when* Pete *comes out of the room.)*

Pete. Harvey? *(He goes after him quickly.* Harvey *stops, turns, and looks at* Pete *innocently.)*

Pete. Why?

Words to Know and Use | **engrossed** (en grōst′) *adj.* completely occupied; absorbed **engross** *v.*

Harvey. Look, I quit, that's all. What's the difference whether I write a crummy column or not?

(Pete *looks at him, trying to read his mood.*)

Pete. Why come and tell me, then—if it doesn't make any difference?

Harvey. I just thought you had a right to know, since it was your idea in the first place.

Pete. What happened, Harvey?

Harvey. Nothing happened. Why are you trying to make a big deal out of it?

Pete. I'm not—I'm just interested in knowing why this sudden change of attitude.

Harvey. Well, you see, it's this way—I've been offered this better job, see . . . Humor editor for *The National Geographic*. (Pete *doesn't smile.*) Oh, come on, sir . . . that deserves at least a little smile, doesn't it? Just a teeny little . . . (*With his fingers he pushes the corner of his own mouth into a smile.*)

Pete. You can still come Friday night if you want to. I figure the columns you've written are worth the price of dinner for two.

Harvey. Ah, well, you see . . . now that's another problem. I haven't been able to find the girl to bring to that affair who measures up to my own incredibly high standards.

Pete (*understanding*). You don't have to bring a date, Harvey.

Harvey. You're not suggesting, sir . . . Mr. Dixon, sir . . . that I haven't been able to get a date, are you, sir?

Pete. Harvey, it just isn't necessary . . .

Harvey (*cuts in*). Isn't necessary? Of course it's necessary! I don't want you going around with the impression that I can't get a date! Fat people *do* date, sir. You see, that's one of the great things about a school the size of Whitman—no matter how fat and homely you are, there's always somebody bad enough to go out with you. (*He's trying to make the whole thing sound funny and flippant, but his tear ducts betray him.* Harvey *turns his head so that* Pete *can't see the tears.*)

Pete. Harvey.

Harvey. Mr. Dixon . . . *please* . . . (Harvey *stands there, humiliated, wiping away the tears, unable to face* Pete.)

Harvey. I'm *not* gonna be the only one there without a date!

Pete (*gently*). Hey . . . would it really be so bad?

(*His back still turned.* Harvey *nods his head emphatically.*)

Pete. Isn't what you're doing to yourself worse? Isn't *this* worse?

(Harvey *says nothing.*)

Pete. Harvey, give yourself a chance. (*pause*) Try accepting yourself as you are . . . and maybe other people will.

Harvey. Easy to say.

Pete (*with the heat of conviction*). I *know* it's not easy. But it's up to you. Anybody tries to make contact . . . you give 'em a joke . . . you make 'em laugh . . . but you

---

Words to Know and Use | **flippant** (flip′ ənt) *adj.* lacking in seriousness; silly and disrespectful

don't let anybody get close . . . *(pause)* Try giving people a chance. Let 'em know who you really are!

(Shot of Harvey's face as Pete stands behind him trying to reach him. The camera moves in for a close shot.)

Interior of banquet room, Friday night. The junior-class members of The Blue and Gold *staff and their dates are noisily assembled in a typical banquet room in a small Italian restaurant. Pete and Liz are sitting together at one end of the table. A boy, Neil, is staring at the menu as a waiter awaits his order.*

For the stage: In center stage, actors and stagehands bring on a large restaurant table with chairs and settings for nine people. There is an empty seat next to Marge. When the table is ready, the actors take their seats.

Neil. What's this? Veal piccolini?

Waiter. That's thin slices of veal sauteed in Marsala wine . . . covered with prosciutto ham and mozzarella cheese.

Neil *(shakes his head).* I don't like veal.

(Camera pans to Richie and his date. Richie is staring at the menu.)

Richie *(to date).* What's a sweetbread?

Richie's Date. Beats me.

Richie. Hey, Mr. Dixon. What's a sweetbread?

Pete. A sweetbread? Well, it's a . . . *(tries to describe it with his hands)* . . . they're . . . *(to Liz)* What's a sweetbread?

Liz *(no hesitation).* Sweetbreads are the thymus glands of a young calf.

(A disgusted look crosses everyone's face.)

Richie. I think I'll have a pizza. *(suddenly looks up)* Hey, look who's here!

(Angle shot of doorway. Harvey Butcher is standing there a bit self-consciously. Everyone turns and looks and sees Harvey. He is greeted with laughs and cheers and assorted cries of "Harvey!" . . . "Hey, man" . . . "We didn't think you were coming," and so on. Harvey is all dressed up and looks about ninety-five percent better than we have ever seen him look. Grinning, he grabs an extra chair and pushes it toward the table as room is made for him. Close-up of Harvey. As he sits down, he glances down the table toward Pete. Pete catches Harvey's glance and gives him a smile of encouragement. As Harvey sits there, looking around, slightly ill at ease, everyone is expectant, waiting for him to say something funny.)

Boy's Voice. Hey, Harvey . . . how come you're late?

(A couple of laughs, anticipating his answer . . . Harvey looks around at the faces . . .)

Harvey *(long pause).* I almost didn't come at all . . . because I couldn't get a date.

(Camera moves to Pete and Liz. Pete turns and looks at Harvey; Liz looks pained by his candid admission. Shot of various students as they react to Harvey's admission, not with pity or embarrassment, but with a sort of respect for his honesty . . .)

Harvey. But somebody told me I should . . . *(He glances over at Pete.)* I really wanted to come anyway . . . I like doing the column . . . and I like being on the staff . . . with everybody . . . so I decided to come tonight . . .

(The room is very quiet . . . All the kids watching Harvey . . . *)*

Marge. We're glad you did . . .

(Others join in agreeing. Shot of Harvey *looking at* Pete. *Fade out.)*

Fade in: Interior of teachers' cafeteria, Monday noon. Mr. Kaufman *is just taking a tray near the end of the line as* Pete *comes up behind him.*

For the stage: This scene may be omitted. For television, it is a kind of wind-up scene which may follow the final commercial. For the purposes of the drama itself, the play ends satisfactorily with The Blue and Gold *banquet. If the scene is used, all of the actors but* Pete Dixon *exit, and* Dixon *joins* Mr. Kaufman *stage left in the faculty room, where a small cafeteria table has been set up.*

Pete. I had a message you wanted to see me.

Kaufman. I got the bill from your Emilio's Restaurant for your Junior Class Achievement orgy. I wanted to go over a few things with you. *(He takes a bill out of his pocket as he and* Pete *inch forward in the line along the steam table.)*

Kaufman. Which one of the students had the double martini?

Pete *(grins)*. That was for the waiter. Believe me, he needed it.

Kaufman *(consulting bill)*. How many in your party altogether?

Pete. Let's see . . . fifteen students, Liz, and myself.

Kaufman. Seventeen. You got charged for eighteen dinners.

Pete. Harvey Butcher had two.

(Kaufman nods as if this makes sense and puts the bill back in his pocket. He takes a jello salad on a single leaf of lettuce.)

Kaufman. How was the food?

Pete. Good. I had veal scallopini and mushrooms.

(Kaufman's eyes glaze slightly as he lapses into a sort of glutton's reverie. He is snapped back to reality by the voice of the serving lady behind the steam table.)

Serving Lady. Tuna surprise or franks and beans, Mr. Kaufman?

Kaufman. No surprises for me today, thanks.

Serving Lady. Franks and beans, then?

(Kaufman nods glumly, and she slaps the rubbery frankfurter and soggy beans on a plate and hands it to him.)

Kaufman *(to* Pete*)*. The next time you decide to have another one of your achievement dinners . . .

Pete. Yes?

Kaufman. Please take me with you. *(He picks up his tray and ambles disconsolately off, and we fade out.)* ❧

"Funny Boy"
written by Allan Burns
from the series entitled "ROOM 222" © 1969
Twentieth Century Fox Film Corporation.
All rights reserved.

---

*Words
to Know
and Use* | **reverie** (rev′ ər ē) *n.* a daydream

Responding to Reading

First Impressions

1. How do you feel about Harvey? Write your response in your journal or notebook.

Second Thoughts

2. In your opinion, what are Harvey's biggest strengths and his biggest weaknesses?

3. How much do you think Harvey has changed by the end of the play? Explain your opinion.

   Think about
   - whether he has accepted himself as he is
   - how he uses humor
   - how Pete Dixon helps him

4. How would you react to Harvey if he were in your class?

5. Do you think *Funny Boy* is realistic in its portrayal of students and teachers? Explain.

Broader Connections

6. After reading this play, do you think you would enjoy being a teacher? Why or why not?

Literary Concept: Exposition

The part of the play that provides background information and introduces the characters, setting, and plot is called the **exposition.** Where in *Funny Boy* is the exposition, and what does it explain?

Concept Review: Humor   Consider your prereading discussion about humor. How many examples of different kinds of humor can you find in the play?

Writing Options

1. Harvey wrote the humor column for his school newspaper. Write your own **humor column** about something going on at your school.

2. Write a **character analysis** of either Harvey or Pete. Be sure to describe their characteristics, strengths, and weaknesses.

3. Based on what you learned about them during the play, write a **letter of advice** to Mr. Walters, Mr. Kaufman, or Alice.

4. Write a **scenario,** or quick plot summary, of the next episode of the series featuring Harvey.

Vocabulary Exercise

Exercise   On a separate sheet of paper, identify each pair of words as *Synonyms* or *Antonyms*.

1. flippant—serious
2. girth—circumference
3. amiably—disagreeably
4. bemused—confused
5. alienate—befriend
6. engrossed—absorbed
7. insolent—disrespectful
8. relinquish—keep
9. militant—agitator
10. reverie—daydream

*Words
to Know
and Use*

**alienate
amiably
bemused
engrossed
flippant
girth
insolent
militant
relinquish
reverie**

Options for Learning

1 • **Act Funny** With other students, choose a scene from *Funny Boy* to perform. Pay close attention to the stage directions in order to set the scene properly. If you have a camcorder available, try the television version of the play and videotape it to show to the class; otherwise, perform the stage version.

2 • **Historic Humor** For his test, Harvey wrote a humorous sketch that thrust Benjamin Franklin into today's world. With classmates, take another historical figure and create a humorous skit in which that person encounters problems typical of today's society. Practice and perform your skit for the class.

3 • **Hip Threads** This episode was first broadcast around 1970. Research magazines from this time to discover what students wore then. Sketch or wear appropriate clothing and hairstyles of the period. Explain these styles to the class.

4 • **Sketch a Scene** A storyboard includes a series of rough sketches of a drama's important scenes. Choose a scene from this play and draw a storyboard of the action. Share your storyboard with others.

 FACT FINDER HISTORY

Harvey jokes about the Mason-Dixon line. What was it?

Allan P. Burns
1935-

The screenplay *Funny Boy* is only one example of the award-winning career Allan Burns has had in television and film. Born in Baltimore, Burns has lived and attended school in Hawaii and Oregon.

Burns began writing and producing television series right after college. His writing talent was first recognized in 1968 when he won an Emmy Award for the show *He and She*. He won a Writers Guild Award for *Funny Boy* as the Best Comedy Script in 1970. With producer and director James L. Brooks, he created and produced the very popular television series *The Mary Tyler Moore Show, Rhoda,* and *Lou Grant.* During these years, Burns won five more Emmy Awards for writing and producing.

In the late 1970s, Burns extended his writing talents to movie scripts. He received an Oscar nomination for his screenplay for the 1979 movie *A Little Romance.* Burns presently lives in southern California with his wife, who is also a writer.

WRITER'S WORKSHOP

WRITING ABOUT LITERATURE/PERSUASION

As a group, you have shared and discussed the literary selections that have been presented in this book. Now it's time for you to share a book of your own choosing with your classmates. For this assignment you will create an advertising poster that promotes your favorite book. Your goal will be to "sell" your book to your classmates—to interest them enough in your book to make them want to read it. You will combine writing about literature with persuasive writing. Just like other kinds of advertisements, your advertisement will also contain visual images to capture your audience's attention and help promote the book.

Here is one writer's PASSkey to this assignment.

GUIDED ASSIGNMENT: ADVERTISING POSTER

Create an advertising poster that promotes your favorite book.

P URPOSE: To persuade others to read a book
A UDIENCE: Classmates
S UBJECT: A favorite book
S TRUCTURE: Poster

Prewrite and Explore

1 **Find the good parts**   You can choose any book that you enjoy and would like to write about. If you skim it again, you'll recall the parts you like best. You might jot words and phrases to remind yourself which parts these are and what you like about them.

2 **Look at possibilities**   Book covers and jacket flaps, back covers of paperbacks, posters in bookstore windows, supermarket book displays, and magazines are all good places to find examples of book advertisements. Notice the visual elements—the illustrations, the design, the style and size of lettering—as well as the verbal elements of the advertisements. Study the student model on the facing page to see another example of a book advertisement.

> "Playing with time and space is a dangerous game...."

DANGER! MYSTERY! COURAGE!

from the award-winning author of *A Wind in the Door*

MADELEINE L'ENGLE

comes the riveting tale of a journey beyond time and space

A WRINKLE IN TIME

"Wild nights are my glory," confides the stranger who blows into the Murry family's kitchen one stormy night. She then transports Meg Murry, Meg's little brother Charles Wallace, and their friend Calvin far beyond our galaxy. There Meg and Charles Wallace find their father, a scientist who had vanished five years earlier. He is being held prisoner by an evil force that wants to control everyone's mind.

Meg has always been different. She has often been in trouble in school, and she is unhappy with herself. Now, with others' help, Meg learns that her faults can be strengths. She and the boys manage to rescue her father. However, the evil force captures Charles Wallace. Meg knows that only she can save her brother. She just doesn't know how. The end of the story surprises everyone.

Madeleine L'Engle won the Newbery Award for this book, and it's easy to see why. Whether or not you like fantasy or science fiction, you'll like *A Wrinkle in Time*. Just don't expect it to be like anything else you've ever read. It's the story of a journey to distant worlds, but even more, it's the story of a journey into people's hearts and minds.

—by Francine Robinson

STUDENT MODEL

The writer quotes an exciting line from the book.

Descriptive language captures readers' interest.

The writer explains the main conflicts in the plot.

The writer mentions the author's credentials.

Persuasive language urges the audience to read the book.

3 **Sketch a plan and gather material** Taking off from what you've seen, you can plan your poster. Then you can gather the information that you will include on it. Keep in mind that although most posters do not contain extended sections of text, yours will.

GATHERING INFORMATION

Try closing your eyes for a minute to visualize your poster. Then sketch out your plan, with notes about what goes where. Think of things that will appeal to your classmates: attention-grabbing art and lettering, surprising quotes and details from the book, facts about the author, an idea of the plot, "teaser" words and phrases. Look at Francine's plan for her text below.

quotes and details: "Playing with time and space is a dangerous game." "Wild nights are my glory." Stranger blows in during storm, transports them to distant galaxy.

teasers: courage, danger, mystery, riveting

about the author: Also wrote A Wind in the Door. Won Newbery Medal.

conflict summary: Meg and others rescue her father; she must rescue Charles Wallace.

how it's unique: Meg's not like a hero. She's in trouble a lot, unpopular. Also, not the usual space stuff. More about people.

Draft and Discover

WRITER'S CHOICE
If you get an idea that's not in your sketch, don't be afraid to try it. It may be just the touch you need.

1 **Get into gear** To get yourself going, write a short paragraph tracing key action in your book. If your book is nonfiction, write an overview of its main ideas. Include enough detail to give readers a taste of the book—but leave them wanting more.

2 **Sell it** To persuade your audience, you need to appeal to their logic as well as their emotions. The best way to appeal to logic is to present facts as clearly as possible. Your facts include information about the book and the author. Your opinion is supported by those facts. You can appeal to emotions through the words that express your own enthusiasm and the visuals you choose.

3 **Make it shine**   You can use your own photos, drawings, or paintings to underscore your words, or you can cut pictures from magazines. As you select or plan your pictures, think about the impact they will have on your audience. Be creative—the more fun you have designing your poster, the better your audience will respond.

COMPUTER TIP

You may be able to add computer graphics to your written text. Try different sizes and fonts for your lettering.

Revise Your Writing

1 **Lay it out**   Now you can arrange your material as it will appear in your poster. Work with it until it satisfies you. Don't forget that it's fine to break up your writing into sections between art elements, to enclose some sections in boxes, and to vary your lettering.

IN OTHER CLASSES

In art class you can try similar ways of fusing visual elements with words. For example, you might include written material in a collage.

2 **Check your wording**   This is a good time to look at the words you've used. Try focusing on verbs. For example, Malcolm X doesn't write that he *read* literature but that he *devoured* literature. Francine Robinson doesn't write that the stranger *comes* in but that she *blows* in. Could you replace any ordinary verbs with ones that create more vivid images? Could you replace any with verbs whose connotations—emotional overtones—reflect your feelings better?

NEED MORE HELP?

See the Vocabulary Workshop on denotation and connotation, page 465.

3 **Work with a peer**   Using the lists of questions below, you and a peer can take turns responding to each other's posters.

Revision Questions

For You

1. Have I given a good idea of the content of the book?
2. Have I chosen words and visuals that strengthen each other?
3. Would any changes generate more excitement about the book?

For a Peer Reader

1. Which part of my poster caught your interest first?
2. What do you think you'd like about this book?
3. How might I increase the impact of my wording or design?

THE EDITOR'S EYE: VERB TENSES

Avoid unnecessary shifts in verb tense.

Verbs change form, or **tense,** to show changes in time. In some of your sentences and paragraphs, all the action occurs in the same time period. Then you need to keep all your verbs in the same tense.

Problem	He is being held prisoner by an evil force that wanted to control everyone's mind.
Revised	He is being held prisoner by an evil force that wants to control everyone's mind.
Also Correct	He was being held prisoner by an evil force that wanted to control everyone's mind.

.... **NEED MORE HELP?**
See the Language Workshop on pages 517–519.

Proofread

Check your poster carefully, correcting errors in spelling, punctuation, and grammar. Pay special attention to verb tenses.

Publish and Present

Here is a suggestion for promoting your book to your classmates.

Book Share Fair   Find an area in your classroom where you can display your poster and stand next to it to give a "sales pitch." As your classmates walk by, use your poster and try to talk them into reading your book. List titles and authors of books that your classmates convince you to read as well!

Reflect on Your Writing

.... FOR YOUR PORTFOLIO ▶

Write your answers to the questions below. Attach them to your poster when you place it in your portfolio.

1. How did you feel when you saw others' responses to your poster?
2. What did you enjoy most about designing your poster?

LANGUAGE WORKSHOP

VERB TENSES

As you know, verbs tell about actions or states of being. Verbs also tell about time. All verbs change form, or **tense,** to show changes in time. When you write, be sure your tense changes make sense. Otherwise your readers will end up wondering what happened when.

Verb tenses are formed from the **principal parts** of verbs: the **present,** the **past,** the **present participle,** and the **past participle.** These basic forms may be combined with helping verbs such as *will* and *have.* The chart below shows time spans that verb tenses cover.

Tense	Example	Use
• **Present**	she walks	for action that is happening now
• **Past**	she walked	for action that was completed in the past
• **Future**	she will walk	for action that will happen in the future
• **Present Perfect**	she has walked	for action that began in the past and continues into the present, or for action completed at an indefinite time in the past
• **Past Perfect**	she had walked	for action in the past that was completed before another action in the past

◀ **GRAMMAR TIP**

Verb-tense changes are made in three ways: the addition of an ending: *walk, walked;* a change in spelling: *bring, brought;* a change in helping verbs: *has walked, will walk.*

Exercise 1 Concept Review Make two columns. Label the first *Verbs* and the second *Verb Tenses.* In the first, write each verb in the sentences below. In the second, write the tense of each verb.

1. Finally, spring has arrived.
2. In his expensive suit, the businessman feels proud.
3. A beggar has stopped the successful businessman.
4. The businessman asks about the beggar's story.

◀ **REMINDER**

An adverb, such as *not, always,* or *usually,* sometimes comes between parts of a verb. It is not part of the verb.

5. An accident injured the beggar fourteen years ago.
6. Because of the accident he will never see again.
7. The beggar had gone to work as usual on the day of the accident.
8. The factory exploded into an inferno of burning chemicals.
9. To his horror, the chemicals burned him badly.
10. He will always remember the sight of the factory in flames.

Avoiding Unnecessary Shifts in Tense

> Use the same tense to show two or more actions that occur in the same time period.

In some of your writing, all the action in a sentence or a paragraph takes place in one time period. To show this kind of consistent action, use the same tense for all the verbs in the sentence or paragraph.

Incorrect   Malcolm X *stays* in his cell and *studied.*
Correct   Malcolm X *stays* in his cell and *studies.*
Correct   Malcolm X *stayed* in his cell and *studied.*

You do need to change tenses when you write about a chain of events. For example, the sentence below tells about two actions in the past. One, however, finished before the other. Notice how the change in verb tense reflects the flow of time.

The day *ended* (past), and Malcolm X *had copied* (past perfect) the entire first page of the dictionary.

When you proofread, check the verb tenses you've used. Make sure that you haven't shifted—changed—tenses without reason. Often you can tell "by ear" whether a tense shift makes sense.

ASK FOR HELP

When you are unsure about tense shifts in your writing, ask a peer to read the passage for clarity.

Exercise 2 Concept Review   Rewrite each sentence to correct shifts in verb tense.

1. Alex Haley helped Malcolm X with an autobiography, and later Haley becomes famous for his own book *Roots.*
2. Malcolm X writes most of his own material, but Haley had helped him to shape it.
3. Haley researches *Roots* for years and even traveled to West Africa in search of information.

4. There he will visit villages and has learned more about his heritage.

5. Certain mysterious words and stories had been in his family for generations, and he discovers their meanings.

Exercise 3 Proofreading Skill   Work in groups to revise the paragraph below. Look carefully at each verb in italics, and decide how to correct unneeded tense shifts. Write the corrected paragraph.

Malcolm X's autobiography *tells* about his childhood struggles with poverty and hunger. Bright but indifferent, he *dropped* out of school. The unfairness of his life *makes* him angry. As a teenager, he *sells* drugs and *burglarized* houses. His life *will spiral* out of control, and his prison sentence *has* almost *seemed* like a relief to him. In prison he *will concentrate* for the first time on learning. He *improves* his shaky reading and writing skills. The more he *reads* and *wrote,* the more clearly he *had thought.* Finally he *has regained* control of his life. Once freed, Malcolm X *becomes* a powerful figure in the fight against inequality.

Exercise 4 Looking at Style   Reread the second paragraph of the excerpt from *The Autobiography of Malcolm X* on page 472. How do the changing verb tenses show the different periods of time discussed in the paragraph?

Exercise 5 Revising Your Writing   Reread your advertising poster, and lightly underline each verb you used. Check your tenses carefully. Be sure your tense shifts make sense, and correct any that do not.

LANGUAGE HANDBOOK
. . . .
For review and practice: Section 6, Using Verbs, pages 743–746.

READER'S WORKSHOP

FACT AND OPINION

> A **fact** is a statement that can be proved. An **opinion** cannot be proved.

Fact   *Funny Boy* was written by Allan Burns.
Opinion   *Funny Boy* is a hilarious play.

You could prove the first statement by looking in a reference book or by asking Allan Burns himself. The second statement, however, expresses what a person thinks—it is an opinion, not a fact. In some kinds of writing, such as news reports, sticking to facts is crucial. In others, such as editorials, reviews, and advertisements, opinions are important. However, opinions must be supported by facts.

Opinions often contain **judgment words**—words that express personal feelings. See if you can add any judgment words to the list below.

wonderful	horrible	ridiculous	great	silly
awful	boring	excellent	terrible	

WRITING TIP
Although judgment words sometimes signal faulty logic, a well-supported opinion can strengthen an appeal to emotion.

▶ When you read and write, notice which statements are facts and which are opinions. Ask yourself whether enough facts are presented to support the opinions.

Exercise   For each sentence below, write *F* for a fact or *O* for an opinion. If the sentence is a fact, write a way it could be proved. If the sentence is an opinion, list any judgment words you find in it.

1. Alice Walker wrote a poem called "Without Commercials."
2. It's silly for people to try to change the way they look.
3. Alice Walker was the daughter of sharecroppers.
4. No U.S. poet is greater than Alice Walker.
5. People should accept themselves as they are.
6. *Funny Boy* was an episode of the television series *Room 222*.
7. Allan Burns won a Writer's Guild Award for *Funny Boy*.
8. Allan Burns is an excellent writer.
9. Few things are more important than the ability to read.
10. A love of reading made Malcolm X aware of new ideas.

NEED HELP?
For more about appeals to emotion and faulty logic, see the Reader's Workshop on page 347.

DOORS OF UNDERSTANDING

Doors have often been used as metaphors to describe the workings of the mind and heart. We open the door to new ideas and new relationships, but close it to people we do not like. An open door suggests an inviting attitude; a closed door implies "Do not disturb!"

In this group of selections, you will meet fictional characters and real people who pass through various doors of understanding. Some of the doors are opened freely. Others have to be pushed open, at times against great resistance.

As you read, decide which doors are being opened—or closed—and what is learned as a result.

Fiction

Last Cover

PAUL ANNIXTER

Examine What You Know

Do you know someone who feels an especially strong attachment to his or her pet? Why do you think some people develop such close ties with animals? What can a pet offer that another human cannot? Discuss your ideas about pets with your classmates.

Expand Your Knowledge

In this story two boys who live near the woods adopt a red fox as their pet. The red fox is the most common fox in the world. Red foxes are clever and quick. They are excellent hunters who feed on anything from rodents to the carcasses of large animals. A fox and its mate may travel thirty miles to find a hunting territory, which may be the size of seventy city blocks. In turn, foxes are often hunted for their fur, for sport, or because their raids on chicken houses are a nuisance to farmers.

In a fox hunt, dogs are used to find the fox in its hiding place. When found, the cries of the dogs signal the fox's location to the hunters on horseback, who follow the dogs.

Enrich Your Reading

Context Clues As you read "Last Cover," you may come across unfamiliar words or phrases. Often you can discover their meaning if you make use of context clues—words or sentences around a term that help explain its meaning. Use a chart like the one below to record unfamiliar words and phrases, their context clues, and probable meanings.

Word or Phrase	Context Clues	Probable Meaning
kit	tiny, pet fox Colin and I raised	a baby fox
pine		
pranking		

■ *Author biography on Extend page*

Last Cover

PAUL ANNIXTER

I'm not sure I can tell you what you want to know about my brother; but everything about the pet fox is important, so I'll tell all that from the beginning.

It goes back to a winter afternoon after I'd hunted the woods all day for a sign of our lost pet. I remember the way my mother looked up as I came into the kitchen. Without my speaking, she knew what had happened. For six hours I had walked, reading signs, looking for a delicate print in the damp soil or even a hair that might have told of a red fox passing that way—but I had found nothing.

"Did you go up in the foothills?" Mom asked.

I nodded. My face was stiff from held-back tears. My brother, Colin, who was going on twelve, got it all from one look at me and went into a heartbroken, almost silent, crying.

Three weeks before, Bandit, the pet fox Colin and I had raised from a tiny kit, had disappeared, and not even a rumor had been heard of him since.

"He'd have had to go off soon anyway," Mom comforted. "A big, lolloping fellow like him, he's got to live his life same as us. But he may come back. That fox set a lot of store by you boys in spite of his wild ways."

"He set a lot of store by our food, anyway," Father said. He sat in a chair by the kitchen window, mending a piece of harness. "We'll be seeing a lot more of that fellow, never fear. That fox learned to pine for table scraps and young chickens. He was getting to be an egg thief, too, and he's not likely to forget that."

"That was only pranking when he was little," Colin said desperately.

From the first, the tame fox had made tension in the family. It was Father who said we'd better name him Bandit, after he'd made away with his first young chicken.

"Maybe you know," Father said shortly. "But when an animal turns to egg sucking, he's usually incurable. He'd better not come pranking around my chicken run again."

It was late February, and I remember the bleak, dead cold that had set in, cold that was a rare thing for our Carolina hills. Flocks of sparrows and snowbirds had appeared, to peck hungrily at all that the pigs and chickens didn't eat.

"This one's a killer," Father would say of a morning, looking out at the whitened barn roof. "This one will make the shoats[1] squeal."

A fire snapped all day in our cookstove and another in the stone fireplace in the living room, but still the farmhouse was never

---

1. **shoats** (shōts): young pigs.

Words to Know and Use | **bleak** (blēk) *adj.* harsh and dreary

warm. The leafless woods were bleak and empty, and I spoke of that to Father when I came back from my search.

"It's always a sad time in the woods when the seven sleepers are under cover," he said.

"What sleepers are they?" I asked. Father was full of woods lore.

"Why, all the animals that have got sense enough to hole up and stay hid in weather like this. Let's see, how was it the old rhyme named them?

Surly bear and sooty bat,
Brown chuck and masked coon
Chippy-munk and sly skunk,
And all the mouses
'Cept in men's houses.

"And man would have joined them and made it eight, Granther Yeary always said, if he'd had a little more sense."

"I was wondering if the red fox mightn't make it eight," Mom said.

Father shook his head. "Late winter's a high time for foxes. Time when they're out deviling, not sleeping."

My chest felt hollow. I wanted to cry like Colin over our lost fox, but at fourteen a boy doesn't cry. Colin had squatted down on the floor and got out his small hammer and nails to start another new frame for a new picture. Maybe then he'd make a drawing for the frame and be able to forget his misery. It had been that way with him since he was five.

I thought of the new dress Mom had brought home a few days before in a heavy cardboard box. That box cover would be fine for Colin to draw on. I spoke of it, and Mom's glance thanked me as she went to get it. She and I worried a lot about Colin. He was small for his age, delicate and blond, his hair much lighter and softer than mine, his eyes deep and wide and blue. He was often sick, and I knew the fear Mom had that he might be predestined.[2] I'm just ordinary, like Father. I'm the sort of stuff that can take it—tough and strong—but Colin was always sort of special.

Mom lighted the lamp. Colin began cutting his white cardboard carefully, fitting it into his frame. Father's sharp glance turned on him now and again.

"There goes the boy making another frame before there's a picture for it," he said. "It's too much like cutting out a man's suit for a fellow that's, say, twelve years old. Who knows whether he'll grow into it?"

Mom was into him then, quick. "Not a single frame of Colin's has ever gone to waste. The boy has real talent, Sumter, and it's time you realized it."

"Of course he has," Father said. "All kids have 'em. But they get over 'em."

"It isn't the pox[3] we're talking of," Mom sniffed.

"In a way it is. Ever since you started talking up Colin's art, I've had an <u>invalid</u> for help around the place."

Father wasn't as hard as he made out, I knew, but he had to hold a balance against all Mom's frothing.[4] For him the thing was the land and all that pertained to it. I was follow-

---

2. predestined (prē des' tind): describing someone whose fate is decided beforehand, by God; in this case, chosen for an early death.

3. pox: a contagious disease causing skin eruptions.

4. frothing (frôth' iŋ): light, meaningless talking.

Words to Know and Use | **invalid** (in' və lid) *n.* a sickly or disabled person

CORKSCREW BOG   1987   William Nichols   Courtesy, OK Harris Works of Art, New York.

ing in Father's footsteps, true to form, but Colin threatened to break the family tradition with his leaning toward art, with Mom "aiding and abetting[5] him," as Father liked to put it. For the past two years she had had dreams of my brother becoming a real artist and going away to the city to study.

It wasn't that Father had no understanding of such things. I could remember, through the years, Colin lying on his stomach in the front room making pencil sketches and how a good drawing would catch Father's eye halfway across the room; and how he would sometimes gather up two or three of them to study, frowning and muttering, one hand in his beard, while a great pride rose in Colin, and in me too. Most of Colin's drawings were of the woods and wild things, and there Father was a master critic. He made out to scorn what seemed to him a passive "white-livered" interpretation of nature through brush and pencil instead of rod and rifle.

---

5. **aiding and abetting:** helping and urging.

Words to Know and Use | **passive** (pas' iv) *adj.* inactive, but receiving action; lacking in energy or willpower

At supper that night, Colin could scarcely eat. Ever since he'd been able to walk, my brother had had a growing love of wild things; but Bandit had been like his very own, a gift of the woods. One afternoon a year and a half before, Father and Laban Small had been running a vixen through the hills with their dogs. With the last of her strength, the she-fox had made for her den, not far from our house. The dogs had overtaken her and killed her just before she reached it. When Father and Laban came up, they'd found Colin crouched nearby, holding her cub in his arms.

The fox became Colin's whole life.

Father had been for killing the cub, which was still too young to shift for itself, but Colin's grief had brought Mom into it. We'd taken the young fox into the kitchen, all of us, except Father, gone a bit silly over the little thing. Colin had held it in his arms and fed it warm milk from a spoon.

"Watch out with all your soft ways," Father had warned, standing in the doorway. "You'll make too much of him. Remember, you can't make a dog out of a fox. Half of that little critter has to love, but the other half is a wild hunter. You boys will mean a whole lot to him while he's kit, but there'll come a day when you won't mean a thing to him, and he'll leave you shorn."[6]

For two weeks after that, Colin had nursed the cub, weaning it from milk to bits of meat. For a year they were always together. The cub grew fast. It was soon following Colin and me about the barnyard. It turned out to be a patch fox, with a saddle of darker fur across its shoulders.

I haven't the words to tell you what the fox meant to us. It was far more wonderful owning him than owning any dog. There was something rare and secret, like the spirit of the woods, about him; and back of his calm, straw-gold eyes was the sense of a brain the equal of a man's. The fox became Colin's whole life.

Each day, going and coming from school, Colin and I took long side trips through the woods, looking for Bandit. Wild things' memories were short, we knew; we'd have to find him soon, or the old bond would be broken.

Ever since I was ten, I'd been allowed to hunt with Father, so I was good at reading signs. But, in a way, Colin knew more about the woods and wild things than Father or me. What came to me from long observation Colin seemed to know by instinct.

It was Colin who felt out, like an Indian, the stretch of woods where Bandit had his den, who found the first slim, small fox-print in the damp earth. And then, on an afternoon in March, we saw him. I remember the day well, the racing clouds, the wind rattling the tops of the pine trees and swaying the Spanish moss. Bandit had just come out of a clump of laurel; in the maze of leaves behind him, we caught a glimpse of a slim red vixen, so we knew he had found a mate. She melted from sight like a shadow, but Bandit turned to watch us, his mouth open, his tongue lolling as he smiled his old foxy smile. On his thin chops, I saw a telltale chicken feather.

---

6. **shorn**: cut off, like hair; forsaken.

Colin moved silently forward, his movements so quiet and casual he seemed to be standing still. He called Bandit's name, and the fox held his ground, drawn to us with all his senses. For a few moments he let Colin actually put an arm about him. It was then I knew that he loved us still, for all of Father's warnings. He really loved us back, with a fierce, secret love no tame thing ever gave. But the urge of his life just then was toward his new mate. Suddenly, he whirled about and disappeared in the laurels.

Colin looked at me with glowing eyes. "We haven't really lost him, Stan. When he gets through with his spring sparking,[7] he may come back. But we've got to show ourselves to him a lot, so he won't forget."

"It's a go," I said.

"Promise not to say a word to Father," Colin said, and I agreed. For I knew by the chicken feather that Bandit had been up to no good.

A week later the woods were budding, and the thickets were rustling with all manner of wild things scurrying on the love scent. Colin managed to get a glimpse of Bandit every few days. He couldn't get close though, for the spring running was a lot more important to a fox than any human beings were.

Every now and then Colin got out his framed box cover and looked at it, but he never drew anything on it; he never even picked up his pencil. I remember wondering if what Father had said about framing a picture before you had one had spoiled something for him.

I was helping Father with the planting now, but Colin managed to be in the woods every day. By degrees, he learned Bandit's range, where he drank and rested and where he was likely to be according to the time of day. One day he told me how he had petted Bandit again and how they had walked together a long way in the woods. All this time we had kept his secret from Father.

As summer came on, Bandit began to live up to the prediction Father had made. Accustomed to human beings, he moved without fear about the scattered farms of the region, raiding barns and hen runs that other foxes wouldn't have dared go near. And he taught his wild mate to do the same. Almost every night they got into some poultry house, and by late June, Bandit was not only killing chickens and ducks but feeding on eggs and young chicks whenever he got the chance.

*B*andit was not only killing chickens and ducks but feeding on eggs.

Stories of his doings came to us from many sources, for he was still easily recognized by the dark patch on his shoulders. Many a farmer took a shot at him as he fled, and some of them set out on his trail with dogs, but they always returned home without even sighting him. Bandit was familiar with all the dogs in the region, and he knew a hundred tricks to <u>confound</u> them. He got

---

7. **spring sparking**: an old slang term referring to the mating period of certain animals.

Words to Know and Use | **confound** (kən found′) *v.* to bewilder; confuse

527

FOXES 1886 Bruno Liljefors The Gothenburg Art Gallery, Göteborg, Sweden.

a reputation that year beyond that of any fox our hills had known. His confidence grew, and he gave up wild hunting altogether and lived entirely off the poultry farmers. By September, the hill farmers banded together to hunt him down.

It was Father who brought home that news one night. All time-honored rules of the fox chase were to be broken in this hunt; if the dogs couldn't bring Bandit down, he was to be shot on sight. I was stricken and furious. I remember the misery of Colin's

face in the lamplight. Father, who took pride in all the ritual of the hunt, had refused to be a party to such an affair, though in justice he could do nothing but sanction any sort of hunt; for Bandit, as old Sam Wetherwax put it, had been "purely getting in the Lord's hair."

The hunt began next morning, and it was the biggest turnout our hills had known. There were at least twenty mounted men in the party and as many dogs. Father and I were working in the lower field as they

Words to Know and Use | **sanction** (saŋk′ shən) *v.* to give approval for

passed along the river road. Most of the hunters carried rifles, and they looked ugly.

Twice during the morning I went up to the house to find Colin, but he was nowhere around. As we worked, Father and I could follow the progress of the hunt by the distant hound music on the breeze. We could tell just where the hunters first caught sight of the fox and where Bandit was leading the dogs during the first hour. We knew as well as if we'd seen it how Bandit roused another fox along Turkey Branch and forced it to run for him and how the dogs swept after it for twenty minutes before they sensed their mistake.

Noon came, and Colin had not come in to eat. After dinner Father didn't go back to the field. He moped about, listening to the hound talk. He didn't like what was on any more than I did, and now and again I caught his smile of satisfaction when we heard the broken, angry notes of the hunting horn, telling that the dogs had lost the trail or had run another fox.

I was restless, and I went up into the hills in midafternoon. I ranged the woods for miles, thinking all the time of Colin. Time lost all meaning for me, and the short day was nearing an end when I heard the horn talking again, telling that the fox had put over another trick. All day he had deviled the dogs and mocked the hunters. This new trick and the coming night would work to save him. I was wildly glad as I moved down toward Turkey Branch and stood listening for a time by the deep, shaded pool where for years we boys had gone swimming, sailed boats, and dreamed summer dreams.

Suddenly, out of the corner of my eye, I saw the sharp ears and thin, pointed mask of a fox–in the water almost beneath me. It was Bandit, craftily submerged there, all but his head resting in the cool water of the pool and the shadow of the two big beeches that spread above it. He must have run forty miles or more since morning. And he must have hidden in this place before. His knowing, crafty mask blended perfectly with the shadows and a mass of drift and branches that had collected by the bank of the pool. He was so still that a pair of thrushes flew up from the spot as I came up, not knowing he was there.

Bandit's bright, <u>harried</u> eyes were looking right at me. But I did not look at him direct. Some woods instinct, swifter than thought, kept me from it. So he and I met as in another world, indirectly, with feeling but without sign or greeting.

Suddenly I saw that Colin was standing almost beside me. Silently as a water snake, he had come out of the bushes and stood there. Our eyes met, and a quick and secret smile passed between us. It was a rare moment in which I really "met" my brother, when something of his <u>essence</u> flowed into me, and I knew all of him. I've never lost it since.

My eyes still turned from the fox, my heart pounding, I moved quietly away, and Colin moved with me. We whistled softly as we went, pretending to busy ourselves along the bank of the stream. There was magic in it, as if by will we wove a web of protection

Words to Know and Use | **harried** (har′ ēd) *adj.* worried; distressed **harry** *v.*
essence (es′ əns) *n.* the basic nature of a thing

529

about the fox, a ring-pass-not that none might penetrate. It was so, too, we felt, in the brain of Bandit, and that doubled the charm. To us he was still our little pet that we had carried about in our arms on countless summer afternoons.

Two hundred yards upstream, we stopped beside slim, fresh tracks in the mud where Bandit had entered the branch. The tracks angled upstream. But in the water the <u>wily</u> creature had turned down.

We climbed the far bank to wait, and Colin told me how Bandit's secret had been his secret ever since an afternoon three months before, when he'd watched the fox swim downstream to hide in the deep pool. Today he'd waited on the bank, feeling that Bandit, hard pressed by the dogs, might again seek the pool for <u>sanctuary</u>.

We looked back once as we turned homeward. He still had not moved. We didn't know until later that he was killed that same night, by a chance hunter, as he crept out from his hiding place.

That evening Colin worked a long time on his framed box cover that had lain about the house untouched all summer. He kept at it all the next day too. I had never seen him work so hard. I seemed to sense in the air the feeling he was putting into it, how he was *believing* his picture into being. It was

evening before he finished it. Without a word he handed it to Father. Mom and I went and looked over his shoulder.

It was a delicate and <u>intricate</u> pencil drawing of the deep branch pool; and there was Bandit's head, and watching, fear-filled eyes hiding there amid the leaves and shadows, woven craftily into the maze of twigs and branches as if by nature's art itself. Hardly a fox there at all, but the place where he was—or should have been. I recognized it instantly, but Mom gave a sort of incredulous sniff.

"I'll declare," she said, "it's mazy as a puzzle. It just looks like a lot of sticks and leaves to me."

Long minutes of study passed before Father's eye picked out the picture's secret, as few men's could have done. I laid that to Father's being a born hunter. That was a picture that might have been done especially for him. In fact, I guess it was.

Finally he turned to Colin with his deep, slow smile. "So that's how Bandit fooled them all," he said. He sat holding the picture with a sort of tenderness for a long time, while we glowed in the warmth of the shared secret. That was Colin's moment. Colin's art stopped being a pox to Father right there. And later, when the time came for Colin to go to art school, it was Father who was his solid backer. ❧

Words to Know and Use

wily (wī′ ē) *adj.* crafty; sly
sanctuary (saŋk′ chōō er′ ē) *n.* shelter; protection
intricate (in′ tri kit) *adj.* elaborately detailed

Responding to Reading

First Impressions

1. What were your thoughts at the end of the story? Describe your reaction in your journal.

Second Thoughts

2. In your opinion, why are the doors of understanding opened between Colin and his father?

> **Think about**
> • why the father changes his mind about Colin's art
> • what Colin and his father have in common

3. Why do you think Bandit is so important to the two boys?

> **Think about**
> • how a wild animal is different from a tamed one
> • your previous discussion of what pets do for people

4. Which family member do you think shows the most understanding of Colin? Explain your opinion.

5. Why do you think Colin leaves the framed box cover blank for the entire summer?

6. What do you think the title of the story means?

Broader Connections

7. Based on this story and your own experience, do you think people should raise wild animals as pets? Do you think wild animals should be raised in zoos? Give reasons for your answers.

Literary Concept: Flashback

The events in a story's plot usually occur in the order in which they happen. Sometimes, however, writers interrupt the flow of events to describe an episode that happened before the beginning of the story. This is called a **flashback.** Find a flashback in "Last Cover." What does the flashback contribute to your understanding of the story?

Concept Review: Narrator How does the narrator's opinion of his brother come through in his story?

Writing Options

1. Imagine that Colin is holding his first exhibition of paintings. Write an **advertising flyer** about his art and background to get people to come to his exhibition.

2. Imagine that you are a neighbor of the two brothers. Write a **letter** to the local paper in which you voice your approval or disapproval of the fox hunt.

3. Write a **comparison-contrast paper** that explains the differences and the similarities between the two brothers.

4. Find out more about fox hunts. Write a **feature article** to report your findings and to explain what happens on the hunt.

Vocabulary Practice

Exercise   On your paper, write the word from the list that is most closely related to the meaning of the boldfaced word or phrase.

1. Bandit found **safety** in his hiding place.

2. The boys' father did not **encourage** the idea of keeping a wild fox as a pet.

3. Like all foxes, Bandit proved himself to be a **clever** trickster.

4. The winter proved to be **cheerless** and bitterly cold.

5. Colin's avoidance of chores led his father to compare him to a **sickly, bedridden person.**

6. The fox was able to **confuse** the dogs during the hunt.

7. A person who is **lacking in spirit or force** would not please Colin's father.

8. To understand Colin's **true character,** his father needed to understand his art.

9. The farmers were **troubled** by Bandit's constant attacks on their livestock.

10. Colin's picture showed **complex** use of details.

> *Words to Know and Use*
>
> **bleak**
> **confound**
> **essence**
> **harried**
> **intricate**
> **invalid**
> **passive**
> **sanction**
> **sanctuary**
> **wily**

E X T E N D

Options for Learning

1 • Nature's Art Colin created an intricate pencil drawing of Bandit's hiding place. Using a different medium, such as paint, chalk, ink, fabric, clay, or whatever you choose, create your own interpretation of the scene he presented. Before you begin, skim the story to find relevant details.

2 • The Lay of the Land Skim "Last Cover" and list the sites where the action takes place. Use this information and your imagination to make a map of the area.

3 • Call of the Wild Read *Call of the Wild* by Jack London, *Rascal* by Sterling North, *Born Free* by Joy Adamson, or another book of your choice about taming wild animals. Give an oral book report in which you draw comparisons to Bandit's response toward taming.

4 • Fox Facts Find out about any foxes that live in your area. Then create a poster that provides interesting facts about these foxes, including pictures if possible.

 FACT FINDER SCIENCE

Name a hibernating animal that is not among the seven mentioned in the father's rhyme.

Paul Annixter
1894–1985

Paul Annixter is a pen name that Howard A. Sturtzel used for the more than five hundred short stories he published. Most of these stories are about wildlife.

When he was nine, Sturtzel and his mother were left alone, having to earn a living for themselves and his paralyzed grandmother. Sturtzel sold newspapers and candy and later worked as a hotel bellhop. When he was sixteen, he traveled across the United States and Canada, living the life of a hobo.

Eventually, Sturtzel settled a timber claim in northern Minnesota, where he lived alone for one and a half years and began to write.

After attending college, he married the daughter of his favorite writer and tutor, Will Levington Comfort. He and his wife Jane worked together to produce more than twenty novels for young people, including *The Phantom Stallion* (1961) and *Windigo* (1963). "Where one may have a weakness," he said of himself and his wife, "the other is apt to have a strength."

Poetry

ᴬ *Minor Bird*
ROBERT FROST

ᵀʰᵉ *Time We Climbed Snake Mountain*
LESLIE MARMON SILKO

Examine What You Know

Are you the sort of person who feels responsibility toward animals? Or do you feel that the needs of animals should be secondary to those of humans? Rate yourself on the following scale and compare your views to those of your classmates.

Animal Attitude Scale					
	Strongly disagree			Strongly agree	
	1	2	3	4	5
I like being around animals.					
I feel a strong link to animals.					
People should be judged by how they treat animals.					
Animals have rights that people abuse.					

Expand Your Knowledge

These poems show two speakers' responses to animals found in their natural environments. Those environments, or settings, are very different. Robert Frost's poem, like most of his poetry, is set in the isolated New England countryside where Frost lived and worked. Leslie Marmon Silko's poem is set in the West, where the speaker is part of a mountain-climbing expedition. Silko lives on the Laguna Pueblo Reservation in mountainous New Mexico. Her writing often reflects the experiences and beliefs of her Native American culture.

Write Before You Read

■ *Author biographies in Reader's Handbook*

In your journal or notebook, write about a personal experience you have had that involved an animal.

A Minor Bird

ROBERT FROST

I have wished a bird would fly away,
And not sing by my house all day;

Have clapped my hands at him from the door
When it seemed as if I could bear no more.

5 The fault must partly have been in me.
The bird was not to blame for his key.

And of course there must be something wrong
In wanting to silence any song.

Responding to Reading

First Impressions of "A Minor Bird"

1. What did you think about the speaker as you read this poem?
Describe your thoughts in your journal or notebook.

Second Thoughts on "A Minor Bird"

2. How do you think the speaker judges himself? Do you agree with
him? Explain your opinion.

3. Based on your own experiences, do you find the speaker's irritation
with the bird to be a normal response? Explain.

4. Explain what you think the title of the poem means.

The Time We Climbed Snake Mountain

LESLIE MARMON SILKO

Seeing good places
    for my hands
I grab the warm parts of the cliff
        and I feel the mountain as I climb.
5 Somewhere   around here
      yellow spotted snake is sleeping   on his rock
      in the sun.

So
  please, I tell them
10   watch out,
don't step on the spotted yellow snake
      he lives here.
The mountain is his.

THE MOUNTAIN, NEW MEXICO
1931   Georgia O'Keeffe
Oil on canvas, 30 x 36 inches.
Collection of the Whitney Museum of
Art, New York. Photograph by Sheldon
C. Collins, New Jersey.

Responding to Reading

First Impressions of "The Time We Climbed Snake Mountain"

1. What mental pictures did you form while reading this poem? Describe them in your journal or notebook.

Second Thoughts on "The Time We Climbed Snake Mountain"

2. What does the poem reveal about the speaker's attitude toward the snake?

3. Do you agree or disagree with the speaker's claim that the mountain belongs to the snake? Explain your opinion.

Comparing the Poems

4. Do you think both poems share a common theme? Give reasons for your answer.

5. In your opinion, how would each speaker respond to the Animal Attitude Scale? Compare and contrast their ratings to your own.

6. Which of the two poems do you think would mean more to Colin in "Last Cover"? Explain your choice.

Broader Connections

7. In recent years, animal rights activists have taken action on various issues, ranging from the killing of animals for fur to the use of animals in scientific experiments. What is your opinion of the animal rights movement? How do you think the speakers in the two poems would react to it?

Writing Options

1. Work with a partner to come up with an animal **bill of rights.** List what you believe are the most important rights.

2. Write a **poem** that reflects your feelings and ideas about a particular animal, such as a snake or bird.

Nonfiction

Primary Lessons
from Silent Dancing

JUDITH ORTIZ COFER

Examine What You Know

Think about your first experiences with formal schooling, which probably took place in kindergarten or first grade. Looking back, how would you rate your first teacher and school? If you could change anything about your first classroom experience, what would it be? Write your thoughts in your journal or notebook.

Expand Your Knowledge

Judith Ortiz Cofer, a poet and novelist, shares her earliest memories of school in this essay from her collection *Silent Dancing: A Partial Remembrance of a Puerto Rican Childhood*. At the age of six, Cofer moved from Paterson, New Jersey, back to her birthplace, Puerto Rico, along with her mother and brother. They lived in her grandmother's house while her father, a member of the U.S. Navy, was stationed in Europe. Later, the family reunited in Paterson when his ship returned to New York. The family's cycle of moving from the mainland to Puerto Rico and back continued for over twenty years.

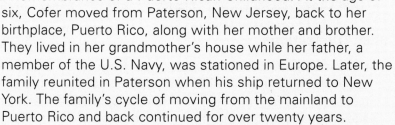

Cofer's homeland, Puerto Rico, is an island in the Caribbean Sea about a thousand miles southeast of Florida. Puerto Rico is a commonwealth; its people are U.S. citizens with limited rights. For example, they have no voting representative in Congress, and they cannot vote in U.S. presidential elections. The island has a mixture of ethnic groups, the largest being Spanish and African. First claimed for Spain by Christopher Columbus in 1493, Puerto Rico remained a Spanish colony until 1898, when the United States took possession after winning the Spanish-American war.

Enrich Your Reading

■ *Author biography on Extend page*

Identifying an Opinion As you read, determine Cofer's opinions about her school in Puerto Rico and the school system as a whole.

Primary Lessons

from Silent Dancing

JUDITH ORTIZ COFER

My mother walked me to my first day at school at La Escuela Segundo Ruiz Belvis, named after the Puerto Rican patriot born in our town. I remember yellow cement with green trim. All the classrooms had been painted these colors to identify them as government property. This was true all over the Island. Everything was color-coded, including the children, who wore uniforms from first through twelfth grade. We were a midget army in white and brown, led by the hand to our battleground. From practically every house in our barrio[1] emerged a crisply ironed uniform inhabited by the savage creatures we had become over a summer of running wild in the sun.

At my grandmother's house, where we were staying until my father returned to Brooklyn Yard in New York and sent for us, it had been complete <u>chaos</u>, with several children to get ready for school. My mother had pulled my hair harder than usual while braiding it, and I had dissolved into a pool of total self-pity. I wanted to stay home with her and Mamá, to continue listening to stories in the late afternoon, to drink *café con leche*[2] with them, and to play rough games with my many cousins. I wanted to continue living the dream of summer afternoons in Puerto Rico, and if I could not have it, then I wanted to go back to Paterson, New Jersey, back to where I imagined our apartment waited, peaceful and cool, for the three of us to return to our former lives. Our gypsy lifestyle[3] had convinced me, at age six, that one part of life stops and waits for you while you live another for a while—and if you don't like the present, you can always return to the past. Buttoning me into my stiff blouse while I tried to squirm away from her, my mother attempted to explain to me that I was a big girl now and should try to understand that, like all the other children my age, I had to go to school.

"What about him?" I yelled, pointing at my brother who was lounging on the tile floor of our bedroom in his pajamas, playing quietly with a toy car.

"He's too young to go to school; you

---

1. barrio (bär′ ē ō): a neighborhood in a Latin American city.
2. *café con leche* (kä fā′ kôn le′ chā) *Spanish:* coffee with milk.
3. gypsy lifestyle: a way of life in which one continually moves from place to place.

Words to Know and Use | **chaos** (kā′ äs′) *n.* a state of disorder and confusion

know that. Now stay still." My mother pinned me between her thighs to button my skirt, as she had learned to do from Mamá, from whose grip it was impossible to escape.

"It's not fair, it's not fair. I can't go to school here. I don't speak Spanish." It was my final argument, and it failed miserably because I was shouting my defiance in the language I claimed not to speak. Only I knew what I meant by saying in Spanish that I did not speak Spanish. I had spent my early childhood in the United States, where I lived in a bubble created by my Puerto Rican parents in a home where two cultures and languages became one. I learned to listen to the English from the television with one ear while I heard my mother and father speaking in Spanish with the other. I thought I was an ordinary American kid—like the children on the shows I watched—and that everyone's parents spoke a secret second language at home. When we came to Puerto Rico right before I started first grade, I switched easily to Spanish. It was the language of fun, of summertime games. But school—that was a different matter.

I made one last desperate effort to make my mother see reason: "Father will be very angry. You know that he wants us to speak good English." My mother, of course, ignored me as she dressed my little brother in his play clothes. I could not believe her indifference to my father's wishes. She was usually so careful about our safety and the many other areas that he was forever reminding her about in his letters. But I was right, and she knew it. Our father spoke to us in English as much as possible, and he corrected my pronunciation constantly—not "jes" but "y-es." Y-es, sir. How could she send me to school to learn Spanish when we would be returning to Paterson in just a few months?

But, of course, what I feared was not language but loss of freedom. At school there would be no playing, no stories, only lessons. It would not matter if I did not understand a word, and I would not be allowed to make up my own definitions. I would have to learn silence. I would have to keep my wild imagination in check. Feeling locked into my stiffly starched uniform, I only sensed all this. I guess most children can intuit[4] their loss of childhood's freedom on that first day of school. It is separation anxiety[5] too, but mother is just the guardian of the "playground" of our early childhood.

The sight of my cousins in similar straits comforted me. We were marched down the hill of our barrio where Mamá's robin's-egg-blue house stood at the top. I must have glanced back at it with yearning. Mamá's house—a place built for children—where anything that could be broken had already been broken by my grandmother's early batch of offspring (they ranged in age from my mother's oldest sisters to my uncle, who was six months older than me). Her house had long since been made childproof. It had been a perfect summer place. And now it was September—the cruelest month for a child.

La Mrs., as all the teachers were called, waited for her class of first graders at the door of the yellow and green classroom. She too wore a uniform: it was a blue skirt and a white blouse. This teacher wore black high

---

4. intuit (in to͞o′ it): to understand without conscious thought.

5. separation anxiety (aŋ zī′ ə tē): the emotional disturbance caused by being separated from a parent.

SARO & AITA   1949   Julio Rosado del Valle   Collection of Mrs. F. Monserrate, Puerto Rico   Photography by John Betancourt.

heels with her "standard issue." I remember this detail because when we were all seated in rows, she called on one little girl and pointed to the back of the room where there were shelves. She told the girl to bring her a shoe box from the bottom shelf. Then, when the box had been placed in her hands, she did something unusual. She had the little girl kneel at her feet and take the pointy high heels off her feet and replace them with a pair of satin slippers from the shoe box. She told the group that every one of us would have a chance to do this if we behaved in her class. Though confused about the prize, I soon felt caught up in the competition to bring *La Mrs.* her slippers in the morning. Children fought over the privilege.

Our first lesson was English. In Puerto Rico, every child has to take twelve years of English to graduate from school. It is the law. In my parents' school days, all subjects were taught in English. The U.S. Department of Education had specified that as a United States territory, the Island had to be "Americanized," and to accomplish this task, it was necessary for the Spanish language to be replaced in one generation through the teaching of English in all schools. My father began his school day by saluting the flag of the United States and singing "America" and "The Star-Spangled Banner" by <u>rote</u>, without understanding a word of what he was saying. The logic behind this system was that though the children did not understand the English words, they would remember the rhythms. Even the games the teacher's manuals required them to play

became absurd <u>adaptations</u>. "Here We Go Round the Mulberry Bush" became "Here We Go Round the Mango Tree." I have heard about the confusion caused by the use of a primer[6] in which the sounds of animals were featured. The children were forced to accept that a rooster says *cock-a-doodle-doo* when they knew perfectly well from hearing their own roosters each morning that in Puerto Rico a rooster says *cocorocó*. Even the vocabulary of their pets was changed; there are still family stories circulating about the bewilderment of a first grader coming home to try to teach his dog to speak in English. The policy of assimilation by immersion[7] failed on the Island. Teachers <u>adhered</u> to it on paper, substituting their own materials for the texts, but no one took their English home. In due time, the program was <u>minimized</u> to the one class in English per day that I encountered when I took my seat in *La Mrs.*'s first-grade class.

Why aren't the Spanish-speaking children able to learn English?

review

Catching us all by surprise, she stood very straight and tall in front of us and began to sing in English:

Pollito—Chicken
Gallina—Hen
Lápiz—Pencil
Y Pluma—Pen.

---

6. **primer** (prim′ ər): a schoolbook for teaching reading.
7. **assimilation by immersion** (ə sim′ ə lā′ shən, im mʉr′ shən): learning a language by being exposed to it all the time.

Words to Know and Use

rote (rōt) *n.* memorization without understanding
adaptation (ad′ əp tā′ shən) *n.* a thing changed to suit new conditions
adhere (ad hir′) *v.* to be loyal
minimize (min′ ə mīz′) *v.* to reduce to the smallest possible amount

"Repeat after me, children: Pollito—Chicken," she commanded in her heavily accented English that only I understood, being the only child in the room who had ever been exposed to the language. But I too remained silent. No use making waves or showing off. Patiently *La Mrs.* sang her song and gestured for us to join in. At some point it must have dawned on the class that this silly routine was likely to go on all day if we did not "repeat after her." It was not her fault that she had to follow the rule in her teacher's manual stating that she must teach English *in* English, and that she must not translate but merely repeat her lesson in English until the children "begin to respond" more or less "unconsciously." This was one of the vestiges[8] of the regimen followed by her predecessors in the last generation. To this day I can recite "Pollito—Chicken" mindlessly, never once pausing to visualize chicks, hens, pencils, or pens.

I soon found myself crowned "teacher's pet" without much effort on my part. I was a privileged child in her eyes simply because I lived in "Nueva York" and because my father was in the navy. His name was an old one in our pueblo, associated with once-upon-a-time landed people and long-gone money. Status is judged by unique standards in a culture where, by definition, everyone is a second-class citizen. Remembrance of past glory is as good as titles and money. Old families living in decrepit old houses rank over factory workers living in modern comfort in cement boxes—all the same. The professions raise a person out of the dreaded "sameness" into a niche of status, so that

teachers, nurses, and everyone who went to school for a job were given the honorifics[9] of *El Míster* or *La Mrs.* by the common folks, people who were likely to be making more money in American factories than the poorly paid educators and government workers.

What kinds of people are respected in this society?

review

My first impressions of the hierarchy began with my teacher's shoe-changing ceremony and the exaggerated respect she received from our parents. *La Mrs.* was always right, and adults scrambled to meet her requirements. She wanted all our schoolbooks covered in the brown paper now used for paper bags (used at that time by the grocer to wrap meats and other foods). That first week of school, the grocer was swamped with requests for paper, which he gave away to the women. That week and the next, he wrapped produce in newspapers. All school projects became family projects. It was considered disrespectful at Mamá's house to do homework in privacy. Between the hours when we came home from school and dinner time, the table was shared by all of us working together, with the women hovering in the background. The teachers communicated directly with the mothers, and it was a matriarchy[10] of far-

---

8. vestiges (ves′ tij əz): traces of something that is now gone.
9. honorifics (än′ ər if′ iks): titles or words used to show respect.
10. matriarchy (mā′ trē är′ kē): a social group in which women rule.

Words to Know and Use | **predecessor** (pred′ ə ses′ ər) *n.* a person who comes before
niche (nich) *n.* the place a person occupies in society
hierarchy (hī′ ər är′ kē) *n.* a group of people organized according to rank or authority

543

QUEBRADILLAS   Luis G. Cajiga   Courtesy, Instituto de Cultura Puertorriqueno, San Juan, Puerto Rico.

reaching power and influence.

There was a black boy in my first-grade classroom who was also the teacher's pet but for a different reason than I: I did not have to do anything to win her favor; he would do anything to win a smile. He was as black as the cauldron that Mamá used for cooking stew, and his hair was curled into tight little balls on his head--*pasitas,*[11] like little raisins glued to his skull, my mother had said. There had been some talk at Mamá's house about this boy; Lorenzo was his name. I later gathered that he was the grandson of my father's nanny. Lorenzo lived with Teresa, his grandmother, having been left in her care when his mother took off for "Los Nueva Yores" shortly after his birth. And they were poor. Everyone could see that his pants were too big for him—hand-me-downs—and his shoe soles were as thin as paper. Lorenzo seemed unmindful of the giggles he caused when he jumped up to erase the board for *La Mrs.* and his baggy pants rode down to his thin hips as he strained up to get every stray mark. He

----

11. ***pasitas*** (pä sē′ täs) *Spanish:* small raisins.

seemed to <u>relish</u> playing the little clown when she asked him to come to the front of the room and sing his phonetic[12] version of "o-bootifool, forpashios-keeis," leading the class in our <u>incomprehensible</u> tribute to the American flag. He was a bright, loving child, with a talent for song and mimicry that everyone commented on. He should have been chosen to host the PTA show that year instead of me.

At recess one day, I came back to the empty classroom to get something. My cup? My nickel for a drink from the kiosk[13] man? I don't remember. But I remember the conversation my teacher was having with another teacher. I remember because it concerned me and because I memorized it so that I could ask my mother to explain what it meant.

"He is a funny *negrito*,[14] and, like a parrot, he can repeat anything you teach him. But his mamá must not have the money to buy him a suit."

"I kept Rafaelito's First Communion suit; I bet Lorenzo could fit in it. It's white with a bow tie," the other teacher said.

"But Marisa," laughed my teacher, "in that suit Lorenzo would look like a fly drowned in a glass of milk."

Both women laughed. They had not seen me crouched at the back of the room, digging into my school bag. My name came up then.

"What about the Ortiz girl? They have money."

"I'll talk to her mother today. The superintendent, *El Americano* from San Juan, is coming down for the show. How about if we have her say her lines in both Spanish and English."

The conversation ends there for me. My mother took me to Mayagüez and bought me a frilly pink dress and two crinoline petticoats[15] to wear underneath so that I looked like a pink and white parachute with toothpick legs sticking out. I learned my lines, "*Padres, maestros,* Mr. Leonard, *bienvenidos*[16]/Parents, teachers, Mr. Leonard, welcome . . ." My first public appearance. I took no pleasure in it. The words were formal and empty. I had simply memorized them. My dress pinched me at the neck and arms and made me itch all over.

I had asked my mother what it meant to be a *"mosca en un vaso de leche,"* a fly in a glass of milk. She had laughed at the image, explaining that it meant being "different," but that it wasn't something I needed to worry about. 🐦

---

12. **phonetic** (fō net′ ik): based on the way words are pronounced.
13. **kiosk** (kē′ äsk′): an open stand where things are sold.
14. *negrito* (ne grē′ tô) *Spanish:* a small black boy.
15. **crinoline petticoats** (krin′ ə lin′): underskirts of coarse, stiff cloth that make a skirt stand out.
16. *Padres, maestros . . . bienvenidos* (pä′ dres, mä es′ trôs, byem ve nē′ dôs) *Spanish.*

Words to Know and Use

relish (rel′ ish) *v.* to enjoy
incomprehensible (in′ käm′ prē hen′ sə bəl) *adj.* not capable of being understood

545

Responding to Reading

First Impressions

1. What is your first impression of the author? Jot down your reaction in your journal or notebook.

Second Thoughts

2. Do you think Cofer is proud of her Puerto Rican heritage? Explain.

3. What is Cofer's opinion of the school and its methods of instruction? Do you think she is being fair?

    Think about
    - your opinion of the way English was taught
    - your reaction to the teacher's shoe-changing ceremony
    - why the community supported the school

4. What doors of understanding are opened—or closed—as a result of Cofer's school experience?

5. How is Cofer's first experience with school similar to or different from your own first experience?

Broader Connections

6. Some people believe that all instruction in U.S. schools should be in English. Others believe that non-English-speaking students should be taught first in their native language (a method called bilingual education). Which method makes more sense to you? Consider Cofer's experience in your response.

Literary Concept: Title

Often, the title of a selection hints at the main idea, or theme. Why do you think Cofer titled this essay "Primary Lessons"? What are the different meanings of the title?

Concept Review: Description Find at least two sentences in the essay that you think provide good descriptions. What makes these descriptions effective?

Writing Options

1. Imagine that you are an advisor to the superintendent of schools in this selection. Write a **memo** to him, giving your advice on how to improve Cofer's school.

2. Write **notes** for a chapter in your own autobiography about your first experience at school. What were your "primary lessons"?

3. Write your own **opinion** of the teachers' decision to have the narrator host the PTA show.

4. With a partner, research bilingual education in the United States. Find out about the arguments for and against it. Write a **short report** to share your findings.

Vocabulary Practice

Exercise A Write the letter of the word that is most nearly *opposite* in meaning to the capitalized word.

1. RELISH: (a) enjoy (b) dislike (c) favor (d) please (e) annoy

2. CHAOS: (a) order (b) confusion (c) noise (d) loudness (e) silence

3. ADHERE: (a) support (b) speak (c) betray (d) multiply (e) stick

4. MINIMIZE: (a) reduce (b) restrict (c) increase (d) fail (e) loosen

5. INCOMPREHENSIBLE: (a) mysterious (b) silly (c) large (d) understandable (e) chaotic

Words to Know and Use

adaptation
adhere
chaos
hierarchy
incomprehensible
minimize
niche
predecessor
relish
rote

Exercise B Write the letter of the word that is *least* like the other words in the set.

1. (a) grandparent (b) ancestor (c) predecessor (d) friend

2. (a) place (b) position (c) niche (d) absence

3. (a) hierarchy (b) order (c) structure (d) disorder

4. (a) permanence (b) adaptation (c) alteration (d) change

5. (a) rote (b) repetition (c) routine (d) creativity

Options for Learning

1 • Who's on Top? Cofer describes the hierarchy of her Puerto Rican town. Create a chart or diagram that shows the hierarchy in your community. Which people and which jobs are most valued? Which are least valued? Present your chart to the class.

2 • A Fifty-first State Some people would like to see Puerto Rico become a state. In a group of four, research the pros and cons of this issue. Then stage a debate, with two people arguing for statehood and two taking the opposing side.

3 • Migration Map Draw or copy a map and trace the route between Puerto Rico and Paterson, New Jersey. Estimate how many miles separate the two locations.

4 • Primary Focus Schools have changed since Cofer was in primary school. Interview other adults, especially any who attended school outside the United States, to find out about their primary-school experiences. Share their experiences with your class, and contrast these experiences with those in your own community.

 FACT FINDER SOCIAL STUDIES

About how many Puerto Ricans live in the mainland United States?

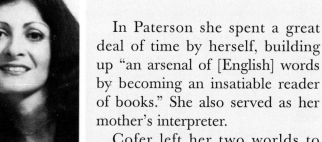

Judith Ortiz Cofer
1952–

As a child, Judith Cofer grew up in two different worlds, her native Puerto Rico and Paterson, New Jersey. Cofer's two homes, which shifted according to her father's assignments in the U.S. Navy, both contributed to her writing.

In Puerto Rico, she listened to her grandmother's stories in Spanish under a giant mango tree, surrounded by the women and children of her extended family. It was there, Cofer says, "that I first began to feel the power of words."

In Paterson she spent a great deal of time by herself, building up "an arsenal of [English] words by becoming an insatiable reader of books." She also served as her mother's interpreter.

Cofer left her two worlds to attend college. She later taught at the Universities of Miami and Georgia and at Macon College before receiving a poetry fellowship from the National Endowment for the Arts in 1989. Cofer's poems, essays, and reviews appear in literary magazines and anthologies. A novel, *The Line of the Sun,* was nominated for a Pulitzer Prize. She now lives in Georgia.

Nonfiction

Oh Broom, Get to Work

YOSHIKO UCHIDA (yō' shē kō yōō chē' dä)

Examine What You Know

This selection describes how a young girl tries to rid her household of a frequent guest whom she does not like. How would you deal with an unwanted guest? With your classmates, come up with creative solutions to this problem.

Expand Your Knowledge

As a young girl, Yoshiko Uchida, a novelist and writer of children's books, found herself constantly in the company of household guests. Her parents, both born and educated in Japan, had settled in Berkeley, California, near her father's workplace in San Francisco. Graduates of Japan's Doshisha University, her parents often opened their home to Japanese students who came to the United States to study religion at the University of California at Berkeley or the Pacific School of Religion.

These students were engaged in graduate work, the advanced courses taken by those who have already received a college or university degree. Their studies, made more difficult by living in a foreign and unwelcoming land, were in preparation for Christian ministry.

Write Before You Read

Think of times when you have tried to avoid someone's company—without letting him or her know what you were doing. What strategies did you employ to avoid spending time with that person? Did your strategies succeed without hurting that person's feelings? Write about your experience in your journal or notebook.

■ *Author biography in Reader's Handbook*

Oh Broom, Get to Work

YOSHIKO UCHIDA

Of the many visitors who came to our home in Berkeley during my childhood, I remember Mr. Okada because I disliked him most and because he was the target of the only successful bit of Oriental sorcery I ever practiced.

I first met Mr. Okada one cold and rainy afternoon when I answered the hesitant twinge of our front doorbell. I opened the door to find a thin, hatless stranger in a shabby overcoat, holding a carefully furled black umbrella still trickling water from its ferrule.[1]

I looked at him silently and waited for him to speak, but he only returned my silence, staring at me with sad, sullen eyes that peered from a pallid face. I had never seen him before and thought he might be another peddler my mother had befriended. I knew the Watkins Man, whose small black bag divulged thick, creamy chocolate bars and slim bottles of vanilla and lemon extract. I also knew the Real Silk Lady, who came calling with stockings and silk underwear stuffed inside her sample case.

I looked now to see if this stranger carried a valise[2], but he had nothing to redeem his presence on a gloomy afternoon besides his enormous sopping umbrella.

Seeing that I was not about to break the silence or to let him in, he cleared his throat and spoke in a soft voice, totally unbecoming a man, I thought. "Is your mama at home?" he asked.

I had been cautioned against unlatching the screen door to strangers and kept my hand pressed firmly on the hook. "Wait a minute, I'll call her," I said, and took the added precaution of closing the door noisily in his face.

"There's a funny-looking man at the door," I called to my mother in the kitchen, and with only that cryptic description to enlighten her, she hurried to see who had come.

I heard her open the door and then quickly unlatch the screen. "*Mah,* Okada-san,"[3] she said. "Such a miserable day. *Dozo,*[4] please, do come in." And taking his umbrella, she quickly urged him toward the seat by the fire. "I am so sorry my daughter kept you waiting in the rain," she apologized.

---

1. ferrule (fer′ əl): a metal band protecting the end of an umbrella.

2. valise (və lēs′): a small suitcase or traveling bag.

3. *mah, Okada-san* (mä o kä dä sän) *Japanese:* The word *mah* expresses surprise. The word ending *-san* is added to a person's name as a polite form of address.

4. *dozo* (dō zō) *Japanese:* please.

Words to Know and Use

sorcery (sôr′ sər ē) *n.* magic
pallid (pal′ id) *adj.* pale; lacking normal color
divulge (də vulj′) *v.* to reveal
cryptic (krip′ tik) *adj.* puzzling; mysterious

I hated having my mother apologize on my behalf. "Why didn't he tell me he was your friend?" I asked the moment he left. "I thought he was a peddler. Besides, he looks like he has TB."[5]

At supper that night, Mother told how she had met Mr. Okada, a seminary student from Japan, at a recent WCTU[6] meeting in Mrs. Toda's home. My mother went to the monthly meetings of this organization partly because she believed in its precepts but mostly because its president, Mrs. Toda, was one of our dearest friends and neighbors. Whenever Mother sought to withdraw from its membership, she was drawn back not only by the covey of Japanese ladies who discussed temperance over steaming cups of green tea but by Mrs. Toda, whose quiet zeal she could not escape. It seemed incredible that a man could be trapped into attending one of these meetings.

"You mean he was the only man there?" I asked.

"He's just come from Japan, and he's terribly lonely."

"Poor fellow," my father interjected.

"But you mean he was really the only man there?" I persisted.

When my mother confirmed this fact, my opinion of Mr. Okada fell to new and terrible depths.

"What a sad case," I said, and believed at the time that I had dismissed him from further thought.

Lonely and homesick people were not unknown to me by any means. Living just across the bay from San Francisco where ships from the Orient deposited their store of lonely students and travelers, our family was a ready source of solace. My parents were graduates of a well-known university in Japan, and it seemed that every alumnus arriving in California came directly to our home as though reporting in to an alumni office. They came in growing numbers over the years, to do graduate work at the university or at the divinity school, and whenever they longed to unburden themselves in their native tongue or sip a bowl of steaming bean-curd soup, they found both a willing ear and a generous table at our home.

On every major holiday my parents would call the seminary and invite the dozen or more students from Japan who had nowhere to go. Reeking of pomade,[7] polished and stiff in their squeaky shoes and their Sunday suits, they would crowd into our house and consume vast quantities of baked ham, roast turkey, or sukiyaki[8].

Mr. Okada was always included in these groups and never failed to accept an invitation. Although the other men came in groups of three or four, he always came alone. He was often the first to arrive, offering only a shy smile as he stepped inside, and he usually sat on the hassock[9]

---

5. **TB:** tuberculosis, a wasting disease of the lungs.
6. **WCTU:** Woman's Christian Temperance Union, an organization known for its fight against abuse of alcohol.
7. **pomade** (päm ād'): a scented hair oil.
8. **sukiyaki** (soo' kē yä' kē): a Japanese dish of meat and vegetables, cooked in soy sauce.
9. **hassock:** a thick, soft cushion used as a low seat or a footstool.

Words to Know and Use

seminary (sem' ə ner' ē) *n.* a school where people are trained to become ministers, priests, or rabbis
precept (prē' sept') *n.* a rule of conduct
zeal (zēl) *n.* enthusiasm; eagerness
solace (säl' is) *n.* comfort
alumnus (ə lum' nəs) *n.* a graduate of a particular school; *plural*—**alumni** (ə lum' nī')

551

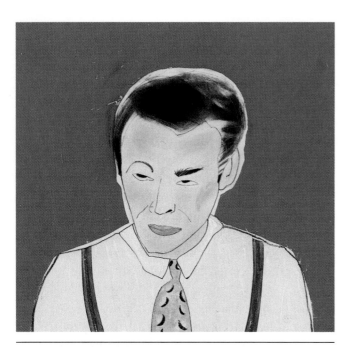
Illustration by Gary Mele.

beside the fireplace. On chilly days when an oak log sputtered in the fireplace, he would lean toward it, neck thrust forward, hands outstretched, as though communing with some spirit in the fire. He seldom spoke more than four or five sentences during an entire evening, and then usually in a voice so low they were lost in the chatter and laughter that filled the room.

The one time he spoke up with some force was to suggest that I play the piano for the assembled group. Pretending that I hadn't heard him, I carefully inspected a spot on my shoe. But the men urged me on with encouraging words, and finally they began to clap. I wanted to pitch Mr. Okada into the fire for forcing me into the kind of performance I detested, but I knew the thing had to be done. I got off to a fumbling start of "The Skylark" and had to stop in the middle to get the music from inside the piano bench and then begin again. It was a miserable show, and I blamed it entirely on Mr. Okada, whose attempt to be sociable had only resulted in my humiliation.

As the months went by, Mr. Okada not only accepted every invitation, he began to come uninvited. He had a distasteful habit of coming in the late afternoon and staying until my mother had to prepare supper and, consequently, felt obliged to ask him to stay.

One afternoon I had run all the way home with a stiff-feathered creature in my hands. "Mama, I found a dead sparrow," I shouted as I burst indoors. "Come help me bury it."

But I found my mother busy entertaining Mr. Okada in the living room. She sat calmly knitting a pair of black wool socks, and seated across from her, pale and morose in a rumpled sweat shirt and a baggy pair of pants, was Mr. Okada.

"Come in, Yo-chan,"[10] my mother called to me, but seeing Mr. Okada, I turned and fled.

I wrapped the small, stiff bird in a piece of red silk and laid it inside an empty candy box lined with foil. Then I buried it carefully in a hole which I dug beneath the flowering peach in our back yard. A chill tingled down my spine as I shaped the earth into a burial mound, and I hurried back inside

---

10. **Yo-chan** (yō chän): the first part of the author's name, with the word ending -*chan,* a Japanese form often used when speaking to a child.

Words to Know and Use | **communing** (kə myōōn' iŋ) *adj.* talking together privately **commune** *v.*
morose (mə rōs') *adj.* in low spirits; gloomy

hoping that by now my mother might be free.

This time I found her in the kitchen getting the tea things from the cupboard. She was placing the cups on small wooden coasters and arranging them with the pot on her best cherry-wood tray.

"Oh, Mama," I wailed, "you're not giving him tea, are you? He'll never go home if you do."

But my mother just gave me a quick smile and told me she couldn't send him away without a cup of hot tea. I knew she was right. After all, she even served tea to the Real Silk Lady after viewing her wares.

"Did you bury your little bird?" she asked gently.

But the thought of Mr. Okada staying on for supper had already swept aside the sweet-sad dream of a bird funeral.

I ran outside simmering with frustration and decided to go see Mrs. Toda. I swung through the narrow wooden gate to their back yard and found Mr. Toda sitting in his canvas chair, wearing an old green eyeshade and dozing beneath its protective celluloid[11]. He started as I banged the gate shut, and shouted a loud welcome as though I were just as deaf as he.

"Come to see us at last, have you?" he shouted, although I had been there just two days before. "Would you like to see my carp?" he asked generously. If I had even expressed a halfhearted desire, he would have roused himself creakily and ruffled the murky depths of the pool with his stiff fingers to let me see his speckled gray carp flash to the surface.

But today I had no time for carp. I had to unburden myself to someone, and Mrs. Toda, since she had introduced Mr. Okada to my mother in the first place, seemed an excellent person on whom to fling my misery.

I let myself in from the back door and found the kitchen filled with the smell of nutmeg and spices sprinkled over hot custard. I sniffed happily.

"Sah, sah,[12] you are just in time," Mrs. Toda clucked, and quickly placed before me a large green cup of custard, still warm and steaming. By the time I had spooned up the last mouthful of slippery sweetness, my tale of woe was not quite so strident. Still, I had few kind thoughts.

"I hate and despise that horrible Mr. Okada," I blurted out.

"Mah! Tell me, what has he done?"

With Mrs. Toda's sympathetic sighs to urge me on, I quickly told her how often he came uninvited; how he came late and always stayed for supper; how I couldn't talk to Mama while he sat there; and finally, as his most unforgivable sin, I added, "And he never says anything. He just sits—like a mushroom!"

"Ah, he is a troublesome one," Mrs. Toda agreed. "And your poor mama busy with so many callers."

---

11. **celluloid:** (sel' yōo loid') a tough plastic.
12. *sah, sah:* (sä sä) *Japanese:* well, well.

Words to Know and Use | **strident** (strīd' 'nt) *adj.* having a harsh sound

553

SHADOWS ON THE DOOR   1968   Jiro Takamatsu   Collection of the Tokyo Metropolitan Museum.

She pursed her lips as she pondered the shape and size of my problem. Then she licked the remnants of custard from her fingertips, wiping them carefully on one corner of her big white apron.

The two of us sat at the round table in her kitchen as the last of the afternoon sun slanted in from the window. I studied the full, curved bins of her worktable, where Mrs. Toda stored her supplies of rice and flour. She studied her pet canary as it hopped restlessly in its golden cage.

"What can we do?" she murmured. Then, suddenly, she brightened. "I have an idea," she said, chuckling at the wickedness of it. "Now listen carefully and do exactly as I tell you."

"What? Tell me," I urged.

"The next time Mr. Okada comes, get your mama's broom and set it upside down on its handle."

She looked to see if I understood. I nodded.

"And then put a dust cloth over the sweeping end."

"And then?"

"Then, just wait for him to leave."

"That's all? Will it really make him go?"

Mrs. Toda nodded. "It is an old Japanese superstition. I've tried it once or twice myself."

"And did it work for you?"

"Always," she said confidently.

I didn't wait to hear any more. If Mr. Okada was still sitting in our living room, I might just have time before Mama had to start supper.

I ran home, went to the crack at the door, and looked into the living room from the kitchen. Mr. Okada was still there. He was staring moodily into his teacup, and my mother was patiently knitting, waiting for him to say something or take his leave.

I flung open the broom closet and quickly set up my silent oblation[13] to Mrs. Toda's antisocial deity. "Oh broom," I whispered. "Get to work!"

In the next fifteen minutes I made dozens of trips between the broom closet and the crack at the door. Still, Mr. Okada sat. Finally, I decided that the broom couldn't exert its occult powers over anything while shut up inside a closet. It would have to be moved as close to Mr. Okada as possible without my actually marching into the living room with it. I decided to set it up at the crack of the door. This obstructed my own

view, but I was willing to put up with this small inconvenience for the sake of expediency. Stooping down low to cast my own evil eye on Mr. Okada as well, I caught a narrow glimpse of him, looking now in my direction.

"Oh broom," I muttered, "get to work!"

In a very few minutes Mr. Okada rose, bowed to my mother, and thanked her for the tea. "I must go now," he said.

"You will not stay to supper then?" she asked.

"Thank you, no," he murmured. And he was gone.

"Mama! Mama!" I shouted as I plummeted into the living room. "I did it! It worked. I got rid of him for you. It really worked!"

My mother didn't know what I was talking about. I knew she was puzzled by Mr. Okada's unexpected departure, but I knew she was not displeased.

I danced around and around the living room, freed at last from Mr. Okada's murky presence. Overwhelmed with my new-found powers and filled with joy over my small triumph, it never once occurred to me that the crack at the door afforded a view into the kitchen as well as out or that poor Mr. Okada might have known a few old Japanese superstitions himself. ॐ

---

13. **oblation** (ə blā′ shən): a sacrifice to a god.

Words to Know and Use

deity (dē′ ə tē) *n.* a god; a divine being
occult (ə kult′) *adj.* supernatural
expediency (ek spē′ dē ən sē) *n.* suitability for the purpose at hand

555

E X P L A I N

Responding to Reading

First Impressions

1. Jot down your first impression of the narrator in your journal.

Second Thoughts

2. Do you think the narrator was too hard on Mr. Okada? Explain.

3. Why do you think Mrs. Toda shows more sympathy to the narrator than the narrator's mother does?

4. What is your opinion of how the mother handled Mr. Okada's visits? Should she have done anything differently?

5. Do you think Mrs. Toda really believes in the broom superstition?

Writing Options

1. What if this selection were adapted for a television comedy? Write a **plot capsule** for a television magazine.

2. Write a **character sketch** of the narrator from Mr. Okada's viewpoint. Describe how he sees her and what he thinks of her.

Vocabulary Practice

Exercise   Replace each numbered word or phrase with the word from the list that is closest in meaning. Use each word once.

1. He is a **(1) depressed (2) graduate** of a **(3) religious college.**

2. Sal showed **(4) great enthusiasm** by shouting a **(5) rule of conduct** in a **(6) shrill** voice.

3. For the sake of **(7) getting the job done efficiently,** she will **(8) reveal** a **(9) puzzling** clue to the identity of the **(l0) god.**

4. Some, **(11) talking privately** with **(12) supernatural** spirits, use **(13) magic.**

5. Give **(14) comfort** to your **(15) pale** friend.

Words to Know and Use

alumnus
communing
cryptic
deity
divulge
expediency
morose
occult
pallid
precept
seminary
solace
sorcery
strident
zeal

Fiction

The *Medicine Bag*

VIRGINIA DRIVING HAWK SNEVE

Examine What You Know

Most people in the United States can trace their roots to one or several ethnic groups. Their ethnic heritage may lead to a country in Africa, Europe, or Latin America, or perhaps to a Native American people. How important is your ethnic background to you? Do you take pride in your ethnic heritage, or are you unconcerned about it? Do you know what your ethnic heritage is? Jot down your thoughts in your journal or notebook.

Expand Your Knowledge

The narrator in this story traces part of his heritage to the Sioux, a Native American people. The Sioux are North American Plains Indians who gained fame for their skill in hunting and battle (their chiefs included Sitting Bull and Crazy Horse).

During the 1800s the Sioux gradually lost their land—and their independence—to white settlers.

Site of Sioux ceremonial Sun Dance near Rosebud, South Dakota.

After being defeated by the U.S. Army, the Sioux were herded onto reservations where they were forced to change their way of living and where many of their customs gradually died out. Today most of the Sioux still live on reservations in North and South Dakota, Montana, and Nebraska. Their lives are far different from those of their ancestors, and many of them live in poverty. The great-grandfather in this story comes from the Rosebud Reservation in South Dakota, where eighteen thousand Sioux live.

Enrich Your Reading

Making Connections   As you read, think about how the narrator's experiences with his relatives and friends compare with your own. Try to remember situations from your own life that may help you understand the narrator's feelings.

■ *Author biography on Extend page*

The Medicine Bag

VIRGINIA DRIVING HAWK SNEVE

My kid sister Cheryl and I always bragged about our Sioux grandpa, Joe Iron Shell. Our friends, who had always lived in the city and knew about Indians only from movies and TV, were impressed by our stories. Maybe we exaggerated and made Grandpa and the reservation sound glamorous, but when we'd return home to Iowa after our yearly summer visit to Grandpa, we always had some exciting tale to tell.

We always had some authentic Sioux article to show our listeners. One year Cheryl had new moccasins that Grandpa had made. On another visit he gave me a small, round, flat rawhide drum that was decorated with a painting of a warrior riding a horse. He taught me a real Sioux chant to sing while I beat the drum with a leather-covered stick that had a feather on the end. Man, that really made an impression.

We never showed our friends Grandpa's picture. Not that we were ashamed of him, but because we knew that the glamorous tales we told didn't go with the real thing. Our friends would have laughed at the picture because Grandpa wasn't tall and stately like TV Indians. His hair wasn't in braids but hung in stringy gray strands on his neck, and he was old. He was our great-grandfather, and he didn't live in a tepee but all by himself in a part log, part tar-paper shack on the Rosebud Reservation in South Dakota. So when Grandpa came to visit us, I was so ashamed and embarrassed I could've died.

There are a lot of yippy poodles and other fancy little dogs in our neighborhood, but they usually barked singly at the mailman from the safety of their own yards. Now it sounded as if a whole pack of mutts were barking together in one place.

I got up and walked to the curb to see what the commotion was. About a block away I saw a crowd of little kids yelling, with the dogs yipping and growling around someone who was walking down the middle of the street.

I watched the group as it slowly came closer and saw that in the center of the strange procession was a man wearing a tall black hat. He'd pause now and then to peer at something in his hand and then at the houses on either side of the street. I felt cold and hot at the same time as I recognized the man. "Oh, no!" I whispered. "It's Grandpa!"

I stood on the curb, unable to move, even though I wanted to run and hide. Then I got mad when I saw how the yippy dogs were growling and nipping at the old man's baggy pant legs and how wearily he poked them away with his cane. "Stupid mutts," I said as I ran to rescue Grandpa.

When I kicked and hollered at the dogs to get away, they put their tails between their legs and scattered. The kids ran to the curb where they watched me and the old man.

"Grandpa," I said and felt pretty dumb when my voice cracked. I reached for his beat-up old tin suitcase, which was tied shut with a rope. But he set it down right in the street and shook my hand.

"*Hau, Takoza,* Grandchild," he greeted me formally in Sioux.

All I could do was stand there with the whole neighborhood watching and shake the hand of the leather-brown old man. I saw how his gray hair straggled from under his big black hat, which had a drooping feather in its crown. His rumpled black suit hung like a sack over his stooped frame. As he shook my hand, his coat fell open to expose a bright red satin shirt with a beaded bolo tie under the collar. His get-up wasn't out of place on the reservation, but it sure was here, and I wanted to sink right through the pavement.

"Hi," I muttered with my head down. I tried to pull my hand away when I felt his bony hand trembling and looked up to see fatigue in his face. I felt like crying. I couldn't think of anything to say, so I picked up Grandpa's suitcase, took his arm, and guided him up the driveway to our house.

Mom was standing on the steps. I don't know how long she'd been watching, but her hand was over her mouth, and she looked as if she couldn't believe what she saw. Then she ran to us.

"Grandpa," she gasped. "How in the world did you get here?"

CHESTER MEDICINE CROW IN HIS RESERVATION HAT 1973 © James Bama   Courtesy, Big Horn Gallery, Cody, Wyoming.

She checked her move to embrace Grandpa, and I remembered that such a display of affection is unseemly to the Sioux and would embarrass him.

"*Hau,* Marie," he said as he shook Mom's hand. She smiled and took his other arm.

As we supported him up the steps, the door banged open and Cheryl came bursting out of the house. She was all smiles and

Words to Know and Use

fatigue (fə tēg′) *n.* extreme weariness or exhaustion
unseemly (un sēm′ lē) *adj.* not decent or proper

559

was so obviously glad to see Grandpa that I was ashamed of how I felt.

"Grandpa!" she yelled happily. "You came to see us!"

Grandpa smiled, and Mom and I let go of him as he stretched out his arms to my ten-year-old sister, who was still young enough to be hugged.

"Wicincala, little girl," he greeted her and then collapsed.

He had fainted. Mom and I carried him into her sewing room, where we had a spare bed.

After we had Grandpa on the bed, Mom stood there helplessly patting his shoulder.

"Shouldn't we call the doctor, Mom?" I suggested, since she didn't seem to know what to do.

"Yes," she agreed with a sigh. "You make Grandpa comfortable, Martin."

I reluctantly moved to the bed. I knew Grandpa wouldn't want to have Mom undress him, but I didn't want to, either. He was so skinny and frail that his coat slipped off easily. When I loosened his tie and opened his shirt collar, I felt a small leather pouch that hung from a thong around his neck. I left it alone and moved to remove his boots. The scuffed old cowboy boots were tight, and he moaned as I put pressure on his legs to jerk them off.

I put the boots on the floor and saw why they fit so tight. Each one was stuffed with money. I looked at the bills that lined the boots and started to ask about them, but Grandpa's eyes were closed again.

Mom came back with a basin of water. "The doctor thinks Grandpa is suffering from heat exhaustion," she explained as she bathed Grandpa's face. Mom gave a big sigh, *"Oh, hinh,* Martin. How do you suppose he got here?"

We found out after the doctor's visit. Grandpa was angrily sitting up in bed while Mom tried to feed him some soup.

"Tonight you let Marie feed you, Grandpa," spoke my dad, who had gotten home from work just as the doctor was leaving. "You're not really sick," he said as he gently pushed Grandpa back against the pillows. "The doctor said you just got too tired and hot after your long trip."

Grandpa relaxed, and between sips of soup, he told us of his journey. Soon after our visit to him, Grandpa decided that he would like to see where his only living descendants lived and what our home was like. Besides, he admitted sheepishly, he was lonesome after we left.

I knew that everybody felt as guilty as I did—especially Mom. Mom was all Grandpa had left. So even after she married my dad, who's a white man and teaches in the college in our city, and after Cheryl and I were born, Mom made sure that every summer we spent a week with Grandpa.

I never thought that Grandpa would be lonely after our visits, and none of us noticed how old and weak he had become. But Grandpa knew, and so he came to us. He had ridden on buses for two and a half days. When he arrived in the city, tired and stiff from sitting so long, he set out, walking, to find us.

Words to Know and Use

reluctantly (ri luk′ tənt lē) *adv.* unwillingly
descendant (dē sen′ dənt) *n.* an immediate or remote offspring of a person

He had stopped to rest on the steps of some building downtown, and a policeman found him. The cop, according to Grandpa, was a good man who took him to the bus stop and waited until the bus came and told the driver to let Grandpa out at Bell View Drive. After Grandpa got off the bus, he started walking again. But he couldn't see the house numbers on the other side when he walked on the sidewalk, so he walked in the middle of the street. That's when all the little kids and dogs followed him.

I knew everybody felt as bad as I did. Yet I was so proud of this eighty-six-year-old man who had never been away from the reservation, having the courage to travel so far alone.

"You found the money in my boots?" he asked Mom.

"Martin did," she answered, and roused herself to scold. "Grandpa, you shouldn't have carried so much money. What if someone had stolen it from you?"

Grandpa laughed. "I would've known if anyone had tried to take the boots off my feet. The money is what I've saved for a long time—a hundred dollars—for my funeral. But you take it now to buy groceries so that I won't be a burden to you while I am here."

"That won't be necessary, Grandpa," Dad said. "We are honored to have you with us, and you will never be a burden. I am only sorry that we never thought to bring you home with us this summer and spare you the discomfort of a long trip."

Grandpa was pleased. "Thank you," he answered. "But do not feel bad that you didn't bring me with you, for I would not have come then. It was not time." He said this in such a way that no one could argue

with him. To Grandpa and the Sioux, he once told me, a thing would be done when it was the right time to do it, and that's the way it was.

"Also," Grandpa went on, looking at me, "I have come because it is soon time for Martin to have the medicine bag."

We all knew what that meant. Grandpa thought he was going to die, and he had to follow the tradition of his family to pass the medicine bag, along with its history, to the oldest male child.

"Even though the boy," he said, still looking at me, "bears a white man's name, the medicine bag will be his."

I didn't know what to say. I had the same hot and cold feeling that I had when I first saw Grandpa in the street. The medicine bag was the dirty leather pouch I had found around his neck. "I could never wear such a thing," I almost said aloud. I thought of having my friends see it in gym class or at the swimming pool and could imagine the smart things they would say. But I just swallowed hard and took a step toward the bed. I knew I would have to take it.

But Grandpa was tired. "Not now, Martin," he said, waving his hand in dismissal. "It is not time. Now I will sleep."

So that's how Grandpa came to be with us for two months. My friends kept asking to come see the old man, but I put them off. I told myself that I didn't want them laughing at Grandpa. But even as I made excuses, I knew it wasn't Grandpa that I was afraid they'd laugh at.

Nothing bothered Cheryl about bringing her friends to see Grandpa. Every day after school started, there'd be a crew of giggling little girls or round-eyed little boys crowded around the old man on the patio, where he'd gotten in the habit of sitting every afternoon.

Grandpa would smile in his gentle way and patiently answer their questions, or he'd tell them stories of brave warriors, ghosts, and animals; and the kids listened in awed silence. Those little guys thought Grandpa was great.

I was so proud of him and amazed at how respectfully quiet my buddies were.

Finally, one day after school, my friends came home with me because nothing I said stopped them. "We're going to see the great Indian of Bell View Drive," said Hank, who was supposed to be my best friend. "My brother has seen him three times, so he oughta be well enough to see us."

When we got to my house, Grandpa was sitting on the patio. He had on his red shirt, but today he also wore a fringed leather vest that was decorated with beads. Instead of his usual cowboy boots, he had solidly beaded moccasins on his feet that stuck out of his black trousers. Of course, he had his old black hat on—he was seldom without it. But it had been brushed, and the feather in the beaded headband was proudly erect, its tip a brighter white. His hair lay in silver strands over the red shirt collar.

I stared just as my friends did, and I heard one of them murmur, "Wow!"

Grandpa looked up, and when his eyes met mine, they twinkled as if he were laughing inside. He nodded to me, and my face got all hot. I could tell that he had known all along I was afraid he'd embarrass me in front of my friends.

"*Hau, hoksilas,* boys," he greeted and held out his hand.

My buddies passed in a single file and shook his hand as I introduced them. They were so polite I almost laughed. "How, there, Grandpa," and even a "How-do-you-do, sir."

"You look fine, Grandpa," I said as the guys sat on the lawn chairs or on the patio floor.

"*Hanh,* yes," he agreed. "When I woke up this morning, it seemed the right time to dress in the good clothes. I knew that my grandson would be bringing his friends."

"You guys want some lemonade or something?" I offered. No one answered. They were listening to Grandpa as he started telling how he'd killed the deer from which his vest was made.

Grandpa did most of the talking while my friends were there. I was so proud of him and amazed at how respectfully quiet my buddies were. Mom had to chase them home at supper time. As they left, they shook Grandpa's hand again and said to me,

"Martin, he's really great!"

"Yeah, man! Don't blame you for keeping him to yourself."

"Can we come back?"

But after they left, Mom said, "No more visitors for a while, Martin. Grandpa won't admit it, but his strength hasn't returned. He likes having company, but it tires him."

That evening Grandpa called me to his room before he went to sleep. "Tomorrow," he said, "when you come home, it will be time to give you the medicine bag."

I felt a hard squeeze from where my heart is supposed to be and was scared, but I answered, "OK, Grandpa."

All night I had weird dreams about thunder and lightning on a high hill. From a distance I heard the slow beat of a drum. When I woke up in the morning, I felt as if I hadn't slept at all. At school it seemed as if the day would never end, and when it finally did, I ran home.

Grandpa was in his room, sitting on the bed. The shades were down, and the place was dim and cool. I sat on the floor in front of Grandpa, but he didn't even look at me. After what seemed a long time, he spoke.

"I sent your mother and sister away. What you will hear today is only for a man's ears. What you will receive is only for a man's hands." He fell silent, and I felt shivers down my back.

"My father in his early manhood," Grandpa began, "made a vision quest to find a spirit guide for his life. You cannot understand how it was in that time when the great Teton Sioux were first made to stay on the reservation. There was a strong need for guidance from *Wakantanka,* the Great Spirit. But too many of the young men were filled with despair and hatred. They thought it was hopeless to search for a vision when the glorious life was gone and only the hated <u>confines</u> of a reservation lay ahead. But my father held to the old ways.

"He carefully prepared for his quest with a purifying sweat bath, and then he went alone to a high butte[1] top to fast and pray. After three days he received his sacred dream—in which he found, after long searching, the white man's iron. He did not understand his vision of finding something belonging to the white people, for in that time they were the enemy. When he came down from the butte to cleanse himself at the stream below, he found the remains of a campfire and the broken shell of an iron kettle. This was a sign that reinforced his dream. He took a piece of the iron for his medicine bag, which he had made of elk skin years before, to prepare for his quest.

"He returned to his village, where he told his dream to the wise old men of the tribe. They gave him the name Iron Shell, but neither did they understand the meaning of the dream. The first Iron Shell kept the piece of iron with him at all times and believed it gave him protection from the evils of those unhappy days.

"Then a terrible thing happened to Iron Shell. He and several other young men were taken from their homes by the soldiers and sent far away to a white man's boarding school. He was angry and lonesome for his parents and the young girl he had wed before he was taken away. At first Iron Shell resisted the teacher's attempts to change him, and he did not try to learn. One day it was his turn to work in the school's blacksmith shop. As he walked into the place, he

---

1. **butte** (byo͞ot): a flat-topped hill rising from flatland.

Words to Know and Use | **confines** (kän' fīnz') *n.* limits; boundaries

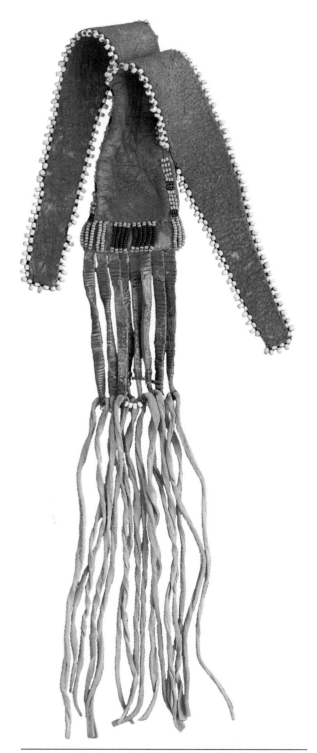

Small beaded pouch   about 1915   Private collection.
Photo by Benson L. Lanford and Robert W. Gilmore.

knew that his medicine had brought him there to learn and work with the white man's iron.

"Iron Shell became a blacksmith and worked at the trade when he returned to the reservation. All of his life he treasured the medicine bag. When he was old and I was a man, he gave it to me, for no one made the vision quest any more."

Grandpa quit talking, and I stared in disbelief as he covered his face with his hands. His shoulders were shaking with quiet sobs, and I looked away until he began to speak again.

"I kept the bag until my son, your mother's father, was a man and had to leave us to fight in the war across the ocean. I gave him the bag, for I believed it would protect him in battle, but he did not take it with him. He was afraid that he would lose it. He died in a faraway place."

Again Grandpa was still, and I felt his grief around me.

"My son," he went on after clearing his throat, "had only a daughter, and it is not proper for her to know of these things."

He unbuttoned his shirt, pulled out the leather pouch, and lifted it over his head. He held it in his hand, turning it over and over as if memorizing how it looked.

"In the bag," he said as he opened it and removed two objects, "is the broken shell of the iron kettle, a pebble from the butte, and a piece of the sacred sage." He held the pouch upside down and dust drifted down.

"After the bag is yours, you must put a piece of prairie sage within and never open it again until you pass it on to your son." He replaced the pebble and the piece of iron and tied the bag.

I stood up, somehow knowing I should. Grandpa slowly rose from the bed and stood upright in front of me holding the bag before my face. I closed my eyes and waited for him to slip it over my head. But he spoke.

"No, you need not wear it." He placed the soft leather bag in my right hand and closed my other hand over it. "It would not be right to wear it in this time and place where no one will understand. Put it safely away until you are again on the reservation. Wear it then, when you replace the sacred sage."

Grandpa turned and sat again on the bed. Wearily he leaned his head against the pillow. "Go," he said. "I will sleep now."

"Thank you, Grandpa," I said softly, and left with the bag in my hands.

That night Mom and Dad took Grandpa to the hospital. Two weeks later I stood alone on the lonely prairie of the reservation and put the sacred sage in my medicine bag. ❧

I N S I G H T

Looking North to Taos

RUDY BANTISTA

I saw the pueblo beneath the blue
mountain, the older
buildings crumbling,
melting into mud. I watched
the old men, their heads
hidden beneath blankets,
and I wondered.

I have heard the round dance songs
from a thousand miles away,
have held the record cover in my
hands and seen the young boys
pictured on the back, their braids
long, their smiles not showing.
And I have wondered.

I sit still in the cool grass
toward evening,
legs crossed and tongue silent,
thinking as I look into the
dancing supper fires, "Am I
an Indian?" And I wonder.

CLIFF DWELLINGS NO. 3   1927
Raymond Jonson   Collection of Jonson Gallery
of the University of New Mexico, Albuquerque.

Responding to Reading

First Impressions

1. What thoughts went through your mind at the end of the story? Describe them in your journal or notebook.

Second Thoughts

2. What doors of understanding were opened for the narrator as a result of Grandpa's actions?

   Think about
   • how his opinion of Grandpa changes
   • why he put the sacred sage in his medicine bag

3. Do you admire Grandpa? Explain why or why not.

4. What connections were you able to make between your own experiences and the narrator's experiences?

5. Do the narrator in "The Medicine Bag" and the speaker in "Looking North to Taos" have similar feelings about their Native American heritage? Explain your answer.

Broader Connections

6. What difficulties do you think Native Americans face in the effort to continue their traditions? Use "The Medicine Bag" and your own knowledge as examples.

Literary Concept: Internal Conflict

An **internal conflict** occurs when a character has a struggle within himself or herself. Explain the internal conflict that the narrator faces. Is the conflict resolved? How?

Concept Review: Exposition   The exposition introduces the setting, the main characters, and the conflict. What do you learn about the narrator's internal conflict from the exposition?

Writing Options

1. Imagine that the narrator grows up and has a son of his own. Write a **dialogue** about the time when he passes the medicine bag to his son.

2. Write a **song lyric** to tell the story of Grandpa and his gift. The lyric should also convey your own feelings about Grandpa.

3. Write a **comparison and contrast paper** that explains the similarities and differences between Grandpa and the "TV Indians" described on page 558.

4. Research the details of a vision quest, which can be found in books about the Sioux. Create a **booklet** to share your findings.

Vocabulary Practice

Exercise Use your understanding of the boldfaced word to complete each of the following sentences. Write the letter of the word or phrase that best completes the sentence.

1. The narrator's **descendant** would be born (a) the same year as he was   (b) before him   (c) after him.

2. If the narrator greeted Grandpa **reluctantly,** his manner would show (a) excitement   (b) a lack of enthusiasm (c) bitter anger.

3. The **confines** of a reservation might be shown by (a) lines on a map   (b) photographs of daily life   (c) the tired faces of residents.

4. Grandpa would regard being hugged by his grown daughter as an **unseemly** display of affection because (a) he is too old for strong feelings   (b) the Sioux are not expected to show feelings toward adults openly   (c) he would be afraid of how it would look.

5. Grandpa's **fatigue** is most obvious when (a) he decides to take a bus trip   (b) he collapses   (c) he tells stories of his past glory.

> *Words to Know and Use*
>
> **confines**
> **descendant**
> **fatigue**
> **reluctantly**
> **unseemly**

Options for Learning

1 • Native American Update With a partner, investigate living conditions among modern Native Americans. What special problems and challenges do they face? What is being done to help them? Report your findings, using the format of a radio news show.

2 • Ethnic Profile As an extension of your prereading activities, work in a small group to conduct an ethnic poll in your class. Identify the different ethnic heritages in your classroom, and find out how important each student's ethnic background is to him or her. Your poll can take the form of a questionnaire or of individual interviews. When the poll is completed, give an oral report on the results.

3 • Keeping the Past Interview one of your grandparents or someone else's grandparent. Find out what objects or mementos hold a special meaning in his or her life and why. Report your findings to the class.

4 • Your Own Medicine Bag Choose three or four ordinary objects that you think represent your life or your destiny. Then make a bag for them, complete with a string or rope. Explain the significance of the objects to the class.

 FACT FINDER GEOGRAPHY

What two large rivers run through the Rosebud Reservation in South Dakota?

Virginia Driving Hawk Sneve
1933–

Virginia Driving Hawk Sneve grew up in a family she describes as "secure, warm, and loving" on the Sioux Rosebud Reservation in South Dakota. "I never realized that I was an Indian," she reports, "until I went to college at South Dakota State University. It was a shock to realize I was different. People expected me not to speak English well and to wear feathers and beads."

Sneve began to write as a way of correcting people's misconceptions of Native Americans. Her first book, *Jimmy Yellow Hawk,* was awarded the Interracial Council for Minority Books for Children Award. The award gave her the confidence to continue writing. Since then, she has gone on to write eleven more books. "The Medicine Bag" is based on the experience of a friend whose grandmother left her reservation for the first time to visit her family in Minneapolis.

Sneve writes in the summer and works as a counselor at Rapid City Central High School in South Dakota during the school year.

INFORMATIVE WRITING

Doors of understanding open when we learn about the customs of others. In this subunit you've read about traditions in Puerto Rico, a superstition from Japan, and customs of the Sioux. Now you can deepen your understanding as you **research**—use outside sources to locate information about—a custom that interests you. You'll use **informative** writing—writing that explains facts and ideas—to prepare a brief report about the custom you've chosen.

USE INFORMATIVE
WRITING FOR
reports
histories
biographies
instructions
explanations
analyses

Here is one writer's PASSkey to this assignment.

GUIDED ASSIGNMENT: RESEARCH REPORT

Write an informative report about an interesting custom of a specific group of people.

PURPOSE: To inform

AUDIENCE: Classmates, teachers, and friends

SUBJECT: An interesting custom

STRUCTURE: Research report

The Prophet's Birthday
by Michael Deddeh

A new star shone in the sky the night he was born. Angels gathered, and his mother received a gift of gold. These tales commemorate Maulid-an-Nabi, the birthday of the prophet Muhammad. Muslims in Lebanon especially enjoy celebrating this traditional holiday.

Muhammad believed in generosity. He was born in the Arabian city of Mecca, around A.D. 570. As he grew up, the things that happened to poorer people upset him. He went into the mountains to meditate about the problem. There, in a vision, an angel said Muhammad was to be God's prophet. The angel gave Muhammad messages, which were later

STUDENT MODEL

Before you write, read how one student responded to the assignment.

The custom and people are identified in the introduction.

recorded in the Koran, a holy book. The Koran says people should give to the poor. Over the years Muhammad had more visions and founded a new religion, Islam. Muslims around the world now celebrate his birthday in September.

In Lebanon, Maulid-an-Nabi brings nine days of fun and generosity in honor of Muhammad. There are parades and fairs. People give gifts and food to the needy. Families invite friends to share huge meals that start with tabbouleh, a salad of chopped mint, parsley, onions, tomatoes, and cooked wheat. Next comes roast chicken with a special stuffing of ground lamb, rice, and spices. For dessert, there is baklava, a pastry with honey and pine nuts. Later in the evenings, people tell the story of Muhammad's birth.

The story says that a bright star appeared over Mecca on that night long ago. Seven thousand angels brought a beautiful gift: a golden bowl of dew for Muhammad's mother to bathe him in. This story shows the spirit of happiness and generosity that Lebanese Muslims feel on the prophet's birthday.

Bibliography

Adams, Charles J. "Islam." The World Book Encyclopedia. 1990 ed.

Dooley, Leticia. Customs Around the World. New York: Grove, 1982.

Khoury, C. "September in Lebanon." Junior Scholastic Sept. 1992: 19-21.

The transitions *later, over the years,* and *now* keep readers oriented in time.

A topic sentence states the main idea of the paragraph.

Details support the main idea.

The conclusion sums up feelings about the custom.

Now that you've read Michael's paper, it's time to begin your own.

Prewrite and Explore

1 **Browse around**   If you need a writing idea, a trip to the library can help you find customs to write about. Since many customs are based on religious beliefs, you might locate an encyclopedia and look up a specific religion, such as Judaism, Hinduism, or Buddhism.

The article you find may have headings for customs and celebrations. You also might browse through books shelved under the Dewey Decimal number 394. These deal with customs and traditions. As you browse, you can make a list of customs that interest you.

2 Make a choice and research it   From your list, choose the custom that interests you most. Skim books and articles that might contain information on your topic. When you come to facts and details you can use, slow down and take notes on index cards.

3 Take notes   Begin by recording information about each reference source you use: title, author (if named), name of article (for magazines and encyclopedias), date. This information will be used in the bibliography at the end of your report. Then begin taking notes about your topic, using one note card for each fact or idea that you might want to use in your report. When you take notes, don't copy. Write the ideas in your own words. If you want to record specific words from your source, put them in quotation marks.

4 Get organized   After you gather information, you will be ready to organize it. If you scan your notes, you'll see that most of them relate to a few main ideas. Try grouping your note cards according to these main ideas. You might make an outline of your main ideas and details.

◄ **WRITER'S CHOICE** . . . .
Customs can be associated with holidays, seasons, coming of age, marriage, birth, and death.

◄ **REMINDER** . . . .
Try using the *Readers' Guide* to locate magazine articles about your topic.

◄ **WRITER'S CHOICE** . . . .
What if a card doesn't relate to any of your main ideas? You may want to use it as a starting point for researching a new idea, or you may decide not to use it at all.

◄ **STUDENT MODEL** . . . .

◄ **IN OTHER CLASSES** . . . .
In social studies you can use outlining to organize class notes and information from your textbook when you study for essay tests.

ORGANIZING INFORMATION

When you make an outline, you arrange ideas in a logical order. The main idea of each note-card group can become a main heading in your outline. The supporting facts on each note card can become subheadings. Study the portion of Michael's outline below.

```
The Prophet's Birthday
   I. Introduction
  II. Muhammad's belief in generosity
      A. Sympathy for the suffering of the poor
      B. Koran's commandment to help the needy
 III. Fun and treats on Muhammad's birthday
      A. Parades and fairs
      B. Gifts to the poor
      C. Family feasts
      D. Storytelling
```

Draft and Discover

NEED MORE HELP?
For more about topic sentences and supporting details, see the Reader's Workshop on page 577.

1 **Use your outline to plan paragraphs** Your outline is a blueprint for paragraphs. Each main heading suggests a topic sentence, and subheadings suggest the details that will complete a paragraph. Don't, however, let your outline stop your thinking. As you write, you may get good ideas that aren't part of your outline. It's fine to include them. If you want to stop writing and do more research first, go ahead.

COMPUTER TIP
Some computer programs have a split-screen feature. You can use it to keep your outline on the screen for reference as you draft.

2 **Use transitions** In your outline, numbers and letters show how ideas relate. When you turn your outline into an essay, you need to replace the numbers and letters with **transitions**—words and phrases that show relationships of time, space, or logic.

3 **Name your sources** At the end of your draft, add a list of the sources you used. This list, referred to as either a **bibliography** or **works cited,** backs up your facts and lets readers find more information if they want to. For bibliography guidelines, see Research and Report Writing in the Writer's Handbook.

Revise Your Writing

WRITING TIP
Remember, you can do more research at any time.

1 **Adjust the focus** As you reread your draft, decide your main feeling about the custom. With that focus in mind, you can fine-tune the organization of your report. You may decide to insert key words, rearrange paragraphs, add more details to some parts, or omit parts. Next, write a short introduction, perhaps using attention-catching details related to your focus.

2 **Wrap it up** Your conclusion may be a brief paragraph summing up the main ideas in your report, emphasizing the importance of the custom, or describing your feelings about it.

IT'S THE LAW!
Plagiarism, the use of someone else's words as if they were your own, is against the law. Even when you've named your sources, be sure to state ideas in your own words.

3 **Listen for smoothness** You do not want your report to sound like an encyclopedia article. Instead, your sentences should reflect your own writing voice. They should flow naturally. Consider combining sentences or sentence parts to smooth out choppy places. When you're ready, ask a peer to read your draft. Use the checklists below.

Revision Questions

For You	For a Peer Reader
1. Have I included the details I found most interesting?	**1.** Which parts of my report are most vivid to you?
2. Could I add transitions to help my readers stay oriented?	**2.** Do all parts of my report reflect my own writing voice?
3. Could I combine sentences to make my report smoother?	**3.** What did you learn from my report?

Proofread

Check your report carefully for errors in grammar and mechanics.

THE EDITOR'S EYE: PROOFREADING

To proofread for spelling errors, start at the end of your paper and work toward the beginning. Proofreading symbols make it easy to note needed changes.

Problem Muhammad beleived in generousity.
Revised Muhammad believed in generosity.

NEED MORE HELP?
See the Language Workshop on pages 574-576.

Publish and Present

Custom Fair   With your teacher's help, plan a custom fair. Class members can bring appropriate illustrations, costumes, objects, or foods to display with their reports.

Reflect on Your Writing

Answer the following questions on a separate sheet of paper, then add the paper to your report. Place your report in your portfolio.

FOR YOUR PORTFOLIO

1. If you had more time, what would you change in your report?
2. Did you prefer the research or the writing?

PROOFREADING SKILLS

When you proofread, you focus on correcting errors. You look at grammar, spelling, punctuation, and capitalization. For a research report you also double-check your facts, dates, statistics, and source information.

▶ When you proofread, you should have a dictionary handy so you can check the spelling of words you're not sure of. You may find it easier to proofread several times, looking for a different kind of problem each time. To avoid being distracted by content, begin proofreading at the end of your paper and work toward the beginning.

The list below shows nine common types of errors. Make a habit of double-checking those that crop up often in your writing.

COMPUTER TIP

Some software has a feature that checks spelling. It can be fooled by words that sound alike, so double-check these. (See the Language Workshop on pages 344–346.)

PROOFREADING CHECKLIST

1. Do all my data (facts, statistics, and so on) match what I have in my notes?

2. Have I avoided sentence fragments and run-on sentences?

3. Do all my verbs agree with their subjects? Do my tense shifts make sense?

4. Do I use the correct subject and object forms of pronouns?

5. Each time I've joined two complete sentences, have I used a comma and an appropriate conjunction?

6. Is the first sentence in each of my paragraphs indented?

7. Do all sentences and proper nouns begin with capital letters?

8. Have I used commas, periods, and quotation marks correctly?

9. Have I checked my spelling, including words that sound alike?

PUNCTUATION TIP

▶ Watch out for unnecessary commas! Review the rules for using commas in the Language Handbook, pages 775–780. Then be sure to use commas only where they're needed.

Proofreading Symbols

The following symbols can remind you of changes to make when you recopy your draft.

Symbol	Meaning	Example
∧	Add letters or words.	1) He walked. *(slowly inserted)*
⊙	Add a period.	2) He walked slowly⊙
≡	Capitalize a letter.	3) His name was muhammad.
⌒	Close up space.	4) They serve fruit cakes.
⌃	Add a comma.	5) On his way back, he stopped.
/	Make a capital letter lowercase.	6) He looked at the Shrine.
¶	Begin a new paragraph.	7) at night. Usually, the journey
∼	Switch the positions of letters or words.	8) He never has been wrong.
℘	Take out letters or words.	9) We welcomed him gladly.

Michael used the symbols when he proofread his final paragraph.

> The story says that a bright star appeared over
> mecca on that night long ago. Seven thousand
> angles brought a beautiful gift: golden a bowl of dew
> for Muhammad's mother to bathe him in. This story
> shows the spirit of happiness and generosity that
> Lebanese Muslims feel on the prophet's birthday.

◀ STUDENT MODEL ....

After you've proofread and marked a draft, you can recopy it, being sure to make all the corrections indicated. Then check the new copy—sometimes new errors creep in. A friend may be able to spot them more easily than you can at this point.

Exercise 1   Concept Check   Use the proofreading checklist to find mistakes in the paragraph below. (Hint: There are fourteen errors.) Then recopy the paragraph, correcting each error you found. Double-check your copy to be sure there are no new errors, and correct any you find.

In Denmark the custom of wearing costumes on the last monday before Lent have been popular for centuries. Schools are closed on this special day. Called Fastelavn. The night before Fastelavn, families buy or bake big, round rolls made with butter, sugar, raisins, pieces of candied fruit peel. On the morning of Fastelavn, children dress in they're masks and costumes and go from door to door as U.S. children do on Halloween night. They carry small money boxes. At each door they sang a traditonal song, threatening to make mischeif if they were not given sweet rolls to eat and money to put in their boxes. Later they use the money to buy candy, pastries, and soda. That evening, everybody eats their fill at big family dinners. Long ago, this was a last feast before the long fasting period of Lent. Few Danes today still give up his or her favorite foods during Lent, all Danish children still celabrate Fastelavn.

Exercise 2   Proofreading Your Writing   Using the checklist in this workshop, proofread the research report you wrote for the Writer's Workshop on pages 569–573. Use the proofreading symbols to mark errors. Then make a clean copy of your report, correcting your errors.

Exercise 3   Proofreading Your Writing   Using the proofreading checklist and symbols, proofread two other papers in your portfolio. Then answer the questions and follow the directions below.

1. In which of the nine problem areas did you find errors in your research report?
2. In the three papers you proofread, what is the total number of errors you found in each problem area?
3. Based on the number of errors you found in each area, list three areas you think you should focus on when proofreading your work in the future.

MAIN IDEAS AND SUPPORTING DETAILS

Informative writing deals with ideas. Each paragraph is a group of sentences about one idea—the **main idea.** Often the main idea of a paragraph is stated in a **topic sentence.** The other sentences contain **supporting details,** or details that relate to the main idea. When you revise reports and other informational pieces, you need to decide exactly what main idea each of your paragraphs is presenting. Then you will be able to figure out which kinds of details and transitions will strengthen the paragraph. Delete any sentences that don't refer to the main idea. Also, be sure to start a new paragraph when you begin to write about a new idea.

Writers often state the main idea at the beginning of a paragraph. The supporting details follow, explaining or illustrating the main idea. However, some paragraphs (such as this one) start with supporting details and build toward a main idea in the last sentence. The topic sentence, then, may come either first or last in a paragraph.

In some cases, a paragraph does not contain a topic sentence. The main idea is not stated directly; it is **implied,** or suggested, by the details in the paragraph. Writers use this technique to emphasize a main idea and to encourage readers to think about it for themselves.

◀ **EXCEPTION**
When a paragraph about one idea gets very long, you can give your readers a mental and visual rest by dividing it into two paragraphs.

◀ **READING TIP**
To understand an implied main idea, you must make an inference based on the details in the paragraph. For more about making inferences, see the Reader's Workshop on page 66.

Exercise 1   For each paragraph listed below, write the sentence that states the main idea and the sentences that contain supporting details. Be ready to explain your decisions.

1. Paragraph 7 of "Primary Lessons," on page 540.
2. Paragraph 11 of "The Medicine Bag," on page 559.

Exercise 2   Reread the last paragraph of "Primary Lessons," on page 545, and answer the questions below.

1. What details appear in the paragraph?
2. How would you state the main idea implied by the paragraph?
3. How might the effect of the paragraph have been different if the author had stated the main idea directly?

Exercise 3   Looking at Your Writing   Reread the report you wrote for the Writer's Workshop on pages 569–573. On a sheet of paper, write the main idea of each of your paragraphs. Then list the supporting details that develop each idea.

Reading on Your Own

Suggested Novels for Unit Five

In the novels introduced on these pages, "A Question of Identity" arises for everyone—even the reader!

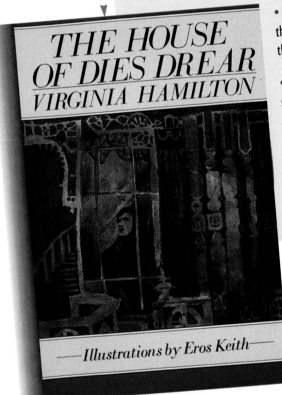

THE HOUSE OF DIES DREAR

VIRGINIA HAMILTON ©1968

Very odd things are happening in the old mansion called Drear House. Built before the Civil War, and once a stopping point on the Underground Railroad, the house has become a new home for a family named Small. However, it seems that someone is not happy that they have moved in. The secret passages behind every wall are filled with a strange sighing noise, and the ancient caretaker, Pluto, is rumored by the local people to be the devil himself! Share young Thomas Small's adventures as he tries to unravel questions of identity. As you read this mystery, think about these questions:

- Are ghosts causing the disturbances in the house?

- What secret is the strange little neighbor girl hiding?

- Could Thomas be running into hidden danger?

THE HOUSE OF DIES DREAR
VIRGINIA HAMILTON

—Illustrations by Eros Keith—

RISK N' ROSES

JAN SLEPIAN ©1990

What would you do to become a member of the "in" crowd? Skip Berman's new idol Jean wants to find out. In this novel set in New York in the 1940s, Jean rules the playground, and her daring makes her extremely attractive and popular. However, she sets up dares as tests for Skip to join the group. When Skip's family embarrasses Skip in front of her new friend, Skip tries to declare her independence from them and ends up questioning her own identity. Jean's interest in Skip's handicapped sister, Angela, causes Skip to decide how far she will go to keep Jean's loyalty. As you read, ask yourself these questions:

* How outrageous will Jean's demands become?

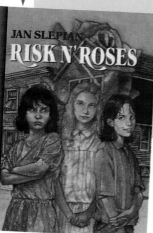

* Will Skip be able to resist Jean's dares?

* Can Skip protect Angela?

THE ADVENTURES OF TOM SAWYER

MARK TWAIN © 1876

This timeless classic is about a young boy in Missouri before the Civil War. Tom Sawyer and his friends hide out on an island, intending to lead new lives as pirates even though their families and the town think that they have drowned. They return home when, unable to resist the temptation, they arrive at their own funerals! In further adventures, Tom and his sweetheart Becky are lost in a cave that holds a murderous secret. Read to find out . . .

* whether Tom's daring will prove to be disaster for his friends

* what Tom does when he becomes a witness to a murder

* how Tom rescues Becky from the cave

Other Recommended Books

Thunderwith by Libby Hathorn (© 1991). In this contemporary novel set in the Australian outback, a girl faces new and difficult relationships. After her mother's death, she must live with her father and his unfriendly wife and children. With the help of a dog, doors of understanding open.

Good Night, Mr. Tom by Michelle Magorian (© 1981). This historical novel is set in England during World War II, when children were being brought to the country to escape the bombing in London. An abused boy learns to live with a gruff but kindly old man.

Dogsong by Gary Paulsen (© 1985). In this contemporary realistic novel, a fourteen-year-old Eskimo boy searches for self-knowledge on a 1400-mile journey by dog sled, alone, across the tundra. On this long journey he finds his own song.

Waiting to Waltz: A Childhood by Cynthia Rylant (© 1984). This book of poetry follows the author's search for her own identity as she grows up in a small town in West Virginia.

579

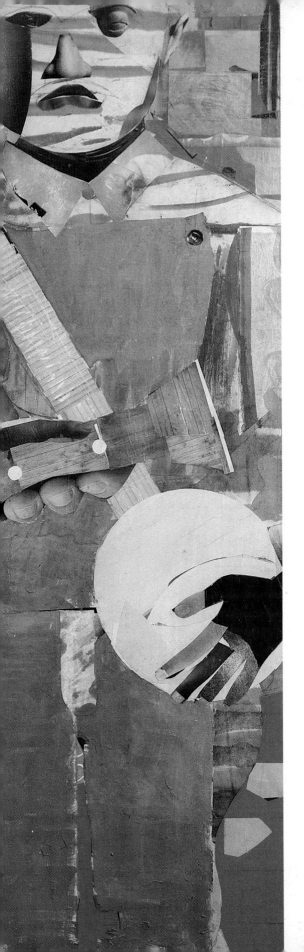

THEMES IN WORLD FOLKLORE

These are the stories that never, never die, that are carried like seed into a new country.

Meridel Le Sueur

THREE FOLK MUSICIANS   1967
Romare Bearden   Courtesy, The Estate of
Romare Bearden and ACA Galleries, New York.

UNIT PREVIEW

The unit you are about to read is set apart from the other units in two ways.

Folklore All the selections in this unit are classified as folklore—traditional literature that was passed along by word of mouth before being written down. You will learn more about such literature in Elements of Folklore on pages 584–585.

Thematic Links to Previous Units The folklore in this unit is divided into five groups. The selections in each group relate to the theme of a previous unit in this book. For example, the first group of folklore selections extends the theme of Unit One, "A Matter of Perspective."

Elements of
FOLKLORE

Folklore can be defined as all the traditions, customs, and stories that are passed along by word of mouth in a culture. The stories of folklore have their beginnings in spoken language, not the written word. Because stories are passed along from teller to teller, generation to generation, their authorship cannot be traced to any one person. A single story may undergo frequent changes as each storyteller adds his or her special twist. Typically, folklore stories are collected and written down only after they have been told for many years, perhaps centuries. The stories you will read in this unit were not originated by the authors named but were retold or translated by them.

When storytellers weave their tales they offer more than entertainment. Their stories **keep the past alive,** introducing young people to the history, beliefs, and religion of their society. The stories **teach moral lessons** and **illustrate qualities that are valued by the society,** such as kindness and courage. They also **warn against negative qualities,** like greed and foolishness.

Very often, the same basic story appears in different cultures. For example, hundreds of versions of the Cinderella story have been found in places ranging from Canada to Africa to Japan. The similarities in these stories point to values that many cultures hold in common.

Folklore stories can be grouped into four major categories: **myths, folk tales, fables, and legends.**

Myths

Myths are stories that were created to answer basic questions about the world, the gods, and human life. Myths tell about events from the distant past and were considered truthful and often sacred by the societies that told them.

Many myths offer explanations of natural events. For example, you will read Greek myths that explain how deserts were formed and why voices sometimes echo. Almost all cultures have **creation myths,** which explain how the world came into being or how humans were created.

Myths usually tell about the adventures of gods or of human beings who come into contact with them. These gods and goddesses have extraordinary powers. The gods of ancient Greece, for instance, were all immortal—they could not die. Each god or goddess had his or her own special areas of power: Aphrodite governed love, Poseidon controlled the sea, Demeter ruled agriculture, and so on. Yet divine powers were not unlimited. Even Zeus, the ruler of the Greek gods, could not always get his way. In the myths of many cultures, the gods possess all the emotions and personality traits of human beings. Greek myths tell about the jealousy of Aphrodite and the impatience of Poseidon. In Norse mythology (the body of myths from Scandinavia), Thor is famous for his temper, and Loki is known for his trickery and deceit.

Folk Tales

In contrast to myths, folk tales are not about the gods, nor are they about the origins of the world. Told primarily for entertainment, folk tales are not taken as truthful or factual by their audience.

The characters in folk tales are usually ordinary humans or animals that act like humans. Typically, the humans are peasants or other members of lowly classes; often, they are portrayed as having better values than the rich and powerful.

These tales are told in a simple style, sometimes with each character representing one human trait (greed, curiosity, kindness, and so on). Many folk tales feature a kind or cruel supernatural being, such as a giant or a fairy godmother. Magic and enchantment may play a key role in these stories.

The themes of folk tales are usually simple—the reward of good, the punishment of evil, the exposing of a fool. Some folk tales teach practical lessons for living; others illustrate moral truths or offer warnings about dangers to avoid.

Many folk tales are comical and poke fun at human weaknesses, such as the **trickster tales** found in most cultures. In a trickster tale a smart person or animal outwits or takes advantage of some fool.

Fables

Fables are very short tales that illustrate a clear, often directly stated, **moral**—a principle of right and wrong behavior. The characters are often animals that act like humans. Often these characters have human faults.

Legends

Legends are considered factual by those who tell them, and many have some basis in historical fact. For example, the legends surrounding King Arthur, Joan of Arc, and John Henry are based upon people who actually existed. These stories tend to be set in a past more recent than that of myths. Legends often include elements of magic and the supernatural.

Strategies for Reading Folklore

1. **Enjoy** the tale. These stories are fun because they are filled with action and adventure. As you read, imagine the stories being repeated through many generations.

2. **Think about the purpose** of the story. Is its purpose to explain a mystery of nature, to teach a lesson, or poke fun at human weaknesses?

3. **Look for values and customs** of the culture from which the story comes. What is virtuous behavior, and how is it rewarded? What traits are admired and respected? Which are negative?

4. **Decide who holds the power** in the story. Do humans control their own fate, or are the gods or some supernatural power in charge?

5. **Compare** the story with others that you know about, perhaps from other cultures. What do the stories have in common?

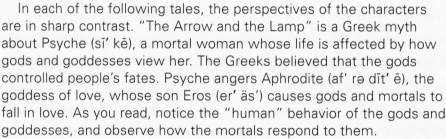

A Matter of Perspective

**Links to
Unit One**

The Arrow and the Lamp   MARGARET HODGES

Lazy Peter and His Three-Cornered Hat   RICARDO E. ALEGRIA

The Force of Luck   RUDOLFO A. ANAYA

*E*xamine *What You Know*

The way you judge someone else depends on your perspective—where you are standing and what your own situation is. Folklore shows us that this truth has been understood by all peoples. In small groups discuss why people's perspectives cause their opinions to differ so greatly. For example, why does a farmer's point of view differ from a city dweller's? a poor person's from a rich person's?

*E*xpand *Your Knowledge*

In each of the following tales, the perspectives of the characters are in sharp contrast. "The Arrow and the Lamp" is a Greek myth about Psyche (sī′ kē), a mortal woman whose life is affected by how gods and goddesses view her. The Greeks believed that the gods controlled people's fates. Psyche angers Aphrodite (af′ rə dīt′ ē), the goddess of love, whose son Eros (er′ äs′) causes gods and mortals to fall in love. As you read, notice the "human" behavior of the gods and goddesses, and observe how the mortals respond to them.

Tricksters use the perspectives—and sometimes the weaknesses—of others to fool them. "Lazy Peter and His Three-Cornered Hat" is a typical trickster tale that comes from Puerto Rico. The folklore of Puerto Rico has roots in the Orient, Arabia, Spain, and West Africa. As you read about ordinary human characters in this tale, notice how each represents one point of view.

Your own perspective will determine your answer to the question posed in "The Force of Luck." This folk tale comes from the U.S. Southwest. Like tales from Puerto Rico, tales from the Southwest reflect a mixture of cultures, including Hispanic and Native American. Notice what values are upheld in this tale of a hard-working miller.

*W*rite *Before You Read*

■ *Author biographies
on Extend page*

Write about a time when your perspective on something was quite different from someone else's. Why were your viewpoints different? Did you ever end up agreeing?

The Arrow and the Lamp:

The Story of Psyche

Retold by MARGARET HODGES

Once a king and a queen had three daughters. All three were beautiful, but the youngest, Psyche, was different. Her sisters were content to know what they were told. Psyche always wanted to know more. She was so lovely that men called her a new Aphrodite, a young goddess of love and beauty, but no man dared to marry a goddess. So while the two older sisters found husbands and went away to live in their own homes, Psyche stayed on alone with her father and mother.

Now all might have been well if golden, sweet-smiling Aphrodite had not heard of Psyche. The goddess came up out of the sea to find out whether men were really leaving her temples empty and silent and throwing flowers in the streets where Psyche walked. And when Aphrodite saw that it was true, she no longer smiled. She was furious, and she said to herself, "This girl is mortal. Beautiful she may be, but like all mortals she will die, and until she dies, she must never have a happy day. I shall see to that."

Then she called her favorite child, Eros, and he came flying to her. This young god, as fair as his mother, had golden wings on which he moved swiftly and unseen on his mysterious errands, often doing mischief. He carried a golden bow and a quiver filled with arrows.

"Go to this girl, this Psyche," said Aphrodite. "Wound her with one of your arrows. Pour bitterness on her lips. Then find her the <u>vilest</u> husband in the world—mean, bad tempered, ugly—and make her fall in love with him."

There were two springs of water in Aphrodite's garden—one bitter, the other sweet. Carrying water from both springs, Eros flew off, invisible.

He found Psyche asleep. Her beauty moved him to pity, but, obeying his mother's command, he poured bitter water on her lips and touched her side with one of his arrows. Psyche felt the pain and opened her eyes. She could not see Eros, but as he looked into her eyes, the arrow trembled in his hand, and by chance he wounded himself. He poured a little of the sweet water on her forehead and flew away.

Still no lovers came to ask for Psyche's hand in marriage, so the king and the queen, guessing that their daughter had somehow angered one of the gods, asked an oracle[1] to look into the future and tell them what could be done to find a husband for her.

The oracle answered with frightening words: "Dress your daughter for her funeral. She will never marry a mortal man but will be the bride of a creature with wings, feared even by the gods. Take Psyche to the stony top of the mountain that looks down on your city, and leave her there alone to meet her fate."

When they heard this prophecy, all the people wept with Psyche's father and mother. But Psyche said, "Tears will not help me. I was doomed from the moment when you called me the new Aphrodite. It must be Aphrodite herself whom I have angered. Obey the oracle before the goddess punishes all of you. I alone must bear her anger."

Psyche led the way to the mountaintop and said good-bye to her weeping parents and the crowd of folk who had sadly followed her. When all were gone, she sat down, trembling and afraid, to wait. But no monster husband came. Instead, the warm west wind began to blow and, raising her gently in the air, carried her down the far side of the mountain to a green and flowering meadow in a hidden valley.

Psyche fell peacefully asleep in the soft grass. When she woke, she saw a grove of tall trees watered by a clear stream. In the grove stood a marvelous palace, its golden pillars topped with a roof of carved sandalwood and ivory.

She entered through the open doorway, wondering at the light that flashed from silver walls. Surely only a god could have made such a palace! Psyche passed from room to room, walking on floors made of precious stones, until she came to a marble pool filled with scented water.

Then a voice spoke to her: "Lady, all of this is yours. Ask for whatever you like." Unseen hands led her to the bath and afterward clothed her in a robe of fine silk. A table appeared, spread with delicious food, and Psyche ate and drank while invisible servants waited on her and the air was filled with the sound of sweet voices singing.

When darkness fell, Psyche found a bed ready for her and lay down to rest. But in the night she woke, feeling the presence of someone standing beside her bed, and she was full of fear. Then a voice said, "Do not be afraid, Psyche. I am the husband you have been waiting for. Trust me. No harm will come to you. Only do not try to see me." Psyche's husband stayed with her all night long, but before daylight he was gone.

For some months Psyche lived in the palace, surrounded by beauty and comfort. The unseen servants answered all her wishes, and when her unseen husband came at night, he was always kind. She began to long for the sound of his voice and very soon fell deeply in love with him. Still, the days seemed empty and she often felt lonely.

One night her husband said to her, "Psyche, your sisters are looking for you. If you hear them calling, do not answer."

Psyche promised to obey, but she wished more and more to see a face. The clear waters of the pool reflected only her own face, and the palace now seemed like a prison. At last her husband found her

---

1. **oracle:** in ancient Greece, a priest who consulted the gods in order to foretell the future

LOVE AND THE MAIDEN   John Roddam Spencer-Stanhope   Private collection.   Bridgeman/Art Resource, New York.

weeping and, taking her in his arms, said, "Well, my love, have your wish, even if it brings trouble. The west wind shall carry your sisters here." And Psyche thanked him with grateful kisses.

The next day she heard her sisters calling to her from the mountaintop, and she called back to them. Then the west wind carried them down into the valley, and when they found Psyche safe and well, they embraced her joyfully. But their joy turned to jealousy as she showed them her palace and they saw how she was dressed and waited on like a queen.

When Psyche confessed that she had never seen her husband, they spoiled her happiness by planting suspicions in her mind: "If your husband will not let you see him, he must be the monster that the oracle said you would marry. He is only biding his time until he is ready to kill you. Take our advice. The next time he comes, have a lamp and a sharp knife hidden at your side. When he is asleep, light the lamp and look at him. If he is a monster, kill him while there is yet time."

The west wind carried the sisters away as safely as they had come, but Psyche was tormented by what they had said. At last she filled a little lamp with oil and found a sharp knife, both of which she hid beside her bed.

That night, when her husband was asleep, she lit the lamp and saw him—not a monster, but the most beautiful of beings, a fair and

ROSES   decorative panel   1909–1916   Ernest Quost
Musée d'Orsay, Paris.

graceful youth with golden wings, smiling even in his sleep. Psyche was moved by a deeper love than she had ever felt. She bent over her husband, and from the lamp a drop of oil, burning hot, fell on his shoulder. Stung by the pain, he opened his eyes and looked at her sternly. "Foolish Psyche," he said, "I knew how it would be. You could not trust me. You had to see for yourself. Now you will lose everything that I could give you, and I must lose you." Too late she knew who he was: Eros, the son of Aphrodite. There was a flash of golden wings and he was gone. The palace too was

gone, and Psyche found herself alone again on the mountaintop.

Psyche was determined to find her lost husband, but although she walked all the roads of the world, she could not discover where he was. He had flown to one of his mother's many palaces, sick at heart and feverish with the burning pain of the oil from Psyche's lamp. Aphrodite was angrier than she had ever been. "You are meant to make mortals fall in love, not to fall in love yourself," she said. "However, you will soon be well and will forget all about that girl." She locked him into a chamber, and there he lay.

As Psyche searched for Eros, she came at last to a faraway river that flowed from a high waterfall. At the edge of the river stood a temple, and in its doorway she saw Aphrodite. She knelt at the feet of the goddess and begged Aphrodite to tell her where she could find Eros. But Aphrodite, jealous of her beauty, answered with a false smile, "I will give Eros back to you if you will do something for me." And when Psyche eagerly agreed, the goddess led her into the temple and showed her a room filled with a great heap of grains: corn and barley, poppy seed, lentils, and beans, all mixed together. "Anyone as ugly as you is fit only to work," Aphrodite said scornfully. "Sort all of these grains into separate piles, and have it done by evening."

When the goddess had left her, Psyche sat down and began to cry. The task was impossible. But as she sat there weeping, she saw a procession of little ants coming out of the earth and running to her rescue. They attacked the heap of grains and carried each kind to a separate pile, never stopping until the work was done. Then they vanished into the earth.

When Aphrodite returned in the evening, she found Psyche sitting with folded hands. All the work was finished. "You do not deceive me, <u>wretched</u> girl," cried the goddess. "Someone has helped you. Tomorrow you must work alone, but your task is easy. Across the river is a field where golden sheep are grazing. Bring me a strand of their fleece."

At dawn Psyche went to the river and stepped into the water. But as she did so, she heard the whispering of the reeds that grew along the shore: "Psyche, the sheep are wild rams, as fierce as the sun's rays. They will batter you with their stony foreheads and pierce you with their sharp horns."

Psyche was ready to sink down into the river, despairing. But the reeds whispered, "Do not give up. Be patient. Things will change. Wait until the sun sinks. Then the rams sleep, and you can easily gather a strand of their golden fleece from the bushes along the edge of the field." Psyche obeyed, and in the evening gave the shining fleece to Aphrodite.

The goddess was enraged. She could not bear to find Psyche still alive. "Tomorrow you must work again," she said. She gave Psyche a crystal jar and pointed to the waterfall that plunged from the mountain peak. "That is where the river Styx comes from Hades, the land of death. Bring me water from the top of the waterfall," she ordered. She thought to herself, "The girl will never return. It is a just punishment for stealing my son's love."

Psyche made her way to the foot of the mountain and climbed the steep and rugged path—up, up, on and on, fearing every moment that she would fall and be dashed to pieces. At last she reached the topmost crag, a rough and slippery rock, and saw that the torrent of water poured out of a cavern guarded by dragons with unwinking eyes. Psyche heard the waters roaring, "Beware!" and stood as if turned to stone by fear. Then, from high in the air above her, there flew down an eagle, the messenger of Zeus, king of the gods. The eagle took the crystal jar in its claws and swooped past the dragons. It hovered at the top of the waterfall until the jar was filled to the brim, then brought it back to Psyche.

That night Aphrodite could hardly believe her eyes when she saw Psyche alive and well, bearing the jar of water in her hands. "I have obeyed all your commands," said Psyche. "I beg you to give me my husband."

"I have only one more task for you," said Aphrodite with a bitter smile. "If you accomplish this, Eros shall be yours forever. Go to the world of the dead and ask Queen Persephone to fill this box with some of her beauty." "For," she thought to herself, "no mortal comes back from Hades."

Psyche took the box. She knew now that Aphrodite wished nothing less than her death, and she climbed a high tower, ready to leap to the ground and so be taken at once to the land of the dead, never to return. But as she looked out from the top of the windy tower, a voice echoed from its walls: "Psyche, do not lose hope. There is a way to accomplish the last of your labors.

Words to Know and Use | **wretched** (rech' id) *adj.* deserving contempt; inferior

591

Near at hand you will find a cave. A path leads through it to the river Styx. Carry two coins in your mouth to pay the ferryman who will row you across the river to Hades and back again. A three-headed dog guards the palace of Hades. Take two barley cakes for the dog. Give him one when you enter, the other when you leave."

Psyche found the cave and followed the dark path that led through it into the secret places of the earth. When she came to the river Styx, the ferryman took one of the coins from her mouth and rowed her across. When the fierce three-headed dog of Hades barked at her, she silenced him with a barley cake and went on to the jeweled palace of Hades. There Queen Persephone came to greet her. And when Psyche saw that gentle face, she knew why even Aphrodite wanted to have some of its beauty. The goddess took the box and put something into it, saying in a voice both soft and kind, "Do not open this, my child. It is not for you."

Gratefully, Psyche took the box and ran from the palace. She gave her last cake to the three-headed dog and her last coin to the ferryman, and hurried up the path. But as she stepped out under the open sky, she thought, "My husband once said that I was beautiful. He may no longer think so, after all my labors. Perhaps I should keep a little of Persephone's beauty for myself." She opened the box. At once a deep sleep came over her, and she lay as if dead.

But even from afar, Eros saw her. He had recovered from his hurt, and his love for her was so strong that he burst open the locked door of his chamber and flew to her, tenderly wiping away the spell of sleep. He closed the box and gave it back to her. Then, with Psyche in his arms, he flew upward. As they neared the top of Mount Olympus, the heavenly radiance shone brighter and brighter, and in the center of the light Psyche saw Zeus, the father of light. He called Aphrodite and all the other gods and goddesses together and spoke to them: "See this mortal girl whom Eros loves. No mortal can have Persephone's beauty, but Psyche has brought some of that beauty to us. So give her the food and drink of gods, and let her be one of us, never to die, never to be separated again from her love."

Finally, even Aphrodite said it should be so. Then from Psyche's shoulders delicate wings, like those of a butterfly, unfolded. And mortals, seeing butterflies in summer fields, remember Psyche and her love. ❧

Responding to Reading

1. Write your first reaction to this myth in your journal or notebook.

2. Compare the **characters** of Aphrodite and Psyche. Consider each character's strengths and weaknesses and the way each loves Eros.

3. Why do you think the gods finally accept Psyche as Eros' wife?

4. In your opinion, why was this myth created? What purposes, messages, and explanations might it have had for the early Greeks?

Lazy Peter and His Three-Cornered Hat

RICARDO E. ALEGRIA
Translated by Elizabeth Culbert

This is the story of Lazy Peter, a shameless rascal of a fellow who went from village to village making mischief.

One day Lazy Peter learned that a fair was being held in a certain village. He knew that a large crowd of country people would be there selling horses, cows, and other farm animals and that a large amount of money would change hands. Peter, as usual, needed money, but it was not his custom to work for it. So he set out for the village, wearing a red three-cornered hat.

The first thing he did was to stop at a stand and leave a big bag of money with the owner, asking him to keep it safely until he returned for it. Peter told the man that when he returned for the bag of money, one corner of his hat would be turned down, and that was how the owner of the stand would know him. The man promised to do this, and Peter thanked him. Then he went to the drugstore in the village and gave the druggist another bag of money, asking him to keep it until he returned with one corner of his hat turned up. The druggist agreed, and Peter left. He went to the church and asked the priest to keep another bag of money and to return it to him only when he came back with one corner of his hat twisted to the side. The priest said fine, he would do this.

Having disposed of three bags of money, Peter went to the edge of the village where the farmers were buying and selling horses and cattle. He stood and watched for a while until he decided that one of the farmers must be very rich indeed, for he had sold all of his horses and cows. Moreover, the man seemed to be a miser who was never satisfied but wanted always more and more money. This was Peter's man! He stopped beside him. It was raining, and instead of keeping his hat on to protect his head, he took it off and wrapped it carefully in his cape, as though it were very valuable. It puzzled the farmer to see Peter stand there with the rain falling on his head and his hat wrapped in his cape.

After a while he asked, "Why do you take better care of your hat than of your head?"

Peter saw that the farmer had swallowed the bait, and smiling to himself, he said that the hat was the most valuable thing in all the world and that was why he took care to protect it from the rain. The farmer's curiosity increased at this reply, and he asked Peter what was so valuable about a red three-cornered hat. Peter told him that the hat worked for him; thanks to it, he never had to work for a living, because whenever he put the hat on with one of the corners turned over, people just handed him any money he asked for.

The farmer was amazed and very interested in what Peter said. As money-getting was his greatest ambition, he told Peter that he couldn't believe a word of it until he saw the hat work with his own eyes. Peter assured him that he could do this, for he, Peter, was hungry, and the hat was about to start working, since he had no money with which to buy food.

With this, Peter took out his three-cornered hat, turned one corner down, put it on his head, and told the farmer to come along and watch the hat work. Peter took the farmer to the stand. The minute the owner looked up, he handed over the bag of money Peter had left with him. The farmer stood with his mouth open in astonishment. He didn't know what to make of it. But of one thing he was sure—he had to have that hat!

Peter smiled and asked if he was satisfied, and the farmer said yes, he was. Then he asked Peter if he would sell the hat. This was just what Lazy Peter wanted, but he said no, he was not interested in selling the hat, because with it, he never had to work and he always had money. The farmer said he thought that was unsound reasoning because thieves could easily steal a hat, and wouldn't it be safer to invest in a farm with cattle? So they talked, and Peter pretended to be impressed with the farmer's arguments. Finally he said yes, he saw the point, and if the farmer would make him a good offer, he would sell the hat. The farmer, who

had made up his mind to have the hat at any price, offered a thousand pesos. Peter laughed aloud and said he could make as much as that by just putting his hat on two or three times.

As they continued haggling over the price, the farmer grew more and more determined to have that hat, until finally he offered all he had realized from the sale of his horses and cows—ten thousand pesos in gold. Peter still pretended not to be interested, but he chuckled to himself, thinking of the trick he was about to play on the farmer. All right, he said, it was a deal. Then the farmer grew cautious and told Peter that before he handed over the ten thousand pesos, he would like to see the hat work again. Peter said that was fair enough. He put on the hat with one of the corners turned up and went with the farmer to the drugstore. The moment the druggist saw the turned-up corner, he handed over the money Peter had left with him. At this the farmer was convinced and very eager to set the hat to work for himself. He took out a bag containing ten thousand pesos in gold and was about to hand it to Peter when he had a change of heart and thought better of it. He asked Peter please to excuse him, but he had to see the hat work just once more before he could part with his gold. Peter said that that was fair enough, but now he would have to ask the farmer to give him the fine horse he was riding as well as the ten thousand pesos in gold. The farmer's interest in the hat revived, and he said it was a bargain!

Lazy Peter put on his hat again, doubled over one of the corners, and told the farmer that since he still seemed to have doubts, this time he could watch the hat work in the church. The farmer was delighted with this, his doubts were stilled, and he fairly beamed thinking of all the money he was going to make once that hat was his.

They entered the church. The priest was hearing confession, but when he saw Peter with his hat, he said, "Wait here, my son," and he went to the sacristy and returned with the bag of money Peter had left with him. Peter thanked the priest, then knelt and asked for a blessing before he left. The farmer had seen everything and was fully convinced of the hat's magic powers. As soon as they left the church, he gave Peter the ten thousand pesos in gold and told him to take the horse also. Peter tied the bag of pesos to the saddle, gave the hat to the farmer, begging him to take good care of it, spurred his horse, and galloped out of town.

As soon as he was alone, the farmer burst out laughing at the thought of the trick he had played on Lazy Peter. A hat such as this was priceless! He couldn't wait to try it. He put it on with one corner turned up and entered the butcher shop.

The butcher looked at the hat, which was very handsome indeed, but said nothing. The farmer turned around, then walked up and down until the butcher asked him what he wanted. The farmer said he was waiting for the bag of money. The butcher laughed aloud and asked if he were crazy. The farmer thought that there must be something wrong with the way he had folded the hat. He took it off and doubled another corner down. But this had no effect on the butcher. So he decided to try it out some other place. He went to the mayor of the town.

The mayor, to be sure, looked at the hat but did nothing. The farmer grew desperate and decided to go to the druggist who had given Peter a bag of money. He entered and stood with the hat on. The druggist looked at him but did nothing.

The farmer became very nervous. He began to suspect that there was something very wrong. He shouted at the druggist, "Stop looking at me and hand over the bag of money!"

The druggist said he owed him nothing, and what bag of money was he talking about, anyway? As the farmer continued to shout about a bag of money and a magic hat, the druggist called the police. When they arrived, he told them that the farmer had gone out of his mind and kept demanding a bag of money. The police questioned the farmer, and he told them about the magic hat he had bought from Lazy Peter. When he heard the story, the druggist explained that Peter had left a bag of money, asking that it be returned when he appeared with a corner of his hat turned up. The owner of the stand and the priest told the same story. And I am telling you the farmer was so angry that he tore the hat to shreds and walked home. ❧

*R*esponding to Reading

1. Jot down your reaction to the story's ending.

2. In your opinion, why does Lazy Peter's trick work?

3. Do you feel sympathy for the farmer? Why or why not?

4. How do you think this tale fits the theme "A Matter of Perspective"? Before you answer, think about each character's point of view or attitude toward life.

The Force of Luck

RUDOLFO A. ANAYA

Once two wealthy friends got into a heated argument. One said that it was money which made a man prosperous, and the other maintained that it wasn't money, but luck, which made the man. They argued for some time and finally decided that if only they could find an honorable man, then perhaps they could prove their respective points of view.

One day while they were passing through a small village, they came upon a miller who was grinding corn and wheat. They paused to ask the man how he ran his business. The miller replied that he worked for a master and that he earned only four bits[1] a day, and with that he had to support a family of five.

The friends were surprised. "Do you mean to tell us you can maintain a family of five on only fifteen dollars a month?" one asked.

"I live modestly to make ends meet," the humble miller replied.

The two friends privately agreed that if they put this man to a test, perhaps they could resolve their argument.

"I am going to make you an offer," one of them said to the miller. "I will give you two hundred dollars, and you may do whatever you want with the money."

"But why would you give me this money when you've just met me?" the miller asked.

"Well, my good man, my friend and I have a long-standing argument. He contends that it is luck which elevates a man to high position, and I say it is money. By giving you this money, perhaps we can settle our argument. Here, take it, and do with it what you want!"

So the poor miller took the money and spent the rest of the day thinking about the strange meeting which had presented him with more money than he had ever seen. What could he possibly do with all this money? Be that as it may, he had the money in his pocket, and he could do with it whatever he wanted.

When the day's work was done, the miller decided the first thing he would do would be to buy food for his family. He took out ten dollars and wrapped the rest of the money in a cloth and put the bundle in his bag. Then he went to the market and bought supplies and a good piece of meat to take home.

On the way home he was attacked by a hawk that had smelled the meat which the miller carried. The miller fought off the bird, but in the struggle he lost the bundle of money. Before the miller knew what was

---

1. **four bits:** a slang term for fifty cents.

happening, the hawk grabbed the bag and flew away with it. When he realized what had happened he fell into deep thought.

"Ah," he moaned, "wouldn't it have been better to let that hungry bird have the meat! I could have bought a lot more meat with the money he took. Alas, now I'm in the same poverty as before! And worse, because now those two men will say I am a thief! I should have thought carefully and bought nothing. Yes, I should have gone straight home, and this wouldn't have happened!"

So he gathered what was left of his provisions and continued home, and when he arrived he told his family the entire story.

When he was finished telling his story, his wife said, "It has been our lot to be poor, but have faith in God, and maybe someday our luck will change."

The next day the miller got up and went to work as usual. He wondered what the two men would say about his story. But since he had never been a man of money, he soon forgot the entire matter.

Three months after he had lost the money to the hawk, it happened that the two wealthy men returned to the village. As soon as they saw the miller, they approached him to ask if his luck had changed. When the miller saw them, he felt ashamed and afraid that they would think that he had squandered the money on worthless things. But he decided to tell them the truth, and as soon as they had greeted each other, he told his story. The men believed him. In fact, the one who insisted that it was money and not luck which made a man prosper took out another two hundred dollars and gave it to the miller.

"Let's try again," he said, "and let's see what happens this time."

The miller didn't know what to think. "Kind sir, maybe it would be better if you put this money in the hands of another man," he said.

"No," the man insisted, "I want to give it to you because you are an honest man, and if we are going to settle our argument, you have to take the money!"

The miller thanked them and promised to do his best. Then, as soon as the two men left, he began to think what to do with the money so that it wouldn't disappear as it had the first time. The thing to do was to take the money straight home. He took out ten dollars, wrapped the rest in a cloth, and headed home.

When he arrived, his wife wasn't at home. At first he didn't know what to do with the money. He went to the pantry, where he had stored a large earthenware jar filled with bran. That was as safe a place as any to hide the money, he thought, so he emptied out the grain and put the bundle of money at the bottom of the jar, then covered it up with the grain. Satisfied that the money was safe, he returned to work.

That afternoon when he arrived home from work, he was greeted by his wife.

"Look, my husband, today I bought some good clay with which to whitewash[2] the entire house."

---

2. **whitewash:** to paint with a lime-and-water mixture.

*Words
to Know
and Use*

598

squander (skwän′ dər) *v.* to spend carelessly

CALLEJON DEL BESO   1957   Archibald J. Motley, Jr.   Kenkeleba House, New York.

"And how did you buy the clay if we don't have any money?" he asked.

"Well, the man who was selling the clay was willing to trade for jewelry, money, or anything of value," she said. "The only thing we had of value was the jar full of bran, so I traded it for the clay. Isn't it wonderful? I think we have enough clay to whitewash these two rooms!"

The man groaned and pulled his hair.

"Oh, you crazy woman! What have you done? We're ruined again!"

"But why?" she asked, unable to understand his anguish.

"Today I met the same two friends who gave me the two hundred dollars three months ago," he explained. "And after I told them how I lost the money, they gave me another two hundred. And I, to make sure the money was safe, came home and hid it inside the jar of bran—the same jar you have traded for dirt! Now we're as poor as we were before! And what am I going to tell the two men? They'll think I'm a liar and a thief for sure!"

"Let them think what they want," his wife said calmly. "We will only have in our lives what the good Lord wants us to have. It is our lot to be poor until God wills it otherwise."

So the miller was consoled, and the next day he went to work as usual. Time came and went, and one day the two wealthy friends returned to ask the miller how he had done with the second two hundred dollars. When the poor miller saw them, he was afraid they would accuse him of being a liar and a spendthrift. But he decided to be

LA MOLENDERA (The grinder) Diego Rivera
Museo Nacional de Art, I.N.B.A. Mexico City.

truthful, and as soon as they had greeted each other, he told them what had happened to the money.

"That is why poor men remain honest," the man who had given him the money said. "Because they don't have money, they can't get into trouble. But I find your stories hard to believe. I think you gambled and lost the money. That's why you're telling us these wild stories."

"Either way," he continued, "I still believe that it is money and not luck which makes a man prosper."

"Well, you certainly didn't prove your point by giving the money to this poor miller," his friend reminded him. "Good evening, you luckless man," he said to the miller.

"Thank you, friends," the miller said.

"Oh, by the way, here is a worthless piece of lead I've been carrying around. Maybe you can use it for something," said the man

Words to Know and Use | **spendthrift** (spend′ thrift′) *n.* a person who wastes money who believed in luck. Then the two men left, still debating their points of view on life.

Since the lead was practically worthless, the miller thought nothing of it and put it in his jacket pocket. He forgot all about it until he arrived home. When he threw his jacket on a chair, he heard a thump, and he remembered the piece of lead. He took it out of the pocket and threw it under the table. Later that night after the family had eaten and gone to bed, they heard a knock at the door.

"Who is it? What do you want?" the miller asked.

"It's me, your neighbor," a voice answered. The miller recognized the fisherman's wife. "My husband sent me to ask you if you have any lead you can spare. He is going fishing tomorrow, and he needs the lead to weight down the nets."

The miller remembered the lead he had thrown under the table. He got up, found it, and gave it to the woman.

"Thank you very much, neighbor," the woman said. "I promise you, the first fish my husband catches will be yours."

"Think nothing of it," the miller said and returned to bed. The next day he got up and went to work without thinking any more of the incident. But in the afternoon when he returned home, he found his wife cooking a big fish for dinner.

"Since when are we so well off we can afford fish for supper?" he asked his wife.

"Don't you remember that our neighbor promised us the first fish her husband caught?" his wife reminded him. "Well, this was the fish he caught the first time he threw his net. So it's ours, and it's a beauty. But you should have been here when I gutted him! I found a large piece of glass in his stomach!"

"And what did you do with it?"

"Oh, I gave it to the children to play with," she shrugged.

When the miller saw the piece of glass, he noticed it shone so brightly it appeared to illuminate the room, but because he knew nothing about jewels, he didn't realize its value and left it to the children. But the bright glass was such a novelty that the children were soon fighting over it and raising a terrible fuss.

Now it so happened that the miller and his wife had other neighbors, who were jewelers. The following morning when the miller had gone to work, the jeweler's wife visited the miller's wife to complain about all the noise her children had made.

"We couldn't get any sleep last night," she moaned.

"I know, and I'm sorry, but you know how it is with a large family," the miller's wife explained. "Yesterday we found a beautiful piece of glass, and I gave it to my youngest one to play with, and when the others tried to take it from him, he raised a storm."

The jeweler's wife took interest. "Won't you show me that piece of glass?" she asked.

"But of course. Here it is."

"Ah, yes, it's a pretty piece of glass. Where did you find it?"

"Our neighbor gave us a fish yesterday, and when I was cleaning it, I found the glass in its stomach."

"Why don't you let me take it home for just a moment. You see, I have one just like it, and I want to compare them."

"Yes, why not? Take it," answered the miller's wife.

So the jeweler's wife ran off with the glass to show it to her husband. When the jeweler saw the glass, he instantly knew it was one of the finest diamonds he had ever seen.

"It's a diamond!" he exclaimed.

"I thought so," his wife nodded eagerly. "What shall we do?"

"Go tell the neighbor we'll give her fifty dollars for it, but don't tell her it's a diamond!"

"No, no," his wife chuckled, "of course not." She ran to her neighbor's house. "Ah, yes, we have one exactly like this," she told the miller's wife. "My husband is willing to buy it for fifty dollars—only so we can have a pair, you understand."

"I can't sell it," the miller's wife answered. "You will have to wait until my husband returns from work."

That evening when the miller came home from work, his wife told him about the offer the jeweler had made for the piece of glass.

"But why would they offer fifty dollars for a worthless piece of glass?" the miller wondered aloud. Before his wife could answer, they were interrupted by the jeweler's wife.

"What do you say, neighbor, will you take fifty dollars for the glass?" she asked.

"No, that's not enough," the miller said cautiously. "Offer more."

"I'll give you fifty thousand!" the jeweler's wife blurted out.

"A little bit more," the miller replied.

"Impossible!" the jeweler's wife cried. "I can't offer any more without consulting my husband." She ran off to tell her husband how the bartering was going, and he told her he was prepared to pay a hundred thousand dollars to acquire the diamond.

He handed her seventy-five thousand dollars and said, "Take this and tell him that tomorrow, as soon as I open my shop, he'll have the rest."

When the miller heard the offer and saw the money he couldn't believe his eyes. He imagined the jeweler's wife was jesting with him, but it was a true offer, and he received the hundred thousand dollars for the diamond. The miller had never seen so much money, but he still didn't quite trust the jeweler.

"I don't know about this money," he confided to his wife. "Maybe the jeweler plans to accuse us of robbing him and thus get it back."

"Oh no," his wife assured him, "the money is ours. We sold the diamond fair and square—we didn't rob anyone."

"I think I'll still go to work tomorrow," the miller said. "Who knows, something might happen, and the money will disappear, then we would be without money and work. Then how would we live?"

So he went to work the next day, and all day he thought about how he could use the money. When he returned home that afternoon, his wife asked him what he had decided to do with their new fortune.

"I think I will start my own mill," he answered, "like the one I operate for my master. Once I set up my business we'll see how our luck changes."

The next day he set about buying everything he needed to establish his mill and to build a new home. Soon he had everything going.

Six months had passed, more or less, since he had seen the two men who had given him the four hundred dollars and the piece of lead. He was eager to see them again and to tell them how the piece of lead had changed his luck and made him wealthy.

Time passed and the miller prospered. His business grew, and he even built a summer cottage where he could take his family on vacation. He had many employees who worked for him. One day while he was at his store, he saw his two benefactors riding by. He rushed out into the street to greet them and ask them to come in. He was overjoyed to see them, and he was happy to see that they admired his store.

"Tell us the truth," the man who had given him the four hundred dollars said. "You used that money to set up this business."

The miller swore he hadn't, and he told them how he had given the piece of lead to his neighbor and how the fisherman had in return given him a fish with a very large diamond in its stomach. And he told them how he had sold the diamond.

"And that's how I acquired this business and many other things I want to show you," he said. "But it's time to eat. Let's eat first, then I'll show you everything I have now."

The men agreed, but one of them still doubted the miller's story. So they ate, and then the miller had three horses saddled, and they rode out to see his summer home. The cabin was on the other side of the river, where the mountains were cool and beautiful. When they arrived the men admired the place very much. It was such a peaceful place that they rode all afternoon through the forest. During their ride they came upon a tall pine tree.

"What is that on top of the tree?" one of them asked.

"That's the nest of a hawk," the miller replied.

"I have never seen one; I would like to take a closer look at it!"

"Of course," the miller said, and he ordered a servant to climb the tree and bring down the nest so his friend could see how it was built. When the hawk's nest was on the ground they examined it carefully. They noticed that there was a cloth bag at the bottom of the nest. When the miller saw the bag, he immediately knew that it was the very same bag he had lost to the hawk which fought him for the piece of meat years ago.

"You won't believe me, friends, but this is the very same bag in which I put the first two hundred dollars you gave me," he told them.

"If it's the same bag," the man who had doubted him said, "then the money you said the hawk took should be there."

"No doubt about that," the miller said. "Let's see what we find."

The three of them examined the old, weather-beaten bag. Although it was full of holes and crumbling, when they tore it apart they found the money intact. The two men remembered what the miller had told them, and they agreed he was an honest and honorable man. Still, the man who had given him the money wasn't satisfied. He wondered what had really happened to the second two hundred he had given the miller.

They spent the rest of the day riding in the mountains and returned very late to the house.

As he unsaddled their horses, the servant in charge of grooming and feeding the horses suddenly realized that he had no grain for them. He ran to the barn and checked, but there was no grain for the hungry horses. So he ran to the neighbor's granary, and there he was able to buy a large clay jar of bran. He carried the jar home and emptied the bran into a bucket to wet it before he fed it to the horses. When he got to the bottom of the jar, he noticed a large lump which turned out to be a rag-covered package. He examined it and felt something inside. He immediately went to give it to his master, who had been eating dinner.

"Master," he said, "look at this package which I found in an earthenware jar of grain which I just bought from our neighbor!"

The three men carefully unraveled the cloth and found the other one hundred and ninety dollars which the miller had told them he had lost. That is how the miller proved to his friends that he was truly an honest man.

And they had to decide for themselves whether it had been luck or money which had made the miller a wealthy man! 🐦

*R*esponding to Reading

1. What words or phrases would you use to describe the miller? Write them down in your journal or notebook.

2. Based on your own perspective and experience, who or what do you think is responsible for the miller's success? Why?

3. What values do you think this story teaches?

Responding to Reading

Comparing the Selections

1. In which story do you think perspective most affects the plot?

2. Which character do you admire most? least? Explain.

Broader Connections

3. In the story of Psyche and in "The Force of Luck," the gods or fate determines the destinies of humans. Do you think that humans control their own destinies? Why or why not?

Literary Concepts: Myths and Folk Tales

In **myths** gods and goddesses have the same emotions and failings that humans possess. What specific human weaknesses are shown by the gods and goddesses in "The Arrow and the Lamp"?

Folk tales often teach lessons. What lesson do you think "Lazy Peter and His Three-Cornered Hat" teaches? Do you think "The Force of Luck" teaches a lesson? Why or why not?

Writing Options

1. Write a short **essay** on whether you believe luck or money is more important in achieving success.

2. Write a **letter of advice** that Lazy Peter might have sent Psyche.

Vocabulary Practice

Exercise   Which word best completes each sentence?

1. In the palace Psyche's __?__ was Eros.

2. The __?__ place that Psyche visited was the river Styx.

3. The farmer felt __?__ when he knew he had been tricked.

4. The miller did not want to seem like a __?__ who would __?__ money carelessly.

Words to Know and Use

**benefactor
spendthrift
squander
vilest
wretched**

Options for Learning

1 • Tales of the Gods   Find and read another Greek myth about Persephone, Aphrodite, Eros, or Zeus. Summarize the myth and share your summary with the class.

2 • Fool's Paradise   Find a tale that describes a greedy fool like the farmer in "Lazy Peter and His Three-Cornered Hat." Illustrate the story as a comic book to share with your class.

Margaret Hodges   1911–

Though Margaret Hodges retired as a university professor in 1978, she has since published more than fifteen books. Hodges's many award-winning books fall into three categories: "real life stories based on the adventures and misadventures of my three sons"; retellings of folk tales and myths, such as *Hauntings: Ghosts and Ghouls from Around the World;* and biographies.

Ricardo Enrique Alegría   1921–

Ricardo Alegría is not only an avid collector of folk tales but also an anthropologist and historian. Alegría became a professor of history at the University of Puerto Rico. He has served as the director of the Institute of Puerto Rican Culture and the archaeological museum and research center at the University of Puerto Rico. He has written many books and articles on the history and folklore of Puerto Rico.

Rudolfo A. Anaya   1937–

Rudolfo Anaya says, "In New Mexico everyone tells stories; it is a creative pastime."

Anaya was born in Pastura, New Mexico. He has lived his entire life in New Mexico and now teaches at the University of New Mexico. He has given readings from his work throughout the Southwest and, in 1980, at the White House. Anaya has won many awards for his fiction and nonfiction, which draw on New Mexico's Hispanic past.

EXPLORE

Scales of Justice

Examine What You Know

What is justice? How could you define *justice* in a way that would satisfy most people in the world? In small groups, work to come up with a definition of *justice*. Then share your definitions and decide which are the most accurate.

Expand Your Knowledge

The theme of justice appears in tales from all over the world. The first two selections you are about to read are fables thought to have been written by Aesop, a Greek slave who lived around the sixth century B.C. The third is an Ashanti fable featuring the tricky spider Anansi, who appears in many tales that originate in Africa. All three fables concern the simplest kind of justice between members of a community.

Justice is also an important theme in "A Blind Man Catches a Bird," from Zimbabwe, a country in southeastern Africa. The people of Zimbabwe represent many cultures and speak a variety of languages. This folk tale reflects the importance of storytelling as a great tradition and art in Africa.

The fifth selection, "The Old Grandfather and His Little Grandson," is a folk tale from Russia that has been told with slightly different twists in many countries. It too concerns simple justice. Leo Tolstoy was a wealthy aristocrat who became a leader of peasants, organizing famine-relief projects and working to educate the poor. Tolstoy collected many folk tales that he heard in peasant homes.

Write Before You Read

■ *Author biographies on Extend page and in Reader's Handbook*

• Think of a real incident or a story you have heard that illustrates your group's definition of *justice*. In your journal, briefly describe the incident or story and explain how it relates to justice.

Aesop's Fables

AESOP

Illustration by Charles Santore.

The Wolf in Sheep's Clothing

A certain wolf could not get enough to eat because of the watchfulness of the shepherds. But one night he found a sheep skin that had been cast aside and forgotten. The next day, dressed in the skin, the wolf strolled into the pasture with the sheep. Soon a little lamb was following him about and was quickly led away to slaughter.

That evening the wolf entered the fold with the flock. But it happened that the shepherd took a fancy for mutton broth that very evening and, picking up a knife, went to the fold. There the first he laid hands on and killed was the wolf.

The evildoer often comes to harm through his own deceit. ❧

The Travelers and the Purse

Two men were traveling in company along the road when one of them picked up a well-filled purse.

"How lucky I am!" he said. "I have found a purse. Judging by its weight it must be full of gold."

"Do not say, '*I* have found a purse,'" said his companion. "Say rather, '*We* have found a purse' and 'How lucky *we* are.' Travelers ought to share alike the fortunes or misfortunes of the road."

"No, no," replied the other angrily. "*I* found it and *I* am going to keep it."

Just then they heard a shout of "Stop, thief!" and looking around saw a mob of people armed with clubs coming down the road.

The man who had found the purse fell into a panic.

"We are lost if they find the purse on us," he cried.

"No, no," replied the other. "You would not say 'we' before, so now stick to your 'I.' Say '*I* am lost.'"

We cannot expect any one to share our misfortunes unless we are willing to share our good fortune also.

Responding to Reading

1. What is your initial reaction to these two fables?

2. Do you think the man who found the purse in "The Travelers and the Purse" should have shared the gold? Why or why not?

3. Think about how you defined *justice* earlier. Which fable do you think more clearly illustrates that definition? Why?

4. In your opinion, are the morals at the end of these fables useful guides to living in today's world? Explain.

Anansi and His Visitor, Turtle

EDNA MASON KAULA

It was almost time for Sun to sink to his resting place when Turtle, tired and dusty from hours of wandering, came to Anansi's house in the middle of a clearing in the woods. Turtle was hungry, and the appetizing aroma of freshly cooked fish and yams drew him to approach Anansi's door and to knock. Anansi jerked the door open. When he saw the tired stranger he was inwardly annoyed, but it was an unwritten law of his country that one must never, no never, refuse hospitality to a passerby.

Anansi smiled grimly and said, "Come in, come in, and share my dinner, Mr. Turtle."

As Turtle stretched out one paw to help himself from the steaming platter, Anansi almost choked on a mouthful of food. In a shocked voice he said, "Turtle, I must remind you that in my country it is ill-mannered to come to the table without first washing. Please go to the stream at the foot of the hill and wash your dusty paws."

Turtle waddled down the hill and waded in the water for a while. He even washed his face. By the time he had trudged back up the trail to Anansi's house, the platter of fish was half empty. Anansi was eating at a furious rate.

Turtle stretched out one paw to help himself to food, but again Anansi stopped him. "Turtle, your paws are still dusty. Please, go wash them."

"It is the dust from the long trail up the hill," Turtle explained in a meek voice. Clearly, it was not Turtle's place to argue if he expected to share the delectable meal, so he crawled down the hill a second time and rewashed his paws. Turtle was careful to walk on the grass beside the dusty trail on the climb back to Anansi's house. He hurried, for by now he was ravenous.

But, oh dear! Anansi had scraped the platter bare of fish and yams. "My, that was a good dinner," he said, wiping the last drop of gravy from his chin.

"Thank you for your wonderful hospitality, Anansi. Some day you must visit me." And Turtle, in a huff, went on home.

Some months later Anansi visited Turtle. After creepy-crawling all day from one tall grass stem to the next, he found Turtle snoozing beside the river.

"Well, well," exclaimed Turtle. "So you have come to share my dinner. Make yourself comfortable, my dear Anansi, while I go below and prepare the food." He plunged into the river with a splash. Anansi was hungry. He paced the shoreline and watched for Turtle's reappearance.

At last, Turtle's head popped above the water. "Dinner is ready," he called as he bit into a huge clam. "Come on down." Then he disappeared from sight.

Anansi dived headfirst into the water, sank a few inches, then floated to the surface. His spindly legs and tiny body prevented him from sinking. He flipped and flapped his puny arms, tried swallow dives and belly-flops, but he could not reach the bed of the river.

Then that cunning spider schemed. He filled the pockets of his jacket with small round pebbles, dived into the river, and sank with a bump that landed him right at the dinner table. Before him was spread the most delicious meal he had ever seen. There were oysters and clams, mussels, slices of eel, and crabs. As a centerpiece, sprays of watercress rested against large pink shrimp. Anansi's eyes widened with pleasure, his stomach rumbled in anticipation.

Turtle, already seated at the table, swallowed a piece of eel, looked at Anansi and said, "Oh, Anansi, I must remind you that in my country it is ill-mannered to come to the table wearing a jacket. Please take it off."

Very slowly Anansi removed his jacket. Very slowly Anansi left the table. Without the weight of the pebbles to hold him down, he floated straight up through the green water and out of sight.

When you set out to outsmart another person to your own advantage, there is usually someone who can outsmart you. ❧

Responding to Reading

1. In your journal write your reaction to the end of this fable.

2. In your opinion, is Anansi or Turtle more responsible for the outcome of the fable? Explain.

3. What do you think this fable says about justice?

A Blind Man Catches a Bird

ALEXANDER McCALL SMITH

A young man married a woman whose brother was blind. The young man was eager to get to know his new brother-in-law, and so he asked him if he would like to go hunting with him.

"I cannot see," the blind man said. "But you can help me see when we are out hunting together. We can go."

The young man led the blind man off into the bush. At first they followed a path that he knew, and it was easy for the blind man to tag on behind the other. After a while, though, they went off into thicker bush, where the trees grew closely together and there were many places for the animals to hide. The blind man now held onto the arm of his sighted brother-in-law and told him many things about the sounds that they heard around them. Because he had no sight, he had a great ability to interpret the noises made by animals in the bush.

"There are warthogs around," he would say. "I can hear their noises over there."

Or "That bird is preparing to fly. Listen to the sound of its wings unfolding."

To the brother-in-law, these sounds were meaningless, and he was most impressed at the blind man's ability to understand the bush although it must have been for him one great darkness.

They walked on for several hours, until they reached a place where they could set their traps. The blind man followed the other's advice and put his trap in a place where birds might come for water. The other man put his trap a short distance away, taking care to disguise it so that no bird would know that it was there. He did not bother to disguise the blind man's trap, as it was hot and he was eager to get home to his new wife. The blind man thought that he had disguised his trap, but he did not see that he had failed to do so and any bird could tell that there was a trap there.

They returned to their hunting place the next day. The blind man was excited at the prospect of having caught something, and the young man had to tell him to keep quiet, or he would scare all the animals away. Even before they reached the traps, the blind man was able to tell that they had caught something.

"I can hear birds," he said. "There are birds in the traps."

When he reached his trap, the young

man saw that he had caught a small bird. He took it out of the trap and put it in a pouch that he had brought with him. Then the two of them walked toward the blind man's trap.

"There is a bird in it," he said to the blind man. "You have caught a bird too."

As he spoke, he felt himself filling with jealousy. The blind man's bird was marvelously colored, as if it had flown through a rainbow and been stained by the colors. The feathers from a bird such as that would make a fine present for his new wife, but the blind man had a wife too, and she would also want the feathers.

The young man bent down and took the blind man's bird from the trap. Then, quickly substituting his own bird, he passed it to the blind man and put the colored bird into his own pouch.

"Here is your bird," he said to the blind man. "You may put it in your pouch."

The blind man reached out for the bird and took it. He felt it for a moment, his fingers passing over the wings and the breast. Then, without saying anything, he put the bird into his pouch and they began the trip home.

On their way home, the two men stopped to rest under a broad tree. As they sat there, they talked about many things. The young man was impressed with the wisdom of the blind man, who knew a great deal although he could see nothing at all.

© 1991 by Robert Vavra.

"Why do people fight with one another?" he asked the blind man. It was a question which had always troubled him, and he wondered if the blind man could give him an answer.

The blind man said nothing for a few moments, but it was clear to the young man that he was thinking. Then the blind man raised his head, and it seemed to the young man as if the unseeing eyes were staring right into his soul. Quietly he gave his answer.

"Men fight because they do to each other what you have just done to me."

The words shocked the young man and made him ashamed. He tried to think of a response, but none came. Rising to his feet, he fetched his pouch, took out the brightly colored bird, and gave it back to the blind man.

The blind man took the bird, felt over it with his fingers, and smiled.

"Do you have any other questions for me?" he asked.

"Yes," said the young man. "How do men become friends after they have fought?"

The blind man smiled again.

"They do what you have just done," he said. "That's how they become friends again." 🐦

Responding to Reading

1. What do you think is the most interesting part of this folk tale?

2. Why do you think the blind man keeps quiet when he first realizes that he has been cheated?

3. What purpose might this tale serve in African society?

The Old Grandfather and His Little Grandson

LEO TOLSTOY

The grandfather had become very old. His legs would not carry him, his eyes could not see, his ears could not hear, and he was toothless. When he ate, bits of food sometimes dropped out of his mouth. His son and his son's wife no longer allowed him to eat with them at the table. He had to eat his meals in the corner near the stove.

One day they gave him his food in a bowl. He tried to move the bowl closer; it fell to the floor and broke. His daughter-in-law scolded him. She told him that he spoiled everything in the house and broke their dishes, and she said that from now on he would get his food in a wooden dish. The old man sighed and said nothing.

A few days later, the old man's son and his wife were sitting in their hut, resting and watching their little boy playing on the floor. They saw him putting together something out of small pieces of wood. His father asked him, "What are you making, Misha?"

The little grandson said, "I'm making a wooden bucket. When you and Mamma get old, I'll feed you out of this wooden dish."

The young peasant and his wife looked at each other, and tears filled their eyes. They were ashamed because they had treated the old grandfather so meanly, and from that day they again let the old man eat with them at the table and took better care of him. ❧

Responding to Reading

1. What feelings did you have as you read this story?

2. Why do you think the couple treats the grandfather in the way that they do?

3. How do you think this tale involves "Scales of Justice"?

4. Do you think this tale is relevant today? Explain.

E X P L A I N

Responding to Reading

Comparing the Selections

1. In your opinion, do all of these stories reflect the idea of justice that you discussed before you read? Explain.

2. If you were a judge, which character would you punish most harshly? Explain your choice.

Broader Connections

3. Choose one of the simple truths demonstrated in these stories, and show how it applies to a situation in our nation or in the world today.

Literary Concept: Fables

A brief story written to teach a lesson about human nature is called a **fable.** The characters in fables are often animals that act and talk like humans. What human qualities do Anansi, Turtle, and the wolf in Aesop's fable show?

Concept Review: Setting   How important is the setting in "A Blind Man Catches a Bird" and in "The Old Grandfather and His Little Grandson"? Could either story happen somewhere else?

Writing Options

1. Think of a lesson about life that you have learned. Write a **fable** that illustrates this lesson.

2. Write a **first-person narrative** about an experience you have had that illustrates the moral of one of these stories.

*O*ptions for Learning

1 • **Telling Tales**   Make puppets and use them to retell your favorite folk tale to young children. Practice with your classmates, and then arrange a folk-tale puppet show for a younger class.

2 • **Fable Follies**   Locate a collection of fables, and in a small group, choose one to act out. Act out your fable for the class and have them guess the moral.

*A*esop   620–560 B.C.

So little is known about Aesop that he might be a fable himself. Historians think he may have been an African slave who worked on the island of Samos. How many fables Aesop actually wrote remains a question.

His death even sounds like a folk tale. After Aesop insulted the people of Delphi, the story says, they secretly hid a golden bowl in his belongings as he prepared to leave. He was then arrested for theft and thrown off a cliff.

*A*lexander McCall Smith

Born in Zimbabwe, Alexander McCall Smith returned to his homeland after his education in Scotland. He recorded the stories of both old people and schoolchildren. These tales, he says, are "uniquely the property of the people of Africa."

Smith has published several children's books, plays, and short stories. Many of the stories have been read on the radio in Britain, and one was made into an animated film.

*L*eo Tolstoy   1828–1910

Born to a wealthy family in Russia, the young Leo Tolstoy lived a life of luxury. He wrote his two most famous novels, *War and Peace* and *Anna Karenina,* while living on his large country estate. Later, however, Tolstoy began to question his life. He no longer believed people were entitled to have as much land, money, and power as he had. Eventually, in his old age, he turned over his entire estate to his family and left. A few days later he died at a railroad station in a small town.

Reaching for the Stars

**Links to
Unit Three**

Phaëthon MOIRA KERR / JOHN BENNETT
The People Could Fly VIRGINIA HAMILTON
Kelfala's Secret Something ADJAI ROBINSON

Examine What You Know

A scientist works a lifetime to find the cure for a disease. A man who cannot read goes back to school. A woman runs for political office. Many people struggle against great odds to fulfill their dreams. In small groups discuss the different types of dreams people have and the obstacles that they must overcome to achieve those dreams. For every dream, think of at least one obstacle.

Expand Your Knowledge

A main character in the myth "Phaëthon" is a Greek god, Apollo. Handsome Apollo was the god of the sun, of music, and of healing. He and Clymene (klī' mə nē), a mortal woman, had a son named Phaëthon. In this myth Phaëthon dreams of riding gloriously through the heavens in his father's golden chariot.

The characters in the second story dream not of fame or glory but of freedom. "The People Could Fly" is an American slave tale. Because most slaves were not allowed to learn to read or write, much of their culture was passed down orally. To show this, the author has written her story in the **dialect** that slaves might have used. Tales such as this provided comfort and hope and preserved the history of the lives of slaves and the legends of their African homeland.

The third selection tells of yet another kind of dream. It is a folk tale of the Kikuyu people of Kenya in East Africa. The Kikuyus, Kenya's largest ethnic group, live mostly in the southern central part of the country, near the border of Tanzania. The Kikuyus in this story live near Mount Kilimanjaro, the highest mountain in Africa. Among the Kikuyus, the traditions and instructions of parents and elders are binding, almost like laws.

Write Before You Read

■ *Author biographies
on Extend page*

Have you ever had a dream or goal that was frustrated when someone or something got in the way? In your journal describe your dream and explain how you fought for it.

Phaëthon

MOIRA KERR / JOHN BENNETT

One day the fair youth Phaëthon, whose father was the sun god, Apollo, was taunted about his parentage by Epaphus[1], a youth of the same age whose father was the mighty Zeus.

Stung with shame, Phaëthon reported the insults to his mother, Clymene.

"I am unable to answer them. If my father is really a god, as you have told me, give me proof of my noble birth, and let me take my place in heaven."

Clymene was moved.

"It would not take you long to visit your father's dwelling place. If you wish to do so, go and question the sun himself, for Apollo is indeed your father."

Apollo's <u>abode</u> was a lofty palace of glittering gold and bronze. Its towering columns, supporting a roof of polished ivory, shone like fire. Its double doors reflected the light from their silver surfaces.

After climbing the steep approach, Clymene's son was ushered into the presence of his father, who was dressed in a purple robe and was sitting on a throne of shining emeralds. But Phaëthon could not approach too close, for he could not bear the blinding light.

"What do you want in this citadel[2], Phaëthon, my son? Son, I call you, for you are one whom any parent would be proud to acknowledge."

"To prove that I am indeed your son, give me evidence."

"To remove any doubt from your mind, Phaëthon, make any request you wish, and you shall have it from me."

Instantly the lad asked to be allowed for one day to drive his father's sun chariot across the sky.

The words were scarcely spoken when Apollo regretted his oath. A mortal may, perhaps, break his word, but not so a god who had sworn by the waters of the Styx.[3] Apollo knew that the request meant death for a mortal, and he used every argument to <u>dissuade</u> his son from a venture that was suicide.

"You cannot possibly keep the horses under control. I, a god, can scarcely manage them. Even Zeus himself couldn't drive the chariot. The heavens are dangerous. You will have to keep to the path, past the horns

---

1. **Epaphus** (ə paf′ əs): the son of Zeus and the mortal woman Io.
2. **citadel**: a fortress
3. **Styx** (stiks): in Greek mythology, the river around Hades across which dead souls are ferried.

Words to Know and Use

abode (ə bōd′) *n.* a home
acknowledge (ak näl′ ij) *v.* to recognize the status or rights of
dissuade (di swād′) *v.* to persuade not to do something

619

From *Favorite Greek Myths* retold by Mary Pope Osborne,
illustrated by Troy Howell. Illustrations copyright © 1989 by Troy Howell.
Reprinted by permission of Scholastic, Inc.

of the hostile Bull, past the Thracian Archer and the paws of the raging Lion, past the Scorpion's cruel pincers and the clutching claws of the Crab.[4] Release me from my promise. Ask anything else and I shall grant it."

But Phaëthon, full of confidence, would not change his mind, and the reluctant Apollo had the swift Hours yoke his team, lead the four fire-breathing steeds from the stable, and fasten on the jingling harness.

No sooner had the proud youth leaped into the chariot and taken the reins in his hands than the horses knew they had not the firm hands of their master to guide them. Feeling their burden was too light, off they raced, out of control. The lad was panic-stricken. He did not know the path, he did not even know the names of the horses, and he was not able to manage the horses, even had he known. He could only cling helplessly to the sides of the swaying chariot as it plunged hither and thither through the sky.

---

4. Bull, Thracian (thrā′ shən) **Archer, Lion, Scorpion, Crab:** the constellations known as Taurus, Sagittarius, Leo, Scorpio, and Cancer.

For the first time, the cold stars of the Northern Plough grew hot, and the Serpent,[5] which lay close to the icy pole, was roused to fury as it sweltered in the heat. Phaëthon's terror mounted as he sighted the Scorpion and the other monstrous beasts sprawling over the face of the high heavens. Then the horses went plunging downward toward the earth. The heat of the sun's rays <u>seared</u> the ground, destroying vegetation and drying up rivers and seas. Great cities perished, and whole nations were reduced to ashes. So close did the chariot come to Africa that Libya became a desert.

Everywhere the ground gaped open, and great beams of light descended even to Tartarus,[6] frightening the king of the underworld and his queen. Three times did Poseidon try to emerge above the waters, but the fiery air was too much for him.

It was then that the alarmed Zeus had to interfere, or the whole world would have perished in flame. Mounting to the highest point of heaven, he let fly a powerful thunderbolt against the young charioteer, which dashed the luckless Phaëthon to earth.

His body fell into the Po River, and the Italian nymphs buried it on the bank. On a rock, they set this inscription:

*"Here Phaëthon lies: his father's car
  he tried—
Though proved too weak, he greatly
  daring died."*

---

5. **Northern Plough** (plou), **Serpent**: the constellations known as the Big Dipper and Draco.
6. **Tartarus** (tär′ tə rəs): in Greek mythology, another name for Hades, the world of the dead.

Responding to Reading

1. What adjectives would you use to describe Phaëthon? Jot them down in your journal.

2. In your opinion, who is most to blame for Phaëthon's death?
   Think about
   • the reason behind Phaëthon's requests
   • the roles of Apollo and Zeus in the story

3. What purposes do you think this myth served in Greek society? Before answering, review Elements of Folklore on pages 584–585.

Words to Know and Use | **sear** (sir) *v.* to burn the surface; scorch

The People Could Fly

VIRGINIA HAMILTON

They say the people could fly. Say that long ago in Africa, some of the people knew magic. And they would walk up on the air like climbin' up on a gate. And they flew like blackbirds over the fields. Black, shiny wings flappin' against the blue up there.

Then, many of the people were captured for Slavery. The ones that could fly shed their wings. They couldn't take their wings across the water on the slave ships. Too crowded, don't you know.

The folks were full of misery, then. Got sick with the up and down of the sea. So they forgot about flyin' when they could no longer breathe the sweet scent of Africa.

Say the people who could fly kept their power, although they shed their wings. They kept their secret magic in the land of slavery. They looked the same as the other people from Africa who had been coming over, who had dark skin. Say you couldn't tell anymore one who could fly from one who couldn't.

One such who could was an old man, call him Toby. And standin' tall, yet afraid, was a young woman who once had wings. Call her Sarah. Now Sarah carried a babe tied to her back. She trembled to be so hard worked and scorned.

The slaves labored in the fields from sunup to sundown. The owner of the slaves callin' himself their Master. Say he was a hard lump of clay. A hard, glinty coal. A hard rock pile, wouldn't be moved. His Overseer on horseback pointed out the slaves who were slowin' down. So the one called Driver cracked his whip over the slow ones to make them move faster. That whip was a slice-open cut of pain. So they did move faster. Had to.

Sarah hoed and chopped the row as the babe on her back slept.

Say the child grew hungry. That babe started up bawling too loud. Sarah couldn't stop to feed it. Couldn't stop to soothe and quiet it down. She let it cry. She didn't want to. She had no heart to <u>croon</u> to it.

"Keep that thing quiet," called the Overseer. He pointed his finger at the babe. The woman scrunched low. The Driver cracked his whip across the babe anyhow. The babe hollered like any hurt child, and the woman fell to the earth.

The old man that was there, Toby, came and helped her to her feet.

"I must go soon," she told him.

"Soon," he said.

Sarah couldn't stand up straight any longer. She was too weak. The sun burned

---

*Words
to Know
and Use* | **croon** (krōōn) *v.* to sing softly

From *The People Could Fly: American Black Folktales* told by Virginia Hamilton and illustrated by Leo and Diane Dillon. Illustration copyright © 1985 by Leo and Diane Dillon. Reprinted by permission of Alfred A. Knopf, Inc.

her face. The babe cried and cried, "Pity me, oh, pity me," say it sounded like. Sarah was so sad and starvin', she sat down in the row.

"Get up, you black cow," called the Overseer. He pointed his hand, and the Driver's whip snarled around Sarah's legs. Her sack dress tore into rags. Her legs bled onto the earth. She couldn't get up.

Toby was there where there was no one to help her and the babe.

"Now, before it's too late," panted Sarah. "Now, Father!"

"Yes, Daughter, the time is come," Toby answered. "Go, as you know how to go!"

He raised his arms, holding them out to her. *"Kum . . . yali, kum buba tambe,"* and more magic words, said so quickly, they sounded like whispers and sighs.

The young woman lifted one foot on the air. Then the other. She flew clumsily at first, with the child now held tightly in her arms. Then she felt the magic, the African mystery. Say she rose just as free as a bird. As light as a feather.

The Overseer rode after her, hollerin'. Sarah flew over the fences. She flew over the woods. Tall trees could not snag her. Nor could the Overseer. She flew like an eagle now, until she was gone from sight. No one dared speak about it. Couldn't believe it. But it was, because they that was there saw that it was.

Say the next day was dead hot in the fields. A young man slave fell from the heat. The Driver come and whipped him. Toby come over and spoke words to the fallen one. The words of ancient Africa once heard are never remembered completely. The young man forgot them as soon as he heard them. They went way inside him. He got up and rolled over on the air. He rode it awhile. And he flew away.

Another and another fell from the heat. Toby was there. He cried out to the fallen and reached his arms out to them. *"Kum kunka yali, kum . . . tambe!"* Whispers and sighs. And they too rose on the air. They rode the hot breezes. The ones flyin' were black and shinin' sticks, wheelin' above the head of the Overseer. They crossed the rows, the fields, the fences, the streams, and were away.

"Seize the old man!" cried the Overseer. "I heard him say the magic *words*. Seize him!"

The one callin' himself Master come runnin'. The Driver got his whip ready to curl around old Toby and tie him up. The slave owner took his hip gun from its place. He meant to kill old black Toby.

But Toby just laughed. Say he threw back his head and said, "Hee, hee! Don't you know who I am? Don't you know some of us in this field?" He said it to their faces. "We are ones who fly!"

And he sighed the ancient words that were a dark promise. He said them all around to the others in the field under the whip, "... *buba yali* ... *buba tambe* ..."

There was a great outcryin'. The bent backs straightened up. Old and young who were called slaves and could fly joined hands. Say like they would ring-sing. But they didn't shuffle in a circle. They didn't sing. They rose on the air. They flew in a flock that was black against the heavenly blue. Black crows or black shadows. It didn't matter, they went so high. Way above the plantation, way over the slavery land. Say they flew away to *Free-dom.*

And the old man, old Toby, flew behind them, takin' care of them. He wasn't cryin'. He wasn't laughin'. He was the seer. His gaze fell on the plantation where the slaves who could not fly waited.

"Take us with you!" Their looks spoke it, but they were afraid to shout it. Toby couldn't take them with him. Hadn't the time to teach them to fly. They must wait for a chance to run.

"Goodie-bye!" the old man called Toby spoke to them, poor souls! And he was flyin' gone.

So they say. The Overseer told it. The one called Master said it was a lie, a trick of the light. The Driver kept his mouth shut.

The slaves who could not fly told about the people who could fly to their children. When they were free. When they sat close before the fire in the free land, they told it. They did so love firelight and *Free-dom,* and tellin'.

They say that the children of the ones who could not fly told their children. And now, me, I have told it to you. ❧

*R*esponding to Reading

1. To what part of this story did you react most strongly? Why?

2. Why do you think the slaves who can fly take so long to do so?

3. Why do you think only some of the slaves in this story can achieve the dream of flying?

4. Do you think the storytellers who retold this story believed that people actually flew? Explain.

5. What reasons might slaves have had for telling this story?

Kelfala's Secret Something

ADJAI ROBINSON

Listen, children, do you know the Gituyu? It is such an animal that in Kenya it is said that even the dogs will not eat its meat for supper, nor the hyena, nor even the wildcat—and never the poorest of people. That is tradition. This you must know.

But the story . . .

On the steep slopes of the Kilimanjaro stood a tiny village of very hardy people. Mountain climbers were they all, and their gardens of tea and pyrethrum[1] and coffee were as dear to their hearts as the cap of snow shielding the head of their father mountain. The men and women had strong hands and great mountain strides. They were a happy people with warm hearts. And they were a people faithful to their traditions.

The young fellow, Kelfala, was one of these. Kelfala, the clown. People used to say that he was funny from the time he entered his mother's womb. He could make a thousand and one faces with his one fleshy face. His lips he could twist and curl, and even if you wanted to hiss, your hissing would turn to laughing. If you listened to Kelfala's stories, I tell you, you would see and hear all the animals in the forest in this one Kelfala. And he sprang surprises as fast as he spinned yarns, on everything around.

Kelfala, the clown, was like his grandfather before him. He was funny. He was clever. Oh, he was a charming darling. It seemed that nothing or no one could resist Kelfala.

No one, except the beautiful Wambuna. She would not even turn his way.

Before, as children, these two had played together, laughed together, teased together. But Wambuna had gone into the girl's society, as all girls of the village do. There, the old women had taught her how to wash and care for babies, how to prepare leaves and herbs for simple cures, how to sing the village songs, how to cook meats and yams and vegetables. Her roasted peanuts were always brown and tasty. And if you ate her sauces, you would lick your fingers as if you were going to bite them, too. Her graces were admired even by other young girls. And when she came out, she was given the oath: that from that time on, if she talked to any man outside her family, she was bound to marry him. That was tradition.

Kelfala would sit in the bush and watch this darling Wambuna. Her skin was as

---

1. **pyrethrum** (pī reth′ rəm): a flowering plant that is used to make insecticide.

smooth as a mirror. Her mahogany-brown arms swayed gracefully by her sides, keeping time with her swaying hips. When she laughed, she showed ivory-white teeth. And just a smile from Wambuna sent warm thrills through clownish Kelfala. Her head she carried erect, and the rings sat on her neck like rows of diamonds on a crown. The more Kelfala watched, the more he wanted Wambuna for his own.

But she had an endless stream of suitors. (If you could have seen her, you would not mind even being last, as long as you were in line.) Some of these young men went to her father to ask for Wambuna. That was tradition. But many had heard his loud "No-No" and tried to trick Wambuna, instead. But do you think she talked to the young men around? Well! You wait and see.

Always they paid their visits to her at the garden, always when the elders were having their rest from the hot midday sun.

"Wambuna, let me get you water from the stream."

"Ay'ee, Wambuna, I hit my toe against a stone. It is gushing out blood!"

"Wambuna, your plants are not growing at all. You are so lazy. Yambuyi's plants are better than yours, lazy you!"

"Wambuna, hear your father? He is snoring so hard under this hot sun, he has driven all the animals away!"

But Wambuna's lips were sealed, and all this teasing and coaxing only kept her lips tighter. She would not even raise her head to smile. She worked in silence, and if she talked at all, she only whispered kind things to her plants.

Now Kelfala joined the line, too. And—

tradition or not—he would not risk the father's "No-No." Why? He, Kelfala, the clown? Kelfala, who could coax words and laughter out of trees? He would get Wambuna to speak!

He tried his hippopotamus face, to get her to shout in fear. He turned into a leopard, springing into Wambuna's path when she was alone, so she would cry for help. He hid behind a clump of trees and became Wambuna's mother, asking questions and questions and questions that needed answers.

But Wambuna's lips were sealed.

The stream of suitors grew smaller, like the village stream itself, shrinking and shrinking in the dry season when the rains have stopped. But Kelfala did not give up. Finally, he confided in two friends that he had a something that would win Wambuna for him. A secret something. (He did not tell them what.)

For two weeks Kelfala and his two friends, Shortie Bumpie and Longie Tallie, trailed Wambuna and her family as they went to the farm. Then Kelfala's day came. They spied Wambuna going alone to the farm with her basket balanced on her head. He and Shortie Bumpie and Longie Tallie set out behind her, *kunye, kunye, kunye,* as if they were treading on hot coals. They stood behind the trees and bushes, unseen by anyone but themselves, and waited.

On this day, Kelfala had put on his best dress. But if you had seen him, you would think that he was the most unlikely suitor for a young girl. His dress was rags and tatters. He had rubbed grease all over his body, mud on his head, and funny chalk marks on his face. He also had painted his front teeth with red-black clay.

© 1991 by Robert Vavra.

The birds were twitting happily as they caught worms on the dewy grass. Nearby, the stream was flowing by, its waters dazzling in the early morning sunlight. From time to time Kelfala opened his sack, touched his something, and smiled to himself.

Wambuna started working hard and fast. Indeed, she was racing the sun. By the time the sun got halfway on its journey, she hoped to have gotten to the end of hers. She only stopped her work for a moment, went to the stream with her calabash[2] for water, then returned and kindled a fire. She took some yams from her little basket, put them on the hot coals, and returned to her plants. She was weeding the new grasses on her tea beds.

Kelfala's opportunity had come. Soon, Kelfala, the clown, Kelfala, the funny one, would be married to the most beautiful, the most gentle, the mildest lady on Kilimanjaro. At least, that is what Kelfala thought.

Kelfala spied here, there, and everywhere from his hiding, stepped out into the open, and hopped and skipped to the fireplace. Out of his sack he pulled his something and placed it on the hot coals beside Wambuna's yams. Then he squatted on the largest fire stone and poled the red-hot coals. Shoving Wambuna's yams aside, he uttered a throaty chuckle, which he quickly trapped with his hands. He glanced again at the

---

2. **calabash** (kal′ ə bash′): the dried hollow shell of a gourd, used as a bowl.

fireplace, and like a cock ready to peck at the yams, he tittered quietly to himself. But again he quickly stopped himself.

But only for a moment, for suddenly more chuckles escaped, and Kelfala howled like a ruffled owl. He hooted the monkeys out of the tree tops. He rolled himself into a ball as he rolled and rolled with laughter. Kelfala, the laughing clown. He laughed and he laughed and he laughed.

Now, the bush came alive. Shortie Bumpie and Longie Tallie poked their heads out to see what was happening. At first they twitched their faces and cocked their ears. But as Kelfala rolled on and on, and the laughter rolled on and on, it dragged the two young men with it.

Wambuna—who had to poke her fire—tried to sneak past the hooting trio, but the loud roars quickly sank into *her* bones. Oh, how silly those three idle friends! Kelfala, that clown Kelfala! But as she watched them, her grin turned into a broad smile, *her* smile turned into a shy laugh, and without realizing it, she became one of the howling trio. She was all fits of laughter. Oh! How the tears ran down Wambuna's eyes.

All four laughed and laughed, laughed and laughed and laughed.

When all at once Kelfala stood, with arms akimbo[3] and stomach shot forward, and pointed to Wambuna's fireplace.

"A beautiful girl like you," he laughed, "proud as the cotton tree and the greatest cook in the village, you, you roast a Gituyu with your yams!"

Wambuna turned around.

There by the giant firestone, on the ashes, was Kelfala's something. A shrunken, old, burnt Gituyu!

Wambuna caught her breath, looked from Kelfala to his friends, and cried out between tears and laughter. "A Gituyu! It cannot be. It cannot . . ."

But at that Kelfala threw up his arms. "Aha! You have spoken to Kelfala. Kelfala, the great, Kelfala, the clown! Kelfala, the cunning one. Kelfala, the proud husband of a proud wife!"

The laughter was mine, see, I started it.

"Wait a minute, Kelfala," one of his friends said. "Kelfala, I tell you now, she doesn't belong to you."

"Oh no, you Shortie Bumpie? The trick was mine, see?" and with that, Kelfala hopped.

"The plan was mine, see?" and with that, Kelfala skipped.

"The secret was mine, see?" and with that, he jumped.

"The Gituyu was mine, see? My secret something! And the laughter was mine, see, I started it." And with that, he laughed and laughed and laughed. . . .

Wambuna stood, amazed, but she soon found support in Shortie Bumpie and Longie Tallie.

"I know that a man has had three wives, but never on this whole mountain has ever a woman shared three husbands," retorted Shortie Bumpie.

---

3. akimbo (ə kim′ bō) : with hands on hips and elbows bent outward.

"Yes, Kelfala, this girl either belongs to all of us . . . or none of us," cried the other friend.

You could see Kelfala's heart heaving.

"What did you say? You, Longie Tallie?"

Wambuna lifted her eyes.

"Yes," Longie Tallie went on. "Wambuna laughed at you. She cried at you. She mumbled, she grumbled at you. She laughed-cried. She laughed-mumbled-cried at you. But she talked to all three of us!"

Wambuna pressed her lips together in a quiet, sly smile and looked into Kelfala's eyes. Then she walked back to her plants with her head raised up like a large pink rose in early spring.

Kelfala just looked, his head bowed like a weeping willow. But then he tapped his bag and grinned. "Today is only for today. There is still tomorrow. There will always be another secret."

That was tradition, too. ❧

Responding to Reading

1. Jot down your first impression of Kelfala.

2. Do you think Kelfala earns the right to fulfill his dream and marry Wambuna? Why or why not?

3. On the basis of this story, what qualities in men and women do you think the Kikuyu people value?

4. In what ways are Kelfala and Lazy Peter similar? How are they different?

E X P L A I N

Responding to Reading

Comparing the Selections

1. In your opinion, which of the characters' dreams should have been easiest to fulfill? Which should have been hardest? Why?

2. What do you think is the purpose of each story? How do the purposes differ?

3. How are Phaëthon and Kelfala alike and different?

Literary Concept: Symbol

A **symbol** is a person, a thing, or an event that stands for something beyond itself, such as an idea or a group of people. For example, in Greek mythology, Zeus carries a thunderbolt, which is a symbol of his power. In "The People Could Fly," what might flying be a symbol of?

Writing Options

1. Think of a character in Unit 3 who tried to fulfill a dream. In a brief **essay,** contrast this character with Phaëthon.

2. Write an **article** for the *Kikuyu News,* headlined "Flash! Wambuna Speaks!" Then, using your imagination, tell the story of how Kelfala finally wins the right to marry Wambuna.

Vocabulary Practice

Exercise   Write the word from the list that is closest in meaning to the boldfaced word.

1. Her baby cried, but Sarah had no heart to **sing.**
2. Apollo's **home** was a palace of glittering gold.
3. He was happy to **admit** that Phaëthon was his son.
4. Apollo couldn't **discourage** his son from wanting to drive the chariot.
5. Phaëthon didn't mean to **burn** the earth.

> *Words
> to Know
> and Use*
> ───
> **abode
> acknowledge
> croon
> dissuade
> sear**

E X T E N D

Options for Learning

1 • **Myth Maker** Create a myth to explain the origin of a natural occurrence, such as a volcano eruption. You may use Greek gods or gods you create. Share your myth with your classmates.

2 • **Cover Art** Design a book jacket for a book containing one of these tales. Create an inviting illustration and share your drawing with the class.

Moira Kerr   1938–

Moira Kerr wrote her own versions of myths when her students did not enjoy the versions they were reading. She joined her artist friend John Bennett to create an illustrated book, *Myth*.

Born in Canada, Kerr taught for several years in Toronto. She now works in Oklahoma as a psychologist and is studying for her doctorate in ministry. "Much of my interest in life," Kerr says, "has been exploring the deep wisdom which lies within all of us."

Virginia Hamilton   1936–

Virginia Hamilton's future brightened when she received a college scholarship. Later, she began working on a children's story she had started in college, which became *Zeely,* her first book. In 1975 she became the first black writer to win the Newbery Medal, for her book *M. C. Higgins, the Great.* She speaks from her own family's experience when she writes about escaping slaves. Hamilton's great-grandmother is said to have been a conductor on the Underground Railroad.

Adjai Robinson   1932–

Growing up in Sierra Leone, Adjai Robinson listened to storytellers recount wonderful tales. Later, he began to record folk tales and became a storyteller on the radio. Robinson came to the United States to lead workshops about African folklore and to attend Columbia University. In 1975 he moved to Nigeria to become principal education officer at the Nigeria Teachers Institute. Robinson has since published a number of children's books.

E X P L O R E

Person to Person

Links to
Unit Four

Prometheus   BERNARD EVSLIN
Where the Girl Saved Her Brother   RACHEL STRANGE OWL
How Odin Lost His Eye   CATHARINE F. SELLEW

Examine What You Know

Almost every culture has myths and legends about people or gods who sacrifice themselves for others, or who risk doing so. Can you think of any myths or legends about great sacrifice? Why are such stories appealing or important? Discuss your ideas with your class.

Expand Your Knowledge

"Prometheus" (prō mē′ thē əs) tells about the sacrifice made by a Greek god to serve humanity. Prometheus and his brother Epimetheus (ep′ ə mē′ thē əs) belonged to the oldest generation of gods, the giant Titans. They were the only two Titans who had sided with Zeus in his battle against his father Cronus (crō′ nəs), another Titan, to become supreme ruler. After his victory Zeus ordered Prometheus to create human beings. As you will see, Prometheus and Zeus disagreed about how to treat the humans.

"Where the Girl Saved Her Brother" describes a woman who risked her own life for her brother. This Native American legend is about the Battle of the Rosebud, which took place in southern Montana on June 17, 1876. This version is told by Rachel Strange Owl, a present-day Cheyenne. Such legends have been used as a way of passing along Native American history.

"How Odin Lost His Eye" is a myth that tells about the efforts of the mightiest Norse (Scandinavian) god to protect human beings. Odin lived with other Norse gods in a heavenly realm called Asgard. From his tall throne he watched over the humans whom he had created. Odin hoped to guard humans from his enemies, the evil frost giants, who roamed an icy realm called Jotunnheim.

Write Before You Read

■ *Author biographies*
on Extend page

What is the most memorable story of sacrifice for the good of others that you have heard? Summarize the story in a few sentences. As you read, compare that story with the selections.

Prometheus

BERNARD EVSLIN

Prometheus was a young Titan, no great admirer of Zeus. Although he knew the great lord of the sky hated explicit questions, he did not hesitate to beard[1] him when there was something he wanted to know.

One morning he came to Zeus and said, "O Thunderer, I do not understand your design. You have caused the race of man to appear on earth, but you keep him in ignorance and darkness."

"Perhaps you had better leave the race of man to me," said Zeus. "What you call ignorance is innocence. What you call darkness is the shadow of my decree. Man is happy now. And he is so framed that he will remain happy unless someone persuades him that he is unhappy. Let us not speak of this again."

But Prometheus said, "Look at him. Look below. He crouches in caves. He is at the mercy of beast and weather. He eats his meat raw. If you mean something by this, enlighten me with your wisdom. Tell me why you refuse to give man the gift of fire."

Zeus answered, "Do you not know, Prometheus, that every gift brings a penalty? This is the way the Fates[2] weave destiny–by which gods also must abide.

Man does not have fire, true, nor the crafts which fire teaches. On the other hand, he does not know disease, warfare, old age, or that inward pest called worry. He is happy, I say, happy without fire. And so he shall remain."

"Happy as beasts are happy," said Prometheus. "Of what use to make a separate race called man and endow him with little fur, some wit, and a curious charm of unpredictability? If he must live like this, why separate him from the beasts at all?"

"He has another quality," said Zeus, "the capacity for worship. An aptitude for admiring our power, being puzzled by our riddles and amazed by our caprice.[3] That is why he was made."

"Would not fire, and the graces he can put on with fire, make him more interesting?"

"More interesting, perhaps, but infinitely more dangerous. For there is this in man too: a vaunting pride that needs little sustenance to make it swell to giant size. Improve his lot, and he will forget that

---

1. **beard**: to face up to.
2. **Fates**: in Greek mythology, the three goddesses who decide the course of people's lives.
3. **caprice** (kə prēs'): the quality of acting impulsively.

Words to Know and Use	**explicit** (eks plis' it) *adj.* plain; straightforward **endow** (en dou') *v.* to provide with a quality or a talent **aptitude** (ap' tə tōōd') *n.* a natural ability **sustenance** (sus' tə nəns) *n.* nourishment; assistance

PROMETHEUS CARRYING FIRE Jan Cossiers The Prado, Madrid Bridgeman/Art Resource, New York.

a reed filled with a dry fiber; he thrust it into the sunrise until a spark smoldered. Then he put the reed in his tunic and came down from the mountain.

At first men were frightened by the gift. It was so hot, so quick; it bit sharply when you touched it, and for pure spite made the shadows dance. They thanked Prometheus and asked him to take it away. But he took the haunch[4] of a newly killed deer and held it over the fire. And when the meat began to sear and sputter, filling the cave with its rich smells, the people felt themselves melting with hunger and flung themselves on the meat and devoured it greedily, burning their tongues.

"This that I have brought you is called 'fire,'" Prometheus said. "It is an ill-natured spirit, a little brother of the sun, but if you handle it carefully, it can change your whole life. It is very greedy; you must feed it twigs, but only until it becomes a proper size. Then you must stop, or it will eat everything in sight—and you too. If it escapes, use this magic: water. It fears the water spirit, and if you touch it with water, it will fly away until you need it again."

He left the fire burning in the first cave, with children staring at it wide-eyed, and then went to every cave in the land.

Then one day Zeus looked down from the mountain and was amazed. Everything had changed. Man had come out of his cave. Zeus saw woodmen's huts, farmhouses, villages, walled towns, even a castle or two. He saw men cooking their food, carrying torches to light their way at night. He saw forges blazing, men beating out

which makes him pleasing—his sense of worship, his humility. He will grow big and poisoned with pride and fancy himself a god, and before we know it, we shall see him storming Olympus. Enough, Prometheus! I have been patient with you, but do not try me too far. Go now and trouble me no more with your speculations."

Prometheus was not satisfied. All that night he lay awake making plans. Then he left his couch at dawn and, standing tiptoe on Olympus, stretched his arm to the eastern horizon where the first faint flames of the sun were flickering. In his hand he held

---

4. **haunch:** the hip and leg of an animal.

ploughs, keels, swords, spears. They were making ships and raising white wings of sails and daring to use the fury of the winds for their journeys. They were wearing helmets, riding out in chariots to do battle, like the gods themselves.

Zeus was full of rage. He seized his largest thunderbolt. "So they want fire," he said to himself. "I'll give them fire—more than they can use. I'll turn their miserable little ball of earth into a cinder." But then another thought came to him, and he lowered his arm. "No," he said to himself, "I shall have vengeance—and entertainment too. Let them destroy themselves with their new skills. This will make a long, twisted game, interesting to watch. I'll attend to them later. My first business is with Prometheus."

He called his giant guards and had them seize Prometheus, drag him off to the Caucasus,[5] and there bind him to a mountain peak with great chains specially forged by Hephaestus[6]—chains which even a Titan in agony could not break. And when the friend of man was bound to the mountain, Zeus sent two vultures to <u>hover</u> about him forever, tearing at his belly and eating his liver.

Men knew a terrible thing was happening on the mountain, but they did not know what. But the wind shrieked like a giant in torment and sometimes like fierce birds.

Many centuries he lay there—until another hero was born brave enough to defy the gods. He climbed to the peak in the Caucasus and struck the shackles[7] from Prometheus and killed the vultures. His name was Heracles. ❧

---

5. **Caucasus** (kô′ kə səs): a mountainous region in southeastern Europe, between the Black and Caspian seas.
6. **Hephaestus** (hē fes′ təs): in Greek mythology, the god of fire and metalworking.
7. **shackles:** metal bands for holding the ankles or wrists of a prisoner.

*R*esponding to Reading

1. What were your first impressions of Zeus and Prometheus? In your journal write down words and phrases to describe them.

2. Prometheus views fire as a great gift, while Zeus focuses on the "penalty" that such a gift brings. In your opinion, which god makes the most sense in his views on human beings and fire?

   Think about
   - the changes that Prometheus' gift brings to people's lives
   - Zeus' dark predictions about humans
   - whether fire brings humans greater happiness

3. Prometheus knows that it is dangerous to anger Zeus. Why do you think he risks so much to help humans?

Words to Know and Use | **hover** (huv′ ər) *v.* to fly or flutter over a place as if suspended

Where the Girl Saved Her Brother

Told by RACHEL STRANGE OWL

Almost exactly a hundred years ago, in the summer of 1876, the two greatest battles between soldiers and Indians were fought on the plains of Montana. The first fight was called the Battle of the Rosebud. The second battle, which was fought a week later, was called the Battle of the Little Big Horn, where General Custer was defeated and killed. The Cheyennes call the Battle of the Rosebud the fight "Where the Girl Saved Her Brother." Let me tell you why.

But first let me explain what is meant when an Indian says, "I have counted coup." "Counting coup" is gaining war honors. The Indians think that it is easy to kill an enemy by shooting him from ambush. This brings no honor. It is not counting coup. But to ride up to an enemy, or walk up to him while he is still alive, unwounded and armed, and then to hit him with your feathered coup stick, or touch him with your hand, this brings honor and earns you eagle feathers. This is counting coup. To steal horses in a daring raid can also be counting coup. But one of the greatest honors is to be gained by dashing with your horse into the midst of your enemies to rescue a friend, surrounded and unhorsed, to

take him up behind you and gallop out again, saving his life by risking your own. That is counting coup indeed, counting big coup.

Well, a hundred years ago, the white men wanted the Indians to go into prisons called "reservations," to give up their freedom to roam and hunt buffalo, to give up being Indians. Some gave in tamely and went to live behind the barbed wire of the agencies, but others did not.

Those who went to the reservations to live like white men were called "friendlies." Those who would not go were called "hostiles." They were not hostile, really. They did not want to fight. All they wanted was to be left alone to live the Indian way, which was a good way. But the soldiers would not let them. They decided to make a great surround and catch all "hostiles," kill those who resisted, and bring the others back as prisoners to the agencies. Three columns of soldiers entered the last stretch of land left to the red man. They were led by Generals Crook, Custer, and Terry. Crook had the most men with him, about two thousand. He also had cannon and Indian scouts to guide him. At the Rosebud he met the united Sioux and Cheyenne warriors.

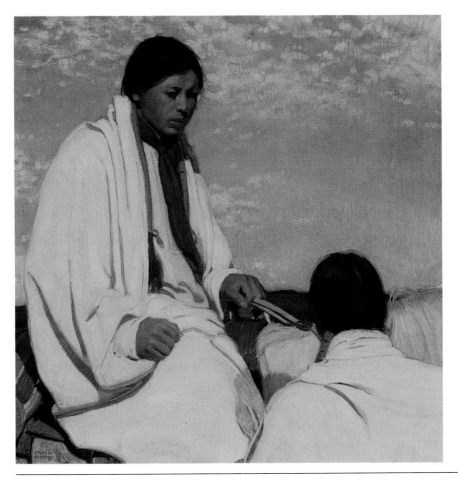

THE ENCOUNTER © 1920 Ernest Martin Hennings Courtesy, The Anschutz Collection, Denver.

The Indians had danced the sacred Sun Dance. The great Sioux chief Sitting Bull had been granted a vision telling him that the soldiers would be defeated. The warriors were in high spirits. Some men belonging to famous warrior societies had vowed to fight until they were killed, singing their death songs, throwing their lives away, as it was called. They painted their faces for war. They put on their finest outfits so that, if they were killed, their enemies should say, "This must have been a great fighter or chief. See how nobly he lies there."

The old chiefs instructed the young men how to act. The medicine men prepared the charms for the fighters, putting gopher dust on their hair, or painting their horses with hailstone designs. This was to render them invisible to their foes, or to make them bulletproof. Brave Wolf had the most admired medicine—a mounted hawk that he fastened to the back of his head. Brave Wolf always rode into battle blowing on his eaglebone whistle—and once the fight started, the hawk came alive and whistled too.

Many proud tribes were there besides the Cheyenne—the Hunkpapa, the Minniconjou, the Oglala, the Burned Thighs, the Two Kettles—and many famous chiefs and brave warriors—Two Moons, White Bull, Dirty Moccasins, Little Hawk, Yellow Eagle, Lame White Man. Among the Sioux was the great Crazy Horse, and Sitting Bull—their holy man still weak from his flesh offerings made at the Sun Dance—and the fierce Rain-in-the-Face. Who can count them all, and what a fine sight they were!

Those who earned the right to wear war bonnets were singing, lifting them up. Three times they stopped in their singing, and the fourth time they put the bonnets on their heads, letting the streamers fly and trail behind them. How good it must have been to see this! What would I give to have been there!

Crazy Horse of the Oglala shouted his famous war cry, "A good day to die, and a good day to fight. Cowards to the rear, brave hearts—follow me!"

The fight started. Many brave deeds were done, many coups counted. The battle swayed to and fro. More than anybody else's, this was the Cheyenne's fight. This was their day. Among them was a brave young girl, Buffalo Calf Road Woman, who rode proudly at the side of her husband, Black Coyote. Her brother, Chief Comes-in-Sight, was in the battle too. She looked for him and at last saw him. His horse had been killed from under him. He was surrounded. Soldiers were aiming their rifles at him. Their white Crow scouts circled around him, waiting for an opportunity to count cheap coups upon him. But he fought them with bravery and skill.

If their women fight like this, what will their warriors be like?

Buffalo Calf Road Woman uttered a shrill, high-pitched war cry. She raced her pony right into the midst of the battle, into the midst of the enemy. She made the spine-chilling, trilling, warbling sound of the Indian woman encouraging her man during a fight. Chief Comes-in-Sight jumped up on her horse behind his sister. Buffalo Calf Road Woman laughed with joy and with the excitement of battle. Buffalo Calf Road Woman sang while she was doing this. The soldiers were firing at her, and their Crow scouts were shooting arrows at her horse— but it moved too fast for her or Chief Comes-in-Sight to be hit. Then she turned her horse and raced up the hill from which the old chiefs and the medicine men watched the battle. The Sioux and Cheyenne saw what was being done. And then the white soldiers saw it too. They all stopped fighting and just looked at that brave girl saving her brother's life. The warriors raised their arms and set up a mighty shout—a long, trilling, undulating war cry that made one's hairs stand on end. And even some of the soldiers threw their caps in the air and shouted "Hurrah" in honor of Buffalo Calf Road Woman.

The battle was still young. Not many men had been killed on either side, but the white general was thinking, "If their women fight like this, what will their warriors be like? Even if I win, I will lose half my men." And so General Crook retreated a hundred miles or so. He was to have joined up with Custer, Old Yellow Hair, but when Custer had to fight the same Cheyennes and Sioux again a week later, Crook was far away and Custer's army was wiped out. So Buffalo Calf Road Woman in a way contributed to the winning of that famous battle too.

Many who saw what she had done thought that she had counted the biggest coup—not taking life but giving it. That is why the Indians call the Battle of the Rosebud "Where the Girl Saved Her Brother."

The spot where Buffalo Calf Road Woman counted coup has long since been plowed under. A ranch now covers it. But the memory of her deed lives on—and will live on as long as there are Indians. This is not a fairy tale, but it is a legend. ❧

Responding to Reading

1. What was your favorite part of the story? Jot down your thoughts in your journal or notebook.

2. As you know, a legend may be based on a real person or event. What parts of this story could be true? What parts seem imaginary?

3. Why do you think the story of Buffalo Calf Road Woman continues to be told more than a hundred years after the event?

How Odin Lost His Eye

CATHARINE F. SELLEW

Once when the world was still very young, Odin sat on his throne in the most beautiful palace in Asgard. His throne was so high that he could see over all three parts of the world from where he sat. On his head he wore a helmet shaped like an eagle. On his shoulders perched two black ravens called Memory and Thought. And at his feet crouched two snarling wolves.

The great king gazed thoughtfully down on the earth below him. He had made the green land that stretched out before his eyes. With the help of the other gods, he had made men and women who lived on that earth. And he felt truly like the All-father he was called.

The fair elves had promised they would help his children of the earth. The elves were the tiny people who lived between heaven and earth. They were so small that they could flit about doing their work unseen. Odin knew that they were the artists who painted the flowers and made the beds for the streams. They took care of all the bees and the butterflies. And it was the elves who brought the gentle rain and sunshine to the earth.

Even the ugly dwarfs, who lived in the heart of the mountains, agreed to help.

They forged iron and metals, made tools and weapons. They dug gold and silver and beautiful jewels out of the earth. Sometimes they even cut the grain and ground the flour for the farmers on the earth.

All seemed to be going well. Odin found it hard to think of evil times. But he knew that the frost giants were only waiting for a chance to bring trouble to his children. They were the ones who brought cold and ice to the world and shook the earth in anger. They hated Odin and all the work of the gods.

And from high on his throne, Odin looked down beyond the earth, deep into the gloomy land of his enemies. He saw dark figures of huge men moving about. They looked like evil shadows. He, the king of the gods, must have more wisdom. It was not enough just to see his enemies. He must know more about them.

So Odin wrapped his tall figure in a blue cloak. Down from his throne he climbed. Down the broad rainbow bridge he strode, and across the green earth till he came to one of the roots of the great evergreen tree. There, close by the tree, was a well full of clear water. Its surface was so still it was like a mirror. In it one could see pictures of things that had happened and things that were going to happen.

But beside the well sat an old man. His face was lined with the troubles of the world. His name was Mimir, which means "memory." No one, not even the great Odin, could see the pictures in the well unless he first drank some of its water. Only Mimir could give the magic drink.

"Aged Mimir," Odin said to the old man, "you who hold the knowledge of the past and future in your magic waters, let me have but one sip. Then I can know enough to protect the men and women of the earth from the hate of the giants."

Mimir looked kindly at Odin, but he did not smile. Although he spoke softly, his voice was so deep it reminded Odin of the distant roar of the ocean.

"The price of one drink from this well is not cheap," Mimir said. "And once you have drunk and gazed into the mirror of life, you may wish you had not. For sorrow and death as well as joy are pictured there. Think again before you ask to drink."

But once the king of the gods had made up his mind, nothing could change it. He was not afraid to look upon sorrow and death.

"What is your price, aged Mimir?" Odin asked.

"You are great and good, Odin," answered Mimir. "You have worked hard to make the world. Only those who know hard work may drink from my well. However, that is not enough. What have you given up that is very dear to you? What have you sacrificed? The price of a drink must be a great sacrifice. Are you still willing to pay the price?"

What could the king of the gods sacri-

fice? What was most dear to him? Odin thought of his handsome son, Balder, whom he loved most in the world. To give up his son would be like giving up life and all that was wonderful around him. Odin stood silent before Mimir. Indeed that would be a high price!

Then Mimir spoke again. He had read Odin's thoughts.

"No, I am not asking for your dear son. The Fates say his life must be short, but he has time yet to live and bring happiness to the gods and the world. I ask for one of your eyes."

© Hulton Deutsch.

Odin put his hands up to his bright blue eyes. Those two eyes had gazed across the world from his high throne in the shining city of the gods. His eyes had taught him what was good and beautiful, what was evil and ugly. But those eyes had also seen his children, the men and women of the earth, struggling against the hate of the giants. One eye was a small sacrifice to win knowledge of how to help them. And without another thought, Odin plucked out one of his blue eyes and handed it to Mimir.

Then Mimir smiled and gave Odin a horn full of the waters of his well.

"Drink deeply, brave king, so you may see all that you wish in the mirror of life."

Odin lifted the horn to his lips and drank. Then he knelt by the edge of the well and watched the pictures passing across its still and silent surface. When he stood up again, he sighed, for it was as Mimir had said. He had seen sorrow and death as well as joy. It was only the glorious promise at the end, that gave him courage to go on.

So Odin, the great king of the gods, became one-eyed. If you can find Mimir's well, you will see Odin's blue eye resting on the bottom. It is there to remind men and women of the great sacrifice he made for them. ❧

*R*esponding to Reading

1. What was your reaction to Odin's sacrifice of his eye? Record your thoughts in your journal or notebook.

2. Odin wants to protect people from the frost giants. Why do you think he seeks knowledge instead of some other kind of help?

   Think about
   • what Odin might see in the well
   • how knowledge could help him

3. What do you think is the "glorious promise" that Odin sees in the well?

4. Why do you think this myth was first told? What message might its creators have wanted to share?

E X P L A I N

Responding to Reading

Comparing the Selections

1. What do the two myths and the legend reveal about the traits or qualities that are admired in each society? Consider why each character is considered heroic.

2. Compare these three tales with the stories of sacrifice that you discussed before reading. What do all the stories have in common?

Broader Connections

3. Do you think humanity is making progress, as Prometheus believed we would; or is the human race going downhill, as Zeus predicted; or is humanity somewhere in the middle, as Odin seemed to believe?

Literary Concept: Hero/Heroine

A **hero** or **heroine** is a character whose actions win great admiration. In myths and legends the heroes represent the qualities that societies most admire. Which character do you consider most heroic—Prometheus, Odin, or Buffalo Calf Road Woman? Why?

Concept Review: Symbol What do you think fire symbolizes in "Prometheus"? Work with a partner to explore your ideas.

Writing Options

1. Write a **myth** about a modern Prometheus who wants to save humanity by giving it one more gift.

2. Write a **dialogue** between Prometheus, Odin, and Buffalo Calf Road Woman in which they discuss their frightening experiences.

Vocabulary Practice

Exercise Write a word from the list to fill in each blank.

Zeus had the power to __1__ humans with the ability, or __2__, to cook food for their own __3__. He might have chosen to give them __4__ instructions and to __5__ over them to make sure they used fire correctly.

> **Words to Know and Use**
>
> ---
>
> **aptitude**
> **endow**
> **explicit**
> **hover**
> **sustenance**

Options for Learning

1 • Art for the Ages Illustrate one of the stories. Draw a series of sketches to illustrate the entire piece or draw a detailed version of one key scene.

2 • History Hunt Find out more about either the Battle of the Rosebud or the Battle of the Little Bighorn. Report your findings to the class.

Bernard Evslin 1922–

When Bernard Evslin's wife asked for advice on how to interest her students in mythology, he wrote his own version of a Greek myth. The students loved his story and asked for more, which Evslin supplied. He went on to write more than thirty books for young people, including *The Greek Gods and Heroes.* Over six million copies of his works are in print.

Evslin has also written award-winning television documentaries and two plays. One of his books, *The Green Hero,* was nominated for a National Book Award.

Rachel Strange Owl 1947–

Rachel Strange Owl, a Cheyenne Indian, lives on the Northern Cheyenne Lame Deer Reservation in Montana. In the early 1970s she told the legend "Where the Girl Saved Her Brother" to Richard Erdoes, a collector of Native American myths and legends. She first heard the story, which is based on actual events, from her mother.

Today, Strange Owl lives on the reservation with her husband and several of her seven children. She supervises artists who bead high-fashion clothes with Cheyenne and Cree designs.

Catharine F. Sellew 1922–1982

As a child, Catharine Sellew loved to listen as her mother read myths. Sellew later studied mythology and went on to publish her first collection of ancient Greek myths, *Adventures with the Gods.*

She then retold Norse myths in *Adventures with the Giants* and *Adventures with the Heroes.* She also retold stories from the Old Testament and wrote a novel for teenagers entitled *Torchlight.*

A Question of Identity

Examine What You Know

Beauty is a key issue in a number of myths and folk tales. In many cases beauty is tied very closely to a character's identity. With a small group of classmates, list as many tales as you can—some of which may have been turned into animated movies—that deal with beauty. Compare your list with those of your classmates and discuss why beauty so often plays a role in such stories.

Expand Your Knowledge

"Echo and Narcissus" tells the story of a Greek youth, Narcissus (när sis' əs), who was famous for his beauty. The myth really begins with Zeus, who never lost his desire for pretty women, despite his marriage to Hera. Zeus often roamed the forests of the earth looking for nymphs—minor nature goddesses in the form of beautiful women. His jealous wife usually came looking for him, causing problems for anyone who got in her way. Hera never showed mercy to any nymph, including Echo.

"The Emperor's New Clothes" focuses not on beautiful faces but on beautiful clothes. This folk tale by Hans Christian Andersen of Denmark offers a humorous look at people's concern about their appearance.

"The Fatal Flower," a folk tale that originated in China, gives another view of beauty. Though the Chinese admire physical beauty, the desire for loveliness may be offset by the need to conform to society's roles. This thought is expressed by an old Chinese proverb, "The nail that sticks out gets hammered." Chinese immigrants to the United States told this tale to their children as a warning.

Write Before You Read

Write your own proverb—a wise saying—about beauty. An example of such a proverb is "Beauty is only skin deep, but ugly goes to the bone." As you read, compare your proverb with the lessons of the stories.

■ *Author biographies on Extend page*

GREEK MYTH

Echo and Narcissus

MOIRA KERR / JOHN BENNETT

Not many men, or even gods, were as handsome as young Narcissus. So fair was he that almost everyone who saw him fell in love with him that very moment.

One day, as Narcissus roamed the forests with his hunting companions, he was spied by the watchful eye of the nymph Echo. She had once been a great chatterer, ready to talk to any passerby on any subject at any time, and on several occasions she had detained the goddess Hera with hours of casual talk, just as Hera was on the point of stumbling upon Zeus with one of his illicit[1] loves. Eventually Hera grew so annoyed that she put a curse on Echo, and from that time on the unfortunate nymph could say nothing but the last few words that she had heard.

Trembling, Echo followed Narcissus through the trees. She longed to go closer to him, to gaze upon the beauty of his face, but she feared that he would laugh at her silly speech. Before long Narcissus wandered away from his companions, and when he realized he was lost, he called in panic, "Is there anybody here?"

"Here!" called Echo.

Mystified by this reply, Narcissus shouted, "Come!"

"Come!" shouted Echo.

Narcissus was convinced that someone was playing tricks on him.

"Why are you avoiding me?" he called. The only answer he heard was his own question repeated from the woods.

"Come here, and let us meet!" pleaded Narcissus.

"Let us meet!" Echo answered, delighted.

She overcame her shyness and crept from her hiding place to approach Narcissus. But he, satisfied now that he had solved the mystery of the voice, roughly pushed her away and ran.

"I would die before I would have you near me!" he shouted mockingly over his shoulder.

Helpless, Echo had to call after him, "I would have you near me!"

The nymph was so embarrassed and ashamed that she hid herself in a dark cave and never came into the air and sunlight again. Her youth and beauty withered away, and her body became so shrunken and tiny that eventually she vanished altogether. All that was left was the pathetic voice which still roams the world, anxious to talk, yet able only to repeat what others say.

---

1. **illicit** (il lis′ it): against custom or law

Poor Echo was not the only one to be treated brutally by Narcissus. He had played with many hearts, and at last one of those he had scorned prayed to the gods that Narcissus would some day find himself scorned by one he loved. The prayer was heard and granted.

Tired and thirsty from his hunting, Narcissus threw himself down beside a still, clear pool to drink. As he leaned over the shining surface, he saw reflected the most beautiful face he had ever seen. His heart trembled at the sight, and he could not tear himself away from it—his own image.

For a long time Narcissus remained there beside the pool, never raising his eyes from the surface, and from time to time murmuring words of love. At last his body withered away and became the stem of a flower, and his head, the lovely gold and white blossom that still looks into quiet pools, and is called the narcissus. ❧

From *Favorite Greek Myths* retold by Mary Pope Osborne, illustrated by Troy Howell. Illustrations copyright © 1989 by Troy Howell. Reprinted by permission of Scholastic, Inc.

*R*esponding to Reading

1. Which character, Echo or Narcissus, made a bigger impression on you? Describe your thoughts in your journal or notebook.

2. Do you think the punishments given to Echo and Narcissus are fair?

   Think about
   • what each does to anger the gods
   • whether Echo or Narcissus deserves punishment
   • whether the punishments fit the offenses

3. How do you think Narcissus' identity is related to his appearance?

4. Myths can have more than one purpose. What are the purposes of this myth?

The Emperor's New Clothes

HANS CHRISTIAN ANDERSEN

Many years ago there was an Emperor who was so excessively fond of new clothes that he spent all his money in dress. He did not trouble himself in the least about his soldiers; nor did he care to go either to the theater or the chase, except for the opportunities they afforded him for displaying his new clothes. He had a different suit for each hour of the day; and as of any other king or emperor one is accustomed to say, "He is sitting in council," it was always said of him, "The Emperor is sitting in his wardrobe."[1]

Time passed away merrily in the large town which was his capital; strangers arrived every day at the court. One day two rogues, calling themselves weavers, made their appearance. They gave out that they knew how to weave stuffs of the most beautiful colors and elaborate patterns, the clothes manufactured from which should have the wonderful property of remaining invisible to everyone who was unfit for the office he held, or who was extraordinarily simple in character.

"These must indeed be splendid clothes!" thought the Emperor. "Had I such a suit, I might at once find out what men in my realm are unfit for their office, and also be able to distinguish the wise from the foolish! This stuff must be woven for me immediately." And he caused large sums of money to be given to both the weavers, in order that they might begin their work directly.

So the two pretended weavers set up two looms and affected[2] to work very busily, though in reality they did nothing at all. They asked for the most delicate silk and the purest gold thread, put both into their own knapsacks, and then continued their pretended work at the empty looms until late at night.

"I should like to know how the weavers are getting on with my cloth," said the Emperor to himself, after some little time had elapsed. He was, however, rather embarrassed when he remembered that a simpleton, or one unfit for his office, would be unable to see the manufacture. To be

---

1. **wardrobe:** the place in which clothing is kept in a royal household.
2. **affected:** pretended.

Words to Know and Use | **excessively** (ek ses′ iv lē) *adv.* overly; too much
rogue (rōg) *n.* a rascal
realm (relm) *n.* a kingdom

sure, he thought, he had nothing to risk in his own person, but yet he would prefer sending somebody else to bring him intelligence about the weavers and their work before he troubled himself in the affair. All the people throughout the city had heard of the wonderful property the cloth was to possess; and all were anxious to learn how wise, or how ignorant, their neighbors might prove to be.

"I will send my faithful old Minister to the weavers," said the Emperor at last, after some deliberation. "He will be best able to see how the cloth looks; he is a man of sense, and no one can be more suitable for his office than he is."

So the honest old Minister went into the hall, where the knaves[3] were working with all their might at their empty looms. "What can be the meaning of this?" thought the old man, opening his eyes very wide; "I cannot discover the least bit of thread on the looms!" However, he did not express his thoughts aloud.

The impostors requested him very courteously to be so good as to come nearer their looms, and then asked him whether the design pleased him and whether the colors were not very beautiful, at the same time pointing to the empty frames. The poor old Minister looked and looked; he could not discover anything on the looms for a very good reason: there was nothing there. "What!" thought he again. "Is it possible that I am a simpleton? I have never thought so myself, and at any rate if I am

so, no one must know it. Can it be that I am unfit for my office? No, that must not be said either. I will never confess that I could not see the stuff."

"Well, sir Minister!" said one of the knaves, still pretending to work. "You do not say whether the stuff pleases you."

"Oh, it is admirable!" replied the old Minister, looking at the loom through his spectacles. "This pattern, and the colors— yes, I will tell the Emperor without delay how very beautiful I think them."

"We shall be much obliged to you," said the impostors, and then they named the different colors and described the patterns of the pretended stuff. The old Minister listened attentively to their words in order that he might repeat them to the Emperor; and then the knaves asked for more silk and gold, saying that it was necessary to complete what they had begun. However, they put all that was given them into their knapsacks and continued to work with as much apparent diligence as before at their empty looms.

The Emperor now sent another officer of his court to see how the men were getting on and to ascertain whether the cloth would soon be ready. It was just the same with this gentleman as with the Minister: he surveyed the looms on all sides but could see nothing at all but the empty frames.

"Does not the stuff appear as beautiful to you as it did to my lord the Minister?" asked the impostors of the Emperor's second ambassador, at the same time making the same gestures as before and talking of

---

3. **knaves** (nāvz): sly, dishonest people.

*Words
to Know
and Use* | **diligence** (dil′ ə jəns) *n.* constant effort

THE SERMON (detail)   1566   Pieter Bruegel the Elder   National Gallery of Art, Budapest, Hungary.

the design and colors which were not there.

"I certainly am not stupid!" thought the messenger. "It must be that I am not fit for my good, profitable office! That is very odd; however, no one shall know anything about it." And accordingly he praised the stuff he could not see and declared that he was delighted with both colors and patterns. "Indeed, please Your Imperial Majesty," said he to his sovereign when he returned, "the cloth which the weavers are preparing is extraordinarily magnificent."

The whole city was talking of the splendid cloth which the Emperor had ordered to be woven at his own expense.

And now the Emperor himself wished to see the costly manufacture while it was still on the loom. Accompanied by a select number of officers of the court, among whom were the two honest men who had already admired the cloth, he went to the crafty impostors, who, as soon as they were aware of the Emperor's approach, went on working more diligently than ever, although they still did not pass a single thread through the looms.

"Is not the work absolutely magnificent?" said the two officers of the crown already mentioned. "If Your Majesty will only be pleased to look at it! What a splendid design! What glorious colors!" and at the same time they pointed to the empty frames, for they imagined that everyone but themselves could see this exquisite piece of workmanship.

"How is this?" said the Emperor to himself. "I can see nothing! This is indeed a terrible affair! Am I a simpleton? Or am I unfit

Words to Know and Use

sovereign (säv′ rən) *n.* a monarch; royal ruler
exquisite (eks′ kwi zit) adj. beautiful; outstanding

to be an emperor? That would be the worst thing that could happen. Oh, the cloth is charming!" said he aloud. "It has my entire approbation."[4] And he smiled most graciously and looked at the empty looms, for on no account would he say that he could not see what two of the officers of his court had praised so much. All his retinue[5] now strained their eyes, hoping to discover something on the looms, but they could see no more than the others; nevertheless they all exclaimed, "Oh! How beautiful!" and advised His Majesty to have some new clothes made from this splendid material for the approaching procession. "Magnificent! Charming! Excellent!" resounded on all sides, and everyone was uncommonly gay. The Emperor shared in the general satisfaction and presented the impostors with the riband[6] of an order of knighthood to be worn in their buttonholes, and the title of "Gentlemen Weavers."

The rogues sat up the whole of the night before the day on which the procession was to take place, and had sixteen lights burning so that everyone might see how anxious they were to finish the Emperor's new suit. They pretended to roll the cloth off the looms, cut the air with their scissors, and sewed with needles without any thread in them. "See!" cried they at last. "The Emperor's new clothes are ready!"

And now the Emperor, with all the grandees of his court, came to the weavers; and the rogues raised their arms as if in the act of holding something up, saying, "Here are Your Majesty's trousers! Here is the scarf! Here is the mantle![7] The whole suit is as light as a cobweb; one might fancy one

has nothing at all on when dressed in it; that, however, is the great virtue of this delicate cloth."

"Yes, indeed!" said all the courtiers, although not one of them could see anything of this exquisite manufacture.

"If Your Imperial Majesty will be graciously pleased to take off your clothes, we will fit on the new suit in front of the looking glass."

The Emperor was accordingly undressed, and the rogues pretended to array him in his new suit, the Emperor turning round from side to side before the looking glass.

"How splendid His Majesty looks in his new clothes, and how well they fit!" everyone cried out. "What a design! What colors! These are indeed royal robes!"

"The canopy which is to be borne over Your Majesty in the procession is waiting," announced the Chief Master of the Ceremonies.

"I am quite ready," answered the Emperor. "Do my new clothes fit well?" asked he, turning himself round again before the looking glass in order that he might appear to be examining his handsome suit.

The lords of the bedchamber, who were to carry His Majesty's train, felt about on the ground as if they were lifting up the ends of the mantle, and pretended to be carrying something; for they would by no means betray anything like simplicity or unfitness for their office.

So now the Emperor walked under his

---

4. **approbation** (ap′ rə bā′ shən): official approval.
5. **retinue** (ret′ 'n yoo′): a group of attendants or servants.
6. **riband** (rib′ band′): a decorative ribbon.
7. **mantle:** a royal robe.

high canopy in the midst of the procession, through the streets of his capital; and all the people standing by, and those at the windows, cried out, "Oh, how beautiful are our Emperor's new clothes! What a magnificent train there is to the mantle! And how gracefully the scarf hangs!" In short, no one would allow that he could not see these much-admired clothes, because in doing so, he would have declared himself either a simpleton or unfit for his office. Certainly, none of the Emperor's various suits had ever excited so much admiration as this.

"But the Emperor has nothing at all on!" said a little child. "Listen to the voice of innocence!" exclaimed his father, and what the child had said was whispered from one to another.

"But he has nothing at all on!" at last cried out all the people. The Emperor was vexed, for he knew that the people were right; but he thought, "The procession must go on now!" And the lords of the bedchamber took greater pains than ever to appear holding up a train, although in reality there was no train to hold. ❧

Responding to Reading

1. Jot down your reaction to the ending of this tale.

2. In your opinion, why is a child the one who tells the truth about the Emperor's new clothes?

3. Why do you think the Emperor and his court continue their procession even after the truth is known?

4. Why do you think the rogues are able to carry out their scheme?
    Think about
    • which people they say can see the clothes
    • why they target the Emperor for their scheme
    • how the other members of court react

5. What common human failings does the story portray?

Words to Know and Use | **vexed** (vekst) *adj.* troubled **vex** *v.*

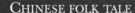

The Fatal Flower

LAURENCE YEP

Long ago in a faraway kingdom there was a girl called Gem who hated the way she looked. She was so ashamed that she refused to leave the house. Instead, she would stand in her little courtyard and peek through the gates at the other girls as they passed by in the village lane. "What pretty eyes she has," she would sigh. "Why can't I have eyes like that?" Or she would stare enviously at someone else. "Look at how graceful she is. Why can't I walk like that?"

Her exasperated mother would tell her that she looked fine. "You should go outside. You've got two eyes and a nose and a mouth, all in the right place. Why do you have to complain all the time?"

"Because other girls have their eyes, noses, and mouths arranged much better than me," Gem insisted. "I'm so repulsive that they'll just laugh."

"It's different flowers for different eyes," her mother said. Though her mother coaxed and scolded, Gem remained inside trying to make herself beautiful.

From herbs her family gathered for her, she tried to make all sorts of pills, lotions, and ointments. Some were to make her skin smooth as silk. Others were to make her

hair shiny and full. Whichever one she tried, she was always disappointed; and the smells from all her brews almost drove her family from the house. Eyes watering from the smoke and holding his nose against the stench, her father found her by the stove getting ready to throw out her latest failure. "I can't stand it anymore. They say there's a wise woman who has the power to change things. Maybe she can make you into what you want to be. Follow the river to the hill."

By now, Gem was desperate enough to try anything. The next morning before sunrise, she sneaked out with a piece of cloth wrapped around her head as a veil.

Keeping to the high riverbank, she followed the wide, muddy river until she reached the hill. The wise woman's hut sat upon the top, surrounded by terraced fields where herbs grew in neat, well-tended rows. Harvested herbs and flowers sat drying on the hut's roof or were hanging inside from the ceiling, so the hill smelled like a dusty garden of flowers.

Outside the little hut was a woman with black skin. She was winnowing rice—separating the harvested grains from the chaff and bits of straw. She would lay out handfuls of the harvest on a big, flat, round

Words to Know and Use

repulsive (ri pul' siv) *adj.* offensive; disgusting
stench (stench) *n.* a strong, foul smell

653

tray woven from bamboo and toss the contents into the air. The grain, still in its brown hulls, would rattle down, while the breeze would blow the chaff and straw away.

Kneeling before the wise woman, Gem bowed. "I look like a monster, but I hear you have the power to change me into someone beautiful."

The wise woman calmly poured the winnowed rice into a basket. "First, let's see what I have to work with."

"You've been warned." Trembling, Gem unwrapped her veil. "Just look at me. I'm too gruesome to live."

The wise woman put another handful of harvested grain upon the tray. With a powerful jerk of her arms, she tossed it up into the air. Once again, the brown rice pattered down upon the tray like hard drops of rain. "Rice is ugly, but it fills the belly." Then she nodded to the chaff and bits of straw that shone like flakes of gold as they whirled

around in the breeze. "While that fluff is pretty but useless."

Gem touched her forehead against the dirt, pleading with the wise woman to help her. With a sigh, the wise woman put her tray down and patted Gem on the shoulder. "Deep in the mountains there once lived a king and his daughter. The king was also a powerful wizard, and his daughter was almost as magical. When she died, she changed into a creeper with thin vines from which grow tiny yellow flowers like five-pointed stars. If your heart is set upon becoming beautiful, you must bring me a flower from that vine, and I will grant your wish."

So Gem traveled beside the river until it had narrowed into a cold, steely blue ribbon and the land had slanted upward into steeper and steeper hills. Though she looked everywhere, she saw nothing. Just as she was about to turn back in discouragement, she heard a voice. "Why are you wearing that veil?"

She looked all around, but she saw no one.

"Are you

MALLOWS, ASTERS,
BEETLE AND BUTTERFLY
1735 Chen Shu Chengxun
tang collection, Hong Kong.

deaf?" the voice repeated from overhead.

Leaning her head back, she saw a little woman perched on the branch of a tree. She wore an embroidered blouse and skirt, and Gem could see a pair of bird's claws peeking out from the dress as the strange little woman clung to a tree branch.

The little woman leaned her head to one side like a bird and studied Gem. "What's wrong?"

"Everything," the girl said, and explained her quest. "Do you know where the flowers grow?"

The little woman folded her arms smugly. "I certainly do."

Gem clung to the trunk of the tree. "Oh, please tell me."

The little woman leaned down and felt the veil. "First, you must bring me a piece of cloth as long as the river."

Gem thought long and hard while the bird-woman watched expectantly. Finally, Gem broke off a straight twig from a nearby branch. With a sharp rock, she made an elaborate show of marking the stick into ten equal units. Then she presented her home-made ruler to the bird-woman. "First, you must tell me the exact length of the river."

The bird-woman waved the ruler in annoyance. "I can't measure the whole river."

"Then I can't make a cloth as long as it. But," Gem said, and unwound her veil, "until you can measure the river, why don't you keep this as a sample gift?"

The bird-woman took the cloth, drawing it back and forth in her hands as she stared at Gem. "If I were a human, I'd be more ashamed of my fat, sloppy feet than my face."

Gem glanced at the woman's great, ugly claws but said only, "Where are the flowers?"

The bird-woman wrapped the cloth around her shoulders. "I'll show you." Leaping lightly to the ground, she began to hop along like a bird. Gem followed her among the trees until they came to a shadowy place where red pine trees grew in a circle. Though the scent of the pine was thick, Gem could smell another sweet fragrance that she could not name.

And in the center of the clearing was a tree about Gem's height around which grew a tangle of slender vines without any roots. Tiny yellow flowers rose from the tips of the vines like constellations of stars.

Excited, Gem was going to pluck hand-fuls of the flower, but the bird-woman stopped her. "If I can have only a sample cloth, you can take only a sample flower."

Gem tried to hide her disappointment, because the flowers were so small. "Well," she sighed, "one flower will have to do." Carefully, she selected the largest of the flowers. Tucking it away safely in a sleeve, Gem reached the wise woman late in the afternoon.

"Now, please keep your promise," Gem said triumphantly.

The wise woman took the tiny stalk between her fingers. "Remember. Beauty does not always bring happiness. Do you still wish it?"

"With all my heart."

"To my mind, a girl who is clever enough to find the flower does not need to be beautiful too." The wise woman shrugged. "But so be it. Fetch me some water from the well."

TWO BEAUTIFUL LADIES: LADY WITH FAN (detail)   1863   Ju Qing
Art Gallery, Institute of Chinese Studies, The Chinese University of Hong Kong.

Gem found a bucket and brought the water as the wise woman had asked. In the meantime, the wise woman had started a fire beneath a small stove. At the wise woman's directions, the eager girl filled a pot with water and placed it upon the top of the stove.

Then, murmuring a spell, the wise woman began to twirl the flower between her palms, faster and faster, harder and harder, until she squeezed the juice from the flower. Instantly, the hut was filled with a sweet scent that overpowered all the other fragrances. When she had wrung out the last drop, she threw the flower itself into the hole beneath the stove where the fire burned. The crushed flower disappeared in a flash of light.

Under the wise woman's watchful eye, Gem kept feeding the fire until the whole pot had almost boiled away. Carefully pouring the remaining contents into a small jar, the wise woman handed it to Gem.

"Wash your face with the first drop," the wise woman instructed. "Rub any warts and moles with the second. Swallow the third."

As the sun set, Gem skipped home clutching the jar to her chest. People turned to stare at the stranger, because no one but her own family had ever seen her. Soon, Gem said to herself, they will all be wishing they could be me.

She burst into her home, holding the jar triumphantly in the air. "I found the wise woman," she told her astounded family.

With elaborate caution, Gem poured the first drop onto her palm and washed her cheeks. Though it was only a drop, the fluid kept spreading magically until her whole face felt cool and tingly.

The second drop she massaged onto any bumps on her face, and wherever she touched, the spot burned with a pleasant warmth.

Then, raising the jar and closing her eyes, she drank the third drop. "Ai yah. Ai yah," she murmured.

"Are you feeling sick?" her mother asked anxiously.

"No." Gem hugged herself. "At least I don't think so." She gave a shiver. "But I feel as though there's lightning bouncing around inside. And each bit of lightning is tiny as an ant and they're all racing around under my skin. What kind of evil trick has the wise woman played on me?"

Terrified, Gem put her hands to her face and began to cry.

"Quick," her worried mother said. "We'll go to a doctor." The mother grabbed her wrists and tried to pull Gem toward the door.

As her mother tugged at her, Gem was forced to lower her hands. When the mother saw her daughter, she stopped in midstep.

"How terrible is it?" Gem asked. When her mother could only gape, Gem turned to her father. "Am I even more hideous?" When he only stared too, she begged her brothers to tell her, but they were as stunned as their parents.

Desperately Gem flung some water into a bowl and stared down, waiting for the water to calm down enough so she could see her reflection. She blinked when she saw the beautiful stranger gazing up at her. The stranger's face had eyebrows like the leaf of the willow, eyes like kernels of apricots, a mouth like a cherry, a face shaped like a melon seed.

As the sun set, Gem skipped home clutching the jar to her chest.

Cautiously, hardly daring to believe, she raised a hand to touch her face. Upon the surface of the water, the lovely stranger also raised a delicate hand.

"It worked," she said. "It worked!"

Word of her beauty quickly spread through the countryside, for there was no one as lovely as she.

About that time, though, the king of the land fell sick with a terrible fever that burned through his body like flames through an old log. Hurriedly his doctors examined him and, after a lengthy consultation among themselves, went to his heir, the prince. "Everyone has the elements of yin and yang.[1] His Highness burns because he has too much fiery yang and must be cooled with yin. Because his illness is so severe, it must be quickly countered with a powerful dose."

"What are you waiting for?" the prince demanded. "Do it!"

The doctors bowed deeply, and their chief hardly dared to look up at the angry prince. "We regret to inform you that yin is most concentrated in the heart of a beautiful girl. We must cut it out."

The prince paled. "Is there no other way?"

The chief doctor apologized and said, "It would take too long to gather it from other sources. He must have a broth made from such a heart as soon as possible, or His Highness will surely die."

The prince took a breath and then nodded. "So be it." That very night he sent men racing from the palace across the kingdom to fetch back the most beautiful girls.

In her village, Gem woke to the frightened cries and the wailing. Her sleepy father staggered into the lane to find out what was happening. Hastily he scurried back, wide-eyed with the news. "Everyone with a pretty daughter is telling the king's men to come here for you. They want to cut out your heart."

"Quickly. Go hide in the hills," her mother ordered her daughter. "We'll put up a fuss and distract them for as long as we can."

Gem slid out of the courtyard gate and darted away from the lights by the village gates. Moving a cart against the village walls, she managed to climb to the top of a wall. To her dismay, she saw men with torches ringing the village.

She dropped back down within the village and tried to hide, but the other villagers, fearing for the lives of their own daughters, pointed at Gem and called to the king's men. Not knowing where else to go, she stumbled into the temple of the goddess of mercy. As she heard the mob coming toward her, she collapsed in despair.

The next instant there was a flash of light, and the wise woman was standing there with her arms folded in front of her. With a cry, Gem crawled on her hands and knees toward the wise woman. "Save me. This cursed beauty will be my death."

The wise woman looked down at her sternly. "Make up your mind. Are you too beautiful or too ugly to live?"

However, as the terrified girl begged for help, the wise woman's expression softened. From her sleeve, she produced another small jar. "I thought you might be needing this, so I saved the last three drops. Use them as before."

Shaking with fright, Gem took the jar from the wise woman, who disappeared just

---

1. **yin and yang:** in Chinese philosophy, the two primary forces in the universe. The first is passive and negative; the second, active and positive.

Words to Know and Use | **consultation** (kän′ səl tā′ shən) *n.* a meeting to discuss or decide something

as quickly as she had come. Hastily Gem rubbed one drop on her face, dotted her face with the second, and swallowed the third.

As the mob burst into the temple, they found Gem cowering upon the floor of the temple. Sure that they had found the most beautiful girl, they yanked her to her feet; but when they saw her, they became angry. "She's just an ordinary girl," their captain said. "They've just been playing a trick on us."

And kicking and slapping the villagers who had led them there, the soldiers left Gem alone in the temple.

As it turned out, the king's fever broke that night and he recovered. And when he was well and heard what had almost happened, he dismissed all his old doctors and hired new ones.

As for Gem, she found her looks were adequate for her needs. ❧

Responding to Reading

1. What feelings did you have about Gem? Jot down your reactions in your journal or notebook.

2. What do you think are Gem's strengths and weaknesses?

3. What does the story reveal about Chinese values?

   Think about
   • why it is dangerous to stand apart from the crowd
   • the advice given to Gem by her mother and the wise woman

4. If you could become more handsome or more beautiful, as Gem did, would you? Explain your feelings.

*R*esponding to Reading

Comparing the Selections

1. On the basis of what you learned from these tales, how are the Greek and Chinese attitudes towards beauty alike and different?

2. In your opinion, which selection is more critical of those in power, "The Emperor's New Clothes" or "The Fatal Flower"?

Broader Connections

3. What modern products do you think would tempt Narcissus, the Emperor, and Gem?

*L*iterary Concept: Literary Folk Tale

Although Hans Christian Andersen relied on the folklore of Denmark for many of his tales, he also invented new stories and gave new twists to old ones. His works are called **literary folk tales** because they have their origin in writing, not oral retellings. Andersen's stories were written for children. What do you think children would like about this story?

*W*riting Options

1. In a **letter** from Gem to the organizers of a beauty pageant, express her thoughts about the pageant's effects on contestants.

2. Choose a well-known person for the Narcissus "I Love Myself" Prize. Write a **testimonial** explaining that person's qualifications.

*V*ocabulary Practice

Exercise   Recopy the paragraph below, replacing each boldfaced word with a word from the list.

King Elmer was a most **offensive ruler.** He was a selfish **crook** with an **overly** bad **odor.** He became so **annoyed** with his **beautiful** wife, who worked with **persistence** in a **meeting** with his enemies, that he threw her out of his **kingdom.**

Words to Know and Use

consultation
diligence
excessively
exquisite
realm
repulsive
rogue
sovereign
stench
vexed

Options for Learning

1 • Rogue's Business Imagine that the two rogues in "The Emperor's New Clothes" set up shop in your town. Work in a small group to devise products they might sell, and create a brochure about the products.

2 • The Selling of Beauty Create a television ad in which either Gem or Narcissus endorses a beauty product, such as "Gem Lotion." Act out your ad in class.

Hans Christian Andersen   1805–1875

At the age of fourteen, Hans Christian Andersen, the son of a poor washerwoman and a shoemaker, went to Copenhagen, the capital of Denmark, hoping to win fame in the theater. He failed as an actor, a dancer, and a singer before he finally found patrons who arranged for his education.

Later, he turned to writing. In 1835 he published a cheap booklet called *Tales Told for Children*. His tales became immensely popular, gaining him fame across Europe. Andersen went on to write 168 tales, including "The Princess and the Pea," and "The Ugly Duckling."

Interestingly, Andersen never thought highly of his tales, perhaps because he always hoped his success would come in the theater. Also, he had no particular liking for children.

Laurence Yep   1948–

Yep published his first short story as a college freshman. When only twenty-five, he published his first book. Two years later he wrote his second book, *Dragonwings,* which won ten awards, including a Newbery Medal Honor Award. He has written over seventeen books and two plays, many of them reflecting his Chinese heritage.

His books, such as *Child of the Owl* and *Sea Glass,* often focus on characters caught between two cultures. Yep says that his books are popular among teenagers because "I'm always pursuing the theme of being an outsider—an alien—and many teenagers feel they're aliens."

Yep has also taught at various schools, including the University of California at Berkeley, where he was a writer in residence.

■ *A biography of Moira Kerr can be found on page 631.*

WRITER'S WORKSHOP

WRITER'S CHOICE

As you discovered in this unit, the forms of folklore are many and varied. In this workshop your writing opportunities are varied as well. You can pick a format of your choice—one that you've enjoyed before. You can make your own PASSkey and create your own steps. So go ahead! Choose the assignment you like best, loosen up your writing arm, and let your imagination fly.

A. Narrative Writing: Where Did It Come From?

It's hard to imagine, but long ago when the world was young, there were no VCR's, microwave ovens, soft drink machines, or even blow dryers. How did these miraculous devices originate? Which gods or goddesses, heroes or heroines, might have been responsible? Write a myth that explains the "origin" of a modern technological device.

NEED MORE HELP?

A **myth** is a story—a narrative. For more about writing a narrative, see the Writer's Workshop on pages 174–178.

Prewrite and Explore   You might start by listing six to eight technological devices you use or see others use daily. Then you can choose a device and brainstorm, perhaps with friends, about its "mythical" origin. Feel free to make up new gods and heroes, giving them appropriate names, duties, and supernatural powers.

Draft and Discover   You can write your myth in chronological order. As you write, think about causes and effects. For example, the device you've chosen is an effect, and the actions of your characters are its causes. Make the effects of actions clear.

NEED MORE HELP?

For more about cause and effect, see the Reader's Workshop on page 182.

Revise Your Writing   Use the checklist on page 177 to revise your work. Ask a classmate to help.

B. Descriptive/Informative Writing: As Great-Grandma Used to Say . . .

Every family has its own stories and sayings, just as every culture has its own folklore. Some stories feature things that family members have done or seen. Other favorites may spring from a family's ethnic heritage. Write about the place that stories and sayings have in your family. Describe the people who recite them and the ways that other family members respond.

Prewrite and Explore Try jotting notes about *who* tells your family's folklore and *when, where, why,* and *how* it's told. Then you can rough out one or two general statements about the importance of this folklore to your family.

Draft and Discover You might open with a description of a family storyteller in action. Then, in two or three paragraphs, you can explain your ideas about the role of folklore in your family. Include examples and anecdotes, and don't forget to state your own feelings.

Revise Your Writing Use the checklists for descriptive writing, page 112, and informative writing, page 573, as revision guides.

◀ **NEED HELP?**

For more about descriptive writing, see the Writer's Workshop on pages 109–113. For more about informative writing, see the Writer's Workshop on pages 569–573.

C. Writing About Literature: Watch That Trickster!

Talk about sly! You have to get up pretty early in the morning to outwit tricksters like Lazy Peter, Anansi the spider, and Anansi's friend Turtle. Find and read more trickster tales from several cultures. Then write a paper comparing and contrasting two of the tricksters.

Prewrite and Explore You might make a chart to help you explore the two tricksters' likenesses and differences. Chart areas like *looks, personality,* and *powers.* As you fill in the spaces with the tricksters' traits, include supporting details from the tales.

◀ **NEED HELP?**

For more on writing about literature, see the Writer's Workshop on pages 457–461.

Draft and Discover One approach is to describe the first trickster in a paragraph, covering each area in your chart. In the next paragraph, describe the second trickster, covering the same areas and noting the tricksters' likenesses and differences. Another approach is to use one paragraph for likenesses and differences in both tricksters' looks, a second for likenesses and differences in their personalities, and so on. Include transitions such as *on the other hand, like, unlike, in the same way,* and *in contrast.*

Revise Your Writing Look at the checklist on page 461. Then, with a friend, create a checklist for a comparison-and-contrast paper.

D. Narrative Writing: Lights, Camera, Action!

What if the tales from this unit were made into modern movies? Can you picture Phaëthon in his father's chariot, pulling up for a drive-through burger and fries? Update a tale from this unit by rewriting it as a movie script. Give your script a modern setting, and feel free to add modern twists.

NEED HELP?

For more about writing
a script, see the
Writer's Workshop on
pages 237–241.

▶ **Prewrite and Explore**   Choose a tale to dramatize, and list its main events. Each main event can become a scene in your script. You can use scene charts to plan details about each scene's modern setting, characters, and action. Consider working in a small group.

Draft and Discover   Follow standard drama format, beginning with a cast of characters. Then, scene by scene, write dialogue and stage directions.

Revise Your Writing   Have friends "walk through" your script, reading it aloud. Make needed changes so that the tale will work as drama.

E. Informative Writing: What Caused That Tale?

Although legends, myths, and folk tales are entertaining, they also pass along history and cultural values. Choose a tale from this unit, and do some detective work. First, speculate about the reasons that might have caused the people to tell that tale. Then research the culture from which the tale comes in order to support your theory. Finally, in a cause-and-effect essay, explain why and how the tale probably originated.

NEED HELP?

For more about writing
an informative report,
see the Writer's
Workshop on pages
339–343.

▶ **Prewrite and Explore**   Which story's origins and purpose can you form a theory to explain? For example, do you have a good idea of why "The People Could Fly" was told? Choose a tale and write a statement that expresses why you think it was told. Then head for the library to track down information about the culture that told it. Look for facts or statistics that support your theory—or change your theory to fit the facts you find. Take notes, including bibliography notes.

Draft and Discover   You are explaining the cause of an effect—the tale you chose. State your main idea clearly at the beginning. Then support your theory with several reasons, using facts and details from your notecards. Conclude with a powerful restatement of your main idea. Add a list of your sources.

Revise Your Writing   Use the checklist on page 342. Ask a friend to read your draft and respond to it.

F. Persuasive Writing: Get Out the Vote!

In this unit, you've met characters with great personal strengths as well as those with supernatural powers. Choose one whose strengths or powers would be useful in modern politics. Then write a campaign pamphlet urging people to elect your character president.

Prewrite and Explore   You might create a chart with spaces to list the strengths and powers of several "candidates." Choose the one best suited to the job, and try a focused freewriting about why he or she would be a good president. Then sketch a layout for your pamphlet, including both verbal and visual elements.

Draft and Discover   Draft the text of your pamphlet, using ideas and words from your freewriting. Introduce your candidate at the beginning. Use logic to explain his or her strong points, and choose words that have connotations that will help persuade readers.

Revise Your Writing   Check the text of your pamphlet for errors in reasoning, and write a call to action for the conclusion. Then add illustrations and other visual elements to create a finished product.

◄ NEED HELP?
· ·
For more about persuasive writing, see the Writer's Workshops on pages 388–392 and 512–516.

G. Narrative Writing: Fix-It Time

"The People Could Fly" uses fantasy to deal with a real problem. The fantasy may not offer a practical solution—but it makes the problem clear and unforgettable. Think of a current problem that you care about, and come up with a fantasy solution. Then write the story of what happens once your solution is used.

◄ NEED HELP?
· ·
For more on writing about problems and solutions, see the Writer's Workshop on pages 339–343.

Prewrite and Explore   Freewrite to focus your observations of a problem that you care about. Next, brainstorm for fantasy solutions. Then close your eyes for a moment. Form detailed mental pictures of what might happen if your fantasy solution came true.

Draft and Discover   As you write the tale of what happens when your solution is used, keep your imagination humming. Reach for descriptive, sensory details to bring your mental pictures to life. Be sure you clearly show the problem as well as the solution.

Revise Your Writing   Find a "grabber" action scene to open your story. Be sure you show readers why the problem concerns you. See if you can add transitions to make the order of events clearer to your readers. Then create a satisfying conclusion.

Final Revision

No matter which assignment you chose, be sure to give your draft another look. Before you proofread for errors in grammar, spelling, punctuation, and capitalization, look for ways you can add life to your writing. Try varying sentence beginnings, as shown in the box at the top of the next page.

THE EDITOR'S EYE: VARYING SENTENCE BEGINNINGS

Your writing can sound immature when all your sentences start with their subjects. Instead, try starting some sentences with an adverb or a prepositional phrase.

Problem   *Coyote* is the loner among all the animals. *He* often disagrees with the others. *No one* can predict what he'll do.

Improved   *Among all the animals,* Coyote is the loner. *Often* he disagrees with the others. No one can predict what he'll do.

NEED MORE HELP?
See the Language Workshop on pages 668–670.

Publish and Present

Here are some suggestions for sharing your work with others.

Face Value   Make a mask that represents a central character in your writing. Decorate it with colors, designs, and objects related to the character. Read your work and display the mask to classmates.

Variety Show   With others who have done the same assignment, create a group presentation. Read your writings for class members and play appropriate background music during your presentation.

Reflect on Your Writing

Write brief answers to the following questions. Attach them to your paper when you put it in your portfolio.

FOR YOUR PORTFOLIO ▶

1. How did you decide which assignment you would complete?
2. How did your writing process for this paper differ from the processes you followed in previous Writer's Workshops?

WRITER'S WORKSHOP

SELF-ASSESSMENT

Portfolio Review

Guided Assignment   Write a one-page essay in which you explain your achievements this year as a writer.

Prewrite and Explore   Read through your Portfolio, taking notes. Choose the writings you feel best about, and pinpoint what you like about your work. Decide which aspects of your writing were weakest at the beginning of the year. Where do you see improvement now? Then list two or three aspects of your writing that you'd like to strengthen. Consider your level of comfort with each part of the writing process (prewriting, drafting, revising, proofreading, and publishing).

Draft and Discover   Using your notes and lists, draft your essay. You might begin either with your strengths or with areas you'd like to improve. Use examples from your own work to explain your points.

Revise Your Writing   Find the organization that's emerging in your draft, and work to make it clear. Keep reshaping your paragraphs and sentences until they say exactly what you think and feel, and they're easy for readers to follow. Then add an introduction that will catch readers' attention and a conclusion that will give readers a sense of completion. Design a checklist that a friend can use to offer helpful responses and a checklist that you can use on your own.

Proofread   Find and correct any errors in grammar, spelling, and mechanics. A friend might help. Then make a clean copy of your essay.

Publish and Present   Share your essay with a small group of classmates. As a group, discuss what you enjoy most—and least—about writing.

SENTENCE VARIETY

Have you ever read a story by a third grader? The plot may be wild, but the sentences are usually tame: short, simple, subject-verb-object. Even a hair-raising story gets dull when it's told in a monotonous way. Mature writers learn to vary their sentence lengths and structures—and so can you.

Varying Sentence Beginnings

You can add variety by changing the beginnings of some of your sentences.

1. Begin with an **appositive,** a phrase that identifies the subject.

> *The young fellow,* Kelfala, was a clown.
> *His friends,* Shortie Bumpie and Longie Tallie, followed Kelfala.

2. Begin with a **prepositional phrase.** Prepositions, words such as *with, over, on, in,* and *at,* show relationships in space or time.

> *With Wambuna,* Kelfala had no success.
> Even *after failure,* he wouldn't give up.

3. Begin with an **adverb** or adverb phrase. Adverbs modify verbs and may end in *-ly.*

> *Finally* he asked two friends for help.
> *A week later,* his chance came.

4. Begin with a **participial phrase.** A participle is an adjective formed by adding *-ing* to a verb.

> *Carrying a mysterious packet,* Kelfala set out.
> *Trailing Wambuna silently,* he followed her to a stream.

5. Begin with a **quote.**

> *"Wait a minute, Kelfala,"* one of his friends said.
> *"The trick was mine, see?"* and with that, Kelfala hopped.

Varying Sentence Structure

Changing the inner structures of some of your sentences is another way to avoid monotony.

1. Put the object or complement first.

> *This* the young men admired about Wambuna.
> *Her head* she carried erect.

2. Combine sentence ideas by using words like *when, if, while, because,* or *although.*

> *When she laughed,* she showed ivory-white teeth.
> Kelfala loved her *because she was clever and beautiful.*

Varying Sentence Length

When you have too many short sentences in a row, you can join some of them, changing the rhythm of your writing.

1. Join simple sentences with a comma and a conjunction.

> Kelfala's trick worked. He didn't marry Wambuna.
> Kelfala's trick worked, *but* he didn't marry Wambuna.

2. Create compound subjects, verbs, or objects.

> Wambuna smiled. The young men smiled too. Then they laughed.
> Wambuna and the young men smiled and laughed.

3. Insert a phrase from one sentence into another sentence.

> Wambuna sauntered off. She was heading toward her garden.
> Wambuna sauntered off toward her garden.

◀ NEED MORE HELP?
See the Language Workshop on pages 462–464.

Exercise 1   Concept Check   Revise each of the following sentences five times. Add a different kind of beginning each time. Use details from "Where the Girl Saved Her Brother."

1. The Cheyenne girl rescued her brother.
2. Her people have never forgotten her bravery.

Exercise 2   Revision Skill   You wouldn't write a paragraph as monotonous as the one below. Work with a group of friends to revise it. Vary sentence beginnings, sentence structures, and sentence lengths.

> The girl called Gem looked fine. She thought she looked ugly. She would not leave the house. She talked to a wise woman. She learned of a magic flower. It could make her beautiful. She found the flower. It grew in a distant forest. She became beautiful. Beauty was a curse for her. That was a surprise. Soldiers almost killed her. She wanted to be plain again. The wise woman helped her. Gem learned a lesson. The story is interesting. It shows a complicated kind of vanity. Gem was conceited in reverse. She was also greedy. She was greedy for beauty. She wanted more than she needed.

Exercise 3   Looking at Style   Look at Leo Tolstoy's "The Old Grandfather and His Little Grandson," on page 615. Then follow the directions.

1. From the story, copy an example of each sentence variety technique listed below.

    a. a short, simple sentence followed by a long, intricate sentence

    b. two sentence ideas combined by using *when*

    c. a sentence that begins with an adverb phrase, followed by two sentences that begin with their subjects

2. Rewrite the story so that each sentence starts with its subject. How is the effect different from the effect of the original?

Exercise 4   Revising Your Writing   Reread the paper you wrote for the Writer's Workshop on pages 662–666. Revise it by adding variety to your sentence beginnings, sentence structures, and sentence lengths.

VOCABULARY
WORKSHOP

GREEK ROOTS

The ancient Greeks passed on not only their myths but some of their language as well. Many of our English words are based on Greek **roots,** or combining forms.

A root may appear at the beginning, in the middle, or at the end of a word. A prefix or suffix may be added to it. For example, the suffix *-ic* is used to form adjectives. The Greek root *phobia* (fear), with this suffix added, gives us the word *phobic,* "fearful." Roots are sometimes joined with other roots. *Graph* (writing) plus *logy* (study of) gives us *graphology,* "the study of handwriting." Study the Greek roots below. They can help you figure out the meanings of many words.

phobia—fear	psycho—mind	graph—writing
genes—origin	hydro—water	patri—father
stere—strong	techni—skilled	anthropo—human
phon—sound	pyro—fire	philo—to love
arch—first	zoo—animal	logi, logy—reason, study of
soph—wisdom	typos, typi—type, example	
biblio—book		

Exercise   The following words are made from the Greek roots above. By thinking like a detective, you can guess their meanings. First, copy the word on your paper and draw lines between the parts to separate the roots. Next, write the roots' meanings. Then write your guess of each word's meaning. Check your guesses in a dictionary.

Example: zoo/phobia   animal + fear = fear of animals

1. hydroplane	**6.** logical	**11.** photograph	**16.** technology
2. psychology	**7.** philanthropy	**12.** bibliography	**17.** pyrogenic
3. stereophonic	**8.** philosophy	**13.** bibliophile	**18.** genealogy
4. archetype	**9.** zoology	**14.** pyrotechnics	**19.** patriarch
5. archeology	**10.** stereotype	**15.** anthropology	**20.** phonograph

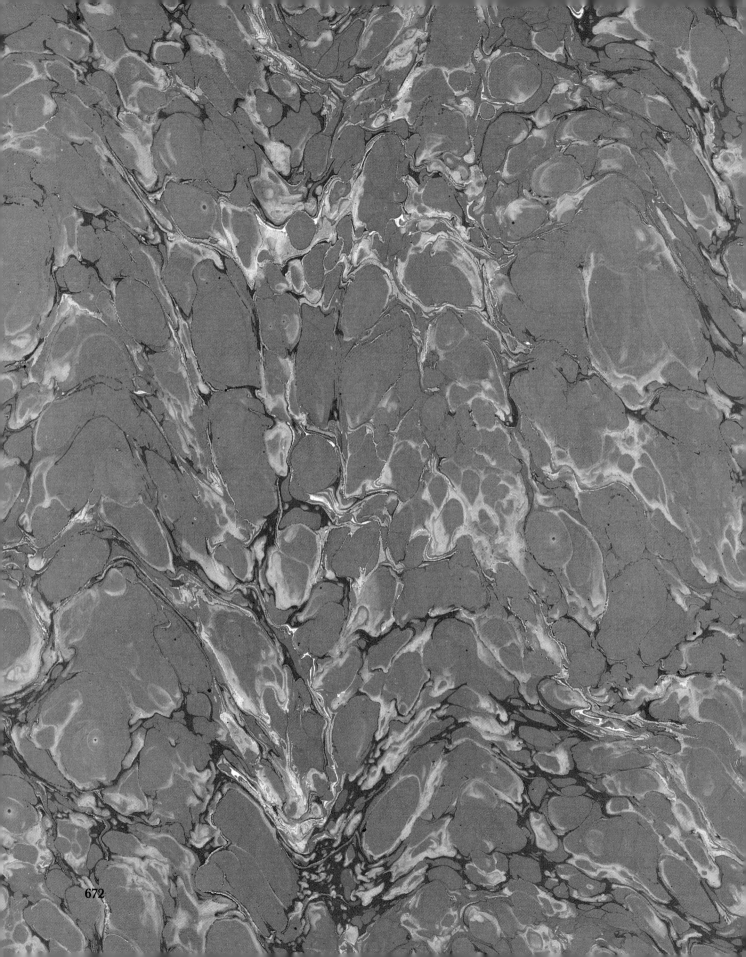

Handbook Contents

GLOSSARY

The **glossary** is an alphabetical listing of words from the selections, with meanings. The glossary gives the following information:

1. The entry word broken into syllables.

2. The pronunciation of each word. The **respelling** is shown in parentheses. The Pronunciation Key below shows the symbols for the sounds of letters and key words that contain those sounds.

A **primary accent** ′ is placed after the syllable that is stressed the most when the word is spoken. A **secondary accent** ′ is placed after a syllable that has a lighter stress.

3. The part of speech of the word. These abbreviations are used:

n. noun   *v.* verb   *adj.* adjective
adv. adverb   *prep.* preposition

4. The meaning of the word. The definitions listed in the glossary apply to selected ways a word is used in these selections.

5. Related forms. Words with suffixes such as *-ing*, *-ed*, *-ness*, and *-ly* are often listed under the base word.

1. entry word
2. respelling
3. part of speech
4. meaning

def er en tial (def′ ər en′ shəl)
adj. showing courteous regard or respect

Pronunciation Key

Symbol	Key Words	Symbol	Key Words	Symbol	Key Words	Symbol	Key Words
a	at, gas	o͞o	tool, crew	∫a	in ago	ch	chin
ā	ape, day	o͝o	look, pull	e	in agent	sh	she
ä	car, lot	yo͞o	use, cute, few	ə ∫i	in insanity	th	thin
e	elf, ten	yo͝o	cure	o	in comply	*th*	then
ē	even, me	oi	oil, coin	u	in focus	zh	leisure
i	is, hit	ou	out, sour			ŋ	ring
ī	bite, fire	u	up, cut			′	able (ā′ b′l)
ō	own, go	ʉr	fur, bird				
ô	law, horn	er	perhaps, murder				

Foreign Symbols

a	salle	*n*	mon
ë	coer	δ	abuelos
ö	feu	*r*	gringos
ü	rue		

From *Webster's New World Dictionary, Third Edition,* Copyright © 1988 by Simon & Schuster Inc.

A

a bode (ə bōd′) *n.* a home

a bra sion (ə brā′ zhən) *n.* a scrape on the skin

a brupt ly (ə brupt′ lē) *adv.* suddenly

ac com mo da tion (ə käm′ ə dā′ shən) *n.* a room and food in hotels, ships, trains, etc.

ack nowl edge (ak näl′ ij) *v.* to recognize the status or rights of

ac qui si tion (ak′ wə zish′ ən) *n.* the act of getting something

ad ap ta tion (ad′ əp tā′ shən) *n.* a thing changed to suit new conditions

ad here (ad hir′) *v.* to be loyal

al ien ate (āl′ yən āt′) *v.* to cause someone to become unfriendly

al lot (ə lät′) *v.* to give out as a share or portion

a lum nus (ə lum′ nəs) *n.* a graduate of a particular school; *plural*—**alumni** (ə lum′ nī′)

a mi a bly (ā′ mē ə blē) *adv.* agreeably; pleasantly

an guished (aŋ′ gwisht) *adj.* filled with pain, mental or physical; extremely upset **anguish** *v.*

an tag o nism (an tag′ ə niz′ əm) *n.* hostility; unfriendliness

ap pal ling (ə pôl′ iŋ) *adj.* horrifying; dreadful **appall** *v.*

ap ti tude (ap′ tə tood′) *n.* a natural ability

ar chive (är′ kīv) *n.* a storehouse for records of the past

a ris to crat ic (ə ris′ tə krat′ ik) *n.* wealthy, privileged people

ar tic u late (är tik′ yoo lit) *adj.* able to express oneself clearly in words

as cer tain (as′ ər tān) *v.* to find out

au di tion (ô dish′ ən) *n.* a test of skill or ability, usually of a musician or actor; a tryout

B

base less (bās′ lis) *adj.* having no foundation in fact

beck on (bek′ ′n) *v.* to summon or call someone, usually by a gesture or nod

be mused (bē myoozd′) *adj.* confused; bewildered **bemuse** *v.*

ben e fac tor (ben′ ə fak′ tər) *n.* a person who provides money or help

binge (binj) *n.* a period of uncontrolled eating or drinking

bleak (blēk) *adj.* harsh and dreary

brash ness (brash′ nəs) *n.* recklessness; foolish daring

brood ing (brood′ iŋ) *adj.* full of worry; troubled **brood** *v.*

C

cap size (kap′ sīz′) *v.* to be overturned or upset

caul dron (kôl′ drən) *n.* a large kettle

cha os (kā′ äs′) *n.* a state of disorder and confusion

cher ish (cher′ ish) *v.* to hold dear; treasure

cla mor (klam′ ər) *n.* a loud noise; uproar

com bat ant (kəm bat′ ′nt) *n.* fighter

com mun ing (kə myoon′ iŋ) *adj.* talking together privately **commune** *v.*

com pas sion ate (kəm pash′ ən it) *adj.* showing concern or sympathy

com pe tence (käm′ pə təns) *n.* a state of being capable

com pet i tive (kəm pet′ ə tiv) *adj.* relating to rivalry among businesses, groups, or individuals

con cus sion (kən kush′ ən) *n.* a strong shaking

con fines (kän′ fīns′) *n.* limits; boundaries

con found (kən found′) *v.* to bewilder; confuse

con sen sus (kən sen′ səs) *n.* an opinion shared by most; general agreement

con sul ta tion (kän′ səl tā′ shən) *n.* a meeting to discuss or decide something

con sump tion (kən sump′ shən) *n.* the act of eating or drinking

con temp tu ous (kən temp′ choo əs) *adj.* lacking respect; scornful

con tort ed (kən tôrt′ əd) *adj.* twisted or pulled out of shape **contort** *v.*

con vic tion (kən vik′ shən) *n.* a strong belief

cow er (kou′ ər) *v.* crouch or shrink down in fear

cringe (krinj) *v.* to shrink back from something unpleasant

croon (kroon) *v.* to sing softly

cryp tic (krip′ tik) *adj.* puzzling; mysterious

cu bi cle (kyoo′ bi kəl) *n.* a small compartment used for work or sleep

cull (kul) *v.* to remove from a group something or someone that is not as good as the rest

cul ti vat ed (kul′ tə vāt′ id) *adj.* planted or prepared for planting as opposed to wild, **cultivate** *v.*

cyn i cal (sin′ i kəl) *adj.* mistrustful of others′ sincerity

D

de fi ant (dē fī′ ənt) *adj.* refusing to obey or act in a way acceptable to others

de i ty (dē′ ə tē) *n.* a god; a divine being

de lib er ate (di lib′ ər āt′) *v.* to carefully consider

de mol ish (di mäl′ ish) *v.* to wreck; destroy

der i va tion (der′ ə vā′ shən) *n.* origin; source

de scend ant (dē sen′ dənt) *n.* an immediate or remote offspring of a person

des o la tion (des′ ə lā′ shən) *n.* feeling of loneliness and misery

des per ate ly (des′ pər it lē) *adv.* acting in a manner that shows extreme need or hopelessness

de ten tion (di ten′ shən) *n.* punishment of being held against one′s will, as in having to stay after school

dex ter ous ly (deks′ tər əs lē) *adv.* skillfully

dil i gence (dil′ ə jəns) *n.* constant effort

din gy (din′ jē) *adj.* somewhat dark and unclean; shabby

dis a bled (dis ā′ bəld) *n.* people with an illness or physical handicap that limits their activities

dis creet ly (di skrēt′ lē) *adv.* in a polite way; tactfully

dis si pate (dis′ ə pāt′) *v.* to gradually disappear

dis suade (di swād′) *v.* to persuade not to do something

dis tinc tive (di stiŋk′ tiv) *adj.* different from others; characteristic

di vert (də vʉrt′) *v.* to shift; to turn aside

di vulge (də vulj′) *v.* to reveal

drawl (drôl) *v.* to speak in a slow manner, stretching the vowel sounds

du bi ous ly (doō′ bē əs lē) *adv.* in a doubtful way; skeptically

E

e lec tive (ē lek′ tiv) *n.* a school subject or course chosen by the student rather than assigned

e lite (ā lēt′) *n.* a group regarded as the best

e lo quence (el′ ə kwəns) *n.* forceful, convincing speech

e lude (ē loōd′) *v.* to avoid or get away from by being sly or quick

em u late (em′ yoō lāt′) *v.* to imitate or copy

en dow (en dou′) *v.* to provide with a quality or a talent

en dure (en door′) *v.* to withstand; put up with; tolerate

en grossed (en grōst′) *adj.* completely occupied; absorbed **engross** *v.*

en ter pris ing (ent′ ər prī′ ziŋ) *adj.* adventurous; energetic

es sence (es′ əns) *n.* the basic nature of a thing

et i quette (et′ i kit) *n.* the proper way to behave toward others; good manners

e va sion (ē vā′ zhən) *n.* the act of avoiding or escaping from

e vic ted (ē vikt′ ′d) *adj.* to be forced to move from a rented house or apartment **evict** *v.*

ex as per a tion (eg zas′ pər ā′ shən) *n.* annoyance; irritation

ex ces sive ly (ek ses′ iv lē) *adv.* overly; too much

ex ot ic (eg zät′ ik) *adj.* strange; unusual

ex pe di en cy (ek spē′ dē ən sē) *n.* suitability for the purpose at hand

ex pire (ek spīr′) *v.* to die

ex plic it (eks plis′ it) *adj.* plain; straightforward

ex qui site (eks′ kwi zit) *adj.* beautiful; outstanding

F

fa tigue (fə tēg′) *n.* extreme weariness or exhaustion

feign (fān) *v.* to pretend

fe roc i ty (fə räs′ ə tē) *n.* extreme fierceness; savagery

fe ver ish ly (fē′ vər ish lē) *adv.* in a highly emotional or nervous way

flip pant (flip′ ənt) *adj.* lacking in seriousness; silly and disrespectful

flour ish (flʉr′ ish) *v.* to thrive; grow vigorously

flus tered (flus′ tərd) *adj.* nervous or confused **fluster** *v.*

G

gen ial ly (jēn′ yəl lē) *adv.* in a friendly way

girth (gᵤrth) *n.* the distance around something

glim mer (glim′ ər) *v.* to give off a flickering dim light

glow er (glσu′ ər) *v.* to stare in an angry way; scowl

grope (grōp) *v.* to touch or feel about in search of something

gruff (gruf) *adj.* rough and husky

gul li ble (gul′ ə bəl) *adj.* easily fooled or tricked

H

har ried (har′ ēd) *adj.* worried; distressed **harry** *v.*

heft (heft) *v.* to lift something to see how heavy it is

hi er ar chy (hī′ ər är′ kē) *n.* a group of people organized according to rank or authority

hoax (hōks) *n.* a trick or deception

hov er (huv′ ər) *v.* to fly or flutter over a place as if suspended

hu mil i ty (hyσο mil′ ə tē) *n.* lack of pride

I

i di o syn cra sy (id′ ē ō′ siŋ′ krə sē) *n.* a personal way of acting; odd mannerism

im mense (im mens′) *adj.* very large; enormous

im mense ly (im mens′ lē) *adv.* very much; enormously

im merse (im mᵤrs′) *v.* to involve oneself completely

im paled (im pāld′) *adj.* pierced through **impale** *v.*

im per a tive (im per′ ə tiv) *adj.* absolutely necessary

im promp tu (im prämp′ tσο′) *adj.* without preparation; on the spur of the moment

in ad e quate (in ad′ i kwət) *adj.* not enough

in com pre hen si ble (in′ käm′ prē hen′ sə bəl) *adj.* not capable of being understood

in con sol a ble (in′ kən sōl′ ə bəl) *adj.* brokenhearted; not able to be comforted

in cred u lous (in krej′ σο ləs) *adj.* unable or unwilling to believe something

in crim i nate (in krim′ i nāt′) *v.* to cause someone to appear guilty

in def i nite ly (in def′ ə nit lē) *adv.* for an unlimited length of time

in dif fer ence (in dif′ ər əns) *n.* a lack of interest or concern

in dig nant (in dig′ nənt) *adj.* angry because of an action that seems wrong

in ev i ta ble (in ev′ i tə bəl) *adj.* sure to happen; unavoidable

in scrip tion (in skrip′ shən) *n.* a brief message permanently marked or engraved on a surface

in sin u a tion (in sin′ yσο ā′ shən) *n.* a suggestion or hint intended to insult

in so lent (in′ sə lənt) *adj.* boldly showing no respect

in tense (in tens′) *adj.* firm; very serious

in ter ven ing (in′ tər vēn′ iŋ) *adj.* coming between **intervene** *v.*

in trep id (in trep′ id) *adj.* very brave

in tri cate (in′ tri kit) *adj.* elaborately detailed

in val id (in′ və lid) *n.* a sickly or disabled person

i rate (ī rāt′) *adj.* angry

J

jeer ing (jir′ iŋ) *adj.* mocking; rude, taunting **jeer** *v.*

L

le git i mate (lə jit′ ə mət) *adj.* normal; according to the rules

lib er a tion (lib′ ər ā′ shən) *n.* the state of freedom reached after a struggle

lin ger (liŋ′ gər) *v.* to continue to stay; delay leaving

loath some (lōth′ səm) *adj.* deserving of hate; disgusting

M

ma lig nant (mə lig′ nənt) *adj.* wishing or causing evil; very harmful

mil i tant (mil′ i tənt) *n.* a person fighting for a cause

mim i cry (mim′ ik rē) *n.* an act of imitation

min i mize (min′ ə mīz′) *v.* to reduce to the smallest possible amount

mor bid ly (môr′ bid lē) *adv.* in a gloomy, depressed way

mo rose (mə rōs′) *adj.* in low spirits; gloomy

N

niche (nich) *n.* the place a person occupies in society

nov el ty (näv′ əl tē) *n.* something new, original, or unusual

O

ob scured (əb skyoord′) *adj.* hidden from view **obscure** *v.*

ob sessed (əb sest′) *adj.* greatly preoccupied with something **obsess** *v.*

oc cult (ə kult′) *adj.* supernatural

o men (ō′ mən) *n.* an event or sign believed to point toward a future happening

om in ous ly (äm′ ə nəs lē) *adv.* in a threatening or evil way

op ti mis tic (äp′ tə mis′ tik) *adj.* hopeful about the future; confident

P

pains tak ing (pānz′ tāk′ iŋ) *adj.* very careful

pal lid (pal′ id) *adj.* pale; lacking normal color

pas sive (pas′ iv) *adj.* inactive, but receiving action; lacking in energy or willpower

pend ing (pen′ diŋ) *prep.* while waiting for; until

per pet u al (pər pech′ oo əl) a*dj.* endless; lasting forever

per sist ent (pər sist′ ənt) *adj.* refusing to stop; continuing stubbornly

pig men ta tion (pig mən tā′ shən) *n.* a skin color

pil fer ing (pil′ fər iŋ) *n.* stealing **pilfer** *v.*

plac id (plas′ id) *adj.* calm; at peace

pon der (pän′ dər) *v.* to think deeply; carefully consider

pre cept (prē′ sept′) *n.* a rule of conduct

pred e ces sor (pred′ ə ses′ ər) *n.* a person who comes before

pre lim i nary (prē lim′ ə ner′ ē) *n.* a match or competition before the main contest; *plural* **preliminaries**

pre oc cu pa tion (prē äk′ yoo pā′ shən) *n.* a state of being wrapped up or engrossed in something

pri or i ty (prī ôr′ ə tē) *n.* something that must receive attention first

prod i gy (präd′ ə jē) *adj.* of a child with extraordinary talent or genius

pro lif ic (prō lif′ ik) *adj.* producing many children

prom in ent (präm′ ə nənt) *adj.* well-known; widely recognized

proph e cy (präf′ ə sē) *n.* a prediction; foretelling of future events

Q

quiv er (kwiv′ ər) *v.* to tremble or shake

R

ra tion al ize (rash′ ən əl īz′) *v.* to explain or make excuses for

rav age (rav′ ij) *v.* to violently attack, causing severe damage

realm (relm) *n.* a kingdom

re coil (ri koil′) *v.* to draw back from something distasteful or painful

ref uge (ref′ yooj) *n.* a safe place

re ha bil i ta tion (rē′ hə bil′ ə tā′ shən) *n.* the restoring of a person's ability to lead a useful life

re lin quish (ri liŋ′ kwish) *v.* to give up

rel ish (rel′ ish) *v.* to enjoy

re luc tant ly (ri luk′ tənt lē) *adv.* unwillingly

re plen ished (ri plen′ ishd) *adj.* added to; resupplied **replenish** *v.*

re pris al (ri prī′ zəl) *n.* an injury done in response to an injury received; retaliation

re pul sive (ri pul′ siv) *adj.* offensive; disgusting

re sil ient (ri zil′ yənt) *adj.* flexible and springy

re tal i ate (ri tal′ ē āt′) *v.* to get revenge; get even

rev er ie (rev′ ər ē) *n.* a daydream

re vive (ri vīv′) *v.* to regain consciousness; wake up

rogue (rōg) *n.* a rascal

rote (rōt) *n.* memorization without understanding

S

sanc tion (saŋk′ shən) *v.* to give approval for

sanc tu ar y (saŋk′ choo er′ ē) *n.* shelter; protection

sa vor (sā′ vər) *v.* to take great pleasure in

scheme (skēm) *v.* to plot or plan in a secretive way

scowl (skoul) *v.* to look angry by drawing the eyebrows together and frowning

sear (sir) *v.* to burn the surface; scorch

sem i nar y (sem′ ə ner′ ē) *n.* a school where people are trained to become ministers, priests, or rabbis

se nile (sē′ nīl′) *adj.* showing the mental confusion sometimes found in old people

shrewd ly (shro͞od′ lē) *adv.* wisely; in a clever way

slack en (slak′ ən) *v.* to lessen; let up

sloth (slôth) *n.* laziness

slug gish (slug′ ish) *adj.* moving at a slow pace

sneer ing (snir′ iŋ) *adj.* having a mocking smile **sneer** *v.*

snip ing (snīp′ iŋ) *n.* attacking someone in a sly or deceitful way **snipe** *v.*

sol ace (säl′ is) *n.* comfort

sor cer y (sôr′ sər ē) *n.* magic

sov er eign (säv′ rən) *n.* a monarch; royal ruler

spec u lat ing (spek′ yo͞o lāt′ iŋ) *adj.* thinking about different possibilities; guessing what might happen **speculate** *v.*

spell bound (spel′ bound′) *adj.* as if in a trance; fascinated

spend thrift (spend′ thrift′) *n.* a person who wastes money

squan der (skwän′ dər) *v.* to spend carelessly

stark (stärk) *adv.* entirely; completely

stench (stench) *n.* a strong, foul smell

strick en (strik′ ən) *adj.* suddenly affected by pain; wounded

stri dent (strīd′ ′nt) *adj.* having a harsh sound

stu pen dous (sto͞o pen′ dəs) *adj.* huge; tremendous

sub con scious ly (sub kän′ shəs lē) *adv.* without being fully aware

suit or (so͞ot′ ər) *n.* a man seeking a woman's love

sul len (sul′ ən) *adj.* gloomy; acting moody

su per flu ous (sə pʉr′ flo͞o əs) *adj.* unnecessary; not important

surge (sʉrj) *v.* to suddenly push forward in a violent way

sur plus (sʉr′ plus′) *adj.* extra

sus te nance (sus′ tə nəns) *n.* nourishment; assistance

swarth y (swôr*th*′ ē) *adj.* having darkish skin

T

tac tic (tak′ tik) *n.* a method used to accomplish something; a strategy

taunt (tônt) *v.* to make fun of; jeer

te di ous (tē′ dē əs) *adj.* boring; dull

trans fixed (trans fikst′) *adj.* unable to move because of awe or fear **transfix** *v.*

trans for ma tion (trans′ fər mā′ shən) *n.* a change

trib ute (trib′ yo͞ot) *n.* an action or gift that honors a deserving individual

tu mul tu ous ly (to͞o mul′ cho͞o əs lē) *adv.* in a wild and disorderly way

ty rant (tī′ rənt) *n.* a ruler with unlimited power

U

ul ti mate (ul′ tə mit) *adj.* final; most important

un nerve (un nʉrv′) *v.* to take away courage; to make nervous

un seem ly (un sēm′ lē) *adj.* not decent or proper

up hol ster y (up hōl′ stər ē) *n.* the soft fabric covering furniture

V

van quish (vaŋ′ kwish) *v.* to conquer, defeat

ven om (ven′ əm) *n.* bitterness; hatred

ve ran da (və ran′ də) *n.* a long open porch, usually with a roof

vexed (vekst) *adj.* troubled **vex** *v.*

vil est (vīl′ ist) *adj.* most horrible or unpleasant

W

wield ing (wēld′ iŋ) *adj.* handling and using **wield** *v.*

wil y (wīl′ ē) *adj.* crafty; sly

wretch ed (rech′ ′d) *adj.* deserving contempt; inferior

Z

zeal (zēl) *n.* enthusiasm; eagerness

LITERARY AND READING TERMS

Act   An act is a major section of a play. Each act may be further divided into smaller sections called **scenes.** *The Monsters Are Due on Maple Street* has two acts.
   See *Drama* and *Scene.*

Alliteration   Alliteration is the repetition of consonant sounds at the beginnings of words. Writers use alliteration to emphasize certain words and to give their writing a musical quality. Note the repetition of the c sound in this line from "The Highwayman":

"Over the cobbles he clattered and clashed"

Allusion   An allusion is a reference to a famous person, place, event, or other work of literature. In "Aunt Millicent," Grandma makes an allusion to the story "Rikki-tikki-tavi."

Analysis   Analysis is the process of breaking something down into its elements and examining each one. When you analyze a literary work, you examine its various parts in order to understand the work as a whole.

Author's Purpose   An author's purpose may be to entertain, to explain or inform, to express an opinion, or to persuade readers to do or believe something. The author may combine two or three purposes, but one is usually most important.

Autobiography   An autobiography is a form of nonfiction in which one person tells the story of his or her life. *Nadja on My Way* is an example of autobiography.
   See *Nonfiction.*

Biography   A biography is the story of a person's life written by another person. The subjects of biographies are often famous people, as in Jacobs's "Eleanor Roosevelt."
   See *Nonfiction.*

Cast of Characters   In a drama, the cast of characters is given at the beginning of the script. It is a list of all the characters in the play, usually in order of appearance.
   See *Drama.*

Cause and Effect   Events are often related by cause and effect. This relationship occurs when one event brings about a second event. The first event in time is the cause; the second event is the effect. This statement from "The Noble Experiment" shows a cause and effect: "He pointed out that I couldn't play for a few days anyhow because of my bum arm."

Character   A character is a person, an animal, or an imaginary creature that takes part in the action of a literary work. Generally, a work focuses on one or more **main characters.** Less important characters are called **minor characters.**

Characterization   Characterization refers to the techniques a writer uses to create and develop a character. There are four basic methods of developing a character: 1) a physical description of the character; 2) the character's thoughts, speech, or actions; 3) the thoughts, speech, and actions of other characters; 4) direct comments on a character's nature.

Chronological Order   Chronological order refers to the order in which events happen in time. The biography "Eleanor Roosevelt" follows chronological order, beginning with Eleanor's birth and ending with her death.

Climax   The climax, or turning point, is the high point of interest in the plot of a story or play. At the climax, the conflict is resolved and the outcome of the plot becomes clear. The climax of "The Smallest Dragonboy," for example, occurs when Keevan Impresses the dragon at the hatching.
   See *Plot.*

Comparison   The process of identifying similarities is called comparison. In "All Summer in a Day," the writer compares Margot to "an old photograph dusted from an album, whitened away." Both Margot and the photograph are pale and fragile.

Conflict   Conflict is a struggle between two opposing forces. In an **external conflict,** such as the battle between Rikki and the cobras in "Rikki-tikki-tavi," a character struggles against some outside person or force. **Internal conflict** occurs when the struggle is within a character. Martin in "The Medicine Bag" experiences internal conflict when caught between feelings of shame and pride toward his grandfather.
    See *Plot*.

Connecting   The process of relating the content of a literary work to the reader's own knowledge or experience is called connecting. For example, in *Nadja on My Way* when the author describes her feelings before competing, the reader may remember similar feelings in his or her own experience.

Connotation   Connotation refers to the suggestions and associations that go along with a given word, stretching well beyond its dictionary meaning. For example, the word *mother* is defined as "a female parent," but the word suggests images of love, warmth, and security.

Context Clues   Context clues are the words or phrases before or after an unfamiliar word that help explain its meaning. Context clues may define the word, give a synonym for it, give an example of its meaning, provide comparisons or contrasts, or enable readers to infer the meaning.

Contrast   The pointing out of differences between two or more things is called contrast. In "Last Cover" the narrator contrasts himself with his brother Colin:

I was following in my father's footsteps, true to form, but Colin threatened to break the family tradition.

Denotation   Denotation is the dictionary definition of a word.
    See *Connotation*.

Description   Description is a picture, in words, of a scene, a character, or an object. A description might appeal to the reader's senses or provide detailed information about characters or events.

Dialect   Dialect is a form of language as it is spoken in a certain place or among a certain group of people. A dialect has its own pronunciations, spellings, and expressions. Mrs. Pratchett in *Boy* speaks the dialect of the British working class: "Let's 'ave a look at some of them titchy ones."

Dialogue   A conversation between two or more characters is called dialogue. In most literary forms, dialogue is set off by quotation marks. In plays, however, dialogue simply follows the name of the character who is speaking and does not require quotation marks.

Drama   A drama, or play, is a form of literature meant to be performed by actors before an audience. In drama, the story is told through the dialogue and the actions of the characters.
    See *Act*, *Cast of Characters*, *Dialogue*, *Scene*, and *Stage Directions*.

Drawing Conclusions   Combining several pieces of information to make a decision is called drawing a conclusion. Conclusions can be drawn from a combination of stated facts and inferences the reader makes.
    See *Inference*.

Essay   A short nonfiction work that deals with one subject is called an essay. Some essays emphasize personal feelings, such as "Homeless." Others focus more on the presentation of information, as in "America the Not-so-Beautiful."

See *Nonfiction.*

Evaluating   Evaluating is the process of judging the worth of something or someone. A work of literature or its elements may be evaluated by standards such as entertainment, believability, originality, or emotional power.

Exaggeration   The extreme overstating of an idea is called exaggeration. In *Driving Miss Daisy,* Florine exaggerates, "I told you a million times."

Exposition   Exposition is the beginning of a plot in a story or play. It introduces main characters, describes the setting, and often establishes the conflict. For example, the opening paragraphs of "Old Sly Eye" provide the exposition for the story.

External Conflict   See *Conflict.*

Fable   A fable is a brief story that teaches a lesson about human nature. Many fables feature animals that act and speak like humans. Fables often end with a stated moral that summarizes the lesson. "The Wolf in Sheep's Clothing" is an example of a fable.

See *Moral.*

Fact and Opinion   A fact is a statement that can be proved, such as "April has thirty days." In contrast, an opinion is a statement that cannot be proved, such as "April is the nicest month of the year." Opinions usually reflect personal beliefs and are often debatable.

Fantasy   A fantasy is a type of fiction that takes place in an unreal, invented world, such as Pern in "The Smallest Dragonboy." Fantasies often involve magic or characters with extraordinary powers.

Fiction   Fiction is prose writing that tells an imaginary story. The term usually refers to novels and short stories. Writers of fiction may invent the entire work, or they may loosely base their story on real people or events.

See *Character, Conflict, Plot, Setting, Theme.*

Figurative Language   Figurative language goes beyond dictionary meanings of words to create fresh and original descriptions. In a figurative expression, the words are not literally true, and one thing may be described in terms of another. For example, the speaker in "For My Father" says of her father that "the desert had dried his soul." The three most common forms of figurative expressions are the simile, the metaphor, and personification.

See *Metaphor, Simile,* and *Personification.*

Flashback   In a literary work a flashback is a scene that interrupts the present action to describe an event that took place at an earlier time. For example, a flashback in "Last Cover" explains how Colin found Bandit.

Foil   A character who provides a striking contrast to a main character is called a foil. A foil helps make the personal qualities of the main character more obvious. For example, in "The Revolt of the Evil Fairies," Rat Joiner is a foil to the narrator.

Folk Tale   A folk tale is a simple story that has been handed down by word of mouth from one generation to another. The characters in folk tales may be animals, humans, or superhumans. Folk tales usually occur in the distant past and may involve supernatural events. "The Force of Luck" is a folk tale.

Folklore   The traditions, customs, and stories that are passed along by word of mouth within a culture are known as its folklore. Folklore includes various forms of literature, such as legends, folk tales, myths, and fables.

Foreshadowing   Foreshadowing refers to a writer's use of hints that suggest events that will occur later in a story. For example, in "Old

Sly Eye" the father warns Alben, "I wouldn't want to come home and find Old Sly Eye had done to us what he's done to others." His comments foreshadow the confrontation between Alben and the panther.

Form   Form is a term that describes a literary work's structure or organization. In poetry, form describes the physical arrangement of words and lines on a page. Some poems follow a very predictable pattern with the same number of syllables in each line and the same number of lines in each stanza. Other poems, like E. E. Cummings's "old age sticks," have an irregular form.

Free Verse   Poetry with no regular patterns of rhyme, rhythm, or line length is called free verse. Poets use free verse to capture the sounds and rhythms of ordinary language. "I'll Walk the Tightrope" is written in free verse.
   See *Poetry.*

Generalization   A generalization is a broad statement made about an entire group, such as "Novels take longer to read than short stories." Not all generalizations are true. Some are too broad or not backed up by evidence, like the statement "All seventh graders are tall."

Genre   The term used to identify the major categories of literature is called genre. There are four main literary genres: fiction, nonfiction, poetry, and drama.

Hero   A hero is a character whose actions win great admiration, often for his or her courage or nobility. A hero can be a real person, such as Jackie Robinson or Eleanor Roosevelt, or a fictional creation, such as Keevan in "The Smallest Dragonboy."

Imagery   Words and phrases that appeal to the reader's senses are known as imagery. Writers use details to help the reader imagine how things look, feel, smell, sound, and taste.

Note the imagery in these lines from "Looking North to Taos."

I saw the pueblo beneath the blue
mountain, the older
buildings crumbling,
melting into mud.

Inference   An inference is a logical guess or conclusion based on evidence. Based on details in selections and their own experience, readers can figure out more than the words say. For example, in "The Emperor's New Clothes" the Emperor is described as "so excessively fond of new clothes that he spent all his money in dress. He did not trouble himself in the least about his soldiers." From these details and their own knowledge, readers could infer that the Emperor is vain and concerned only about himself.

Internal Conflict   See *Conflict.*

Irony   Irony is a contrast between what is expected and what actually exists or happens. For example, most readers of "A Man Who Had No Eyes" believe that the successful and prosperous Mr. Parsons is sighted, only to discover at the end that he is blind.

Jargon   A specialized vocabulary used by those in a certain profession is called jargon.

Legend   A legend is a story handed down from the past about a specific person, usually someone of heroic accomplishments. Legends usually have some basis in historical fact. "Where the Girl Saved Her Brother" is an example of a legend.

Main Idea   The main idea is the central point that a writer is making. Usually, the term is used in discussions of nonfiction. The main idea may refer to the central message of the entire work or simply the topic sentence of a paragraph.

Metaphor   A comparison of two unlike things that have something in common is called a metaphor. A metaphor does not use direct words of comparison such as *like* and *as.* The following metaphor from "All Summer in a Day" describes Margot: "If she spoke at all, her voice would be a ghost."
   See *Figurative Language.*

Minor Character   See *Character.*

Mood   The mood, or atmosphere, is the feeling created in the reader by a literary work. In "All Summer in a Day," Ray Bradbury creates a mood of tension and anticipation. Writers use many techniques to establish the mood, such as word choice, dialogue, description, and plot events.

Moral   A moral is the lesson taught by a story. Morals are often stated directly in fables.
   See *Fable.*

Motivation   A motivation is a reason that explains why a character acts, feels, or thinks a certain way. Gem in "The Fatal Flower" is motivated by her desire for beauty.

Myth   A myth is a traditional story, usually of unknown authorship, that tells about the actions of gods or heroes or explains how something came to be. Myths may explain such things as human nature, the origin of the world, mysteries of nature, or social customs. Most myths were once believed to be true and were tied to a particular society's religious beliefs. "Phaëthon" is an example of a myth.

Narrative   Any writing that tells a story is called a narrative. The events in a narrative may be real or imagined. Narratives dealing with real events include biographies and autobiographies. Fictional narratives include myths, short stories, novels, and narrative poems.

Narrative Poetry   Poetry that tells a story is called narrative poetry. Like any story, narrative poetry has characters, setting, and plot. Narrative poems also have elements of poetry, such as rhyme, rhythm, imagery, and figurative language. "The Highwayman" is an example of narrative poetry.

Narrator   The narrator is the teller of a story.
   See *Point of View.*

Nonfiction   Writing that tells about real people, places, and events is called nonfiction. Types of nonfiction include biographies, autobiographies, articles, and essays.

Novel   A novel is a work of fiction which is longer and more complex than a short story. The setting, plot, and characters of a novel are developed in detail.

Onomatopoeia   Onomatopoeia is the use of words that by their sound suggest their meaning. *Whirr, buzz, pop,* and *sizzle* are examples of onomatopoeia. In "The Highwayman" the words *tlot-tlot* imitate the sound of horse hooves hitting the road.

Personification   The giving of human qualities to an animal, object, or idea is called personification. In "Anansi and His Visitor, Turtle," for example, the spider and turtle converse as if they were human.

Persuasion   Persuasion is a type of writing that is meant to sway the reader's feelings, beliefs, or actions. Persuasion normally is used to appeal to both the mind and emotions of the reader.

Play   See *Drama.*

Plot   Plot is the sequence of related events that make up a story; it is the action, or what happens in the story. Most plots follow a regular pattern. The **exposition** introduces the characters and the conflict they face. Complications set in as the characters try to resolve the conflict. Eventually, the plot reaches a **climax,** the highest point of interest or suspense. The final stage is the **resolution,** in which loose ends are tied up and the story is brought to a close.

Poetry   Poetry is a type of literature that expresses ideas and feelings in compact, imaginative, and musical language. Poets combine words in patterns to touch the reader's senses, emotions, and mind. Normally, poems are written in lines, which are often grouped in stanzas. Many poems contain a regular rhythm and some use rhyme.

See *Alliteration, Figurative Language, Form, Free Verse, Imagery, Narrative Poetry, Rhyme, Rhythm,* and *Stanza.*

Point of View   The perspective from which a story is told is called its point of view. The most common points of view are first person, third-person omniscient, and third-person limited.

In the **first-person** point of view, the narrator is one of the characters in the story and uses first-person pronouns such as *I, me,* and *we.* The reader sees the events of the story and other characters only through the eyes of the narrator. "Lose Now, Pay Later" uses first-person point of view.

In the **third-person** point of view, the narrator is not in the story and relates the story using third-person pronouns such as *he, she,* or *it.* In the **third-person omniscient,** or all-knowing, point of view, the narrator knows everything about the characters and can see into their minds. "The Emperor's New Clothes," which brings us into the minds of the Emperor and his advisors, is an example of omniscient narration.

In the **third-person limited** point of view, the narrator brings us into the mind of only one character. "The Smallest Dragonboy," which limits its focus to Keevan's thoughts and actions, is an example of this type of narration.

Predicting   Using what you know to guess what will happen in the future is called predicting. Good readers gather information as they read and combine that information with prior knowledge to predict the events in a story.

Problem Solving   The process of identifying a problem and considering possible solutions is known as problem solving. First, the problem is defined. Second, the causes of the problem are identified. Third, a list of possible solutions is made and possible outcomes of each of the solutions are considered. Finally, a solution is chosen and applied.

Prose   Prose is the ordinary form of spoken and written language, that is, language that does not possess the regular rhythmic pattern of poetry.

Questioning   The process of raising questions while reading is called questioning. Good readers ask themselves questions in an effort to understand characters and events. They look for the answers as they continue to read.

Repetition   Repetition is the repeated use of any element of language—a sound, a word, a phrase, a line, or a grammatical structure. Writers use repetition to stress important ideas and to create memorable sound effects, as in these lines from "The Charge of the Light Brigade."

Theirs not to make reply,
Theirs not to reason why,
Theirs but to do and die;

Resolution   See *Plot.*

Reviewing   The process of pausing while reading to recall previous events and check understanding is called reviewing. Readers stop to reflect on what they know, to make some inferences about what is happening, and to better understand what they are reading.

Rhyme   Rhyme is the repetition of identical or similar sounds. Two words rhyme when their accented syllables and all the sounds following these syllables sound the same. *Dog* and *log* are rhymes, as are *letter* and *better.*

The most common form of rhyme is **end rhyme,** where the rhyme occurs at the end of the lines of poetry. **Internal rhyme** takes place when rhymes occur within lines. Note both the internal and end rhymes found in these lines from "Wishes."

> I want to <u>sail</u> on a swallow's <u>tail</u> and
>   peep through the sky's blue <u>glass</u>.
> I want to <u>see</u> if the dreams in <u>me</u> shall
>   perish or come to <u>pass</u>.
> See *Poetry.*

Rhythm   The pattern of stressed and unstressed syllables in poetry is called rhythm. When the stressed syllables—the syllables that are emphasized—are arranged in a consistent pattern, the poem has a regular beat. Note the rhythm in these lines from "If I Can Stop One Heart from Breaking." The stressed syllables are marked by ⁄; the unstressed ones by ⌣ .

> ⌣ ⁄ ⌣ ⁄ ⌣ ⁄ ⌣ ⁄ ⌣
> If I can stop one Heart from breaking

> ⌣ ⁄ ⌣ ⁄ ⌣ ⁄
> I shall not live in vain
> See *Poetry.*

Satire   Satire is a literary technique that makes fun of foolish behaviors or ideas. A satire usually offers a humorous criticism of something that needs to be changed for the good of society. For example, "Upon the Waters" makes fun of the bureaucracy of the welfare system.

Scanning   In reading, scanning is the process of searching for a particular fact or piece of information. When you scan, your eyes sweep across a page, looking for key words that may lead you to the information you want.

Scene   A scene is a unit of action in a play that takes place in one setting at one time. For example, in *Driving Miss Daisy* one scene takes place in Daisy's kitchen; the next occurs at Boolie's workplace. Each scene of the play presents an episode in the plot.

Science Fiction   Science fiction is fiction based on real or imagined scientific developments. These stories are often set in imaginary places and usually take place in the future. "Lose Now, Pay Later" is science fiction.

Screenplay   A script from which a movie is produced is called a screenplay. Screenplays often have more scenes than stage plays because it is easier to show changes in time or place on film than on a stage. Consequently, screenplays tend to have many stage directions and often include camera instructions. The version of *Driving Miss Daisy* in this book is a screenplay.

Setting   Setting is the time and place of the action of a story, poem, or play. Sometimes the setting is clear and well-defined; at other times, it is left to the reader's imagination. Setting may include geographic location, the historical period (past, present, or future), season, time of day, and customs and manners of the society.
  See *Fiction.*

Short Story   A work of fiction that can generally be read in one sitting is called a short story. Short stories usually focus on one or two main characters who face a single problem or conflict.
  See *Fiction.*

Simile   A simile is a comparison of two unlike things that have some quality in common. Similes make a direct comparison, using words such as *like, as,* or *resembles.* Note the following simile from *Boy:* "What is left looks rather like a gigantic black pancake."
  See *Figurative Language.*

Skimming   Skimming is reading quickly to find the main idea or to get an overview. When you skim, you read only the title, the headings, the words in special type, and the first sentence of each paragraph. You also read charts, graphs, and time lines.

Sound Effects See *Alliteration, Onomatopoeia, Poetry, Repetition, Rhyme,* and *Rhythm.*

Speaker The speaker in a poem is the voice that talks to the reader. The speaker is comparable to a narrator in a work of fiction. In some poems, the speaker expresses the feelings of the poet, as in "There Is No Word for Goodbye." In other poems the speaker and poet are not the same.

Stage Directions Instructions to the actors, director, and stage crew in a play script are called stage directions. These instructions may suggest scenery, lighting, music, sound effects, and how actors should move or speak. In this book, stage directions appear within parentheses in italic type.

See *Drama.*

Stanza A group of lines in poetry is called a stanza. A stanza is like a paragraph in prose. "The Charge of the Light Brigade," for example, has seven stanzas.

See *Poetry.*

Stereotype A broad generalization about something or someone that leaves no room for individual differences is called a stereotype. A stereotype is often used to judge people unfairly on the basis of race, ethnic background, or physical appearance.

Style Style is the way in which a piece of literature is written. Style refers to *how* something is said rather than to *what* is said. Many elements contribute to style, including word choice, sentence length, tone, and figurative language. The style of *Boy,* for example, can be described as playful, relying on exaggeration, humor, and colorful words.

Summarizing To summarize means to tell briefly in your own words the main ideas of a piece of writing, omitting unimportant details.

Surprise Ending An unexpected twist in the plot at the end of a story is called a surprise ending. "Hearts and Hands" is an example of a story with a surprise ending.

Suspense The feeling of growing tension and excitement felt by a reader is called suspense. Writers create suspense by raising questions in the readers' minds about what might happen in the plot. For example, a suspenseful moment occurs in "Old Sly Eye" when Alben is trapped in the loft.

Symbol A symbol is a person, a place, an object, or an action that stands for something outside itself. The bald eagle, for example, is a symbol of the United States.

Literary symbols take on their meaning within the context of the work of literature. In "Dream Deferred," for instance, the "raisin in the sun" might be a symbol of dreams that have been denied, lost, or forgotten.

Teleplay A play written for television is called a teleplay. In a teleplay, the stage directions usually include camera instructions.

Theme A theme is the message about life or human nature communicated by a work of literature. In most cases the reader must infer the theme. One way of figuring out a theme is to apply the lessons learned by the main characters to all people. For example, one theme of "The Christmas Hunt" is that a child's parents sometimes know best.

Tone A writer's attitude toward his or her subject is called tone. A writer's tone may be amused, objective, angry, or any number of other attitudes. The tone of "Formula" might be considered dreamy or escapist.

Visualizing The process of forming a mental picture from a written description is called visualizing. Good readers use details supplied by the writer to picture characters, settings, and events in their mind.

BIOGRAPHIES OF THE AUTHORS*

JAMES BERRY

Sherwood Anderson *(1876–1941)* grew up in Ohio. After serving in the Spanish-American War, he managed a paint factory in Ohio, even though he had very little formal education. One day he pretended to lose his mind and walked out. He then moved to Chicago and began writing. With the help of Carl Sandburg and others, he published his first notable work, *Winesburg, Ohio,* which brought him national recognition.

James Berry *(1924–)* grew up in Jamaica but emigrated to England in 1948. Currently he divides his time between the two countries. A well-known poet and critic, Berry won first prize in the National Poetry Competition of Great Britain in 1981. His collections of poetry include *Chain of Days* and *Fractured Circles.* Of Jamaica, Berry says, "No one has reported our stories, or the way we saw things. It's the function of writers and poets to bring in the left-out side of the human family."

RAY BRADBURY

Ray Bradbury *(1920–)* was writing stories by the age of twelve, and in high school he put out his own magazine. Bradbury says about his early writing, "I was in love with everything I did. I did not warm to a subject, I boiled over." Bradbury tries to write one thousand words each day and at least one story a week. Though he writes about future technology and space travel, he has never learned to drive a car and rarely flies in airplanes. His favorite way to get around is by bicycle.

Russell Gordon Carter *(1892–1957)* was a young political writer for Woodrow Wilson's presidential campaign and fought in the First World War before he began to write for *Youth's Companion,* a magazine for adolescents. He quickly became popular for stories based on historical events, such as "Brothers of the Frontiers" and "A Patriot Lad of Old Boston." In his lifetime, he published over fifty books and hundreds of stories.

SANDRA CISNEROS

Sandra Cisneros *(1954–)* grew up with six brothers in a Mexican-American family in Chicago. For her, books were an escape from poverty and loneliness. Today, she mixes the Spanish she heard as a child into poems, short stories, and novels about everyday Hispanic life. *The House on Mango Street,* from which "Bums in the Attic" is taken, won the Before Columbus Book Award. She has won many other honors and grants, including two National Endowment for the Arts fellowships.

*These pages provide author biographies for literature lessons that do not already include this information.

Lucille Clifton *(1936–)* is the great-great-granddaughter of a woman who was brought from West Africa as a slave in 1830. Clifton published her first book in 1969 and has written poetry and prose for children and adults ever since. Her writing focuses on black urban families. She was Poet Laureate of Maryland from 1979 to 1982, and in 1984 she won the Coretta Scott King Award for her children's book *Everett Anderson's Goodbye.*

LUCILLE CLIFTON

Margaret Danner *(1915–1984)* began writing poetry in middle school and won first prize in a poetry competition when she was in the eighth grade. After college she became the first African-American assistant editor at *Poetry,* a magazine that publishes works of many great poets. *Poetry* published some of Danner's poems. She received several awards that allowed her to travel to Africa, and much of her poetry is about that continent.

Julia Fields *(1938–)* grew up in Bessemer, Alabama. Later, she taught high school English in Birmingham and wrote poetry on the side. In 1968, she received a grant from the National Endowment for the Arts and also released her first volume of work, *Poems.* She has since been poet-in-residence at several colleges and universities, helping others to find their own poetic voices and continuing to write and publish her own work.

ROBERT FROST

Robert Frost *(1874–1963)* drew his inspiration from his life in rural New England. His poems reflect the spirit of New England's independence and stubbornness. He claimed that he started out as such a poor student that he didn't read a book until he was fifteen. Yet at the end of his life, he was the only poet ever to have won four Pulitzer Prizes and participate in a presidential inauguration; he recited a poem when John F. Kennedy was sworn in as president. On his eighty-eighth birthday, he received a Congressional Gold Medal and had a mountain in Vermont named after him. "One can never tell how the race will turn out until the end," he said. "I'm a lucky man."

O. Henry *(1862–1910),* whose real name was William Sydney Porter, left school at the age of fifteen and worked as a pharmacist, a ranch hand, a newspaper columnist, a publisher, and a bank teller. He was convicted of embezzling from the bank and spent three years in jail. O. Henry spent the last eight years of his life in New York City, where his career as a writer prospered. He wrote more than 250 short stories and several novels. His stories are famous for their surprise endings, irony, and humor.

O. HENRY

© 1987 Layle Silbert

LANGSTON HUGHES

Langston Hughes *(1902–1967)* was at different times a janitor, a teacher, a farmer, a cook, a waiter, a doorman, a sailor, a busboy, and a poet. While a busboy, he left his poems on the table of Vachel Lindsay, a well-known poet. Hughes became famous overnight. He wrote poems, short stories, novels, plays, songs, and a newspaper column. He is best known for his poetry about African Americans; their search for justice and a better life; and their beauty, strength, and heritage. He founded three theaters, taught at several universities, and won many awards for his work.

Ana Maria Iza *(1941–)* was born in Quito, Ecuador, and attended its Universidad Central. However, she so enjoyed the time she spent singing at the music conservatory there that she switched her attention to music. She became a soprano with the choir of the prestigious Ecuadorian Casa de la Cultura. Iza has received several prizes and awards in Ecuadorian poetry competitions, and she published her first volume of poetry, *Pedaza de Nada* (Bits of Nothing), when she was only twenty-eight.

Shirley Jackson *(1919–1965)* was born and raised in California. After attending Syracuse University, she settled in Vermont with her husband. She wrote many humorous stories about her husband and four children, fictionalizing their lives in *Life Among the Savages* and *Raising Demons*. However, she is best known for writing horror stories such as "The Lottery" and the novels *The Haunting of Hill House* and *We Have Always Lived in the Castle*. Many of Jackson's stories have been made into plays, movies, and television dramas.

GEORGIA DOUGLAS JOHNSON

Georgia Douglas Johnson *(1886–1966)* helped pave the way for later African-American poets, including Langston Hughes and Mari Evans. In Washington, D.C., Johnson started a weekly open house for young poets, which Hughes attended. She was active in the pan-Africa movement, worked for women's and minority rights, and served as a commissioner at the U.S. Department of Labor. Johnson was also a playwright, but some producers refused to stage three of her plays about a lynching of a black person by a white mob.

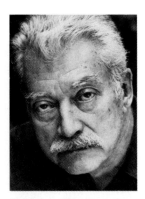

MACKINLAY KANTOR

MacKinlay Kantor *(1904–1977)* was encouraged to write by his mother, a newspaper editor. However, it was years before Kantor found a successful market for his work in the "pulps," cheap popular magazines. Often paid only a penny a word, Kantor quickly produced stories with surprise endings and melodramatic climaxes. He also wrote murder mysteries. In 1956, Kantor won the Pulitzer Prize for *Andersonville*, a novel about the conditions in a southern Civil War prison camp. Kantor's last historical novel, *Valley Forge*, was published in 1975 in honor of the nation's bicentennial.

Edna Mason Kaula *(1906–   )* has lived in Australia, New Zealand, Indonesia, Holland, Central Africa, and the United States. She studied to be an artist in Holland and later added writing to her skills. She has made lengthy visits to many countries in Africa. On some of her visits, she witnessed ceremonies never before seen by a non-African. She has written and illustrated many popular books for adults and children about the places she has been.

JANICE MIRIKITANI

Janice Mirikitani says that "For My Father," written to her stepfather, describes the pain of "being an Asian-American in a country that treated you as a foreigner." This pain clearly fueled a desire to help others as well as to express her own feelings. Mirikitani is president of the Glide Foundation in San Francisco, California, which feeds the poor, houses the homeless, and helps victims of drugs, battering, and AIDS. She continues to publish her own work, and her efforts on the behalf of other writers and artists have resulted in many awards. These include California's Woman of the Year and San Francisco's Woman Warrior in Arts and Culture.

Pat Mora *(1942–   )* is the author of three poetry collections, two of which have received Southwest Book Awards. Much of her writing describes both the visual beauty and cultural diversity of the Southwest, and the harmony that exists in nature and among Mexican and Anglo peoples. Her work has appeared in many textbooks and has been translated into Spanish, Italian, and Bengali. She presently lives in Ohio, continues to write, and gives readings of her poetry, essays, and children's books.

PAT MORA

Alfred Noyes *(1880–1958)* was born and raised in Wolverhampton, England. While still an undergraduate in college, he published his first collection of poems. By 1910 he had written his first biography and eight full books of poetry. Noyes wrote "The Highwayman" in only two days. His readers so loved his ballads and narrative poetry that he soon became the most popular poet in England. Noyes continued writing until 1942, when glaucoma took his eyesight.

ANNA QUINDLEN

Anna Quindlen *(1952–   )* published her first story in *Seventeen* magazine in 1974, the year she graduated from Barnard College. In 1981 she began writing columns for *The New York Times,* which have made her famous. In 1991 she won a Pulitzer Prize for her syndicated weekly column, "Public and Private." Quindlen says that mixing up fact and fiction, being too curious, and asking too many questions are "the kinds of things you are not supposed to do at fifteen, but get you a Pulitzer Prize at thirty-nine."

ANDREW A. ROONEY

Andrew A. Rooney *(1919–   ),* born in Albany, New York, won writing prizes and wrote for magazines in high school and college. During World War II he wrote for the military newspaper *Stars and Stripes.* In 1949 Rooney began his career with CBS. When he read "An Essay on War" on television in 1971, not only did the essay win an award, but Rooney began his on-camera career. In 1978 he joined the popular CBS news program *60 Minutes.* He has written ten books, won four Emmy awards, and six Writers Guild Awards.

Juan A. A. Sedillo *(1902–1982)* had a long, distinguished career in law and government. From 1932 to 1936 he served in the New Mexico state senate but then left New Mexico for Europe, where he practiced law. He joined the U.S. Army and fought in World War II, in which he was awarded a Bronze Star and five battle stars. After the war, Sedillo became a chief defense counsel for the German war crimes trials, then chief legal officer for the U.S. military government in Germany. Next he was a judge in the American Zone in Berlin, then a State Department advisor, and finally a staff member with the U.S. diplomatic corps in Morocco. In later life, Sedillo returned to New Mexico to become a judge.

JUAN A. A. SEDILLO

Leslie Marmon Silko *(1948–   )* was born in Albuquerque, New Mexico. Her ancestry is a mixture of Laguna Pueblo Indian, Mexican, and European. She grew up on the Laguna Pueblo Reservation and still lives there. Silko wrote many short stories and poems before her first novel, *Ceremony,* won her fame as a Native American writer in 1977. Silko has received several grants and awards for her writing, including a MacArthur Foundation five-year grant. Silko feels that Native American rituals and traditions are seeds of renewal and identity.

Mary TallMountain *(1918–   )* was three years old when her mother, a member of the Koykon-Athabascan people of Nulato, Alaska, was fatally stricken with tuberculosis. The Nulato village council approved Mary's adoption by a white couple. After her adoptive parents died, TallMountain moved to San Francisco in 1945 where she ran her own business. A bout with illness left her almost penniless, and she nearly became homeless. TallMountain decided to become a voice for the homeless. She moved to one of the poorest parts of the city and wrote about the people there. She still lives in California and writes about her heritage.

LESLIE MARMON SILKO

Alfred, Lord Tennyson *(1809–1892)*   found fame only after much misfortune. He and his family were plagued by poverty, his earliest poetry received terrible reviews, and his best friend, Arthur Hallam, died suddenly. Tennyson became so depressed he did not publish anything for the next nine years. In 1850, Tennyson's luck changed. His poem *In Memoriam,* written in honor of Arthur Hallam, became hugely popular. Queen Victoria so liked his work that she made him Poet Laureate of England and Lord Tennyson.

ALFRED, LORD TENNYSON

Yoshiko Uchida *(1921–1992)*   wrote stories on brown wrapping paper when she was ten. When she attended college in Berkeley, California, she found much prejudice against Japanese Americans. During World War II her family was imprisoned along with thousands of other Japanese-American families. Finally, Uchida was allowed to leave to study at Smith College. In 1952 she received a Ford Foundation Fellowship to collect folk tales in Japan. Uchida wrote more than twenty-five books, including *Journey Home, The Best Bad Thing, A Jar of Dreams,* and the award-winning *Journey to Topaz.*

YOSHIKO UCHIDA

THE WRITING PROCESS

Writing is a process—a series of steps taken to create a finished product. The process a writer uses is unique to him or her and may not be the same for every writing experience. You need to develop your own writing process, one that works best for you.

Many writers focus their thinking and writing in stages similar to the ones outlined on these pages and shown in the graphic below. Use these stages as a guide, but feel free to go backward or forward in the procedure and to shorten or even skip some stages if you are comfortable doing so.

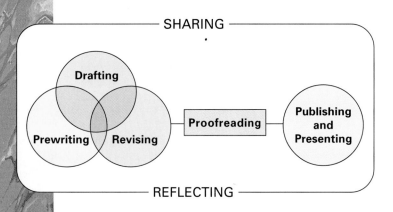

Prewriting and Exploring

Before you write, you think and plan. The following steps might help you get started:

1. Clarify the Assignment

When you are given a writing assignment, make sure you understand what you are being asked to write. To clarify your task, fill out as much of a PASSkey as you can for the assignment by answering the following questions:

P = Purpose
Is the purpose stated in the assignment?
Do I want to express ideas or feelings? to inform? to entertain? to analyze? to persuade?

A = Audience
Who will read my writing?
How much about the subject do my readers know?
How much more do they need to know?
What might they find interesting?
How do I want my audience to respond?

S = Subject
Has a topic been assigned?
What topic do I know about or want to explore?
What topic can I handle well in the length that has been assigned?

S = Structure
Has a structure or form been assigned?
What organization would help me accomplish my purpose?
What should the final product look like?

2. Get Ideas for a Topic

Try some of these different ways of finding topics:

Recalling   Remember events and scenes from your past. Look through family photo albums, scrapbooks, diaries, or your journal to jog your memory. Talk to family members or old friends. Think of the first time you did something.

Brainstorming   With a partner or a small group of classmates, think of and jot down as many ideas as possible. One person's ideas will spur another's. Keep the atmosphere positive and don't stop to evaluate. Ideas should be generated, not judged.

Listing Write a topic or category at the top of a page and list every idea you can think of that relates to it. Go in as many different directions as your imagination will allow.

Freewriting Choose a topic you want to explore and write the first thing that pops into your head. For about three minutes, keep writing everything that comes into your mind. Don't worry about grammar, spelling, or punctuation, and don't stop to read what you've written. After a few minutes, stop writing, read what you wrote, and pick out any ideas that you want to explore further.

Webbing Write a central idea in the middle of your page and circle it. Outside the circle write related ideas. Circle each and draw a line connecting it to the central idea. Do the same for each related idea, as in the idea web below.

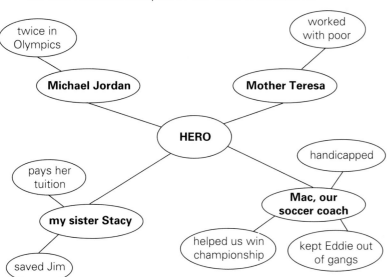

3. Choose and Limit Your Topic

Choose a topic that excites you—one you know about or would like to learn about. Narrow your topic to a size you can deal with in the length of your paper. For example, "my family" is too broad a topic to cover in a short composition, but a topic like "my brother's funny habits" could be handled easily.

4. Gather Information

Although different kinds of writing require you to gather information in different ways, most writing involves doing some research and/or using your imagination. If you write an informative or persuasive paper, you must do research to get facts and statistics. If you write about your own experience, you will delve into your memory. If you create fiction or drama, you will use your imagination, but you might do research as well. When you write about literature, you study the literary work itself. For whatever type of writing you do, make notes on a piece of paper, index cards, or a computer screen to record your thoughts .

5. Organize Your Ideas

After you have all the information and ideas you need, organize your notes into the order in which you wish to present your ideas. You can organize by outlining, numbering, using graphic devices, arranging index cards, or moving sections of notes around on a computer screen.

Draft and Discover

When you draft, you begin to put your ideas on paper, following any notes, graphics, or outlines you have made. Drafting is a time to let ideas flow without concern for spelling and punctuation. Errors can be corrected later.

Revise Your Writing

When you revise, you judge the strengths and weaknesses of your paper. You can do this by yourself or with a peer reader. Try to improve what you said and how you said it.

Look for ways you can improve your writing by asking yourself questions about the content. The revision questions on the next page will help you get started.

Revision Questions

- Are the ideas clear and focused on the topic?
- Is the purpose of the writing clear?
- Do any parts need more details?
- Do the ideas flow in a logical order?
- Is the tone consistently the way I want it?
- Will this produce the response I want from the audience?
- Can I add a more exciting beginning?
- Does the piece end in a satisfying way?

When you are satisfied with the content of your writing, check for mistakes in grammar, usage, capitalization, punctuation, and spelling. Use proofreading symbols to mark these errors. Then make a clean, corrected copy of your paper.

Proofreading Symbols

Symbol	Meaning	Example
∧	insert	leson
≡	capitalize	douglass
/	lowercase	History
∼	transpose	veiw
ℓ	take out	lots of
¶	paragraph	¶ The
⊙	add a period	slavery⊙
⌄	add a comma	Finally⌄

Publish and Present

You communicate with others by sharing your writing. Here are a few possible ways to do this.

- Read your writing aloud to classmates.
- Trade papers with a classmate so that you can read each other's work.
- Publish everyone's work in your own magazine.
- Submit your writing to a school newspaper.
- Tape-record a reading of your work.
- Videotape classmates acting out your writing.

Reflect on Your Writing

After you have completed your writing, think about it and the process you went through to complete it. What have you discovered about your own writing process? Should you change your method the next time around? By learning from what you do each time, you will constantly improve your personal writing process.

TIPS FOR BETTER PARAGRAPHS

Paragraphs are the building blocks of writing. Whether a paragraph stands by itself or is part of a longer composition, such as an essay or a story, it needs to be solidly constructed.

The following information will help you understand paragraphs and give you tips for constructing better paragraphs.

What Is a Paragraph?

A **paragraph** is a group of related sentences that work together to develop a main idea or accomplish a single purpose. Each paragraph that follows has a single main idea or purpose. In the model below, the first sentence states the main idea.

> Away from Allenswood, Eleanor's old uncertainty about her looks came back again. She saw herself as too tall, too thin, too plain. She worried about her buckteeth, which she had thought made her look horselike. The old teasing began again, especially on the part of Uncle Ted's daughter, "Princess" Alice Roosevelt, who seemed to take pleasure in making Eleanor feel uncomfortable.
>
> William J. Jacobs, "Eleanor Roosevelt"

In the next model paragraph, no one sentence states the main idea. Instead, all the sentences work together for a single purpose—to describe Rikki-tikki-tavi, a mongoose.

> He was a mongoose, rather like a little cat in his fur and his tail, but quite like a weasel in his head and his habits. His eyes and the end of his restless nose were pink. He could scratch himself anywhere he pleased with any leg, front or back, that he chose to use. He could fluff up his tail till it looked like a bottle brush, and his war cry as he scuttled through the long grass was *Rikk-tikk-tikki-tikki-tchk!*
>
> Rudyard Kipling, "Rikki-tikki-tavi"

Unity and Coherence

Well-written paragraphs, such as the previous models, reflect two characteristics: unity and coherence. A paragraph has **unity** when all the sentences tell about one main idea or serve a single purpose. In the example below, one of the sentences strays from the topic. Can you tell which one?

> I never saw my sister in better form. Sarah hit every note in the songs, and her acting was superb. The woman sitting next to me in the audience cried when Sarah gave her farewell speech. I noticed other people in the audience with tears in their eyes. Sometimes boys get embarrassed when they cry, but I don't know why they should. The audience belonged to Sarah that night.

The sentence that begins "Sometimes boys get embarrassed" has nothing to do with the description of Sarah's performance. The sentence breaks the unity of the paragraph. It strays from the point and may confuse readers.

A paragraph has **coherence** when the sentences flow smoothly and logically from beginning to end. In a well-written paragraph, the relationship between the sentences is clear to the reader. Compare the following two paragraphs. Which has more coherence?

> Theaters in ancient Athens were built outside, nestled in the hills. A circular stone floor, called the orchestra, served as the performing stage. The stone seats were set into the hillside. There stood a large building called a skene. This was just a building that the actors used for costume changes. It served as a scenic background for the action of a play. Everything was done on a grand scale to entertain the thousands of people in the audience.

> Theaters in ancient Athens were built outside, nestled in the hills. *At the bottom* of the hills, a circular stone pit, called the orchestra, served as the performing stage. Stone seats, *rising above* the orchestra, were

set into the hillside. *Behind* the orchestra, there stood a large building called a skene. *Originally,* this was just a building that the actors used for costume changes. *Later,* it served as a scenic background for the action of a play. Everything was done on a grand scale to entertain the thousands of people in the audience.

The second paragraph in the pair is more coherent because it makes use of **transitions,** the words in italic type. Transitions are the connecting words that let readers know how the details in a paragraph are related.

Some common transitions show relationships of time and space. Others point out comparison and contrast and other logical relationships.

When you revise your paragraphs, check to make sure that your sentences are clearly connected to one another. When necessary, add transition words to help make the relationships clearer.

The chart below lists words and phrases commonly used as transitions.

Transition Words and Phrases

Time Order	before	after	next
	then	meanwhile	yesterday
	during	first	second
Spatial Order	above	below	behind
	around	to the left	on top of
	inside	outside	in front of
Order of Importance	first	most important	strongest
	second	less important	most significant
	third	least important	weakest
Comparison	as	than	like
	similarly	in the same way	by comparison
	neither/nor	either/ or	also
Contrast	yet	but	however
	unlike	instead	in contrast
	nevertheless	on the contrary	on the other hand
Cause and Effect	because	therefore	for this reason
	if/then	thus	so
	as a result	since	due to

Making Your Main Idea Clear

There are two ways of getting across the main idea of your paragraph. One way is to come right out and state your main idea in a **topic sentence.** A topic sentence identifies your topic and tells what you want to say about it. Often, writing that explains or persuades makes use of topic sentences.

The topic sentence may be the first sentence of the paragraph, as in the example below.

> Whenever the white man treats an Indian as they treat each other, then we shall have no more wars. We shall all be alike—brothers of one father and mother, with one sky above us and one country around us and one government for all. Then the Great Spirit Chief who rules above will smile upon this land and send rain to wash out the bloody spots made by brothers' hands from the face of the earth. For this time the Indian race are waiting and praying. I hope that no more groans of wounded men and women will ever go to the ear of the Great Spirit Chief above, and that all people may be one people.
>
> Chief Joseph, "Chief Joseph Speaks"

A topic sentence may appear elsewhere in a paragraph. Sometimes, the second sentence in a paragraph serves as the topic sentence. At other times, it may be the last sentence of the paragraph.

A good topic sentence does more than state the main idea of a paragraph. It also catches readers' interest and makes them want to read on. Compare the following topic sentences.

> I am going to explain the second reason why our class should "adopt" a family for the holidays.

> Besides helping the "adopted family," our holiday basket project will build class spirit.

The second sentence is more interesting and more specific than the first. It tells readers what the paragraph will be about and makes them curious to find out more. Use the checklist below to improve your own topic sentences.

Topic Sentence Checklist

1. Does the sentence tell what the paragraph is about?

2. Is the main idea stated clearly?

3. Is the sentence interesting enough to catch the reader's attention?

4. Is the main idea narrow enough to be developed in one paragraph?

5. Does the sentence cover all the related ideas in the paragraph?

Another way of getting across main ideas is to use an **implied main idea.** Unlike a topic sentence, an implied main idea is not stated directly but is communicated by all the paragraph's sentences working together.

Narrative and descriptive writing often make use of implied main ideas. In the following model, all the sentences work together to describe the lonely appearance of Margot, the main character in the story.

> Margot stood alone. She was a very frail girl who looked as if she had been lost in the rain for years, and the rain had washed out the blue from her eyes and the red from her mouth and the yellow from her hair. She was an old photograph dusted from an album, whitened away, and if she spoke at all her voice would be a ghost. Now she stood, separate, staring at the rain and the loud, wet world beyond the huge glass.
>
> Ray Bradbury, "All Summer in a Day"

Elaboration

A well-constructed paragraph needs details that support its main idea or help to accomplish its purpose. The chart below lists some common types of **elaboration,** or ways of adding supporting details, that you might use to develop your paragraphs.

A well-developed paragraph feels complete. It doesn't leave out important information or state ideas without explaining them. Do you think the following paragraph is well developed?

> You probably don't care much about fruit flies. However, plenty of scientists do. Thousands of experiments have been conducted with fruit flies. They are a valuable source of scientific knowledge.

This paragraph leaves too many questions unanswered. Why do scientists conduct experiments with fruit flies? What have scientists learned from them? Now read another version of the paragraph, one with more elaboration.

> You probably don't care much about fruit flies. However, plenty of scientists do. Fruit flies are a perfect subject for genetics, the branch of biology that deals with heredity. A fruit fly only lives about two weeks. In the course of a year, twenty-seven generations of fruit flies are born and die. Their short life cycle gives scientists a unique opportunity to study how and why traits are passed on to other generations. As a result, fruit flies have contributed more to the study of genetics than any other animal.

When you revise your paragraphs, look for places where you need more information or details.

Types of Elaboration

Type	Definition	Example
Facts/Statistics	Statements that can be proved	The capital of Cameroon is Yaoundé.
Sensory Details	Words that appeal to the five senses	The canary with the silky orange feathers sang loudly in a staccato rhythm.
Reasons	Logical statements to support an idea	Rita deserved to win. She offered the best plan for improving the school. She also worked very hard and listened to everyone's ideas.
Examples	Specific cases or instances that illustrate a main idea	Picking wildflowers and littering are two ways that people ruin national parks.
Quotations	Someone's exact words	"Women who smoke face a greater risk of cancer," said Dr. Peavy.

Paragraphing

When you begin drafting, you often do not know how many paragraphs you will write or what the main idea of each paragraph will be. The following guidelines will help you organize your ideas into effective paragraphs.

Guidelines for Paragraphing

As you draft:

- **Look for related details.**
  Group them together as a paragraph.

- **Look for changes in main ideas.**
  Start a new paragraph with each new idea.

- **Recognize changes in setting or speaker.**
  Whenever the setting or speaker changes, begin a new paragraph.

As you revise:

- **Look for overloaded or overly long paragraphs.**
  Break these down into smaller paragraphs, each focusing on one main idea.

- **Look for strings of short paragraphs.**
  These paragraphs may need to be grouped together or need further elaboration.

- **Make sure each paragraph has a main idea or clear purpose.**
  If you can't tell what the main idea is, how will your reader be able to?

- **Watch out for paragraphs that overlap one another.**
  If two paragraphs cover the same topic, revise one or both of them.

RESEARCH AND REPORT WRITING

This section gives you a brief overview of the steps involved in writing research papers and reports. For further help in this area, consult the Writer's Workshop on Informative Writing on page 569.

Finding a Topic

These tips on finding an idea can make writing easier:

1. Choose a topic that truly interests you. That way you won't get bored and your work will be easier to finish.

2. Check the library. See whether there are enough books and articles available for you to adequately research your subject.

3. Limit your topic. Many topic ideas start out too big. A topic like diabetes may be too large because there is simply too much to say. Choose a smaller topic, such as juvenile diabetes, the causes and treatment of diabetes, or the discovery and history of diabetes. A smaller topic makes a report more manageable.

4. Jot down major points you think you might cover in your report. You may need to look through books to get some general ideas for what you might write about. These general ideas will help you focus your research.

Using the Library

After choosing and focusing your topic, begin your search for information. Like most researchers, you will probably begin with the resources in the library. However, research can also include interviews, TV programs, and many other nonprint sources.

The Card Catalog The card catalog lists all the materials in the library and tells you where to find them. There are three cards for every book: a **title card,** an **author card,** and a **subject card.** Begin by looking up your subject, but don't panic if you can't find what you want right away. You may need to look under a different heading.

Computerized Catalogs Most public libraries now have computerized catalogs. Instructions for using them are usually posted next to the terminals. Generally, you type in your subject; the title of the book; or the last name, then first name, of the author.

Call Numbers Most libraries arrange nonfiction books according to the Dewey Decimal System. The Dewey Decimal System assigns every book a number in one of ten categories. This **call number** is usually printed on the spine of the book. The books are then arranged on the library shelves in numerical order. When you use a card catalog or computer, you are given the call numbers to help you locate the book. Find the area of the library containing those numbers, and search for your book.

Reference Section

The reference section of your library contains all kinds of books that provide facts and statistics, including the different types of materials mentioned below. Ask the librarian for help if you have trouble finding any source.

Readers' Guide to Periodical Literature This journal lists, by subject, articles in current magazines and newspapers. Find the most current *Readers' Guide* and look up the subject of your report. After you find an article that looks promising, write the name and date of the magazine and the page number. Then go to the magazine area and ask the librarian for the issue of the magazine you need. For more information about using the *Readers' Guide,* see page 390.

General Encyclopedias Encyclopedias are often a good place to start your research, since they give a general overview of a subject.

Beware of depending on them, however. If you use only an encyclopedia entry, you haven't done any serious research. You need to find more current and detailed information by using other sources as well.

Specialized Dictionaries and Encyclopedias These books focus on a particular area of knowledge. You can find dictionaries for ballet, biographies, and slang, for example, and encyclopedias on science, sports, and so on.

Almanacs and Yearbooks Since these books are published yearly, they have up-to-date facts and statistics. Check the table of contents and the index of the most current almanac to find your subject.

Atlases These books of maps also contain information on other geographical topics, such as population, temperature, and weather.

Parts of a Book

With the help of a card catalog or computer, you will find many nonfiction books on your topic. By scanning the parts of a book, you can decide immediately whether the book will be useful to you or not.

Title Page This gives the full title of a book, the place of publication, and the names of authors, editors, and publishers.

Copyright Page This page has the publication date, so you can decide how current the information in the book is. A 1972 book on Russia, for instance, will not discuss the breakup of the Soviet Union.

Foreword, Preface, or Introduction These pages contain important background information, such as the author's purpose for writing or the method used to collect the information.

Table of Contents This is a summary of the contents of the book, arranged in order of appearance. These pages are especially important because they may quickly show you

whether the book discusses your topic and whether the coverage is detailed enough for your purposes.

Text This is the body of the book. A quick look can help you decide whether the book is too simple or too technical for your needs.

Glossary This is a dictionary at the back of the book that defines technical terms used in the text.

Index Found at the back of the book, this is an alphabetical list of the subjects in the book, together with the page numbers where they can be found. Check the index to see how many pages are devoted to your topic.

Taking Notes

When you find facts and details you can use, take notes. Using index cards can make note-taking easy for you.

Begin by recording important information about each source you use on a **source card** or **bibliography card.** Include the author or editor, last name first; the title of the book or name of the article (for magazines and encyclopedias); the city and publisher; the year (or date for a magazine) of publication; and the library call number (for nonfiction books). You will use the information on these cards later, when you compile your **bibliography** or list of **works cited.** Notice the example below.

Source Card

362.196462
D.

Dolger, Henry, M.D., and Bernard Seeman. <u>How to Live with Diabetes</u>. New York: Norton, 1977.

Then use one note card for each fact or idea you might want to include in your report. On the first line, write the title of the source. On the second line, write the page numbers. Then write the fact. You will use these cards to organize your outline and write your paper. To see how note cards look, see the example below.

Note Card

<u>How to Live with Diabetes</u>	**Title**
36–37	**Pages**
	Information
In juvenile diabetes, the pancreas does not produce enough insulin. Without insulin injections, patients can die.	

When to Take a Note   As you read, keep your topic in mind. When you find information that will help you get your ideas across, stop and take a note. Look for the following:

- details about the main ideas you plan to cover in your paper
- important dates and facts
- important people
- interesting events or examples
- conflicting opinions
- special terms or jargon

Summarizing and Quoting   Whenever you can, summarize information in your own words. If you want to include someone else's idea, be sure you say whose idea it is. You might choose to quote someone's exact words because they are clever, famous, or memorable. If so, copy them word for word, and mark the beginning and end with quotation marks.

Remember that **plagiarism** is the use of someone else's words or ideas without giving

that person credit. Plagiarism is against the law. Always give credit to your sources.

If your teacher requires you to credit sources within your report, put the source in parentheses at the end of the passage that contains someone else's words or ideas. Use these guidelines:

Crediting Sources Within Your Paper

- **Work by one author**   At the end of your sentence, put the author's last name and the page number in parentheses.
(Pray 234)

- **Work by more than one author**   Put all the last names and the page number in parentheses.
(Dolger and Seeman 32)

- **Works with no author**   Put the title or a shortened version of the title and the page number in parentheses.
("Diabetes" 12)

- **Nonprint works**   Put the name of the person interviewed, the television program, or other nonprint work in parentheses.
(Curtis)

Outlining

An outline helps you organize your main points and supporting details in logical order. Begin by reviewing your note cards. Group the cards into separate piles, putting together those that are about similar ideas. Then review the groups, thinking about what they have in common. Your groups can help you organize your outline into headings and subheadings.

In a topic outline, use phrases, not complete sentences, in a form similar to that shown on the next page.

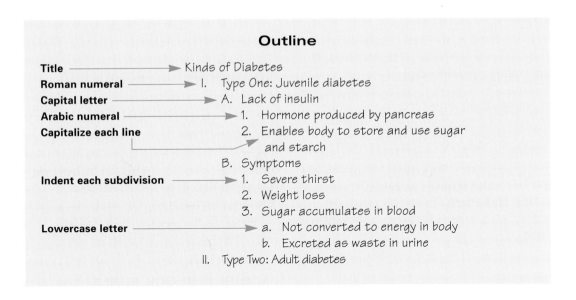

Outline

Title → Kinds of Diabetes

Roman numeral → I. Type One: Juvenile diabetes

Capital letter → A. Lack of insulin

Arabic numeral → 1. Hormone produced by pancreas

Capitalize each line → 2. Enables body to store and use sugar and starch

　　　　　　　　　　B. Symptoms

Indent each subdivision → 1. Severe thirst

　　　　　　　　　　　2. Weight loss

　　　　　　　　　　　3. Sugar accumulates in blood

Lowercase letter → a. Not converted to energy in body

　　　　　　　　　　　　b. Excreted as waste in urine

　　　　　　　II. Type Two: Adult diabetes

Guidelines for Listing Works Cited

On a separate sheet of paper at the end of your report, you must list the sources you used while writing. This list is sometimes called a **bibliography.** You can compile the information from your source cards. List sources in alphabetical order by the name of the author. The guidelines and examples below show the correct format and punctuation for several different kinds of sources. Remember to underline any information that appears in italics.

Books　Author or editor, last name first; book title; city and publisher; year of publication

Covelli, Pat. *Borrowing Time: Growing Up with Juvenile Diabetes.* New York: Crowell, 1977.

Dolger, Henry, M.D., and Bernard Seeman. *How to Live with Diabetes.* New York: Norton, 1977.

Magazine articles　Author, if one is named; article title; name and date of magazine; page numbers

"Diabetes to Go." *Prevention* Apr. 1992: 12–13.

Encyclopedia articles　Author, if listed; title of the entry; encyclopedia name; year of publication

Roth, Jesse. "Diabetes." *The World Book Encyclopedia.* 1988 ed.

Interviews　Name of person interviewed; type of interview (personal or telephone); date

Curtis, Frank. Personal interview. Sept. 25, 1992.

Television programs　Name of program; narrator or other person providing information; name of series; network; local station; date

"A Desert Blooming." Writ. Marshall Riggan. *Living Wild.* PBS. WTTW, Chicago. 29 Apr. 1984.

Recordings　Artist; title of work; title of recording; type of recording; manufacturer; catalog number; year

U2. "MLK." *The Unforgettable Fire.* Audiocassette. RCA, 90231-4, 1984.

WRITING LETTERS

Business Letters

A business letter is written for a specific purpose—for example, requesting information or ordering a product. It requires a formal writing style and a specific format. Business letters have six parts: the **heading,** the **inside address,** the **salutation,** the **body,** the **closing,** and the **signature.** These six parts can be arranged in either **block form** or **modified block form.**

Block Form and Modified Block Form

For any business letter, use plain white 8 1/2" X 11" paper, whether you type the letter or write it by hand. In **block form** all parts begin at the left margin. Use this form only when you type a letter. In **modified block form** the heading, the closing, and the signature are aligned near the right margin, and the other parts are at the left margin. With this form new paragraphs may be indented.

BLOCK FORM

```
37254 Breezeway Terrace
Spokane, Washington 77777     Heading
October 8, 19—


United States Forest Service
Gifford Pinchot National Forest
P.O. Box 8944                 Inside
Vancouver, Washington 98668   Address

Dear Sir or Madam:           Salutation
                             Body
During my vacation I spoke with
Ms. Julie Pizarro, a ranger stationed
in the Gifford Pinchot National
Forest. I told her that I was
interested in a career in the Forest
Service in your area. She suggested
that I write to you for information.

Please send me any material you have
that describes the qualifications I
would need to join the Forest Service.
Thank you for your time and attention.

Yours truly,                 Closing

Maya Garber
                             Signature
Maya Garber
```

MODIFIED BLOCK FORM

```
                   451 Pine Street
Heading            Ames, Iowa 55555
                   June 6, 19—


Credit Manager
Threads Express, Inc.
P.O. Box 14367               Inside Address
Ithaca, New York 11111


Dear Sir or Madam:           Salutation

  I shop regularly at one of your    Body
stores, and I saw a report on our
local television news about your new
credit line for young people.

  Please send me an application form
for your special "Kid's Charge" card.
I understand that my parents must
cosign the application. Thank you for
your prompt response.

Closing            Sincerely,

Signature          Mark O'Neill
                   Mark O'Neill
```

Heading   The heading of a letter tells where and when you are writing. It gives your street address on the first line; your city, state, and ZIP code on the second line; and the month, day, and year on the third line. The heading should be placed about an inch below the top of the page.

Inside Address   The inside address tells to whom the letter is being sent. Place the inside address at the left margin at least four lines below the heading. On the first line you should place the name of the receiver (if you know the person's name). If there is room, place the person's title on the same line, separated from the name by a comma. Otherwise, place the title on the next line. If you do not know the name of the person who will receive the letter, use the person's title or the name of the department. On the following lines, place the name and address of the organization or company, including the city, state, and ZIP code.

Salutation   The salutation of a business letter is the way you greet the person to whom you are writing. The salutation should be positioned two lines below the inside address. Begin with the word *Dear,* follow it by the name of the person, and end with a colon. Use only the person's last name, preceded by a title such as *Mr., Mrs., Ms., Dr.,* or *Professor.* If you do not know the person's name, use a general salutation such as *Ladies and Gentlemen.* Another alternative is to write to a department or to a position within a company. The following forms are acceptable:

Dear Mr. Allen: Dear Sir or Madam:
Dear Ms. Kreutzer: Dear Customer
Dear Mrs. Jackson: Service Department:
                         Dear Editor:

Body   The body, the main part of the letter in which you write your message, begins two spaces below the salutation. The body may contain a single paragraph or several paragraphs. Leave a space between each paragraph.

Closing   The closing is placed two lines below the body, in line with the heading. Closings commonly used for business letters include *Sincerely, Sincerely yours,* and *Very truly yours.* Note that only the first word is capitalized and that the closing ends with a comma.

Signature   Type or print your name four spaces below the closing, and sign your name in the space between.

Friendly Letters

A friendly letter has all the parts of a business letter except the inside address. Notice that a friendly letter is not formal in tone; its salutation might read *Hey Susie!* or *Howdy, John,* while its closing might read *Your pal* or *Missing you.* Notice that the salutation is followed by a comma instead of the colon that is used in a business letter. Indent each paragraph, and write clearly so that your reader can follow what you are saying.

Heading   813 King Drive, #2
                               Dallas, Texas 33333
                               March 12, 19—

Dear José,   **Salutation**
                                        Body
I am very sorry I can't accept your invitation to visit you at your summer place in Michigan. I have already signed up to go to scuba-diving camp during that week in June! Maybe you could go to the camp with me, and we could go to Michigan from there. Could you ask your parents? Hurry and write me back to tell me what they say.

Closing   Take it easy,
Signature   Stan

LANGUAGE
HANDBOOK

WORD ORIGINS

The words *grammar* and *glamour* are related. Back in the Middle Ages, when few people could read and write, learning was often associated with magic. A *glamorous* person was one who possessed the secrets of magic because he or she knew *grammar*—the art of reading and writing.

USING THE LANGUAGE HANDBOOK

Think of this handbook as your owner's manual for the English language. The handbook gives you basic information about how our language works. It explains the most common terms for describing the parts and functions of the language. It also helps you to avoid common errors so that you can improve your writing and speaking.

SECTION 1: PARTS OF SPEECH PREVIEW

All words in our language are classified into eight different groups called the *parts of speech*.

Each part of speech plays a different role in a sentence. Before you learn what each role is, learn to recognize what part of speech a word is. The examples below show how one part of speech differs from another.

Noun   A noun is a word that names a person, a place, a thing, or an idea.

> Examples: student   Cleveland   soccer   cooperation
> The *students* went to *Cleveland* to play a *game* of *soccer*.

Pronoun   A pronoun is a word used in place of a noun or another pronoun.

> Examples: he   it   ourselves   everybody   whom   that   I
> The coach made sure *everybody* was on the bus before *he* got on.

Verb   A verb is a word that expresses an action or a state of being. The forms of verbs usually change to show the time of the action.

> Examples: borrow   snicker   invent   do   is   look
> When Jeff *lost* Jim's shinguards, Jim *was* angry.

Adjective   An adjective is a word that modifies, or defines by describing, a noun or a pronoun. It tells *which one, how many, what kind,* or *how much.* Often, it comes before the noun it modifies.

> Examples: silly   monstrous   purple   strong   shiny   few
> Bill used *two elastic* bandages to wrap his *sore* shin.

Adverb An adverb is a word that modifies, or defines by describing, a verb, an adjective, or another adverb. It tells *where, when, how,* or *to what extent.*

>Examples: never quite frequently soon happily here
>*Often* the losing team *valiantly* tries to make a comeback.

Preposition A preposition is a word that shows how the noun or pronoun that follows it is related to some other word in the sentence. Many prepositions show direction, position, or relation in time.

>Examples: at during between from after of to
>The ball rolled *toward* the goal *in* the last minute *of* the game.

Conjunction A conjunction is a word that connects words or groups of words.

>Examples: and or but yet because although
>Both Marius *and* I tried to prevent the goal, *but* we were too slow.

Interjection An interjection is a word or group of words that shows strong or sudden emotion. An interjection can stand by itself.

>Examples: gee oh oops look out wow
>*Oh!* The loss was so disappointing!

DID YOU KNOW?
. . . .
The parts of speech were described over two thousand years ago by language experts in ancient India.

Parts of Speech at a Glance

Every word in a sentence is a particular part of speech. Notice the following illustration.

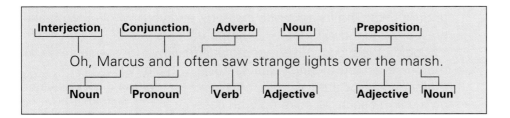

You will be learning more about each of the parts of speech in later sections of this handbook. For now, see how many you can recognize in the following exercises.

Exercise 1   Concept Check

Identifying Parts of Speech   Write the part of speech of each italicized word.

1. The Underground Railroad *was* not a *real* railroad; it had no trains, no engines, and no steel tracks.
2. It was a network of escape routes used by slaves trying *courageously* to reach freedom in the free states and in *Canada.*
3. The people who *helped* the *runaway* slaves were called conductors.
4. The conductors *secretly* led the slaves from one stopping place, *or* station, to another along the route.
5. Benjamin Baker was a Quaker *from* New York *who* acted as a conductor.
6. *Oh!* He risked everything—his money, his freedom, and his life—to help *complete* strangers make their way to freedom.
7. A former slave, Harriet Tubman, *rightly* gained fame for her *work* as a conductor on the Underground Railroad.
8. Because of her *success* in leading slaves to the "Promised Land" of freedom, she *became* known as the "Moses" of her people.
9. *Nobody* knows how many slaves used the Underground Railroad *then.*
10. A *low* estimate is forty thousand people, *and* a high estimate is one hundred thousand.

Exercise 2   Application in Literature

Parts of Speech   Write the part of speech of each italicized word.

LITERARY MODEL
· · · · · · · · · · · · · ·
from "Lose Now, Pay Later" by Carol Farley

▶

(1) Swoodies aren't cold like ice cream or warm like cooked *pudding,* (2) *but* they're a blending of both in temperature and texture.   (3) The flavor melts *instantly,* and your whole mouth and brain are flooded with tastes and impressions.   (4) Like that *first* swoodie I tried, coconut-almond-marshmallow; (5) suddenly, as my mouth separated the individual tastes, my brain burst into memories associated *with* each flavor.   (6) I felt as if I were lying on a *warm* beach, all covered with coconut suntan oil (7)—then I heard myself giggling and singing as a group of *us* roasted marshmallows around a campfire (8)—then I relived the long-ago moments of biting *into* the special Christmas cookies my grandmother made with almonds when I was little.

(9) *"Wow!"* Trinja looked at me, and I see that she had just experienced the same kind of reactions.   (10) We scarfed up the rest of that *swoodie* in just a few more bites, and we moved on to another flavor.

Exercise 3   Drafting Skill

Adding Words   On your paper, write words to complete the following paragraphs. Choose the most exciting words you can think of, but be sure to use the parts of speech indicated on the blanks.

When Mika heard the soldiers' (1) __(noun)__ , she felt
(2) __(adjective)__ at first. But (3) __(adverb)__ her courage
(4) __(verb)__ . She grasped her (5) __(noun)__ firmly and hid
(6) __(preposition)__ the kitchen cupboard. Suddenly, the shouting
stopped, (7) __(conjunction)__   the voices seemed farther away.

(8) " __(interjection)__ !" she thought. "Now (9) __(pronoun)__
can (10) __(verb)__ !"

SECTION 2: UNDERSTANDING SENTENCES

A *sentence* is a group of words that expresses a complete thought. A sentence must have a *subject* and *predicate*.

Subjects and Predicates

The **subject** tells whom or what a sentence is about, and the **predicate** tells what the subject does or is. The complete subject and the complete predicate together contain all the words in the sentence.

Complete Subject	Complete Predicate
Gloria Cooper	edited a book.
The book	listed funny mistakes from headlines.
The mistakes	had appeared in newspapers around the country.

Simple Subjects and Verbs

In every sentence there are a few words that are more important than the rest. These key words are the simple subject and the simple predicate, or verb. The **simple subject** is the key word in the complete subject. The **simple predicate,** or **verb,** is the key word in the complete predicate. Consider this sentence:

A dark mysterious *shadow*   suddenly *appeared* in the doorway.

Shadow is the key word in the complete subject. It names the thing that appeared. The simple subject is a noun or pronoun, not a modifier. *Appeared* is the key word in the complete predicate; it tells what the shadow did. *Appeared* is the verb.

Subjects and Verbs at a Glance

The **complete subject** includes all the words that identify the person, place, thing, or idea the sentence is about.	The **complete predicate** includes all the words that tell or ask something about the subject.

Bright yellow **daffodils** **cheer** the patients in the ward.

The **simple subject** tells whom or what the sentence is about. It may be one or several words, but it does not include modifiers.	The **simple predicate,** or **verb,** tells what the subject does or is. It may be one word or several, but it does not include modifiers.

Exercise 1   Concept Check

Subjects and Predicates   Copy the sentences below. Draw a line to separate the complete subject from the complete predicate. Circle the simple subject, and draw two lines under the verb.

1. Apollo drove an incredible chariot.
2. The magnificent chariot sparkled in the sunlight.
3. Phaëthon begged for his own ride.
4. His father feared the outcome.
5. The new driver felt confident at first.
6. He grabbed the reins.
7. The mighty horses snorted fire.
8. The inexperienced Phaëthon suddenly zoomed through the sky.
9. The foolish boy fell out of the chariot.
10. The story ended in tragedy.

Finding the Verb

A verb can express an action, state that something exists, or link the subject to another word that describes the subject.

To understand a sentence, you must find the verb. Here are some guidelines that tell you what verbs do.

An **action verb** says what the subject of the sentence does. The action may or may not be something you can see.

> Armand *jumped* six feet.
> Robin *said* no.
> Jill *loves* classical music.

A **linking verb** links the subject of the sentence with a word in the predicate that renames or modifies the subject. It does not refer to an action.

> A pizza *is* a cheese pie. (links *pizza* with *pie*)
> The pizza *is* huge. (links *pizza* with *huge*)

The most common linking verbs are *am, are, were, being, is, was, be,* and *been.* Other familiar linking verbs include *look, appear, seem, become, remain, feel, sound, taste, grow,* and *smell.* Many linking verbs can also be used as action verbs.

> That face *looked* mean. (linking verb)
> Those eyes *looked* right through me. (action verb)

A **helping verb** helps the main verb express meaning. Some forms of verbs such as *is, has,* and *do* can be used to help other verbs. When they are used in this way, they are called **helping verbs.** The verb they help is called the **main verb.** Together, the helping verb and the main verb make up a **verb phrase.**

I *do love* pizza.   *Have* you *seen* Marie?

Helping Verbs and Main Verbs at a Glance

The parts of a verb phrase often appear next to one another. However, sometimes the parts of the verb phrase are separated by words that are not part of the verb phrase.

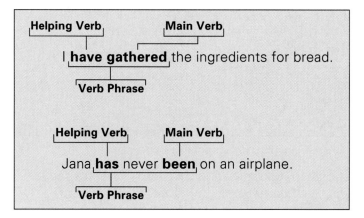

> **QUICK TIP**   To find the verb of a sentence, use these methods:
>
> 1. Look for a word that tells the main action, expresses a state of being, or links the subject with a description.
> 2. Look for helping verbs. Examples are *is, am, are, was, were, be, been, have, has, had, do, does, did, shall, will, should, would,* and *could.*
> 3. Look for all the verbs that make up the verb phrase.

Exercise 2   Concept Check

Identifying Verbs   Write the verb or verb phrase in each of the following sentences. Tell whether the verb or verb phrase shows action or is a linking verb. Be sure to include any helping verbs.

1. In March of 1987, a tugboat from New York became famous.
2. It was towing a barge of garbage.

3. A barge is a large flat-bottomed boat.

4. It can hold a great deal of cargo.

5. This barge carried 3,186 tons of New York's garbage.

6. According to the original plan, North Carolina would buy the rotten garbage for its methane gas.

7. However, officials in North Carolina changed their minds.

8. They would no longer accept New York's garbage.

9. The smelly barge traveled to different places for two months.

10. Finally it returned, still full, to New York City.

Compound Sentence Parts

A *compound subject* or a *compound verb* has two or more parts.

This sentence has a compound subject:

> *Clams* and *shrimp* are shellfish.

This sentence has a compound verb:

> The sailboat *pitches* and *rolls* in the bay.

QUICK TIP   You can make your writing more concise and less repetitive and choppy by using compound subjects and verbs, as follows:

Choppy	The bridge heaved. The bridge swayed.
Improved	The bridge heaved and swayed.

Exercise 3   Concept Check

Compound Subjects and Verbs   Write the compound subject or compound verb in each of the following sentences. Tell whether it is a compound subject or a compound verb.

1. Eng and Chang were the original Siamese twins.

2. The twins were joined at birth and were never separated.

3. They looked alike but had different personalities.

4. The connective ligament between their chests stretched and grew with them.

5. Tragically, their father and five of their brothers and sisters died of the deadly disease cholera.

Exercise 4   Revision Skill

Combining Sentences   Combine the sentences in each item into a single sentence with either a compound subject or compound verb. You may add, change, or delete words as necessary.

Example   The twins had to find work. Their mother had to find work too.

Answer   The twins and their mother had to find work.

1. Robert Hunter discovered the twins in Siam. He made them famous.
2. The twins could run. The twins could dive. They could swim.
3. Hunter managed the twins. Hunter exhibited them in the United States.
4. Audiences were fascinated by the twins. Doctors were also fascinated by them.
5. The twins performed tricks for the audience. They answered questions for the audience.
6. Their American shows were sold out. Their European exhibitions were sold out.
7. They were unhappy with their new manager. They fired him. They became their own managers.
8. Later, Chang became a successful farmer. Eng also became a successful farmer.
9. Both men fell in love with sisters. They married the sisters.
10. The Siamese twins achieved a fairly normal life. Their twenty-one children had a normal life too.

Kinds of Sentences

One way to make your writing and speech interesting is to use different kinds of sentences. You can use all of these four types of sentences.

A *declarative sentence* makes a statement.

The book *Stolen Continents* tells about the European invasion of the Americas.

An *interrogative sentence* asks a question.

How many people lived in America before the Europeans came?

An *imperative sentence* makes a request or commands someone to do something.

Tell me what happened to all those people.

An *exclamatory sentence* expresses strong feeling.

Oh, how terribly the people suffered!

An **end mark** is the punctuation at the end of a sentence. The end mark you use depends on what kind of sentence you write. Use a period (**.**) after a declarative sentence, a question mark (**?**) after an interrogative sentence, a period (**.**) after an imperative sentence, and an exclamation point (**!**) after an exclamatory sentence.

Exercise 5   Concept Check

Kinds of Sentences   On your paper, write *Declarative, Interrogative, Imperative,* or *Exclamatory* to show what kind each sentence is. Then write the correct punctuation mark.

1. Washington, D.C., is a very exciting city to visit
2. Can you imagine the sense of history a visit will give you
3. Oh, what a weird feeling you get at Ford's Theatre, where Lincoln was shot
4. Did you know you can watch money being printed in Washington
5. Be sure to see the Federal Bureau of Investigation
6. What an impressive sight the Washington Monument is
7. The Vietnam Veterans Memorial is the most-visited monument
8. The wall evokes more emotion than other monuments do
9. What would you say if you met a politician in the Capitol
10. When you visit Washington, just dress casually

Exercise 6   Revision Skill

Revising Sentences   Rewrite each sentence from Exercise 5 as a different kind of sentence. Tell what kind of sentence the new sentence is. Add or delete words as necessary.

Sentence Fragments

A *sentence fragment* is a group of words that does not express a complete idea.

A fragment leaves out important information such as the subject or the verb.

Fragment   Colonies on the moon. (There is no verb.)

Sentence   Colonies on the moon are being planned.

Fragment   Trapped several miles beneath the earth's surface.
                 (There is no subject.)

Sentence   The miners were trapped several miles beneath the
                 earth's surface.

Exercise 7   Concept Check

Identifying Fragments   Write *Sentence* or *Fragment* on your paper for
each of the following. Then change all the fragments to complete
sentences.

1. Mountain lions are beautiful wild animals.
2. Most of them live in rugged high country.
3. Also called cougars, panthers, or pumas.
4. Unlike lions and tigers, cannot roar.
5. In some areas, mountain lions are nearly extinct.
6. Wildlife sanctuaries important.
7. Some states do not allow hunters to kill the animals.
8. Can kill animals eight times their size.
9. Fight each other to the death.
10. Mountain lions usually will not attack humans.

Exercise 8   Proofreading Skill

Correcting Fragments   Rewrite the following paragraph and turn any
fragments into complete sentences. Add correct punctuation.

(1) There are thirty-seven different species of dolphins
(2) Some are among the most intelligent animals in the world
(3) Dolphins our friends (4) Like us, mammals, not fish
(5) Seem to develop ties with humans (6) Conservationists are
working to protect the dolphins (7) Being killed by people fishing
for tuna (8) Get caught in the huge nets and drown (9) Fishing
fleets used to kill 250,000 dolphins every year (10) New laws have
been passed to protect the dolphins

Run-on Sentences

**A *run-on sentence* occurs when two or more sentences are
written as one.**

Sometimes, when people are in a hurry, they incorrectly write two
sentences as one. The result is a **run-on sentence.** The end mark may

accidentally be left off the end of the first sentence. Sometimes a comma is incorrectly used to separate the sentences. This is known as a **comma splice.**

Run-on	A deer stood by the roadside it was blinded by our headlights.
Corrected	A deer stood by the roadside. It was blinded by our headlights.
Run-on **(comma splice)**	Maria is from Peru, she speaks fluent Spanish.
Corrected	Maria is from Peru. She speaks fluent Spanish.

To correct a run-on, use one of the methods described below.

Correcting Run-on Sentences

- Add an end mark to the first sentence and begin the second sentence with a capital letter.
- Add a semicolon after the first sentence.
- Add a comma after the first sentence and use a conjunction such as *and, or, nor, for, but, so,* or *yet* to begin the second.

Run-on	Maria is from Peru, she speaks fluent Spanish.
Corrected	Maria is from Peru; she speaks fluent Spanish.
Corrected	Maria is from Peru, and she speaks fluent Spanish.

◀ PUNCTUATION NOTE
· · · · · · · · · · · · · · ·
When you combine two sentences using a conjunction, always place a comma before the conjunction.

Exercise 9   Concept Check

Run-ons   Decide if each of the following is a correct sentence or a run-on. If it is correct, write *Correct* on your paper. If it is a run-on, rewrite it correctly.

1. I enjoy history; it is my favorite subject.
2. History teaches us about people in the past those ancient guys did some wonderful and terrible things.
3. I'm learning that people really haven't changed that much over the ages.
4. Incan history is fascinating, Incas were amazing people.
5. Have you learned about the Incas let me tell you about them.

Exercise 10　Revision Skill

Correcting Run-ons　Each sentence below is a run-on. Correct each sentence in two different ways.

Example　Manco Capac was the first Incan emperor, Atahualpa was the last.

Separate　Manco Capac was the first Incan emperor. Atahualpa was the last.

Combined　Manco Capac was the first Incan emperor, and Atahualpa was the last.

1. The Incas were great architects, they were masterful road builders.

2. The main Incan royal road began at Quito it ended at Cuzco.

3. The Incas had impressive roads, they had no horses or vehicles.

4. Atahualpa had golden ornaments in his hair, he wore an emerald necklace.

5. The Incas were brave soldiers they were destroyed by smallpox and civil war.

Exercise 11　Revision Skill

Sentence Review　Rewrite the following paragraph, correcting all sentence fragments and run-ons.

(1) The first computers were huge, took an entire room to hold them. (2) Today they are small many people have them at home. (3) Home computers useful, fun. (4) Some people use them for work, thousands of new businesses are started each year by home computer users. (5) Play games. (6) They can be used for shopping they can also be used for banking and paying bills. (7) Even talk to other people all over the country. (8) Computers are especially helpful with school work, they allow you to easily correct typing errors. (9) Entire encyclopedia on compact disc. (10) What other uses are there for a home computer you can probably name several.

SECTION 3: PREPOSITIONS, CONJUNCTIONS, AND INTERJECTIONS

Prepositions show relationships. Conjunctions link words together. Interjections express feelings.

Three Parts of Speech at a Glance

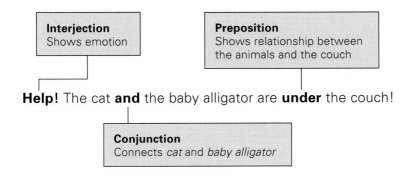

Interjection
Shows emotion

Preposition
Shows relationship between the animals and the couch

Help! The cat **and** the baby alligator are **under** the couch!

Conjunction
Connects *cat* and *baby alligator*

Prepositions and Prepositional Phrases

A *preposition* is a word that shows the relationship of its object to some other word in the sentence.

The word *preposition* can be divided into two parts: *pre,* meaning "before," and *position.* A preposition is a word that is *positioned before* its object to show how that object relates in time or space to some other word in the sentence. The **object of a preposition** is a noun or a pronoun. The examples below are **prepositional phrases:** the preposition plus its object.

> *on* the hook *(on* is a preposition; *hook* is its object)
>
> *during* the storm *(during* is a preposition; *storm* is its object)

The job of a preposition is to show how its object relates to another word in the sentence, usually a word that comes before the prepositional phrase.

> The coat *on* the hook belongs *to* me. *(Hook* is connected to *coat* by the preposition *on; me* is connected to *belongs* by the preposition *to.)*

◄ WRITING TIP
. . . .
When you write, try beginning some sentences with a prepositional phrase to add an interesting twist.

Many prepositions show relationships in **space.** (The sign is *above* the door.) Others show relationships in **time.** (We went to the movies *after* dinner.)

Words Often Used as Prepositions

about	below	from	past
above	beneath	in	through
across	beside	inside	to
after	between	into	toward
against	beyond	near	under
along	but (except)	of	underneath
among	by	off	until
around	down	on	up
as	during	out	with
before	except	outside	within
behind	for	over	without

WRITING TIP

Make sure when you write that your prepositional phrases are close to the words they tell about.
Unclear: Ali stared at the huge spider with a terrified look.
Clear: With a terrified look, Ali stared at the huge spider.

QUICK TIP   Remember that a preposition must have an object. In a sentence, if one of the words in the list is used without an object, it is an adverb. Prepositions always have objects; adverbs never do.

Preposition   He fell *down* the steps.
Adverb   He fell *down.*

Exercise 1   Concept Check

Prepositional Phrases   Write the prepositional phrases that appear in the following sentences. Draw one line under each preposition. Draw two lines under its object. There may be more than one phrase in a sentence.

Example   Mother Teresa saved many lives in Calcutta.
Answer   in Calcutta

1. Mother Teresa won the Nobel Peace Prize for her work with homeless people.
2. Born in Yugoslavia, Mother Teresa joined a religious order, which sent her to Calcutta.

3. With three million inhabitants, Calcutta has one of the largest populations in the world.

4. Most Calcuttans live below an average American's standard of living.

5. Many poor Calcuttans without homes live from day to day.

6. Through Mother Teresa's efforts, however, schools and hospitals have been established for the needy.

7. She has helped lepers beyond hope and poor people near death.

8. Orphanages and youth centers were created under her supervision.

9. Until her arrival, it seemed that no one cared about these people.

10. Mother Teresa focused international attention on the poor within big cities around the world.

Exercise 2   Drafting Skill

Using Prepositional Phrases   Complete the following story by writing prepositional phrases to fit the blanks.

(1) Last night I dreamed about traveling __?__ . (2) My best friend, Kim, went __?__ . (3) __?__ , Kim and I saw many new things. (4) At first we just strolled __?__ , looking __?__ . (5) Then we rode a boat __?__ . (6) Later we hiked __?__ . (7) We enjoyed talking __?__ . (8) Kim stayed __?__ the whole time. (9) We went __?__ and did not return __?__ . (10) When I woke up, I saw my suitcase __?__ .

IN THE END

Ending sentences with prepositions is a practice that some people just won't put up with. Other people feel that prepositions at the ends of sentences are just fine. Check with your teacher to see what his or her view is.

Conjunctions and Interjections

A *conjunction* is a word that connects words or groups of words.

An *interjection* is a word or short group of words used to express feelings such as anger, fear, joy, or surprise.

Conjunctions can be used to combine sentences or sentence parts.

Two Sentences	Gossip is sometimes fun. Gossip is often hurtful to people.
Combined Sentence	Gossip is sometimes fun, *but* it is often hurtful to people.
Combined Sentence Parts	Gossip can be both fun *and* hurtful at the same time.

Common conjunctions include *and, or, nor, for, but, so,* and *yet.*

An interjection expresses feeling. If an interjection expresses strong emotion, it is punctuated with an exclamation point. An interjection that expresses only mild emotion is punctuated by a comma.

> *Help!* I'm falling! (strong emotion)
>
> *Oh,* I guess I'll live. (mild emotion)

Common interjections include *oh, ah, alas, gee, gosh, oops, well, wow, help, so, whew, hooray, hey,* and *yeah.*

Exercise 3   Concept Check

Conjunctions and Interjections   Write the conjunctions and interjections in the following sentences. Tell whether each is a conjunction or an interjection.

1. Hey, isn't that a scarab beetle charm around your neck?
2. Yeah, such ornaments, made of stone or metal, were popular in ancient Egypt.
3. Egyptians had gold, but they had to import silver and iron.
4. Wow! Did you know that Egyptians pioneered in the fields of mathematics, medicine, astronomy, and architecture?
5. Gee, I never knew how much the Egyptians influenced our culture, yet they lived so long ago.

Exercise 4   Revision Skill

Adding Interest to Your Writing   Rewrite the following paragraph. Make it more lively by adding prepositional phrases, conjunctions, and interjections. Underline each addition you make and, in the margin of your paper, write what part of speech the addition is. You may combine sentences and add words if necessary.

> I enjoy mystery stories. I also enjoy stories about ancient cultures. One story that combines both is the story of Atlantis. No one knows exactly where Atlantis was. No one knows if it even existed. However, this ancient city is mentioned by the ancient Greek philosopher Plato. According to Plato, Atlantis was a powerful, wealthy city. It was on an island in the Mediterranean Sea. Its power did not last. Plato says that earthquakes caused Atlantis to disappear into the sea. Modern science has confirmed that the ancient island of Thera was destroyed by a volcano. That must have been some explosion! Could Thera be Atlantis? No one really knows. I find the mystery fascinating.

SECTION 4: USING NOUNS

A *noun* is a word that names a person, a place, a thing, or an idea.

Persons	Eleanor Roosevelt, baby, host, Aladdin, vice-president
Places	Houston, park, arcade, rain forest
Things	concert, skateboard, television, football
Ideas	cooperation, friendship, wonder, honor

QUICK TIP   To find out whether a word is a noun, simply see if it makes sense in one of these blanks:

_____ is   _____ are

Nouns	*Houston* is	*friends* are
Not Nouns	*to* is	*see* are

Types of Nouns

If a noun names a particular person, place, thing, or idea, it is a *proper noun*.

Michael Jordan	EPCOT Center	Nile
Florida	Felicia	Hinduism

If a noun names a kind of person, place, thing, or idea, it is a *common noun*.

player	auditorium	river
state	woman	religion

A noun made up of more than one word is called a *compound noun*.

You may have noticed that some nouns—like *vice-president, rain forest, football,* and *Michael Jordan*—are made up of more than one word.

spacewalk	great-grandfather	time capsule
basketball	Zuni Pueblo	Lake Ontario

QUICK TIP   A compound noun might be spelled as one word, like *spacewalk;* with a hyphen, like *great-grandfather;* or as two words, like *Zuni Pueblo.*

◀ **PLACE NAMES**

Many place names in the Americas come from Native American languages. *Mexico* comes from the name of Mexítli, an Aztec war god. *Missouri* comes from words meaning "people of the big canoes"; *Mississippi,* from words meaning "big river."

Exercise 1   Application in Literature

Types of Nouns   Write the nouns in the following passage. Label the three proper nouns and the two compound nouns.

LITERARY MODEL
. . . .
from "Seventh Grade"
by Gary Soto

▶

(1) In homeroom, roll was taken, emergency cards were passed out, and they were given a bulletin to take home to their parents. (2) The principal, Mr. Belton, spoke over the crackling loudspeaker, welcoming the students to a new year, new experiences, and new friendships. (3) The students squirmed in their chairs and ignored him. (4) Victor sat calmly, thinking of Teresa, who sat two rows away, reading a paperback novel. (5) This would be his lucky year.

Exercise 2   Concept Check

Proper Nouns   On your paper write a proper noun that names an example of the person or thing named by each common noun.

Example	mountain	**Answer**	Mount Everest

1. actor

2. city

3. planet

4. nation

5. game

6. singer

7. university

8. car

9. teacher

10. company

Using Nouns

Nouns are used as *subjects, direct objects, indirect objects, predicate nouns,* and *objects of prepositions*.

Think of the **subject** as naming the actor in a sentence—whom or what the sentence is about. The **direct object** names the thing or person who *receives* the action.

Bill threw the ball.

Bill names the actor, so it is the subject. To determine the direct object, ask yourself *what* he threw. The direct object is *ball*.

An **indirect object** names a person or thing to whom something is done or given.

Bill threw Jack the ball.

You already know what Bill threw (direct object)—the ball. To whom did he throw it? The indirect object is *Jack*. To have an indirect object, a sentence must have a direct object. However, a sentence can have a direct object without an indirect object.

When the noun after the verb refers to the subject, it is called a **predicate noun.**

> Bill is our best pitcher.

Since *pitcher* renames the subject *Bill, pitcher* is a predicate noun. It is a noun in the predicate that names the same person, place, thing, or idea as the subject.

You remember that a preposition takes an object. A noun can function as the **object of a preposition.**

> Bill is the best pitcher on our team.

Team is the object of the preposition *on.*

Uses of Nouns at a Glance

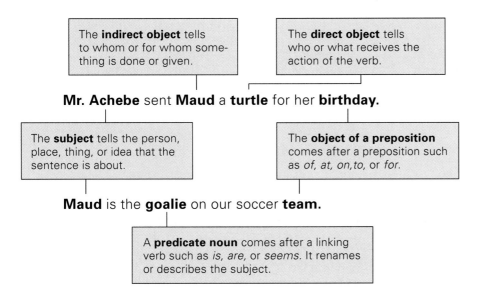

The **indirect object** tells to whom or for whom something is done or given.

The **direct object** tells who or what receives the action of the verb.

Mr. Achebe sent **Maud** a **turtle** for her **birthday.**

The **subject** tells the person, place, thing, or idea that the sentence is about.

The **object of a preposition** comes after a preposition such as *of, at, on, to,* or *for.*

Maud is the **goalie** on our soccer **team.**

A **predicate noun** comes after a linking verb such as *is, are,* or *seems.* It renames or describes the subject.

Exercise 3   Concept Check

Uses of Nouns   Decide what job each italicized noun is doing in the sentence. Write *Subject, Direct Object, Indirect Object, Object of a Preposition,* or *Predicate Noun.*

1. For my *birthday,* Dad gave me plane *tickets.*

2. He also gave my *sister tickets.*

3. My *dad* was a *winner* on a television quiz show.

4. Dad won the *prize* in a lucky *spin* of the wheel.

5. I sent *Jane* the good *news.*

Exercise 4   Drafting Skill

Nouns in Sentences   Think of an interesting noun that can be used to complete each sentence. Write the noun on a sheet of paper. Then identify the noun as *Subject, Direct Object, Indirect Object, Object of a Preposition*, or *Predicate Noun*.

Example   ___?___ is a large city.

Answer   San Juan, Subject

1. Puerto Rico is a beautiful ___?___ .
2. We will stay there for a ___?___ .
3. I will buy my ___?___ a gift in Old San Juan.
4. Tourism is an important ___?___ here.
5. You can reach Puerto Rico by ___?___ .
6. One afternoon we visited a ___?___ .
7. The ___?___ was covered with beautiful white sand.
8. We ate fresh ___?___ almost every day.
9. The ___?___ include scuba diving, swimming, and fishing.
10. I sent my ___?___ a postcard.

Using Plural Forms of Nouns

A noun is *singular* if it names one person, place, thing, or idea. It is *plural* if it names more than one person, place, thing, or idea.

1. To form the plurals of most nouns, add *-s*.

| bicycle | hairstyle | pet | kitchen |
| *bicycles* | *hairstyles* | *pets* | *kitchens* |

2. When a singular noun ends in *s, sh, ch, x,* or *z*, add *-es*.

| gas | bush | couch | box |
| *gases* | *bushes* | *couches* | *boxes* |

3. For most singular nouns that end in *o*, add *-s*. For a few nouns that end in *o* preceded by a consonant, add *-es*.

| stereo | radio | potato | hero |
| *stereos* | *radios* | *potatoes* | *heroes* |

CONFUSED?
· · · · · · · · · ·
How did we get so many rules? Over time, the English language has borrowed words and rules from many other languages. That's why our spellings and plurals are so mixed up.

4. **If a singular noun ends in *y* with a consonant before it, change the *y* to *i* and add *-es.* If the noun ends in *y* with a vowel before it, add *-s* to form the plural.**

comedy	baby	joy	donkey
comedies	*babies*	*joys*	*donkeys*

5. **For some nouns ending in *f,* add *-s.* For other nouns ending in *f* or *fe,* change the *f* to *v* and add *-es* or *-s.* Since there is no rule, you must memorize such words.**

chief	roof	life	thief
chiefs	*roofs*	*lives*	*thieves*

6. **Some nouns are spelled the same in the singular and in the plural.**

sheep	quail	deer	tuna

7. **The plurals of some nouns are formed in ways that are unusual.**

ox	woman	child	mouse
oxen	*women*	*children*	*mice*

8. **For a compound noun written as one word, form the plural by changing the last word in the compound to its plural form.**

grandfather	butterfly	stepchild	snowstorm
grandfathers	*butterflies*	*stepchildren*	*snowstorms*

◀ **ANIMAL NAMES**
A number of nouns that name animals can be the same in the singular and the plural. Here are just a few:

bass	elk
carp	deer
fish	grouse
moose	pike
quail	salmon
sheep	shrimp
trout	tuna

Exercise 5 Concept Check

Plural Nouns Write the correct plural form of each noun.

1. country
2. fish
3. studio
4. cave
5. box
6. child
7. belief
8. stitch
9. bridge
10. shelf
11. woman
12. calf
13. hobby
14. shrimp
15. turkey
16. porch
17. building
18. lady
19. fox
20. photo

◀ **HOW DO YOU KNOW?**
Most dictionaries show the plurals of nouns when the plurals are formed in unusual ways. If you are unsure how to spell the plural of a noun, look the noun up in a dictionary.

Exercise 6   Revision Skill

Plural Nouns   Rewrite the following sentences. Change the italicized singular nouns to their correct plural forms.

1. My parents and I love *rodeo*.
2. Last year two *family* went to a rodeo in Arizona.
3. Luckily, the *highway* between here and there were good.
4. At one stop we had a chance to pet some tame *deer*.
5. We brought along some *sandwich* to eat.
6. Some contestants roped *calf*.
7. My *hero* were the bull riders.
8. People stamped their *foot* and cheered.
9. Of course, everyone loves to see the *clown*.
10. Rodeo clowns often save the *life* of contestants.

Using Possessive Forms of Nouns

A *possessive noun* **is one that shows ownership or belonging.**

▶ **1. If a noun is singular, add 's to form the possessive.**

a flower's petals   Juanita's luck

2. If a noun is plural and already ends in s, add an apostrophe.

the wolves' territory   six years' time

3. If a noun is plural and does not end in s, add 's.

the geese's feathers   the deer's tracks

EXCEPTIONS

A few proper nouns ending in *s* may take the apostrophe only: Jesus', Moses', and many names from Greek mythology that end in *s*, such as Zeus', Narcissus', and so on.

WRITING TIP

Sometimes a possessive noun can be replaced with a prepositional phrase. You can say *the truck's bumper* or *the bumper of the truck, the river's mouth* or *the mouth of the river.*

Exercise 7   Concept Check

Possessive Nouns   On a separate piece of paper, write the possessive forms of these nouns.

1. Steve	6. baby	11. children
2. twins	7. families	12. doctors
3. mouse	8. box	13. sheep
4. piano	9. thieves	14. class
5. fish	10. horses	15. men

Exercise 8   Revision Skills

Possessive Nouns   Rewrite the following sentences. Change the italicized nouns to their correct possessive forms.

1. I like Victoria *Chess* illustrations.

2. The *woman* travels took her all over the world.

3. She observed the world with an *artist* eye.

4. Her *pens* points are made of metal.

5. Many *illustrators* backgrounds include art school.

6. You should see *viewers* reactions to her lizard drawings!

7. Her *cats* names are Mrs. Bloom, Zazou, and Pearl.

8. *Pearl* specialty is hunting.

9. According to Chess, *children* laughter inspires her.

10. Two books illustrated by her are on our *library* shelves.

Exercise 9   Revision Skill

Noun Usage Review   Each sentence below has one error in the form of a plural or possessive noun. Find the error and write the word correctly on your paper.

1. The earthes closest neighbor is the moon.

2. Today we know that our planets orbit takes it around the sun.

3. Early people, though, had different believes.

4. Six planets orbits are larger than the earth's orbit.

5. Today, big telescopes can study valley's on the moon.

6. Telescopes show that Marses surface has dark areas, bright areas, and polar caps.

7. Scientists have spotted Mars's giant canal's.

8. During World War II, noise's were interfering with radio communication.

9. At first scientists thought the noises came from other radioes.

10. They thought their enemy's were making the sounds.

11. Imagine those scientists surprise!

12. Studys show that the noises were made by sunspots.

13. They look like dark patches on the sun's surface.

14. A sunspots surface is cooler than the rest of the surface of the sun.

15. Men's and womens's knowledge about the planets grows daily.

SECTION 5: USING PRONOUNS

A *pronoun* is a word that is used in place of a noun or another pronoun.

Noun	Take the *clothes* to the shelter for the homeless.
Pronoun	Take *them* to the shelter for the homeless.
Noun	*Belia* is working there today.
Pronoun	*She* is working there today.

Personal Pronouns

A *personal pronoun* refers to a particular person, place, object, or idea.

Like the nouns they replace, pronouns have different jobs in a sentence. Personal pronouns have three forms: **subject, object,** and **possessive.** The form of a personal pronoun depends on its job in a sentence. For example, *I* is used as a subject, *me* as an object, and *my* or *mine* as a possessive.

Forms of Personal Pronouns

	Subject	Object	Possessive
Singular	I	me	my, mine
	you	you	your, yours
	she, he, it	her, him, it	her, hers, his, its
Plural	we	us	our, ours
	you	you	your, yours
	they	them	their, theirs

Exercise 1   Application in Literature

Identifying Pronoun Forms   Write all the personal pronouns in the following passage. Write *S* above the subject pronouns, *O* above the object pronouns, and *P* above the possessive pronouns.

LITERARY MODEL
. . . .
from "Hearts and Hands" by O. Henry

▶

(1) "Don't you worry about them, miss," said the other man. (2) "All marshals handcuff themselves to their prisoners to keep them from getting away. (3) Mr. Easton knows his business." (4) "Will we see you again soon in Washington?" asked the girl. (5) "Not soon, I think," said Easton. (6) "My butterfly days are over, I fear."

Personal Pronouns at a Glance

She wrote the poem.

> A subject pronoun can be used as the **subject** of a sentence.

The poet was **she.**

> A subject pronoun can be used as a **predicate pronoun** after a linking verb.

We gave **him** the idea.

> An object pronoun can be used as an **indirect object.**

The idea came from **us.**

> An object pronoun can be used as the **object of a preposition.**

My friend welcomed **me.**

> Possessive pronouns are used to show ownership or possession.

> An object pronoun can be used as a **direct object.**

Using the Subject Form

The subject form of a pronoun (*I, you, he, she, it, we,* and *they*) is used as the subject of a sentence or as a predicate pronoun. A **predicate pronoun,** like a predicate noun, is one that follows a linking verb and renames or identifies the subject of a sentence.

Subject	**Predicate Pronoun**
She won first prize.	The winner was *she.*
Tina and *I* were cheerleaders.	The cheerleaders were Tina and *I.*

> **QUICK TIP**   A sentence with a predicate pronoun will still make sense if you reverse the order of the subject and pronoun:
> The winner was *she. She* was the winner.

Using the Object Form

The object form of a pronoun (*me, you, him, her, it, us,* and *them*) is needed if the pronoun is used as a direct object, an indirect object, or an object of a preposition.

Direct Object	The coach called *her.*
Indirect Object	The boy gave *her* the money.
Object of Preposition	The cook gave samples to *them.*

Exercise 2   Concept Check

Using Subject and Object Pronouns   Write the correct pronoun.

1. (I, Me) was surprised to learn that *Frankenstein* was written in 1816 by Mary Shelley.
2. It was (she, her) who married the famous poet, Percy Bysshe Shelley.
3. She would probably be surprised to learn that her story is still popular with (we, us).
4. However, there is one point that (we, us) often confuse.
5. Most people call the monster "Frankenstein," but in the book no name is given to (he, him).
6. Frankenstein is the name of the mad scientist who created (he, him).
7. In most movies the monster is evil; people are terrified of (he, him).
8. In the novel the monster is kind toward others until (they, them) become hostile toward him.
9. Because of their hostility, (he, him) becomes a true monster.
10. Actually, (I, me) found the story to be sad, not scary.

Exercise 3   Proofreading Skill

Correcting Pronoun Forms   Rewrite the following paragraph, correcting all pronoun errors.

    (1) Mary Godwin was born in London in 1797. (2) When she was sixteen, the poet Percy Bysshe Shelley fell in love with she. (3) The two of they ran away to Italy and married in 1816. (4) Life was adventurous for the Shelleys, but many did not approve of they and their wild lifestyle. (5) When Percy drowned in 1822, Mary was devastated. (6) Her husband had left she no money, and she had young children to raise. (7) It was her who wrote *Frankenstein*. (8) However, it did not earn much for she while she was alive.

Using the Possessive Form

    Possessive pronouns show ownership or belonging. Unlike possessive nouns (such as *student's*), possessive pronouns do not contain an apostrophe.

    Do not confuse possessive pronouns with contractions that sound similar. If the word you are writing takes the place of two words, it is a contraction and needs an apostrophe.

| **Possessive Pronouns** | its | your | their |
| **Contractions** | it's (it is) | you're (you are) | they're (they are) |

Exercise 4   Revision Skill

Pronouns and Contractions   Rewrite each sentence, correcting errors in the use of pronouns and contractions. If a sentence is already correct, write *Correct*.

1. Your always going to get disagreements about which boxing match was the greatest fight of the century.

2. Some people would cast they're vote for the fight between Joe Louis and Max Schmeling in 1938.

3. The fight gained international attention because of it's participants.

4. The Germans, under the rule of Adolf Hitler, felt confident that their boxer, Schmeling, would win.

5. Louis had already lost one match to Schmeling, but Louis's fans never lost they're belief in his ability.

6. Its hard for some people to forget that night in New York City.

7. When Louis entered the ring, one fan yelled, "You're victory will be for the U.S.A., Joe!"

8. Another fan screamed, "It's going to be a sad trip back to Germany for Schmeling!"

9. The announcer predicted, "Your going to remember this great fight!"

10. The crowd voiced it's approval for Louis; in two minutes and four seconds, he knocked out Schmeling.

Pronouns in Compounds

Sometimes two pronouns, or a pronoun and a noun, are joined by *and, or,* or *nor* to form a compound. Don't let a compound confuse you. Remember that the way a pronoun is used always determines its form. A pronoun in a compound subject must be in the subject form. A pronoun in a compound object must be in the object form.

Compound Subject
   Toshiro and *I* disagreed about the meaning of the poem.

Compound Predicate Pronoun
   The co-captains of the debate team are *she* and *I*.

Compound Direct Object
   The school sent *Yolanda* and *me* to the state finals.

Compound Indirect Object
   The teacher gave *Raheem* and *me* two tickets.

Compound Object of a Preposition
   This is a special evening for *you* and *me*.

> **QUICK TIP**   To decide which pronoun to use in a compound, try each pronoun separately with the verb. *This is a special evening for I* sounds wrong. *This is a special evening for me* is correct.

Exercise 5   Revision Skill

Compound Pronouns   Read each sentence. If the italicized pronoun is correct, write *Correct*. If the pronoun is incorrect, rewrite it correctly.

1. Pam, Ravi, and *me* worked together on a paper about Norse myths.
2. *Her* and Ravi suggested that we research Loki, the trickster.
3. The librarian and *us* searched the card catalog until we found information about Loki and other Norse gods.
4. Finding out about Loki's two wives surprised neither Pam nor *I.*
5. The librarian also told Ravi and *she* about the travels of Loki and Thor, the god of thunder.
6. When Thor's hammer was missing, *him* and Loki knew that the giant Thrym had taken it.
7. Two gods planned to recover the hammer; they were Thor and *him.*
8. Pam drew attention to Thor disguising himself as a bride; Ravi and *she* enjoyed that part.
9. Thrym thought that Thor was a goddess; he invited Loki and *"she"* into his home.
10. Thrym was tricked by Thor and *he;* the two gods left with the hammer.

Interrogative Pronouns: Who and Whom

> ***Interrogative pronouns* are used to ask a question.**

The interrogative pronouns are *who, whom, whose, which,* and *what.* Two of these pronouns, *who* and *whom,* are often confused. *Who* is a subject pronoun. It is used as a subject or as a predicate pronoun.

Subject	*Who* is coming to dinner?
Predicate Pronoun	The captain of the team is *who?*

Whom is an object pronoun. It is used as a direct object, an indirect object, or an object of a preposition.

Direct Object	*Whom* do you admire most?
Indirect Object	She gave *whom* the pen?
Object of a Preposition	To *whom* was the pen given?

QUICK TIP   To tell whether *who* or *whom* should be used, try answering the question with a statement that uses a personal pronoun.

Who is coming to dinner?	*She* is coming to dinner.
Whom do you admire most?	You admire *him* the most.
To whom was the pen given?	The pen was given to *her*.

If your answer contains a subject pronoun, use *who* in your question. If the answer contains an object pronoun, use *whom* in your question.

◀ WHO CARES ABOUT *WHOM?* . . . . . .

Many people seldom use *whom* in conversation. They break grammatical rules by saying *"Who do you like best?"* and *"Who should I call next?"* Most experts think that such talk is fine in conversation, but they advise that *whom* should be used in formal writing and speaking.

Exercise 6   Revision Skill

Who **and** ***Whom***   Write the correct pronouns.

1. In your opinion, (who, whom) is the better journalist, Connie Chung or Diane Sawyer?

2. (Who, Whom) do you prefer as an interviewer?

3. (Who, Whom) was featured on the cover of *Vogue,* which caused a stir among other journalists?

4. (Who, Whom) did Marlon Brando once embarrass during an interview?

5. After Richard Nixon resigned as president, (whom, who) did he allow to interview him?

Pronouns and Their Antecedents

Pronouns usually refer back to a noun or to another pronoun. The noun or pronoun that a pronoun stands for is the pronoun's **antecedent.**

◀ PRONOUNS WITHOUT ANTECEDENTS . . . .

Most pronouns need a clear antecedent. However, some do not, as in the following examples:
Who went to the game?
It looks like rain.
What was the question?

Have you read the story of *Gilgamesh? He* was a king of ancient Sumer. (The antecedent of *He* is *Gilgamesh.*)

The *story* of Gilgamesh has *its* roots in oral literature. (The antecedent of *its* is *story.*)

The antecedent may appear before the pronoun in the same sentence, or it may be in a preceding sentence, as in the first example above.

Exercise 7   Concept Check

Pronouns and Their Antecedents   Write the pronouns in the following sentences. Then write the antecedent of each pronoun.

>   **Example**   George Washington Carver was born in Missouri; his mother was a slave.
>
>   **Answer**   *his, George Washington Carver*

1. As a boy, Carver was fascinated by plants and rocks; he studied botany in college.
2. His research focused on agriculture. It led to many profitable new crops for farmers in the South.
3. Carver created hundreds of products from peanuts. They included soap, fertilizer, cosmetics, and fabric.
4. Carver joined Tuskegee Institute in Alabama after Booker T. Washington hired him.
5. Carver's success was legendary. It inspired countless people.

Indefinite Pronouns

An *indefinite pronoun* is one that does not refer to a particular person or thing.

The following chart lists singular and plural indefinite pronouns:

Singular Indefinite Pronouns

another	each	everything	nothing
anybody	either	neither	one
anyone	everybody	nobody	somebody
anything	everyone	no one	someone

Plural Indefinite Pronouns

both	few	many	several

An indefinite pronoun must agree in number with its antecedent.

The singular possessive pronouns *his, her,* and *its* are used with singular indefinite pronouns.

>   *Someone* lost *her* purse. (The antecedent of the possessive pronoun is *someone,* which is singular. Therefore, the singular form *her* is correct.)

His or her may be used when the person referred to could be either male or female, as in the following example:

> *Someone* must have forgotten *his or her* book.

The plural possessive *their* is used with plural indefinite pronouns.

> *Few* were willing to change *their* plans. (The antecedent of the possessive pronoun is *few. Few* is plural. Therefore, the plural form *their* is correct.)

> **QUICK TIP**   Don't be fooled by words that come between a possessive pronoun and its antecedent.
>
> *One* of them left *his or her* coat there. (The antecedent of *his or her* is the singular pronoun *one*, not the plural *them.)*
>
> *Many* in the audience voiced *their* displeasure. (The antecedent of *their* is the plural pronoun *Many*, not the singular noun *audience.)*

◄ NONSEXIST LANGUAGE
In the old days, the masculine pronouns *he, him,* and *his* were used to refer to all people, as in this sentence: *A firefighter needs to take good care of his equipment.* Nowadays, masculine pronouns are often replaced with phrases such as *he or she* and *his or her,* as in this sentence: *A firefighter needs to take good care of his or her equipment.*

Exercise 8   Revision Skill

Agreement with Indefinite Antecedents   Write the correct possessive pronouns.

1. Each of my aunts has extended (her, their) invitation for lodging when we visit Montreal next month.
2. Both will be pleased to open (her, their) homes to us.
3. Either should have a spare room in (her, their) house.
4. Anyone would want to spend (his or her, their) time seeing a Montreal Canadiens hockey game.
5. Many in the crowd at the Forum show (its, their) appreciation by cheering wildly.
6. We may also visit McGill University; somebody there may show us (his or her, their) room.
7. Each of the metro stations has good maps on (its, their) walls.
8. Those men probably work in the Underground City because neither is carrying (his, their) coat.
9. Several stores in Montreal have beautiful exhibits in (its, their) windows.
10. We will meet new people everywhere; perhaps a few will show us (his or her, their) hospitality.

Exercise 9 Revision Skill

Pronoun Usage Most of the following sentences contain an error in the use of a pronoun or a contraction, or in pronoun agreement. Rewrite the sentences that need correction. If a sentence has no error, write *Correct.*

1. Each of us must choose their topic by Wednesday.
2. This book was written by Isaac Asimov; its a good one.
3. Ms. Washington suggested it to Kai, Jenny, and I.
4. At the library, Kai and me learned about Asimov's work as a scientist, teacher, and writer.
5. When he was three, his family moved to the United States; at seven, he taught his sister to read.
6. Both must have studied his or her books constantly.
7. "Who did he write for?" I asked the librarian.
8. The librarian said, "Your going to be surprised at how many books he has written."
9. If I had to choose my favorite writer, I would have a hard time deciding between he and Anne McCaffrey.
10. The author of this book about comets was him.
11. His wife and him wrote a number of books together.
12. Many children's books were written by she and him.
13. He and Robert Silverberg also wrote a book together.
14. It's title is *Nightfall.*
15. They're work is still in print, along with dozens of other Asimov books.

SECTION 6: USING VERBS

A *verb* expresses action or a state of being.

> The new model airplane *flew* beautifully.
> These paintings *are* strange.
> I *was* in class.

Action verbs* are verbs that tell what a subject does.

> Sabrina *stamped* her foot.   Everyone *laughed*.

A *linking verb* connects the subject of the sentence to a word that renames or describes the subject.

> Jane *is* brilliant.   The water *felt* cold.
> Bill *was* the writer.   The Robs *became* parents.

All the forms of the verb *be* are linking verbs. These include *am, is, are, was, were, be, been,* and *being*. Other common linking verbs are *appear, become, feel, grow, look, seem, smell, sound,* and *taste*.

QUICK TIP   Some words can be either action verbs or linking verbs. To see whether a verb is a linking verb, try replacing it with a form of *be*. If the sentence still makes sense, the verb is a linking verb. If it does not, then the verb is an action verb.

> The trumpet player *sounded* terrible. (*The trumpet player is terrible* makes sense, so *sounded* is a linking verb here. *Terrible* modifies *trumpet player*.)

> The fire chief *sounded* the siren. (*The fire chief is the siren* does not make sense. *Sounded* is an action verb here.)

Exercise 1   Concept Check

Types of Verbs   Write the verbs in the following sentences. After each verb, write *A* for action or *L* for linking.

1. Antoine-Joseph Sax lived in Brussels, Belgium.
2. He worked with his father, a maker of instruments.
3. His father built wind and brass instruments, as well as pianos, harps, and guitars.
4. Antoine-Joseph Sax was a talented inventor.
5. One of his best-known inventions is the saxophone.
6. Sax invented several other instruments as well.

7. The general public first heard the saxophone in 1844.
8. Sax performed a musical selection by the composer Berlioz.
9. Sax never became rich during his lifetime.
10. Today, however, many people play the saxophone.

Verb Phrases

A *verb phrase* consists of a main verb and one or more helping verbs.

Often the **main verb** of a sentence appears with one or more **helping verbs.** A main verb with one or more helping verbs is called a **verb phrase.** Notice the helping verbs in italics below.

will ride   *could be* growing   *had been* looking

The following chart names the most common helping verbs.

Helping Verbs	
Forms of *be*	am, is, are, was, were, be, been, being
Forms of *do*	do, does, did
Forms of *have*	have, has, had
Other Verbs	can will shall may must could would should might

Verbs at a Glance

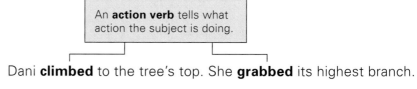

An **action verb** tells what action the subject is doing.

Dani **climbed** to the tree's top. She **grabbed** its highest branch.

A **linking verb** connects a subject (*Clay*) to a word in the predicate (*hoarse*).

Clay **has sounded** hoarse since his performance.

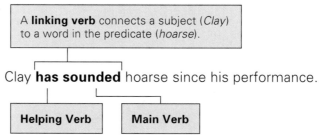

Helping Verb   Main Verb

Exercise 2   Concept Check

Types of Verbs   Write the complete verb in each sentence. Underline the helping verb once and the main verb twice. Then write *A* if the verb shows action and *L* if the verb links the subject to a word in the predicate.

1. For hundreds of years, Shanghai has been a major seaport.
2. On a map of China, you can see the city's key position on the East China Sea.
3. Shanghai must be one of the busiest places in the world!
4. The Communist government of mainland China has ruled Shanghai since 1949.
5. Shanghai has continued its trade with the non-Communist world.

Exercise 3   Drafting Skill

Helping Verbs   Add a helping verb to complete the meaning of each sentence.

1. Next week my sister ___?___ return from Shanghai.
2. She ___?___ written me about the city several times.
3. "You ___?___ see the Temple of the Jade Buddha," she wrote.
4. "That temple ___?___ be the most wonderful place in the city."
5. I ___?___ like to see the jade statue inside that temple.

The Tenses of Verbs

Every verb has several different forms that are used to refer to different times. These forms are called the *tenses* of the verb.

Tenses of Verbs

Present   Shows an action that happens now or that happens regularly or constantly

> Now: Lisa *walks* the dog.
> Regularly: He *sets* the alarm every night.
> Constantly: Marie *lives* in Paris.

Past   Shows an action that was completed in the past

> Roberto *changed* the tire.

Future   Shows an action that will happen in the future

> Lorena *will call* me tomorrow.

There are three ways
to change the tense of
a verb: (1) change the
ending—*walk, walked;*
(2) change the
spelling—*see, saw,
seen;* (3) change the
helping verb—*will
play, has played.*

Present Perfect	Shows an action that was completed at an indefinite time in the past or that began in the past and continues into the present
	We *have ridden* these horses all summer.
Past Perfect	Shows a past action that came before another past action
	Lee *had bought* his gifts before he left.

Exercise 4   Concept Check

Identifying Tenses   Identify the verb and its tense in each sentence.

1. Yes, I have heard of William Tell.
2. My Swiss cousin calls him a national hero.
3. Gessler, a cruel man, ruled Switzerland.
4. He had made life miserable for his subjects.
5. Now you will learn about heroic William Tell.

Exercise 5   Drafting Skill

Using Tenses   Complete the following sentences with the verb forms given in parentheses. Write the complete sentences.

1. A man said, "This man (present perfect of *break)* a law!"
2. William Tell (past perfect of *refuse)* to kneel before Gessler's hat.
3. Gessler (past of *order)* him to prove his skill with a crossbow.
4. In this picture, Tell (present of *shoot)* an apple off his son's head.
5. In the next chapter he (future of *escape)* from Gessler's soldiers.
6. Tomorrow we (future of *read)* about other legendary heroes.
7. Yesterday I (past of *view)* a great film about Robin Hood.
8. For years, people (present perfect of *relate)* stories about King Arthur.
9. When I was younger, I (past of *believe)* most of the stories.
10. Recently I really (present perfect of *enjoy)* stories about knights.

Principal Parts of Verbs

Every verb has four *principal parts.* The principal parts of verbs are the *present,* the *present participle,* the *past,* and the *past participle.*

The principal parts of verbs are used to make the verb tenses. Most verbs are regular, like those in the chart below. **Regular verbs** add -*ed* or -*d* to the present form to show the past tense. The past form never uses a helping verb. The past participle is the same as the past form, but it always uses a helping verb.

Regular Verbs

Present	Present Participle	Past	Past Participle
walk	(is) walking	walked	(have) walked
clap	(is) clapping	clapped	(have) clapped
wait	(is) waiting	waited	(have) waited

Verbs that do not form the past tense by adding -*ed* or -*d* are **irregular verbs.** In some cases the past and the past participle are the same, but in many cases they are not. Learn as many of the irregular forms as you can from the chart below.

REMEMBER!
The past form **never** uses a helping verb. The past participle **always** uses a helping verb.

Irregular Verbs

Present	Past	Past Participle	Present	Past	Past Participle
begin	began	(have) begun	ride	rode	(have) ridden
break	broke	(have) broken	ring	rang	(have) rung
bring	brought	(have) brought	rise	rose	(have) risen
choose	chose	(have) chosen	run	ran	(have) run
come	came	(have) come	say	said	(have) said
do	did	(have) done	see	saw	(have) seen
drink	drank	(have) drunk	sing	sang	(have) sung
eat	ate	(have) eaten	speak	spoke	(have) spoken
fall	fell	(have) fallen	steal	stole	(have) stolen
freeze	froze	(have) frozen	swim	swam	(have) swum
give	gave	(have) given	take	took	(have) taken
go	went	(have) gone	teach	taught	(have) taught
grow	grew	(have) grown	throw	threw	(have) thrown
have	had	(have) had	wear	wore	(have) worn
know	knew	(have) known	write	wrote	(have) written

Exercise 6   Concept Check

Irregular Verbs   Write the correct verb form.

1. Last week my father and I (ride, rode) up to Vermont.
2. On the way we played games and (sung, sang) songs.
3. On our first night in Vermont, we stayed in a motel and (swam, swum) in the pool.
4. The next morning we got back on the road, and by 9 A.M. we had (begun, began) to see signs for Jericho.
5. I have long (knew, known) about Jericho because of "Snowflake" Bentley.
6. Wilson Bentley (grew, grown) up in Jericho, Vermont.
7. When the school bell (rang, rung), Bentley ignored it.
8. His mother, a teacher, had (chose, chosen) to teach him at home.
9. When he was young, his parents (gave, given) him a microscope.
10. During snowstorms, Bentley (went, gone) outside with a camera.
11. He took pictures of snowflakes that had (froze, frozen) on a black tray.
12. If the snowflake had (broke, broken), he didn't photograph it.
13. Bentley (did, done) other artistic work as well.
14. Some days he (rose, risen) early to study dew or frost on windows.
15. He has (wrote, written) a book that has hundreds of his pictures.

Confusing Verb Pairs

The following verb pairs are sometimes confused.

Let means "to permit or allow." *Leave* means "to cause or allow to remain."

> *Let* me help you.
> *Leave* those books with me.

Lie means "to rest in a flat position." *Lie* never has a direct object. *Lay* means "to place." It almost always takes a direct object.

> Mom will *lie* down on the hammock this afternoon.
> *Lay* those packages on the table.

Sit means "to occupy a seat." *Sit* never has a direct object. *Set* means "to place." *Set* almost always has a direct object.

> Please *sit* down.
> Please *set* the groceries on the counter over there.

Rise means "to go upward." It never has a direct object. *Raise* means "to lift" or "to make something go up." It usually has a direct object.

We shall *rise* tomorrow morning at ten o'clock.
The mechanic *raised* the hood of the car.

	Present	**Past**	**Past Participle**
Let and *Leave*	let	let	(have) let
	leave	left	(have) left
Lie and *Lay*	lie	lay	(have) lain
	lay	laid	(have) laid
Sit and *Set*	sit	sat	(have) sat
	set	set	(have) set
Rise and *Raise*	rise	rose	(have) risen
	raise	raised	(have) raised

MORE CONFUSION · · · · · · · ·
Two other verbs that are sometimes confused are *learn* and *teach*. *Learn* means "to gain knowledge or skill." *Teach* means "to help someone learn."
Today we *learned* to yodel.
Ms. Montalva *taught* us how to yodel.

Exercise 7   Concept Check

Confusing Verbs   Write the correct verb form.

1. Even in these polluted times, many fascinating creatures (lie, lay) at the bottoms of tide pools.

2. (Leave, Let) me tell you about a few of them.

3. (Sitting, Setting) beneath rocks or clumps of seaweed, small crabs hide from sea gulls and other predators.

4. The globe-shaped sea urchins are covered with spines that cause predators to (let, leave) them alone.

5. (Lie, Lay) an urchin on your hand and watch it cling to your palm.

6. If you (sit, set) a crab down on the sand, it scuttles off in a peculiar sideways motion.

7. Other creatures such as starfish and sand dollars are (lying, laying) in tide pools.

8. When the tide (rises, raises), sea water floods into the tide pools, bringing food to the inhabitants.

9. The tiny barnacles open their hard shells and (rise, raise) their legs to move particles of food toward their mouths.

10. Tide pools are fragile ecosystems, so feel free to look at the creatures in them, but then (let, leave) them alone.

Exercise 8   Proofreading Skill

Verb Review   Each of the following sentences contains one error in verb usage. Write the correct verb.

1. Angela Bates has wrote an excellent article in *National Parks* magazine about Nicodemus, Kansas.
2. In her article she has gave a brief history of the town.
3. Leave me tell you what her article says.
4. The small town of Nicodemus, Kansas, sets on Highway 24.
5. After the Civil War, many former slaves go to that town.
6. They had chose new lives on the Kansas frontier.
7. They had took the name Nicodemus from an African prince, the first slave in the United States to buy his freedom.
8. These former slaves believed that they could rise crops in Kansas.
9. The African-American pioneers faced many hardships, but the town growed nonetheless.
10. In 1973 the U.S. government gived Nicodemus the status of National Historic Landmark.

Exercise 9   Revision Skill

Verb Usage Review   Rewrite the following paragraph, correcting any errors in verb usage.

(1) The great white shark was laying on the sandy bottom, ready to raise to attack any unsuspecting prey. (2) Allan, a scuba diver who weared a tank and flippers, swimmed closer and closer to the shark. (3) He had just began his dive when he suddenly seen the shark. (4) Allan knowed that great whites are called "man-eaters" because they attack more people than any other shark. (5) Allan slowly began to back away. (6) Whenever possible, he never breaked his rule, "Leave sleeping sharks lay."

SECTION 7: USING ADJECTIVES AND ADVERBS

Understanding Adjectives

An *adjective* is a word that modifies a noun or a pronoun.

golden apples   *furry* critters   *silly* conversation
unbelievable story   *perfect* alibi   *old* clothes

Articles

The most widely used of all adjectives are the words *a, an,* and *the.* These adjectives are called **articles.** *The* is the **definite article** because it points to specific persons, places, things, or groups.

the Buddhist temple   *the* open window   *the* Laplanders

A and *an* are **indefinite articles** because they do not refer to specific items. Use *a* before a consonant sound. Use *an* before a vowel sound.

a tangerine   *an* honor   *an* orange

Common and Proper Adjectives

***Proper adjectives* are adjectives that are formed from proper nouns.**

A **proper noun,** you may recall, is a word that names a particular person, place, thing, or idea. Here are some examples of proper nouns and adjectives:

Proper Noun	Proper Adjective	Example
Russia	Russian	Russian dance
England	English	English tea
Texas	Texas	Texas chili
Sunday	Sunday	Sunday brunch

Notice that some proper nouns change their form when they become adjectives. For example, *Asia* becomes *Asian.* However, some proper nouns and adjectives, like *Texas,* have the same form.

All other adjectives, except articles, are called **common adjectives.** Examples of common adjectives include *blue, clear, extraordinary, final, fluffy, lovable, quiet, round, salty,* and *weird.*

PRONOUNS AS ADJECTIVES

The demonstrative pronouns *this, these, that,* and *those* can act as adjectives and modify nouns: *this* plant or *those* islands. Some possessive pronouns can also act as adjectives: *my* family or *their* car.

Exercise 1   Concept Check

Identifying Adjectives   Write the adjectives in the following sentences on your paper. Then label each one *P* for proper adjective or *C* for common adjective. Ignore the articles.

Example   Volcanoes are spectacular and dangerous.

Answer   spectacular, C   dangerous, C

1. One fine day in February of 1943, a Mexican farmer went out to plow his fields.
2. As he worked, he heard a strange sound coming from the ground.
3. The solid ground burst open, and an enormous mound of hot ash appeared.
4. By the next morning, a volcano stood where the farmer's field had been.
5. This dramatic eruption occurred in Paricutín, a small town in western Mexico.
6. The Paricutín volcano is one of several unusual eruptions that have happened in the past few decades.
7. For example, an American volcano made headlines in May of 1980.
8. Mount St. Helens, in the state of Washington near the Oregon border, caused tremendous damage when it erupted.
9. The violent blast laid waste to hundreds of miles of land.
10. Gray clouds rose from the site and blocked out the sun in Washington and in nearby states.

Predicate Adjectives

REMINDER
. . . .
Linking verbs include forms of the verb *to be* (*is, am, are, was, were, be, been,* and *being*) and verbs like *become, feel, grow, look, seem, smell,* and *taste.*

▶   **When an adjective is separated from the noun or pronoun it modifies by a linking verb, it is a *predicate adjective.***

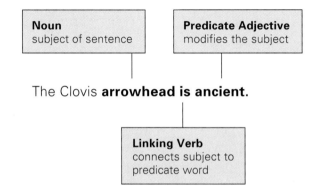

| **Noun** subject of sentence | **Predicate Adjective** modifies the subject |

The Clovis **arrowhead is ancient.**

Linking Verb connects subject to predicate word

Exercise 2   Concept Check

Predicate Adjectives   Write each sentence on your paper. Circle the linking verb. Underline the subject once. Then underline the predicate adjective or adjectives twice.

1. Central Italy is beautiful throughout the year.
2. Of all the cities in central Italy, Rome is the most famous.
3. In the late afternoon, the shadows around the ancient monuments grow long.
4. At that time of day, Rome looks even more splendid than usual.
5. Visitors become thoughtful and dream about Rome's past.
6. Visitors to Rome's underground catacombs are sometimes frightened.
7. This network of underground passages, built by early Christians, is dark and eerie.
8. Because tombs for the dead were cut into the walls, the walls are full of skeletons.
9. These burial places were sacred.
10. When the Romans persecuted the Christians, these tombs became useful for holding secret meetings.

WRITING TIP

Varying the positions of adjectives can make your writing more interesting. Adjectives can appear before or after the words they modify. A *young, spindly* colt stood in the corral; or, a colt, *young* and *spindly*, stood in the corral.

Understanding Adverbs

An *adverb* modifies a verb, an adjective, or another adverb.

Modifying Verbs	works *slowly*	runs *there*
Modifying Adjectives	*very* little	*extremely* hot
Modifying Adverbs	*so* clearly	*too* easily

Adverbs tell *how, where, when,* or *to what extent* about the words they modify. As you can see from the following examples, adverbs can make writing more specific and more interesting.

How	grew *rapidly*	calls *loudly*	jumps *high*
Where	came *here*	went *back*	ran *out*
When	called *yesterday*	stop *now*	*never* ask
To What Extent	*almost* ready	*quite* often	*too* slow

Many adverbs are formed by adding *-ly* to an adjective.

crisp + *-ly* = crisply   neat + *-ly* = neatly

Commonly used adverbs that do *not* end in *-ly* are listed in the chart on the next page.

Questionable Adverbs

Some adverbs are used to ask questions. These adverbs are known as **interrogatives.** *How* does a plane fly? *When* is the first day of spring? *Where* do meteorites come from? *Why* do stars twinkle?

Commonly Used Adverbs

afterward	hard	never	so	very
almost	here	next	soon	well
already	how	not	still	when
also	instead	now	straight	where
back	late	often	then	why
even	long	quick	there	yes
far	low	rather	today	yesterday
fast	more	seldom	tomorrow	yet
forth	near	slow	too	

Exercise 3   Concept Check

Finding Adjectives and Adverbs   Make two columns on your paper. In one column write all the adjectives (except articles) you find in the following paragraph. Write all the adverbs in the second column.

(1) The phoenix is a famous bird in Greek mythology. (2) Supposedly, only one of these amazing golden creatures actually existed at any one time. (3) It lived for exactly five hundred years. (4) Then, the old phoenix would burn itself to death. (5) Amazingly, a new phoenix would immediately rise from the warm ashes. (6) Because the bird continually re-created itself, it is now used as a powerful symbol of rebirth, determination, and survival.

Adjective or Adverb?

Sometimes people confuse adverbs and adjectives. Remember that an adjective modifies a noun or a pronoun. An adverb modifies a verb, an adjective, or another adverb.

Adjective   These are *good hockey* skates. (*good* and *hockey* modify the noun *skates*.)

Adverb   Pedro skates *well*. (*well* modifies the verb *skates*)

An adjective, not an adverb, is used after a linking verb such as *is, am, was, were, be, looks, feels, grows, sounds, smells, tastes, becomes,* or *seems.* The linking verb connects the adjective to a noun or pronoun that it modifies.

Adjective after a linking verb   That song sounds *beautiful*.
Adverb modifying an action verb   Marika sings *beautifully*.

752   LANGUAGE HANDBOOK

Do not use an adverb after a linking verb.

Incorrect   She sounds *angrily.*

Correct   She sounds *angry.*

Incorrect   The food here tastes *badly.*

Correct   The food here tastes *bad.*

Do not use an adjective to modify a verb, an adjective, or another adverb.

Incorrect   John writes *careless.*

Correct   John writes *carelessly.*

Incorrect   Many TV programs are *real* boring.

Correct   Many TV programs are *really* boring.

Exercise 4   Concept Check

Choosing the Correct Modifier   Write the modifier that is correct.

1. Vice-President Al Gore has studied the environment for a (real, really) long time.
2. He believes that solving environmental problems is (terrible, terribly) important to our future.
3. In his book *Earth in the Balance,* Mr. Gore writes (forceful, forcefully) about these issues.
4. Dumping toxic wastes into the air and water is (bad, badly) policy for the future.
5. Mr. Gore sounds (angry, angrily) when he speaks about those who have broken laws meant to protect our resources.

Exercise 5   Proofreading Skill

Using Modifiers Correctly   Decide whether the italicized modifiers in the following paragraph are used correctly. If the modifier is correct, write *Correct* on your paper. If the modifier needs to be changed, write the correct form on your paper.

(1) Some people think that it's *extreme* late to start to clean up our nation's waterways. (2) Our rivers, streams, and lakes once smelled and tasted *sweet.* (3) Now, the water in many of our major waterways tastes *badly.* (4) It also smells *real* funny. (5) We *sure* can do something about this situation! (6) We can move *quick* to ban the dumping of wastes into the water.

Avoiding Double Negatives

Do not use two negative words together in the same sentence.

Some of the most commonly used adverbs are the negative words *no, not, none, nothing,* and *never.* Other negatives include the adverbs *hardly* and *scarcely* and contractions that contain *n't,* the shortened form of *not: can't, don't, doesn't, won't, wouldn't, isn't,* and *aren't.* If two of these words are used in a sentence when only one is needed, the result is a **double negative.**

Double Negative	I *don't* have *nothing* to lose.
Correct	I don't have anything to lose.
Correct	I have nothing to lose.
Double Negative	You *can't* have *none* of that food.
Correct	You can't have any of that food.
Correct	You can have none of that food.
Double Negative	Those boys *won't never* come back.
Correct	Those boys won't ever come back.
Correct	Those boys will never come back.

Exercise 6   Proofreading Skill

Correcting Double Negatives   Rewrite the following sentences, correcting all double negatives.

1. Some people might think that there weren't hardly any black soldiers who fought in the Civil War.

2. This could not be no further from the truth.

3. In fact, there weren't scarcely any eligible African-American men who stayed out of the war.

4. These men felt that there wasn't nothing else they could do but fight against the system that had enslaved them.

5. They did not want to let no one else do their fighting.

6. Many had come from the South and didn't never want to return.

7. However, rather than say to themselves, "We're not never going back there," they willingly put on their uniforms.

8. They never had no second thoughts about fighting for freedom.

9. One can't think of nothing more noble than a willingness to risk death or a return to slavery in order to free others.

10. We won't never forget their bravery.

Adjectives and Adverbs in Comparisons

When you use a modifier to compare one thing with another, use the *comparative form.*

When you use a modifier to compare one thing with more than one other thing, use the *superlative form.*

Modifier	That math test was hard.
Comparative Form	That math test was harder than the science test.
Superlative Form	That math test was the hardest test I ever took.

Short modifiers such as the adjective *thin* and the adverb *soon* change their forms by adding *-er* for the comparative and *-est* for the superlative. Notice in the examples below that words ending in *n* and *y* may undergo slight spelling changes when *-er* or *-est* is added.

Modifier	Comparative Form	Superlative Form
thin	thinner	thinnest
soon	sooner	soonest
happy	happier	happiest
slow	slower	slowest

Longer modifiers such as the adjective *wonderful* and the adverb *cautiously* add the word *more* to make the comparative, and they add *most* to make the superlative.

Modifier	Comparative Form	Superlative Form
wonderful	more wonderful	most wonderful
cautiously	more cautiously	most cautiously
important	more important	most important
practical	more practical	most practical

Never use *more* and the *-er* ending together, or *most* and the *-est* ending together.

Incorrect	more prettier	most beautifullest
Correct	prettier	most beautiful

Exercise 7 Revision Skill

Comparison of Modifiers Find the errors in adjective and adverb forms in the following sentences. Write the correct forms on your paper.

1. Of all the stories that I have read, "All Summer in a Day" is probably the sadder.

2. In this story the main character, Margot, is the most shyest child in the class.

3. The story takes place on Venus, where it rains more frequentlier than it does on Earth.

4. In the story, a group of children have gathered on the most thrillingest day of their life.

5. This day is most exciting than any other day because the sun will come out for an hour.

6. No child in the class has greatest expectations than Margot because she alone remembers how the sun looks and feels.

7. Margot's envious classmates behave most cruelly than anyone could imagine: they lock Margot in a closet.

8. Then they run outside where the sun feels gloriouser than anything else they could dream of.

9. Suddenly, the sadder sound they ever heard begins: it is the dripping of the rain.

10. The student who acts most courageously than the rest of the class will open the closet door.

Unusual Form Changes

Some modifiers change their forms completely and use different words for the comparative and superlative.

Modifier	Comparative Form	Superlative Form
good	better	best
bad	worse	worst
badly	worse	worst
well	better	best
much	more	most
little	less	least

Exercise 8 Concept Check

Unusual Forms Find the errors in modifier forms in the following sentences. Write the modifiers correctly.

1. The United States has the bestest basketball players on earth.
2. That U.S. basketball players are more better than their competitors was proved in the 1992 Olympics.
3. The U.S. Olympic team was so better that people called them "the Dream Team."
4. Even the less skilled player on the U.S. team was still very talented.
5. It might seem useless to challenge a team of the world's very better players.
6. What could be worst than to play against a team of such greats as Michael Jordan, Larry Bird, and Magic Johnson?
7. However, other teams actually played their better game against the Americans.
8. No matter how badlier they played, other teams still enjoyed being on the same court with "the Dream Team."
9. The actual game was least important to them than the joy of playing against the best.
10. The more difficult problem they had was getting autographs from the U.S. players!

Using Demonstrative Adjectives

A **demonstrative pronoun,** such as *this, that, these,* or *those,* points out a specific person or thing. When such a word is used as a modifier, it becomes a **demonstrative adjective.**

This and *that* modify singular nouns. *These* and *those* modify plural nouns.

this book	*these* books
that brick	*those* bricks

Kind and *sort* are singular. They are used with the demonstrative adjectives *this* and *that. Kinds* and *sorts* are plural and are used with the demonstrative adjectives *these* and *those.*

this kind	*these* kinds	*that* sort	*those* sorts

Never use *here* or *there* with demonstrative adjectives.

Incorrect	*This here* water is salty.
Correct	*This* water is salty.

Exercise 9   Revision Skill

Demonstrative Adjectives   Rewrite the following paragraph, correcting the errors that you find.

(1) This here invention of mine is bound to catch on. (2) After all, we need these sort of thing. (3) With my invention those pen you are now using will not be needed. (4) These kind of writing tool will be outdated. (5) Here's how this here invention works. (6) To use the invention, you first put on these here headphones. (7) Then you concentrate on those there ideas you want to write about. (8) Magically, that ideas appear on paper. (9) Of course, this here idea of mine is just a fantasy right now. (10) However, these kind of wild ideas have come true in the past. Who knows what the future might bring!

Exercise 10   Revision Skill

Modifier Review   All of the following sentences contain errors in the use of modifiers. Rewrite the sentences correctly.

1. Benjamin Franklin was a eminent America statesman, scientist, and inventor.

2. These here are just a few of his inventions: the lightning rod, bifocals, and the Franklin stove.

3. As a boy, he dreamed of going to sea, but his father said it wouldn't get him nowhere.

4. At age twelve, he became a apprentice printer, but he wanted to do importanter work.

5. When he was seventeen, he thought he could do no worst on his own.

6. When he arrived in Philadelphia, he was terrible poor.

7. He began publishing a newspaper and *Poor Richard's Almanack,* one of the much popular books ever printed.

8. The success of that there book helped him become famous.

9. Most of us remember Franklin for the kite experiment, which was perhaps his dangerousest scientific investigation.

10. He seemed to be most happyest when he was busy.

11. He was known to be a honest man.

12. One of his most proud achievements was signing both the Declaration of Independence and the U.S. Constitution.

13. Franklin thought mail was delivered more slower than it should have been; he became the country's first postmaster general.

14. Franklin was a real extraordinary person.

15. We can't never have enough of this kind of ingenuity in the world.

SECTION 8: SUBJECT—VERB AGREEMENT

Singular and Plural

**A noun that names one person, place, thing, or idea is *singular*.
A noun that names more than one is *plural*.**

Singular	**Plural**
spaceship	spaceships
country	countries
notebook	notebooks

Verbs also have singular and plural forms.

Singular	**Plural**
I dream	we dream
you dream	you dream
he, she, or it dreams	they dream

Some verbs have special singular or plural forms, as shown in the
following chart.

	Be	**Have**	**Do**
Singular Forms	is, am, was	has, had	does, did
Plural Forms	are, were	have, had	do, did

Exercise 1　Concept Check

Identifying Singular and Plural Words　Tell whether the italicized
word in each sentence is singular or plural.

1. I have seen *bats* flying around at night above the trees in my yard.
2. Bats are nocturnal animals—that is, they *come* out only at night.
3. *Do* you know that a single bat can eat its weight in insects?
4. One bat *eats* about twenty thousand bugs in a week.
5. I read once that bats *are* the only mammals capable of true flight.
6. Bats *migrate* to warmer climates in the winter.
7. The largest bat in the world actually *has* a six-foot wingspan.
8. Bats are not really blind; that *is* a myth.
9. They *depend* on their hearing more than on their sight, however.
10. *People* think bats are nasty, but most are actually quite harmless.

◀ AN ODD COUPLE
. . . .
The pronouns *I* and
you are a bit strange.
I always refers to one
person. *You* can refer
to one person or to
more than one person.
Even when they refer
to only one person,
both pronouns are
used with plural verbs
(except in the
expressions *I am* and
I was):

I *do*	I *have*
you *do*	you *have*

Agreement of Subject and Verb

A verb must agree with its subject.

In a sentence the verb must agree with its subject. If the subject is singular, the verb must be singular. If the subject is plural, the verb must be plural.

> A <u>scrapbook</u> <u><u>is</u></u> a place for storing memories. (The subject, *scrapbook,* is singular. Therefore, a singular verb, *is,* is used.)

> <u>Journals</u> <u><u>are</u></u> good places to record your ideas. (The subject, *journals,* is plural. Therefore, a plural verb, *are,* is used.)

> My <u>journal,</u> my <u>scrapbook,</u> and my <u>sketchbook</u> <u><u>are</u></u> very important to me. (The subject—*journal, scrapbook, and sketchbook*—is plural. Therefore, a plural verb, *are,* is used.)

QUICK TIP Sometimes a prepositional phrase appears between a subject and its verb. Remember, however, that a verb never agrees with a word that appears in a prepositional phrase.

> <u>One</u> (of the explorers) <u><u>claims</u></u> to have seen a sea serpent. (The verb *claims* agrees with *one,* the subject of the sentence. It does not agree with *explorers,* which is part of a prepositional phrase.)

> Some <u>parts</u> (of the space shuttle) <u><u>were</u></u> faulty, and they are what caused the explosion. (The verb *were* does not agree with *space shuttle,* which appears in a prepositional phrase. Instead, it agrees with its real subject, *parts.*)

Exercise 2   Drafting Skill

Making Subjects and Verbs Agree   Write the correct verbs.

1. The pictures on my wall (is, are) of Parguera, a fishing village on Puerto Rico, an island in the West Indies.
2. My parents (was, were) born in San Juan, the capital of Puerto Rico.
3. The people of this island (is, are) known for the beautiful baskets, pottery, and straw rugs that they make.
4. The United States and Puerto Rico (hasn't, haven't) always been friendly.
5. Puerto Ricans (was, were) having problems cooperating with the United States until Luis Muñoz Marín became friendly with people in Franklin D. Roosevelt's administration.

6. The U.S. Congress and Harry Truman (is, are) credited with allowing Puerto Rico to become a commonwealth of the United States in 1952.

7. Now Puerto Rico (is, are) a place that attracts tourists from all over the world.

8. Many people in Puerto Rico (works, work) in the clothing industry.

9. One of the island's most beautiful places (is, are) El Yunque, a mountain covered by a rain forest.

10. My family and I (is, are) going to Puerto Rico in June.

Agreement with Compound Subjects

A subject made up of two or more parts is known as a *compound subject*.

A compound subject with parts joined by the conjunction *and* is plural and always takes a plural verb.

> <u>Flutes and drums</u> <u>are</u> the most common instruments around the globe.

If the parts of a compound subject are joined by *or* or *nor,* the verb agrees with the part that is closest to the verb.

> <u>An afghan or some other handmade item</u> <u>makes</u> a nice gift. (The singular verb *makes* agrees with the nearer noun, *item.*)
>
> <u>Neither the earth nor the other planets</u> <u>have existed</u> forever. (The plural verb *have existed* agrees with the nearer noun, *planets.*)
>
> <u>Neither the other planets nor the earth</u> <u>has existed</u> forever. (The singular verb *has existed* agrees with the nearer noun, *earth.*)

Exercise 3   Drafting Skill

Choosing the Correct Verb   Write the correct verb.

1. The other students in my geography class and I (has, have) learned that the Amazon alone carries one-fifth of the world's river water.

2. Neither the Nile River nor the Mississippi River (has, have) as much water as the Amazon.

3. The Amazon and the Nile (is, are) the two longest rivers in the world.

4. When my father visited the Amazon years ago, either a large excursion boat or small guide boats (was, were) available to take people down the river.

5. A large Amazonian crocodile or flesh-eating Amazonian piranhas (is, are) frightening to come across in the wild.

Agreement with Indefinite Pronouns

Singular indefinite pronouns are used with singular verbs.

Plural indefinite pronouns are used with plural verbs.

Some indefinite pronouns are plural in some sentences and singular in others.

Indefinite Pronouns

Singular			**Plural**
another	either	nobody	both
anybody	everybody	no one	few
anyone	everyone	one	many
anything	everything	somebody	several
each	neither	someone	

Singular *Each* of these tornadoes *has caused* terrible destruction.

Plural *Both* of these tornadoes *have caused* terrible destruction.

These indefinite pronouns are plural in some sentences and singular in others: *all, any, most, none,* and *some.*

Singular Is *any* of the pie left on the plate?

Plural Are *any* of the cookies left in the bag?

Exercise 4   Proofreading Skill

Agreement with Compound Subjects and Indefinite Pronouns
Rewrite the following paragraph, correcting any agreement errors.

(1) The ancient Greeks and Romans was very inventive people. (2) One of their myths and legends concern a strange people who live in a faraway land. (3) In the story neither men nor any boy are ever allowed to live in that distant country. (4) All of the inhabitants is women. (5) These women and their daughters is known as Amazons. (6) Each of the Amazons are allowed to interact with societies that contain men. (7) Often everybody hunts together. (8) However, none of the males can stay in the land of the Amazons. (9) Many myths and stories about the Amazons has been told over the centuries. (10) Some historians and other scholars believes that the explorer Francisco de Orellana named South America's largest river the Amazon because of fierce women whom he met there.

Agreement in Inverted Sentences

In most sentences the subject comes before the verb. However, sometimes the subject and the verb are switched around, or **inverted.**

Regular Order   The jumbo jet taxied onto the runway.
(The subject, *jet,* comes before the verb, *taxied.*)

Inverted Order   Onto the runway taxied the jumbo jet.
(The subject, *jet,* comes after the verb, *taxied.*)

Subjects and verbs are often inverted in questions.

Are bats really mammals? (The subject is *bats.* The verb is *are.*)

Is the moray eel or the crown-of-thorns starfish dangerous? (The compound subject is *the moray eel or the crown-of-thorns starfish.* The verb is *is.*)

The words *there, where,* and *here* often begin sentences. Their job is to get the sentence moving. When *there, where,* or *here* begins a sentence, look for the subject later in the sentence.

There is the entrance to the space museum. (The subject is *entrance.* The verb is *is.*)

Where do fish go in the winter? *(Fish* is the subject of the verb *do go.)*

A verb must always agree with its subject, even if the subject and the verb are inverted.

Incorrect   On the wall <u>hangs</u> <u>photos</u> of Mr. Guzman when he was a little boy in Puerto Rico.

Correct   On the wall <u>hang</u> <u>photos</u> of Mr. Guzman when he was a little boy in Puerto Rico.

Incorrect   Here <u>is</u> the <u>tickets</u> you ordered.
Correct   Here <u>are</u> the <u>tickets</u> you ordered.

Exercise 5   Proofreading Skill

Agreement in Inverted Sentences   Rewrite the following paragraph, correcting agreement errors.

(1) Where does the oceans come from? (2) Scientists has thought about this question for many years. (3) There are now a good theory to explain the origin of oceans. (4) According to modern geologists, the early earth was a ball of rock. (5) All over

WRITING TIP
· · · · · · · · · · · · · · · ·
One way to make your writing more interesting is to vary the kinds of sentences you use. From time to time, try changing the order of ideas in your sentences. Instead of writing "A lone wolf howled deep in the woods," write "Deep in the woods howled a lone wolf."

the surface of the earth was hundreds of thousands of volcanoes that were constantly erupting. (6) Continually hitting the earth was hundreds of thousands of meteorites. (7) So where does the oceans come in? (8) Quite simply, thrown into the sky by these mighty blasts were a lot of water vapor. (9) This vapor cooled and turned into droplets of liquid water. (10) In the skies all over the earth was enormous clouds made up of these tiny droplets. (11) Eventually, there was tremendous rainstorms, all over the earth. (12) These rains became the oceans of today.

Exercise 6   Drafting Skill

Review of Subject-Verb Agreement   Write the correct verb.

1. Televisions, radios, and motion pictures (has, have) brought about great changes in the past century.
2. A typhoon in Guam or hungry people in Somalia (is, are) brought directly into our homes over the airwaves.
3. Now new inventions and new discoveries (is, are) promising to bring about even greater changes.
4. Neither television nor motion pictures (has, have) the far-reaching potential of personal computers.
5. Letters and numbers (is, are) stored by computers in a special format that is known as "digital."
6. The music on compact discs (is, are) also in digital form.
7. A digital machine like a computer or a compact disc player (converts, convert) information into 1s and 0s.
8. These 1s and 0s (is, are) easily sent between machines over telephone wires.
9. Today, along telephone wires (goes, go) digital signals carrying all kinds of information.
10. In a flash (arrives, arrive) information sent from across the city or across the world.
11. There (is, are) a strong possibility that in the future all movies, telephone calls, news, photographs, money transactions, and orders for goods and services will travel between homes and businesses over telephone lines.
12. Where (does, do) the digital revolution seem to be taking us?
13. Thinkers in many different fields (is, are) considering this question.
14. Here (is, are) one widely accepted answer.
15. Computers and telephone networks (has, have) the potential of bringing all people of the world closer together.

SECTION 9: CAPITALIZATION

Proper Nouns and Proper Adjectives

Capitalize proper nouns and proper adjectives.

A **common noun** is the name of a whole class of persons, places, things, or ideas. A **proper noun** is the name of a particular person, place, thing, or idea. A **proper adjective** is an adjective made from a proper noun. Proper nouns and proper adjectives are capitalized, but common nouns and common adjectives are not.

Common Noun	hero	continent
Proper Noun	**H**ercules	**A**frica
Common Adjective	heroic	continental
Proper Adjective	**H**erculean	**A**frican

Names and Titles of People

Capitalize the names of persons and initials that stand for names.

Lucille **C**lifton   **T**oni **C**ade **B**ambara   **R**obert **D**. **B**allard

Capitalize titles and abbreviations for titles that appear before people's names. Capitalize abbreviations such as _Jr._ that appear after a name.

Rev. Martin Luther King, **J**r.   **M**s. Rylant   **D**r. Asimov

Capitalize such words as _mother, father, aunt,_ and _uncle_ when these words are used as names or when they come just before a name.

Hey, **A**unt Flores, look at the swans!
Here are the car keys, **D**ad.
This painting was done by **U**ncle Tiu.

Do not capitalize words that name family members if these words are preceded by a possessive, such as _your_ or _my,_ or by an article such as _a_ or _the._

My **a**unt loves swans.   His **u**ncle did that painting.

The Pronoun I

Capitalize the pronoun *I*.

I read some poems by Derek Walcott.

Religions, Sacred Beings, and Sacred Writings

Capitalize words that name religions, sacred beings, or religious scriptures. Also capitalize adjectives formed from these names.

Allah	**J**ehovah	the **T**orah	the **B**ible
Brahma	**I**sis	the **V**irgin **M**ary	the **V**edas
Christian	**I**slam	**I**slamic	**C**onfucian

Races, Ethnic Groups, Languages, and Nationalities

Capitalize the names of races, ethnic groups, languages, and nationalities. Also capitalize adjectives formed from such names.

Hispanics	**K**enyan coffee	**F**rench food	**I**talian
African **A**merican	**S**wahili	**O**riental art	**S**ioux

Exercise 1   Concept Check

Using Capital Letters   Write the following sentences using correct capitalization.

1. i enjoy listening to uncle amit tell about his childhood in bombay, india.

2. i love hearing the stories from those sacred hindu books: the vedas, the ramayana, and the mahabharata.

3. In hinduism, my uncle's religion, the supreme being is brahma.

4. My uncle suggested that i read a book by dr. mary s. mistri and ms. emily grant about the hindu religion.

5. According to dr. mistri and ms. grant, brahma has three different forms.

6. At times, brahma appears as brahama, the creator; the other two forms are vishnu, the preserver, and shiva, the destroyer.

7. Many people in asia practice the hindu faith.

8. Perhaps the most famous hindu of our century was mohandas k. gandhi.

9. dr. gandhi used the principle of nonviolent action to force the british to give up control of india.

10. In the united states, gandhi's principle of nonviolent action was practiced by rev. martin luther king, jr.

Geographical Names

Capitalize each important word in a geographical name. Do not capitalize prepositions, such as *in* or *of,* or the articles *a, an,* or *the.*

Bodies of Water	the **P**acific **O**cean, the **P**o **R**iver, **G**ulf of **M**exico
Continents	**A**ntarctica, **E**urope, **S**outh **A**merica
Land Forms.	**M**ississippi **D**elta, **C**ape **A**nn, the **G**obi **D**esert, **M**ount **C**armel, **C**hallenger **D**eep
Objects in the Universe	**J**upiter, **V**enus, **M**ilky **W**ay
Political Units	**L**atvia, the **E**uropean **E**conomic **C**ommunity, **T**exas, **M**onroe **C**ounty, the **C**herokee **N**ation
Public Areas	**M**uir **W**oods, **B**oston **C**ommon, **Y**ellowstone **N**ational **P**ark
Roads, Highways	**R**oute 66, **S**kyline **D**rive, **P**ennsylvania **A**venue
World Regions	the **F**ar **E**ast, the **S**outhern **H**emisphere, the **B**alkans, **M**icronesia

Directions and Sections

Capitalize names of sections of the United States or the world. Also capitalize any adjectives that come from those names.

The **N**orth had many more factories than the **S**outh.
The **W**estern nations agreed to offer aid by way of **W**est **A**frica.

Do not capitalize nouns or adjectives that merely indicate compass directions or locations.

Walk three blocks **n**orth to the Korean Meeting House.

Organizations, Institutions, Buildings, and Structures

Capitalize all important words in the names of organizations, institutions, buildings, and structures.

Organizations and Institutions	the Libertarian Party, the United Negro College Fund, Oxfam America, Bolivar High School
Buildings	Grand Central Station, the Taj Mahal, the Monadnock Building, the Forbidden Palace
Structures	the Holland Tunnel, the Vietnam Veterans Memorial, Hoover Dam, the Great Wall of China

Events, Documents, and Periods of Time

Capitalize all important words in the names of historical events, documents, and periods of time.

Events	King Philip's War, the 1992 Winter Olympics, Macy's Thanksgiving Day Parade, the California Gold Rush
Documents	the Emancipation Proclamation, the Magna Carta, the Declaration of Independence, the Treaty of Versailles
Periods of Time	the Heroic Age, the Enlightenment, the Mesozoic Era, the Great Depression, the Middle Ages

Months, Days, and Holidays

Capitalize the names of months, days, and holidays, but not the names of seasons.

October	Thursday	Yom Kippur	winter

Time Abbreviations

Capitalize the abbreviations B.C., A.D., A.M., and P.M.

Please be at the bus by 7:30 A.M.
The first makeup was worn about 4000 B.C.
Pompeii was buried by lava in A.D. 79.

Exercise 2 Concept Check

Using Capital Letters Write the words and abbreviations in the following sentences that should be capitalized. Begin them with a capital letter.

1. mom and dad were busy preparing for our new year's eve party, so I went for a bike ride down moonwalk avenue.
2. it was almost 3004 a.d., and we had just bought another house in the northern hemisphere of saturn.
3. Only two years ago last spring, we were citizens of Earth, living in new york city near the chrysler building.
4. we were planning to move to a cottage by the gulf of mexico.
5. One morning, however, we read that the interspace treaty had been signed by president shirley pankhurst and by members of congress.
6. "This will allow human beings to live on other friendly planets by labor day," dad said.
7. We had to travel to the capitol in washington, d.c., and apply for space housing.
8. the day before we left, i took pictures of the empire state building and the duck pond in central park.
9. My brother and I now attend saturn high school monday through friday, from eight a.m. to two p.m.
10. I still look through my high-powered telescope at Earth in order to keep an eye on north america.

Sentences and Poetry

Capitalize the first word of every sentence.

Roberto peeled peanuts delicately.

Capitalize the first word of every line of poetry.

And of course there must be something wrong
In wanting to silence any song.

◀ EXCEPTION
. . . .
Sometimes, especially in modern poetry such as "in the inner city" (page 33) and "For My Father," (page 90) a poet chooses not to capitalize the first word of every line.

Quotations

Capitalize the first word of a direct quotation.

Borey said, "**A**ll roads, howsoe'er they diverge, lead to Rome."

When a quotation is interrupted, it is called a **divided quotation.** Do not capitalize the second part unless it starts a new sentence.

"Close your booklet," said Mr. Suarez, "and go to lunch."
"Remind me tomorrow," Sarah said. "I have to go now."

Parts of a Letter

In the greeting of a letter, capitalize all important words.

Dear Dr. Simington: Dear Sir or Madam:

In the closing of a letter, capitalize only the first word.

Yours truly,   Sincerely yours,

Outlines and Titles

Capitalize the first word of each item in an outline and the letters that introduce major subsections.

I. Cars
   A. Sedans
      1. Convertibles
      2. Hardtops
   B. Sports cars

Capitalize the first word, the last word, and all other important words in titles.

Book	*Boy: Tales of Childhood*
Newspaper	*The Los Angeles Times*
Play	*The Monsters Are Due on Maple Street*
Television Series	*Murder, She Wrote*
Short Story	"Hearts and Hands"
Song	"Simple Gifts"
Work of Art	*Twittering Machine*

The word *the* at the beginning of a title and the word *magazine* are capitalized only when they are part of the formal name.

The Boston Globe   *The New York Times Magazine*
Time magazine

Exercise 3   Concept Check

Using Capital Letters   Copy the following letter, correcting each error in capitalization.

---

521 jefferson ave.
evanston, illinois 60202
may 10, 19—

dear ms. eliot,

I'm sorry that I've missed so many school days because of the flu. I will soon finish reading the novel julie of the wolves. By the end of the week, I also hope to complete my paper on the story "all summer in a day."

Here is the beginning of an outline for my essay on orchestras:
 I. instruments
  A. woodwinds
   1. flutes
   2. clarinets

Finally, I have chosen the poem I want to read at the memorial day parade: robert frost's "mending wall." I especially love the line at the end that says, "good fences make good neighbors."

I hope to be back to school soon.

yours truly,

marlena lopez

Exercise 4   Proofreading Skill

Using Capital Letters   Write the following sentences with correct capitalization.

1. i have been reading a wonderful book by diane ackerman.

2. the book is called *the moon by whale light*.

3. it was recommended to me by dad. My mom also loved it.

4. did you know that ms. ackerman writes for *the new yorker*?

5. that's a well-known magazine published in new york city.

6. Her book tells about her travels to patagonia, a region of argentina, in the southern hemisphere, where she studied whales.

7. the whales come down the atlantic coast to the very tip of the south american continent.

8. ms. ackerman gives a lively account of the time she swam with a mother whale named fang.

9. she also tells about observing whales from a boat called *morning watch* and from a plane called *love juicy.*

10. in her opinion, no answer has been found to the question, what do whales do with the largest brains on earth?

11. the author even showed her sense of humor: one day she went to a halloween party dressed as a thunderstorm.

12. I made an outline of the animals she discussed in her book:
   I. bats
   II. crocodilians
   III. whales
   IV. penguins

13. her book inspired me to write a poem.
   bats are not like rats.
   they're more like me.
   they fill the night
   with mystery.

14. She discusses the differences between the constellations in the southern hemisphere and those that appear in the north.

15. i recommended this book and another book by ackerman, *a natural history of the senses,* to emily, my sister.

SECTION 10: PUNCTUATION

Imagine trying to get around a large department store without any signs to guide you. Now imagine trying to read a story that contains no punctuation marks. Punctuation marks, like signs, help people to avoid becoming confused.

End Marks

The punctuation marks that show where a sentence ends are called end marks. The three **end marks** are the period, the question mark, and the exclamation point.

The Period

A period is used in each of the following ways:

- at the end of a **declarative** sentence
- at the end of most **imperative** sentences
- after an **indirect question**
- after an **abbreviation** or an **initial**
- after a **number** or **letter** used to label a part of an outline or an item in a list

A **declarative sentence** is one that makes a statement.

> Custer graduated last in his class at West Point.

An **imperative sentence** is one that gives a command or makes a request.

> Please be careful with that Ming Dynasty vase.

An **indirect question** tells that someone has asked a question but does not contain the exact words of the question.

> Yolanda asked whether the violin or the clarinet was harder to learn how to play.

An **abbreviation** is a shortened version of a word.

Mon. (Monday)	Sr. (Sister)
Gov. (Governor)	U.S. (United States)
Co. (Company)	A.D. (*anno Domini*)

STOP!
In British English, a period is referred to as a full stop.

DON'T OVERDO IT!
If an abbreviation comes at the end of a sentence that ends with a period, use one period, not two.
Incorrect Malcolm was born at 3:30 P.M..
Correct Malcolm was born at 3:30 P.M.

SHORTEST NAMES OF ALL
. . . .
Some people have names that consist of single letters. One-letter names are not written with periods because they are not initials. Examples include Malcolm X and U Thant, a Burmese secretary-general of the United Nations.

▶ An **initial** is the first letter of a name, used by itself.

Robert D. Ballard   Juan A. A. Sedillo   E. E. Cummings

In an **outline** or **list,** periods are used to mark divisions or items.

I. Poetry	Ingredients
A. Epic poetry	1. 1/2 pound cooked wild rice
B. Lyric poetry	2. 1/2 pound roasted chestnuts
C. Dramatic poetry	3. 1/4 pound dried mixed fruit

Exercise 1   Concept Check

Using Periods Correctly   Copy the following items, adding periods where needed.

1. The Presidio in San Francisco, Calif, will soon be a national park
2. Special Features
   1 Hundreds of buildings
   2 Airfield and parade ground
   3 National cemetery
3. I Physical Features
   A Size
      1 Bigger than Central Park in N Y
      2 Total size 1,487 acres
4. U S representative Phillip Burton helped save the Presidio
5. Show me where Crissy Field is
6. The U S Army took over the Presidio in 1846
7. I asked if the Presidio had been damaged by the earthquake that hit at 5:13 A M on Apr 18, 1906
8. I've seen the parks in New Orleans, La, and in Lowell, Mass
9. On Sept 5, Ms West and I visited the area around 6:30 P M
10. I wonder if the Dept of Defense still owns the Presidio

The Question Mark and the Exclamation Point

Use a question mark at the end of an interrogative sentence.

An **interrogative sentence** asks a question.

Didn't Geronimo write an autobiography**?**
Wasn't Crazy Horse a great hero**?**

Remember that a period is used at the end of an indirect question.

> We asked whether Geronimo wrote an autobiography.

Use an exclamation point at the end of an exclamatory sentence.

An **exclamatory sentence** expresses strong feelings.

> Your performance was excellent!   These socks are filthy!

Use an exclamation point at the end of an imperative sentence that expresses excitement. Other imperative sentences should be followed by a period.

> Watch out!   Call the dentist and change your appointment.

Use an exclamation point at the end of a strong interjection.

> Hooray!   Good grief!

Exercise 2   Concept Check

Using Question Marks and Exclamation Points   Copy the following sentences and add the proper end marks.

1. What beautiful pictures those are in your living room
2. Where did you find such unusual works
3. Raoul wondered if the pictures were Japanese woodblock prints
4. Look at these antique portraits by the artist Sharaku
5. Wow Were these women also drawn by the same artist
6. I wondered if you liked the scenes that Hiroshige drew
7. I heard that Van Gogh was a fan of Hiroshige's work
8. When were the first color woodblock prints made
9. Didn't an artist named Harunobu create those first prints
10. We should ask the librarian for a book on Japanese prints

Commas in Compound Sentences and in Series

Use a comma before the conjunction that joins the parts of a compound sentence.

A **compound sentence** contains independent sentences joined with a conjunction such as *and, or, nor, for, but, so,* or *yet.*

> A well-known cowboy film star died in the fire in the Coconut Grove nightclub, **and** over four hundred others died too.

QUICK TIP   Don't confuse compound sentences with compound sentence parts. In a compound sentence, each main part has both a subject and a verb.

Compound Sentence	Raheem wrote the musical, and he directed it too.
Compound Sentence Parts	Raheem wrote the musical and directed it too.

Use commas to separate items in a series.

A **series** contains three or more items. The commas should appear after each item in the series except the last.

> Common birds of the Atlantic seacoast include the cormorant, the sanderling, and the herring gull.

> The pilot put on his helmet, climbed into the cockpit, and waved goodbye to the crowd.

> Marissa held Scruffy, Walter brushed the dog with soapy water, and I rinsed him with the hose.

Use commas between two or more adjectives of equal rank that modify the same noun.

> It was a dark, dreary night.

To decide whether adjectives are of equal rank, try placing the word *and* between them. If *and* sounds natural and if you can reverse the order of the adjectives without changing the meaning, then a comma is needed.

Exercise 3   Proofreading Skill

Commas in Compound Sentences and Items in Series   Rewrite the following paragraph, adding commas where needed.

(1) Water can be a solid a liquid or a gas. (2) Solid water is known as ice and gaseous water is known as water vapor. (3) Tanya, Pablo and I did a simple interesting experiment. (4) Our water-pressure experiment required water a can and a nail. (5) Tanya found a hammer and punched holes in the can. (6) One hole was near the top one was near the middle and one was near the bottom. (7) Pablo found thick black tape and covered the holes. (8) Then Tanya filled the can with water. (9) I removed the tape and water spurted from all three holes. (10) The water pressure near the bottom was the greatest so water from the lowest hole squirted the farthest.

Commas with Introductory Elements

Use a comma to separate an introductory word or phrase from the rest of a sentence.

> So, is the hive full of honey yet?
> Tumbling out of bed, the toddler bumped his head.
> Due to heavy snow, there were many accidents on Route 22.

Commas with Interrupters

Use a comma before and after a word or group of words that interrupts a sentence.

> This is, by the way, why we call crazy people lunatics.
> In ancient days, if you can believe it, people thought that craziness had a lunar, or moon-related, cause.

Use a comma to set off nouns used in direct address.

A **noun of direct address** is the name of the person you are speaking to.

> Well, Thor, what's the news from Asgard?

Use a comma after most appositives.

An **appositive** is a word or group of words that renames or identifies the person or thing referred to before it.

> Mount Ararat, a mountain mentioned in the Bible, is in Turkey.

◀ SPEAKING OF PHRASES

A comma usually isn't needed after a single introductory prepositional phrase: *In the garage* I saw a 1932 Ford.
A comma *is* needed after two or more introductory prepositional phrases: *In the garage at the end of our street,* I saw a 1932 Ford.

Exercise 4   Concept Check

Using Commas Correctly   Copy the following sentences, adding commas where needed.

1. Apollo the son of Zeus was the god of light.
2. Yes he rode across the sky each day from east to west.
3. At night I believe he took a boat back to the east.
4. Just today Melvin I heard the story of Clytie a wood nymph.
5. Well she was really in love with Apollo.
6. He however paid her no attention.
7. All day long she would sit and watch Apollo the sun god.
8. As his chariot moved across the sky she followed with her eyes.
9. Clytie just pined away Pat and was turned into a heliotrope.
10. That flower by the way always keeps turned toward the sun.

Commas in Quotations

Use a comma to set off a direct quotation from the rest of a sentence.

A **direct quotation** is one that gives the exact words of a speaker. An explanatory phrase, such as *he said,* may come before the quotation, after it, or in the middle of it. If the explanatory phrase comes first, put the comma right after it.

> John said, "We must unite."

If the phrase comes last, put the comma inside the quotation marks that end the quotation.

> "We must unite," John said.

If the explanatory words come in the middle of the quotation, use commas both before (inside the quotation marks) and after the explanatory words.

> "We must unite," John said, "or we will be defeated."

Do not use a comma to set off an indirect quotation. An **indirect quotation** is one that does not give the speaker's exact words but restates them in different words.

> Ulysses S. Grant said that persons of African descent would make excellent soldiers.

Commas in Dates, Addresses, and Letters

Use commas to separate the parts of dates and addresses.

In writing dates, use a comma between the day of the month and the year. If no day of the month is given, it is not necessary to use a comma between the month and the year.

> On May 20, 1992, Chris won the championship.
> The concert was on Friday, June 2, 1993.
> The celebration took place in November 1993.

In writing addresses, use a comma after the name of the street and after the name of the city. Do not use a comma before the ZIP code. Study the following examples:

> Her address is 735 Halsted Street, Chicago, Illinois 60604.
> She lived in Cairo, Egypt, after leaving Tulsa, Oklahoma.
> We arrived at 525 East Fiftieth Street, New York City.

Use a comma after the salutation of a friendly letter. Use a comma after the closing of a friendly or a business letter.

Dear Jackie**,**   Sincerely yours**,**   Your pal**,**

Exercise 5   Concept Check

Correct Comma Usage   Copy the following sentences, adding commas where needed.

1. "You know" said Jade "I'd like to travel a lot."
2. In July 1990 she made this announcement.
3. Last week she returned from a week in Tangier Morocco.
4. She said "Many places there are named for Ibn Batuta."
5. On June 13 1325 Ibn Batuta left Morocco on his first journey.
6. Before he was through his travels had taken him 75,000 miles!
7. He traveled as far as Quanzhou China I think.
8. "For twenty-nine years he traveled through the known world" said Jade.
9. After returning Ibn Batuta dictated his life story.
10. A library in Paris France has his manuscript.

Exercise 6   Proofreading Skill

Checking for Comma Errors   Write the following paragraph, correcting all errors in comma usage.

(1) Yes our summer's trip will certainly be a welcome treat. (2) This year, my family will visit Spain, Algeria and Morocco. (3) We will not be sightseeing however. (4) My mother a history teacher wants to do some research. (5) Much of it centers on Casablanca Morocco. (6) I asked her why she wanted to go there. (7) She said that Casablanca is very historic, and she told me why. (8) In January 1943, an important meeting took place there. (9) President Franklin D. Roosevelt met there I believe with Winston Churchill. (10) The meeting took place I have read, during World War II.

Exercise 7   Revision Skill

Using Commas and End Marks   Copy the following sentences, adding end marks and commas as needed.

1. Emile said "Stop I want to take a picture"
2. I asked if he had ever seen an iceberg before

3. He hadn't and he wanted a picture of one
4. Icebergs can be dangerous, you know
5. On April 14 1912, a terrible accident happened
6. Didn't the *Titanic* the world's biggest passenger ship hit an iceberg and sink
7. While photographing Emile asked, "How are icebergs formed"
8. Many icebergs are near the North Pole Greenland and Antarctica
9. What a lot of icebergs Cape Farewell, Greenland has
10. "Well it's not surprising," said Mr. Wong our science teacher
11. "The icebergs Emile break off of the Greenland icecap" he said
12. Every spring, thousands of new icebergs form and some of them are huge
13. Emile asked how big an iceberg could get
14. "A really big one" said Mr. Wong "might be a mile long"
15. Wow I'd like to see an iceberg that size

The Semicolon

Use a semicolon (;) to join the parts of a compound sentence if no conjunction is used.

We looked outside the tent; it was still raining.

Use a semicolon to separate items in a series if the items contain commas.

The expedition's leaders were from Beijing, China; from Katmandu, Nepal; and from London, England.

The Colon

Use a colon (:) to introduce a list of items.

A sentence containing a word or phrase such as *these, the following,* or *here* is often followed by a colon. The colon only follows a complete sentence; it never comes directly after a verb.

Incorrect	The winning dogs are: Rover, Fido, and Rex.
Correct	These are the winning dogs: Rover, Fido, and Rex.

Use a colon between hours and minutes when given as numbers.

12:00 A.M.   4:46 P.M.

Exercise 8 Concept Check

Using Semicolons and Colons Read each sentence. If no additional punctuation is needed, write *Correct.* If the sentence needs a semicolon or a colon, write the sentence correctly.

1. Annie hurried to the museum she, Takao, and I were meeting there at 300.
2. There were the following three exhibits one of photography, one of Chinese art, and one of paintings by the artist Velázquez.
3. "Velázquez" was only part of his name; his full name was Diego Rodríguez de Silva y Velázquez.
4. He was connected to the court in the following way he was the king's painter, and he and his family lived at court.
5. Look at the people in this painting the artist, the princess, and the courtiers.
6. The museum stays open late on Thursdays it doesn't close until 900 P.M.
7. I had a chance to see my favorite picture it's called *The Infanta Margarita.*
8. Velázquez painted it early in his career; it was his first portrait of the Spanish royal princess.
9. This may not be his best-known work *Las Meninas,* or *The Maids of Honor*, is probably more famous.
10. Tonight at 800 there is a television show about Velázquez.

The Hyphen

Use a hyphen (-) to show a word break at the end of a line. Be sure to break words between syllables.

> Writing a report can be an excellent coopera-
>   tive learning project.

◀ REMINDER
If you're not sure how to break a word between syllables, look up the word in a dictionary.

Use a hyphen between the words that make up a compound modifier used before a noun.

> Paolo wrote a sixteen-line poem.
> I have a king-size headache.

Use hyphens in compound nouns.

> editor-in-chief   stick-in-the-mud
> great-grandchild   ex-president

Use hyphens in compound numbers from twenty-one to ninety-nine.

seventy-six trombones   ninety-nine bottles

Use a hyphen in a fraction.

one-half   six-tenths   two-thirds

Exercise 9   Concept Check

Using Hyphens   Write the words that need hyphens in the following sentences, adding the hyphens that are needed.

1. My blue eyed cat cannot hear sounds.
2. My great grandfather wears a hearing aid.
3. Dogs can hear high pitched sounds that we don't hear.
4. Sounds too high for humans to hear are called ultra sonic sounds.
5. About two thirds of the students know that vibrations cause sound.
6. Listen to this king size rubber band vibrate when I pluck it.
7. When sound waves hit our eardrums, our eardrums begin to vi brate.
8. I tried an experiment with the twenty six students in my class.
9. The vice president of the class held up her wristwatch.
10. Everyone saw it, but only four fifths of the students in the room could hear it.

The Apostrophe

Use an apostrophe (') to make the possessive form of a noun.

Make the possessive of a singular noun by adding an apostrophe and s even if the noun already ends in s.

the boss**'s**   my friend**'s**   a chimpanzee**'s**

Make the possessive of a plural noun that ends in s by adding just an apostrophe.

the countries**'** borders   the boys**'** locker room

Make the possessive of a plural noun that does not end in s by adding an apostrophe and s.

the oxen**'s** salt lick   the children**'s** toys

Use an apostrophe to show that one or more letters have been left out of a contraction.

don't (do not)   wouldn't (would not)   could've (could have)

Use an apostrophe and *s* to show the plurals of a letter or a word referred to as a word.

There are six *and*'**s** in that sentence!
How many *i*'**s** are there in the word *Mississippi?*

Exercise 10   Concept Check

Using Apostrophes   Write the words and letters that need apostrophes in the following sentences. Add the needed apostrophes.

1. My brother and I both attend my fathers high school.
2. Kondo is trying out for the mens soccer team.
3. He said, "Its a popular sport."
4. His grades are all As and Bs.
5. Our parents wont let him play if his grades fall.
6. Our parents trophies show that they were both competitive swimmers.
7. Some students interests are limited to one area.
8. My brothers and sisters arent like that.
9. There are no *cant*s in their vocabularies.
10. My youngest sisters interests include track and computers.

Exercise 11   Proofreading Skill

Using Punctuation Correctly   Write correctly any sentences that need additional punctuation in the following paragraph. If a sentence needs no additional punctuation, write *Correct.*

(1) At the age of twenty five, Jim Thorpe was called "the finest all-around athlete in the world." (2) He excelled in a number of sports football, track, and baseball. (3) The boys early education was rugged. (4) His school day began at 545 A.M. and ended at 900 P.M. (5) His first school taught Thorpe more than academic subjects it also taught him sports. (6) The boy would watch the players at practice. (7) Later, he tried to imitate the players moves. (8) Thorpe's reputation as a good player grew. (9) Then the following series of problems struck his father was injured in an accident; the boy left school; Jims mother and brother died. (10) Shortly thereafter, Jim returned to school. (11) This time, he went to Pennsylvania's Carlisle Indian School. (12) This school had a first rate football coach named Glenn S. "Pop" Warner.

Exercise 12 Revision Skill

Using Semicolons, Colons, Hyphens, and Apostrophes Write the following sentences, adding any needed punctuation.

1. The Grimm brothers stories are full of numbers.
2. "I didnt notice that," said Fatima.
3. Listen to these titles "The Six Swans," "The Twelve Brothers," and "The Wolf and the Seven Goats."
4. Those fairy tales titles are amazing.
5. They are some of the best known fairy tales in the world.
6. I like "The Frog Prince" that's the story where a princess kisses a frog.
7. A frog finds the toy she lost she kisses him, and he turns into a prince.
8. My father and mother collect old childrens books.
9. My parents collection includes several books of fairy tales from around the world.
10. Mother said, "These books aren't just for kids; even middle aged people enjoy them."

Quotation Marks

Use quotation marks (" ") at the beginning and the end of a direct quotation.

> The kids in the haunted house yelled, "Let us out of here!"

▶ Capitalize the first word of a quotation. Separate the quotation from the rest of the sentence with one or more commas. A comma or period before a quotation comes before the quotation marks. A comma or period after a quotation goes inside the quotation marks.

REMINDER
. . . .
Remember, commas and periods are too little to be outside quotation marks alone!

> Mr. Sandoz said, "Now you're on your own," just as we got to the mouth of the cave.
> "Help!" said Timothy. "I can't see anything in here."

A question mark or exclamation point goes inside the quotation marks if it is part of the quotation; it goes outside the quotation marks if it is not part of the quotation.

> Ms. Lee asked, "How many planets are there in the solar system?"
> Did Ms. Lee say, "There are nine known planets"?

Use quotation marks around both parts of a divided quotation.

Do not capitalize the first letter of the first word of the second part of a divided quotation unless it begins a new sentence.

> "Listen!" said Mr. Sandoz. "**Y**ou can hear the bats down there."
> "Can you imagine," said Mr. Sandoz, "**h**ow many of them there must be?"

When punctuating dialogue, begin a new paragraph to indicate a new speaker.

> "Hello, class," said Ms. Lee. "You'll probably want to know something about me. Any questions?"
> "Yes," said Sue Washington. "What did you do before you were a teacher?"
> "I spent thirty years as a professional astronomer."

Exercise 13 Concept Check

Using Quotation Marks and Other Punctuation Write the following sentences, adding quotation marks and other punctuation as needed.

1. What an exciting photograph exclaimed Carlos
2. This picture he said shows the eruption of a volcano
3. Did Carlos say This picture shows the eruption of a volcano
4. Our science teacher said The center of the earth is extremely hot
5. How hot is it asked Coretta
6. Mr. Red Deer said It can reach 13,000 degrees Fahrenheit
7. Is the hot melted rock called magma I asked
8. Yes said Mr. Red Deer The magma bursts through the earth's crust
9. What did Mr. Red Deer say asked Coretta, about a ring of fire
10. The Ring of Fire said Carlos, is an area with many active volcanoes

Exercise 14 Revision Skill

Punctuating Dialogue Rewrite the following passage using correct paragraphing and punctuation.

> Oh, nuts I spilled liquid soap all over my blouse said Barbara. Sue replied Im sure you can wash it out Yes complained Barbara but then my blouse will be wet for the rest of the day I think Id better go home and start this week over If this is only Monday, what will Friday be like

Punctuating Titles

Use quotation marks to set off the titles of short stories, poems, essays, magazine articles, chapters, television episodes, reports, and songs.

Short Story	"Charles," by Shirley Jackson
Poem	"A Dream Deferred," by Langston Hughes
Essay	"Homeless," by Anna Quindlen
Song	"Ave Maria," by Franz Schubert
Television Episode	"The Trouble with Tribbles"

IN PRINT
. . . .
Titles and names that are underlined in writing appear in italics in print.

▶ **Underline the titles of books, newspapers, magazines, movies, television series, plays, works of art, and long musical compositions.**

Book	Kipling's <u>Jungle Book</u>
Newspaper	<u>The Boston Globe</u>
Movie	<u>Malcolm X</u>
Television Series	<u>Star Trek</u>
Long Musical Composition	Puccini's <u>La Bohème</u>

Underline the names of planes, trains, and ships.

the <u>Titanic</u>   <u>Air Force One</u>

Exercise 15   Concept Check

Punctuating Titles   Write the titles given in the following sentences. Underline them or use quotation marks as needed.

1. I just finished reading a book called Trains.
2. I need it for my report, which is titled Art and the Train.
3. I've always wanted to ride on a train like the Orient Express.
4. I know there's a book called Murder on the Orient Express by Agatha Christie.
5. There are lots of songs about trains, including City of New Orleans.
6. Didn't Emily Dickinson write a poem called The Railway Train?
7. I read an article about train whistles in an old issue of Cricket magazine.
8. The article was called The Language of Train Whistles.
9. I know that Key, Lock, and Lantern is a periodical about trains.
10. In your bibliography did you include Toby's story Lost in Grand Central Station?

Exercise 16   Proofreading Skill

Using Quotation Marks and Punctuating Titles   Write the following passage, correcting any errors in punctuation or paragraphing that you find.

(1) Omar and I just finished writing a report called Early Trains. (2) We included drawings, maps, and early railroad songs, such as I've Been Working on the Railroad. (3) Was I surprised when I read, "Early trains were rather slow!" (4) In 1829 the fastest train in the world was the Rocket. (5) "I think" said Omar "that its top speed was thirty-five miles an hour." (6) I said, "Is that what we wrote in our report?" (7) My teacher said that "he liked our approach." (8) "This report shows a lot of work, he said. (9) "I want to put it in the library. (10) I'll put it next to that book called "Railroads."

Exercise 17   Revision Skill

Using Punctuation Marks Correctly   Write the following sentences, correcting any errors in punctuation.

1. On May 27 1907 Rachel Carson was born in Springdale Pennsylvania
2. Juanita said, Wasnt she an environmentalist
3. What a difference she made in this world exclaimed Walt
4. She did part time work for the Bureau of Fisheries and she later got a full time job.
5. Was Under the Sea Wind her first book
6. I asked if Ms Carsons next book was successful
7. Thats the book that was published on July 2 1951
8. The book The Sea Around Us was a huge success it stayed on the best-seller list for eighty six weeks.
9. Carson had several concerns the sea its life forms and the use of pesticides
10. Pesticides were used frequently and Carson wondered if they were safe
11. She worked with several experts, including Dr Wilhelm C Huepner of the National Cancer Institute.
12. Some critics made fun of Carsons warnings an article in Time magazine called her book "unfair"
13. Over a two year period however the U S government stopped using the most dangerous pesticide.
14. She wrote an article called Teach Your Child to Wonder but I havent read it.
15. Rachel Carson was extraordinary she was a good writer and a gifted scientist.

Index of Fine Art

Index of Skills

Literary Terms

*R*eading and Critical Thinking Skills

*G*rammar, Usage, and Mechanics

*W*riting Skills, Modes, and Formats

Salutation, in letters, 706–707
Self-assessment, 62, 113, 178, 241, 290, 343, 346, 392, 461, 516, 573, 666, 667 , 696
Sensory details, 109, 111, 112, 266, 269, 665, 700
Signal words, 174, 177
   see also Transitions
Signature, in letters, 706–707
Statistics
   used in elaboration, 700
   in persuasive writing, 388, 390, 391
Supporting details, 459, 664
Supporting an opinion, 111, 391, 455, 514
Thesis statement, 460
Topic sentence, 699
Transitions, 289, 342, 570, 572, 663, 665, 698
   see also Signal words
Unity, in writing, 697
Word choice, 344, 391, 513, 515
Words often confused, 344–46
Writing about literature, 366, 457–61, 512–16, 663
   analyzing character, 83, 457–61, 510
   analyzing a poem, 89
   analyzing theme, 272
   character sketch, 556
   comparing and contrasting characters, 190, 209, 477, 532, 567, 592, 630
   comparing and contrasting selections, 386
   personal response, 34, 106, 171, 218, 234, 265, 269, 272, 365, 385, 405, 454, 476, 488, 509, 531, 537, 547, 566, 592, 611, 629, 639, 652
   responding to characters, 23, 24, 55, 140, 152, 172, 208, 209, 283, 313, 317, 336, 419, 556, 604, 621, 635, 642, 647, 659
   responding to speaker, 320, 371, 535
Writing letters
   business letters, 706–707
   friendly letters, 707
Writing process, 694–701
   coherence in, 697–98
   conclusions, 342, 458, 460, 570, 665, 667
   details, 61, 62, 111
   elaboration in, 699–700
   implied main idea in, 699
   introductions, 61, 112, 289, 341, 569, 665, 667
   main idea in, 697, 699–700, 701
   organization, 59, 60, 61, 106, 111, 177, 286, 289, 391

paragraphs in, 697–701
topic sentence in, 699
transitions, 289, 342, 570, 572, 663, 665, 698
unity in, 697
writing with computers, 61, 112, 177, 240, 290, 341, 515, 572, 574
   see also Drafting; Prewriting; Proofreading; Publishing and presenting; Revising; Self-assessment

Vocabulary Skills

Analogies, 303, 477
Antonyms, 56, 76, 386, 510, 547
Briticisms, 222, 236
Connotation, 465, 515, 665, 681
   negative, 465
   neutral, 465
   positive, 465
Context clues, 24, 107, 117, 141, 190, 235, 314, 406, 465, 522, 567, 605, 643, 681
   antonyms, 56, 76, 386, 510, 547
   definition and restatement, 117, 681
   example, 117, 681
   inference, 35, 117, 284, 337, 366, 681
   synonyms, 76, 153, 172, 266, 386, 510, 532, 556, 630, 660, 681
Denotation, 209, 465, 681
Dialect, 26, 234, 420, 618, 681
Dictionaries, 131
   specialized, 703
Glossary, 703
Homonyms, 343, 344
Jargon, 93, 683
Loaded language, 520
Persuasion, language of, 347
Prefixes, 671
Restatement clues. *See* Context clues
Roots, Greek, 671
Specialized vocabulary. *See* Jargon
Suffixes, 671
Synonyms, 76, 153, 172, 266, 386, 510, 532, 556, 630, 660, 681
There, They're, and *Their,* 343

*R*esearch and Study Skills

Speaking, Listening, and Viewing

Index of Titles and Authors

Page numbers that appear in italics refer to biographical information.

Acknowledgments

(continued from page iv)

Estate of Margaret Danner: "I'll Walk the Tightrope" by Margaret Danner. Reprinted by permission of Naomi Washington for the Estate of Margaret Danner.

Dell Books, a division of Bantam Doubleday Dell Publishing Group, Inc.: "Lose Now, Pay Later" by Carol Farley; copyright © 1991 by Carol Farley, from *2041: Twelve Short Stories About the Future* by Jane Yolen, Editor. Used by permission of Dell Books, a division of Bantam Doubleday Dell Publishing Group, Inc.

Mari Evans: "The Rebel," from *I Am a Black Woman* by Mari Evans, published by William Morrow & Co., 1970. By permission of the author.

Farrar, Straus & Giroux, Inc., and Murray Pollinger, Literary Agent: "The Bicycle and the Sweetshop," "The Great Mouse Plot," and "Mr. Coombes," from *Boy* by Roald Dahl; copyright © 1984 by Roald Dahl. English editions published by Jonathan Cape Limited and Penguin Books Ltd. "Charles," from *The Lottery and Other Stories* by Shirley Jackson; copyright 1948, 1949 by Shirley Jackson, renewal copyright © 1976, 1977 by Laurence Hyman, Barry Hyman, Mrs. Sarah Webster, and Mrs. Joanne Schnurer. Reprinted by permission of Farrar, Straus & Giroux, Inc.

Julia Fields: "Aardvark" by Julia Fields, from *Nine Black Poets*. By permission of the author.

Harcourt Brace Jovanovich, Inc.: "Seventh Grade," from *Baseball in April and Other Stories* by Gary Soto; copyright © 1990 by Gary Soto. "Without Commercials," from *Horses Make a Landscape Look More Beautiful* by Alice Walker; copyright © 1984 by Alice Walker. Reprinted by permission of Harcourt Brace Jovanovich, Inc. "What Do We Do with a Variation," from *When I Dance* by James Berry; copyright © 1991, 1988 by James Berry. Reprinted by permission of Harcourt Brace Jovanovich, Inc., and June Hall Literary Agency Ltd., a division of Peters, Fraser & Dunlop Ltd.

HarperCollins Publishers: "The Fatal Flower," from *Tongues of Jade* by Laurence Yep; text copyright © 1991 by Laurence Yep. Chapter ll from *The Endless Steppe* by Esther Hautzig; copyright © 1968 by Esther Hautzig. Reprinted by permission of HarperCollins Publishers.

Lawrence Hill Books: "Last Cover," from *The Best Nature Stories of Paul Annixter* by Paul Annixter; copyright © 1974 Jane and Paul Annixter. By permission of the publisher, Lawrence Hill Books (Brooklyn, New York).

Henry Holt and Company, Inc.: "A Minor Bird," from *The Poetry of Robert Frost* by Robert Frost, edited by Edward Connery Lathem; copyright 1928, © 1969 by Holt, Rinehart and Winston, copyright © 1956 by Robert Frost. "Upon the Waters" (pp. 187–197), from *Rites of Passage* by Joanne Greenberg; copyright © 1966, 1967, 1968, 1969, 1970, 1971, 1972 by Joanne Greenberg. Reprinted by permission of Henry Holt and Company, Inc.

Houghton Mifflin Company: "Aunt Millicent" by Mary Steele, from *Dream Time,* edited by Gascoigne, Goodman, and Tyrrell; copyright © 1989 by Mary Steele. Reprinted by permission of Houghton Mifflin Co. All rights reserved.

Interlink Publishing Group, Inc.: "A Blind Man Catches a Bird," from *Children of Wax: African Folk Tales* by Alexander McCall Smith; copyright © 1990 Alexander McCall Smith.

Estate of MacKinlay Kantor: "A Man Who Had No Eyes" by MacKinlay Kantor. By permission of Tim Kantor and Layne Shroder, children of deceased author.

Virginia Kidd, Literary Agent for Anne McCaffrey: "The Smallest Dragonboy" by Anne McCaffrey; copyright © 1973 by Anne McCaffrey, first appeared in *Science Fiction Tales*. Reprinted by permission of the author and the author's agent, Virginia Kidd.

Little, Brown and Company: "How Odin Lost His Eye," from *Adventures with the Giants* by Catharine F. Sellew; copyright 1950 by Catharine F. Sellew, copyright © renewed 1978 by Catharine F. Sellew. *The Arrow and the Lamp: The Story of Psyche* retold by Margaret Hodges; text copyright © 1989 by Margaret Hodges. By permission of Little, Brown and Company.

Liveright Publishing Corporation: "old age sticks," from *Complete Poems, 1913-1962* by E. E. Cummings; copyright © 1923, 1925, 1931, 1935, 1938, 1939, 1940, 1944, 1945, 1946, 1947, 1948, 1949, 1950, 1951, 1952, 1953, 1954, 1955, 1956, 1957, 1958, 1959, 1960, 1961, 1962 by the Trustees for the E. E. Cummings Trust, copyright © 1961, 1963, 1968 by Marion Morehouse Cummings.

Macmillan Publishing Company: Excerpts from "Eleanor Roosevelt," from *Great Lives: Human Rights* by William Jay Jacobs; copyright © 1990 William Jay Jacobs. Reprinted with the permission of Charles Scribner's Sons, an imprint of Macmillan Publishing Company.

Janice Mirikitani: "For My Father," from *Awake in the River; Poetry and Prose* by Janice Mirikitani, Isthmus Press, 1978, San Francisco, CA. By permission of the author.

Museum of New Mexico Press: "The Force of Luck," from *Cuentos: Tales from the Hispanic Southwest* by José Griego y Maestas and Rudolfo Anaya; copyright © 1980. Reprinted with permission of the Museum of New Mexico Press.

Hugh Noyes for Literary Estate of Alfred Noyes: "The Highwayman" by Alfred Noyes. Permission of Hugh Noyes, for Trustees of Alfred Noyes Literary Estate.

Harold Ober Associates, Inc.: "Stolen Day" by Sherwood Anderson; copyright © 1941 by United Newspapers Magazine Corp., copyright renewed © 1968 by Eleanor Copenhaver Anderson. Reprinted by permission of Harold Ober Associates, Inc.

Penguin Books Canada Limited: Excerpts from *Little by Little* by Jean Little; copyright © 1987 Jean Little. Reprinted by permission of Penguin Books Canada Limited.

The Putnam Publishing Group: "Kelfala's Secret Something" by Adjai Robinson, from *Three African Tales*; copyright © 1979 by Adjai Robinson. Reprinted by permission of The Putnam Publishing Group. "Anansi and His Visitor, Turtle," from *African Village Folk Tales* by Edna Mason Kaula; copyright © 1968 by Edna Mason Kaula. Reprinted by permission of Philomel Books.

Random House, Inc.: "Where the Girl Saved Her Brother" told by Strange Owl, from *The Sound of Flutes and Other Indian Legends*, edited by Richard Erdoes; copyright © 1976 by Richard Erdoes. Reprinted by permission of Pantheon Books, a division of Random House, Inc. "Dream Deferred," from *The Panther and the Lash* by Langston Hughes; copyright © 1951 by Langston Hughes. "Homeless," from *Living Out Loud* by Anna Quindlen; copyright © 1987 by Anna Quindlen. "America the Not-so-Beautiful," from *Not That You Asked* by Andrew A. Rooney; copyright © 1989 by Essay Productions. Excerpts from *The Autobiography of Malcolm X* by Malcolm X with Alex Haley; copyright © 1964 by Alex Haley and Malcolm X. Copyright © 1965 by Alex Haley and Betty Shabazz. Reprinted by permission of Random House, Inc. "The People Could Fly," from *The People Could Fly: American Black Folktales*, told by Virginia Hamilton; text copyright © 1985 by Virginia Hamilton. Reprinted by permission of Alfred A. Knopf, Inc. Excerpts from *Nadja on My Way* by Nadja Salerno-Sonnenberg; copyright © 1989 by Nadja Salerno-Sonnenberg. Reprinted by permission of Crown Publishers, Inc.

Marian Reiner, Literary Agent: "The Women's 400 Meters," from *The Sidewalk Racer and Other Poems of Sports and Motion* by Lillian Morrison; copyright © 1965, 1967, 1968, 1977 by Lillian Morrison. Reprinted by permission of Marian Reiner for the author.

Scholastic, Inc.: "Prometheus," from *Heroes, Gods and Monsters of the Greek Myths* retold by Bernard Evslin; copyright © 1966 by Scholastic, Inc. Chapters 2 and 3 from *Exploring the Titanic* by Robert D. Ballard; copyright © 1991 by The Madison Press Ltd. Reprinted by permission of Scholastic, Inc.

The Rod Serling Trust: *The Monsters Are Due on Maple Street* by Rod Serling; copyright © 1960 Rod Serling; © 1988 Carolyn Serling, Jodi Serling, and Anne Serling. Reprinted by permission of the Rod Serling Trust. All rights reserved.

Virginia Driving Hawk Sneve: "The Medicine Bag," by Virginia Driving Hawk Sneve, first printed in *Boys' Life*, March 1975. Reprinted by permission of the author.

Mary TallMountain: "There Is No Word for Goodbye" by Mary TallMountain, from *The Blue Cloud Quarterly*. Reprinted by permission of the author.

Twentieth Century Fox Film Corp.: "Funny Boy" by Allan Burns, from the series entitled *Room 222*; copyright © 1969 Twentieth Century Fox Film Corporation. All rights reserved.

Estate of Yoshiko Uchida: "Oh Broom, Get to Work" by Yoshiko Uchida; copyright © 1977, 1990 by Cynthia Rylant. Reprinted with permission of Orchard Books, New York. Reprinted by permission of the Estate of Yoshiko Uchida.

Franklin Watts, Inc.: "A Crush," from *A Couple of Kooks and Other Stories About Love* by Cynthia Rylant; copyright © 1990 by Cynthia Rylant. Reprinted with permission of Orchard Books, New York.

Western Publishing Company, Inc.: "Old Sly Eye" by Russell Gordon Carter, from *Story Parade*; copyright © 1945 Story Parade, renewed © 1973. Used by permission of Western Publishing Company, Inc.

Wylie, Aiken & Stone: "The Time We Climbed Snake Mountain" by Leslie Marmon Silko; copyright © 1972 by Leslie Marmon Silko. By permission of Sarah Chalfant, Literary Agent of Wylie, Aiken & Stone for the author.

The Zanuck Company and Scholastic, Inc.: Adaptation of *Driving Miss Daisy* by Alfred Uhry, from *Literary Cavalcade Magazine*, January 1990. By permission of The Zanuck Company and Scholastic, Inc.

The authors and editors have made every effort to trace the ownership of all copyrighted selections found in this book and to make full acknowledgment for their use.

Illustrations

Illustrations by Rich Lo: 475, 611, 610. Illustrations by Jerry Nelson: 15, 42, 84, 155, 584. Maps by Robert Voigts: 17, 192, 222, 377, 538, 587, 593, 597, 608, 610, 612, 615, 619, 622, 625, 633, 636, 640, 646, 648, 653.

Author Photographs

AP/Wide World Photos: Alfred Uhry 456, MacKinlay Kantor 690 bottom, Andrew A. Rooney, 692 top. © Archive Photos: Rod Serling 173. Arte Publico Press: Judith Ortiz Cofer 548, Pat Mora 691 top. Avon Books: Carol Farley 77. © Sophie Baker: Roald Dahl 236. The Chicago Defender: Alfred Ducket 154. Cox Studios: Virginia Hamilton 631 middle. Culver

Pictures: Rudyard Kipling 338, Hans Christian Andersen 661 top, Alfred Lord Tennyson 693 top. Richard Erdoes: Rachel Strange Owl 644 middle. Bernard Evslin: 644 top. © June Finfer, Filmedia Ltd.: Yoshiko Uchida 693 bottom. Historical Pictures/Stock Montage: Emily Dickinson 372 top, Leo Tolstoy 617 bottom, Aesop 617 top, O. Henry, 689 bottom. By permission of the Houghton Library, Harvard University: e.e. cummings 221 bottom. © 1987 Elizabeth Gilliland: Lillian Morrison 321 top. The Granger Collection, New York: Malcolm X 478, Langston Hughes 690 top. Rubén Guzmán: Sandra Cisneros 688 bottom. Virginia Kidd, literary agent: Anne McCaffrey 267. Photo by Jay Kay Klein: Ray Bradbury 688 middle. © 1991 George T. Kruse: Janice Mirikitani 691 top. Photo by Michael LeRoy: Allan Burns 511. © Lee Marmon: Leslie Marmon Silko 692 bottom. Photo by Jim Marshall: Alice Walker 483. Photo by Margaret Miller: Cynthia Rylant 407. Courtesy, Moorland-Spingarn Research Center, Howard University, Washington, D.C.: Georgia Douglas Johnson 690 bottom. Collection of the National Palace Museum, Taipei, Taiwan, Republic of China: Po Chü-i 372 bottom. National Portrait Gallery, Smithsonian Institution, Washington, D.C./Art Resource, New York: Robert Frost 689 middle. Photo by Barbara Nitke: Robert Ballard 108. Courtesy, *The New York Times*: Anna Quindlen 691 bottom. NYT Pictures: Frank Horne 321 bottom. Photo by Christian Steiner: Nadja Salerno-Sonnenberg 315. Schomburg Center for Research in Black Culture, The New York Public Library, Astor, Lenox and Tilden Foundations: Toni Cade Bambara 36, Ted Poston 191. Photo by Bob Tradelius: Joanne Greenberg 142. Photo by Ian West: Mary Steele 210. Photo by K. Yep: Laurence Yep 661, bottom.

Miscellaneous Art Credits

viii STOP LIGHT 1986 © C. J. Yao. Courtesy, Styria Studio, New York. x DAKOTA PIPE CLAN MAGIC Oscar Howe Courtesy, Mr. and Mrs. Peter A. Hassrick. xii THE STARRY NIGHT 1889 Vincent van Gogh Oil on canvas, 29 x 36 1/4 inches (73.4 x 92.1 cm). Collection, The Museum of Modern Art, New York. Acquired through the Lillie P. Bliss Bequest. Photograph © 1992 The Museum of Modern Art, New York. xiv THE BOATING PARTY 1893-94 Mary Cassatt National Gallery of Art, Washington, D.C. Chester Dale Collection. xvi YO Y MI FUTURO (I and my future) 1951 Jesús Guerrero Galván Collection, Pascual Gutiérrez Roldán. xviii THREE FOLK MUSICIANS 1967 Romare Bearden Courtesy, the estate of Romare Bearden and ACA Galleries, New York. 3 The Hermitage, St. Petersburg, Russia. 4 top EXOTIC LANDSCAPE 1910 Henri Rousseau (1844-1910) Oil on canvas 45 3/4 x 64 inches Norton Simon Foundation, Pasadena, California; bottom Small beaded pouch, about 1915. Photo 1989 Benson L. Lanford and Robert W. Gilmore. 5 top © 1988 from *Exploring the Titanic* by Robert D. Ballard. A Scholastic/Madison Press Book, bottom LE PETIT DEJEUNER 1986 Jennifer Hornyak Courtesy, Gallery Claude Lafitte, Montreal, Canada. 14 Mural in Philadelphia (detail) 1992 Meg Fish. Courtesy of the artist. 17 © 1991 H. Richard Johnson/FPG. 26 PAINTED BRONZE 1960 © Jasper Johns/VAGA, New York Courtesy, Leo Castelli Gallery, New York. 37 Underwood Photo Archives. 38 The Bettmann Archive. 44 AP/Wide World Photos. 48 © 1991 Michael Simpson/FPG. 67 Illustration by Lynn Rowe Reed. 68 © Barry Seidman/The Stock Market. 78 © 1987 Tom Bean/The Stock Market. 86 The Hermitage, St. Petersburg, Russia. 90 Courtesy, California Historical Society. 91 H. Armstrong Roberts. 93, 94, 96-97, 100, 103 © 1988 From *Exploring the Titanic* by Robert D. Ballard. A Scholastic/Madison Press Book. 95 Joseph Carvalho collection. 99 Courtesy, 7C's Press/Titanic Historical Society, Inc., Old Orchard, Mass. 118 *Monkey Island* by Paula Fox. Copyright © 1991 by Paula Fox. Jacket painting copyright © 1991 by Rene Ade. Reproduced with permission of the publisher, Orchard Books, New York. 119 From *The Witch of Blackbird Pond* by Elizabeth George Speare. Copyright © 1958 by Elizabeth George Speare. Reprinted by permission of Houghton Mifflin Company. All rights reserved. 119 *Against the Storm* by Gaye Hicyilmaz. Copyright © 1992 by Little, Brown and Company, Inc. Used by permission. 122 UPI/Bettmann. 123 From *The World*

Book Encyclopedia © 1992 World Book, Inc. By permission of the publisher. 131 D. Lada/H. Armstrong Roberts. 143 Courtesy AU Sports Memorabilia. 147 inset UPI/Bettmann. 157 Culver Pictures. 183 SHIFTING EMBRACE (detail) 1990 Philemona Williamson Collection of Mr. and Mrs. Clarence Otis, photo by Manu Sassoonian, Courtesy, June Kelly Gallery, New York. 184 © James van der Zee Institute. 211 © John Running. 217 UPI/Bettmann. 229 THE APPRENTICE 1981 Terry Mimnaugh bronze, edition of 15 from a series "What Little Boys Are Made Of." 246 From *Roll of Thunder, Hear My Cry* by Mildred D. Taylor, jacket illustration by Jerry Pinkney. Copyright © 1976 by the Dial press. Used by permission of Dial Books for Young Readers, a division of Penguin Books USA Inc. 247 *Maniac Magee* by Jerry Spinelli. Copyright © 1990 by Little, Brown and Company, Inc. Used by permission. 247 From *Brother Eagle, Sister Sky* by Susan Jeffers. Copyright © 1991 by Susan Jeffers. Used by permission of Dial Books for Young Readers, a division of Penguin Books USA, Inc. 250 RECLINING WOMAN (detail) Will Barnet © 1992 Will Barnet/VAGA, New York. 251 From *The Dragonlover's Guide to Pern* by Jody Lynn Nye with Anne McCaffrey, illustrations by Todd Cameron Hamilton. Copyright © 1989 by Bill Fawcett and Associates. Reprinted by permission of Ballantine Books, a division of Random House, Inc. 268 Illustration by Judy Pedersen. 273 Franklin Roosevelt Library. 295 LORD OF THE RIMROCK (detail) Leon Parson Print from National Wildlife Galleries, Fort Myers Florida. 296 The Bettmann Archive. 304 H. Abernathy/H. Armstrong Roberts. 316 © 1990 David Madison/Duomo. 322 © Norman Myers/Bruce Coleman Inc. 348 *The Hobbit* by J.R.R. Tolkien. © 1938. Reprinted with permission of Houghton Mifflin Company. All rights reserved. 349 Jacket illustration by Eric Velasquez from *The Gift of the Girl Who Couldn't Hear* by Susan Shreve. Text copyright © 1991 by Susan Shreve. Illustration copyright © by Eric Velasquez. By permission of Tambourine Books, a division of William Morrow & Company, Inc. 349 *Anpao* by Jamake Highwater. Cover reprinted by permission of HarperCollins Publishers. 352 Photo copy by Peter Schaff. 353 © Joe McDonald/Animals, Animals. 368 H. Armstrong Roberts. 373 © David Woodfall/TSW. 375 © Matt Lambert/TSW. 397 Illustration by Patsy Dryden. 398 © Greenlar/The Image Works. 400, 401 Illustrations © 1992 by Norman Green. 408 Original illustration by Charles Mikolaycak for *The Highwayman*. Courtesy of the Kerlan Collection at the University of Minnesota. Used with permission of the illustrator and Lathrop, Lee and Shepard Publishers. 415 D. Degnan/H. Armstrong Roberts. 420 © Stephen Ellison/Shooting Star. 424, 451 © Shooting Star. 431 Globe Photos © Rangefinders. 437, 440 Photofest. 466 *The Flawed Glass* by Ian Strachan. Copyright © 1990 by Little, Brown Inc. Used by permission. 467 Reprinted with permission of Bradbury Press, an Affiliate of Macmillan, Inc., from *One-Eyed Cat* by Paula Fox. Jacket Illustration by Neil Waldman. Copyright © 1984 Bradbury Press. 467 Jacket illustration by Susan Bonners from *The Clay Marble* by Minfong Ho. Jacket illustration copyright © 1991 by Susan Bonners. Reprinted by permission of Farrar, Straus & Giroux, Inc. 470 THE LIBRARIES ARE APPRECIATED (detail) 1943 Jacob Lawrence Philadelphia Museum of Art, Louis A. Stern Collection. 471 UPI/Bettmann. 479 Bill Bachman/Leo de Wys. 484 © Steve Leonard/TSW. 521, 522 © Brian Milne/Animals, Animals. 534 © Michael Dich/Animals, Animals. 549 The Bancroft Library, University of California, Berkeley. 557 AP/Wide World Photos. 578 Reprinted with the permission of Macmillan Publishing Company from *The House of Dies Drear* by Virginia Hamilton. Illustrated by Eros Keith. Copyright © 1968 Macmillan Publishing Company. 579 *The Adventures of Tom Sawyer* by Mark Twain. By permission of Tom Doherty Associates/Tor Books. 579 *Risk n' Roses* by Jan Slepian. © 1977 Reprinted with permission of Philomel Books, a division of Putnam. 582, 586 © Michael Holford. 582, 607 The Granger Collection, New York. 583, 618 A DRAWING BASED ON A SPIRITUAL 1958 Charles White Courtesy, Heritage Gallery, Los Angeles. 583, 632 Arapaho spear. Oklahoma Museum of Natural History, University of Oklahoma, Norman. 583, 615, 645 © Carmine Fantasia. 595 International Procession, from Girard Foundation Collection in the Museum of International Folk Art, a unit of The Museum of New Mexico, Santa Fe. Photograph by Michel Monteaux.